Lecture Notes in Computer Science

Vol. 352: J. Díaz, F. Orejas (Eds.), TAPSOFT '89. Volume 2. Proceedings, 1989. X, 389 pages. 1989.

Vol. 353: S. Hölldobler, Foundations of Equational Logic Programming. X, 250 pages. 1989. (Subseries LNAI).

Vol. 354: J.W. de Bakker, W.-P. de Roever, G. Rozenberg (Eds.), Linear Time, Branching Time and Partial Order in Logics and Models for Concurrency. VIII, 713 pages. 1989.

Vol. 355: N. Dershowitz (Ed.), Rewriting Techniques and Applications. Proceedings, 1989. VII, 579 pages. 1989.

Vol. 356: L. Huguet, A. Poli (Eds.), Applied Algebra, Algebraic Algorithms and Error-Correcting Codes. Proceedings, 1987. VI, 417 pages. 1989.

Vol. 357: T. Mora (Ed.), Applied Algebra, Algebraic Algorithms and Error-Correcting Codes. Proceedings, 1988. IX, 481 pages. 1989.

Vol. 358: P. Gianni (Ed.), Symbolic and Algebraic Computation. Proceedings, 1988. XI, 545 pages. 1989.

Vol. 359: D. Gawlick, M. Haynie, A. Reuter (Eds.), High Performance Transaction Systems. Proceedings, 1987. XII, 329 pages. 1989.

Vol. 360: H. Maurer (Ed.), Computer Assisted Learning – ICCAL '89. Proceedings, 1989. VII, 642 pages. 1989.

Vol. 361: S. Abiteboul, P.C. Fischer, H.-J. Schek (Eds.), Nested Relations and Complex Objects in Databases. VI, 323 pages. 1989.

Vol. 362: B. Lisper, Synthesizing Synchronous Systems by Static Scheduling in Space-Time. VI, 263 pages. 1989.

Vol. 363: A.R. Meyer, M.A. Taitslin (Eds.), Logic at Botik '89. Proceedings, 1989. X, 289 pages. 1989.

Vol. 364: J. Demetrovics, B. Thalheim (Eds.), MFDBS 89. Proceedings, 1989. VI, 428 pages. 1989.

Vol. 365: E. Odijk, M. Rem, J.-C. Syre (Eds.), PARLE '89. Parallel Architectures and Languages Europe. Volume I. Proceedings, 1989. XIII, 478 pages. 1989.

Vol. 366: E. Odijk, M. Rem, J.-C. Syre (Eds.), PARLE '89. Parallel Architectures and Languages Europe. Volume II. Proceedings, 1989. XIII, 442 pages. 1989.

Vol. 367: W. Litwin, H.-J. Schek (Eds.), Foundations of Data Organization and Algorithms. Proceedings, 1989. VIII, 531 pages. 1989.

Vol. 368: H. Boral, P. Faudemay (Eds.), IWDM '89, Database Machines. Proceedings, 1989. VI, 387 pages. 1989.

Vol. 369: D. Taubner, Finite Representations of CCS and TCSP Programs by Automata and Petri Nets. X. 168 pages. 1989.

Vol. 370: Ch. Meinel, Modified Branching Programs and Their Computational Power. VI, 132 pages. 1989.

Vol. 371: D. Hammer (Ed.), Compiler Compilers and High Speed Compilation. Proceedings, 1988. VI, 242 pages. 1989.

Vol. 372: G. Ausiello, M. Dezani-Ciancaglini, S. Ronchi Della Rocca (Eds.), Automata, Languages and Programming. Proceedings, 1989. XI, 788 pages. 1989.

Vol. 373: T. Theoharis, Algorithms for Parallel Polygon Rendering. VIII, 147 pages. 1989.

Vol. 374: K.A. Robbins, S. Robbins, The Cray X-MP/Model 24. VI, 165 pages. 1989.

Vol. 375: J.L.A. van de Snepscheut (Ed.), Mathematics of Program Construction. Proceedings, 1989. VI, 421 pages. 1989.

Vol. 376: N.E. Gibbs (Ed.), Software Engineering Education. Proceedings, 1989. VII, 312 pages. 1989.

Vol. 377: M. Gross, D. Perrin (Eds.), Electronic Dictionaries and Automata in Computational Linguistics. Proceedings, 1987. V, 110 pages. 1989.

Vol. 378: J.H. Davenport (Ed.), EUROCAL '87. Proceedings, 1987. VIII, 499 pages. 1989.

Vol. 379: A. Kreczmar, G. Mirkowska (Eds.), Mathematical Foundations of Computer Science 1989. Proceedings, 1989. VIII, 605 pages. 1989.

Vol. 380: J. Csirik, J. Demetrovics, F. Gécseg (Eds.), Fundamentals of Computation Theory. Proceedings, 1989. XI, 493 pages. 1989.

Vol. 381: J. Dassow, J. Kelemen (Eds.), Machines, Languages, and Complexity. Proceedings, 1988. VI, 244 pages. 1989.

Vol. 382: F. Dehne, J.-R. Sack, N. Santoro (Eds.), Algorithms and Data Structures. WADS '89. Proceedings, 1989. IX, 592 pages. 1989.

Vol. 383: K. Furukawa, H. Tanaka, T. Fujisaki (Eds.), Logic Programming '88. Proceedings, 1988. VII, 251 pages. 1989 (Subseries LNAI).

Vol. 384: G.A. van Zee, J.G.G. van de Vorst (Eds.), Parallel Computing 1988. Proceedings, 1988. V, 135 pages. 1989.

Vol. 385: E. Börger, H. Kleine Büning, M.M. Richter (Eds.), CSL '88. Proceedings, 1988. VI, 399 pages. 1989.

Vol. 386: J.E. Pin (Ed.), Formal Properties of Finite Automata and Applications. Proceedings, 1988. VIII, 260 pages. 1989.

Vol. 387: C. Ghezzi, J.A. McDermid (Eds.), ESEC '89. 2nd European Software Engineering Conference. Proceedings, 1989. VI, 496 pages. 1989.

Vol. 388: G. Cohen, J. Wolfmann (Eds.), Coding Theory and Applications. Proceedings, 1988. IX, 329 pages. 1989.

Vol. 389: D.H. Pitt, D.E. Rydeheard, P. Dybjer, A.M. Pitts, A. Poigné (Eds.), Category Theory and Computer Science. Proceedings, 1989. VI, 365 pages. 1989.

Vol. 390: J.P. Martins, E.M. Morgado (Eds.), EPIA 89. Proceedings, 1989. XII, 400 pages. 1989 (Subseries LNAI).

Vol. 391: J.-D. Boissonnat, J.-P. Laumond (Eds.), Geometry and Robotics. Proceedings, 1988. VI, 413 pages. 1989.

Vol. 392: J.-C. Bermond, M. Raynal (Eds.), Distributed Algorithms. Proceedings, 1989. VI, 315 pages. 1989.

Vol. 393: H. Ehrig, H. Herrlich, H.-J. Kreowski, G. Preuß (Eds.), Categorical Methods in Computer Science. VI, 350 pages. 1989.

Vol. 394: M. Wirsing, J.A. Bergstra (Eds.), Algebraic Methods: Theory, Tools and Applications. VI, 558 pages. 1989.

Vol. 395: M. Schmidt-Schauß, Computational Aspects of an Order-Sorted Logic with Term Declarations. VIII, 171 pages. 1989 (Subseries LNAI).

Vol. 396: T.A. Berson, T. Beth (Eds.), Local Area Network Security. Proceedings, 1989. IX, 152 pages. 1989.

Vol. 397: K.P. Jantke (Ed.), Analogical and Inductive Inference. Proceedings, 1989. IX, 338 pages. 1989 (Subseries LNAI).

Vol. 398: B. Banieqbal, H. Barringer, A. Pnueli (Eds.), Temporal Logic in Specification. Proceedings, 1987. VI, 448 pages. 1989.

Vol. 399: V. Cantoni, R. Creutzburg, S. Levialdi, G. Wolf (Eds.), Recent Issues in Pattern Analysis and Recognition. VII, 400 pages. 1989.

Vol. 400: R. Klein, Concrete and Abstract Voronoi Diagrams. IV, 167 pages. 1989.

Vol. 401: H. Djidjev (Ed.), Optimal Algorithms. Proceedings, 1989. VI, 308 pages. 1989.

Vol. 402: T.P. Bagchi, V.K. Chaudhri, Interactive Relational Database Design. XI, 186 pages. 1989.

Vol. 403: S. Goldwasser (Ed.), Advances in Cryptology – CRYPTO '88. Proceedings, 1988. XI, 591 pages. 1990.

Vol. 404: J. Beer, Concepts, Design, and Performance Analysis of a Parallel Prolog Machine. VI, 128 pages. 1989.

Vol. 405: C.E. Veni Madhavan (Ed.), Foundations of Software Technology and Theoretical Computer Science. Proceedings, 1989. VIII, 339 pages. 1989.

Vol. 406: C.J. Barter, M.J. Brooks (Eds.), AI '88. Proceedings, 1988. VIII, 463 pages. 1990 (Subseries LNAI).

Vol. 407: J. Sifakis (Ed.), Automatic Verification Methods for Finite State Systems. Proceedings, 1989. VII, 382 pages. 1990.

Lecture Notes in Computer Science

Edited by G. Goos and J. Hartmanis

469

I. Guessarian (Ed.)

Semantics of Systems of Concurrent Processes

LITP Spring School on Theoretical Computer Science
La Roche Posay, France, April 23–27, 1990
Proceedings

Springer-Verlag Berlin Heidelberg GmbH

Volume Editor

Irène Guessarian
Université Paris VI
LITP, Tour 45–55, 4 place Jussieu
F-75252 Paris Cedex 05, France

CR Subject Classification (1987): F.3–4, D.4, C.1.2, H.2.4

ISBN 978-3-540-53479-2 ISBN 978-3-540-46897-4 (eBook)
DOI 10.1007/978-3-540-46897-4

Originally published by Springer-Verlag Berlin Heidelberg New York in 1990

2145/3140-543210 – Printed on acid-free paper

FOREWORD

The present volume contains the proceedings of the 1990 Spring School of Theoretical Computer Science which was devoted this year to the Semantics of Concurrency. The School was organized jointly by the LITP (Laboratoire d'Informatique Théorique et Programmation, Paris) and IRIT (Institut pour la Recherche en Informatique de Toulouse). The talks were divided into two series:
- tutorial talks, which introduced the subject to neophytes;
- advanced talks, which presented a survey of recent achievements in Semantics of Concurrency.

The following is a detailed list of the tutorial talks given: Transitions systems and the semantics of communicating processes (*A. Arnold*), Process algebra: CCS and MEIJE (*G. Boudol*), Mobile processes (*R. Milner*), Testing equivalences (*M. Hennessy*), An introduction to metric semantics (*J. W. de Bakker*), Parallelism and computability (*Ph. Darondeau*), CCS and Petri nets (*U. Goltz*), Specification and verification of process properties (*J. Sifakis and A. Arnold*), Event structures (*I. Castellani*), Categories for parallelism (*U. Montanari*). Most of these talks are not contained in the present proceedings, or only very briefly covered, with references to the existing literature, because they are already very well documented in various papers.

The advanced talks, on the other hand, are contained in the present volume. These talks center around four main themes:
- Models for concurrent and distributed systems: this area includes pomsets and metric semantics (J. W. de Bakker, J. H. A. Warmerdam), event structures (G. Boudol, I. Castellani), causal trees (Ph. Darondeau, P. Degano), partial orders and languages (B. Rozoy), fixpoints and languages (I. Guessarian), trace monoids (G. Duchamp, D. Krob, P. Gastin), CCS and Petri nets (U. Goltz), categorical models (U. Montanari, S. Kasangian, A. Labella, A. Pettorossi).
- Observation and bisimulation equivalences: this part includes observational semantics and abstract data types (E. Astesiano, A. Giovini, G.Reggio), preservation of equivalences by refinements (R. J. van Glabbeek).
- Logics for concurrency: this area contains computability notions for operational specifications (Ph. Darondeau), for fairness (L. Priese), bisimulation logics (R. De Nicola, F. Vaandrager).
- Applications to distributed systems: this part covers the following: parallel languages for SIMD connection machines (L. Bougé), problems of distributed systems such as byzantine generals (J. Beauquier), or notions of clock (B. Charron).

I would like to thank the members of the program committee of the school, which consisted of *André Arnold, Joffroy Beauquier, Gérard Boudol, Philippe Darondeau, Irène Guessarian* and *Maurice Nivat*. Special thanks are due to *Maurice Nivat*, who for 20 years has consistently animated and each time given a new spirit to the spring schools. Special thanks also go to *Colette Ravinet* and *Patrick Sallé* who most efficiently managed all practical problems before and during the conference, for their perfectly equal and amiable temper throughout all events. Thanks are due also to the City Hall, the Syndicat d'Initiative of La Roche Posay, and the managers and employees of the hotel de l'Esplanade.

Thanks are due finally to the Département Sciences Physiques pour l'Ingénieur of the CNRS, the PRC Mathématiques et Informatique, and most specially (last but not least) the GRECO Communication, Concurrence, Coopération, whose financial support made this school possible. The proceedings of the last five schools have also been published in the Springer-Verlag LNCS series (Vols. 192, 242, 316, 377 and 386).

Paris, October 1990 Irène Guessarian

TABLE OF CONTENTS

Processes as Data Types: Observational Semantics and Logic*
(Extended Abstract)

Egidio Astesiano Alessandro Giovini Gianna Reggio
Department of Mathematics
University of Genova - Italy

Introduction

We present here an attempt towards a unifying approach for the semantics of concurrency, abstracting from the particular language used for describing processes. The original motivation of this work was the integration of process specifications into the general schema of algebraic specifications of abstract data types (see [AR,AGR2] for the general approach). In this area abstraction from the language is essential. Indeed whenever some data are processes, in order to keep a reasonable level of abstraction, processes are to be specified just as special elements in some algebraic structure and moreover their semantics has to fit into the overall semantics of the specification. Now it is rather well-known that the classical notions of semantics for algebraic specifications turn out to be not adequate for expressing sensible semantics for processes. Our approach is to learn and abstract from the fundamental studies on calculi like *CCS* some basic ideas, showing how they can be lifted to a treatment not depending on the language and accomodating a variety of semantics.

Processes are here abstractly viewed as elements of observable sort in an algebraic structure (in secion 1 we briefly introduce some examples of this approach, viewing processes as algebraic transition systems; but note that this view is not essential for the following theory). In order to define a semantics we embody in the algebraic structure an observational viewpoint, obtaining what we call an *observational structure* (section 2).

Essentially an observational structure consists of an algebra equipped with

- *experiments*: possibly infinitary first order contexts for observable elements;
- a *similarity law* for experiments: a function which, given a (similarity) relation on the elements of the algebra, generates a similarity relation on experiments;
- a *propagation law* for relations: a function which propagates a (similarity) relation on the observable elements to a (similarity) relation on elements of the other sorts.

*Work partially funded by COMPASS–Esprit Basic Research Group No. 3264 and by CNR–PF–Sistemi Informatici e Calcolo Parallelo.

With each observational structure an *observational equivalence* is associated, which is an abstract version of the well-known bisimulation equivalence of [P] for transition systems. In order to explore further this correspondence, we introduce the notion of *representable observational structure*: essentially a structure where the similarity law for experiments is representable by families of patterns of experiments. The main result of the paper shows how to associate with a representable observational structure a set of *modal observational logic formulas* (section 3), such that an abstract version of the Hennessy-Milner theorem holds: two observable elements are observationally equivalent iff they satisfy the same set of such formulas.

It is shown that interesting examples (not only strong and weak, but also distributed and branching bisimulation) can be seen as instances of representable observational structures, and so we get a corresponding modal observational logic. Throughout the paper we use variations of *CCS* to illustrate ideas, definitions and applications.

The problem of a sensible generalization of the notion of bisimulation has been first tackled in [AW], where a lattice of simulation relations is defined, whose greatest element can be seen as a possible generalization of Park and Milner's notion of bisimulation in an algebraic framework; in [AGR1] a different generalization closer to the original definition is proposed; in [GR] it is shown that this generalization is indeed quite natural, and are given also sufficient conditions for the maximum observational relation to be a congruence and generate a model. Applications of the notion of generalized bisimulation to concurrency can be found in [AR] (where a family of parametric concurrent calculi integrating processes, functions and abstract data types is defined and its properties are studied) and in [AGR2] (where several examples of processes used as data types are given); while applications to the semantics of abstract data types can be found in [AGR1]. Our work, together with generalizing the Hennessy-Milner work (see [M2]) to general algebraic structures, is clearly much related to the work by De Nicola and Hennessy on testing equivalences (see [DH]), and the relationship will be partly clarified in the paper. We also feel that in the framework of observational structures it is possible to formalize and deal with the hierarchies of semantics for concurrent processes presented by Abramsky in [A]; this will be the subject of further work.

Arnold and Dicky [AD] and Ferrari and Montanari [FM] work in a similar direction to ours, aiming at a general framework for the semantics of concurrency. Their approaches are however different; they define classes of models (Φ-algebras in [AD], the $\mathcal{U}CCS$ category in [FM]) and of morphisms (quasi-saturating homomorhpisms in [AD], abstraction homomorphisms in [FM], a notion introduced in [C]) and get the notion of maximum observational equivalence via terminality. A deeper analysis of the relationship between our and their work would probably be of interest. Also, it is a research topic to be examined whether with each observational structure can be associated a category such that the observational equivalence (or, the maximum congruence contained in it) can be obtained via terminality; some preliminary investigations can be found in [GR].

In this paper we do not deal with the application of the theory of observational structures to algebraic specifications in general; for this we refer to a full paper which includes also the proofs of all the results (see [AGR3]).

1 Processes as Data Types

In this section we briefly show how processes can be formally described as data types in an algebraic style, adopting the view of *CCS* that processes are labelled transition systems; however this viewpoint is not essential to the following theory, where processes are just modelled by algebras. The examples, centered around *CCS*, will be used throughout the paper.

1.1 The algebraic framework

We briefly summarize our formal framework, which is that of *total algebras with predicates.* The basic definitions and results can be found in [GM]; here we repeat just the essential notions.

A *signature* Σ consists of a set of *sorts* (S), a family of *operation symbols* ($F = \{F_{\omega,s}\}_{\omega \in S^*, s \in S}$) and a family of *predicate symbols* ($P = \{P_\omega\}_{\omega \in S^*}$); moreover we indicate by

- $f: s_1 \times \cdots \times s_n \to s$ the fact that $f \in F_{s_1 \ldots s_n, s}$;
- $p: s_1 \times \cdots \times s_n$ the fact that $p \in P_{s_1 \ldots s_n}$;
- $T_\Sigma(X)$ the *term algebra* on Σ and the S-sorted family of variables $X = \{X_s\}_{s \in S}$ and we write $t: s$ for $t \in (T_\Sigma(X))_s$;
- $\mathcal{FOF}_\Sigma(X)$ the set of the *first order formulas* (with possibly infinitary conjunctions) on Σ and X; if $\phi \in \mathcal{FOF}_\Sigma(X)$, then $fv(\phi)$ denotes the set of the *free variables* of ϕ.

A Σ-*algebra* A is a triple $(\{A_s\}_{s \in S}, \{f^A\}_{f \in F}, \{p^A\}_{p \in P})$ such that for all $s \in S$, A_s is a set, for all $f: s_1 \times \cdots \times s_n \to s$, $f^A: A_{s_1} \times \cdots \times A_{s_n} \to A_s$ is a total function and for all $p: s_1 \times \cdots \times s_n$, $p^A \subseteq A_{s_1} \times \cdots \times A_{s_n}$. If $\phi \in \mathcal{FOF}_\Sigma(X)$ and A is a Σ-algebra, we indicate as usual $A \models \phi$ the fact that ϕ holds in A.

A Σ-algebra is said *term generated* iff each element of a carrier is the interpretation of a ground term.

1.2 Some Examples

Here we give some examples adopting the well-known and accepted technique of viewing a process as a labelled transition system (see [M1]). A *labelled transition system* is a triple $TS = (S, L, \longrightarrow)$ where S is a set of *states*, L is a set of *labels* (or *flags*) and $\longrightarrow \subseteq S \times L \times S$ is the *transition relation*; as usual we write $s \xrightarrow{l} s'$ for $(s, l, s') \in \longrightarrow$.

Labelled transition systems can be seen as algebras on a signature having the sorts *state*, *label* and a predicate $\longrightarrow$: *state* $\times$ *label* $\times$ *state*; we call them *algebraic transition systems* (shortly, *ats*).

As a first example we rephrase the well-known (finite) *CCS* calculus of [M1] as an ats.

Example *CCS*0: **Finite** *CCS*
The signature of *CCS*0 is the following, where we use the "–"-notation for defining mixfix operations:

$$
\begin{array}{l}
\textbf{sig } \Sigma_{CCS0} = \\
\quad \textbf{sorts } be, act \\
\quad \textbf{opns} \\
\qquad \text{nil}: \to be \\
\qquad - \cdot -: act \times be \to be \\
\qquad - + -: be \times be \to be \\
\qquad - \mid -: be \times be \to be \\
\qquad \{a: \to act \mid a \in ACT\} \\
\qquad \overline{-}: act \to act \\
\quad \textbf{preds} \\
\qquad - \xrightarrow{-} -: be \times act \times be
\end{array}
$$

where ACT is a set of operation symbols for actions such that $\tau \in ACT$.

The "usual" operational model for *CCS*0 is just the *term-generated algebra* over the signature Σ_{CCS0} such that all and only the identifications which can be inferred from the equalities $\overline{\overline{a}} = a$ for all a: *act*, and $\overline{\tau} = \tau$ hold, and such that the interpretation of the predicate $\longrightarrow$ is given by the following inductive rules (where a: *act* and b, b', b'', b_1, b'_1: *be*):

$$a \cdot b \xrightarrow{a} b$$

$$\frac{b \xrightarrow{a} b'}{b + b'' \xrightarrow{a} b'} \qquad \frac{b \xrightarrow{a} b'}{b'' + b \xrightarrow{a} b'}$$

$$\frac{b \xrightarrow{a} b'}{b|b'' \xrightarrow{a} b'|b''} \qquad \frac{b \xrightarrow{a} b'}{b''|b \xrightarrow{a} b''|b'}$$

$$\frac{b \xrightarrow{a} b_1 \quad b' \xrightarrow{\bar{a}} b'_1}{b|b' \xrightarrow{\tau} b_1|b'_1} \qquad \text{for } \alpha \neq \tau.$$

In the sequel we indicate this model simply by *CCS*0. **End of Example**

Thus in an ats processes are just a data type and so it is possible to formally describe systems where processere are exchanged as values, where there are functions taking as parameters and/or returning (values containing) processes and so on (see [AGR2]); as an example we give a simple variation of *CCS*.

Example CCS^+: **a Higher Order** *CCS*
We extend *CCS*0 by allowing handshaking communication with exchange of behaviours (see [AR,T]); formally we add to the signature of *CCS*0 an operation *SEND*: *be* $\to$ *act*; a behaviour b can hence perform a *SEND*(b') action, where b' is another behaviour, and the intuitive meaning is that b' is being sent as a value which can be received by some other process performing a corresponding $\overline{SEND(b')}$ action. **End of Example**

In this framework it is also possible to handle *concurrent systems*, i.e., a particular kind of transition systems in which a state has an internal structure built starting from another transitition system representing the (basic) active components of the state. As an example, here we build a concurrent system whose basic components are just $CCS0$ behaviours.

Example net-CCS: A net of CCS Behaviours
We add to the signature Σ_{CCS0}:

- a new sort *net*, whose elements model nets of $CCS0$ behaviours (inductively defined as a single behaviour or a parallel composition $n_1||n_2$ of two networks) and whose activities proceed in a free parallel way, except when restricted by the "/" operation;
- a new sort *lab*, whose elements are used to label the network transitions; network labels can be composed in parallel, and we assume to this end a binary operation on labels "$*$";
- a new transition relation $\Longrightarrow : net \times lab \times net$ on nets.

"net-CCS" is just the term-generated algebra over the enriched signature such that:

- all and only identifications on the new elements are due to the fact that: "$||$" and "$*$" are commutative and associative, τ is an identity for "$*$" and $\overline{a}$ is the inverse of a w.r.t. "$*$";
- the interpretation of the predicate $\Longrightarrow$ is given by means of the following inductive rules:

$$\frac{b \xrightarrow{a} b'}{b \overset{a}{\Longrightarrow} b'}$$

$$\frac{n_1 \overset{l}{\Longrightarrow} n_1'}{n_1||n_2 \overset{l}{\Longrightarrow} n_1'||n_2} \qquad \frac{n_2 \overset{l}{\Longrightarrow} n_2'}{n_1||n_2 \overset{l}{\Longrightarrow} n_1||n_2'}$$

$$\frac{n_1 \overset{l_1}{\Longrightarrow} n_1' \quad n_2 \overset{l_2}{\Longrightarrow} n_2'}{n_1||n_2 \overset{l_1 * l_2}{\Longrightarrow} n_1'||n_2'} \qquad \frac{n \overset{l}{\Longrightarrow} n'}{n/l' \overset{l}{\Longrightarrow} n'/l'} \quad l \neq l'.$$

End of Example

2 Observational Structures

In sections 2.1 and 2.2 we motivate the formal definitions given in section 2.3 by means of the examples of section 1.

2.1 Similarity of experiments

Strong Bisimulation for $CCS0$ Consider the ats $CCS0$ given in section 1.2 formally defining CCS.

It is well-known that the above model is not satisfactory as a semantic model for CCS, since it distinguishes too much (for example, $b' + b''$ is different from $b'' + b'$); in this sense one is looking for better semantics for $CCS0$.

In general a semantics of an algebra A is given by means of a congruence on A; a congruence can be seen as an *A-family* satisfying additional constraints, where an *A-family* is couple $(\{R_s\}_{s\in S}, \{R_p\}_{p\in P})$, such that for all $s \in S$, $R_s \subseteq A_s^2$ and for all $p: s_1 \times \cdots \times s_n \in P$, $R_p \subseteq A_{s_1} \times \cdots \times A_{s_n}$. In particular, if R is a congruence on A, then A/R is the algebra modelling the semantics given by R (the *semantic model*).

Hence, in this framework, a semantics for $CCS0$ is a couple $R = ((R_{act}, R_{be}), R_{\longrightarrow})$, where R_{act} and R_{be} are binary relations on $CCS0_{act}$ and $CCS0_{be}$ respectively, and $R_{\longrightarrow} \subseteq\ \longrightarrow^{CCS0}$.

The *strong bisimulation* semantics corresponds to the idea that two $CCS0$ behaviours should be identified if and only if they behave in the same way if we can only observe the actions which label their transitions. As it is well known this semantics is given taking the quotient $CCS0/\sim$, where $\sim$ is the so-called *maximum strong bisimulation relation*.

A $CCS0$-family R is a *(strong) bisimulation relation* (see [P,M1]) iff

i) $b'\ R_{be}\ b''$ implies

- for all a: act, b'_1: be, if $b' \xrightarrow{a} b'_1$ then there exists b''_1: be s.t. $b'' \xrightarrow{a} b''_1$ and $b'_1\ R_{be}\ b''_1$;
- for all a: act, b''_1: be, if $b'' \xrightarrow{a} b''_1$ then there exists b'_1: be s.t. $b' \xrightarrow{a} b'_1$ and $b'_1\ R_{be}\ b''_1$;

ii) R_{act} is the identity relation;

iii) $R_{\longrightarrow} \subseteq\ \longrightarrow^{CCS0}$.

The *maximum strong bisimulation* $\sim$ does exist and is the union of all the strong bisimulations.

Now let us call $x \xrightarrow{a} b$, where x is a variable, an *experiment* for $CCS0$, for every a: act and every b: be; note that $x \xrightarrow{a} b$ is a first order formula, since $\longrightarrow$ is a predicate symbol. Then we can rephrase the definition of bisimulation replacing clause i) with the following:

i) $b'\ R_{be}\ b''$ implies

- for all experiments e' if b' *passes* e', then there exists a *similar* experiment e'', such that b'' *passes* e''
- for all experiments e'' if b'' *passes* e'', then there exists a *similar* experiment e', such that b' *passes* e'.

Clearly, if $e = x \xrightarrow{a} b$, "b' *passes* e" can be formally stated as "$e[b']$ holds in $CCS0$", where $e[b'] = e[b'/x] = b' \xrightarrow{a} b$, since $b' \xrightarrow{a} b$ is a first order formula. In this case we define $x \xrightarrow{a} b'$ to be *similar* to all and only the experiments of the form $x \xrightarrow{a} b''$ with

$b' \; R \; b''$. Notice that the similarity relation between experiments depends on R; hence we introduce a function $\mathcal{C}$, that we call *similarity law*, associating with each R a binary relation $\mathcal{C}(R)$ on experiments; in this case $\mathcal{C}$ is defined by: $x \xrightarrow{a} b' \; \mathcal{C}(R) \; x \xrightarrow{a} b''$ iff $b' \; R \; b''$.

Weak Bisimulation If we decide that some actions, let us say τ actions, should not be observable, then we need a semantic equivalence which is less fine than strong bisimulation, since two behaviours whose activity differ only in the nonobservable actions performed should be made equivalent. This is achieved by defining the well-known *weak bisimulation*, which is obtained by introducing a new predicate $\Longrightarrow: be \times act \times be$ defined by the following inductive rules:

$$\frac{}{b \stackrel{\tau}{\Longrightarrow} b} \qquad \frac{b \xrightarrow{\tau} b' \quad b' \stackrel{a}{\Longrightarrow} b''}{b \stackrel{a}{\Longrightarrow} b''} \qquad \frac{b \stackrel{a}{\Longrightarrow} b' \quad b' \xrightarrow{\tau} b''}{b \stackrel{a}{\Longrightarrow} b''}.$$

This predicate introduces a different kind of experiments having form $x \stackrel{a}{\Longrightarrow} b$. Weak bisimulation is defined using the same definition schema of strong bisimulation by just changing the set of experiments and by using a similiarity relation analogous to the one used for strong bisimulation.

Divergence Sensitive Weak Bisimulation Let us extend $CCS0$ to include also some infinite behaviours (for example, either by means of a fixpoint combinator, or directly by means of recursive equations, as $\tau^\omega = \tau \cdot \tau^\omega$). It is well-known that weak bisimulation does not distinguish properly between terminating and nonterminating behaviours (for example, τ^ω is weakly equivalent to **nil**); to get a finer semantic equivalence we introduce a new kind of experiment, *Stop*, defined by the following infinitary first order formula:

$$Stop = \not\exists \{b_i, a_i\}_{i \in \omega}.(b_0 = x) \wedge (\bigwedge_{i \in \omega} b_i \xrightarrow{a_i} b_{i+1}) \quad .$$

where the b_i's and a_i's are variables of sort *be* and *act* respectively. *Stop* succeeds on all and only the terminating behaviours. To be equivalent we require now that not only two behaviours have to exhibit the same visible actions, but they also have to agree w.r.t. termination. The definition schema of bisimulation rephrased using the concept of experiment handles already this case by taking as experiments $\{x \xrightarrow{a} b \mid a: act, b: be\} \cup \{Stop\}$ (and clearly *Stop* is only similar to itself), since clause i) is quantified on all experiments; the maximum bisimulation relation exists and identifies in this case all behaviours which behave similarly w.r.t. all of these experiments.

Observing Multilevel Parallelism It is useful to slightly generalize the definition schema by allowing several observed sorts, to be able to handle, for example, "net-CCS" (see section 1.2). In this case both the arrows $\rightarrow$ and $\Rightarrow$, representing the transitions of behaviours and of nets, can be used to build experiments for observing behaviours and nets, hence we have experiments of the form $x_{be} \xrightarrow{a} b$ and of the form $x_{net} \stackrel{l}{\Longrightarrow} n$; we want that the semantic identifications are made on behaviours and on nets accordingly to these experiments. It is easy to extend the definition of bisimulation by quantifying clause i) over all observed sorts. Let $O = \{be, net\}$ be the set of *observed sorts*,

$$Exp = \{x_{be} \xrightarrow{a} b, x_{net} \xRightarrow{l} n \mid a\colon act, b\colon be, l\colon lab, n\colon net\}$$

the set of *experiments*, and for all R let $\mathcal{C}(R)$ be the following similarity relation:

$$x_{be} \xrightarrow{a} b' \; \mathcal{C}(R) \; x_{be} \xrightarrow{a} b'' \quad \text{iff} \quad b' \; R_{be} \; b''$$

and

$$x_{net} \xRightarrow{l} n' \; \mathcal{C}(R) \; x_{net} \xRightarrow{l} n'' \quad \text{iff} \quad n' \; R_{net} \; n''.$$

A net-*CCS*-family is a *multilevel bisimulation* iff

i) for all $o \in O$, $t' \; R_o \; t''$ implies for all $e' \in Exp$ with free variable of sort o

- if $e'[t']$ holds, then there exists $e'' \in Exp$ such that $e''[t'']$ holds and $e' \; \mathcal{C}(R) \; e''$;
- if $e'[t'']$ holds, then there exists $e'' \in Exp$ such that $e''[t']$ holds and $e'' \; \mathcal{C}(R) \; e'$;

ii) for all $s \notin O$ R_s is the identity relation;

iii) for all $p \in P$, $R_p \subseteq p^A$.

Since $\mathcal{C}$ is monotonic, then there exists the maximum multilevel bisimulation, which is also the maximum fixed point of an appropriate function.

2.2 Propagating Identities

In the examples introduced in the previous section, the semantics of the objects of the nonobserved sorts *act* and *lab* is fixed: the semantic identifications made on behaviours (and on nets) do not introduce new identifications on actions and labels. Clearly, this is not always the case, and we explain this point by considering the case of CCS^+ (see section 1.2).

In this case we want that, given b' and b'', if b' is semantically equivalent to b'' then also the action $SEND(b')$ should be semantically equivalent to $SEND(b'')$. The propagation of the semantic identifications to other sorts is represented by means of a *propagation function* $\mathcal{P}$, for all $s \in S$, $\mathcal{P}(R)_s$ is the propagation of R to the elements of sort s (we require $\mathcal{P}(R)_o = R_o$ for all $o \in O$). In this case we have that given R, if $b' \; R \; b''$, then $SEND(b') \; \mathcal{P}(R) \; SEND(b'')$, so the propagation law $\mathcal{P}$ is defined for all R as follows:

$$\begin{aligned} \mathcal{P}(R)_{act} &= \{(a,a), (\overline{a},\overline{a}) \mid a \in ACT\} \cup \\ &\quad \{(SEND(b'), SEND(b'')), (\overline{SEND(b')}, \overline{SEND(b'')}) \mid b' \; R_{be} \; b''\}. \end{aligned}$$

To complete the example, we have to define the similarity relation between experiments: it seems reasonable to consider a generic experiment $x \xrightarrow{a} b$ to be equivalent to all the experiments of the form $x \xrightarrow{a'} b'$ with $a\ \mathcal{P}(R)\ a'$ and $b\ R\ b'$. In particular if $a = SEND(b_1)$, then

$$x \stackrel{SEND(b_1)}{\longrightarrow} b \quad \text{is similar to} \quad x \stackrel{SEND(b_2)}{\longrightarrow} b'$$

for all $b\ R\ b'$, $b_1\ R\ b_2$. Hence the similarity law $\mathcal{C}$ can be defined in this case in terms of $\mathcal{P}$ as follows: for all R

$$x \xrightarrow{a} b\ \mathcal{C}(R)\ x \xrightarrow{a'} b'$$

for all a, a', b, b' such that $a\ \mathcal{P}(R)\ a'$, $b\ R\ b'$.

2.3 Observational Structures and their Semantics

The discussions, definitions and examples of the previous sections are collected in the notion of *observational structure* and of *(maximum) observational relation*, which are a general framework for observational semantics which is not only restricted to concurrency (see [AGR1]), even though all the applications shown in this paper are to concurrency.

In this section A denotes a Σ-algebra on a signature $\Sigma = (S, F, P)$, and $O \subseteq S$ denotes the set of the observed sorts. A semantics on A is represented by an *A-family* which is defined as follows.

Def. 2.1 *For $S' \subseteq S$, an (A, S')-*family *is an S'-indexed family $R = \{R_s\}_{s \in S'}$ s.t. for all $s \in S'$ $R_s \subseteq A_s^2$.*

A couple $(R_S, \{R_p\}_{p \in P})$, where R_S is an (A, S)-family and $R_p \subseteq A_{s_1} \times \cdots \times A_{s_n}$ for all $p: s_1 \times \cdots \times s_n \in P$, is called A-family.

If R is an A-family and $S' \subseteq S$, then $R|_{S'}$ indicates the (A, S')-family $\{R_s\}_{s \in S'}$.

A family R is reflexive *iff for all s R_s is reflexive; similarly for* symmetric, transitive *and* an equivalence. □

Def. 2.2 *The set of* experiments *in Σ on O, indicated with $\mathbf{Exp}(\Sigma, O)$, is defined as follows:*

$$\mathbf{Exp}(\Sigma, O) = \{\phi \in \mathcal{FOF}_\Sigma(X) \mid card(fv(\phi)) = 1 \wedge fv(\phi) \subseteq \bigcup_{o \in O} \{x_o\}\}.$$

If $fv(e) = \{x_o\}$ we write $e: o$. □

Given an experiment $e \in \mathbf{Exp}(\Sigma, O)$ such that $e: o$, an element $a \in A_o$ and a valuation v s.t. $v(x_o) = a$, we write $A \models e[a]$ to indicate that e holds in A under the valuation v. Usually we do not insist in specifying the sort of an experiment whenever this is clear from the context.

Def. 2.3 (Similarity Laws)
S-law(A, O) *indicates the set of all monotonic functions from A-families into the set of binary relations on $\mathbf{Exp}(\Sigma, O)$ respecting the sorts of the experiments.* □

Def. 2.4 (Propagation Laws)
P-law(A, O) *indicates the set of all monotonic functions* $\mathcal{P}$ *from* (A, O)*-families into* A*-families s.t.* $\mathcal{P}(R)_o = R_o$ *for all* $o \in O$. □

The fact that similarity and propagation laws are monotonic is needed to prove prop. 2.8.
In section 3.4 we use the notation $\mathcal{P}_A$ to indicate the propagation law s.t.:

- $\mathcal{P}_A(R)_s = \{(a, a) \mid a \in A_s\}$ for all $s \in S - O$;
- $\mathcal{P}_A(R)_p = p^A$ for all $p \in P$.

Def. 2.5 (Observational Structures)
An observational structure *is a 6-uple* $(\Sigma, A, O, Exp, \mathcal{C}, \mathcal{P})$ *where*

- $\Sigma = (S, F, P)$ *is a signature;*
- A *is a* Σ*-algebra (the structure on which we want to define a semantics);*
- $O \subseteq S$ *is a set of sorts (*observed sorts, *the sorts of the objects on which we perform some experiments);*
- $Exp \subseteq \mathbf{Exp}(\Sigma, O)$*;*
- $\mathcal{C} \in$ **S-law**(A, O)*;*
- $\mathcal{P} \in$ **P-law**(A, O). □

In the following we use OS to indicate a generic observational structure $(\Sigma, A, O, Exp, \mathcal{C}, \mathcal{P})$.

Def. 2.6 *An* A*-family* R *is an* observational relation *for* OS *(shortly, an* o-relation*) iff*

i) $\forall o \in O, \forall a', a'' \in A_o\ a'\ R_o\ a''$ *implies*
  $*$ $\forall e' \in Exp$, $A \models e'[a']$ *implies* $\exists e'' \in Exp$ *s.t.* $e'\ \mathcal{C}(R)\ e''$ *and* $A \models e''[a'']$;
  $**$ $\forall e'' \in Exp$, $A \models e''[a'']$ *implies* $\exists e' \in Exp$ *s.t.* $e'\ \mathcal{C}(R)\ e''$ *and* $A \models e'[a']$;

ii) $\forall s \in S - O$, $R_s \subseteq \mathcal{P}(R\mid_O)_s$;

iii) $\forall p \in P$, $R_p \subseteq \mathcal{P}(R\mid_O)_p$. □

As for the case of strong bisimulation, for each OS there is a monotonic function $\mathcal{F}_{OS}$ on A-families, which can be used to characterize the observational relations and whose maximum fixed point (which does always exist) is the maximum observational relation.

Def. 2.7 *For all* A*-families* R,

$$\mathcal{F}_{OS}(R) = \mathcal{P}(\{\{(a', a'') \mid a', a'' \in A_o,\ * \text{ and } ** \text{ hold}\}\}_{o \in O}).$$ □

Prop. 2.8 *The following facts hold:*

1. *an* A*-family* R *is an o-relation iff* $R \subseteq \mathcal{F}_{OS}(R)$*;*
2. $\mathcal{F}_{OS}$ *is monotonic over the complete lattice of* A*-families, ordered by inclusion;*

3. *the (arbitrary) union of o-relations is an o-relation;*

4. $\sim_{OS} =_{\text{def}} \bigcup\{R | R \subseteq \mathcal{F}_{OS}(R)\}$ *is an o-relation and* $\sim_{OS} = \text{maxfix}\, \mathcal{F}_{OS}$. □

Sometimes we indicate $\sim_{OS}$ simply by $\sim$ and call it *the maximum* o-relation of OS.

Notice that $a' \sim a''$ iff there exists an o-relation R s.t. $a'\ R\ a''$; moreover $(a_1, \ldots, a_n) \in \sim_p$ iff there exists an o-relation R s.t $(a_1, \ldots, a_n) \in R_p$.

In general we cannot ensure the maximum o-relation to be either reflexive, or transitive, or symmetric; to this end additional requirements on $\mathcal{P}$ and $\mathcal{C}$ can be made; we show just an example.

Prop. 2.9 *If for all A-families R ve have that* $\mathcal{C}(R^*) = \mathcal{C}(R)^*$ *and if for all equivalences R we have that* $\mathcal{P}(R)$ *is an equivalence, then* $\sim$ *is an equivalence, where* R^* *indicates the smallest equivalence containing R.* □

If $\mathcal{C}$ and $\mathcal{P}$ are as in prop. 2.9, then we say that $\mathcal{C}$ *reflects equivalences* and $\mathcal{P}$ *propagates equivalences.*

Even when $\sim$ is an equivalence, it may be that it is not a congruence (for example, the case of weak bisimulation). Sufficient conditions ensuring $\sim$ to be a congruence can be found for the case of transition systems in [GV] and for the algebraic case in [GR].

In the cases when $\sim$ is not a congruence, one can also proceed in a similar way to what has been done by Milner in [M2] for the case of weak bisimulation, and take the greatest congruence contained in $\sim$; in our framework this corresponds to replacing each experiment $e{:}\ o$ by the set of experiments $e[c[x_{o'}]]$ for all contexts $c[x_{o'}]{:}\ o$, for all $o' \in O$.

Example The observational structure implicitely used in section 1.2 to define strong bisimulation semantics for $CCS0$ is

$$(CCS0, be, \{x \xrightarrow{a} b \mid a{:}\ act, b{:}\ be\}, \mathcal{C}_{CCS0}, \mathcal{P}_{CCS0})$$

where $x \xrightarrow{a} b'\ \mathcal{C}_{CCS0}(R)\ x \xrightarrow{a} b''$ iff $b'\ R\ b''$.

End of Example

2.3.1 Testing Structures

Testing structures are a very simple but important class of observational structures used in section 3 to state and prove the generalized version of Hennessy-Milner theorem. They generalize the framework of testing semantics for processes introduced in [DH] and are essentially observational structures where two experiments are similar iff they are the same experiment.

Def. 2.10 *A testing structure is an observational structure* $(\Sigma, A, O, Exp, \mathcal{ID}, \mathcal{P})$, *where* $\mathcal{ID}$ *is the similarity law defined by* $\mathcal{ID}(R) = \{(e', e'') \mid e', e'' \in Exp$ *logically equivalent*$\}$, *for all R.* □

2.4 A Hierarchy of Approximations

We build a class of A-families $(\cong_\lambda)_{\lambda\in\mathcal{O}}$ (where $\mathcal{O}$ is the class of the ordinals) approximating the maximum o-relation $\sim$. We assume in this section that $\mathcal{C}$ reflects equivalences and $\mathcal{P}$ propagates equivalences. This characterization is used in section 3.

Def. 2.11 *The class* $(\cong_\lambda)_{\lambda\in\mathcal{O}}$ *is defined as follows:*

- $\cong_0 = \mathcal{P}(\{A_o^2\}_{o\in O})$;
- $\cong_{\lambda+1} = \mathcal{F}_{OS}(\cong_\lambda)$ *($\mathcal{F}_{OS}$ is defined in def. 2.7);*
- *if λ is a limit ordinal, then* $\cong_\lambda = \bigcap_{\lambda'<\lambda} \cong_{\lambda'}$.

Finally, $\cong = \bigcap_{\lambda\in\mathcal{O}} \cong_\lambda$. □

Prop. 2.12 *For all ordinal numbers λ, μ:*

1. $\mu < \lambda$ *implies* $\cong_\lambda \subseteq \cong_\mu$;
2. $\cong_\lambda$ *is an equivalence;*
3. $\sim \subseteq \cong_\lambda$;
4. *if* $card(\lambda) > card(A_s)$ *for all* $s \in S$, *then* $\cong_\lambda = \cong$;
5. $\cong = \sim$. □

This proposition implies that in case of carriers of denumerable cardinality the maximum fixed point of $\mathcal{F}$ can be obtained by iterating $\mathcal{F}$ up to the first ordinal whose cardinality is greater than that of ω. In general, as it is well-known, $\cong_\omega$ is *not* a fixed point for $\mathcal{F}_{OS}$. In particular cases however it is sufficient to stop to ω (for transition systems, this class generalizes the class of *finitely branching* transition systems of [M2] (see [AGR3]).

3 Observational Logic and its Properties

In this section we first show how we can define an observational modal logic corresponding to the Hennessy-Milner logic (the basic ideas are in section 3.1; the formal definitions are in section 3.2). Then we introduce in section 3.3 the notion of representability of an observational structure and state the generalized Hennessy-Milner theorem with an application to give observational logics for distributed and branching bisimulations. All the proofs can be found in [AGR3].

3.1 From Experiments to Observational Logic Formulas

We recall the definition of the Hennessy-Milner logic for *CCS* (see [HM] and also [M2]). The set of formulas of the logic $\mathcal{HM}(CCS)$ is inductively defined as follows:

- $\langle a \rangle\phi \in \mathcal{HM}(CCS)$ for all a: *act*, $\phi \in \mathcal{HM}(CCS)$;

- $\neg\phi \in \mathcal{HM}(CCS)$ for all $\phi \in \mathcal{HM}(CCS)$;
- $\bigwedge\Phi \in \mathcal{HM}(CCS)$ for all $\Phi \subseteq \mathcal{HM}(CCS)$;

where, if Φ is a set of formulas, $\bigwedge\Phi$ is the infinitary conjunction of all the formulas in Φ, i.e., $\bigwedge_{\phi\in\Phi}\phi$. Notice that $\bigwedge\emptyset$ corresponds to *true*. The satisfaction relation $\models\subseteq CCS_{be} \times \mathcal{HM}(CCS)$ is so defined:

- $b \models \langle a\rangle\phi$ iff there exists b' such that $b \xrightarrow{a} b'$ and $b' \models \phi$;
- $b \models \neg\phi$ iff $b \not\models \phi$;
- $b \models \bigwedge\Phi$ iff $b \models \phi$ for all $\phi \in \Phi$.

A theorem due to Hennessy and Milner states that $b' \sim b''$ iff for all $\phi \in \mathcal{HM}(CCS)$, $b' \models \phi$ iff $b'' \models \phi$ (recall that $\sim$ is the maximum strong bisimulation).

It is easy to translate all modal formulas of $\mathcal{HM}(CCS)$ into (semantically) equivalent first-order formulas; for example, the formula $\langle a\rangle\phi$ becomes the first-order formula $\exists y.x \xrightarrow{a} y \wedge \phi^*(y)$ (where ϕ^* is the translation of ϕ). This translation enlightens the relationship between formulas and experiments: the formula $x \xrightarrow{a} y$ appearing in the translation can be thought as a *pattern* for generating experiments, since for all behaviours b we have that $x \xrightarrow{a} b$ is an experiment. For an experiment $e = x \xrightarrow{a} b$ let us indicate by $e^*[x,y] = x \xrightarrow{a} y$ the corresponding pattern; the formula $\langle a\rangle\phi$ is then equivalent to $\exists y.e^*[x,y] \wedge \phi^*(y)$. Patterns arise naturally in the definition of the similarity relation between experiments for $CCS0$, where given two experiments $e_1[x]$ and $e_2[x]$ we have that $e_1[x]\ \mathcal{C}(R)\ e_2[x]$ iff $e_1[x] = e_1^*[x,b_1]$, $e_2[x] = e_2^*[x,b_2]$, $b_1\ R\ b_2$ and $e_1^*[x,b_1]$ is logically equivalent to $e_2^*[x,b_2]$ in $CCS0$. In what follows, for $\phi, \psi \in \mathcal{FOF}_\Sigma(X)$, we write $\phi = \psi$ meaning 'ϕ and ψ are logically equivalent'.

In the case of $CCS0$ the set of patterns $\{x \xrightarrow{a} y \mid a\colon act\}$ completely determines the value of $\mathcal{C}$ on all R; we say that $\mathcal{C}$ is *representable* whenever this happens. In order to fully appreciate immediately the central role of representability, it is convenient to anticipate the main result of this section: *whenever in an observational structure $\mathcal{C}$ is representable by a set of patterns $\mathcal{H}$, a Hennessy-Milner theorem holds for a generalized logic generated by $\mathcal{H}$.*

In this case, besides negation and conjunction, a set of patterns $\mathcal{H}$ introduces the set of modal formulas $\langle e^*\rangle\ \phi_1 \cdots \phi_{n_{e^*}}$ for all $e^* \in \mathcal{H}$.

A further example may clarify this point. Consider the calculus CCS^+ (the $CCS0$ calculus where behaviours can be exchanged as values via handshaking communication). In CCS^+ an experiment of the form $e[x] = x \xrightarrow{SEND(b)} b'$ should be seen as instantiation of the pattern $e^*[x,y_1,y_2] = x \xrightarrow{SEND(y_1)} y_2$: the introduction of the extra variable y_1 is needed if we want $\mathcal{C}$ to be representable in the sense now discussed; indeed two experiments $e_1[x] = x \xrightarrow{SEND(b_1)} b_1'$ and $e_2[x] = x \xrightarrow{SEND(b_2)} b_2'$ are similar iff $e_1[x] = e_1^*[x,b_1,b_1']$, $e_2[x] = e_2^*[x,b_2,b_2']$, $e_1^*[x,y_1,y_2] = e_2^*[x,y_1,y_2]$ and $b_1\ R\ b_2$, $b_1'\ R\ b_2'$.

We extend now the logic to include experiments like these ones; starting from patterns we build first-order formulas of the form

$$\exists y_1, \ldots, y_n . e^*[x, y_1, \ldots, y_n] \wedge \phi_1(y_1) \wedge \cdots \wedge \phi_n(y_n)$$

or, using a modal style,

$$\langle e \rangle \phi_1 \cdots \phi_n .$$

In the case of CCS^+ the patterns for experiments are the following:

$$x \xrightarrow{a} y_1 \quad \text{for all } a \text{ s.t. } a \in ACT \text{ or } \overline{a} \in ACT,$$

$$x \stackrel{SEND(y_1)}{\longrightarrow} y_2, \qquad x \stackrel{\overline{SEND(y_1)}}{\longrightarrow} y_2,$$

which generate respectively the modal formulas $\langle a \rangle \phi$, $\langle S \rangle \phi_1 \phi_2$ and $\langle \overline{S} \rangle \phi_1 \phi_2$.

The general notion which comes out from these examples is the following: for an observational structure OS, $\mathcal{C}$ is represented by a set of patterns of experiments $\mathcal{H}$ iff the following condition holds:

$e_1[x] \; \mathcal{C}(R) \; e_2[x]$ iff
$e_1[x] = e_1^*[x, t'_1, \ldots, t'_n]$, $e_2[x] = e_2^*[x, t''_1, \ldots, t''_n]$, $e_1^*[x, y_1, \ldots, y_n] = e_2^*[x, y_1, \ldots, y_n]$ in OS and for $i = 1, \ldots, n \quad t'_i \; R \; t''_i$.

This notion of representability of $\mathcal{C}$ can be slightly generalized.

As it is defined above, an experiment e is similar modulo R to all and only the experiments obtained by instantiating its pattern e^* on R-equivalent observed objects. In general, it can be that $\mathcal{C}$ puts in relation experiments which do not correspond to R-equivalent instances of the same "pattern"; we can generalize the definition of representability to "sets of patterns" as follows: if $\mathcal{H}$ is a family of sets of patterns (i.e., each $H \in \mathcal{H}$ is a set of patterns) we say that $\mathcal{H}$ *represents* $\mathcal{C}$ essentially if $e_1[x] \; R \; e_2[x]$ iff for some $H \in \mathcal{H}$ there are two patterns $e_1^*[x, y_1, \ldots, y_n]$, $e_1^*[x, y_1, \ldots, y_n] \in H$, such that $e_1[x] = e_1^*[x, t'_1, \ldots, t'_n]$, $e_2[x] = e_2^*[x, t''_1, \ldots, t''_n]$ and for $i = 1, \ldots, n$ we have that $t'_i \; R \; t''_i$ (i.e., e_1 and e_2 are R-equivalent instances of two patterns belonging to a same $H \in \mathcal{H}$).

While in the previous cases a representation $\mathcal{H}$ was just a set of patterns, now we replace each pattern e^* with a set of patterns H such that two patterns in H are similar whenever instantiated on R-equivalent objects. The simpler cases correspond thus to the case in which each H is a singleton.

In the following section we develop this idea into the technical details; we just point out that the introduction of a class of patterns has as effect in the definition of the corresponding logic of just replacing the formulas of the form

$$\exists y_1, \ldots, y_n . e^*[x, y_1, \ldots, y_n] \wedge \bigwedge_{i=1}^{n} \phi_i(y_i)$$

also written

$$\langle e \rangle \phi_1 \cdots \phi_n ,$$

with formulas of the form

$$\exists y_1, \ldots, y_n. \bigvee_{e^* \in H} e^*[x, y_1, \ldots, y_n] \wedge \bigwedge_{i=1}^{n} \phi_i(y_i)$$

also written

$$\langle H \rangle\, \phi_1 \cdots \phi_n.$$

The disjunction $\bigvee_{e^* \in H}$ models the fact that since all R-equivalent instances of the patterns in H are similar, we allow an instance of any of them to succeed.

3.2 Observational Logic

Def. 3.1 *A* pattern class *is a set* $\mathcal{H}$ *such that* $H \in \mathcal{H}$ *implies* $H \subseteq \mathcal{FOF}_\Sigma(X)$ *and for all* $\phi \in H$, $fv(\phi) \subseteq \{x, y_1, \ldots, y_{n_H}\}$. *If* $x{:}\,o$, *and* $x_i{:}\,o_i$ *then we say that* H *has* type $o_1 \times \cdots \times o_n \to o$. □

Def. 3.2 *The family* $\mathcal{H}^* = \{\mathcal{H}^*_o\}_{o \in O}$ *of* (typed) observational logic formulas w.r.t. a pattern class $\mathcal{H}$ *is inductively defined as follows:*

- $\exists y_1, \ldots, y_n. \bigvee_{e^* \in H} e^*[x, y_1, \ldots, y_n] \wedge \bigwedge_{j=1}^{n} \phi_j[y_j] \in \mathcal{H}^*_o$, *for all* $H \in \mathcal{H}$ *with type* $o_1 \times \ldots \times o_n \to o$, *for all* $\phi_j \in \mathcal{H}^*_{o_j}$, $j = 1, \ldots, n$;
- $\neg\phi \in \mathcal{H}^*_o$, *for all* $o \in O$, *for all* $\phi \in \mathcal{H}^*_o$;
- $\bigwedge \Phi \in \mathcal{H}^*_o$, *for all* $o \in O$, *for all* $\Phi \subseteq \mathcal{H}^*_o$. □

Clearly, for all $o \in O$, $\mathcal{H}^*_o \subseteq \mathbf{Exp}(\Sigma, O)$.

Equivalently, we may define the following set of formulas:

Def. 3.3 *The family* $\mathcal{OL}(\mathcal{H}) = \{\mathcal{OL}(\mathcal{H})_o\}_{o \in O}$ *of* modal (typed) observational logic formulas w.r.t. a pattern class $\mathcal{H}$ *is inductively defined as follows:*

- $\langle H \rangle\, \phi_1 \cdots \phi_n \in \mathcal{OL}(\mathcal{H})_o$, *for all* $H \in \mathcal{H}$ *with type* $o_1 \times \ldots \times o_n \to o$, *for all* $\phi_j \in \mathcal{OL}(\mathcal{H})_{o_j}$, $j = 1, \ldots, n$;
- $\neg\phi \in \mathcal{OL}(\mathcal{H})_o$, *for all* $o \in O$, *for all* $\phi \in \mathcal{OL}(\mathcal{H})_o$;
- $\bigwedge \Phi \in \mathcal{OL}(\mathcal{H})_o$, *for all* $o \in O$, *for all* $\Phi \subseteq \mathcal{OL}(\mathcal{H})_o$. □

Def. 3.4 *The* satisfaction relation $\models$ *is defined as follows: for all* $o \in O$, $a \in A_o$ *and* $\phi \in \mathcal{OL}(\mathcal{H})$

- $a \models \langle H \rangle\, \phi_1 \cdots \phi_n$ *iff there exist* $e \in H$, $a_1, \ldots, a_n$ *such that* $A \models e[a, a_1, \ldots, a_n]$ *and* $a_k \models \phi_k$ *for* $k = 1, \ldots, n$;
- $a \models \neg\phi$ *iff* $a \not\models \phi$;
- $a \models \bigwedge \Phi$ *iff* $a \models \phi$ *for all* $\phi \in \Phi$. □

From now on, we shall always omit the type information on the logic formulas.

Fact 3.5 $\mathcal{H}^*$ *and* $\mathcal{OL}(\mathcal{H})$ *are logically equivalent, i.e.:*

- *for all* $\phi \in \mathcal{H}^*$ *there exists* $\phi' \in \mathcal{OL}(\mathcal{H})$ *such that* ϕ *and* ϕ' *are equivalent (for all* a, $\phi[a]$ *holds iff* $a \models \phi'$*);*
- *viceversa.* □

3.3 A Generalized Hennessy-Milner Theorem

Def. 3.6 *Given an observational structure OS, a* representation *of $\mathcal{C}$ is a pattern class $\mathcal{H}$ such that:*

- *for all $e \in Exp$ there are a unique $H \in \mathcal{H}$ and a unique $\overline{e}[x, y_1, \ldots, y_n] \in H$ such that $e = \overline{e}[x, v_1, \ldots, v_n]$ for some $v_1, \ldots, v_n$;*
- *for all $e, e' \in Exp$, for all A-families R, $e\ \mathcal{C}(R)\ e'$ iff $\exists v_1, \ldots, v_n, v'_1, \ldots, v'_n$ s.t. $e = \overline{e}[x, v_1, \ldots, v_n]$, $e' = \overline{e'}[x, v'_1, \ldots, v'_n]$ and $v_i\ R\ v'_i$ for $i = 1, \ldots, n$, where $\overline{e}$ and $\overline{e'}$ are the patterns associated with e and e' by the above property.*

We say that $\mathcal{C}$ is representable *if such $\mathcal{H}$ exists.* □

We can now state the main result: for a given observational structure OS admitting a representation by means of a pattern class $\mathcal{H}$, the testing structure (see 2.3.1) $OS_{\mathcal{H}^*}$ having as experiments $\mathcal{H}^*$ (see definition 3.2) originates the same maximum o-relation as OS does.

Many observational structures have a representable $\mathcal{C}$; indeed, if $\mathcal{C}(\sim_{OS})$ is an equivalence relation, then $\mathcal{C}$ is representable by $\mathcal{H} = Exp\ /\mathcal{C}(\sim_{OS})$. Clearly, we are interested in the cases in which each $H \in \mathcal{H}$ is finite and the definition of $\mathcal{H}$ itself "does not depend on $\sim$"; notice that this is the case of all the examples given in the paper, and it is not the case for $\mathcal{H} = Exp\ /\mathcal{C}(\sim_{OS})$.

We use the characterization of the maximum observational relation as a limit of a (transfinite) sequence of approximations introduced in section 2.4. We define for each ordinal λ a testing structure $OS_{\mathcal{H}^\lambda}$ having as experiments the set $\mathcal{H}^\lambda$ of formulas in $\mathcal{H}^*$ having "depth" smaller than λ; then indicating by $\sim_{\mathcal{H}^\lambda}$ the maximum observational relation for $OS_{\mathcal{H}^\lambda}$, we show that for all $\lambda \in \mathcal{O}$, $\cong_\lambda = \sim_{\mathcal{H}^\lambda}$.

Since $\mathcal{H}^* = \cup_{\lambda \in \mathcal{O}} \mathcal{H}^\lambda$ we have clearly

$$\sim_{\mathcal{H}^*} = \bigcap_{\lambda \in \mathcal{O}} \sim_{\mathcal{H}^\lambda} = \bigcap_{\lambda \in \mathcal{O}} \cong_\lambda = \sim.$$

Since in a testing structure two experiments are similar iff they are logically equivalent, $\mathcal{H}^*$ is in that case the observational logic characterizing the maximum o-relation: two objects are equivalent iff they satisfy the same set (modulo logical equivalence) of formulas in $\mathcal{H}^*$ The formal statements follow.

Def. 3.7 *The* Depth *of the observational logic formulas is defined as follows:*

- $\mathrm{Depth}(\langle H \rangle\ \phi_1 \cdots \phi_n) = 1 + \sup_{i=1,\ldots,n} \mathrm{Depth}(\phi_i)$;
- $\mathrm{Depth}(\neg\phi) = \mathrm{Depth}(\phi)$;
- $\mathrm{Depth}(\bigwedge \Phi) = \sup\{\mathrm{Depth}(\phi) \mid \phi \in \Phi\}$. □

Def. 3.8 *For all ordinal numbers λ, $OS_{\mathcal{H}^\lambda}$ indicates the testing structure $(\Sigma, A, O, \mathcal{H}^\lambda, \mathcal{P})$, where $\mathcal{H}^\lambda = \{\phi \mid \phi \in \mathcal{H}^* \wedge \mathrm{Depth}(\phi) \le \lambda\}$ and $\sim_{\mathcal{H}^\lambda}$ its maximum o-relation. Moreover $OS_{\mathcal{H}^*}$ indicates the observational structure $(A, \Sigma, O, \mathcal{H}^*, \mathcal{P})$, and $\sim_{\mathcal{H}^*}$ its maximum o-relation.* □

Theorem 3.9 (Generalized Hennessy-Milner Theorem)
Let OS be an observational structure such that $\mathcal{C}$ is represented by $\mathcal{H}$. The the following facts hold:

i) for all ordinal numbers λ, $\cong_\lambda = \sim_{\mathcal{H}^\lambda}$, i.e., $a' \cong_\lambda a''$ iff for all $\phi \in \mathcal{H}^\lambda$ $\phi[a']$ holds iff $\phi[a'']$ holds;

ii) $\sim = \sim_{\mathcal{H}^*}$, i.e., $a' \sim a''$ iff for all $\phi \in \mathcal{H}^*$ $\phi[a']$ holds iff $\phi[a'']$ holds. □

3.4 Applications

Distributed Bisimulation for *CCS* We show the treatment of *distributed bisimulation* for a *CCS*-like language (see [CH]) using observational structures. We show that not only the basic definition is an instance of our schema, but also that we have a characterization of the maximum distributed bisimulation by a corresponding Hennessy-Milner logic.

We consider, as in [CH], a variation *dCCS* of *CCS*0 obtained by replacing the predicate $\longrightarrow$ by

$$- \overset{-}{\longrightarrow} < -, - >: be \times act \times be \times be$$

defined by the following inductive rules:

$$\frac{}{a \cdot b \overset{a}{\longrightarrow} < b, b >}$$

$$\frac{b \overset{a}{\longrightarrow} < b', b'' >}{b + b_1 \overset{a}{\longrightarrow} < b', b'' >} \qquad \frac{b \overset{a}{\longrightarrow} < b', b'' >}{b_1 + b \overset{a}{\longrightarrow} < b', b'' >}$$

$$\frac{b \overset{a}{\longrightarrow} < b', b'' >}{b|b_1 \overset{a}{\longrightarrow} < b', b''|b_1 >} \qquad \frac{b \overset{a}{\longrightarrow} < b', b'' >}{b_1|b \overset{a}{\longrightarrow} < b', b_1|b'' >}.$$

We refer to [CH] for a detailed discussion of how this predicate can be used to model distribution; here we just recall that $b \overset{a}{\longrightarrow} < b', b'' >$ models the fact that b can perform the action a and produce what are called *the local residual* b' and *the concurrent residual* b''.

Notice that *dCCS* does not model handshaking communication (it is possible to extend the definition of distributed bisimulation to handle communication but here for simplicity we omit its treatment; all the results shown in this section apply also in such cases).

The observational structure for *dCCS* is the following:

$$OS_{dCCS} = (\Sigma_{dCCS}, dCCS, \{be\}, Exp, \mathcal{C}, \mathcal{P}_{dCCS}),$$

where $Exp = \{x \overset{a}{\longrightarrow} < b', b'' > \mid a{:}\, act, b', b''{:}\, be\}$, and for all R and all $b' \; R \; b'_1$, $b'' \; R \; b'_2$

$$x \overset{a}{\longrightarrow} < b', b'' > \mathcal{C}(R) \; x \overset{a}{\longrightarrow} < b'_1, b'_2 >.$$

$\mathcal{C}$ is represented by $\mathcal{H} = \{H_a \mid a{:}\, act\}$, where $H_a = \{x \overset{a}{\longrightarrow} < y_1, y_2 >\}$. The modal formulas introduced by H_a are of the form $\langle a \rangle \phi_1 \phi_2$ and $b \models \langle a \rangle \phi_1 \phi_2$ iff for some b', b'' $x \overset{a}{\longrightarrow} < b', b'' >$ and $b' \models \phi_1$, $b'' \models \phi_2$. For example,

$$a' \cdot \mathbf{nil} \,|a'' \cdot \mathbf{nil} \not\sim a' \cdot a'' \cdot \mathbf{nil} + a'' \cdot a' \cdot \mathbf{nil}$$

since they are distinguished by the formula

$$\langle a \rangle (\langle a \rangle\ true\, true)(\langle a \rangle\ true\, true)$$

which the second behaviour satisfies, while the first does not.

Branching Bisimulation Let TS be an algebraic transition system with transition relation $- \xrightarrow{-} -: be \times act \times be$ and whose signature Σ contains an operation $\tau: \to act$ and a predicate $\Longrightarrow: be \times act \times be$. The interpretation of $\Longrightarrow$ in TS is defined by the following inductive rules

$$\frac{}{b \Longrightarrow b} \qquad \frac{b \xrightarrow{\tau} b' \quad b' \Longrightarrow b''}{b \Longrightarrow b''}.$$

We simply write $b \Longrightarrow b' \xrightarrow{a} b''$ for $b \Longrightarrow b' \wedge b' \xrightarrow{a} b''$.

The following definition is just the rephrasing in our notation of the original definition of branching bisimulation as given in [GW,DV].

Def. 3.10 *A TS-family R is a* branching bisimulation *if it is symmetric and satisfies the following property (called* transfer property*):*

- *if* $r\ R_{be}\ s$ *and* $r \xrightarrow{a} r'$, *then either* $a = \tau$ *and* $r'\ R_{be}\ s$, *or* $\exists s_1, s'$ *such that* $s \Longrightarrow s_1 \xrightarrow{a} s'$, $r\ R_{be}\ s_1$ *and* $b'\ R_{be}\ s'$.
- R_{act} *is the identity on* TS_{act}.
- $R_{\longrightarrow} \subseteq \longrightarrow^{TS}$;
- $R_{\Longrightarrow} \subseteq \Longrightarrow^{TS}$. □

Exactly the same notion can be obtained using the observational structure

$$BR = (\Sigma, TS, \{be\}, Exp, \mathcal{C}, \mathcal{P}_{TS}),$$

where

- $Exp = \{x = b, x = b \wedge x \xrightarrow{a} b', x \Longrightarrow b \xrightarrow{a} b', x \Longrightarrow b \wedge b = b' \mid a: act, b, b': be\}$;
- for all R, $\mathcal{C}(R)$ is the equivalence closure of the relation defined by:

$$\begin{aligned} x = b_1 \wedge x \xrightarrow{\tau} b_1' &\quad \mathcal{C}(R) \quad x = b_2' \quad \text{for } b_1'\ R\ b_2' \\ x = b_1 \wedge x \xrightarrow{a} b_1' &\quad \mathcal{C}(R) \quad x \Longrightarrow b_2 \xrightarrow{a} b_2' \quad \text{for } b_1\ R\ b_2,\ b_1'\ R\ b_2' \\ x \Longrightarrow b_1 \xrightarrow{\tau} b_1' &\quad \mathcal{C}(R) \quad x \Longrightarrow b_2' \wedge b_2 = b_2' \quad \text{for } b_1\ R\ b_2',\ b_1'\ R\ b_2'. \end{aligned}$$

Fact 3.11 *R is a branching bisimulation iff it is an o-relation for BR.* □

It is easily seen that a representation of $\mathcal{C}$ is $\mathcal{H} = \{H_a \mid a\colon act\}$ defined as follows:

$$\begin{aligned} H_\tau &= \{x = y_1 \wedge y_1 \xrightarrow{\tau} y_2, x = y_2, x \Longrightarrow y_1 \xrightarrow{\tau} y_2, x \Longrightarrow y_1 \wedge y_1 = y_2\}, \\ H_a &= \{x = y_1 \wedge y_1 \xrightarrow{a} y_2, x \Longrightarrow y_1 \xrightarrow{a} y_2\} \quad \text{for all } a \neq \tau. \end{aligned}$$

The observational logic formulas introduced by $\mathcal{H}$ are hence $\langle\tau\rangle\phi_1\phi_2$ and $\langle a\rangle\phi_1\phi_2$, for $a \neq \tau$. In particular we have that:

- $b \models \langle\tau\rangle\phi_1\phi_2$ iff either of the following holds:
  - $b \models \phi_1$ and there exists b' such that $b \xrightarrow{\tau} b'$ and $b' \models \phi_2$;
  - $b \models \phi_2$;
  - there exists b', b'' such that $b \Longrightarrow b' \xrightarrow{\tau} b''$ and $b' \models \phi_1$, $b'' \models \phi_2$;
  - there exists b' such that $b \Longrightarrow b'$ and $b' \models \phi_1 \wedge \phi_2$;
- $b \models \langle a\rangle\phi_1\phi_2$ for $a \neq \tau$ iff either of the following holds:
  - $b \models \phi_1$ and there exists b' such that $b \xrightarrow{a} b'$ and $b' \models \phi_2$;
  - there exists b', b'' such that $b \Longrightarrow b' \xrightarrow{a} b''$ and $b' \models \phi_1$, $b'' \models \phi_2$.

This observational modal logic provided by free by our approach is similar but quite less intuitive than the one originally given in [DV]; we think that the one of [DV] can be seen as an optimization of ours as it should be, since our logic is generated in a canonical way. The relationship between the two sets of formulas should be investigated.

References

[A] Abramsky S. "Observation Equivalence as a Testing Equivalence", JTCS 53, 1987[1].

[AD] Arnold A.; Dicky A. "An Algebraic Characterization of Transition Systems Equivalences", *Information and Computation*, Vol. 82, No. 2, August 1989, Academic Press.

[AGR1] Astesiano E.; Giovini A.; Reggio G. "Generalized Bisimulation in Relational Specifications", *STACS '88*, LNCS 294, 1988 [2].

[AGR2] Astesiano E.; Giovini A.; Reggio G. "Data in a Concurrent Environment", *Proc. of Concurrency '88*, LNCS 335, 1988.

[AGR3] Astesiano E.; Giovini A.; Reggio G. *Observational Structures and their Logic*, Internal Report, University of Genova, May 1990. Submitted for publication.

[1] Here and in the following JTCS y, 19XX stands for *J TCS n. y*, North Holland, 19XX.

[2] Here and in the following LNCS y, 19XX stands for Berlin, Springer-Verlag, 19XX, (Lecture Notes in Computer Science n. y).

[AR] Astesiano E.; Reggio G. "SMoLCS Driven Concurrent Calculi", *Proc. TAPSOFT'87*, LNCS 249, 1987.

[AW] Astesiano E.; Wirsing M. "Bisimulation in Algebraic Specifications", *Proc. of the Colloquium on Resolution of Equations in Algebraic Structures*, San Diego, Academic Press, 1989.

[C] Castellani I. "Bisimulation and abstraction homomorphisms", *J. Comp. System Sci.* 34, 1987.

[CH] Castellani I.; Hennessy M. "Distributed Bisimulations", *Journal of the ACM*, October 1989, Vol. 36, n. 4, ACM, New York.

[DH] De Nicola R.; Hennessy M. "Testing Equivalence for Processes", JTCS 34, 1984.

[DV] De Nicola R.; Vaandrager F. "Three logics for Branching Bisimulation", to appear in Proc. of LICS '90.

[FM] Ferrari G. L.; Montanari U. "Towards the Unification of Models for Concurrency", *Proc. CAAP '90*, LNCS ???, 1990.

[GR] Giovini A.; Reggio G. "Bisimulation Models in Algebraic Specifications", *Proc. of the Third Italian Conference on Theoretical Computer Science*, World Scientific, 1989.

[GM] Goguen J.; Meseguer J. "Models and Equality for Logical Programming", *Proc. of TAPSOFT '87*, Berlin, Springer Verlag 1987,LNCS 250, 1987.

[GV] Groote J. F.; Vaandrager F. "Structured Operational Semantics and Bisimulation as a Congruence" *Proc. ICALP '89*, LNCS 372, 1989.

[GW] van Glabbeek R. J. ; Weijland W. P. "Branching Time and Abstraction in Bisimulation Semantics", *Information Processing'89*, North Holland, 1989.

[HM] Hennessy M.; Milner R. "Algebraic Laws for Nondeterminism and Concurrency", *Journal of the ACM*, Vol. 26, n. 1, ACM, New York, 1985.

[M1] Milner R. "Calculi for Synchrony and Asynchrony", JTCS 25, 1983.

[M2] Milner R. *Operational and Algebraic Semantics of Concurrent Processes*, LFCS Report Series, Dept. of Computer Science, University of Edinburgh, ECS–LFCS–88–46, February 1988.

[P] Park D. "Concurrency and Automata on Infinite Sequences", *Proc. 5th GI Conf.*, LNCS 104, 1981.

[T] Thomsen B., "A Calculus of Higher-Order Communicating Systems", *Proc. POPL Conference*, 1989.

Metric Pomset Semantics for a Concurrent Language with Recursion

J.W. de Bakker
J.H.A. Warmerdam

*Centre for Mathematics and Computer Science,
P.O. Box 4079, 1009 AB Amsterdam, The Netherlands*

ABSTRACT: We study the semantics of a simple language with concurrency and recursion. Our semantic domain consists of (sets of) finite and infinite partially ordered multisets (pomsets) in order to model true concurrency (i.e. non-interleaved parallel execution). It will be shown that the set of pomsets can be turned into a complete ultra-metric space. With the induced notion of convergence, it is possible to provide meaning to infinite computations. Operational and denotational semantics for the considered language are provided and their equivalence is established by showing that both are fixed points of a contracting higher order operator. In a final section we give a tentative denotational semantics for an extension of the language with synchronization.

KEY WORDS AND PHRASES: denotational semantics, operational semantics, ω-proof rule, true concurrency, pomsets, metric topology.

1. Introduction

In earlier semantic investigations of the Amsterdam Concurrency Group (e.g. [BZ82, BKMOZ86, BM88, KR88, AR89, B89, BR89]), fruitful use has been made of the framework of complete metric spaces. Computations have a small distance (say 2^{-n}) if they differ only after n steps, and the induced metric turns many functions encountered in the semantic design into *contracting* mappings which have unique fixed points (by Banach's theorem). Elsewhere we have exploited these ideas to

- handle recursion and infinite processes in concurrency,
- establish equivalence of several semantics,
- define semantic operators modeling syntactic operators such as sequential and parallel composition,
- treat advanced language families such as parallel object-oriented and logic programming ([ABKR89, B88]).

In our investigations up to now, we have always adopted the so-called interleaving approach to concurrency (as suggested by the equation $\mathcal{M}(a \| b) = \{ ab, ba \}$). In the present paper, we show how the metric techniques may as well be applied to the noninterleaving (or partial order) approach to concurrency. As a case study, we provide a metric treatment of partially ordered multi sets (or *pomsets*, for short), as introduced and studied by Grabowski [Gr81], Pratt [Pr86], Gischer [Gi84], and Gaifman [Ga89] (for other references see [BRR89]). Our investigation of pomset semantics was inspired by a paper by Meyer and De Vink ([MV89]), where the semantic model is based on an order between pomsets which generalizes the usual stream order, and on the Smyth order between (certain) sets of pomsets.

The emphasis in our paper is on the development of the metric framework for pomsets, rather than on the study of some especially interesting programming language concepts. Therefore, we have chosen to illustrate our techniques firstly on a very simple parallel language, that does not even include a notion of synchronization. Later we include a CCS-style (but noninterleaving!) synchronization to this language. We show that a 'pure' noninterleaving treatment would fail in our setting and propose therefore a what might be called hybrid approach.

After introducing the metric and partial order preliminaries in Section 2, in Section 3 we present the metric framework proper to handle (sets of) pomsets. A distance is introduced which turns the collection of pomsets into a complete metric space. Next, we discuss the usual operators of sequential ('•') and parallel ('$\|$') composition. The pomset setting allows a particularly succinct definition of these. Extension of them to sets of pomsets requires some justification (in comparable situations, e.g. in [BM88], we usually handled this through the use of higher-order operators). A compactness lemma turned out to be useful here (cf. [BBKM84, theorems 2.9, 2.10 for related issues).

Section 4 contains the definition of the operational ($\mathcal{O}$) and denotational ($\mathcal{D}$) semantics. $\mathcal{O}$ is defined in terms of an (SOS-style) transition system with quite simple transitions : they are all of the form $s \xrightarrow{p}_d E$, with s a statement, p a pomset, d a declaration (mapping procedure variables to their bodies) and E the empty (or terminated) statement. On the other hand, the transition system includes some not-so-standard means to handle recursion. We mention here the introduction of a kind of ω-rule into the system. (Further comments will follow in section 4.2.) The denotational semantics $\mathscr{D}$ is obtained as the (unique) fixed point of a higher order contracting mapping Φ. Since we also established that $\mathscr{O}$ satisfies a lemma which may, equivalently, be phrased as $\Phi(\mathscr{O}) = \mathscr{O}$, the desired equivalence $\mathscr{O} = \mathscr{D}$ is direct by Banach's theorem.

Section 5 contains a possible denotational semantics for the language extended with synchronization.

We conclude this introduction with a few words on future work :

- The operational semantics may be refined by also including transitions of the form $s \xrightarrow{p}_d s'$ (and by adapting the way the successive steps are assembled into the operational semantics $\mathscr{O}$).
- The pomset framework is (noninterleaving but) of the linear time variety : it assigns the same meanings to $a;(b_1+b_2)$ and $(a;b_1)+(a;b_2)$. In a paper in preparation, we show how four (systems of) domain equations may be defined which allow to define four pairs of equivalent semantics ($\mathscr{O}_i = \mathscr{D}_i$, $i=1,...,4$), for each of the combinations interleaving / noninterleaving and linear time / branching time.
- We expect (or in some cases, know) that the pomset model may be replaced, without undue complications, by other models such as event structures or (sets of) directed acyclic graphs, preserving essentially the same metric approach.

Acknowledgements. We are indebted to John-Jules Meyer and Erik de Vink who showed us the way into the (erstwhile unknown to us) realm of true concurrency. We are also grateful to Erik de Vink for his detailed and constructive comments on preliminary versions of this paper. The members of the Amsterdam Concurrency Group provided useful comments on earlier presentations of the work.

2. Mathematical preliminaries

First of all we adopt the convention that a phrase like 'let $(x \in)X$ be ...' introduces a set X with variable x ranging over X.

For convenience, we introduce $\mathbb{N} = \{ 1, 2, 3, ... \}$, $\mathbb{N}_0 = \mathbb{N} \cup \{ 0 \}$, $\mathbb{N}^\infty = \mathbb{N} \cup \{ \infty \}$ and $\mathbb{N}_0^\infty = \mathbb{N} \cup \{ 0, \infty \}$.

2.1. Metric spaces

DEFINITION 2.1.1 A *metric space* is a pair (M, d) with M a non-empty set and d a mapping $d : M \times M \to [0, \infty)$, that satisfies the following properties.

(a) $\forall x,y \in M : d(x, y) = 0 \Leftrightarrow x = y$,

(b) $\forall x,y \in M : d(x, y) = d(y, x)$,

(c) $\forall x,y,z \in M : d(x, y) \leqslant d(x, y) + d(y, z)$.

A metric space is called 1-bounded if $d : M \times M \to [0, 1]$ (so the distance never exceeds 1). In the sequel we assume that all metric spaces are 1-bounded.

A metric space is called *ultra-metric* or non-Archimedean if d satisfies $\forall x,y,z \in M : d(x, y) \leqslant \max\{ d(x, y), d(y, z) \}$.

Definition 2.1.2 Let (M, d) be a metric space and let $(x_i)_i$ be a sequence in M.

1. $(x_i)_i$ is called a *Cauchy sequence* if $\forall \epsilon>0 : \exists N \in \mathbb{N} : \forall n,m > N : d(x_n, x_m) < \epsilon$.
2. $(x_i)_i$ is called a *converging sequence* if
   $\exists x \in M : \forall \epsilon>0 : \exists N \in \mathbb{N} : \forall n>N : d(x_n, x) < \epsilon$.
   We say $(x_i)_i$ converges to x or the limit of $(x_i)_i$ is x (which is unique) and write $\lim_i x_i = x$.
3. We call (M, d) *complete* if every Cauchy sequence is a converging sequence.

Definition 2.1.3 Let (M_1, d_1) and (M_2, d_2) be metric spaces. Let $f : M_1 \to M_2$.

1. We call f *continuous* whenever
   $\forall x \in M_1 : \forall \epsilon>0 : \exists \delta>0 : \forall y \in M_1 : d_1(x, y) < \delta \Rightarrow d_2(f(x), f(y)) < \epsilon$ or, equivalently, for all converging sequences $(x_i)_i$ with $\lim_i x_i = x$ we have that $\lim_i f(x_i) = f(x)$.
2. Let $\gamma \geqslant 0$. With $M_1 \to^{\gamma} M_2$ we denote the set of all functions $f : M_1 \to M_2$ such that $\forall x,y \in M_1 : d_2(f(x), f(y)) \leqslant \gamma \cdot d_1(x, y)$. Functions $f \in M_1 \to^1 M_2$ are called *non-distance-increasing* (N.D.I.), functions $f \in M_1 \to^{\epsilon} M_2$ with $\epsilon < 1$ are called *contractions*.

Proposition 2.1.4

1. Let (M_1, d_1) and (M_2, d_2) be metric spaces. For every $\gamma \geqslant 0$ and $f \in M_1 \to^{\gamma} M_2$ we have that f is continuous.
2. (Banach's fixed-point theorem)
   Let (M, d) be a complete metric space and $f : M \to M$ a contraction. Then there exists an $x \in M$ such that the following holds.
   - $f(x) = x$ (x is a fixed point of f),
   - $\forall y \in M : f(y) = y \Rightarrow y = x$ (x is unique),
   - $\forall y \in M : \lim_n f^n(y) = x$, where $f^1 = f$ and $f^{n+1} = f \circ f^n$.

Definition 2.1.5 Let (M, d) be a metric space and let X be a subset of M.

1. X is called *closed*, whenever the limit of every converging sequence in X is an element of X.
2. X is called *compact*, whenever every sequence in X contains a subsequence that converges to an element in X.

3. The *closure* of X is the smallest closed subset in M containing X or, equivalently, the closure of X is the set of all limits of converging sequences in X. We denote the closure of X by $\overline{X}$.

DEFINITION 2.1.6

Let (M, d), (M_1, d_1), ..., (M_n, d_n) be metric spaces and let X be a set.

1. With $X \rightarrow M$ we denote the set of all functions from X to M. We define a metric d_F on $X \rightarrow M$ by $d_F(f_1, f_2) = sup\ \{ d(f_1(x), f_2(x)) \mid x \in X \}$.
2. We define a metric d_P on $M_1 \times ... \times M_n$ by $d_P((x_1, ..., x_n), (y_1, ..., y_n)) = \max \{d_i(x_i, y_i) \mid i = 1, ..., n \}$.
3. Let $\mathcal{P}_{nc}(M)$ denote $\{ X \subseteq M \mid X \text{ is non-empty and closed} \}$. We define a metric d_H on $\mathcal{P}_{nc}(M)$, called the Hausdorff distance, by $d_H(X, Y) = \max \{ sup\ \{ d(x, Y) \mid x \in X \}, sup\ \{ d(y, X) \mid y \in Y \} \}$, where $d(x, Z) = inf\ \{ d(x, z) \mid z \in Z \}$, for $x \in M$ and $Z \subseteq M$.

PROPOSITION 2.1.7

Let (M, d), (M_1, d_1), ..., (M_n, d_n) be metric spaces and let X be a set.

1. If (M, d), (M_1, d_1), ..., (M_n, d_n) are complete metric spaces then $(X \rightarrow M, d_F)$, $(M_1 \times ... \times M_n, d_P)$ and $(\mathcal{P}_{nc}(M), d_H)$ are complete metric spaces.
2. If (M, d), (M_1, d_1), ..., (M_n, d_n) are ultra-metric spaces then $(X \rightarrow M, d_F)$, $(M_1 \times ... \times M_n, d_P)$ and $(\mathcal{P}_{nc}(M), d_H)$ are ultra-metric spaces.

Only the proof of the completeness of $(\mathcal{P}_{nc}(M), d_H)$ is not so elementary. A proof can be found for instance in [BZ82].

If in the sequel we write $X \rightarrow M$, $M_1 \times ... \times M_n$ or $\mathcal{P}_{nc}(M)$ we mean the metric spaces with the metric defined above.

2.2. Partially ordered sets

DEFINITION 2.2.1 A *partially ordered set*, or just *partial order*, is a pair $(X, \leqslant)$ where X is a set and $\leqslant$ is a subset of $X \times X$ (notation : $x \leqslant y$ instead of $(x, y) \in \leqslant$), that satisfies the following conditions.

1. $\forall x \in X : x \leqslant x$,
2. $\forall x,y \in X : x \leqslant y$ and $y \leqslant x \Rightarrow x = y$,
3. $\forall x,y,z \in X : x \leqslant y$ and $y \leqslant z \Rightarrow x \leqslant z$.

We will adopt the notations $x < y$, $x \geqslant y$, $x > y$ for respectively $x \leqslant y \wedge x \neq y$, $y \leqslant x$, $y \leqslant x \wedge x \neq y$.

DEFINITION 2.2.2

1. For a partial order $(X, \leqslant)$ and $x \in X$ we define $lev(x) \in \mathbb{N}^\infty$ by $lev(x) = sup \{ n \mid \exists x_1 \dots x_n \in X : x_1 < x_2 < \dots < x_n = x \}$.
2. For a partial order $(X, \leqslant)$, we define $length((X, \leqslant)) \in \mathbb{N}_0^\infty$ by $length((X, \leqslant)) = sup \{ lev(x) \mid x \in X \}$, which is equal to $sup \{ n \mid \exists x_1 \dots x_n \in X : x_1 < x_2 < \dots < x_n \}$ (with the convention that $sup\ \varnothing = 0$).

DEFINITION 2.2.3 Let $(X, \leqslant)$ be a partial order and $A \subseteq X$.
We call A *downward-closed* if $\forall x \in X : [\exists a \in A : x \leqslant a] \Rightarrow x \in A$.

3. Pomsets

In the first subsection, the notion of pomset is defined, and some technical properties about pomsets are derived. In the second subsection, the set of pomsets is turned into a complete metric space and additionally a compactness property of pomsets is given. The third subsection, contains definitions of some operators on pomsets.

3.1. Definition of pomsets

Let $\mathscr{A}$ be a fixed set (finite or infinite) of atomic actions and $\mathscr{X}$ be a fixed (infinite) set of nodes, also called events.

DEFINITION 3.1.1 A labeled partial order or causality structure σ is a three-tuple $(X, \leqslant, \lambda)$, where X is a subset of $\mathscr{X}$, $\leqslant$ is a partial order on X, satisfying $\forall n \in \mathbb{N} : \{ x \mid lev(x) \leqslant n \}$ is finite and $\forall x \in X : lev(x) < \infty$, and $\lambda : X \rightarrow \mathscr{A}$ is a labeling function. We call $act(\sigma) = \{ \lambda(x) \mid x \in X \}$ the action set of σ.

The intended meaning of a labeled partial order is the following. $\mathscr{X}$ is a set of names of events and $x_1 \leqslant x_2$ means event x_1 has to precede x_2. The meaning of λ is that $\lambda(x)$ is the action of event x or stated otherwise, x is an occurrence of $\lambda(x)$. The two restrictions on the partial order are essential for the proof of proposition 3.1.10 which, in turn, is needed to verify that the distance function, introduced in subsection 3.2 is indeed a metric. Furthermore they imply that every event has only a finite numbers of predecessors. Note that different events (even concurrent ones) may be labeled by the same action (our framework does not exclude so-called auto parallelism).
With a causality structure σ we associate X_σ, $\leqslant_\sigma$, λ_σ and also $x <_\sigma y$, $x \geqslant_\sigma y$, $x >_\sigma y$.
A pomset will be a causality structure modulo renaming of nodes, as introduced in
DEFINITION 3.1.2

1. Two structures σ and ρ are called isomorphic, if there exists a bijection

$\phi : X_\sigma \to X_\rho$ such that $\phi(x) \leqslant_\rho \phi(y) \Leftrightarrow x \leqslant_\sigma y$ and $\lambda_\rho \circ \phi = \lambda_\sigma$.

2. A pomset is an isomorphism class of causality structures. Let $(p, q \in)\mathcal{POM}$ denotes the collection of pomsets. $[\sigma]$ denotes a pomset with representative σ. $act([\sigma])$ is defined by $act(\sigma)$ (which is independent of the representative). The empty pomset $[(\emptyset, \emptyset, \emptyset)]$ is denoted by $[]$.

We will draw pomsets by using Hasse diagrams of the partial order belonging to some representative causality structure, with the labels at the place of the nodes, as in

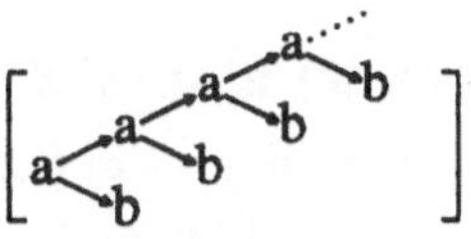

By the length of a structure, we mean the length of the order belonging to that structure. Note that $length(\sigma) < \infty \Leftrightarrow \#X_\sigma < \infty$. We also extend the notion of length to pomsets by taking the length of some representative. (This is independent of the choice of the representative.)
In section 4.2 we need another set of atomic actions (viz. $\mathcal{A}_e$). In that case we will denote $\mathcal{POM}$ w.r.t. $\mathcal{A}$ (resp $\mathcal{A}_e$) by $\mathcal{POM}[\mathcal{A}]$ (resp $\mathcal{POM}[\mathcal{A}_e]$).
We need the notion of truncation for defining a metric on $\mathcal{POM}$ in subsection 3.2.

DEFINITION 3.1.3

1. For a causality structure σ and a downward-closed subset X of X_σ we define $\sigma \upharpoonright X = (X, \leqslant \cap (X \times X), \lambda \upharpoonright X)$. $\sigma \upharpoonright X$ is a causality structure and $lev(x)$ w.r.t. $\sigma \upharpoonright X$ is equal to $lev(x)$ w.r.t. σ.
2. For a causality structure σ and $n \in \mathbb{N}_0$ we define $\sigma[n] = \sigma \upharpoonright \{ x \in X_\sigma \mid lev(x) \leqslant n \}$.
3. $p[n] = \{ \sigma[n] \mid \sigma \in p \} \in \mathcal{POM}$.

EXAMPLE 3.1.4 Let p be the following pomset.

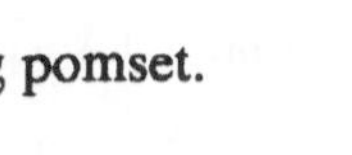

Then $length(p) = 4$, $act(p) = \{ a, b, c \}$ and p has for instance one c at level 3 and one c at level 4. (To be more precise : every representative of p has two nodes labeled with c, one at level 3 and one at level 4.) The truncations $p[0]$, $p[1]$, $p[2]$, $p[3]$, $p[4]$, $p[5]$, ... are respectively

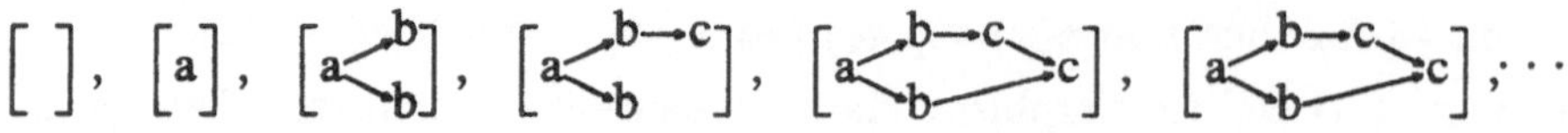

Lemma 3.1.5 Let σ be a structure.

1. If $X \subseteq Y$ downward-closed and $Y \subseteq X_\sigma$ downward-closed then $(\sigma\upharpoonright Y)\upharpoonright X = \sigma\upharpoonright X$.
2. If $X \subseteq X_\sigma$ downward-closed then $(\sigma\upharpoonright X)[n] = (\sigma[n])\upharpoonright(X_{\sigma[n]} \cap X)$.
3. $\sigma[n][m] = \sigma[\min\{ n, m \}]$.
4. For a pomset p we have that $p[n][m] = p[\min\{ n, m \}]$.

Proof

1. Easy verification.
2. $(\sigma\upharpoonright X)[n] = (\sigma\upharpoonright X)\upharpoonright\{ x \in X \mid lev(x)\_w.r.t.\_\sigma\upharpoonright X \leqslant n \} =$
$(\sigma\upharpoonright X)\upharpoonright\{ x \in X \mid lev(x)\_w.r.t.\_\sigma \leqslant n \} = \sigma\upharpoonright\{ x \in X \mid lev(x)\_w.r.t.\_\sigma \leqslant n \} =$
$(\sigma\upharpoonright\{ x \in X_\sigma \mid lev(x)\_w.r.t.\_\sigma \leqslant n \})\upharpoonright(X \cap \{ x \in X_\sigma \mid lev(x)\_w.r.t.\_\sigma \leqslant n \})$
$= (\sigma[n])\upharpoonright(X_{\sigma[n]} \cap X)$.
3. $(\sigma[n])[m] =$
$(\sigma\upharpoonright\{ x \in X_\sigma \mid lev(x)\_w.r.t.\_\sigma \leqslant n \})\upharpoonright\{ x \in X_{\sigma[n]} \mid lev(x)\_w.r.t.\_\sigma[n] \leqslant m \} =$
$\sigma\upharpoonright\{ x \in X_{\sigma[n]} \mid lev(x)\_w.r.t.\_\sigma \leqslant m \} =$
$\sigma\upharpoonright\{ x \in X_\sigma \mid lev(x)\_w.r.t.\_\sigma \leqslant n \wedge lev(x)\_w.r.t.\_\sigma \leqslant m \} =$
$\sigma\upharpoonright\{ x \in X_\sigma \mid lev(x)\_w.r.t.\_\sigma \leqslant \min\{ n, m \} \} = \sigma\upharpoonright[\min\{ n, m \}]$
4. Direct from 3. □

Lemma 3.1.6

Let σ and ρ be structures.

Let $(Y_n)_n$ be a sequence of downward-closed subsets of X_ρ such that $\forall n : Y_n \subseteq Y_{n+1}$.

Let $\phi : X_\sigma \to X_\rho$ be a mapping such that

$\forall n : \phi\upharpoonright X_{\sigma[n]} : \sigma[n] \to \rho\upharpoonright Y_n$ is an isomorphism.

Then $\phi : \sigma \to \rho\upharpoonright(\bigcup_n Y_n)$ is an isomorphism.

Proof Easy verification. Uses the fact that $\bigcup_n X_{\sigma[n]} = X_\sigma$. □

Lemma 3.1.7

Let σ and ρ be structures and let $\phi : X_\sigma \to X_\rho$.

Then $\phi : \sigma \to \rho$ is an isomorphism $\Leftrightarrow$ $\forall n : \phi\upharpoonright X_{\sigma[n]} : \sigma[n] \to \rho[n]$ is an isomorphism.

Proof

"$\Rightarrow$" The only thing to check is $\phi[X_{\sigma[n]}] = X_{\rho[n]}$. This holds since $lev(\phi(x))\_w.r.t.\_\rho$ $= lev(x)\_w.r.t.\_\sigma$.

"$\Leftarrow$" previous lemma : take $Y_n = X_{\rho[n]}$, then $\bigcup_n Y_n = X_\rho$. □

Next we are going to define a partial order $\leqslant$ on $\mathscr{POM}$. We use this partial order to prove Corollary 3.1.11 which, in turn, is needed to verify that the distance function, defined in subsection 3.2 is indeed a metric. Moreover, the partial order makes it possible to express that $\{ p \mid p \leqslant q \}$ is compact (proposition 3.2.5), which is used to prove that the operators, introduced is subsection 3.3, are well-defined.

DEFINITION 3.1.8 We define a relation $\leqslant$ on $\mathscr{POM}$ by putting $p \leqslant q$ iff $\exists \sigma, X : X \subseteq X_\sigma$ downward-closed, $q = [\sigma], p = [\sigma \upharpoonright X]$. In this case we say that p is *initial* to q.

PROPOSITION 3.1.9 "$\leqslant$" is a partial order.

PROOF

(1) If $p = [\sigma]$ then $[\sigma \upharpoonright X_\sigma] = [\sigma] = p$ so $p \leqslant p$.

(2) Assume $p \leqslant q$ and $q \leqslant p$. Let ρ, X_2, σ, X_1 be such that $q = [\rho], p = [\rho \upharpoonright X_2]$, $p = [\sigma]$ and $q = [\sigma \upharpoonright X_1]$. So $\sigma \sim \rho \upharpoonright X_2$ and $\rho \sim \sigma \upharpoonright X_1$, say $\phi : \sigma \to \rho \upharpoonright X_2$ is an isomorphism and $\psi : \rho \to \sigma \upharpoonright X_1$ is an isomorphism. Then also $\phi \upharpoonright X_{\sigma[n]} : \sigma[n] \to (\rho \upharpoonright X_2)[n] = \rho[n] \upharpoonright (X_{\rho[n]} \cap X_2)$ and $\psi \upharpoonright X_{\rho[n]} : \rho[n] \to (\sigma \upharpoonright X_1)[n] = \sigma[n] \upharpoonright (X_{\sigma[n]} \cap X_1)$ are isomorphisms. Since $X_{\sigma[n]}$ and $X_{\rho[n]}$ are finite sets, we can conclude that $X_{\rho[n]} \cap X_2 = X_{\rho[n]}$ and thus $\forall n : \phi \upharpoonright X_{\sigma[n]} : \sigma[n] \to \rho[n]$ is an isomorphism so $\phi : \sigma \to \rho$ is an isomorphism so $p = [\sigma] = [\rho] = q$.

(3) Assume $p \leqslant q$ and $q \leqslant r$. Say $q = [\rho]$ and $p = [\rho \upharpoonright X]$ with $X \subseteq X_\rho$ downward-closed and $r = [\zeta]$ and $q = [\zeta \upharpoonright Y]$ with $Y \subseteq X_\zeta$ downward-closed. Say $\phi : \rho \to \zeta \upharpoonright Y$ is an isomorphism then $\phi \upharpoonright X : \rho \upharpoonright X \to (\zeta \upharpoonright Y) \upharpoonright \phi[X]$ is an isomorphism. So $p = [\rho \upharpoonright X] = [(\zeta \upharpoonright Y) \upharpoonright \phi[X]] = [\zeta \upharpoonright \phi[X]]$, so $p \leqslant r$. □

PROPOSITION 3.1.10 $[\forall n : p[n] \leqslant q] \Rightarrow p \leqslant q$

PROOF

Let $p = [\sigma]$ and $q = [\rho]$.

We will show that there exist a downward-closed subset X of X_ρ and an isomorphism $\phi : \sigma \to \rho \upharpoonright X$, which proves that $p = [\sigma] = [\rho \upharpoonright X]$ or equivalently $p \leqslant q$.

We will make a tree of isomorphisms in the following way.

As nodes we take triples (ϕ, X, n) where (1) $n \in \mathbb{N}_0$, (2) $X \subseteq X_\rho$ is downward-closed, and (3) $\phi : \sigma[n] \to \rho \upharpoonright X$ is an isomorphism.

We put an arc between (ϕ, X, n) and (ϕ', X', n') if (1) $n' = n + 1$, (2) $X' \supseteq X$, and (3) $\phi' \upharpoonright X = \phi$.

First we show that this indeed defines a rooted tree with $(\varnothing, \varnothing, 0)$ as root, as follows. If $(\phi, X, n+1)$ is a node then $\phi : \sigma[n+1] \to \rho\restriction X$ is an isomorphism, so $\phi\restriction X_\sigma[n] : \sigma[n] \to \rho\restriction\phi[X_{\sigma[n]}]$ is an isomorphism thus $(\phi\restriction X_{\sigma[n]}, \phi[X_{\sigma[n]}], n)$ is a node and there is an arc from this node to $(\phi, X, n+1)$.

Next we show that this tree contains infinitely many nodes. In fact we show that $\forall n : \exists\phi, X : (\phi, X, n)$ is a node, as follows. Let us fix some n. Since $p[n] \leqslant q$, by definition there exist ρ' and X' such that $p[n] = [\rho'\uparrow X']$ and $[\rho'] = q$. Let $\phi' : \rho' \to \rho$ be an isomorphism. Also $\phi'\uparrow X' : \rho'\uparrow X' \to \rho\restriction\phi'[X']$ is an isomorphism, so take $X = \phi'[X']$. Then $X \subseteq X_\rho$ is downward-closed and $\sigma[n] \sim \rho'\uparrow X' \sim \rho\restriction X$. So there exists an isomorphism $\phi : \sigma[n] \to \rho\restriction X$ so (ϕ, X, n) is a node.

Since the number of events in $\sigma[n]$ is finite, say m, and there exist only a finite number of downward-closed subsets of X_ρ with m number of elements, we know that the tree is finitely branching. König's Lemma guarantees the existence of an infinite path : $(\phi_n, X_n, n)_{n=0}^{\infty}$ with $X_n \subseteq X_{n+1}$ and $\phi_{n+1}\restriction X_n = \phi_n$. Now take $\phi = \bigcup_{n=0}^{\infty} \phi_n$ and $X = \bigcup_{n=0}^{\infty} X_n$. Then, by lemma 3.1.6 $\phi : \sigma \to \rho\restriction X$ is an isomorphism. □

COROLLARY 3.1.11 $[\forall n : p[n] = q[n]] \Rightarrow p = q$

PROOF

$\forall n : p[n] = q[n] \leqslant q$ so $p \leqslant q$.

Analogous $q \leqslant p$.

So $p = q$. □

3.2. Metric for pomsets

We define a metric on $\mathcal{POM}$ as follows.

DEFINITION 3.2.1 $d : \mathcal{POM} \times \mathcal{POM} \to [0,1]$ is defined by

$$d(p_1, p_2) = inf\{\, 2^{-n} \mid p_1[n] = p_2[n] \,\}$$

PROPOSITION 3.2.2 $(\mathcal{POM}, d)$ is a complete ultra-metric space.

PROOF Proposition 3.1.5.4 and corollary 3.1.11 imply that $(\mathcal{POM}, d)$ is an ultra-metric space. What remains is the verification of the completeness. Let $(p_n)_{n=1}^{\infty}$ be a Cauchy sequence. Take a nondescending chain $(n_m)_{m=1}^{\infty}$ such that $\forall m \in \mathbb{N} : \forall k > n_m : p_k[m] = p_{n_m}[m]$.

Define σ_m, $m \in \mathbb{N}$, recursively such that $\sigma_m \in p_{n_m}[m]$ and $\sigma_{m+1}[m] = \sigma_m$.

(1) Take $\sigma_1 \in p_{n_1}[1]$.

(2) If σ_m has been defined then $\sigma_m \in p_{n_m}[m] = p_{n_{m+1}}[m] = p_{n_{m+1}}[m+1][m]$ so there exists a $\sigma_{m+1} \in p_{n_{m+1}}[m+1]$ with $\sigma_{m+1}[m] = \sigma_m$.

Now define $\sigma = (\bigcup_{i=1}^{\infty} X_{\sigma_i}, \bigcup_{i=1}^{\infty} \leqslant_{\sigma_i}, \bigcup_{i=1}^{\infty} \lambda_{\sigma_i})$ and $p = [\sigma]$.

Then $p_n \to p$ $(n \to \infty)$ because $\sigma_m = \sigma[m]$ so $p_{n_m}[m] = p[m]$ so $\forall k > n_m : p_k[m] = p[m]$ so $\forall m \in \mathbb{N} : \forall k > n_m : d(p_k, p) \leqslant 2^{-m}$. □

See example 4.2.5 for a converging sequence in $\mathcal{POM}$.

Proposition 3.2.3 For $p \in \mathcal{POM} : \lim_n p[n] = p$.

Finally, the semantic domain will be a collection of subsets of $\mathcal{POM}$. The need for *sets of* pomsets in our semantic domain, arises from the presence, in the language to be considered, of the concept of nondeterministic choice.

Definition 3.2.4

Let $(P, Q \in) \mathcal{POM}^*$ is the set of all closed and non-empty subsets of $\mathcal{POM}$ (i.e. $\mathcal{P}_{nc}(\mathcal{POM})$).

$\mathcal{POM}^*$ is a complete (ultra-)metric space if it is endowed with the Hausdorff distance (see proposition 2.1.7).

Next we are going to define a useful compactness property.

Proposition 3.2.5 $\forall q : \{ p \mid p \leqslant q \}$ is compact.

Proof Let $(p_i)_i$ be a sequence with $p_i \leqslant q$. We are going to define $(n_i)_i$ (an increasing sequence of natural numbers) inductively such that if $n_0, \ldots, n_k$ are defined, it holds that

(1) $\forall i,j : i < j \leqslant k : p_{n_j}[i] = p_{n_i}[i]$,

(2) $\#\{ i \mid p_i[k] = p_{n_k}[k] \} = \infty$.

$\underline{k = 0}$: choose n_0 arbitrary. (1) and (2) are trivially satisfied.

$\underline{k \to k+1}$: denote $I = \{ i \mid p_i[k] = p_{n_k}[k] \}$. Since $\forall i : p_i[k+1] \leqslant q[k+1]$ and $q[k+1]$ is finite, there exist only finitely many distinct $p_i[k+1]$, so there exists an $n_{k+1} \in I$ such that $n_{k+1} > n_k$ and $\#\{ i \mid p_i[k+1] = p_{n_{k+1}}[k+1] \} = \infty$. Moreover, $\forall i \leqslant k : p_{n_{k+1}}[i] = p_{n_{k+1}}[k][i] = p_{n_k}[k][i] = p_{n_k}[i] = p_{n_i}[i]$. So (1) and (2) are satisfied.

From (1) we can conclude that $(p_{n_j})_j$ is a Cauchy subsequence, and by proposition

3.1.10 we know that the limit is in $\{ p \mid p \leqslant q \}$, so $\{ p \mid p \leqslant q \}$ is compact. □

3.3. Operators on pomsets

In this subsection we are going to define two operators on pomsets, namely sequential and parallel composition. This is done in the following way. First we define the operators on structures (with disjoint sets of nodes only). Since the isomorphism relation will be a congruence relation with respect to these operators, the operators can be defined on pomsets. Finally, we will define the two operators on pomset-sets. As we go along, we derive some properties of these operators.

DEFINITION 3.3.1 Let σ and ρ be causality structures such that $X_\sigma \cap X_\rho = \emptyset$.

1. $\sigma \bullet \rho = \begin{cases} \sigma, \text{ if } \#X_\sigma = \infty \text{ (or equivalently } \mathit{length}(\sigma) = \infty \text{)}, \\ (X_\sigma \cup X_\rho, \leqslant_\sigma \cup \leqslant_\rho \cup (X_\sigma \times X_\rho), \lambda_\sigma \cup \lambda_\rho), \text{ otherwise.} \end{cases}$
2. $\sigma \parallel \rho = (X_\sigma \cup X_\rho, \leqslant_\sigma \cup \leqslant_\rho, \lambda_\sigma \cup \lambda_\rho)$.

LEMMA 3.3.2

1. if σ is finite then $\mathit{lev}(x)$ w.r.t. $\sigma\bullet\rho = \begin{cases} \mathit{lev}(x) \text{ w.r.t. } \sigma, \text{ if } x \in X_\sigma, \\ \mathit{lev}(x) \text{ w.r.t. } \rho + \mathit{length}(\sigma), \text{ if } x \in X_\rho. \end{cases}$
2. $\mathit{lev}(x)$ w.r.t. $\sigma \parallel \rho = \begin{cases} \mathit{lev}(x) \text{ w.r.t. } \sigma, \text{ if } x \in X_\sigma, \\ \mathit{lev}(x) \text{ w.r.t. } \rho, \text{ if } x \in X_\rho. \end{cases}$
3. $\sigma\bullet\rho$ and $\sigma \parallel \rho$ are causality structures.
4. if $\mathit{length}(\sigma) \geqslant n$ then $(\sigma\bullet\rho)[n] = \sigma[n]$;
   if $\mathit{length}(\sigma) \leqslant n$ then $(\sigma\bullet\rho)[n] = \sigma \bullet \rho[n - \mathit{length}(\sigma)]$.
5. $(\sigma \parallel \rho)[n] = \sigma[n] \parallel \rho[n]$.
6. if σ is finite then $\mathit{act}(\sigma\bullet\rho) = \mathit{act}(\sigma) \cup \mathit{act}(\rho)$;
   if σ is infinite then $\mathit{act}(\sigma\bullet\rho) = \mathit{act}(\sigma)$.
7. $\mathit{act}(\sigma \parallel \rho) = \mathit{act}(\sigma) \cup \mathit{act}(\rho)$.

Now let us define the operators $\bullet$ and $\parallel$ on pomsets.

DEFINITION 3.3.3

$\bullet : \mathcal{POM} \times \mathcal{POM} \to \mathcal{POM}$ and $\parallel : \mathcal{POM} \times \mathcal{POM} \to \mathcal{POM}$ are defined as follows.
If $p = [\sigma]$ and $q = [\rho]$, with $X_\sigma \cap X_\rho = \emptyset$, then $p\bullet q = [\sigma\bullet\rho]$ and $p \parallel q = [\sigma \parallel \rho]$.

REMARK 3.3.4 It is always possible to find representatives with disjoint set of nodes and furthermore the definition is not dependent on the choice of the representatives.

EXAMPLES 3.3.5

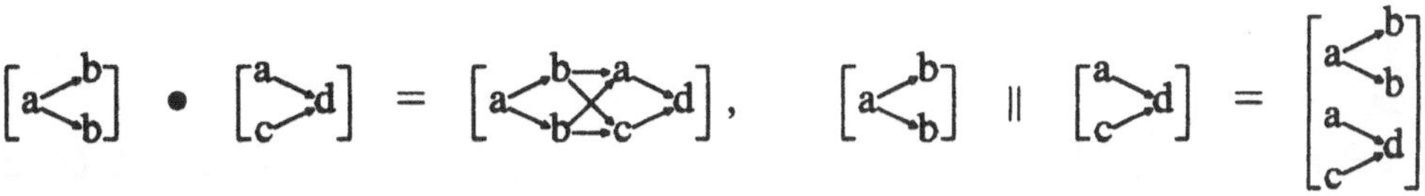

LEMMA 3.3.6

1. if $length(p) \geqslant n$ then $(p \bullet q)[n] = p[n]$;
   if $length(p) \leqslant n$ then $(p \bullet q)[n] = p \bullet q[n - length(p)]$.
2. $(p \,\|\, q)[n] = p[n] \,\|\, q[n]$.
3. if p is finite then $act(p \bullet q) = act(p) \cup act(q)$;
   if p is infinite then $act(p \bullet q) = act(p)$.
4. $act(p \,\|\, q) = act(p) \cup act(q)$.

Now we will define $\bullet$ and $\|$ on $\mathcal{POM}^*$. Also an operator $+$ is defined on $\mathcal{POM}^*$, which is just the set-theoretic union.

DEFINITION 3.3.7

1. $\bullet : \mathcal{POM}^* \times \mathcal{POM}^* \to \mathcal{POM}^*$ is defined by
   $P \bullet Q = \{\, p \bullet q \mid p \in P \text{ and } q \in Q \,\}$.
2. $\| : \mathcal{POM}^* \times \mathcal{POM}^* \to \mathcal{POM}^*$ is defined by
   $P \,\|\, Q = \{\, p \,\|\, q \mid p \in P \text{ and } q \in Q \,\}$.
3. $+ : \mathcal{POM}^* \times \mathcal{POM}^* \to \mathcal{POM}^*$ is defined by
   $P + Q = P \cup Q$.

We need to show that $P \bullet Q$ and $P \,\|\, Q$ are closed. (The fact that $P + Q$ is closed is immediate.) For this purpose, a lemma is given first.

LEMMA 3.3.8

1. $\forall p,q,q' \in \mathcal{POM} : d(p \bullet q, p \bullet q') = 2^{-length(p)} \cdot d(q, q')$.
2. If $\lim_n (p \bullet q_n) = r$ with $length(p) < \infty$, then $\exists q : \lim_n q_n = q$ and $r = p \bullet q$.

PROOF

1. If $length(p) = \infty$ then both sides give 0. Now suppose $length(p) = l < \infty$. $(p \bullet q)[n+l] = (p \bullet q')[n+l] \;\Leftrightarrow\; p \bullet q[n] = p \bullet q'[n] \;\Leftrightarrow\; q[n] = q'[n]$. From this 1. follows immediately.
2. Let $length(p) = l$. Since $d(p \bullet q_n, p \bullet q_m) = 2^{-l} \cdot d(q_n, q_m)$ and $(p \bullet q_n)_n$ is a Cauchy sequence, we have $(q_n)_n$ is a Cauchy sequence, say $q_n \to q$. Then $r = \lim_n (p \bullet q_n) = p \bullet \lim_n q_n = p \bullet q$. □

Proposition 3.3.9

1. $P \bullet Q$ is closed.
2. $P \parallel Q$ is closed.

Proof

1. Let $r = \lim_i r_i$ with $r_i \in P \bullet Q$, say $r_i = p_i \bullet q_i$, with $p_i \in P$ and $q_i \in Q$. Since $r_i \to r$, we have that $\forall l : \exists k_l : r_{k_l}[l] = r[l]$. So $r[l] = (p_{k_l} \bullet q_{k_l})[l]$, so $p_{k_l}[l] \leqslant r[l] \leqslant r$. By the compactness property(3.2.5), there exists an increasing sequence l_m such that $(p_{k_{l_m}}[l_m])_m$ converges, say to $p \in P$. (Note $p \in P$, since also $p_{k_{l_m}} \to p$ and P is closed.)
   If $length(p) = \infty$ then $\forall n : r[n] = \lim_i ((p_i \bullet q_i)[n]) = \lim_m ((p_{k_{l_m}} \bullet q_{k_{l_m}})[n]) = \lim_m p_{k_{l_m}}[n] = p[n]$. So $r = p =$ (for instance) $p \bullet q_0 \in P \bullet Q$.
   If $length(p) < \infty$ then $\exists M : \forall m \geqslant M : p_{k_{l_m}}[l_m] = p$. Moreover, since l_m is increasing, $\exists M' : \forall m \geqslant M' : p_{k_{l_m}} = p$. According to lemma 3.3.8.2, we have that $r = p \bullet q$ with $\lim_m q_{k_{l_m}} = q \in Q$.
2. Let $r = \lim_i r_i$ with $r_i \in P \parallel Q$, say $r_i = p_i \parallel q_i$, with $p_i \in P$ and $q_i \in Q$. Since $r_i \to r$, we have that $\forall l : \exists k_l : r_{k_l}[l] = r[l]$. So $r[l] = r_{k_l}[l] = p_{k_l}[l] \parallel q_{k_l}[l]$. So $p_{k_l}[l] \leqslant r[l] \leqslant r$ and $q_{k_l}[l] \leqslant r[l] \leqslant r$. By the compactness property, there exists an increasing sequence l_m such that $(p_{k_{l_m}}[l_m])_m$ converges, say to $p \in P$. Again by the compactness property, there exists an increasing sequence m_n such that $(q_{k_{l_{m_n}}}[l_{m_n}])_n$ converges, say to $q \in Q$. Now $r = \lim_n r_{k_{l_{m_n}}} = \lim_n (p_{k_{l_{m_n}}} \parallel q_{k_{l_{m_n}}}) = (\lim_n p_{k_{l_{m_n}}}) \parallel (\lim_n q_{k_{l_{m_n}}}) = p \parallel q \in P \parallel Q$. □

4. Semantics

In this section a simple language without synchronization $\mathscr{L}$ is introduced and an operational semantics $\mathcal{O}$ and a denotational semantics $\mathscr{D}$ are given and are proved to be equal.

4.1. The language

First we introduce the language. For this we need two basic sets. Let $(a,b,c,... \in) \mathscr{A}$ be a (finite or infinite) set of atomic actions and let $(x \in) \mathscr{Pvar}$ be a set of procedure variables.

Definition 4.1.1

a. The class $(s \in) \mathscr{L}$ of *statements* is given by

$$s ::= a \mid x \mid s_1;s_2 \mid s_1+s_2 \mid s_1 \| s_2.$$

b The class ($g \in$)$\mathcal{L}^g$ of *guarded statements* is given by

$$g ::= a \mid g;s \mid g_1+g_2 \mid g_1 \| g_2.$$

c. The class ($d \in$)$\mathcal{Decl}$ of *declarations* consists of mappings from $\mathcal{Pvar}$ to $\mathcal{L}^g$.

d. The class ($t \in$)$\mathcal{Prog}$ of *programs* consists of pairs $t \equiv \langle d \mid s \rangle$ with $d \in \mathcal{Decl}$ and $s \in \mathcal{L}$.

A statement is made up from atomic actions and procedure variables, by means of sequential composition, nondeterministic choice and (non-interleaved) parallel composition. A guarded statement is a statement in which every procedure variable is preceded by an atomic action. A declaration is a mapping from procedure variables to guarded statements and finally a program is a declaration plus a statement.

4.2. Operational semantics

The operational semantics is given with the aid of a labeled transition system (l.t.s.). As labels we use pomsets (cf. [BoCa88, Ga89]). In an l.t.s. we encounter, besides statements $s \in \mathcal{L}$, also the special symbol E that we use to indicate the empty (or terminated) statement. In addition, we introduce a special atomic action $e(\notin \mathcal{A})$, used -in a way to be explained below- to handle recursion, and we put $\mathcal{A}_e = \mathcal{A} \cup \{ e \}$. Let $\longrightarrow \subseteq \mathcal{L} \times \mathcal{POM}[\mathcal{A}_e] \times \mathcal{Decl} \times \{ E \}$ to be defined in a moment. Thus, we only employ transitions of a particular simple form, which we shall write as $s \xrightarrow{p}_d E$ (instead of $(s, p, d, E) \in \longrightarrow$). Some explanations follow after definitions 4.2.1 and 4.2.2.

Definition 4.2.1 $\longrightarrow \subseteq \mathcal{L} \times \mathcal{POM}[\mathcal{A}_e] \times \mathcal{Decl} \times \{ E \}$ is the smallest relation satisfying

(1) $a \xrightarrow{[a]}_d E$,

(2) if $g \xrightarrow{p}_d E$ and $d(x) = g$ then $x \xrightarrow{p}_d E$,

(3) if $s_1 \xrightarrow{p_1}_d E$ and $s_2 \xrightarrow{p_2}_d E$ then $s_1;s_2 \xrightarrow{p_1 \cdot p_2}_d E$ and $s_1 \| s_2 \xrightarrow{p_1 \| p_2}_d E$,

(4) if $s_1 \xrightarrow{p}_d E$ then $s_1+s_2 \xrightarrow{p}_d E$ and $s_2+s_1 \xrightarrow{p}_d E$,

(5) if $s \xrightarrow{p_i}_d E$ $(i = 1\ 2\ ...)$ and $\lim_i p_i = p$ then $s \xrightarrow{p}_d E$,

(6) $x \xrightarrow{[e]}_d E$.

Definition 4.2.2

1. $\mathcal{I}_d : \mathcal{L} \rightarrow \mathcal{POM}^*[\mathcal{A}_e]$ is given by $\mathcal{I}_d(s) = \{ p \mid s \xrightarrow{p}_d E \}$.
2. $\mathcal{O}_d : \mathcal{L} \rightarrow \mathcal{POM}^*[\mathcal{A}]$ is given by $\mathcal{O}_d(s) = \mathcal{I}_d(s) \cap \mathcal{POM}[\mathcal{A}]$.
3. $\mathcal{O} : \mathcal{Prog} \rightarrow \mathcal{POM}^*[\mathcal{A}]$ is given by $\mathcal{O}(\langle d \mid s \rangle) = \mathcal{O}_d(s)$.

First we discuss the system for '$\longrightarrow$'. Clauses (1), ..., (4) of definition 4.2.1 should be clear. Clauses (5) and (6) are included in order to enable us to handle possibly infinite computations of recursive procedures. Since we only work with transitions of the form $s \xrightarrow{p}_d E$ (which terminate in one step), we have no means to build up an infinite computation without additional measures. These are provided by (5) and (6) : Axiom (6) provides an arbitrary (cf. Banach's theorem) starting point for the execution of a recursive process. Rule (5) allows us to build up possibly infinite p in a $s \xrightarrow{p}_d E$ step. This set-up would allow e to remain in the final outcome of a computation. Therefore, we obtain the desired operational semantics $\mathcal{O}_d(s)$ by restricting (def. 4.2.2, part 2.) the intermediate semantics $\mathcal{I}_d(s)$ to those outcomes which contain only pomsets involving actions from $\mathcal{A}$. Example 4.2.5 should be helpful to understand our handling of recursion.

Lemma 4.2.3

1. $\mathcal{I}_d$ is well-defined, i.e. $\mathcal{I}_d(s)$ is non-empty and closed.
2. $\mathcal{O}_d(s)$ is non-empty and closed.

Proof

1. By induction on the complexity of s, one can easily show that $\mathcal{I}_d(s) \neq \emptyset$ (use rule (6) in case $s = x$). Because of rule (5), $\mathcal{I}_d(s)$ is closed.
2. $\mathcal{O}_d(s)$ is closed since $\mathcal{I}_d(s)$ is closed. Proving $\mathcal{O}_d(s) \neq \emptyset$ is more involved. We construct a sequence $p_i \in \mathcal{I}_d(s)$ $(i \in \mathbb{N}_0)$ such that $e \notin act(p_i[i])$ and $p_{i+1}[i] = p_i[i]$. From this it follows that $(p_i)_i$ is a Cauchy sequence, say with limit p. $p \in \mathcal{I}_d(s)$ and $\forall n \in \mathbb{N}_0 : e \notin act(p[n])$, so $e \notin act(p)$. We can conclude that $p \in \mathcal{O}_d(s)$.
   The sequence is constructed in the following way. $\mathcal{I}_d(s) \neq \emptyset$, so take a $p_0 \in \mathcal{I}_d(s)$. If $p_k \in \mathcal{I}_d(s)$ with $e \notin act(p_k[k])$ then we can find a $p_{k+1} \in \mathcal{I}_d(s)$ with $p_{k+1}[k] = p_k[k]$ and $e \notin act(p_{k+1}[k+1])$, which is guaranteed by the following lemma. □

Lemma 4.2.4 If $s \xrightarrow{p}_d E$ and $e \notin act(p[n])$ then $\exists p' : s \xrightarrow{p'}_d E$ and $p'[n] = p[n]$ and $e \notin act(p'[n+1])$.

Proof First we remark that $\forall g \in \mathcal{L}^g : \exists p : g \xrightarrow{p}_d E$ and $e \notin act(p[1])$, which can easily be proved by induction on the structure of g and using lemma 3.3.6.

The lemma is proved by transfinite induction on the depth of the proof tree for $s \xrightarrow{p}_d E$, defined in the usual way.

- If $a \xrightarrow{[a]}_d E$ by (1) then we can take $p' = [a]$.
- If $x \xrightarrow{p}_d E$ by rule (2) then $g \xrightarrow{p}_d E$ with $g = d(x)$. By induction $\exists p' : g \xrightarrow{p'}_d E$

with $p'[n] = p[n]$ and $e \notin act(p'[n+1])$. Now also $x \xrightarrow{p'}_d E$.

- If $s_1;s_2 \xrightarrow{p_1 \bullet p_2}_d E$ (resp. $s_1 \| s_2 \xrightarrow{p_1 \| p_2}_d E$) by (3) then $\exists p'_1, p'_2 : s_1 \xrightarrow{p'_1}_d E$ and $s_2 \xrightarrow{p'_2}_d E$ with $e \notin act(p'_1[n+1])$, $e \notin act(p'_2[n+1])$, $p'_1[n] = p_1[n]$ and $p'_2[n] = p_2[n]$. Now $s_1;s_2 \xrightarrow{p'_1 \bullet p'_2}_d E$ (resp $s_1 \| s_2 \xrightarrow{p'_1 \| p'_2}_d E$) and $e \notin act((p'_1 \bullet p'_2)[n+1])$ and $(p'_1 \bullet p'_2)[n] = (p_1 \bullet p_2)[n]$ (resp $e \notin act((p'_1 \| p'_2)[n+1])$ and $(p'_1 \| p'_2)[n] = (p_1 \| p_2)[n]$).
- If $s_1 + s_2 \xrightarrow{p}_d E$ by (4) then $s_i \xrightarrow{p}_d E$ $(i = 1$ or $2)$. By induction $\exists p' : s_i \xrightarrow{p'}_d E$ with $p'[n] = p[n]$ and $e \notin act(p'[n+1])$. Now also $s_1 + s_2 \xrightarrow{p'}_d E$.
- If $s \xrightarrow{p}_d E$ by applying rule (5) then $s \xrightarrow{p_i}_d E$ $(i = 1,2\ldots)$ and $\lim_i p_i = p$. Now $\exists i_0 : p_{i_0}[n] = p[n]$. By induction $\exists p' : s \xrightarrow{p'}_d E$ and $e \notin act(p'[n+1])$ and $p'[n] = p_{i_0}[n] = p[n]$.
- If $x \xrightarrow{[e]}_d E$ by axiom (6) and $d(x) = g$ then $g \xrightarrow{p}_d E$ with $e \notin act(p[1])$ and so $x \xrightarrow{p}_d E$. □

EXAMPLE 4.2.5 Let $d(x) = a;(x \| b);c$ and $s \equiv x$. By applying rules (1), (2), (3), (6), one can derive $s \xrightarrow{p_i}_d E$, for $p_1, p_2, p_3, p_4, \ldots$ equal to

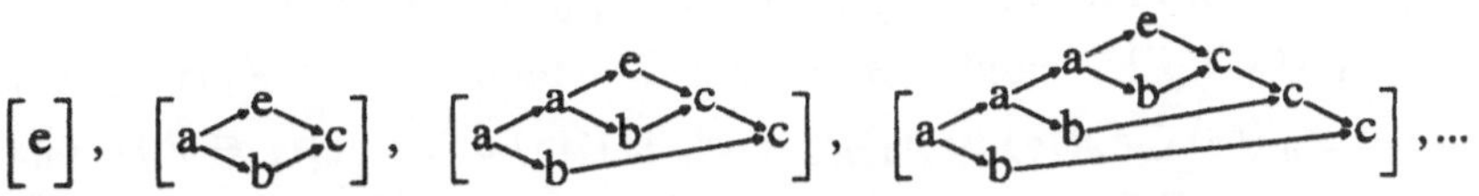

Applying rule (5) gives $s \xrightarrow{p}_d E$ with $p = \lim_i p_i =$

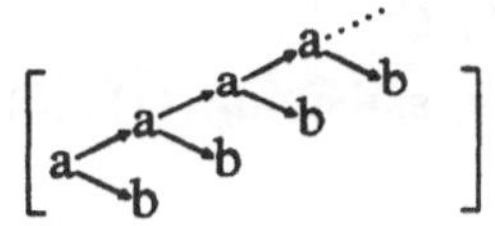

So $\mathcal{I}_d(s)$ is the set of all pomsets listed above and $\mathcal{O}_d(s)$ is only the singleton set with the last pomset, as (only) member.

LEMMA 4.2.6

1.
   a. $\{\,[a]\,\} = \mathcal{I}_d(a)$,
   b. $\mathcal{I}_d(g) \cup \{\,[e]\,\} = \mathcal{I}_d(x)$, if $d(x) = g$,
   c. $\mathcal{I}_d(s_1) \bullet \mathcal{I}_d(s_2) = \mathcal{I}_d(s_1;s_2)$,
   d. $\mathcal{I}_d(s_1) \,\|\, \mathcal{I}_d(s_2) = \mathcal{I}_d(s_1 \| s_2)$,
   e. $\mathcal{I}_d(s_1) \cup \mathcal{I}_d(s_2) = \mathcal{I}_d(s_1 + s_2)$.
2.
   a. $\mathcal{O}_d(a) = \{\,[a]\,\}$,
   b. $\mathcal{O}_d(x) = \mathcal{O}_d(g)$, when $d(x) = g$,
   c. $\mathcal{O}_d(s_1;s_2) = \mathcal{O}_d(s_1) \bullet \mathcal{O}_d(s_2)$,

d. $\mathcal{O}_d(s_1 \| s_2) = \mathcal{O}_d(s_1) \| \mathcal{O}_d(s_2)$,

e. $\mathcal{O}_d(s_1 + s_2) = \mathcal{O}_d(s_1) \cup \mathcal{O}_d(s_2)$.

PROOF

1. First we prove that a ... e hold with "$\subseteq$" instead of "$=$". Only case c. is proved because a. immediately follows from axiom (1) and b. from axiom (6) and rule (2), d. is like c. and e. follows from rule (4).

Let $p \in \mathcal{I}_d(s_1) \bullet \mathcal{I}_d(s_2)$. Then $p = p_1 \bullet p_2$ with $p_1 \in \mathcal{I}_d(s_1)$ and $p_2 \in \mathcal{I}_d(s_2)$. So $s_1 \xrightarrow{p_1}_d E$ and $s_2 \xrightarrow{p_2}_d E$ so (rule(3)) $s_1;s_2 \xrightarrow{p_1 \bullet p_2}_d E$ or equivalently $p \in \mathcal{I}_d(s_1;s_2)$.

To prove "$=$", define $\mathcal{I}_d'$ as follows.

$\mathcal{I}_d'(a) = \{ [a] \}$, $\mathcal{I}_d'(x) = \mathcal{I}_d(g) \cup \{ [e] \}$, when $d(x) = g$,
$\mathcal{I}_d'(s_1;s_2) = \mathcal{I}_d(s_1) \bullet \mathcal{I}_d(s_2)$, $\mathcal{I}_d'(s_1 \| s_2) = \mathcal{I}_d(s_1) \| \mathcal{I}_d(s_2)$ and
$\mathcal{I}_d'(s_1 + s_2) = \mathcal{I}_d(s_1) \cup \mathcal{I}_d(s_2)$.

It follows immediately that $\forall s : \mathcal{I}_d'(s) \subseteq \mathcal{I}_d(s)$ and $\mathcal{I}_d'(s)$ is closed.

Define $\longrightarrow'$ by $s \xrightarrow{p}'_d E \Leftrightarrow p \in \mathcal{I}_d'(s)$

$\longrightarrow'$ satisfies rules (1)...(6) :

(1) trivial.

(2) if $g \xrightarrow{p}'_d E$ and $d(x) = g$ then $p \in \mathcal{I}_d'(g) \subseteq \mathcal{I}_d(g) \subseteq \mathcal{I}_d'(x)$.

(3) if $s \xrightarrow{p_1}'_d E$ and $s \xrightarrow{p_2}'_d E$ then $p_1 \in \mathcal{I}_d'(s_1) \subseteq \mathcal{I}_d(s_1)$ and $p_2 \in \mathcal{I}_d'(s_2) \subseteq \mathcal{I}_d(s_2)$ so $p_1 \bullet p_2 \in \mathcal{I}_d'(s_1;s_2)$ and $p_1 \| p_2 \in \mathcal{I}_d'(s_1 \| s_2)$.

(4) if $s_1 \xrightarrow{p}'_d E$ then $p \in \mathcal{I}_d'(s_1) \subseteq \mathcal{I}_d(s_1) \subseteq \mathcal{I}_d'(s_1 + s_2)$ so $s_1 + s_2 \xrightarrow{p}'_d E$ and similar $s_2 + s_1 \xrightarrow{p}'_d E$.

(5) $\mathcal{I}_d'(s)$ is closed.

(6) $[e] \in \mathcal{I}_d'(x)$ so $x \xrightarrow{[e]}'_d E$.

$\longrightarrow$ is the smallest relation satisfying (1)...(6), so $\longrightarrow \subseteq \longrightarrow'$ or equivalently $\mathcal{I}_d(s) \subseteq \mathcal{I}_d'(s)$.

This proves 1.

2. a. $\mathcal{O}_d(a) = \mathcal{I}_d(a) \cap \mathcal{POM}[\mathcal{A}] = \{ [a] \} \cap \mathcal{POM}[\mathcal{A}] = \{ [a] \}$.

b. $\mathcal{O}_d(x) = \mathcal{I}_d(x) \cap \mathcal{POM}[\mathcal{A}] = \mathcal{I}_d(g) \cap \mathcal{POM}[\mathcal{A}] = \mathcal{O}_d(g)$.

c. $\mathcal{O}_d(s_1;s_2) = \mathcal{I}_d(s_1;s_2) \cap \mathcal{POM}[\mathcal{A}] = (\mathcal{I}_d(s_1) \bullet \mathcal{I}_d(s_2)) \cap \mathcal{POM}[\mathcal{A}] \stackrel{\alpha}{=}$
$(\mathcal{I}_d(s_1) \cap \mathcal{POM}[\mathcal{A}]) \bullet (\mathcal{I}_d(s_2) \cap \mathcal{POM}[\mathcal{A}]) = \mathcal{O}_d(s_1) \bullet \mathcal{O}_d(s_2)$.

Maybe the equality marked with an α needs some explanation.

"$\supseteq$" is trivial : $\mathcal{POM}[\mathcal{A}]$ is closed under $\bullet$.

To prove "$\subseteq$" : $(\mathcal{I}_d(s_1) \bullet \mathcal{I}_d(s_2)) \cap \mathcal{POM}[\mathcal{A}] =$
$\{ p_1 \bullet p_2 \in \mathcal{POM}[\mathcal{A}] \mid p_1 \in \mathcal{I}_d(s_1)$ and $p_2 \in \mathcal{I}_d(s_2) \} = (*)$.

Let $p_1 \bullet p_2 \in (*)$. We have $e \notin act(p_1)$.

If $length(p_1) = \infty$ then

take a $p'_2 \in \mathcal{O}_d(s_2) = \mathcal{I}_d(s_2) \cap \mathcal{POM}[\mathcal{A}]$ ($\mathcal{O}_d(s_2) \neq \varnothing$). So $p_1 \bullet p_2 = p_1 = p_1 \bullet p'_2 \in (\mathcal{I}_d(s_1) \cap \mathcal{POM}[\mathcal{A}]) \bullet (\mathcal{I}_d(s_2) \cap \mathcal{POM}[\mathcal{A}])$.
If $length(p_1) < \infty$ then also $e \notin act(p_2)$ so
$p_1 \bullet p_2 \in (\mathcal{I}_d(s_1) \cap \mathcal{POM}[\mathcal{A}]) \bullet (\mathcal{I}_d(s_2) \cap \mathcal{POM}[\mathcal{A}])$.

d. like c. but now the corresponding equation marked with the α is direct.

e. like d. □

4.3. Denotational semantics

In this section we are going to define a denotational semantics for $\mathcal{L}$. This is done with the aid of some higher-order operator, that will turn out to be a contraction. To prove this, we need the following lemma.

LEMMA 4.3.1

1. $\forall p,q,p',q' \in \mathcal{POM}$: if $p \neq []$ and $p' \neq []$ then
$d(p \bullet q,\ p' \bullet q') \leqslant \max \{ d(p,\ p'),\ \frac{1}{2} d(q,\ q') \}$.
2. $\forall p,q,p',q' \in \mathcal{POM}$: $d(p \,\|\, q,\ p' \,\|\, q') \leqslant \max \{ d(p,\ p'),\ d(q,\ q') \}$.
3. $\forall P,Q,P',Q' \in \mathcal{POM}^*$: if $[] \notin P$ and $[] \notin P'$ then
$d(P \bullet Q,\ P' \bullet Q') \leqslant \max \{ d(P,\ P'),\ \frac{1}{2} d(Q,\ Q') \}$.
4. $\forall P,Q,P',Q' \in \mathcal{POM}^*$: $d(P \,\|\, Q,\ P' \,\|\, Q') \leqslant \max \{ d(P,\ P'),\ d(Q,\ Q') \}$.
5. $\forall P,Q,P',Q' \in \mathcal{POM}^*$: $d(P + Q,\ P' + Q') \leqslant \max \{ d(P,\ P'),\ d(Q,\ Q') \}$.

PROOF

1. If $\max \{ d(p,\ p'),\ \frac{1}{2} d(q,\ q') \} = 1$ then 1. holds trivially.
If $\max \{ d(p,\ p'),\ \frac{1}{2} d(q,\ q') \} \leqslant 2^{-n}$ $(n \geqslant 1)$ then $p[n] = p'[n]$ and $q[n-1] = q'[n-1]$. If $length(p) \geqslant n$ then also $length(p') \geqslant n$ and we have $(p \bullet q)[n] = p[n] = p'[n] = (p' \bullet q')[n]$. If $length(p) < n$ then $p = p'$ and so $(p \bullet q)[n] = p \bullet q[n - length(p)]$ (because $length(p) > 0$) $= p \bullet q'[n - length(p)] = (p \bullet q')[n] = (p' \bullet q')[n]$. So $d(p \bullet q,\ p' \bullet q') \leqslant 2^{-n}$.
2. Similar to 1.
3. This is a consequence of 1. Details can be found in the appendix.
4. Similar to 3.
5. Straightforward verification. □

Now we will define the higher-order mapping.

DEFINITION 4.3.2 $\Phi_d : (\mathcal{L} \to \mathcal{POM}^*) \to (\mathcal{L} \to \mathcal{POM}^*)$ is defined as follows.

Let $F \in \mathcal{L} \to \mathcal{POM}^*$.

$\Phi_d(F)(a) = \{ [a] \}$

$\Phi_d(F)(s_1;s_2) = \Phi_d(F)(s_1) \bullet F(s_2)$
$\Phi_d(F)(s_1 \| s_2) = \Phi_d(F)(s_1) \parallel \Phi_d(F)(s_2)$
$\Phi_d(F)(s_1 + s_2) = \Phi_d(F)(s_1) + \Phi_d(F)(s_2)$
$\Phi_d(F)(x) = \Phi_d(F)(d(x))$

Lemma 4.3.3

1. $\Phi_d(F)$ is well-defined.
2. $[] \notin \Phi_d(F)(s)$
3. Φ_d is a contraction.

Proof 1. and 2. can easily be shown, first for guarded statements and then for general statements, with induction on the complexity of the statements. For 3. one needs to show $\forall s \in \mathscr{L}: d(\Phi_d(F_1)(s), \Phi_d(F_2)(s)) \leqslant \frac{1}{2}d(F_1, F_2)$. Again, this can be shown, first for guarded statements and then for general statements, with induction on the complexity of the statements. We only treat the case $s = s_1;s_2$ as an example.

$d(\Phi_d(F_1)(s_1;s_2), \Phi_d(F_2)(s_1;s_2)) =$
$d(\Phi_d(F_1)(s_1) \bullet F_1(s_2), \Phi_d(F_2)(s_1) \bullet F_2(s_2)) \leqslant$ by part 2. and lemma 4.3.1.3
$\max\{ d(\Phi_d(F_1)(s_1), \Phi_d(F_2)(s_1)), \frac{1}{2}d(F_1(s_2), F_2(s_2)) \} \leqslant$ by induction
$\frac{1}{2}d(F_1, F_2)$ □

Definition 4.3.4

1. $\mathscr{D}_d : \mathscr{L} \to \mathscr{POM}^*$ is defined by $\mathscr{D}_d =$ fixed-point Φ_d.
2. $\mathscr{D} : \mathscr{Prog} \to \mathscr{POM}^*$ is defined by $\mathscr{D}(< d \mid s >) = \mathscr{D}_d(s)$

4.4. Operational semantics = Denotational semantics

Theorem 4.4.1 $\mathscr{O} = \mathscr{D}$

Proof We have to show that $\mathscr{O}_d = \mathscr{D}_d$, for all $d \in \mathscr{Decl}$. Since $\mathscr{D}_d$ is the unique fixed-point of Φ_d, it is sufficient to prove that $\Phi_d(\mathscr{O}_d) = \mathscr{O}_d$. This is a direct consequence of lemma 4.2.6.2. □

5. Synchronization

In this section we incorporate a CCS-style synchronization to our language and give a denotational semantics for this language. The most intuitive approach, where for instance we would define

$$\mathcal{D}(c \,\|\, \bar{c}) = \left\{ \begin{bmatrix} \mathrm{c} \\ \bar{\mathrm{c}} \end{bmatrix}, \; \begin{bmatrix} \tau \end{bmatrix} \right\},$$

leads to a parallel operator that does not satisfy the (necessary, see 4.3) requirement that it be non-distance-increasing.
Consider, for example, the following pomsets.

$$p = \begin{bmatrix} \mathrm{a} \rightarrow \mathrm{c} \end{bmatrix}, \quad p' = \begin{bmatrix} \mathrm{a} \rightarrow \mathrm{d} \end{bmatrix}, \qquad q = q' = \begin{bmatrix} \bar{\mathrm{c}} \end{bmatrix}.$$

If we would define

$$p \,\|\, q = \left\{ \begin{bmatrix} \mathrm{a} \rightarrow \mathrm{c} \\ \bar{\mathrm{c}} \end{bmatrix}, \; \begin{bmatrix} \mathrm{a} \rightarrow \tau \end{bmatrix} \right\}$$

and

$$p' \,\|\, q' = \left\{ \begin{bmatrix} \mathrm{a} \rightarrow \mathrm{d} \\ \bar{\mathrm{c}} \end{bmatrix} \right\}$$

then $d(p \,\|\, q, p' \,\|\, q') = 1$, while $d(p, p') \leqslant \frac{1}{2}$ and $d(q, q') = 0 \leqslant \frac{1}{2}$, showing that the operator '$\|$' fails to be non-distance-increasing.
The solution to this problem that we present here is more or less of a mathematical nature; it doesn't have a very clear semantic intuition. Maybe this approach will be a stepping-stone for a more intuitive solution.
Instead of only delivering 'pure' non interleaved outcomes, we extend the denotational semantics with all interleaved outcomes and all intermediate results.
With p and q as given above, we will have

$$p \,\|\, q = \left\{ \begin{bmatrix} \mathrm{a} \rightarrow \mathrm{c} \\ \bar{\mathrm{c}} \end{bmatrix}, \begin{bmatrix} \mathrm{a} \rightarrow \tau \end{bmatrix}, \begin{bmatrix} \mathrm{a} \begin{smallmatrix} \nearrow \mathrm{c} \\ \searrow \bar{\mathrm{c}} \end{smallmatrix} \end{bmatrix}, \begin{bmatrix} \begin{smallmatrix} \mathrm{a} \searrow \\ \bar{\mathrm{c}} \nearrow \end{smallmatrix} \mathrm{c} \end{bmatrix}, \begin{bmatrix} \mathrm{a} \rightarrow \mathrm{c} \rightarrow \bar{\mathrm{c}} \end{bmatrix}, \begin{bmatrix} \mathrm{a} \rightarrow \bar{\mathrm{c}} \rightarrow \mathrm{c} \end{bmatrix}, \begin{bmatrix} \bar{\mathrm{c}} \rightarrow \mathrm{a} \rightarrow \mathrm{c} \end{bmatrix} \right\}$$

and

$$p' \,\|\, q' = \left\{ \begin{bmatrix} \mathrm{a} \rightarrow \mathrm{d} \\ \bar{\mathrm{c}} \end{bmatrix}, \begin{bmatrix} \mathrm{a} \begin{smallmatrix} \nearrow \mathrm{d} \\ \searrow \bar{\mathrm{c}} \end{smallmatrix} \end{bmatrix}, \begin{bmatrix} \begin{smallmatrix} \mathrm{a} \searrow \\ \bar{\mathrm{c}} \nearrow \end{smallmatrix} \mathrm{d} \end{bmatrix}, \begin{bmatrix} \mathrm{a} \rightarrow \mathrm{d} \rightarrow \bar{\mathrm{c}} \end{bmatrix}, \begin{bmatrix} \mathrm{a} \rightarrow \bar{\mathrm{c}} \rightarrow \mathrm{d} \end{bmatrix}, \begin{bmatrix} \bar{\mathrm{c}} \rightarrow \mathrm{a} \rightarrow \mathrm{d} \end{bmatrix} \right\}$$

making $d(p \| q, p' \| q') = \frac{1}{2}$, solving the problem mentioned above.

In subsection 5.1 we define the extended language. In subsection 5.2 we make the new definition of the parallel operator precise and in subsection 5.3 we prove the fact that this operator is non-distance-increasing. We conclude with the denotational semantics and an example in subsection 5.4.

5.1. A language with synchronization

To extend the language with synchronization, assume $\mathcal{A} = \mathcal{I} \cup \mathcal{C}$: the disjoint union of a set of internal actions $(a,b,... \in)\mathcal{I}$ and a set of synchronization actions $(c \in)\mathcal{C}$. Let $^{-}: \mathcal{C} \rightarrow \mathcal{C}$ (notation : $\bar{c}$ instead of $^{-}(c)$) be a bijection, such that $\bar{\bar{c}} = c$, yielding the matching synchronization action of c. There is some special element $\tau \in \mathcal{I}$ denoting successful synchronization.

DEFINITION 5.1.1

a. The class $(s \in)\mathcal{L}$ of *statements* is given by

$$s ::= a \mid c \mid x \mid s_1;s_2 \mid s_1+s_2 \mid s_1 \| s_2 \qquad a \neq \tau$$

b. The class $(g \in)\mathcal{L}^g$ of *guarded statements* is given by

$$g ::= a \mid c \mid g;s \mid g_1+g_2 \mid g_1 \| g_2 \qquad a \neq \tau$$

c. The class $(d \in)\mathcal{D}ecl$ of *declarations* consists of mappings from $\mathcal{P}var$ to $\mathcal{L}^g$.

d. The class $(t \in)\mathcal{P}rog$ of *programs* consists of pairs $t \equiv \langle d \mid s \rangle$ with $d \in \mathcal{D}ecl$ and $s \in \mathcal{L}$.

5.2. The parallel operator

In order to give a semantics for this language, we need to change the definition of the parallel operator ($\|$). Let $\|_{OLD}$ denote the parallel composition defined in section 3.3. The new parallel composition will be defined by taking the result of the old parallel operator and adding some more results. The additional results will be obtained by transforming old results by two kinds of transformation steps : $\xrightarrow{FUSE}$ and $\xrightarrow{AUG}$. Two nodes in a structure, one labeled with c, the other labeled with $\bar{c}$, are taken together in a $\xrightarrow{FUSE}$ step and the label is replaced by a τ. This step models the real synchronization. To solve the problem mentioned in the introduction of this section, we also add structures obtained by adding more causal dependencies in the structure. For this purpose, we define the $\xrightarrow{AUG}$ steps.

DEFINITION 5.2.1

1. For a structure σ and $x_1, x_2 \in X_\sigma$ independent (i.e. $x_1 \not\leqslant_\sigma x_2 \wedge x_2 \not\leqslant_\sigma x_1$), we define a new structure $\sigma' = (X_\sigma, \leqslant_{\sigma'}, \lambda_\sigma)$, where $\leqslant_{\sigma'} = \leqslant_\sigma \cup$

$\{ (x, y) \mid x \leqslant_\sigma x_1 \wedge x_2 \leqslant_\sigma y \}$. We will use the notation $\sigma \xrightarrow{AUG(x_1,\, x_2)} \sigma'$.

2. We define $\xrightarrow{AUG} \subseteq \mathcal{POM} \times \mathcal{POM}$ by $p \xrightarrow{AUG} p' \Leftrightarrow \exists \sigma, \sigma' : p = [\sigma] \wedge p' = [\sigma'] \wedge \sigma \xrightarrow{AUG(x_1,\, x_2)} \sigma'$ for some pair of independent nodes $x_1, x_2 \in X_\sigma$.

Remarks 5.2.2

1. It is easy to see that σ' is indeed a structure.
2. If $\sigma \xrightarrow{AUG(x_1,\, x_2)} \sigma'$ and $\phi : \sigma \to \rho$ is an isomorphism then $\exists \rho' : \rho \xrightarrow{AUG(\phi(x_1),\, \phi(x_2))} \rho'$ and $\phi : \sigma' \to \rho'$ is an isomorphism.
3. From 2. it follows that $\xrightarrow{AUG}$ is well defined.

Definition 5.2.3

1. Let σ be a structure. We call (x_1, x_2) a matching pair in σ if $x_1 \not\leqslant_\sigma x_2$, $x_2 \not\leqslant_\sigma x_1$ and $\lambda_\sigma(x_1) \in \mathscr{C}$, $\lambda_\sigma(x_2) \in \mathscr{C}$ and $\overline{\lambda_\sigma(x_1)} = \lambda_\sigma(x_2)$.
   We define a new structure $\sigma' = (X_{\sigma'}, \leqslant_{\sigma'}, \lambda_{\sigma'})$ associated with σ and a matching pair (x_1, x_2), where
   $X_{\sigma'} = X_\sigma \setminus \{ x_2 \}$,
   $\leqslant_{\sigma'} = (\leqslant_\sigma \cap (X_{\sigma'} \times X_{\sigma'})) \cup$
   $\{ (x, y) \mid x \leqslant_\sigma x_1 \wedge x_2 <_\sigma y \} \cup \{ (x, y) \mid x <_\sigma x_2 \wedge x_1 \leqslant_\sigma y \}$ and
   $\lambda_{\sigma'}(x) = \lambda_\sigma(x)$, if $x \neq x_1$, and τ otherwise.
   We will use the notation $\sigma \xrightarrow{FUSE(x_1,\, x_2)} \sigma'$.
2. We define $\xrightarrow{FUSE} \subseteq \mathcal{POM} \times \mathcal{POM}$ by $p \xrightarrow{FUSE} p' \Leftrightarrow \exists \sigma, \sigma' : p = [\sigma] \wedge p' = [\sigma'] \wedge \sigma \xrightarrow{FUSE(x_1,\, x_2)} \sigma'$ for some matching pair of nodes $x_1, x_2 \in X_\sigma$.

Remarks 5.2.4

1. It is easy to see that σ' is indeed a structure.
2. If $\sigma \xrightarrow{FUSE(x_1,\, x_2)} \sigma'$ and $\phi : \sigma \to \rho$ is an isomorphism then $\exists \rho' : \rho \xrightarrow{FUSE(\phi(x_1),\, \phi(x_2))} \rho'$ and $\phi \restriction X_{\sigma'} : \sigma' \to \rho'$ is an isomorphism.
3. By 2. we have that $\xrightarrow{FUSE}$ is well defined.

Examples 5.2.5 Let $p_1, \ldots, p_7$ be equal to respectively

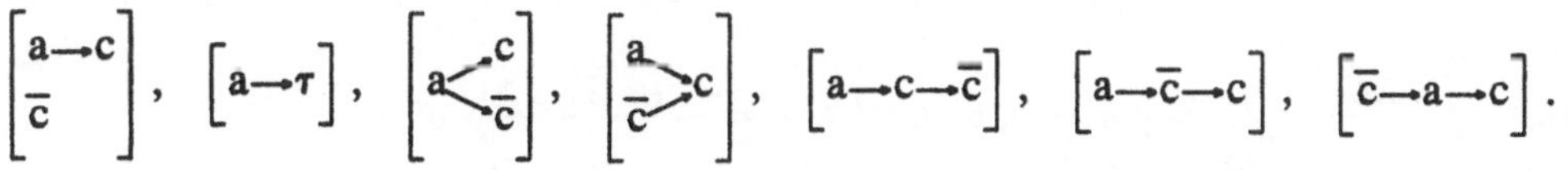

Then $p_2, \ldots, p_7$ are all obtained from p_1 by doing one or more $\xrightarrow{AUG}$ or $\xrightarrow{FUSE}$ steps. For instance p_2 is derived from p_1 by doing a $\xrightarrow{FUSE}$ step, p_3 is obtained from p_1 by doing a $\xrightarrow{AUG}$ step (with (x_1, x_2) equal to (the node belonging to a, the node belonging to c̄)) and p_5 can for instance be produced by doing a $\xrightarrow{AUG}$ step from p_3.

The next lemma states the following. If $n \in \mathbb{N}_0$ is fixed and σ can be transformed to ρ by some transformation step then either $\sigma[n] = \rho[n]$ or $\sigma[n]$ can be transformed to a ρ' that is equal to ρ up to level n ($\rho[n] = \rho'[n]$). This will be needed to prove that the parallel operator is non-distance-increasing.

Lemma 5.2.6 Let $n \in \mathbb{N}_0$ be fixed.

1. Let $\sigma \xrightarrow{AUG(x_1,\, x_2)} \rho$.
   a. If $lev(x_2) > n$ then $\sigma[n] = \rho[n]$.
   b. If $lev(x_1) \leqslant n \wedge lev(x_2) \leqslant n$ then
      $\exists \rho' : \sigma[n] \xrightarrow{AUG(x_1,\, x_2)} \rho' \wedge \rho'[n] = \rho[n]$.
   c. If $lev(x_1) > n \wedge lev(x_2) \leqslant n$ then
      $\exists x_1' : x_1' \not\leqslant_\sigma x_2 \wedge x_2 \not\leqslant_\sigma x_1' \wedge lev(x_1') = n$:
      $\exists \rho' : \sigma \xrightarrow{AUG(x_1',\, x_2)} \rho' \wedge \rho'[n] = \rho[n]$.
2. Let $\sigma \xrightarrow{FUSE(x_1,\, x_2)} \rho$.
   a. If $lev(x_1) > n \wedge lev(x_2) > n$ then $\sigma[n] = \rho[n]$.
   b. If $lev(x_1) \leqslant n \wedge lev(x_2) \leqslant n$ then
      $\exists \rho' : \sigma[n] \xrightarrow{FUSE(x_1,\, x_2)} \rho' \wedge \rho'[n] = \rho[n]$.
   c. If $lev(x_1) > n \wedge lev(x_2) \leqslant n$ then
      $\exists x_1' : x_1' \not\leqslant_\sigma x_2 \wedge x_2 \not\leqslant_\sigma x_1' \wedge lev(x_1') = n$:
      $\exists \rho' : \sigma \xrightarrow{AUG(x_1',\, x_2)} \rho' \wedge \rho'[n] = \rho[n]$
      [Note that a $\xrightarrow{FUSE}$ step is replaced by a $\xrightarrow{AUG}$ step!].

We omit the proof here because it is only technical and does not give any insight. Moreover, for the most difficult case (2.c) we give an example after the next proposition.

Let $\xrightarrow{A\&F} = \xrightarrow{AUG} \cup \xrightarrow{FUSE}$ and let $\xrightarrow{A\&F}{}^*$ denote the reflexive transitive closure of $\xrightarrow{A\&F}$.

Proposition 5.2.7 Let $n \in \mathbb{N}_0$ be fixed.
If $p[n] = q[n]$ and $p \xrightarrow{A\&F} p'$ then $p'[n] = q[n]$ or $\exists q' : q \xrightarrow{A\&F} q' \wedge p'[n] = q'[n]$.

Proof

Case I : $p \xrightarrow{AUG} p'$. Say $\sigma \in p$, $\sigma' \in p'$ and $\sigma \xrightarrow{AUG(x_1,\, x_2)} \sigma'$.

If $lev(x_2) > n$ then $\sigma'[n] = \sigma[n]$ so $p'[n] = p[n] = q[n]$.

Assume now that $lev(x_2) \leqslant n$. If also $lev(x_1) \leqslant n$ then $\sigma[n] \xrightarrow{AUG(x_1,\, x_2)} \sigma''$ with $\sigma''[n] = \sigma'[n]$. Let $\rho \in q$ and $\phi : \sigma[n] \sim \rho[n]$. Since x_1 and x_2 are incomparable in σ we also have that $\phi(x_1)$ and $\phi(x_2)$ are incomparable in ρ so

$p \xrightarrow{AUG(\phi(x_1),\, \phi(x_2))} p'$, say, and since $lev(\phi(x_1)) \leqslant n \wedge lev(\phi(x_2)) \leqslant n$, $p[n] \xrightarrow{AUG(\phi(x_1),\, \phi(x_2))} p''$ with $p''[n] = p'[n]$. Since $\sigma[n] \sim p[n]$ we have $\sigma'' \sim p''$ so $\sigma'[n] = \sigma''[n] \sim p''[n] = p'[n]$. If now $q' = [p']$ then $q \xrightarrow{A\&F} q'$ and $p'[n] = [\sigma'[n]] = [p'[n]] = q'[n]$.

The last case is $lev(x_1) > n$ and $lev(x_2) \leqslant n$. Then $\exists x_1' : lev(x_1') = n$ and $\sigma \xrightarrow{AUG(x_1',\, x_2)} \sigma''$ and $\sigma''[n] = \sigma'[n]$. So this reduces this case to the previous one.

Case II : $p \xrightarrow{FUSE} p'$. Say $\sigma \in p$, $\sigma' \in p'$ and $\sigma \xrightarrow{FUSE(x_1,\, x_2)} \sigma'$.

If $lev(x_1) \leqslant n$ and $lev(x_2) \leqslant n$ then $\sigma[n] \xrightarrow{FUSE(x_1,\, x_2)} \sigma''$ and $\sigma''[n] = \sigma'[n]$. Let $\rho \in q$ and $\phi : \sigma[n] \sim \rho[n]$. Since (x_1, x_2) is a matching pair in σ, we have that $(\phi(x_1), \phi(x_2))$ is a matching pair in ρ so $\rho \xrightarrow{FUSE(\phi(x_1),\, \phi(x_2))} \rho'$, say, and since $lev(\phi(x_1)) \leqslant n \wedge lev(\phi(x_2)) \leqslant n$, $\rho[n] \xrightarrow{FUSE(\phi(x_1),\, \phi(x_2))} \rho''$ with $\rho''[n] = \rho'[n]$. Since $\sigma[n] \sim \rho[n]$ we have $\sigma'' \sim \rho''$ so $\sigma'[n] = \sigma''[n] \sim \rho''[n] = \rho'[n]$. If now $q' = [\rho']$ then $q \xrightarrow{A\&F} q'$ and $p'[n] = [\sigma'[n]] = [\rho'[n]] = q'[n]$.

If $lev(x_1) > n$ and $lev(x_2) \leqslant n$ then $\exists x_1' : lev(x_1') = n$ and $\sigma \xrightarrow{AUG(x_1',\, x_2)} \sigma''$ and $\sigma''[n] = \sigma'[n]$. Case I "$\leqslant$" "$\leqslant$" gives $\exists \rho' : \rho \xrightarrow{AUG(\phi(x_1'),\, \phi(x_2))} \rho'$ and $\sigma''[n] = \rho'[n]$ so $\sigma'[n] \sim \rho'[n]$. If now $q' = [\rho']$ then $q \xrightarrow{A\&F} q'$ and $p'[n] = [\sigma'[n]] = [\rho'[n]] = q'[n]$.

Case $lev(x_1) \leqslant n$ and $lev(x_2) > n$: analogous.

If $lev(x_1) > n$ and $lev(x_2) > n$ then $\sigma'[n] = \sigma[n]$ so $p'[n] = p[n] = q[n]$. □

Example 5.2.8 We give a little explanation about lemma 5.2.6 and proposition 5.2.7 for the most difficult case namely 5.2.6.2.c and the corresponding Case II "$>$" "$\leqslant$" of proposition 5.2.7. Let p, p', q, q' be equal to respectively

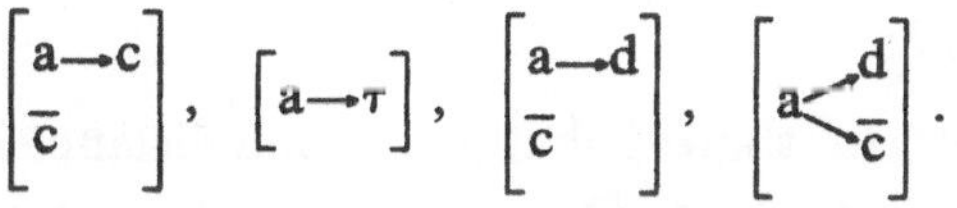

We have $p \xrightarrow{FUSE} p'$ and $p[1] = q[1]$ and since $p'[1] \neq q[1]$ lemma 5.2.7 guarantees the existence of a q' such that $q \xrightarrow{A\&F} q'$ and $p'[1] = q'[1]$. Indeed the q defined above satisfies $q \xrightarrow{AUG} q'$ and $p'[1] = q'[1]$.

Definition 5.2.9

1. $syn : \mathcal{POM} \to \mathcal{POM}^*$ is defined by $syn(p) = \overline{\{\, q \mid p \xrightarrow{A\&F}{}^* q \,\}}$.
2. $syn : \mathcal{POM}^* \to \mathcal{POM}^*$ is defined by $syn(P) = \overline{\bigcup \{\, syn(p) \mid p \in P \,\}}$.

3. $\| : \mathcal{POM}^* \times \mathcal{POM}^* \to \mathcal{POM}^*$ is defined by $\| \; = syn \circ \|_{OLD}$.

The closures are taken to get closed sets and thus elements of $\mathcal{POM}^*$. Moreover, pomsets that contain infinitely many synchronizations are added in this way (see example 5.4.1).

5.3. The parallel operator is non distance increasing

PROPOSITION 5.3.1 $syn : \mathcal{POM} \to \mathcal{POM}^*$ is non distance increasing.

PROOF Let $p, q \in \mathcal{POM}$ such that $p[n] = q[n]$. It suffices to show that $d(\{ p' \mid p \xrightarrow{A\&F}{}^* p' \}, \{ q' \mid q \xrightarrow{A\&F}{}^* q' \}) \leq 2^{-n}$ or equivalently $p \xrightarrow{A\&F}{}^* p' \Rightarrow \exists q' : q \xrightarrow{A\&F}{}^* q' \wedge p'[n] = q'[n]$ and vice versa. This is done by induction on the number of steps in which p' is obtained from p. Let us denote this by $p \xrightarrow{A\&F}{}^k p'$. If $k = 0$ then $p' = p$, so we can take $q' = q$. If $p \xrightarrow{A\&F}{}^{k+1} p'$ then $\exists p_k$ such that $p \xrightarrow{A\&F}{}^k p_k \xrightarrow{A\&F} p'$. By induction there exists a $\overline{q'}$ such that $q \xrightarrow{A\&F}{}^* \overline{q'}$ and $p_k[n] = \overline{q'}[n]$. By proposition 5.2.7 we have that either $p'[n] = \overline{q'}[n]$, in which case we can take $q' = \overline{q'}$, or there exists a q' such that $\overline{q'} \xrightarrow{A\&F} q'$ and $q'[n] = p'[n]$. The symmetric case is similar. □

PROPOSITION 5.3.2 $syn : \mathcal{POM}^* \to \mathcal{POM}^*$ is non distance increasing.

PROOF This is a consequence of proposition 5.3.1 and a small adaptation of the appendix. □

PROPOSITION 5.3.3 $\| : \mathcal{POM}^* \times \mathcal{POM}^* \to \mathcal{POM}^*$ is non distance increasing.

PROOF The composition of two N.D.I. mappings is again N.D.I. □

5.4. Denotational semantics

In the previous subsection we showed that $\|$ is a non-distance-increasing mapping. So lemmas 4.3.1.3, 4.3.1.4, and 4.3.1.5 hold in the new setting. We can now give the denotational semantics for the extended language in the same way as we did in subsection 4.3 by substitution of the old $\|$ by the new $\|$.

EXAMPLE 5.4.1 Let $d(x) = a;(b \| c);x$ and $d(y) = a;(\overline{c} \| d);y$. Then $\mathcal{D}(< d \mid x >)$ contains for instance :

and $\mathscr{D}(< d \mid y >)$ contains for instance :

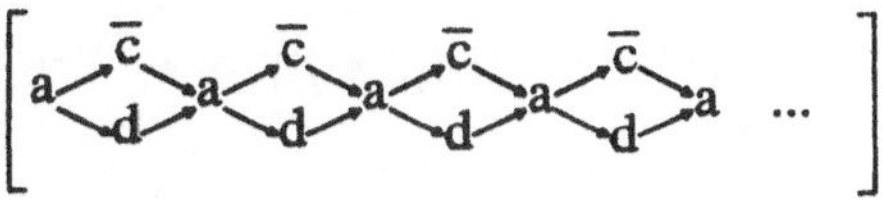

So $\mathscr{D}(< d \mid x \| y >)$ contains for instance :

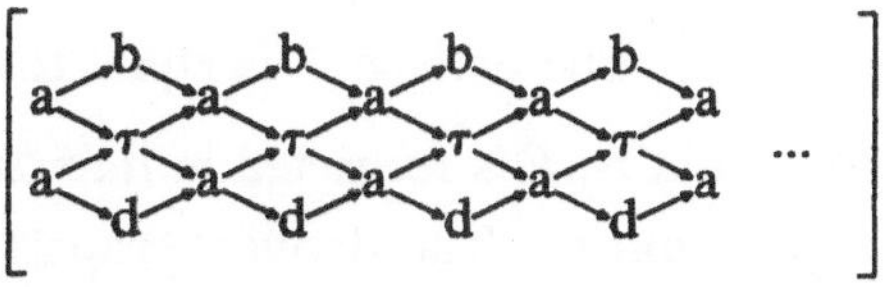

but also :

$$\left[a \to b \to c \to a \to b \to c \to a \to b \to c \to a \to b \to c \to a \ \ldots \right]$$

6. Appendix

In this appendix, it is shown that lemma 4.3.1.3 is a consequence of lemma 4.3.1.1 by applying some metric techniques.

Lemma 6.1 Let $M_1, \ldots, M_n$ and M be metric spaces.
Let $f : M_1 \times \ldots \times M_n \to M$ with $\lambda x_i . f(x_1, \ldots, x_i, \ldots, x_n) : M_i \to^{\gamma_i} M$.
Then $F : \mathscr{P}_{nc}(M_1) \times \ldots \times \mathscr{P}_{nc}(M_n) \to \mathscr{P}_{nc}(M)$ defined by
$F(A_1, \ldots, A_n) = \overline{\{ f(a_1, \ldots, a_n) \mid a_i \in A_i \, , \, i = 1, \ldots, n \}}$ satisfies
$\lambda A_i . F(A_1, \ldots, A_i, \ldots, A_n) : \mathscr{P}_{nc}(M_i) \to^{\gamma_i} \mathscr{P}_{nc}(M)$.

Proof We have to show that

$$d(F(A_1, \ldots, A_i, \ldots, A_n), F(A_1, \ldots, A'_i, \ldots, A_n) \leqslant \gamma_i \cdot d(A_i, A'_i)$$

or equivalently :

$$\forall \epsilon > 0 : d(F(A_1, \ldots, A_i, \ldots, A_n), F(A_1, \ldots, A'_i, \ldots, A_n) \leqslant \gamma_i \cdot d(A_i, A'_i) + \epsilon.$$

Let $x \in F(A_1, \ldots, A_i, \ldots, A_n)$. We will show that there exists an $y \in F(A_1, \ldots, A'_i, \ldots, A_n)$ such that $d(x, y) \leqslant \gamma_i \cdot d(A_i, A'_i) + \epsilon$ (the other part is analogous).

Since $x \in \overline{\{ f(a_1, \ldots, a_n) \mid a_i \in A_i \, , \, i = 1, \ldots, n \}}$, there exist $a_1, \ldots, a_n$ such that $d(x, f(a_1, \ldots, a_n)) \leqslant \frac{\epsilon}{2}$. By the definition of the Hausdorff distance, $\exists a'_i \in A'_i : d(a_i, a'_i) \leqslant \frac{\epsilon}{2\gamma_i + 1} + d(A_i, A'_i)$. Take $y = f(a_1, \ldots, a'_i, \ldots, a_n)$.

Now $d(x, y) \leq d(x, f(a_1, ..., a_n)) + d(f(a_1, ..., a_i, ..., a_n), f(a_1, ..., a'_i, ..., a_n))$

$$\leq d(x, f(a_1, ..., a_n)) + \gamma_i \cdot d(a_i, a'_i)$$

$$\leq \frac{\epsilon}{2} + \gamma_i \cdot (\frac{\epsilon}{2\gamma_i + 1} + d(A_i, A'_i)) \leq \epsilon + \gamma_i \cdot d(A_i, A'_i). \qquad \square$$

To show lemma 4.3.1.3, let $M_1 = \mathcal{POM} \setminus \{[]\}$ and $M_2 = M = \mathcal{POM}$ and let $f = \bullet\restriction(M_1 \times M_2) : M_1 \times M_2 \to M$. By lemma 4.3.1.1 f satisfies the premise of the lemma with $\gamma_1 = 1$ and $\gamma_2 = \frac{1}{2}$. The derived F is equal to $\bullet$ on $\mathcal{POM}^* \times \mathcal{POM}^*$ restricted to $\mathcal{P}_{nc}(M_1) \times \mathcal{POM}^*$. That is, F is restricted in its first argument to pomset-sets that do not contain the empty pomset. The derived property of F is exactly the one formulated in lemma 4.3.1.3, since $\mathcal{POM}^*$ is an ultra-metric space.

7. References

[ABKR89] P. America, J.W. de Bakker, J.N. Kok, J.J.M.M. Rutten, *Denotational semantics of a parallel object-oriented language,* Information and Computation, Vol. 83, pp. 152-205, 1989.

[AR89] P. America, J.J.M.M. Rutten, *Solving reflexive domain equations in a category of complete metric spaces,* Journal of Computer and System Sciences, Vol 39, nr. 3, pp.343-375, 1989.

[B88] J.W. de Bakker, *Comparative semantics for flow of control in logic programming without logic,* Report CS-R8840, Centre for Mathematics and Computer Science, Amsterdam (1988), to appear in Information and Computation.

[B89] J.W. de Bakker, *Designing concurrency semantics,* in: Information Processing 89, G.X. Ritter (ed.), Elsevier, pp. 591-598, 1989.

[BBKM84] J.W. de Bakker, J.A. Bergstra, J.W. Klop, J.-J.Ch. Meyer, *Linear time and branching time semantics for recursion with merge,* Theoretical Computer Science 34 (1984) 135-156.

[BKMOZ86] J.W. de Bakker, J.N. Kok, J.-J.Ch. Meyer, E.-R. Olderog, J.I. Zucker, *Contrasting themes in the semantics of imperative concurrency,* in Current Trends in Concurrency: Overviews and Tutorials (J.W. de Bakker, W.P. de Roever, G. Rozenberg, eds.), Lecture Notes in Computer Science, Vol. 224, Springer (1986) 51-121.

[BM88] J.W. de Bakker, J.-J.Ch. Meyer, *Metric semantics for concurrency,* BIT 28, pp. 504-529, 1988.

[BRR89] J.W. de Bakker, W.P. de Roever, G. Rozenberg (eds.), *Linear Time, Branching Time and Partial Order,* Proc. REX School/Workshop,

Noordwijkerhout, June 1988, Lecture Notes in Computer Science, Vol. 354, Springer 1989.

[BR89] J.W. DE BAKKER, J.J.M.M. RUTTEN, *Concurrency semantics based on metric domain equations,* Report CS-R8954, Centre for Mathematics and Computer Science, Amsterdam (1989).

[BZ82] J.W. DE BAKKER, J.I. ZUCKER, *Processes and the denotational semantics of concurrency,* Information and Control 54 (1982) 70-120.

[BoCa88] G. BOUDOL, I. CASTELLANI, *Concurrency and atomicity,* Theoretical Computer Science 59 (1988) 25-84.

[Ga89] H. GAIFMAN, *Modeling concurrency by partial orders and nonlinear transition systems,* in Proc. REX School/Workshop, Noordwijkerhout, June 1988, (J.W. de Bakker, W.P. de Roever, G. Rozenberg, eds.), *Linear Time, Branching Time and Partial Order,* Lecture Notes in Computer Science, Vol. 354, Springer (1989), 467-488.

[Gi84] J. GISCHER, *Partial orders and the axiomatic theory of shuffle,* Ph.D. thesis, Stanford University, 1984.

[Gr81] J. GRABOWSKI, *On partial languages,* Fundamenta Informaticae IV.2 (1981) 427-498.

[KR88] J.N. KOK, J.J.M.M. RUTTEN, *Contractions in comparing concurrency semantics,* in Proc. 15th ICALP (T. Lepistö, A. Salomaa, eds.), Lecture Notes in Computer Science, Vol. 317, Springer (1988), 317-332. (To appear in Theoretical Computer Science.)

[MV89] J.-J.Ch. Meyer, E.P. de Vink, *Pomset semantics for true concurrency with synchronization and recursion (extended abstract),* in Proc. MFCS '89 (A Kreczmar & G. Mirkowska, eds.), Lecture Notes in Computer Science, Vol. 379, Springer (1989), 360-369.

[Pr86] V. PRATT, *Modelling concurrency with partial orders,* Int. Journal of Parallel Programming 15 (1986) 33-71.

Fault-tolerant naming and mutual exclusion

Joffroy BEAUQUIER[1]
LRI-CNRS Orsay (France)

Abstract

We present solutions to two classical problems concerning distributed systems in which some sites or processes can possibly have byzantine faulty behavior.
We first study the naming problem (how to give each site of a network an unique identifier). We are naturally led to make some supplementary assumptions about the synchrony of message passing, the connectivity of the underlying graph and the existence of a special site, provided with a digital signature, for initiating the protocol. The solution that we present uses three waves of messages between the initiator and any other site.
Then, we solve the mutual exclusion problem with particular assumptions about the behavior of byzantine processes. The solution implements each critical section as a separate segment, whose address (necessary to access it) is "hidden". A process must reconstruct this address before entering its critical section, involving the cooperation of a number of other processes.
For the two problems, protocols are given and their complexity is estimated.

Key words: distributed algorithms, fault tolerance, byzantine process, synchronous and asynchronous message passing, naming problem, mutual exclusion problem.

I. Introduction

In this paper we will consider two classical problems concerning distributed systems, under the assumption that some sites or some processes can possibly have a faulty behavior. The first one is the naming problem and the second one the mutual exclusion problem. We will briefly present them and discuss about the assumptions that we make.
Almost all distributed algorithms assume as a precondition that each site has an unique identifier. Under usual hypothesies, giving each site an identifier is straightforward, even if each site does not know about the entire network. For example, a circulating token containing an integer can perform a traversal of the network, starting with the value 1, and increasing it by 1, each time it leaves a site for the first time [Hélary and Raynal 88]. Each site choses as its unique identifier the integer in the token at its first arrival. This method, like some others ([Cheung 83], [Segall 83]), depends on the fact that each site transmits the token and increases its value correctly. If a given site decreases the value of the token instead of increasing it, two (correct) sites would receive the same identifier. And what about a site keeping the token forever!
In this paper, we will be interested in the (non-trivial) problem of giving each site an unique identifier, assuming that some sites can have byzantine behavior [Lamport, Shostak and Pease 80]. That means that, roughly speaking, the bad sites can perform anything: send false messages or not send messages at all, have a correct behavior, stop then restart, etc.. A site that permanently follows its protocol is called correct.
Without some supplementary, rather strong, assumptions, the naming problem has no solution. We will not present a formal treatment yielding results of indecidability, but simply describe the wrong situations that can possibly occur.

---

[1]LRI-CNRS, Université Paris Sud, Bâtiment 490, F91405 ORSAY Cedex, FRANCE.
This research has been supported by the PRC C^3.

Firstly, let us consider the network in Figure 1.

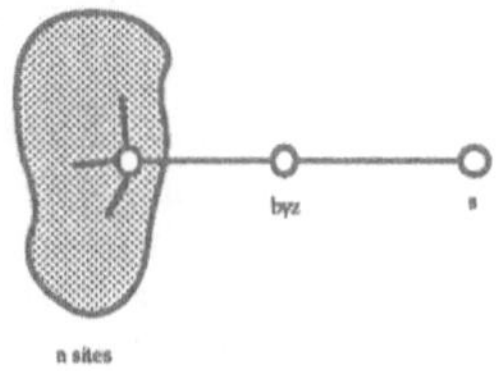

Fig. 1.

If the site s can only communicate with the rest of the network through the byzantine site byz, it cannot necessarily distinguish between the situation above and the situation in Figure 2.

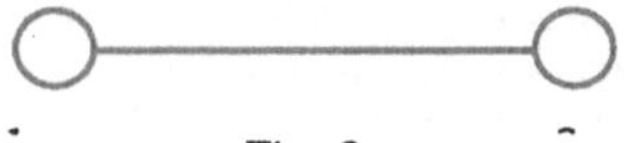

Fig. 2.

Thus, if a deterministic algorithm for solving the naming problem did exist, it must give s an identifier independent of those given to the n other sites. Then the uniqueness of the identifiers would not be ensured.
Such a paradox also appears when a site is "surrounded" by byzantine sites or when two or more correct sites cannot communicate without avoiding a byzantine one.
So, we are naturally led to an assumption about the connectivity degree of the network.
Let k be a strict upper bound to the number of possible byzantine processes. We will assume that the network is k-connected. That is there are at least k+1 disjoint paths connecting two correct sites. Among these k+1 disjoint paths, at least one goes through only correct processes.
The most general and difficult hypothesis about message passing is asynchrony. When the network is not known, asynchrony does not allow to detect the termination of an algorithm. We will assume here that each site knows an upper bound to the maximal lenght of an elementary path between two sites in the network.
The third assumption concerns asymmetry. The naming problem has no solution even if all sites are correct, if the sites are perfectly symmetrical and, therefore, indistinguishable.
In order to prove that *ab absurdo*, consider the network below, in which the two sites are identical.

Fig. 3.

Since the two sites follow the same protocol at the same time, they receive the same information from the other and then chose the same identifier.
So we will assume that there exists a particular site, the initiator, that starts the naming algorithm. Each site knows whether it is the initiator or not, and there is an unique initiator.
We assume that the initiator is always correct and that the messages it sends are authentificated. This requirement can be achieved, for instance, by a cryptographic digital signature [Rivest, Shamir and Adleman 78].
The problem of the mutual exclusion is another classical problem concerning the synchronization of concurrent or distributed processes. Each process is given with a special part of its code, called the critical section and a protocol must be designed, to ensure that, at any

time, at most one process is executing inside its critical section. Moreover, the protocol must yield some fairness, absence of starvation and deadlock requirements. This problem appears, in particular, when an exclusive access to a resource, like a printer, must be imposed.
In a large network, with a number of host computers, the correctness of all the processes running in the network cannot be guaranteed at the same level. For instance, processes running on micro-computers or small computers are supposed to be less reliable than those on large mainframes, where a control system does exist. But the mutual exclusion condition for some access must be guaranteed, whatever the processes do. Some solutions to the problem of mutual exclusion have been presented in the case of crash faults ([Ricart and Agrawala 81], [Buckley and Silberschatz 84]). But, in contrast with crash faults, a faulty byzantine process cannot generally be detected. The difficulty is thus to design a protocol that deals with byzantine faults.
It is not hard to see that such a protocol does not exist for the mutual exclusion problem and that supplementary assumptions must be made, in order to obtain partial solutions. The main difficulty that we are faced to is: when a correct process is executing in its critical section, how can we avoid that a faulty process enters its own critical section? The idea for solving it is to use a mechanism analogous to a capability. If the critical section is implemented as a separate segment and if the access to this segment requires the knowledge of its address, this address should be given to any process only under distributed control. In our solution, a process wanting to enter its critical section must reconstruct the required address from pieces of information sent by the other processes, after they have agreed on him. Schematically, the protocol for a process is:

- ask the other processes for their pieces of information for reconstructing the address of the critical section segment,
- wait until this address can be reconstructed,
- enter the critical section, then leave it,
- send acknowledgments to all other processes (the exit section).

In this paper, we will consider processes that can exhibit byzantine behavior everywhere in their code, except during the execution of some special parts of the protocol, namely the critical and the exit sections. We will call such processes, as in [Beauquier 88], locally byzantine processes. Note that this hypothesis is absolutely necessary, for avoiding a byzantine process to remain forever in its critical section or not to notify its exiting to the other processes.

II. The naming problem with faulty processes

II.a. Preliminaries

Let G_i, $1<i<n$ be processes. Assume that every G_i can directly exchange messages with some other G_j (its neighbors), that message passing is synchronous and that no message is modified or lost. G_i only knows about its neighbors and nothing else about the network topology. Assume topology is fixed.
The naming problem is to design a protocol P_i that G_i may use to obtain an unique identifier. The protocol P_i involves exchanging messages with its neighbors. As long as G_i computes according to P_i, it is called correct. Once a process G_i deviates from P_i, it becomes faulty (or byzantine) and is considered to remain faulty, even if, later on, it reverts back to following P_i.
Initially, each site knows its adjacent communication lines and knows them by a local name (a number).
We also assume that a particular process has the role of initiating the protocols. So each process initially knows whether it is the initiator or not. The initiator is assumed to be correct.
At the end, we suppose that there is a public key cryptographic system, allowing the initiator to use a digital signature [Rivest, Shamir and Adleman 78]. Let s be the digital signature of the initiator and s(m) a signed message.

II.b. The protocol

We will only sketch how the protocol works. At the beginning, the initiator numbers its neighbors and for all numbers i, sends to i the (signed) message S("initialization", i). Each neighbor, receiving such a message, checks for the digital signature of the initiator (in case of failure, the message is rejected), numbers its own neighbors, for each of them concatenates the number to the message, then sends it to the related neighbor. Such a message has the form (S("initialization", i), j), where j is the neighbor number. In a general manner, we call **valid** any message endorsed by the digital signature of the initiator. During the whole protocol, correct sites only accept valid messages.

When a correct site s receives a valid message, it knows how its neighbor has numbered the communication line between them. If this number is j and if s has itself numbered the communication line by i, s registers that $i^{-1} = j$. If, after this first numbering, s receives from the same neighbor conflicting information about the number of the line, it simply does not accept any other message from this neighbor.

The first time a correct site s receives a valid message, it starts a watchdog timer, initialized to the value 3 * D *d, where d is the maximum transmission delay between two adjacent sites and D the maximal lenght of an elementary path between two sites (recall that message passing is synchronous).

At this point, it should be noticed that byzantine sites can possibly relay messages endorsed by the initiator, after having modified some unencoded information.

In the sequel, each site receiving a valid initialization message relays it to its numbered neighbors, after having appended its number to the message. Moreover, each site manages a list, containing the valid messages already received. Each time a valid message is accepted, the list is searched to check that the message is not a looping message (more precisely, it is searched whether a left prefix of the message is already in the list, as a complete message). Looping messages are rejected. So correct sites progressively delete valid messages.

It should be noticed that a correct site can possibly accept and relay a message that contains false information. Figure 4 shows such a situation.

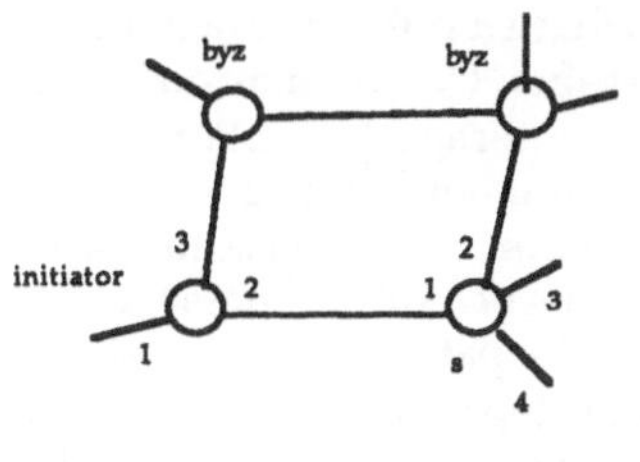

Fig. 4.

The first byzantine site receives S("initialization", 3) from the initiator. It relays it to the other byzantine site without change. This one appends 1 and sends the message (S("initialization", 3), 1) to the correct site. So, s can think that the network is:

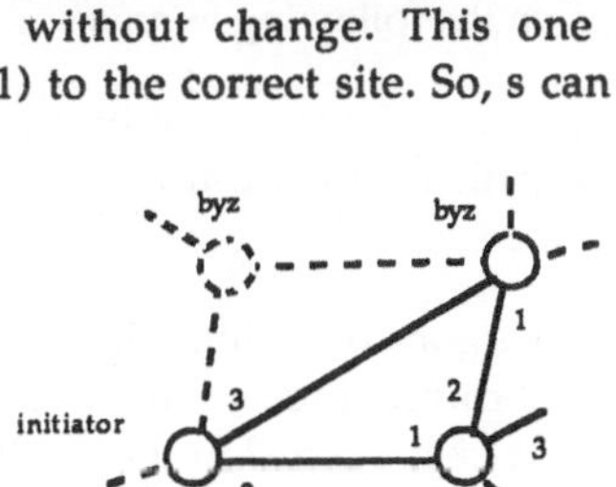

Fig. 5.

Now, we introduce the notion of **confirmation**. Each time a site accepts a valid message, it returns to the initiator a return message, by the reverse path. For that it uses the inverse of the numbers of its outgoing communications lines as registered previously.

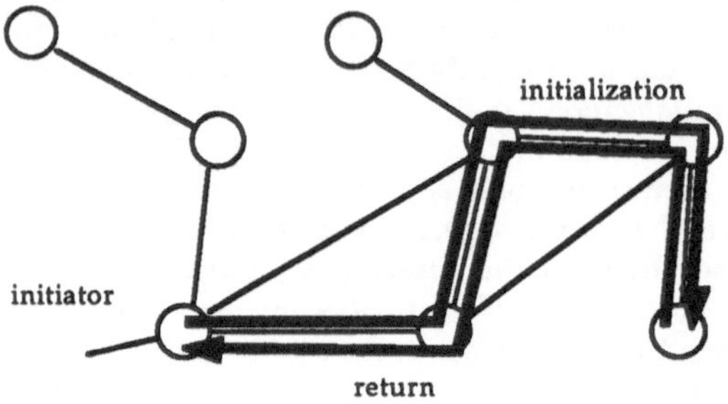

Fig. 6.

As a matter of fact, the actual reverse path is followed only if the message does not go through a byzantine site deviating it. A return message is identical to an initialization message, except that it has a first field "return" (unsigned). A return message is relayed by the correct sites toward the initiator and a pointer shows at what step the message has arrived. For instance, ("return", s("initialization", 3), 1, $\underline{\mathbf{3}}$, 3, 2) is a return message that has followed back a line numbered 2^{-1} and a line numbered 3^{-1}.
Each time the initiator receives a return message, it erases the fields "return" and "initialization", signs the rest of the message, adds the message in clear with a pointer on the first number and a field "confirmation". For instance, such a confirmation message is: ("confirmation", s(3, 1, 3, 3, 2), ($\underline{\mathbf{3}}$,1,3,3,2)). Then the confirmation message is transmitted by the correct sites, according to the included path, until arriving at the destination. At each step, the digital signature of the initiator is checked. Moreover, the pointer is checked and updated, indicating at what step the message has arrived. For instance, this is a circulating confirmation message: ("confirmation", s(3, 1, 3, 3, 2), (3,1,3,$\underline{\mathbf{3}}$,2)), indicating that, from the initiator, the message has followed the lines 3, 1, 3 and 3 and that the destination will be reached by following line 2.
When a confirmation message arrives at its destination, the site checks the digital signature of the initiator, checks whether or not the message is already in its list of valid messages and, if so, stores the value of the path in a table.
After the delay 3 6 D 6 d, a correct site stops and concatenates in a string all the values of paths that are stored in the table (using a separator). Then it choses the result of the concatenation as an identifier.
Note that all protocols do terminate, since the clock interrupts have a finite delay.

The corectness of the solutions depends on the following lemmas.

Lemma 1. Any correct process receives at least one initialization message and one confirmation message with the same path information that have only passed through correct processes.

We call **normal** for P_i any message that has gone only through correct processes between the initiator and P_i. Lemma 1 states that any correct process receives normal initialization and confirmation messages. Moreover, any message normal for P_i is valid for P_i.

Lemma 2. Let P_1 and P_2 be two distinct correct processes and let m_1 and m_2 be two normal messages, respectively for P_1 and P_2. Then m_1 and m_2 are different.

Lemma 3. Let P_1 and P_2 be two distinct correct processes and let m be a normal message for P_1. Then m cannot be a valid message of P_2.

Lemma 4. Two distinct correct processes accept (at least) two distinct valid messages.

The main result of this part is:
Theorem 1.
At the end of the protocols, two distincts correct processes have distinct identifiers.
Proof.
Since the identifier consists of the concatenation of valid messages separated by a marker, they differ, from lemma 4, by at least one message.

II.c. Complexity

Let m be the maximum degree of the graph (maximum number of outgoing lines from a site). Since each correct process stops after the delay $3 * D * d$ and sends at most m messages per d time units, for each accepted message, an upper bound of the total number of exchanged messages is: $3^* D^* m^D$.
The time complexity is obviously: $3^* D^* d$.

III. The mutual exclusion problem with faulty processes

III.a. Preliminaries

Let G_i, $1<i<n$ be processes. Assume that every G_i can directly exchange messages with every other G_j, that communications are asynchronous and that, whenever a process G_i sends a message to G_j, the message eventually reaches G_j.
Each G_i executes a program, that has a section of code, called its critical section. When one process is executing in its critical section, no other process is allowed to execute in its own critical section. The critical section problem is to design a protocol P_i, which G_i may use to cooperate. The protocol P_i involves exchanging messages with other G_j's, deciding when enter the critical section and when to wait for entering it. As long as G_i computes according to P_i, it is called correct. Once a process G_i deviates from P_i, it becomes faulty and is considered to remain faulty, even if, later on, it reverts back to following P_i. P_i also includes the code that G_i executes to request permission to enter its critical section. The section of code implementing this request is called the entry section. The critical section is followed by an exit section. The remaining code is the remainder section, that can be divides into two parts.
A solution to the mutual exclusion problem must satisfy three requirements:
i) Mutual exclusion. If process G_i is executing in its critical section, no other process can be executing in its own critical section.
ii) Progress. If no process is executing in its critical section and there exists some process that wishes to enter its critical section, it cannot be delayed by processes executing forever in their remainder sections.
iii) Bounded waiting. Once all processes are aware of the intention of a process G to enter its critical section, there must exist a bound on the number of times that other processes are allowed to enter their critical section before G's request is granted.
We make the important assumption that the entry and exit sections are always correctly executed, and that a process never crashes in its critical section. In any other part of its protocol, a process can become faulty. Even after becoming faulty, it correctly executes its critical and exit sections. Such a faulty process is called a locally faulty process.
The underlying idea to practically implement this assumption is that each G_i must be a process executing under control of the operating system of an host computer. The critical section is implemented as a separate segment, in its own memory locations. For executing this segment, a process must necessarily know its address (for instance own a capability for the segment).
In the sequel, we will drop these implementation details and keep in mind that the three

sections are always correctly executed.
We will also suppose that the distributed system has a public key cryptographic system, yielding digital signatures [Rivest, Shamir and Adleman 78]. We note s_i the digital signature of the process G_i and $s_i(m)$ a signed message. All messages will be implicitly signed by the sender, so that we will always omit s_i and simply write m for a signed message.

III.b. The protocol

The solution that we will present uses some data structures and primitives, that will be part of each protocol (thus, variables are local to a site, but some are also global to procedures on a same site). They are given in annexe 2.
The solution consists in a main program and two interrupt-handlers, that are the same for all G_i's.
The main program is made of three procedures that are concurrently executed.

```
Program Mutual_exclusion; {for Gi}
var     s: address;
        in: boolean;
begin
allocate (critical_section, s);   {loads the procedure segment in main
                                          memory}
in:= false;        {in is local to Gi}
cobegin
        Listening;
        Byz_cons;
        Local_prog
coend
end.
```

Local_prog is any specific program that G_i is supposed to execute. The only thing that it is assumed about this program is its general structure:

```
Program Local_prog;
procedure critical_section;
begin
repeat
        <remainder section 1>;
        svc(ask_for_critical_section);
        <remainder section 2>
forever
end.
```

A FIFO message buffering system is assumed to exist on each site. The procedure Listening receives the arriving messages (from the buffering system), implicitly checks that they are correctly signed and manages two information tables, ask and acq of type control.
The record ask[j] (of type note) is used to memorize the last message "ask for entering" (setting flag to the value true) with its date (the value of counter) and the corresponding value $I_j(s)$ (coded as an integer).
The record acq[j] is used to memorize the date of the last message "exit". The records ask[j] and acq[j] are both local to G_i. The fields flag are initialized to false and date and info to 0. It must be noticed that only the last messages "ask for entering" and "exit", with their dates, are saved. We consider only solutions to the problem that use finite storage. Thus, since communication is asynchronous, we cannot store all untreated messages, because their number is unbounded.
The procedure Listening treats an inbound message atomically. The text of Listening is quite straightforward and we will omit it.

The procedure byz_cons is used to obtain a consensus among the G_i's, on the particular G_j that should be allowed to enter its critical section. It uses as a primitive the procedure byzantine_agreement of [Rabin 83], that gives the agreement with an expected number of four rounds. As in [Rabin 83] a correct "dealer" is assumed to provide to each G_i an infinite sequence of shadows (in the sense of threshold schemes, Cf. [Denning 83]) of random bits. The reconstruction of the secret bit, indexed by the value of the variable cons_counter, is supposed to be part of byzantine_agreement. An important point of Rabin's technique is that, when a process stops the agreement protocol, it has the proof that all correct processes will stop it in the same round or one round later.
The parts of the procedure represented underlined are executed atomically, at the local level.

```
Procedure byz_cons; {for Gi}
var     cons_counter: time_stamp;
        i,j:site;
        ask, acq: control;
        m, result: consensus;
        f: message;
begin
        repeat
                cons_counter:= 1;          {cons_counter is local to Gi}
                j:= 1;                     {j is local to Gi}
                        repeat
                                if ask[j].flag= false then
                                m.value:= no_demand
                                else    begin   {Gj is wanting to enter}
        m.value:= j;
        m.counter:= ask[j].date;
        end;
        byzantine_agreement (cons_counter, m, result);
        cons_counter:= cons_counter+1;
        j:= j+1 (modulo n);        {try for another process}
                        until
        result.value<>no_demand  and
        result.value<>default_value;
                        {repeat until a wanting process is chosen}
                        if (result, ask[result].date)= m  and
                        ask[result].date>acq[result].date
                                        {no new demand and no exit during
                                        execution of byzantinc_agreement}
                        then
        begin
        send (f, shadow,i, result,ask[result].counter),I_result(s));
                                        {giving the shadow of the address to the
                                        wanting process}}
        while ask[result].date> acq[result].date  do nil;          {waiting for
                                                                        exit}
        end
                        forever
end;
```

At the end, we present the two interrupt handlers, executed under the control of the local operating system. Recall that execution of a svc causes the processor status word to be put at the top of the stack.

Interrupt-handler for
svc(ask_for_critical_section);

```
var     j: site;
        f: message;
        s: address;
        new_psw: psw;
begin
while in= true do nil;          {Gi already made an svc for entering
                                      without exiting}
treshold(s, n, t+1);      {each Ij(s) is signed by the local system]
counter:= counter+1;
for j:= 1 to n do
        begin
        send(f,ask_for_entering, i, j,
        counter, empty field); {fields are signed by the system}
                send (f, shadow, i, j, counter, Ij(s));      {fields are signed by
                                                                  the system}
        end;
wait until arriving of t+1 answers (shadow, j, i, counter, Ij(s)) from t+1 Gj's;
                {the signatures over Ij(s) and of Gj over (j, i, Ij(s), counter) are checked}
                construct s from the Ij(s); {using Lagrange's interpolation polynomials}
in:= true;
jump_to (s);                    {enter the critical section}
end;
```

Interrupt-handler for

```
svc(exit_critical );
var     i,j: site;
        f: message;
        s: address;
begin
while in= false do nil;         {Gi did not make an SVC for entering}
allocate (critical_section, s);  {system primitive}
for j:= 1 to n do
        begin
        send (f, exit, i, j, counter, empty field);  {just an acknowledgment}
        end;
continue;          {continues with Gi}
end;
```

Recall that it is assumed that the two interrupt handlers are always correctly executed, by any process.

Theorem.- If the number of locally byzantine processes does not exceed n/3, the protocol above solves the mutual exclusion problem.
Proof.
The proof is based upon the three following properties of the protocol.
Mutual exclusion.
Assume that two processes G_i and G_j are simultaneously (for an hypothetical global clock) in their own critical section. Each of them has necessarily entered its critical section by an svc, in some fixed order, for instance G_i first and G_j second. In order to build the address of the segment containing its critical section, G_i has received at least t+1 shadows $I_k(s)$. Among those t+1 responding processes, at least one is a correct one, G_r. Since G_r sent $I_r(s)$ and G_r is correct, G_r obtained, together with all correct processes, an agreement on G_i. Thus, each correct process is executing:

while ask[i].date> acq[i].date **do** nil;

since G_i is still in its critical section.
Consequently, no correct process sent $I_j(s)$ to G_j. So G_j received at most t shadows (from incorrect processes) and, contradictory to the hypothesis, is unable to know the segment address of its critical section.

Progress.

Assume that G_i executes a primitive svc(ask_for_critical_section) and let G_j be the first process to enter its critical section after this system call.
Since the only way for a process to enter its critical section is through the Interrupt handler for svc(ask_for_critical_section), G_j requested to enter its critical section. So, G_i cannot be delayed by processes executing forever in their remainder sections.

Bounded waiting.

Assume that G_i executes the primitive svc(ask_for_critical_section). Since there is no loss of messages, the messages (ask for entering,i, j, counter, empty field) will eventually reach their destinations. When the last of these messages arrives, each correct process G_j has: *ask*[*i*].*flag*:= **true**. With a maximum number of n-1 executions of the inner loop of byz_cons, allowing at most n-1 processes to enter their critical sections, the agreement is reached on (*i*, *ask*[*i*].*date*). So G_i can enter its critical section after at most n-1 other distinct processes enter their critical sections.

III.c. Complexity

The number of exchanged messages necessary for a process that requests to enter its critical section has the same order of magnitude than the number of exchanged messages necessary for reaching a byzantine agreement and is in $O(n^2)$.

IV. Conclusion

We have first presented a method for assigning to each site of a network an unique identifier. This identifier is a rather long character string and can seem not to be of a great practical interest. Nevertheless, there do exist renaming algorithms, that allow a reduction in the size of the initial name space, even if some processes are faulty [Attiya and al. 87] and a sequel to this work should be to merge our solution with such an algorithm. Then, we have given an authenticated solution to the mutual exclusion problem. In [Srikanth and Toueg 83], a methodology is given for deriving non-authenticated algorithms from algorithms using digital signatures. This methodology could possibly be applied here, giving a non-authenticated algorithm that solves the mutual exclusion problem for locally byzantine processes.

Annexe 1.

```
type        message: string of char,
            site: integer;
const       D= ...;        {diameter of the network}
            d = ...;       {maximum transmission delay}
var         identifier: string of char;
            valid: set of message;

procedure timer (delay: integer);
begin {initializes the watchdog timer to the value delay; at the expiration of the delay an
interrupt aborts the calling procedure} end;

procedure send (m: message) to (s: site);
begin {send the message m onto the communication line numbered s} end;
```

Annexe 2.

```
const:          maxlength= ...;           {maximum length of a
                                           mesage}
                memory_max= ...;          {range of the primary
                                  memory of the host computer}
type            bit= 0..1;
                site= 1..n;               {n is the number of sites}
                time_stamp: integer;
                data= packed array [0, maxlength] of bit;
                addr= 1..memory_max;
                svc_type=         (ask_for_critical section,
                                  exit_critical_section);
                                  {types of system call}
                consensus_value= (1, 2,..., n, no_demand,
                                           default_value};
                consensus= record
                        value:consensus_value;
                        counter:time_stamp;
                        end;
                message_kind= (ask_for_entering, exit,
                                  shadow);
                message=          record
                        kind: message_kind;
                        sender: site;
                        destination: site;
                        counter: time_stamp;
                        info: data
                        end;
                note=   record  {for bookkeeping asks and
                                  exitings of critical section }
                        flag: boolean;
                        date: time_stamp;
                        info: data
                        end;
                control_array= array [1..site] of note;
```

procedure svc(**var** t:svc_type);
begin {generates an interrupt and a context-switching, causing the process status word register to be saved on the stack and an interrupt-handler to be executed under control of the local operating system} **end;**
procedure continue;
begin {loads the top value of the stack in the processor status word register, including the program counter, of the host computer} **end;**
procedure allocate (**var** proc: procedure, s: addr);
begin {allocates a new memory segment to the procedure proc and returns the base address in the variable s} **end;**
procedure jump_to (**var** s: addr);
begin {settle the value s in the program counter } **end;**
procedure send (f: message);
begin {transmits the message f to the site f.destination} **end;**
procedure treshold (**var** s: address, t: integer, n: site);
begin {starting from an address s and two integers n and t, t<n, this primitive produces n pieces of information, $I_1(s)$, $I_2(s)$,..., $I_n(s)$, called the shadows of s, such that the knowledge of any set of at least t pieces and of no set of strictly less than t pieces allows to built s. The n shadows of s are signed by the system executing this primitive} **end;**
[Shamir 79] and [Denning 83] give several methods for building this primitive.

procedure byzantine agreement (**var** counter: time_stamp, initial_value, final_value: consensus).
begin {reaches a byzantine agreement, by only considering messages that are time-stamped by the value counter, with initial_value as initial message. The result of the agreement protocol is in final_value. The default value chosen for this primitive will be the string: "default value".} **end;**

Since communications are assumed to be asynchronous, this primitive can be implemented by the probabilistic solution of [Rabin 83] or its improved version [Toueg 84]. These solutions guarantee exact agreement within a finite expected number of rounds, provided the number of incorrect processes does not exceed n/3 (Cf. [Toueg 84]).

Bibliography

[Attiya , Bar-Noy , Dolev, Koller, Peleg and Reischuk 87] "Achievable Cases in a Asynchronous Environment", Proceedings of the 28th Found. of Comput. Science IEEE, pages 337- 347, November 1987.

[Beauquier 88] "Locally byzantine processes", in Proc. of the Workshop IEEE on the future trends of distributed systems in the 1990s, Hong-Kong, pages 232-236, September 1988.

[Buckley and Silberschatz 84] "A failure tolerant centralized mutual exclusion algorithm", in Proc. of the 4th Inter. Conf. on Distributed Comp. Syst., pages 347-356, 1984.

[Denning 83] "Cryptography and data security", Addison-Wesley, 1983.

[Lamport, Shostak and Pease 80] "Reaching agreement in the presence of faults", J.A.C.M., pages 228-234, 1980.

[Cheung 83] "Graph Traversal Techniques and the Maximal Flow Problem in Distributed Computation", IEEE Trans. on SE, SE 9 (4), pages 504-512, 1983.

[Helary and Raynal 88] "Assigning Distinct Identities to Sites of an the Future Trends of Distributed Computing Systems in the 1990s, Hong Kong, pages 82-86, September 1988.

[Lamport , Shostak and Pease 80] "Reaching Agreement in the Presence of Faults", J.A.C.M., pp. 228-234, 1980.

[Rabin 83] "Randomized byzantine generals", 24th F.O.C.S. I.E.E.E., Tucson, pages 403-409, November 1983.

[Ricard and Agrawala 81] "An optimal algorithm for mutual exclusion in computer networks", C.A.C.M., vol. 24, pages 9-17, 1981.

[Rivest, Shamir and Adleman 78] "A Method for Obtaining Digital Signatures and Public-Key Cryptosystems", CACM, vol. 21, pages 120-126, 1978.

[Segall 83] "Distributed Network Protocols", IEEE Trans. on Inf. Theory, IT 29 (1), pages 23-25, 1983.

[Shamir 79] "How to share a secret", C.A.C.M., vol. 22, pages 612-613, 1979.

[Srikanth and Toueg 87] "Simulating authenticated broadcasts to derive simple fault-tolerant algorithms", Distributed Computing, vol. 2, pp. 80-94, 1987.

[Toueg 84] "Randomized asynchronous byzantine agreements", Proc. 3rd Symposium of the principles of Distributed Computing, Vancouver, Canada, Aug. 1984.

Flow Event Structures and Flow Nets

Gérard Boudol

INRIA Sophia-Antipolis

06565-VALBONNE FRANCE

1. Introduction

In this paper we investigate the relationships between two models for concurrent computations, namely Petri nets and Winskel's event structures. A distinctive feature of these models, with respect to transition systems used in the so-called interleaving semantics, is that they provide an adequate account of the *causal* relations between events in a distributed system. At least this is true for event structures, if not as clear for Petri nets. For instance in the net

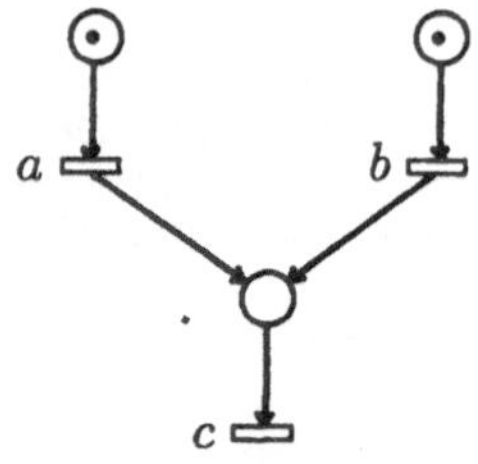

it is not clear whether a and b, when they both occur, are causes of c; this depends on the token that was chosen to fire c. This is a typical example of "non-stable" net. Nevertheless, for some classes of nets, like condition/event systems, one has a definite notion of causality. This is also true for the *occurrence nets* introduced by Nielsen, Plotkin and Winskel in their pioneering paper [13], where a close connection between occurrence nets, *prime event structures* and prime algebraic coherent domains

This work has been partly supported by ESPRIT Basic Research Action 3011 CEDISYS.

was established. Our aim is to generalize their work, so as to be able to compare various semantics for process description languages.

Petri nets have been used to provide a "truly concurrent" semantics for CCS-like languages [12], for instance by Goltz [9,11], Degano, De Nicola and Montanari [6], Olderog [14], van Glabbeek and Vaandrager [8], and Taubner [15]. Similarly, event structure semantics for such languages have been proposed, by Winskel [17,18] using *stable* event structures, and by Goltz [10], Degano, De Nicola and Montanari [7], Vaandrager [16] using *prime* event structures. As a matter of fact, such a semantics also yields a Petri net semantics, at least indirectly by means of the domains of configurations. On the other hand, it seems difficult to relate a net semantics of CCS with an event structure semantics of the same language, unless the nets used are occurrence nets – but these, just like prime event structures, are quite awkward for this purpose.

An advantage of Winskel's semantics, by means of stable structures, is that the events have a clear operational meaning: they are just occurrences of actions in the syntactic tree obtained by unfolding the CCS term. For instance in the term $(a\alpha \mid \bar{\alpha}b)$ the action b corresponds to a unique event, which can be caused in two incompatible ways, either by the action $\bar{\alpha}$ alone, or by the communication action. Stable event structures account for such conflicting causes. In the same spirit, this term can be represented by the net

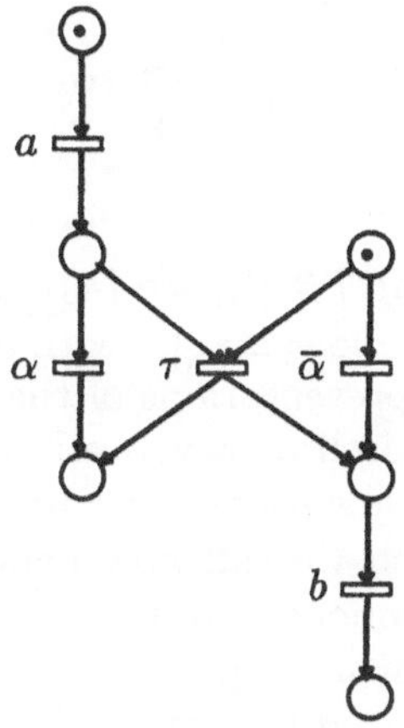

where each possible action of the term is represented by a single event. However this is not an occurrence net, and we do not know how to "extract" it out of a stable event structure, since we do not know which class of nets could correspond to stable event structures. We would like to have a concrete correspondence, preserving the families of configurations – hence in particular the names of the events –, rather than an abstract one which only preserves the domain of configurations, up to isomorphism. Note that the prime event structure semantics of $(a\alpha \mid \bar{\alpha}b)$ gives

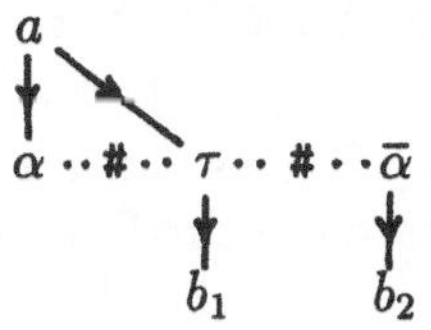

where there are two events b_1 and b_2 representing the possible histories of the same "event" b. Using prime event structures or occurrence nets to interpret other simple terms may be quite painful – try for instance $(\alpha a\beta \mid \bar{\beta} b\bar{\alpha})$ where causality cycles arise.

To moderate these difficulties, we proposed in previous work [1,2] to deal with a more flexible notion of event structure, obtained by relaxing the axiom of conflict heredity. This allowed us to give a "natural" semantics for a CCS-like language. The language was quite restricted, however, since we did not give an event structure semantics for communication. In [3] we introduced another kind of event structures, called *flow event structures*, still similar to prime event structures, but far more relaxed – the price to pay is that the notion of configuration is not so simple as for prime event structures. In a flow event structure the causality ordering is replaced by an irreflexive *flow* relation, which is much like the existence of a place between two events in a Petri net. Moreover there is *no* requirement on the relationships between the flow and the symmetric conflict. With these structures it is fairly easy to interpret CCS terms in a "natural" way. Moreover this flow event structure semantics of CCS has an operational content: we can show that it corresponds to a "truly concurrent" semantics extracted from the usual operational semantics (see [5,3] and also [4]). For instance the term $(a\alpha \mid \bar{\alpha} b)$ is now interpreted as the following flow event structure:

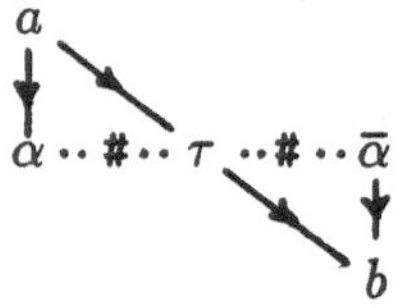

For the "flow" interpretation of $(\alpha a\beta \mid \bar{\beta} b\bar{\alpha})$, see [4]. Here we should also mention that all kinds of event structures – prime, flow, stable (with binary conflict) – are "abstractly" equivalent since they are concrete presentations of the same kind of domains.

In this paper we establish a preliminary result for relating various semantics of CCS-like languages: we show that flow event structures concretely correspond to a new particular class of Petri nets, which we call *flow nets*. These nets have a semantical definition, i.e. by means of firing sequences, but we show that any flow net is equivalent – in the sense of having the same firing sequences – to what we call a *regular* flow net. The regular flow nets are characterized by structural properties, namely:

(1) in a regular flow net a place is of one of the following two kinds:
  (1.1) a *choice* place, which can be forward branched – that is precondition of several events – but cannot be postcondition of any event;
  (1.2) a *causal* place, which can be backward branched, but is precondition of at most one event.
(2) only the choice places can be initially marked.

There is also an additional requirement on causality between events:

(3) if a is a potential cause of b – that is there is a place between a and b – then there is a causal place p between a and b such that any other pre-event e of p shares a precondition with a – that is e is in direct conflict with a.

This last property ensures that in any firing sequence the causal relations between events are unambiguously determined. Therefore the flow nets are "causal" nets, although we cannot claim that any "causal" net is a flow net: there are some (stable) nets where the causality is well-defined but which are not flow nets, like for instance

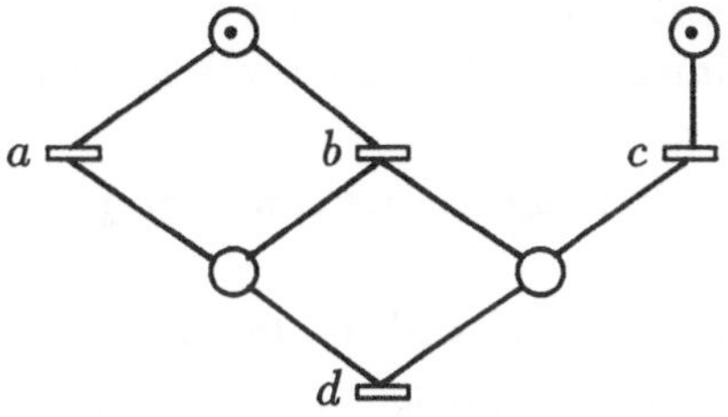

To conclude this presentation, let us state our main result, which establishes a connection between flow event structures and flow nets:

(1) for any flow event structure we can build a flow net such that the sets of events firable in sequence in the net are exactly the configurations of the flow event structure;
(2) conversely for any flow net we can build a flow event structure whose configurations are exactly the sets of events firable in sequence in the net.

This result is a generalization of Nielsen, Plotkin and Winskel's one, since any occurrence net is a flow net – but not conversely –, and any prime event structure is a flow event structure – but not conversely.

2. Event Structures

2.1 Domains and Prime Event Structures

We briefly recall in this section some definitions about partially ordered sets (*cf.* [13] and [18]). Let $(D, \leq)$ be a poset. Then

- two elements x and y of D are *compatible*, in notation $x \uparrow y$, if they have an upper bound:
$$x \uparrow y \;\Leftrightarrow\; \exists z \in D \; x \leq z \;\&\; y \leq z$$
- a subset X of D is *pairwise consistent*, in notation $X\Uparrow$, if every two elements of X are compatible (in D):
$$X\Uparrow \;\Leftrightarrow\; \forall x, y \in X \; x \uparrow y$$
- the poset $(D, \leq)$ is *coherent* if every pairwise consistent subset X of D has a least upper bound $\bigsqcup X$;
- a point x in D is a *complete prime* if for any subset X of D which has a lub $\bigsqcup X$ we have:
$$x \leq \bigsqcup X \;\Rightarrow\; \exists y \in X \; x \leq y$$
We shall denote the set of complete primes of the poset $(D, \leq)$ by $Pr(D, \leq)$ – or simply $Pr(D)$ if there is no ambiguity;
- the poset $(D, \leq)$ is *ω-prime algebraic* if $Pr(D)$ is denumerable(†) and every point of D is the lub of the complete primes it dominates, that is:

(†) a set A is denumerable if it is empty or if there exists an enumeration of A, that is a surjective mapping a from the set of positive integers onto A; in that case we can write $A = \{a_1, \ldots, a_n, \ldots\}$.

$$\forall x \in D\ x = \bigsqcup\{y \mid y \in Pr(D)\ \&\ y \leq x\}$$

We shall denote $\hat{x}$ the set $\{y \mid y \in Pr(D)\ \&\ y \leq x\}$.

- a point x of D is *finite* if it only dominates a finite number of points, that is if the set $\{y \mid y \leq x\}$ is finite. We shall denote the set of finite points of $(D, \leq)$ by $F(D, \leq)$, or simply $F(D)$;
- the poset $(D, \leq)$ is *finitary* if each of its complete prime is finite, that is $Pr(D) \subseteq F(D)$.

The only kind of domain we shall deal with is the following:

DEFINITION (DOMAINS). *A domain is a coherent, ω-prime algebraic and finitary poset.*

Clearly a domain has a least element $\bot = \bigsqcup\emptyset$, since the empty set is pairwise consistent, and if $X \subseteq Y$ then $\bigsqcup X \leq \bigsqcup Y$. One should note that every non empty subset X of a domain D has a greatest lower bound, namely $\bigsqcap X = \bigsqcup\{x \mid \forall y \in X\ x \leq y\}$ (the set $\{x \mid \forall y \in X\ x \leq y\}$ is pairwise consistent since $X \neq \emptyset$). It should also be obvious that if $(D, \leq)$ is a domain, then a subset X of D has a least upper bound if and only if it is bounded (that is $\exists y \in D\ \forall x \in X\ x \leq y$); a bounded set is also called *consistent*.

In the second part of the paper we shall use the fact that the whole structure of a domain $(D, \leq)$ is actually already present in the poset $(F(D), \leq)$ – where we still denote $\leq$ the restriction of the ordering of D on $F(D)$. To see this let us first show that a domain $(D, \leq)$ is isomorphic to the *ideal completion* of $(F(D), \leq)$. An *ideal* of a poset $(F, \leq)$ is a non-empty subset X of F such that:

- X is *directed*, that is:
$$x, y \in X \Rightarrow \exists z \in X\ x \leq z\ \&\ y \leq z$$
- X is a *cone* (or a left-closed or downward-closed subset) of F, that is:
$$x \in X\ \&\ y \leq x \Rightarrow y \in X$$

We denote by $\mathcal{I}(F, \leq)$, or simply $\mathcal{I}(F)$, the set of ideals of the poset $(F, \leq)$. Then the *ideal completion* $(F, \leq)^\infty$ of $(F, \leq)$ is the poset of its ideals, ordered by inclusion, that is $(F, \leq)^\infty = (\mathcal{I}(F), \subseteq)$.

We shall denote by $(D, \leq) \rightleftharpoons (D', \leq')$ the fact that two posets are isomorphic; more precisely, we shall use the notation $(D, \leq) \underset{\psi}{\overset{\varphi}{\rightleftharpoons}} (D', \leq')$ to mean that $\varphi : D \to D'$ and $\psi : D' \to D$ are two inverse poset morphisms.

LEMMA 2.1. *Any domain $(D, \leq)$ is isomorphic to the ideal completion of its poset of finite points: $(D, \leq) \underset{h}{\overset{f}{\rightleftharpoons}} (F(D), \leq)^\infty$ where f and h are given by $f(x) = \{y \mid y \in F(D)\ \&\ y \leq x\}$ and $h(X) = \bigsqcup X$.*

PROOF: let us first show that f and h are well defined: it is obvious that if X is an ideal of $F(D)$ then $\bigsqcup X$ exists, since a directed set is pairwise consistent. It is also clear that for all $x \in D$ the set $f(x) = \{y \mid y \in F(D)\ \&\ y \leq x\}$ is a cone of $F(D)$; moreover $f(x)$ is non-empty since $\bot \in f(x)$. Let us show that $f(x)$ is directed: it is enough to prove

$$x, y \in F(D)\ \&\ x \uparrow y \Rightarrow x \sqcup y \in F(D)$$

Let $u = x \sqcup y$; if $z \in \mathit{Pr}(D)$ is such that $z \leq u$ then we have either $z \leq x$ or $z \leq y$, therefore $\hat{u} = \hat{x} \cup \hat{y}$. Moreover since x and y are finite the set $\hat{u}$ is finite. If $z \leq u$ we have $\hat{z} \subseteq \hat{u}$, and $z = \bigsqcup \hat{z}$ since $(D, \leq)$ is ω-prime algebraic. This shows that there are only finitely many points z such that $z \leq u$, since there are only finitely many subsets of $\hat{u}$; hence $u \in F(D)$.

Since $(D, \leq)$ is finitary we have $\hat{x} \subseteq f(x)$, and since $(D, \leq)$ is ω-prime algebraic we have $x = h(f(x))$ for any $x \in D$ (for $x = \bigsqcup \hat{x} \leq \bigsqcup f(x) \leq x$). Then it is easy to see that $x \leq y \Leftrightarrow f(x) \subseteq f(y)$. It should also be obvious that if $X \in \mathcal{I}(F(D))$ we have $X \subseteq f(h(X))$. Now let $X \in \mathcal{I}(F(D))$ and $x \in F(D)$ be such that $x \leq \bigsqcup X$; then for all $z \in \hat{x}$ there exists $y \in X$ such that $z \leq y$, since z is a complete prime such that $z \leq \bigsqcup X$, hence $z \in X$ since X is a cone. Therefore we have $\hat{x} \subseteq X$; since $\hat{x}$ is finite and X is directed, there exists $y \in X$ such that $z \in \hat{x} \Rightarrow z \leq y$, hence $\bigsqcup \hat{x} \leq y$. Then $x \in X$, since $x = \bigsqcup \hat{x}$ and X is a cone. This shows $f(h(X)) = X$ for any $X \in \mathcal{I}(F(D))$ ☐

Let us see an example of poset, which is not prime algebraic, for which the lemma does not hold; let $(D, \leq)$ be given by

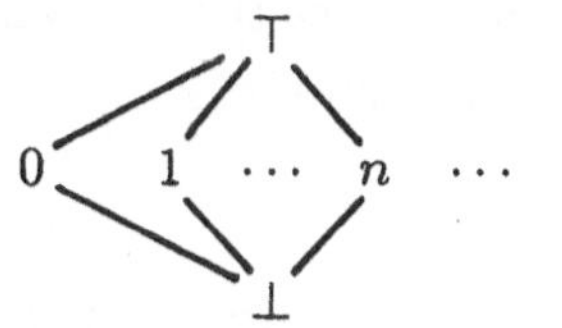

We have $\mathit{Pr}(D) = \emptyset$, and $(F(D), \leq)$ is given by

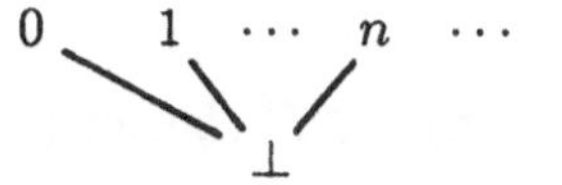

Here the ideal completion of $F(D)$ gives $F(D)$ again. A consequence of the previous lemma is that a domain is fully determined by its poset of finite points:

COROLLARY 2.2. *Two domains $(D, \leq)$ and $(D', \leq')$ are isomorphic if and only if their posets of finite points $(F(D), \leq)$ and $(F(D'), \leq')$ are isomorphic.*

We just saw that a domain is represented as the poset of ideals of its finite points – a *representation* of a poset $(D, \leq)$ is an isomorphism from $(D, \leq)$ to $(\mathcal{F}, \subseteq)$ where $\mathcal{F}$ is a family of subsets of some given set E (i.e. $X \in \mathcal{F} \Rightarrow X \subseteq E$), ordered by inclusion. There is another way to represent a domain $(D, \leq)$ by means of a family over the set of its complete primes. To see this point, let us first observe that for any $x \in D$ the set $\hat{x} \subseteq \mathit{Pr}(D)$ has the following properties:

- $\hat{x}$ is pairwise consistent,
- $\hat{x}$ is a cone of $(\mathit{Pr}(D), \leq)$, where we still denote $\leq$ the restriction of the ordering to $\mathit{Pr}(D)$.

Moreover we have $x \leq y \Leftrightarrow \hat{x} \subseteq \hat{y}$. Then one may wonder whether $(D, \leq)$ is isomorphic to $(\mathcal{F}, \subseteq)$ where $\mathcal{F}$ is the family of pairwise consistent cones of $(\mathit{Pr}(D), \leq)$. However this cannot be quite true: there is something missing in the poset $(Pr(D), \leq)$, namely the compatibility relation of complete primes in $(D, \leq)$. For instance the two domains

$D_0 =$ 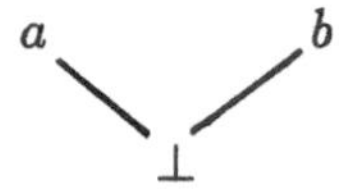

$D_1 =$ 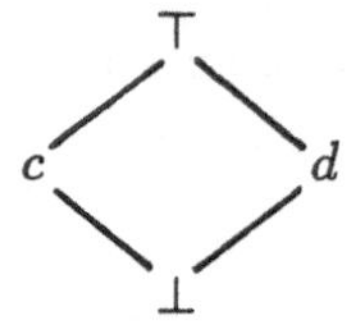

are such that $(Pr(D_0), \leq_0) \rightleftharpoons (\{e_0, e_1\}, \emptyset) \rightleftharpoons (Pr(D_1), \leq_1)$, and the families of pairwise consistent cones of these posets are isomorphic to D_0 itself. In order to get D_1 from $(Pr(D_1), \leq_1)$, we should have kept track of the fact that $c \uparrow d$, while a and b are incompatible in D_0, in notation $a \# b$. Note that this incompatibility relation is irreflexive (that is $x \# y \Rightarrow x \neq y$), symmetric, and satisfies

$$x \# y \;\&\; y \leq z \;\Rightarrow\; x \# z$$

for $x \uparrow z \;\&\; y \leq z \;\Rightarrow\; x \uparrow y$. This motivates the following definition ([13]):

Definition (Prime Event Structures). *A prime event structure is a structure $S = (E, \#, <)$ where*

- *E is the denumerable set of events,*
- *$\# \subseteq E \times E$ is an irreflexive and symmetric relation, the conflict (or incompatibility) relation,*
- *$< \subseteq E \times E$ is a strict ordering, that is an irreflexive and transitive relation,*

satisfying:

(i) the finite causes property: for any $e \in E$ the set $\{e' \mid e' < e\}$ is finite

(ii) the conflict heredity property: $e \# e' \;\&\; e' < e'' \;\Rightarrow\; e \# e''$.

It should be now obvious that we can associate with any domain $(D, \leq)$ a prime event structure, namely $\mathcal{E}(D, \leq) = (Pr(D), \#, <)$ where $\#$ is the incompatibility relation of complete primes in the domain and $<$ the strict ordering determined by $\leq$ on $Pr(D)$. Note that a subset of $Pr(D)$ is pairwise consistent if and only if it is *conflict-free*; for any prime event structure $S = (E, \#, <)$ we shall denote by $Cons_S$ the set of conflict-free subsets of E, that is:

$$X \in Cons_S \;\Leftrightarrow_{\mathrm{def}}\; e, e' \in X \;\Rightarrow\; \neg(e \# e')$$

The next step towards the representation result consists in defining the family of subsets of E determined by the prime event structure $S = (E, \#, <)$, which are called the *configurations* of the structure ([13]):

Definition (Configurations). *Let $S = (E, \#, <)$ be a prime event structure. A configuration of S is a subset X of E such that:*

(i) X is conflict-free: $X \in Cons_S$

(ii) X is a cone: $e \in X \;\&\; e' < e \;\Rightarrow\; e' \in X$.

We shall denote by $\mathcal{F}^\infty(S)$ the set of configurations of the prime event structure S, and by $\mathcal{F}(S)$ the set of finite ones. The poset of configurations defined by S is:

$$\mathcal{D}(S) =_{\mathrm{def}} (\mathcal{F}^\infty(S), \subseteq)$$

We can now state the announced representation result ([13]):

THEOREM (FIRST REPRESENTATION THEOREM). *For any prime event structure S the poset $\mathcal{D}(S)$ is a domain, and any domain $(D, \leq)$ is isomorphic to the poset of configurations of a prime event structure. More specifically we have $(D, \leq) \rightleftharpoons \mathcal{D}(\mathcal{E}(D, \leq))$.*

For a proof, see [13] – in fact we shall prove below a slightly more general result.

2.2 Flow Event Structures

In this paper we regard a domain as the ordered set of computations of some process; from this point of view an event – or a complete prime – may be interpreted as an elementary (irreducible) step of computation, while the ordering represents causality: $e < e'$ means that the event e must occur before e' may occur. Then for the purpose of interpreting the operational semantics of programming constructs, prime event structures turn out to provide too "rigid" a notion (a discussion of this point may be found in [19]). For instance we would like to take into account the fact that a given event may be caused by two incompatible events: in other words, we would like to interpret $(a + b)\,;c$ (where $+$ is non-deterministic choice and ; is the sequential composition) without introducing two distinct events for c. Similarly in $(\mathbf{rec}\, x.(a \,\|\, x))\,;b$ (where **rec** is the fixpoint construct and $\|$ is parallel composition) the event of performing b – which in fact never occurs – should have infinitely many causes. Then we need to introduce a more flexible concrete presentation of domains, ruling out the axioms of finite causes and conflict heredity; in [1] we have introduced such a generalization of prime event structure. Moreover, as we said in the introduction, we need further weakenings of the notion of prime event structures to interpret neatly the operational semantics of CCS. We therefore introduce a new kind of event structure, which we call *flow event structure*:

DEFINITION (FLOW EVENT STRUCTURES). *A flow event structure is a structure $S = (E, \#, \prec)$ where*

- *E is the denumerable set of events,*
- *$\# \subseteq E \times E$ is the symmetric conflict relation,*
- *$\prec \subseteq E \times E$ is an irreflexive relation, the flow relation.*

It should be clear that any prime event structure is a flow event structure. On the other hand, in the definition of flow event structure we do not require the flow relation to be transitive nor acyclic. Note also that the conflict relation is not assumed to be irreflexive: this means that we allow *self-conflicting* – or *inconsistent* – events, that is events $e \in E$ such that $e \# e$ (note also that there are only denumerably many consistent events). We will see that such events cannot in general be removed from a flow event structure without affecting its set of configurations.

The first order flow event structures allow a graphical representation (with two kinds of arcs between events). In this representation we shall draw $e \prec e'$ as $e \rightarrowtail e'$. For instance

N

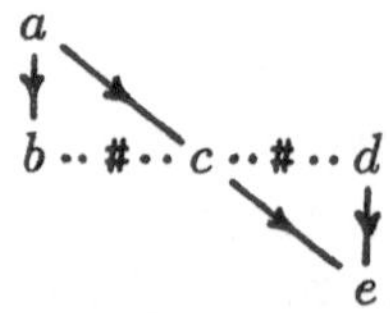

is a flow event structure where $a \prec b$, $b \,\#\, c$, and so on. This structure does not satisfy the conflict heredity property since $c \prec e$, $c \,\#\, d$ and $d \prec e$. Note also that in **N** the flow relation is not transitive since $a \prec e$ does not hold. In a prime event structure, the conflict and flow relations are disjoint; this is not necessarily the case in a flow event structure. For instance

O′

is a structure where $a \prec b$ and $a \,\#\, b$. In the following structure

O

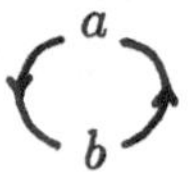

the flow is not acyclic (i.e. the reflexive and transitive closure of $\prec$ is not an ordering). This is also the case for

H

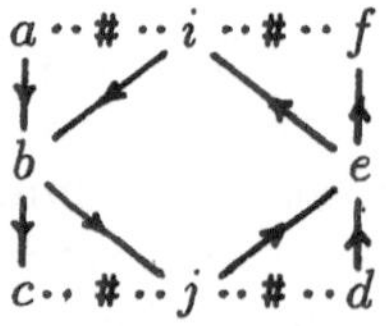

We shall draw self-conflicts as dotted circles around an event. For instance

T

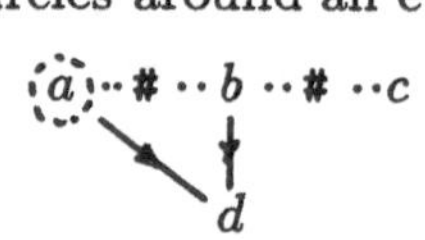

is a flow event structure where a is self-conflicting.

We aim now at showing that flow event structures provide another concrete presentation of domains. To this end we have to define the configurations of a structure $S = (E, \#, \prec)$. Since flow event structures are not very constrained, the definition of configurations is slightly more elaborated than for prime event structures. As we said a configuration represents a computation of the system modelled by S. Since choices are resolved while computing, a configuration will be a conflict-free subset X of E (we still denote by Con_S the set of conflict-free sets of events). Moreover we assume a kind of "causal consistency" property, stating that an event cannot be a strict cause of itself. This property is obviously true in configurations of prime event structures, where there is a global notion of causality, namely $e' < e$ which means "e' is a cause of e". Instead we have the relation $e' \prec e$, which one can interpret as "e' is a condition for e", or "e' is a possible (immediate) cause of e". Then the causal consistency of configurations is expressed by requiring that in a configuration the relation $\prec$ generates a partial order. This (local) *causality* ordering is, denoting as usual by R^* the reflexive and transitive closure of the relation R:

$$\leq_X =_{\text{def}} \prec_X^* \qquad \text{where} \quad \prec_X = \prec \cap (X \times X)$$

This amounts to say that the relation $\prec_X$ is *acyclic*: $e \prec_X^+ e' \;\Rightarrow\; e \neq e'$ (where R^+ denotes the transitive closure of R). Finally, in order to be a configuration a set X of events must satisfy (besides the finite causes property) a "downward-closure" property, meaning that an event cannot occur unless its causes have occurred; this property, expressed in terms of $\prec$, only holds up to the resolution of conflicts. More precisely, this means that if a condition e' for an event $e \in X$ does not appear in X (i.e. $e' \prec e$ and $e' \notin X$), this is because e' is discarded by another condition of e occurring in X. Formally, configurations are defined as follows:

DEFINITION (CONFIGURATIONS). *Let $S = (E, \#, \prec)$ be a flow event structure. A configuration of S is a subset X of E such that:*

(i) X is conflict-free: $X \in \mathit{Con}_S$,

(ii) X does not contain a causality cycle: the relation $\leq_X$ is an ordering,

(iii) for all $e \in X$ the set $\{e' \mid e' \in X \;\&\; e' \leq_X e\}$ is finite,

(iv) for all $e \in X$ if $e' \prec e$ and $e' \notin X$ then there exists $e'' \in X$ such that $e'' \prec e$ and $e' \# e''$.

It should be clear that for prime event structures this definition coincides with the previous one. Then we shall still denote by $\mathcal{F}^\infty(S)$ (resp. $\mathcal{F}(S)$) the set of configurations (resp. finite configurations) of a flow event structure S, and its domain of configurations $(\mathcal{F}^\infty(S), \subseteq)$ by $\mathcal{D}(S)$. Let us see some examples: the structure **O** above has a unique configuration, namely $\emptyset$, while the poset of configurations of **O′** is

The structure **N** has a configuration $X = \{a, c, e\}$ where $a \leq_X e$, while in the configuration $Y = \{a, d, e\}$ the events a and e are not causally related. This example shows that in a flow event structure there is no global causality relation – as it is a case for a prime event structure. In the structure **H** the two events i and j are in a flow cycle ($i \prec^* j \prec^* i$), but they may occur in (different) configurations, namely $\{d, e, i\}$ and $\{a, b, j\}$. The poset of configurations of **T** is:

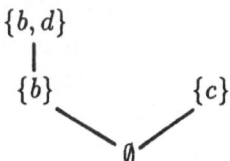

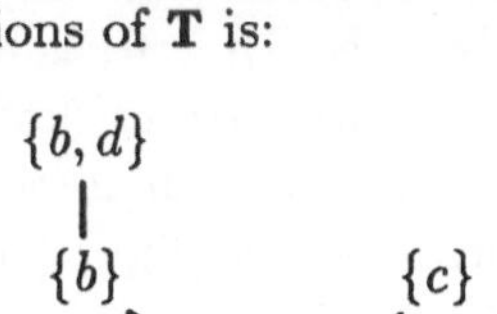

(obviously a self-conflicting event cannot occur in a configuration). Let us see a last example, showing that it may be the case that, although $\{e' \mid e' \prec^* e\}$ is infinite, the event e may occur in a configuration: let

U

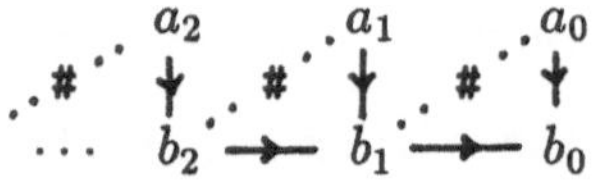

In this "infinite comb" the set $\{e \mid e \prec^* b_i\}$ is infinite for all i, but for instance the set $\{a_{2n}, b_{2n} \mid n \geq 0\}$ is a configuration.

It is in general not so easy to determine whether a given set of events is a configuration of a flow event structure. However we may give an alternative characterization of configurations, which is easier to manage. This characterization formalizes the idea that a computation – i.e. a configuration – may be realized as a sequence of events respecting the causality ordering. Let us introduce the notion of proving sequence with respect to a flow event structure:

DEFINITION (PROVING SEQUENCES). *Given $S = (E, \#, \prec)$, a proving sequence in S is a (finite or infinite) sequence $e_1, \ldots, e_n, \ldots$ of distinct non-conflicting events (i.e. $i \neq j \Rightarrow e_i \neq e_j$ and $\neg(e_i \# e_j)$ for all i, j) satisfying:*

$$\forall i \forall e.\ e \prec e_i \Rightarrow \begin{cases} \exists j < i & e = e_j \quad \text{or} \\ \exists j < i & e \# e_j \prec e_i \end{cases}$$

Remark that any prefix of a proving sequence is a proving sequence. Given $X \subseteq E$, we shall say that a proving sequence $e_1, \ldots, e_n$ is a proof of e in X if $e = e_n$ and $\{e_1, \ldots, e_n\} \subseteq X$. Then we have:

PROPOSITION 2.3. *Given a flow event structure $S = (E, \#, \prec)$, a subset X of E is a configuration of S if and only if*

(i) X is conflict-free, and

(ii) every event $e \in X$ has a proof in X (w.r.t. S).

More precisely, X is a configuration of S if and only if X can be enumerated as $\{e_1, \ldots, e_n, \ldots\}$, where $e_1, \ldots, e_n, \ldots$ is a proving sequence.

Before proving this proposition, let us remark the following: let X be a configuration of S; recall that X, as a subset of E, is denumerable, hence $X = \{x_1, \ldots, x_n, \ldots\}$. Then an obvious idea for enumerating X as a proving sequence $e_1, \ldots, e_k, \ldots$ would be to take at each step the first x_i among minimal events – with respect to the causality ordering of X – which has not been yet enumerated. But this is not sufficient to exhaust X, as shown by the previous example: $\{a_{2n}, b_{2n} \mid n \geq 0\}$ is a configuration of **U** which cannot be enumerated in this way. Therefore we have to devise a more refined technique.

To prove the proposition we first establish some intermediary facts. Let us show that a subset X of a configuration Y is a configuration if and only if it is a cone of Y (with respect to the causality ordering $\leq_Y$ in Y):

LEMMA (THE STABILITY LEMMA) 2.4. *Let X and Y be two configurations of S. If $X \subseteq Y$ then*

$$e \in X \ \&\ e' \leq_Y e \Rightarrow e' \in X$$

Conversely if Y is a configuration of S and X is a cone of Y (w.r.t. $\leq_Y$) then $X \in \mathcal{F}^\infty(S)$.

PROOF: to prove the first point it is enough to show

$$e \in X \;\&\; e' \prec_Y e \;\Rightarrow\; e' \in X$$

Assume the contrary, that is $e' \notin X$: then there should exist $e'' \in X$ such that $e' \# e'' \prec e$, since X is a configuration; but this would imply $Y \notin \mathit{Cons}_S$, for $\{e', e''\} \subseteq Y$.

Conversely if X is a cone of Y, then X clearly satisfies the points (i)-(iii) of the definition of configurations. If $e \in X$ and $e' \prec e$ is such that $e' \notin X$, then we cannot have $e' \in Y$ since X is a cone of Y. Therefore there exists $e'' \in Y$ such that $e' \# e'' \prec e$, and $e'' \in X$ since X is a cone of Y. This shows that X satisfies (iv) ❑

An obvious consequence of this lemma is:

COROLLARY 2.5. *Let S be a flow event structure and X a configuration of S. For $e \in X$ let*

$$\lceil e \rceil_X =_{\text{def}} \{e' \mid e' \in X \;\&\; e' \leq_X e\}$$

Then $\lceil e \rceil_X$ is a (finite) configuration of S.

Recall that for $X, Y \in \mathcal{F}^\infty(S)$ the compatibility relation $X \uparrow Y$ means $\exists Z \in \mathcal{F}^\infty(S)\; X \subseteq Z \;\&\; Y \subseteq Z$.

COROLLARY 2.6. *If $X, Y \in \mathcal{F}^\infty(S)$ then*

$$X \uparrow Y \;\&\; e \in X \cap Y \;\Rightarrow\; \lceil e \rceil_X = \lceil e \rceil_Y$$

PROOF: let Z be a configuration of S such that $X \subseteq Z$ and $Y \subseteq Z$. Let us show that $\lceil e \rceil_X = \lceil e \rceil_Z$ for $e \in X \cap Y$. By definition of the causality ordering $\leq_X$ we have $e' \leq_X e \;\Rightarrow\; e' \leq_Z e$, therefore $\lceil e \rceil_X \subseteq \lceil e \rceil_Z$. Conversely, we know by the previous corollary that $\lceil e \rceil_X$ is a configuration, and $\lceil e \rceil_X \subseteq Z$. Then by the stability lemma $e' \leq_Z e \;\Rightarrow\; e' \in \lceil e \rceil_X$, that is $\lceil e \rceil_Z \subseteq \lceil e \rceil_X$ Similarly $\lceil e \rceil_Y = \lceil e \rceil_Z$, hence $\lceil e \rceil_X = \lceil e \rceil_Y$ ❑

Now we show that two compatible configurations have a least upper bound, which is their union:

COROLLARY 2.7. *Let $X, Y \in \mathcal{F}^\infty(S)$ be two configurations such that $X \uparrow Y$. Then $X \cup Y \in \mathcal{F}^\infty(S)$.*

PROOF: let $Z \in \mathcal{F}^\infty(S)$ be such that $X \subseteq Z$ and $Y \subseteq Z$. Then by the previous lemma X and Y are two cones of Z, and clearly their union $X \cup Y$ is a cone of Z, hence a configuration ❑

The last step towards the proposition is a separation lemma:

LEMMA 2.8. *Let S be a flow event structure and X, Y be two configurations of S such that $X \subset Y$. Then there exists $e \in Y - X$ such that $X \cup \{e\} \in \mathcal{F}^\infty(S)$.*

PROOF: let $e \in Y - X$. Then by corollary 2.5 $\lceil e \rceil_Y$ is a configuration and $\lceil e \rceil_Y \uparrow X$, hence by the previous corollary $Z = \lceil e \rceil_Y \cup X$ is a configuration of S; moreover $Z - X$ is a finite non-empty set of events, since $\lceil e \rceil_Y$ is finite and $e \notin X$. We proceed by induction on the cardinal $k = \#(Z - X)$. If $k = 1$ then $Z - X = \{e\}$ and we are done. If $k > 1$, let $e' \in Z - X$ such that $e' \neq e$. We have $\lceil e' \rceil_Y \subset \lceil e \rceil_Y$ (by corollary 2.6, since $\lceil e \rceil_Y \uparrow Y \;\Rightarrow\; \lceil e' \rceil_{\lceil e \rceil_Y} = \lceil e' \rceil_Y$) and $\lceil e' \rceil_Y \uparrow X$. Then we use the induction hypothesis for $Z' = \lceil e' \rceil_Y \cup X$ ❑

We can now prove the proposition 2.3:

Proof of the **Proposition**: let $X = \{e_1, \ldots, e_n, \ldots\}$ where $e_1, \ldots, e_n, \ldots$ is a proving sequence. Then X is a conflict-free set of events such that every $e \in X$ has a proof in X. Let k_e be the minimal length of a proof of e in X. We show that for $e' \in X$ such that $e' \prec e$ we have $k_{e'} < k_e$. Let $e_1, \ldots, e_n$ be a proof of e in X such that $n = k_e$; then there exists $i < n$ such that $e' = e_i$, otherwise there should exist $j < n$ such that $e' \# e_j$, and this would imply $X \notin \mathit{Con}_S$. Since $e_1, \ldots, e_i$ is a proof of e' in X we have $k_{e'} < k_e$. This shows that $\leq_X$ is an ordering. Moreover given a proof $e_1, \ldots, e_n$ of e in X, it is easy to see by transitivity that $e' \leq_X e \Rightarrow \exists i \leq n\ e' = e_i$ (since $e_1, \ldots, e_j$ is also a proof of e_j in X for all $j \leq n$). Therefore $\{e' \mid e' \leq_X e\}$ is finite. Finally if $e' \prec e$ and $e' \notin X$ (with $e \in X$) then for any proof $e_1, \ldots, e_n$ of e in X there exists $i < n$ such that $e' \# e_i \prec e$, by definition of the notion of proof since $\{e_1, \ldots, e_n\} \subseteq X$ and $e' \notin X$. This shows $X \in \mathcal{F}^\infty(S)$.

Conversely, to show that a configuration X is a conflict-free set of events such that every $e \in X$ has a proof in X, it is enough to prove that X can be enumerated as $\{e_1, \ldots, e_n, \ldots\}$, where the sequence $e_1, \ldots, e_n, \ldots$ is a proving sequence. This is trivial if X is empty. Otherwise since X is a subset of the denumerable set of events, it may be enumerated as $\{x_1, \ldots, x_n, \ldots\}$, in such a way that if $i < j$ and $x_i = x_j$ then $x_m = x_i$ for all $m > i$. Let us define the sequence $(X_n)_{n \geq 1}$ of subsets of X as follows:

$$\begin{cases} X_1 = \lceil x_1 \rceil_X \\ X_{n+1} = X_n \cup \lceil x_{n+1} \rceil_X \quad (\text{for } n > 1) \end{cases}$$

We obviously have $X_n \subseteq X_{n+1}$ and $X = \bigcup\{X_n \mid 1 \leq n\}$. Moreover a simple induction on n shows that every X_n is a finite configuration of S:

- this is true for $n = 1$ by corollary 2.5.
- if $X_n \in \mathcal{F}(S)$, we have $X_n \uparrow \lceil x_{n+1} \rceil_X$ since these two configurations are included into X, hence X_{n+1} is a (finite) configuration by the corollary 2.7.

By the separation lemma 2.8, for any pair of configurations Y, Z such that $Y \subset Z \subseteq X$ there exists $\varepsilon(Y, Z) \in Z - Y$ such that $Y \cup \{\varepsilon(Y, Z)\}$ is a configuration. We can now define the sequence $e_1, \ldots, e_n, \ldots$ as follows, where we let $\overline{X}_n = \{e_1, \ldots, e_n\}$:

$$\begin{cases} e_1 = \varepsilon(\emptyset, X_1) \\ e_{n+1} = \begin{cases} \varepsilon(\overline{X}_n, X_k) & \text{if } \{m \mid \overline{X}_n \subset X_m\} \neq \emptyset \text{ and } k = \mathsf{Inf}\{m \mid \overline{X}_n \subset X_m\} \\ e_n & \text{otherwise} \end{cases} \end{cases}$$

The first point is to check that this sequence is well-defined, i.e. to check that for all n the set $\overline{X}_n$ is a configuration. This is true since if we let $\overline{X}_0 = \emptyset$ then for all $n \geq 0$ either $\overline{X}_{n+1} = \overline{X}_n \cup \{\varepsilon(\overline{X}_n, Z)\}$ for some configuration Z such that $\overline{X}_n \subset Z \subseteq X$, or $\overline{X}_{n+1} = \overline{X}_n$.

Now we prove that $X = \{e_1, \ldots, e_n, \ldots\}$. By definition $e_n \in X$ for all n. Then it is enough to show that for all n there exists m such that $X_n \subseteq \overline{X}_m$. Let us first observe that for all i such that $\overline{X}_i \subset X_n$ we have $e_{i+1} \in X_n - \overline{X}_i$, hence $\overline{X}_i \subset \overline{X}_{i+1} \subseteq X_n$. Therefore the set $\{i \mid \overline{X}_i \subset X_n\}$ is finite since X_n is finite. If there is no i such that $\overline{X}_i \subset X_n$ then we are done since in this case $X_n = \overline{X}_1$ (for $\overline{X}_1 \subseteq X_n$). Otherwise let k be the greatest integer such that $\overline{X}_k \subset X_n$. Then $\{m \mid \overline{X}_k \subset X_m\} \neq \emptyset$, and if $j = \mathsf{Inf}\{m \mid \overline{X}_k \subset X_m\}$

then we have $j \leq n$, hence $e_{k+1} \in X_n - \overline{X}_k$, therefore $\overline{X}_k \subset \overline{X}_{k+1} \subseteq X_n$. Because of our choice for k we have $X_n = \overline{X}_{k+1}$.

Finally we prove that $e_1, \ldots, e_n, \ldots$ is a proving sequence: let $e \in E$ be such that $e \prec e_k$; since $e_k \in \overline{X}_k$ we have either $e \in \overline{X}_k$, in which case there exists $i \leq k$ such that $e = e_i$, and in fact $i < k$ since $\prec$ is irreflexive, or (since $\overline{X}_k$ is a configuration) there exists $e' \in \overline{X}_k$ such that $e \# e' \prec e_k$. In that case we have $e' = e_i$ for some $i < k$ (since $\prec$ is irreflexive). This shows that $e_1, \ldots, e_n, \ldots$ is a proving sequence ❑

2.3 The Representation Theorem

In this section we prove the representation theorem relating domains and flow event structures, and discuss some of its consequences. As a first step, let us relate consistency in the poset $(\mathcal{F}^\infty(S), \subseteq)$ of configurations of S with conflict-freeness in the flow event structure S – recall that for $\mathcal{X} \subseteq \mathcal{F}^\infty(S)$ the pairwise consistency predicate $\mathcal{X}\Uparrow$ means

$$\forall X, Y \in \mathcal{X}\ \exists Z \in \mathcal{F}^\infty(S)\ X \subseteq Z \ \&\ Y \subseteq Z$$

LEMMA 2.9. *Let $\mathcal{X} \subseteq \mathcal{F}^\infty(S)$ be such that $\mathcal{X}\Uparrow$. Then $\bigcup\{X \mid X \in \mathcal{X}\}$ is a configuration of S, which is the least upper bound of $\mathcal{X}$ in $\mathcal{D}(S)$. Moreover $\mathcal{X}\Uparrow$ if and only if $\bigcup\{X \mid X \in \mathcal{X}\} \in$ **Cons**$_S$.*

PROOF: if $e, e' \in \bigcup\{X \mid X \in \mathcal{X}\}$ then there exist $X, Y \in \mathcal{X}$ such that $e \in X$ and $e' \in Y$. Since $\mathcal{X}\Uparrow$ there is a configuration Z such that $X \subseteq Z$ and $Y \subseteq Z$. Therefore $\neg(e \# e')$ since Z is conflict-free, hence $\bigcup\{X \mid X \in \mathcal{X}\} \in$ *Cons*$_S$. Moreover if $e \in \bigcup\{X \mid X \in \mathcal{X}\}$, then $e \in X$ for some $X \in \mathcal{X}$, hence e has a proof in X which is also a proof of e in $\bigcup\{X \mid X \in \mathcal{X}\}$. Then $\bigcup\{X \mid X \in \mathcal{X}\}$ is a configuration of S, and it is obvious that this is the least upper bound of $\mathcal{X}$. The last point to note is that if $\bigcup\{X \mid X \in \mathcal{X}\} \in$ *Cons*$_S$ then $\mathcal{X}\Uparrow$, since $\bigcup\{X \mid X \in \mathcal{X}\}$ is a configuration ❑

THEOREM (SECOND REPRESENTATION THEOREM). *For any flow event structure S the poset $\mathcal{D}(S) = (\mathcal{F}^\infty(S), \subseteq)$ is a domain. Its complete primes are the configurations $\lceil e \rceil_X$ for $X \in \mathcal{F}^\infty(S)$ and $e \in X$, and its finite points are the finite configurations $X \in \mathcal{F}(S)$. Conversely if $(D, \leq)$ is a domain then $(D, \leq)$ is isomorphic to the poset $(\mathcal{F}^\infty(S), \subseteq)$ of configurations of a flow event structure.*

PROOF: the first point to note is that $\mathcal{D}(S)$ is coherent, as shown by the previous lemma.

Let us show that for each configuration X of S and each $e \in X$ the (finite) configuration $\lceil e \rceil_X$ is a complete prime: if $\lceil e \rceil_X \subseteq \bigsqcup \mathcal{X}$ where $\mathcal{X}$ is a (pairwise consistent) set of configurations, then $e \in Y$ for some $Y \in \mathcal{X}$. We have $Y \uparrow \lceil e \rceil_X$ and by the corollary 2.6 this implies $\lceil e \rceil_Y = \lceil e \rceil_{\lceil e \rceil_X} = \lceil e \rceil_X$, hence $\lceil e \rceil_X \subseteq Y$, so $\lceil e \rceil_X$ is a complete prime.

Conversely, let X be a configuration of S. Since $e \in \lceil e \rceil_X$ for all $e \in X$, we obviously have $X = \bigsqcup\{\lceil e \rceil_X \mid e \in X\}$. If X is a complete prime of $\mathcal{D}(S)$ there exists $e \in X$ such that $X \subseteq \lceil e \rceil_X$, hence $X = \lceil e \rceil_X$. To sum up, we have shown that the complete primes of $\mathcal{D}(S)$ are the configurations of the form $\lceil e \rceil_X$, and that $\mathcal{D}(S)$ is ω-prime algebraic (the set of complete primes of $\mathcal{D}(S)$ is denumerable since a complete prime is a finite subset of the denumerable set of events).

This poset is clearly finitary since each $\lceil e \rceil_X$ is a finite set of events. If $X \in \mathcal{F}^\infty(S)$ is finite (as a set of events), then it includes only finitely many configurations. Conversely for $X \in \mathcal{F}^\infty(S)$ if the set $\{Y \mid Y \in \mathcal{F}^\infty(S) \;\&\; Y \subseteq X\}$ is finite, then X is a finite set of events since the set $\{Y \mid Y \in \mathcal{F}^\infty(S) \;\&\; Y \subseteq X\}$ contains the configurations $\lceil e \rceil_X$ for all $e \in X$. Then we have proved:

$$F(\mathcal{F}^\infty(S), \subseteq) = \mathcal{F}(S)$$

Given a domain $(D, \leq)$, we already defined a prime event structure $\mathcal{E}(D, \leq)$ associated with the domain. We let the reader check that from the definition of this structure we have:

$$X \in \mathcal{F}^\infty(\mathcal{E}(D, \leq)) \;\Leftrightarrow\; \exists x \in D \quad X = \hat{x} = \{y \mid y \in Pr(D, \leq) \;\&\; y \leq x\}$$

since $(D, \leq)$ is coherent. Then $\mathcal{D}(\mathcal{E}(D, \leq)) \rightleftharpoons (D, \leq)$ since $(D, \leq)$ is ω-prime algebraic (*cf.* [18,19] for a complete proof) □

We shall regard flow event structures as (semantically, or abstractly) *equivalent* if their domains of configurations are isomorphic:

$$S \cong S' \;\Leftrightarrow_{\text{def}}\; \mathcal{D}(S) \rightleftharpoons \mathcal{D}(S')$$

Then a trivial consequence of the representation theorem (and of corollary 2.2) is:

COROLLARY 2.10. *Two flow event structures S and S' are equivalent if and only if their posets of finite configurations are isomorphic:*

$$S \cong S' \;\Leftrightarrow\; (\mathcal{F}(S), \subseteq) \rightleftharpoons (\mathcal{F}(S'), \subseteq)$$

Another consequence is that for any flow event structure S there exists a prime event structure S' such that $S \cong S'$. As a matter of fact, the representation theorem shows the following equivalences:

$$\mathcal{E}(\mathcal{D}(S)) \cong S \quad \text{for any flow event structure } S$$

$$\mathcal{D}(\mathcal{E}(D, \leq)) \rightleftharpoons (D, \leq) \quad \text{for all domain } (D, \leq)$$

However we will be more interested here in a stronger notion of equivalence, namely "to determine the same sets of configurations", that is:

$$S \equiv S' \;\Leftrightarrow_{\text{def}}\; \mathcal{F}^\infty(S) = \mathcal{F}^\infty(S')$$

Since $X = \bigcup\{\lceil e \rceil_X \mid e \in X\}$ for any configuration X of S we have in fact:

$$S \equiv S' \;\Leftrightarrow\; \mathcal{F}(S) = \mathcal{F}(S')$$

When $S \equiv S'$ we shall say that S and S' are *strongly* (or *concretely*) equivalent. From an operational point of view this notion of equivalence seems to be the right one to use: we think of a domain of configurations as representing the computations of some given distributed system; in such an interpretation the names of events, which are occurrences of elementary actions, are meaningful – for instance one can see that in the interpretation of CCS given in [4], the events are closely related to the syntactic structure of terms. Then if one defines a translation from a given model of distributed computations into another one which "preserves the events", one gets a strong notion of "implementation": a distributed system is thus translated into another one which behaves exactly in the same way. In the next section we shall establish such a concrete relationship between flow event structures and a particular class of Petri nets. Note that the transformation $\mathcal{E} \circ \mathcal{D}$ does not "preserve the events"; this means that we do not have in general $\mathcal{E}(\mathcal{D}(S)) \equiv S$. For instance if $S = (\{e_0, e_1, e_2\}, \#, \prec)$ is the flow event structure represented by:

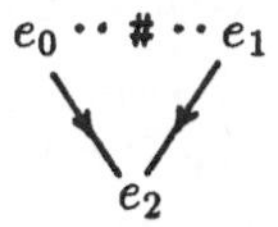

then $\mathcal{E}(\mathcal{D}(S))$ is:

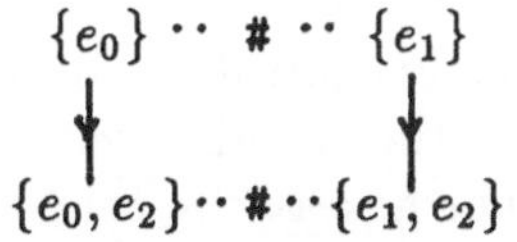

(the mapping $\lceil e \rceil_X \mapsto e$ is not injective in general).

The strong equivalence of flow event structures only requires preservation of the events actually occurring in some configuration. It also preserves the *semantical conflict* relation, meaning that two events cannot occur together in a configuration; given a flow event structure $S = (E, \#, \prec)$, this relation $\#_S$ is defined by:

$$e \, \#_S \, e' \Leftrightarrow_{\mathrm{def}} \forall X \in \mathcal{F}^{\infty}(S) \; \{e, e'\} \not\subseteq X$$

Obviously $e \, \# \, e' \;\Rightarrow\; e \, \#_S \, e'$. We denote by $E(S)$ the set of events which are not semantically inconsistent, that is events which occur in some configuration:

$$e \in E(S) \;\Leftrightarrow_{\mathrm{def}}\; \neg(e \, \#_S \, e) \;\Leftrightarrow\; \exists X \in \mathcal{F}^{\infty}(S) \; e \in X$$

Then we have:

$$S \equiv S' \;\Rightarrow\; \begin{cases} E(S) = E(S') \quad \text{and} \\ e, e' \in E(S) \;\Rightarrow\; e \, \#_S \, e' \;\Leftrightarrow\; e \, \#_{S'} \, e' \end{cases}$$

Following Winskel, we can say that a flow event stucture $S = (E, \#, \prec)$ is *full* if $E = E(S)$, and that S is *faithful* if $\#$ restricted to $E(S)$ coincides with the semantical conflict, and if every semantically inconsistent event is self-conflicting, that is:

$$\begin{cases} \forall e, e' \in E(S) \quad e \, \# \, e' \;\Leftrightarrow\; e \, \#_S \, e' \quad \text{and} \\ e \, \#_S \, e \;\Rightarrow\; e \, \# \, e \end{cases}$$

Note that we do not require a semantically inconsistent event to be conflicting with any other event – that is we do not require $\# = \#_S$. For instance the structure (called ∇' in [2]):

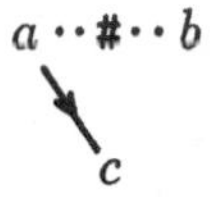

is not faithful. We shall see in the next section that any flow event structure is strongly equivalent to a faithful one. On the other hand, there does not in general exist a full flow event structure strongly equivalent to a given one: in particular one cannot remove the self-conflicting events without affecting the configurations. To see this point, let us prove another consequence of the stability lemma, stating that the causality orderings are in fact inherent to the family of configurations:

LEMMA 2.11. *For any configuration X of a flow event structure S we have*

$$e' \leq_X e \;\Leftrightarrow\; \forall Y \in \mathcal{F}^\infty(S).\; Y \subseteq X \;\&\; e \in Y \;\Rightarrow\; e' \in Y$$

PROOF: let $e' \leq_X e$ and $Y \in \mathcal{F}^\infty(S)$ be such that $Y \subseteq X$ and $e \in Y$. Then by the corollary 2.6 we have $\lceil e \rceil_Y = \lceil e \rceil_X$, hence $e' \in Y$ since $e' \leq_X e \Leftrightarrow e' \in \lceil e \rceil_X$.

Conversely if for any configuration Y such that $Y \subseteq X$ and $e \in Y$ we have $e' \in Y$, then this holds for $Y = \lceil e \rceil_X$, hence $e' \leq_X e$ ❑

A consequence is that for two strongly equivalent flow event structures the local causality relations are the same – note that the covering relation (w.r.t. $\leq_X$) in a configuration X is contained in $\prec_X$, but does not necessarily coincide with this relation, as shown by the following example:

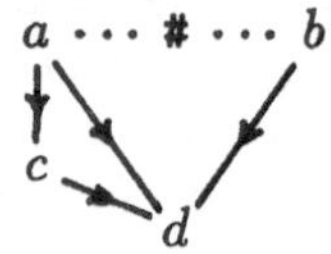

Remark that this structure is strongly equivalent to the following faithful one:

Now let us consider the following flow event structure:

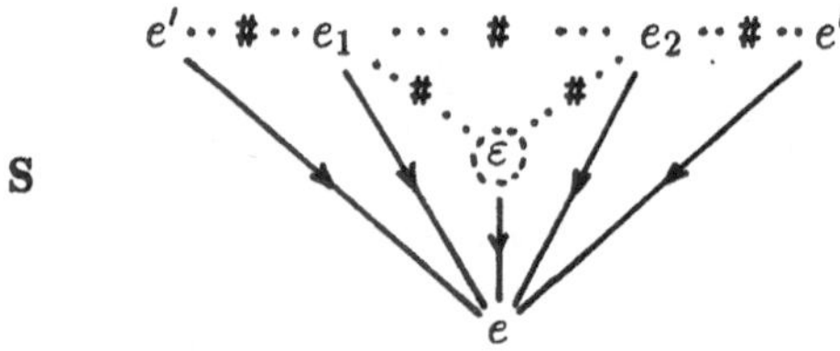

The domain of configurations of **S** is:

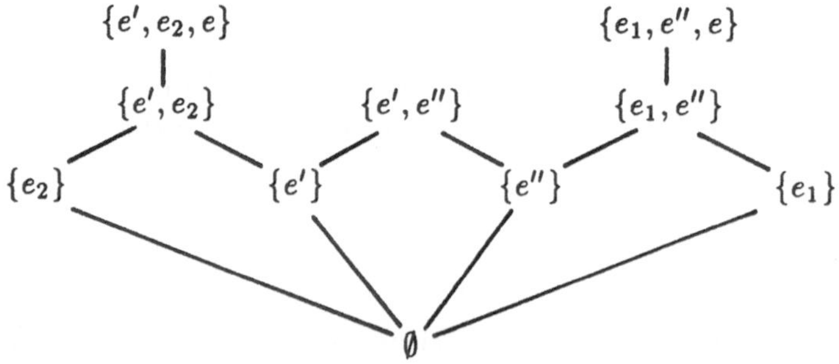

We let the reader convince him/herself (using the previous lemma) that the only possible candidate for a full flow event structure strongly equivalent to **S** is:

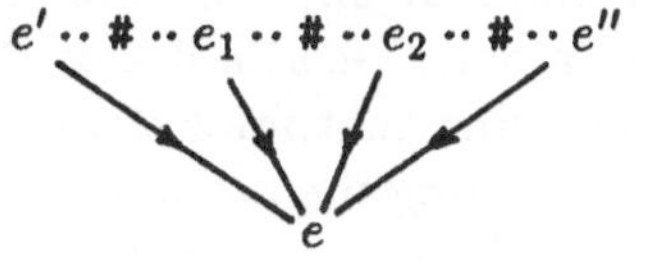

But then $\{e', e'', e\}$ is a configuration of this structure, while it is not a configuration of **S**.

3. Petri Nets

3.1 Flow Nets

In this section we extend the result of [13], establishing the relationship between occurrence nets and prime event structures. We show a correspondence between a class of Petri nets, which is broader than the class of occurrence nets, and the class of flow event structures. The Petri nets we introduce may contain forward and backward conflicts and cycles in the flow relation, but are "semantically" acyclic – roughly speaking this means that in any run of the net a token cannot return in a place which was previously marked (and used as a precondition).

DEFINITION (NETS). *A net is a structure* $N = (B, E, \Phi, \mu_0)$ *where*

- B *is the set of conditions (or places),*
- E *is the denumerable set of events, disjoint from* B,
- $\Phi \subseteq (B \times E) \cup (E \times B)$ *is the flow relation, satisfying: the set* $\{b \mid \exists e, e' \ (e, b) \in \Phi \ \& \ (b, e') \in \Phi\}$ *is denumerable and* $\forall e \in E \ \exists b \in B. \ (b, e) \in \Phi$
- $\mu_0 : B \to \mathbb{N}$ *is the initial marking.*

A condition $b \in B$ is a *precondition* (respectively a *postcondition*) of the event $e \in E$ if $(b, e) \in \Phi$ (resp. $(e, b) \in \Phi$). Note that we require that any event has at least one precondition, but not necessarily a postcondition. The flow relation can also be represented as a mapping

$$\phi : (B \times E) \cup (E \times B) \to \{0, 1\}$$

given by $\phi(x) = 1 \Leftrightarrow x \in \Phi$. We denote by $\varphi(e, e')$ the set of places in between e and e', that is $\varphi(e, e') = \{b \mid \phi(e, b) = 1 = \phi(b, e')\}$. This set is denumerable.

A marking of the net N is any mapping $\mu : B \to \mathbb{N}$. If $\mu(b) > 0$ we shall say informally that the condition b holds at μ (or alternatively that there is a token in the place b). A marking μ *enables* an event e if all the preconditions of e hold in μ, that is $\mu(b) > 0$ for all b such that $(b, e) \in \Phi$ or more formally: $\forall b \in B \ \phi(b, e) \leq \mu(b)$. The net N determines a labelled transition system on its markings, defined as follows:

$$\mu \xrightarrow{e} \mu' \ \Leftrightarrow_{\text{def}} \ \forall b \in B \ \phi(b, e) \leq \mu(b) \ \& \ \mu'(b) = \mu(b) - \phi(b, e) + \phi(e, b)$$

It should be obvious that this transition system is deterministic: if μ enables e then the next marking μ' is uniquely determined. A *firing sequence* of the net N is a finite or infinite sequence of transitions:

$$\mu_0 \xrightarrow{e_1} \mu_1 \cdots \mu_{n-1} \xrightarrow{e_n} \mu_n \cdots$$

We can also say that the sequence $e_1, \ldots, e_n, \ldots$ of events is *firable* in the net N. Let us recall some definitions: a marking μ is reachable if there is a firing sequence such that $\mu = \mu_n$; a place $b \in B$ is called *safe* if at any reachable marking μ there is at most one token in b, that is $\mu(b) \leq 1$, and a net N is *safe* if any place of N is safe.

In this section we aim at showing that for Petri nets of a particular kind one can build a flow event structure *representing* the net in the sense that a (finite) sequence of events is firable in the net if and only if it is a proving sequence in the event structure. Conversely from a flow event structure we shall also build a net representing this structure. It should be clear that this may only hold for nets where the events of a firable sequence are distinct, what we could call *occurrence nets* – a terminology that we shall not officially introduce since it is already overloaded. Moreover the nets we are seeking should be such that one can extract from a firing sequence the causal dependencies between events. For instance we will rule out the net

V

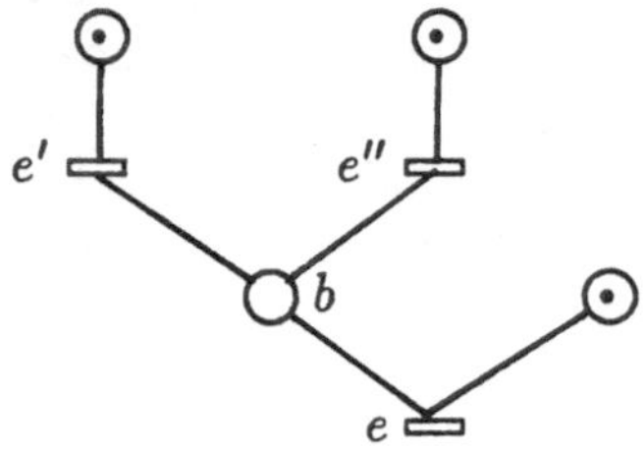

In this net the sequence e', e'', e is firable, but we cannot know what token from b is used to fire e (remark: this net corresponds to the "parallel switch" of [18], example 1.1.7, which is a typical non-stable event structure). Note that this net is not safe.

As a matter of fact, in a safe "occurrence" net one can easily define the causal (immediate) dependency: e depends on e' if there is a place b in between these two events (more precisely $b \in \varphi(e', e)$). However it will turn out that safeness is too strong a requirement for our purpose. To introduce the appropriate class of nets, which we shall call *flow nets*, we first introduce the notion of "strong postcondition" in a net N, which will play the rôle of a safe condition between two events. A place $b \in B$ is a *strong postcondition* of an event $e \in E$ if $\phi(e, b) = 1$ and in any firing sequence $\mu_0 \xrightarrow{e_1} \mu_1 \cdots \mu_{n-1} \xrightarrow{e_n} \mu_n$ where e occurs (i.e. $e = e_j$ for some j), only e can mark b, that is:

$$\mu_0(b) + \sum_{1 \leq i \leq n} \phi(e_i, b) = 1$$

Note that if e really occurs in some firing sequence, then a strong postcondition b of e is initially unmarked ($\mu_0(b) = 0$), and b cannot be a precondition of e (i.e. $\phi(b, e) = 0$, otherwise b should be marked twice in the sequence). We shall use $\widehat{\varphi}(e', e)$ to denote the set of strong postconditions of e' belonging to $\varphi(e', e)$.

DEFINITION (FLOW NETS). *A flow net is a net N satisfying:*

(i) any finite firing sequence $\mu_0 \xrightarrow{e_1} \mu_1 \cdots \mu_{n-1} \xrightarrow{e_n} \mu_n$ is flowing, i.e. a place cannot be used (as a precondition) more than once: $\sum_{1 \leq i \leq n} \phi(b, e_i) \leq 1$ for all $b \in B$,

(ii) for any firing sequence $\mu_0 \xrightarrow{e_1} \mu_1 \cdots \mu_{n-1} \xrightarrow{e_n} \mu_n$ if $\varphi(e_i, e_j) \neq \emptyset$ then $\widehat{\varphi}(e_i, e_j) \neq \emptyset$.

It should be clear that the *occurrence nets* of Nielsen, Plotkin and Winskel ([13,18]) are flow nets. Let us see some consequences of our definition: the first observation is that an event e cannot occur twice in a firing sequence of a flow net (since e has a precondition b, which cannot be used twice). Therefore a flow net is semantically acyclic: in a firing sequence we have $i \neq j \Rightarrow \mu_i \neq \mu_j$. Let us also remark that if two (distinct) events share a precondition (i.e. $\phi(b,e) = 1 = \phi(b,e')$) then they cannot both occur in the same firing sequence. Another direct consequence of the definition is:

FACT 3.1. *If two distinct events e and e' of a flow net share a postcondition b – that is if $\phi(e,b) = 1 = \phi(e',b)$ – which is a strong postcondition of e, then they cannot both occur in the same firing sequence.*

One may remark that in the previous net **V** there is no strong postcondition for e' or e''. On the other hand, we will see that in a flow net the strong postconditions allow us to extract from any firing sequence the actual causal dependencies between the events. Let us see an example of flow net:

W

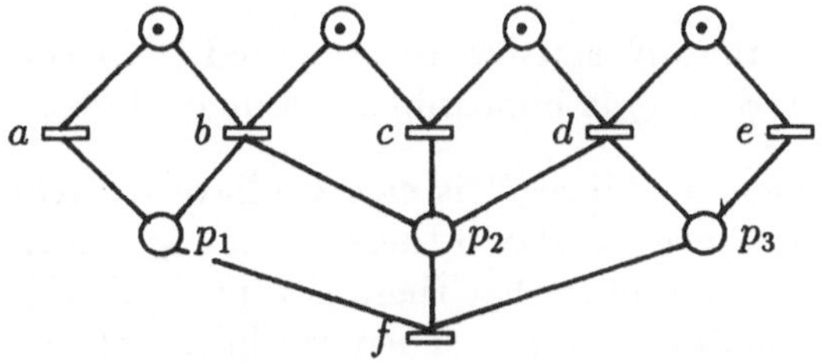

In this net p_1 is a strong postcondition for a and b, p_2 is a strong postcondition for c and p_3 is a strong postcondition for d and e. Note that in the firing sequence

$$\mu_0 \xrightarrow{b} \mu_1 \xrightarrow{d} \mu_2 \xrightarrow{f} \mu_3$$

we have $\mu_2(p_2) = 2$, hence this net is not safe. Remark that the safe flow net

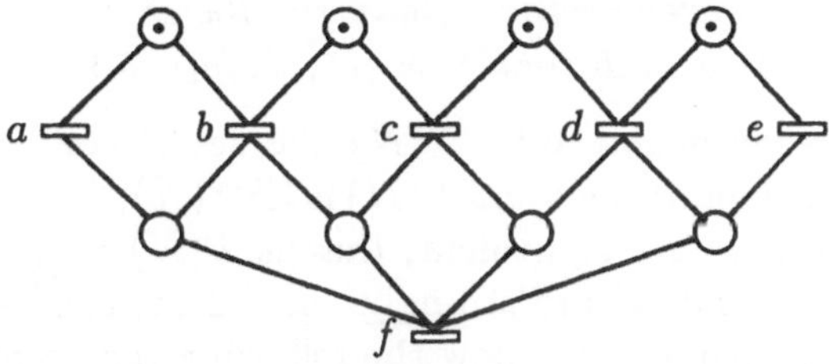

is not equivalent (in the sense of having the same firing sequences) to the previous one: for instance a, d, f and b, e, f are not firable in this net. Onc may characterize safe flow nets as follows:

LEMMA 3.2. *A net N is a safe flow net if and only if for any condition b and for any (finite) firing sequence $\mu_0 \xrightarrow{e_1} \mu_1 \cdots \mu_{n-1} \xrightarrow{e_n} \mu_n$ the following is satisfied: $\mu_0(b) + \sum_{1 \leq i \leq n} \phi(e_i, b) \leq 1$.*

PROOF: let us first remark that if the net N satisfies the property stated in the lemma, then any postcondition in N is a strong postcondition. Moreover such a net is safe since for any firing sequence $\mu_0 \xrightarrow{e_1} \mu_1 \cdots \mu_{n-1} \xrightarrow{e_n} \mu_n$ and for any b the ith marking on b is given by:

$$(*) \qquad \mu_i(b) = \mu_0(b) - \sum_{1 \leq j \leq i} \phi(b, e_j) + \sum_{1 \leq j \leq i} \phi(e_j, b)$$

This formula also gives us $\sum_{1 \leq i \leq n} \phi(b, e_i) = \mu_0(b) - \mu_n(b) + \sum_{1 \leq i \leq n} \phi(e_i, b)$, hence the sequence is flowing.

Conversely let N be a safe flow net; the formula $(*)$ (for $i = n$) can be written:

$$\mu_0(b) + \sum_{1 \leq j \leq n} \phi(e_j, b) = \mu_n(b) + \sum_{1 \leq j \leq n} \phi(b, e_j)$$

Since N is safe we have $\mu_n(b) \leq 1$, and $\sum_{1 \leq j \leq n} \phi(b, e_j) \leq 1$ since N is a flow net. Therefore to show that N satisfies the required property it is enough to prove that $\mu_n(b) = 1 = \sum_{1 \leq j \leq n} \phi(b, e_j)$ is impossible. Assume the contrary, that is $\mu_n(b) = 1$ and $\phi(b, e_j) = 1$ for some j. Since N is safe we have $\mu_{j-1}(b) \leq 1$, but μ_{j-1} enables e_j, hence $\mu_{j-1}(b) = 1$. Since $\mu_n(b) > 0$ there exists $i \geq j$ such that $\phi(e_i, b) = 1$; therefore $\varphi(e_i, e_j) \neq \emptyset$, and this implies that there is a place b' which is a strong postcondition for e_i and a precondition for e_j. Then we have $\mu_0(b') + \sum_{1 \leq l < j} \phi(e_l, b') = 0$, hence $\mu_{j-1}(b') = 0$, which contradicts the fact that μ_{j-1} enables e_j ▭

For flow nets (or more generally for "occurrence nets") the following definition makes sense:

DEFINITION (CONFIGURATIONS). *Given a flow net $N = (B, E, \Phi, \mu_0)$, a configuration of N is a subset X of E such that there exists a sequence*

$$\mu_0 \xrightarrow{e_1} \mu_1 \cdots \mu_{n-1} \xrightarrow{e_n} \mu_n \cdots$$

firing the events of X, that is such that $X = \{e_1, \ldots, e_n, \ldots\}$.

As for event structures we denote by $\mathcal{F}^\infty(N)$ the set of configurations of N; $\mathcal{F}(N)$ denotes the set of finite configurations and $\mathcal{D}(N)$ is $(\mathcal{F}^\infty(N), \subseteq)$. We also denote $N \cong N'$ the fact that these two nets are equivalent, that is $\mathcal{D}(N) \rightleftharpoons \mathcal{D}(N')$, and we still use $N \equiv N'$ to mean that N and N' are strongly equivalent, that is $\mathcal{F}^\infty(N) = \mathcal{F}^\infty(N')$. The main purpose of this paper is to show the following *representation theorem*:

THEOREM. *For any flow net N there exists a flow event structure S such that $\mathcal{F}^\infty(N) = \mathcal{F}^\infty(S)$. Conversely for any flow event structure S there exists a flow net having the same configurations.*

In fact we shall more precisely relate the notion of proving sequence in a flow event structure with the notion of firing sequence in a flow net.

3.2 From Flow Nets to Flow Event Structures

For any flow net $N = (B, E, \Phi, \mu_0)$ we shall define a flow event structure $\mathcal{E}(N)$ whose configurations are exactly the sets of events firable in sequence in N. As a first step, let us build a structure $S(N) = (E, \#_N, \prec_N)$ as follows: two events are conflicting if they cannot both occur in a firing sequence, that is

$$e \,\#_N\, e' \;\Leftrightarrow_{\text{def}}\; \forall X \in \mathcal{F}^{\infty}(N) \quad \{e, e'\} \not\subseteq X$$

Then for instance an event is inconsistent (self-conflicting) if and only if it is not firable (from any reachable marking). For instance if e has a precondition b, i.e. $\phi(b, e) = 1$, which is initially unmarked ($\mu_0(b) = 0$) and which is not a postcondition of another event ($\forall e\ \phi(e, b) = 0$) then e is inconsistent. Note that such an inconsistent event is in conflict with any other event. We have seen previously other examples of conflict, namely:
$\exists b\ \phi(b, e) = 1 = \phi(b, e')\ \&\ e \neq e' \;\Rightarrow\; e \,\#_N\, e'$, a situation which may be drawn:

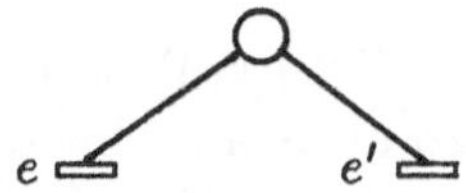

$$\Rightarrow\; e \,\#_N\, e'$$

if $\exists b\ \phi(e, b) = 1 = \phi(e', b)\ \&\ e \neq e'$, that is

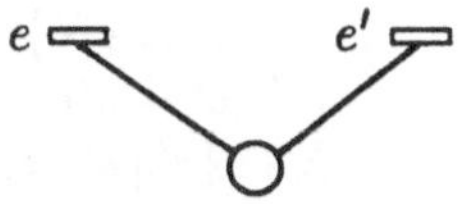

and b is a strong postcondition of e then $e \,\#_N\, e'$.

The flow relation $e' \prec_N e$ of $S(N)$ means that e' and e may both occur in a firing sequence, and that there is a strong postcondition of e' which is a precondition of e:

$$e' \prec_N e \;\Leftrightarrow_{\text{def}}\; \neg(e' \,\#_N\, e)\ \&\ \widehat{\varphi}(e', e) \neq \emptyset$$

Let us define the flow relation $\prec_N^b$ relative to a given place b (initially unmarked) by:

$$e' \prec_N^b e \;\Leftrightarrow_{\text{def}}\; \mu_0(b) = 0\ \&\ \neg(e' \,\#_N\, e)\ \&\ b \in \varphi(e', e)$$

Then it is easy to see that

$$e' \prec_N e \;\Leftrightarrow\; \exists b \in B.\ e' \prec_N^b e$$

Note that the relation $\prec_N$ is irreflexive, since a strong postcondition of a consistent event cannot be a precondition of this event. Therefore $S(N)$ is a flow event structure. However this structure does not quite achieve our purpose; consider for instance the safe flow net:

N 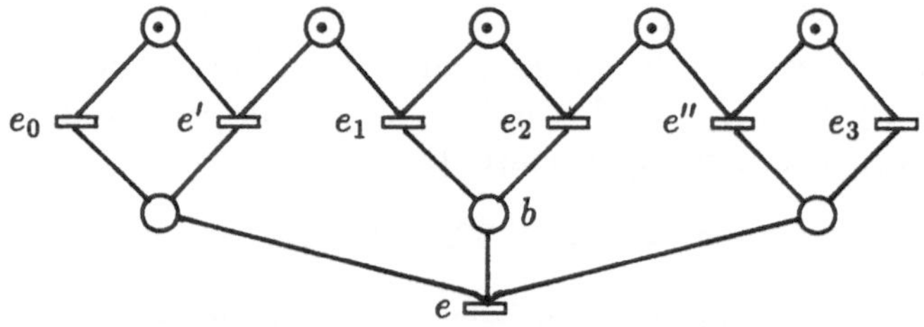

Then in $S(\mathbf{N})$ the conflict relation is the one indicated by the shared initial places, that is $e_0 \#_{\mathrm{N}} e'$, $e' \#_{\mathrm{N}} e_1$, and so on. Similarly it is easily seen that we have $e_0 \prec_{\mathrm{N}} e$, $e' \prec_{\mathrm{N}} e$, and so on. Then $\{e', e'', e\}$ is a configuration of $S(\mathbf{N})$, since for any i the event e_i, which is a possible immediate cause for e, is in conflict with e' or e''. However this should not be the case, since the condition b between e and e_1, e_2 must hold for e to be enabled, and neither e' nor e'' may fill in this place: the set $\{e', e'', e\}$ is not a configuration of $\mathbf{N}$.

The point is that a configuration $X \in \mathcal{F}^\infty(S(N))$ need not intersect all the sets $\{e' \mid e' \prec_N^b e\}$ for $e \in X$ and $b \in \varphi(e', e)$. To overcome this difficulty, we add to $S(N)$ new self-conflicting events. Let us introduce the set Ω_N of triples (X, b, e) which must be discarded, and will be the new events:

$$(X, b, e) \in \Omega_N \Leftrightarrow_{\text{def}} \begin{cases} X \in \mathcal{F}(S(N)) \ \& \ e \in X & \text{and} \\ \{e' \mid e' \prec_N^b e\} \neq \emptyset & \text{and} \\ X \cap \{e' \mid e' \prec_N^b e\} = \emptyset \end{cases}$$

Note that Ω_N is denumerable since we have, denoting $\textit{Fin}(E)$ the set of finite subsets of E:

$$\Omega_N \subseteq \textit{Fin}(E) \times (\{b \mid \exists e, e' \ \phi(e', b) = 1 = \phi(b, e)\}) \times E$$

Let us now define $\mathcal{E}(N) = (E_N, \#_N, \prec_N)$ as follows (we use the same notation as above for the conflict and flow relation since they coincide on the set E of events of the net):

- $E_N = E \cup \Omega_N$ (assuming that $E \cap \Omega_N = \emptyset$); in what follows we shall denote the event (X, b, e) of Ω_N by $\varepsilon_{(X,b,e)}$;

An event $\varepsilon_{(X,b,e)}$ is self-conflicting and in conflict with any event e' which causes e by means of b (that is $e' \prec_N^b e$):

- $e \#_N e' \Leftrightarrow_{\text{def}} \begin{cases} e \in \Omega_N \ \& \ e' = e & \text{or} \\ \exists (X, b, \hat{e}) \in \Omega_N \quad e = \varepsilon_{(X,b,\hat{e})} \ \& \ e' \prec_N^b \hat{e} & \text{or symmetrically} \\ \qquad\qquad e' = \varepsilon_{(X,b,\hat{e})} \ \& \ e \prec_N^b \hat{e} & \text{or} \\ e, e' \in E \ \& \ \forall X \in \mathcal{F}^\infty(N) \quad \{e, e'\} \not\subseteq X \end{cases}$

An event $\varepsilon_{(X,b,e)}$ is a cause for e:

- $e' \prec_N e \Leftrightarrow_{\text{def}} \begin{cases} e, e' \in E \ \& \ \exists b \in B.\ e' \prec_N^b e & \text{or} \\ e' = \varepsilon_{(X,b,e)} \quad \text{for some } X \text{ and } b \end{cases}$

It is obvious that $\mathcal{E}(N)$ is a flow event structure. We shall use the notation Con_N for $\mathit{Con}_{\mathcal{E}(N)}$. Let us see an example; the structure $\mathcal{E}(\mathbf{N})$ built from the net above can be drawn:

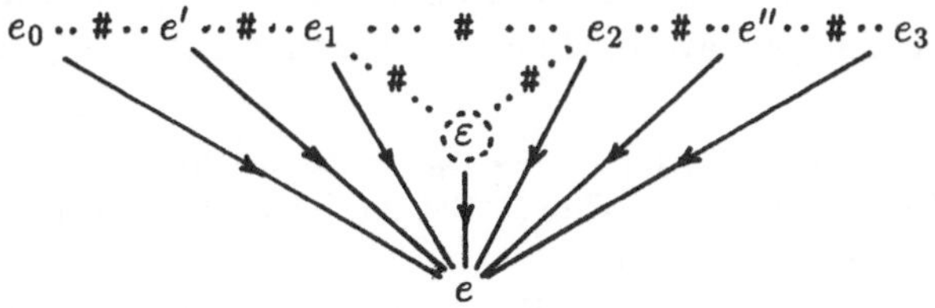

We have:

LEMMA 3.3. *Let $X \in \mathcal{F}(\mathcal{E}(N))$ and $e \in X$. Then for all $b \in B$ such that $\{e' \mid e' \prec^b_N e\} \neq \emptyset$ we have $X \cap \{e' \mid e' \prec^b_N e\} \neq \emptyset$.*

PROOF: let us first check that $\mathcal{F}(\mathcal{E}(N)) \subseteq \mathcal{F}(S(N))$; clearly any subset of E_N which is conflict-free with respect to $\mathcal{E}(N)$ is a subset of E, and is also conflict-free with respect to $S(N)$). If X is a finite configuration of $\mathcal{E}(N)$ then it can be enumerated as in proposition 2.3, that is as a proving sequence $e_1, \ldots, e_n$. Since the restriction to E of the flow relation of $\mathcal{E}(N)$ coincides with the flow relation of $S(N)$, the sequence $e_1, \ldots, e_n$ is also a proving sequence with respect to $S(N)$.

Now let $X \in \mathcal{F}(\mathcal{E}(N))$, $e \in X$ and $b \in B$ be such that $\{e' \mid e' \prec^b_N e\} \neq \emptyset$, and assume that $X \cap \{e' \mid e' \prec^b_N e\} = \emptyset$. Since X is a configuration of $S(N)$ we have $(X, b, e) \in \Omega_N$ by definition, and since $\varepsilon_{(X,b,e)} \prec_N e$ and X is a configuration of $\mathcal{E}(N)$ we have either $\varepsilon_{(X,b,e)} \in X$, but this is impossible since $\varepsilon_{(X,b,e)}$ is inconsistent, or $\exists \hat{e} \in X\ \varepsilon_{(X,b,e)} \#_N \hat{e} \prec_N e$, but then either $\hat{e} = \varepsilon_{(X,b,e)}$, and we just saw that this is impossible, or $\hat{e} \in \{e' \mid e' \prec^b_N e\}$, contradicting the hypothesis $X \cap \{e' \mid e' \prec^b_N e\} = \emptyset$. In any case we get a contradiction, hence $X \cap \{e' \mid e' \prec^b_N e\} \neq \emptyset$ ❑

We can now show that the configurations of the flow event structure $\mathcal{E}(N)$ are the sets of events firable in sequence in N:

PROPOSITION 3.4. *For any flow net N we have $\mathcal{F}^\infty(\mathcal{E}(N)) = \mathcal{F}^\infty(N)$. More precisely a sequence $e_1, \ldots, e_n, \ldots$ is firable in N if and only if it is a proving sequence in $\mathcal{E}(N)$. Moreover the structure $\mathcal{E}(N)$ is faithful.*

PROOF: let X be a configuration of $\mathcal{E}(N)$ (note that $X \subseteq E$ since $X \in \mathit{Con}_N$), and assume that X is enumerated as in the proposition 2.3, that is as a proving sequence $e_1, \ldots, e_n, \ldots$ of $\mathcal{E}(N)$. We show by induction on n that there is a firing sequence $\mu_0 \xrightarrow{e_1} \mu_1 \cdots \mu_{n-1} \xrightarrow{e_n} \mu_n$ (w.r.t. N) such that μ_n enables e_{n+1}:

• since the sequence e_1 is a proving sequence we have $\{e \mid e \prec_N e_1\} = \emptyset$, and e_1 is consistent since X is consistent. Let b be a precondition of e_1. Since e_1 is consistent, it occurs in a firing sequence σ, where b holds. Let us assume that $\mu_0(b) = 0$; then there should exist an event e (occurring in σ) such that $e \prec^b_N e_1$. But this contradicts $\{e \mid e \prec_N e_1\} = \emptyset$, therefore $\phi(b, e_1) \leq \mu_0(b)$ for all $b \in B$.

• let us assume that $\mu_0 \xrightarrow{e_1} \mu_1 \cdots \mu_{n-1} \xrightarrow{e_n} \mu_n$ is a firing sequence, and let $b \in B$ be a precondition of e_{n+1}. We have to show that $\mu_n(b) > 0$. Since e_{n+1} is consistent, it occurs in a firing sequence σ where b holds. Then we have $\mu_0(b) > 0$ or $e \prec^b_N e_{n+1}$ for some e occurring in σ. If $\mu_0(b) > 0$, let us assume that $\mu_n(b) = 0$; then there would exist k $(k \leq n)$ such that $\phi(b, e_k) = 1$, but then $e_k \#_N e_{n+1}$, which does not hold. Therefore

$\mu_0(b) > 0 \Rightarrow \mu_n(b) > 0$. If $\{e \mid e \prec_N^b e_{n+1}\} \neq \emptyset$, by the previous lemma 3.3 we know that $\{e_1, \ldots, e_{n+1}\} \cap \{e \mid e \prec_N^b e_{n+1}\} \neq \emptyset$ since $\{e_1, \ldots, e_{n+1}\}$ is a configuration of $\mathcal{E}(N)$. Then for some $i \leq n$ we have $\phi(e_i, b) = 1$, hence $\mu_i(b) > 0$, and the same argument as above shows that we cannot have $\mu_n(b) = 0$. This shows that any precondition of e_{n+1} holds at μ_n.

Conversely let $\mu_0 \xrightarrow{e_1} \mu_1 \cdots \mu_{n-1} \xrightarrow{e_n} \mu_n \cdots$ be a firing sequence of the net N. By definition we have $\{e_1, \ldots, e_n, \ldots\} \in \mathit{Con}_N$. Let us show by induction on n that $e_1, \ldots, e_n$ is a proving sequence (w.r.t. $\mathcal{E}(N)$):

• let b be a precondition of e_1, that is $\phi(b, e_1) = 1$; then $\mu_0(b) > 0$, hence no precondition of e_1 can be a strong postcondition of some consistent event. Therefore $\{e \mid e \prec_N e_1\} = \emptyset$, thus e_1 is a proving sequence.

• if $e_1, \ldots, e_n$ is a proving sequence, to show that $e_1, \ldots, e_{n+1}$ is a proving sequence we only have to prove that $e \prec_N e_{n+1} \Rightarrow \exists i \leq n \; e = e_i$ or $e \,\#_N\, e_i \prec_N e_{n+1}$. There are two cases:

•• if $e \in \Omega_N$ then for some Y and b we have $e = \varepsilon_{(Y,b,e_{n+1})}$. Then $\phi(b, e_{n+1}) = 1$ and $\{e' \mid e' \prec_N^b e_{n+1}\} \neq \emptyset$, which implies $\mu_0(b) = 0$. Since we have $\mu_n(b) > 0$ there exists $i \leq n$ such that $\phi(e_i, b) = 1$; then it is easy to check that $e_i \prec_N^b e_{n+1}$, and by definition of $\#_N$ we have $e \,\#_N\, e_i$.

•• if $e \in E$ then $e \prec_N e_{n+1} \Rightarrow \neg(e \,\#_N\, e_{n+1})$, hence there exists a firing sequence where both e and e_{n+1} occur. By definition of $e \prec_N e_{n+1}$ there exists a strong post-condition b of e such that $b \in \varphi(e, e_{n+1})$ – recall that this implies $\mu_0(b) = 0$, for e is consistent. Since we have $\mu_n(b) > 0$ there exists $i \leq n$ such that $\phi(e_i, b) = 1$, hence by the fact 3.1 $\phi(e, b) = 1 \Rightarrow e = e_i$ or $e \,\#_N\, e_i$.

Finally it is obvious that $\mathcal{E}(N)$ is faithful since from the previous points for $e, e' \in E(\mathcal{E}(N))$:

$$\exists X \in \mathcal{F}^\infty(\mathcal{E}(N)) \quad \{e, e'\} \not\subseteq X \Leftrightarrow \exists X \in \mathcal{F}^\infty(N) \quad \{e, e'\} \not\subseteq X$$

that is $e \,\#_N\, e'$ by definition; moreover if e does not occur in any configuration of $\mathcal{E}(N)$ then we have either $e \in E$ & $e \,\#_N\, e$ or $e \in \Omega_N$, hence $e \,\#_N\, e$ ☐

One may also note that the structure $\mathcal{E}(N)$ satisfies:

$$e \prec_N e' \Rightarrow \neg(e \,\#_N\, e')$$

3.3 From Flow Event Structures to Flow Nets

Conversely, we may associate with a flow event structure a flow net such that the sets of events firable in sequence are the configurations of the structure. A simple construction of a net associated with a flow event structure $S = (E, \#, \prec)$ could be the following: set a marked precondition for each conflicting pair of events, a marked precondition for each initial event (e such that $\{e' \mid e' \prec e\} = \emptyset$), and a condition (unmarked) between events e and e' if $e \prec e'$. But this is incorrect if the structure does not satisfy a conflict heredity property; for instance if S is the structure:

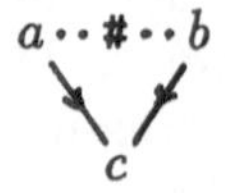

then we would get the net:

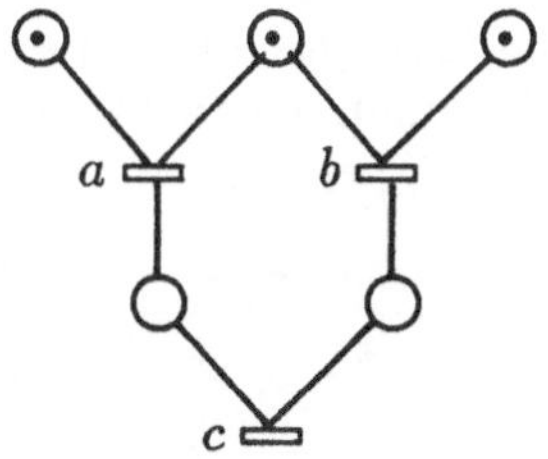

where c is not firable. We then have to refine this simple idea. Somehow a precondition should group together conflicting causes.

Let $S = (E, \#, \prec)$ be a flow event structure. We define the net (having the same events) $\mathcal{N}(S) = (B_S, E, \Phi_S, \mu_S)$ as follows: conditions are sets of events of two types – i.e. $B_S = B'_S \cup B''_S$. The first type is used to solve conflicts; a condition of this type is either the empty set (to inhibit self-conflicting events) or a maximal pairwise conflicting set of events, what we could call a *cell.* Let us denote by Γ_S the set of pairwise conflicting sets of events:

$$F \in \Gamma_S \Leftrightarrow_{\text{def}} F \subseteq E \;\&\; e, e' \in F \;\&\; e \neq e' \;\Rightarrow\; e \# e'$$

This set is ordered by inclusion, and we shall denote by $\bar{\Gamma}_S$ the set of maximal elements of Γ_S, that is

$$F \in \bar{\Gamma}_S \Leftrightarrow_{\text{def}} F \in \Gamma_S \;\&\; (F' \in \Gamma_S \;\&\; F \subseteq F' \;\Rightarrow\; F' = F)$$

It is easily seen, using Zorn's Lemma(†), that for any $F \in \Gamma_S$ there exists $H \in \bar{\Gamma}_S$ such that $F \subseteq H$. Then a condition of the first kind (B'_S) is the empty set or an element of $\bar{\Gamma}_S$, in other words:

$$B'_S =_{\text{def}} \{\emptyset\} \cup \bar{\Gamma}_S$$

Conditions of the second kind (B''_S) are used to record the flow relation of the event structure. These are pairs (G, e) where G is the set of causes for e which are in conflict with (or equal to) a given condition e' for e (if any). Two events of G are not necessarily in conflict; therefore these places will not be safe in general. On the other hand, the place (G, e) will be a strong postcondition for e'. Let us introduce a notation for such G's:

$$\kappa_S(e', e) =_{\text{def}} \{e'\} \cup \{e'' \mid e'' \prec e \;\&\; e'' \# e'\} \qquad \text{for} \quad e' \prec e$$

Then B''_S is given by:

$$(G, e) \in B''_S \Leftrightarrow_{\text{def}} \exists e' \prec e \quad G = \kappa_S(e', e)$$

It should be clear that B''_S is denumerable, since there is a surjective mapping from the subset $\prec$ of $E \times E$ onto B''_S.

(†) Let A be a set and $\mathcal{A}$ a set of subsets of A. The family $\mathcal{A}$ is *inductive* if any chain (totally ordered subset of $\mathcal{A}$, w.r.t. inclusion) is bounded in $\mathcal{A}$. Zorn's Lemma asserts that if $\mathcal{A}$ is inductive, then every element of $\mathcal{A}$ is contained into a maximal element of $\mathcal{A}$.

For instance, with the previous example of flow event structure, besides the empty set there are two conditions of the first type (B'_S), namely $\{a, b\}$ and $\{c\}$, and only one condition of the second type (B''_S) which is $(\{a, b\}, c)$. Let us see another example: for the structure **S** of the previous section, that is:

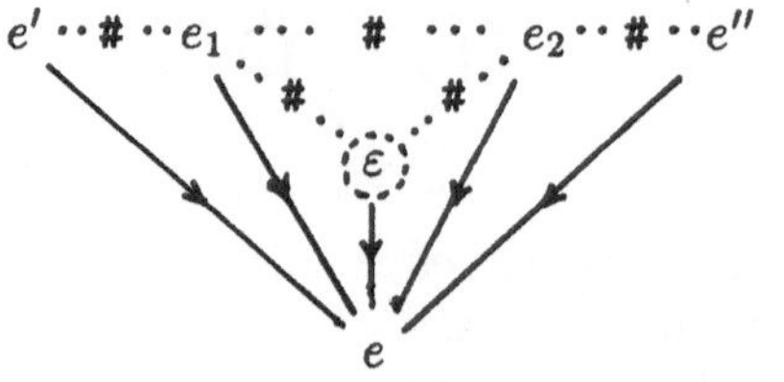

Here the set B'_S consists of $\emptyset$, $b_1 = \{e', e_1\}$, $b_2 = \{e_1, \varepsilon, e_2\}$, $b_3 = \{e_2, e''\}$ and $\{e\}$, while the conditions of B''_S are (b_1, e), $(b_1 \cup b_2, e)$, (b_2, e), $(b_2 \cup b_3, e)$ and (b_3, e).

The flow relation Φ_S of $\mathcal{N}(S)$ is the least one such that:

$$e \# e \;\Rightarrow\; (\emptyset, e) \in \Phi_S$$

$$F \in B'_S \;\&\; e \in F \;\Rightarrow\; (F, e) \in \Phi_S$$

$$(G, e) \in B''_S \;\&\; e' \in G \;\Rightarrow\; (e', (G, e)) \in \Phi_S$$

$$(G, e) \in B''_S \;\Rightarrow\; ((G, e), e) \in \Phi_S$$

Note that a condition of B'_S cannot be a postcondition of an event. In what follows we shall use indexed notations for the mappings related to the flow relation, i.e. ϕ_S and φ_S. Finally the initial marking is given by:

$$\mu_S(b) =_{\text{def}} \begin{cases} 1 & \text{if } b \in B'_S \;\&\; b \neq \emptyset \\ 0 & \text{otherwise} \end{cases}$$

LEMMA 3.5. *For any flow event structure $S = (E, \#, \prec)$ the structure $\mathcal{N}(S)$ is a net.*

PROOF: we already saw (using Zorn's Lemma) that for any $e \in E$ there exists $F \in \Gamma_S$ such that $e \in F$, and by definition $(F, e) \in \Phi_S$. Moreover we saw that $B''_S = \{b \mid b \in B_S \;\&\; \exists e, e' \;\phi_S(e', b) = 1 = \phi_S(b, e)\}$ is denumerable ❑

For instance from the structure

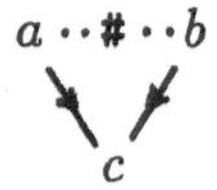

we get the net (omitting the isolated empty condition):

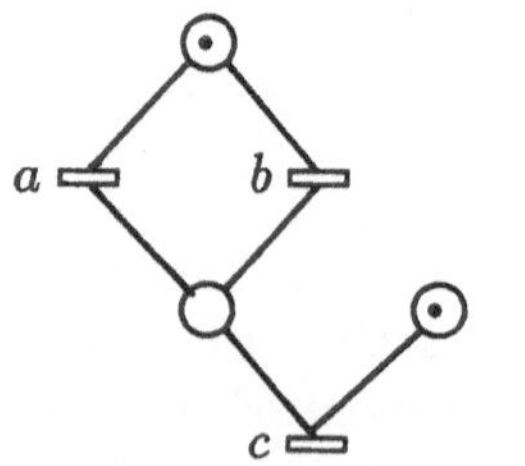

while from **S** we get (omitting the useless precondition $\{e\}$ for e):

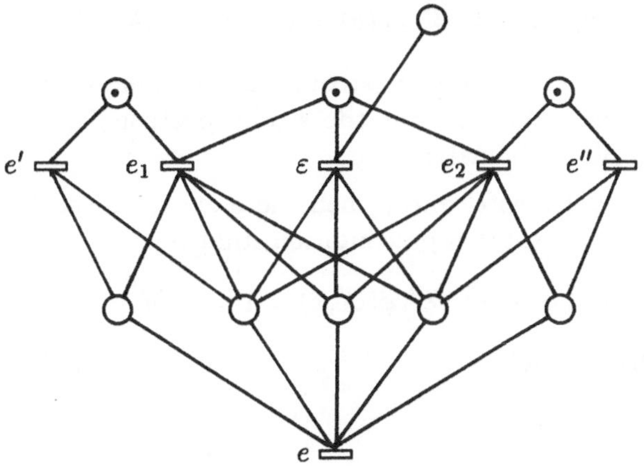

One may observe that the net $\mathcal{N}(S)$ has a "canonical form". Let us see this point in some detail. Remark that in defining flow nets we used *behavioural* properties, that is properties expressed in terms of firing sequences. On the other hand, $\mathcal{N}(S)$ has some remarkable *structural* properties – stated in terms of the "local" flow relation Φ and initial marking μ_0 of a net $N = (B, E, \Phi, \mu_0)$. Roughly speaking, we can distinguish in $\mathcal{N}(S)$ two kinds of places:

• *choice places*: these places are *not* postconditions of any event; on the other hand, one such place b may be *forward branched*, that is $\{e \mid \phi(b, e) = 1\}$ may contain more than one element. In picture:

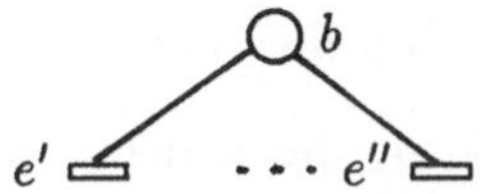

• *causal places*: these places are *both* postconditions and preconditions; one such place b is possibly *backwards branched* – that is $|\{e \mid \phi(e, b) = 1\}| \geq 1$ –, but is precondition of *at most one* event. In picture:

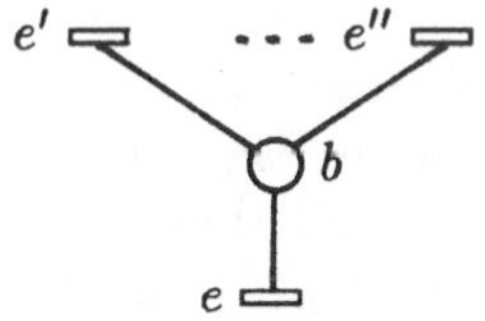

More precisely, $\mathcal{N}(S)$ satisfies the properties:

(i) a forward branched place is a choice place, that is:

$$\exists e', e''\ e' \neq e''\ \&\ \phi(b, e') = 1 = \phi(b, e'') \ \Rightarrow\ \forall e\ \phi(e, b) = 0$$

An equivalent formulation of this property is: if a place $b \in B$ is a postcondition of some event then it is the precondition of at most one event:

$$\exists e\ \phi(e, b) = 1 \ \Rightarrow\ (\phi(b, e') = 1 = \phi(b, e'') \ \Rightarrow\ e' = e'')$$

(ii) only choice places can be initially marked (with at most one token):

$$\mu_0(b) > 0 \Rightarrow \mu_0(b) = 1 \ \& \ \forall e \ \phi(e,b) = 0$$

This property implies that if b is a postcondition of some event, then it is initially unmarked. The last property concerns the strong postconditions, which appear in a rather special way in $\mathcal{N}(S)$, namely:

(iii) if there is a place between e' and e then there exists one such place b such that if $\phi(e'',b) = 1$ then e' and e'' share a precondition, that is:

$$\varphi(e',e) \neq \emptyset \Rightarrow \exists b \in \varphi(e',e) \ \forall e'' \ \phi(e'',b) = 1 \Rightarrow \exists b' \ \phi(b',e') = 1 = \phi(b',e'')$$

This property may be drawn as

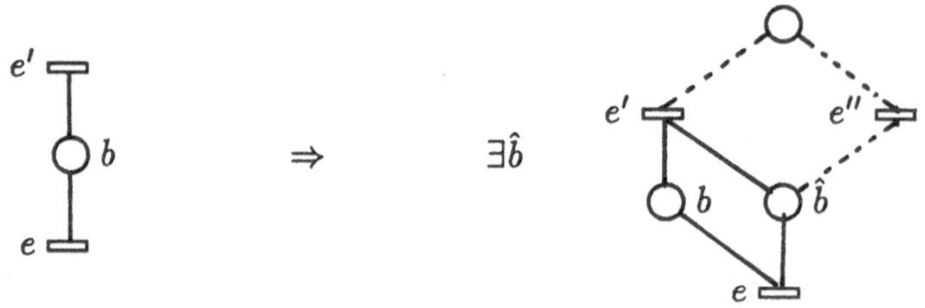

We shall say that a net is a *regular flow net* if it satifies the properties (i)-(iii) above (note: here regularity refers to the fact that the properties are structural, but has nothing to do with the fact that the finite firing sequences of events form a regular language). This terminology is justified by the following:

LEMMA 3.6. *Any regular flow net is a flow net.*

PROOF: let $\mu_0 \xrightarrow{e_1} \mu_1 \cdots \mu_{n-1} \xrightarrow{e_n} \mu_n$ be a firing sequence. Let us first show that if $\phi(b,e_i) = 1 = \phi(b,e_j)$ for some b then $e_i = e_j$: if $e_i \neq e_j$ then b is a forward branched place, hence not a postcondition. Therefore if for instance $i < j$ we have $\mu_0(b) \geq \mu_{i-1}(b) > 0$, hence $\mu_{i-1}(b) = 1$, $\mu_i(b) = 0$ and thus $\mu_{j-1}(b) = 0$, contradicting the fact that e_j is enabled at μ_{j-1}.

Now let us show that $i < j \Rightarrow e_i \neq e_j$; assume the contrary, and let $i = \mathsf{Inf}\{l \mid \exists k > l \ e_k = e_l\}$ There exists $b \in B$ such that $\phi(b,e_i) = 1$, and we have $\mu_{i-1}(b) > 0$. If b is not a postcondition of some event, then b must be initially marked, and then $\mu_0(b) \geq \mu_{i-1}(b)$, hence $\mu_{i-1}(b) = 1$, and thus $\mu_i(b) = 0$. But then we cannot have $\mu_{j-1}(b) > 0$, contradicting the fact that μ_{j-1} enables e_j. Therefore there exists $e \in E$ such that $\phi(e,b) = 1$. In this case we have $\mu_0(b) = 0$, hence there exists $h < i$ such that $\phi(e_h,b) = 1$ since $\mu_{i-1}(b) > 0$. We then have $\varphi(e_h,e_i) \neq \emptyset$, therefore there exists $\hat{b} \in B$ such that $\hat{b} \in \varphi(e_h,e_i)$ and $\phi(e',\hat{b}) = 1 \Rightarrow \exists b' \ \phi(b',e) = 1 = \phi(b',e_h)$. Now for any k if $\phi(e_k,\hat{b}) = 1$ then there is a place b' such that $\phi(b',e_k) = 1 = \phi(b',e_h)$, hence $e_k = e_h$ by the previous point. By the minimality of i this implies $k = h$, but then $\mu_{j-1}(\hat{b}) = 0$ since

$$\begin{aligned}\mu_{j-1}(\hat{b}) &= \mu_0(\hat{b}) - \sum_{1 \leq l < j} \phi(\hat{b},e_l) + \sum_{1 \leq l < j} \phi(e_l,\hat{b}) \\ &= 1 - \sum_{1 \leq l < j} \phi(\hat{b},e_l) \leq 0\end{aligned}$$

contradicting the fact that e_j is enabled at μ_{j-1}.

We have shown that if $\phi(b,e_i) = 1 = \phi(b,e_j)$ then $i = j$, hence the sequence is flowing, and if $\varphi(e_i,e_j) \neq \emptyset$ it is easy to see using the previous points that the place b such that

$$b \in \varphi(e_i,e_j) \ \&\ \forall e\ \phi(e,b) = 1 \ \Rightarrow\ \exists b'\ \phi(b',e) = 1 = \phi(b',e_i)$$

is a strong postcondition for e_i ❑

Let us see an example: the net

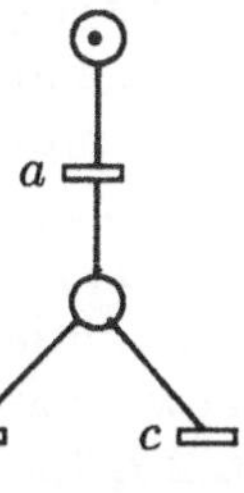

is a flow net which does not satisfies (i); but it is strongly equivalent to the regular net:

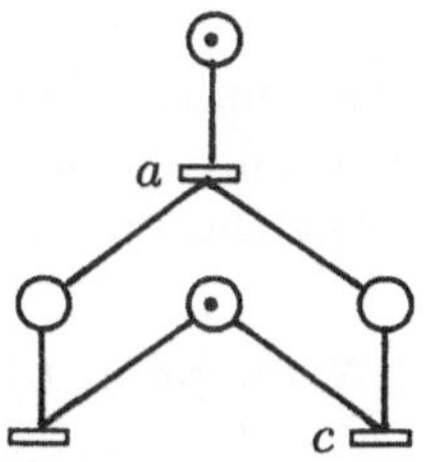

We are now ready to prove the second half of the representation theorem:

PROPOSITION 3.7. *Let $S = (E, \#, \prec)$ be a flow event structure. Then $\mathcal{N}(S)$ is a (regular) flow net such that $\mathcal{F}^\infty(\mathcal{N}(S)) = \mathcal{F}^\infty(S)$. More precisely a sequence $e_1,\ldots,e_n,\ldots$ of events is firable in $\mathcal{N}(S)$ if and only if it is a proving sequence in S.*

PROOF: from the previous lemma we know that $\mathcal{N}(S)$ is a flow net.

Now let X be a configuration of S, enumerated as in the proposition 2.3, that is as a proving sequence $e_1,\ldots,e_n,\ldots$ of S. Note that $\neg(e_i \# e_i)$ since X is conflict-free. We show by induction on n that the sequence $e_1,\ldots,e_n$ may be fired in $\mathcal{N}(S)$. It is enough to prove that (for $n \geq 0$) if $\mu_S = \mu_0 \xrightarrow{e_1} \mu_1 \cdots \mu_{n-1} \xrightarrow{e_n} \mu_n$ is a firing sequence, then μ_n enables e_{n+1}:

• if $F \in B'_S$ is a precondition of e_{n+1}, then clearly we cannot have $F = \emptyset$ since e_{n+1} is consistent. Therefore $e_{n+1} \in F$; let us show that $\mu_n(F) \geq 1$: assume the contrary, that is $\mu_n(F) = 0$; then, since $\mu_S(F) = 1$, there should exist e_i (with $i < n$, hence $e_i \neq e_{n+1}$) such that $e_i \in F$. But this is impossible since we should then have $e_i \# e_{n+1}$, contradicting the fact that X is conflict-free.

• if $(G, e_{n+1}) \in B''_S$, let us show that $\mu_n(G, e_{n+1}) \geq 1$. By definition of the net $\mathcal{N}(S)$ we have $G = \kappa_S(e, e_{n+1})$ for some e such that $e \prec e_{n+1}$. Since $e_1,\ldots,e_{n+1}$ is a proving sequence, there exists $i \leq n+1$ such that $e_i \prec e_{n+1}$ (hence $i \leq n$ in fact) and $e = e_i$ or $e \# e_i$. In any case $e_i \in G$, hence $\phi_S(e_i,(G,e_{n+1})) = 1$, which implies $\mu_i(G,e_{n+1}) > 0$, therefore $\mu_n(G,e_{n+1}) > 0$ since $\mathcal{N}(S)$ is a flow net.

This shows that there is a (unique) sequence of transitions in $\mathcal{N}(S)$ firing the events $e_1, \ldots, e_n, \ldots$ in that order, hence if X is a configuration of S then it is also a configuration of $\mathcal{N}(S)$.

Now let $\mu_0 = \mu_S \xrightarrow{e_1} \mu_1 \cdots \mu_{n-1} \xrightarrow{e_n} \mu_n \cdots$ be a firing sequence in $\mathcal{N}(S)$. We already know that $\forall i, j \; \neg(e_i \# e_j)$ and $i \neq j \Rightarrow e_i \neq e_j$. Let us now show that for any n the sequence (of distinct events) $e_1, \ldots, e_n$ is a proving sequence of e_n, by induction on n:

• if b is a precondition of e_1, that is $\phi_S(b, e_1) = 1$, then $\mu_S(b) > 0$ and this means $b \in B'_S$. Therefore we have $\{e \mid e \prec e_1\} = \emptyset$, and this shows that e_1 is a proving sequence.

• let us assume that $e_1, \ldots, e_n$ is a proving sequence, and that $e \prec e_{n+1}$. By definition of $\mathcal{N}(S)$ if we let $G = \kappa_S(e, e_{n+1})$ then $(G, e_{n+1}) \in B''_S$ and $\phi_S(G, e_{n+1})$. Since μ_n enables e_{n+1} we have $\mu_n(G, e_{n+1}) > 0$, hence there exists $i \leq n$ such that $\phi_S(e_i, (G, e_{n+1})) = 1$ since (G, e_{n+1}) is initially unmarked. By definition of G this implies either $e = e_i$ or $e \# e_i$. This shows that $e_1 \ldots, e_{n+1}$ is a proving sequence.

Consequently, by the proposition 2.3, the set $X = \{e_1, \ldots, e_n, \ldots\}$ (which, as we saw, is conflict-free) is a configuration of S, therefore any configuration of $\mathcal{N}(S)$ is a configuration of S □

This establishes the representation theorem relating flow nets and flow event structures. Let us see some consequences of this result – or more precisely of the constructions we used to prove it. The first one is that the poset of configurations of a flow net is a domain:

COROLLARY 3.8. *For any flow net N the poset $\mathcal{D}(N)$ is a domain.*

Another consequence is that we can now prove that any flow event structure is strongly equivalent to a faithful one:

COROLLARY 3.9. *For any flow event structure S there exists a faithful flow event structure S' such that $S \equiv S'$.*

PROOF: this is true if we let $S' = \mathcal{E}(\mathcal{N}(S))$ □

Recall also that in $\mathcal{E}(\mathcal{N}(S))$ the flow and conflict relations are disjoint; more precisely in this structure we have:

$$e' \prec e \;\Rightarrow\; \neg(e' \# e) \;\&\; \neg(e \# e)$$

Similarly, the transformation $\mathcal{E} \circ \mathcal{N}$ shows that we can find for any flow net a strongly equivalent regular net:

COROLLARY 3.10. *For any flow net N there exists a regular flow net N' such that $N \equiv N'$.*

PROOF: this is true if we let $N' = \mathcal{N}(\mathcal{E}(N))$ □

In fact we can say a little bit more: the structure $\mathcal{E}(N)$ is faithful; then it is easy to see (from the definition of $\mathcal{N}$) that in $\widehat{N} = \mathcal{N}(\mathcal{E}(N))$ we can characterize the semantical conflict as follows:

$$e \#_{\widehat{N}} e' \;\Leftrightarrow\; \begin{cases} e' = e \;\&\; \exists b.\; \mu_0(b) = 0 \;\&\; \phi(b, e) = 1 \;\&\; \forall e''\; \phi(e'', b) = 0 & \text{or} \\ e \neq e' \;\&\; \exists b\; \phi(b, e) = 1 = \phi(b, e') \;\&\; \forall e''\; \phi(e'', b) = 0 \end{cases}$$

In other words, the semantical conflict in $\widehat{N}$ is just the local "immediate" conflict (i.e. the direct conflict of [13]).

Appendix: Stable Event Structures

In [19] Winskel studies another concrete presentation of domains, namely the (second order) stable event structures $I = (E, \#, \vdash)$. Let us recall the definition (with some slight modifications with respect to Winskel's one), where we still denote Con_I the set of conflict-free sets of events:

DEFINITION (STABLE EVENT STRUCTURES). *A stable event structure is a structure* $I = (E, \#, \vdash)$ *where*

- E *is the denumerable set of events,*
- $\# \subseteq E \times E$ *is a symmetric relation, the conflict relation.*
- $\vdash \subseteq P(E) \times E$ *is the enabling relation, satisfying:*

(i) consistency: $F \vdash e \;\Rightarrow\; F \cup \{e\} \in \mathit{Con}_I$

(ii) stability: $F \vdash e \;\&\; G \vdash e \;\&\; F \cup G \in \mathit{Con}_I \;\Rightarrow\; F = G$

In fact this definition involves the *minimal enabling* relation (*cf.* [18,19]), and this induces a slight modification in the definition of the configurations. Let us define a *proving sequence* (w.r.t. I) as a finite conflict-free sequence $e_1, \ldots, e_n$ of distinct events satisfying:

$$\forall i \leq n\; \exists F \subseteq \{e_1, \ldots, e_{i-1}\} \quad F \vdash e_i$$

As before, we say that such a sequence is a proof of e in X if $e_n = e$ and $\{e_1, \ldots, e_n\} \subseteq X$.

DEFINITION (CONFIGURATIONS). *Given an event structure* $I = (E, \#, \vdash)$ *a configuration of* I *is a subset* X *of* E *such that*

(i) X *is conflict-free:* $X \in \mathit{Con}_I$

(ii) every event $e \in X$ *has a proof in* X.

For this variant of Winskel's definition, one can still prove the representation theorem relating domains and stable event structures, (the proof being essentially the same as in [18]). Then with each stable event structure one can associate an equivalent prime event structure. Conversely, given a flow event structure $S = (E, \#, \prec)$, we may define $\vdash_S$ as follows:

$$F \vdash_S e \;\Leftrightarrow_{\mathrm{def}} \begin{cases} F \cup \{e\} \in \mathit{Con}_S \quad \text{and} \\ e' \in F \;\Rightarrow\; e' \prec e \quad \text{and} \\ e' \prec e \;\&\; e' \notin F \;\Rightarrow\; \exists e'' \in F \; e' \# e'' \end{cases}$$

It is trivial to check that $\mathcal{S}(S) = (E, \#, \vdash_S)$ is a stable event structure. Moreover it should be clear that S and $\mathcal{S}(S)$ are strongly equivalent since a sequence $e_1, \ldots, e_n$ is a proving sequence with respect to S if and only if it is a proving sequence with respect to $\mathcal{S}(S)$.

Given a stable event structure $I = (E, \#, \vdash)$ there does not necessarily exist a flow event structure S such that $I = \mathcal{S}(S)$. For instance this is the case for $\mathbf{I} = (\{a, b, c, d\}, \#, \vdash)$ given by:

$a \# c$

$\emptyset \vdash a, b, c$

$\{a\} \vdash d$
$\{b, c\} \vdash d$

The domain of configurations of this structure is:

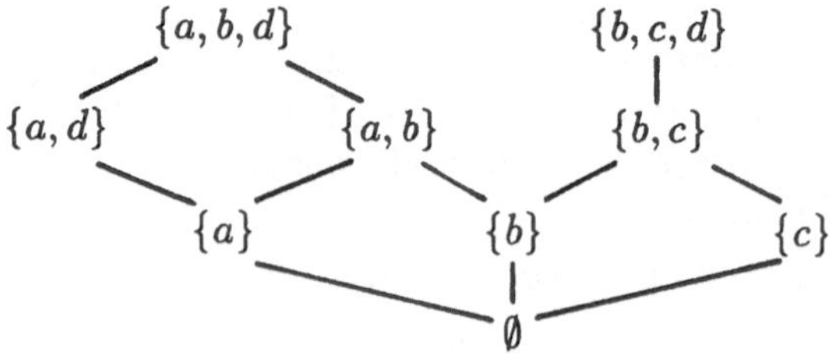

It is not hard to see, using the lemma 2.11, that this family of configurations cannot be that of a flow event structure, since we should have both $b \prec d$ and $b \not\prec d$. Note also that this structure may be represented by a net (which is not a flow net):

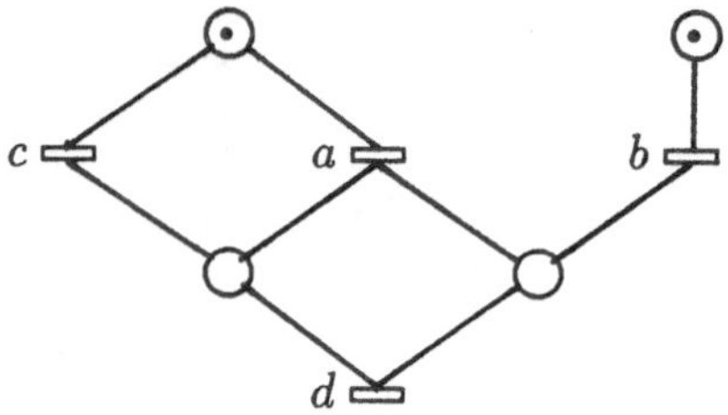

Acknowledgments. Glynn Winskel suggested me to use a direct definition of configurations of a flow event structure, without resorting to stable structures with an enabling relation. This suggestion allowed me to improve a previous draft of this paper.

REFERENCES

[1] G. Boudol, I. Castellani, *On the semantics of concurrency: partial orders and transition systems*, TAPSOFT 87, Lecture Notes in Comput. Sci. 249 (1987) 123-137.

[2] G. Boudol, I. Castellani, *Concurrency and atomicity*, Theoretical Comput. Sci. 59 (1988) 25-84.

[3] G. Boudol, I. Castellani, *Permutation of transitions: an event structure semantics for* CCS *and* SCCS, *in* Linear Time, Branching Time and Partial Orders in Logics and Models for Concurrency, Lecture Notes in Comput. Sci. 354 (1988) 411-427.

[4] G. Boudol, I. Castellani, *Three equivalent semantics for* CCS, this volume (1990).

[5] P. Degano, R. De Nicola, U. Montanari, *Partial ordering derivations for* CCS, FCT 85, Lecture Notes in Comput. Sci. 199 (1985) 520-533.

[6] P. Degano, R. De Nicola, U. Montanari, *A distributed operational semantics for* CCS *based on condition/event systems*, Acta Informatica 26 (1988) 59-91.

[7] P. DEGANO, R. DE NICOLA, U. MONTANARI, *On the consistency of "truly concurrent" operational and denotational semantics,* LICS 88 (1988) 133-141.

[8] R. van GLABBEEK, F. VAANDRAGER, *Petri net models for algebraic theories of concurrency,* Proceedings PARLE Conference, Eindhoven, Lecture Notes in Comput. Sci. 259 (1987) 224-242.

[9] U. GOLTZ, A. MYCROFT, *On the relationship of* CCS *and Petri nets,* ICALP 84, Lecture Notes in Comput. Sci. 172 (1984) 196-208.

[10] U. GOLTZ, R. LOOGEN, *A non-interleaving semantic model for nondeterministic concurrent processes,* Tech. Report 87-15, RWTH Aachen (1987).

[11] U. GOLTZ, *On representing* CCS *programs by finite Petri nets,* MFCS 88, Lecture Notes in Comput. Sci. 324 (1988) 339-350.

[12] R. MILNER, *Communication and Concurrency,* Prentice-Hall International Series in Computer Science (1989).

[13] M. NIELSEN, G. PLOTKIN, G. WINSKEL, *Petri nets, event structures and domains,* Theoret. Comput. Sci. 13 (1981) 85-108.

[14] E.-R. OLDEROG, *Operational Petri net semantics for* CCSP, Advances in Petri Nets 87, Lecture Notes in Comput. Sci. 266 (1987) 196-223.

[15] D. TAUBNER, *Representing* CCS *programs by finite predicate/transition nets,* Acta Informatica 27 (1990) 533-565.

[16] F. VAANDRAGER, *A simple definition for parallel composition of prime event structures,* Tech. Rep. CS-R8903, CWI, Amsterdam (1989).

[17] G. WINSKEL, *Event structure semantics for* CCS *and related languages,* Daimi PB-159, Aarhus University (1983) s.a. 9th ICALP, Lecture Notes in Comput. Sci. 140 (1982) 561-576.

[18] G. WINSKEL, *Event structures,* Advances in Petri Nets 86, Lecture Notes in Comput. Sci. 255 (1987) 325-392.

[19] G. WINSKEL, *An introduction to event structures, in* Linear Time, Branching Time and Partial Orders in Logics and Models for Concurrency, Lecture Notes in Comput. Sci. 354 (1988).

Three Equivalent Semantics for CCS

Gérard Boudol *Ilaria Castellani*
INRIA Sophia-Antipolis
06560-VALBONNE FRANCE

1. Introduction

This work is concerned with non-interleaving models for concurrency, sometimes qualified as "true-concurrency" models because they take the notion of concurrency – or the complementary notion of causality – as fundamental. Typical non-interleaving models are Petri nets [46], event structures [43,58] and Mazurkiewicz traces [38,39].

The other, standard, approach is called the *interleaving* approach because it simulates concurrency with arbitrary interleaving, thus reducing the notion of concurrency to those of nondeterminism and sequentiality: as a result, models have fewer primitive notions and are simpler to deal with. This is why research on the semantics of concurrency has initially concentrated on interleaving models, at least outside the Petri net community. These models, particularly after the appearance of Milner's Calculus of Communicating Systems (CCS) [40] and Plotkin's method of Structural Operational Semantics (SOS) [47], have been mostly developed in relation to CCS or similar algebraic process languages (like TCSP [12], ACP [2] etc.), according to the following two-step schema:

1) first, terms are described operationally – using SOS rules – as *labelled transition systems*, evolving from one state to the other via successive transitions: each transition is labelled by an atomic action, representing an interaction with the environment or an internal computational task.
2) then, transition systems are factored by *behavioural equivalences* (or preorders) to yield a more abstract model. Often axiomatic theories are provided for the behavioural equivalences, as well as logical characterisations. Presentations of various such equivalences and related theories may be found e.g. in [13,22,34,42].

Note that in this two-step semantics, in spite of the variety of behavioural relations and resulting models, there is a general agreement about the first step: the basic operational model is always that of labelled transitions systems.

This work has been partly supported by ESPRIT Basic Research Action 3011 CEDISYS.

Undoubtedly, the interleaving assumption has been useful for the construction of elegant theories of concurrency, with related specification and verification methods. However, this does not mean that concurrency itself is not an essential phenomenon: indeed there are properties of concurrent systems which cannot be specified without a clear distinction between concurrency and nondeterminism (see e.g. [36] for the suitability of non-interleaving models as regards the treatment of *fairness*).

In the field of true concurrency, we find again the two-level schema for semantics, but we have here a variety of basic operational models: we mentioned already Petri nets and event structures, but several other models have been proposed, essentially generalisations of labelled transition systems: transition systems with non-atomic labels, like pomset transition systems [7] (where labels are pomsets, i.e. partially ordered multisets [48]) transition systems with *structured states*, like distributed transition systems (see [14], but also the different notion of [19]), and transition systems satisfying a set of axioms, like asynchronous transition systems [51,1], concurrent transition systems [52] and elementary transition systems [44]. An intensional *tree model* has also been proposed, the causal trees of [17], where arcs are provided with back pointers to their causes. It should be stressed that all these concrete models, here as in the interleaving approach, are operational in nature.

In this paper we shall only be interested in concrete non-interleaving models, that is in the first level of the semantics. In particular we shall not be concerned with equivalence relations respecting concurrency, which have been the subject of much recent research: we will just mention, among others, the work by Van Glabbeek and Vaandrager on equivalence notions for Petri nets [24], and the papers by Van Glabbeek and Goltz on various equivalences for event structures [25,26].

Because of the variety of basic models, an important task in the area of true concurrency is that of *classification and unification* of models. A major contribution in this sense has been provided by Winskel: indeed, event structures were first conceived by Nielsen, Plotkin and Winskel [43] to relate Petri nets with the now classical theory of domains à la Scott. This unifying concern has remained present in most of Winskel's subsequent works on event structures and the theory of concurrency. See for example [57, 59], where different models for parallel computation are specified and related in the framework of category theory. More recently, the comparison and unification of models has also been a main concern of Montanari and Ferrari [31,32]. For the comparison of specific models we could mention Best and Devillers [4], Thiagarajan et al. [54], and Rozoy [50]. When comparing models, a general requirement for considering them *equivalent* is that the resulting *domains of computations* be isomorphic. This is the abstract criterion used in the above-mentioned works [4,54,50]. A more concrete criterion for equivalence of models is that they generate the same *families of computations* – that is computations consisting of the same sets of events. Indeed, this concrete criterion preserves the operational meaning of events, and may be the right one to use when one is interested in a notion of *implementation* of a model into an equivalent one.

Another major issue in true concurrency is the *interpretation of algebraic languages* like CCS or TCSP in non-interleaving models like Petri nets or event structures, and the study of the relations between different such interpretations. Petri nets have been used to give a "truly concurrent" semantics for CCS-like languages for instance by Goltz [29,27,28], Winskel [57], Van Glabbeek and Vaandrager [24], Degano De Nicola and

Montanari [21], Olderog [45] and Taubner [53]. Similarly, event structure interpretations have been proposed, by Winskel [56,58], Goltz and Loogen [30], Degano, De Nicola and Montanari [20], and ourselves [7,8,9]. Now, in order to prove the equivalence of different such interpretations for a language, one has to show that they yield equivalent representations – in one sense or the other – for any term of the language.

The aim of this paper is to contribute to this area of "comparative non-interleaving semantics" for algebraic languages, by establishing the equivalence of three operational models for finite CCS, in a rather concrete sense. The three interpretations we will consider may be summarized as follows:

i) a *semantics by permutations* of concurrent transitions, based on a description of processes as *proved transition systems*: these are labelled transition systems where the labels are *proofs* of transitions, from which a concurrency relation between transitions may be deduced.

ii) a semantics by means of *flow event structures*, which is a variation of Winskel's semantics by stable event structures.

iii) a semantics by means of *flow nets* – a class of Petri nets introduced in [6] – which for finite processes coincides with the "standard" net semantics for CCS, as described by a number of authors [27, 28, 24, 21, 45].

The first two interpretations i) and ii) were already presented in [9]: interpretation i), which is somewhat unusual, will be described in more detail later in this introduction. The third interpretation, iii), is essentially a recasting of the operational Petri net semantics given by Degano, De Nicola and Montanari in [21] (see also Olderog [45]). In particular we take from [21] the idea of defining the places of a net syntactically.

In fact, the particularity of our approach is that all interpretations are given *syntactically*: thus for example the labels of proved transition systems are *proofs* of transitions in the inference system of CCS. Similarly, *events* in event structures and nets have syntactic names which uniquely identify them as occurrences (or pairs of occurrences, for a communication) in the syntactic tree of a term. Moreover the syntax is the same for the three models: the events generated by the proved transition system (see later) for a given term have the same names as the events of the corresponding flow event structure and flow net.

This similarity enables us to carry out a precise comparison of the three models, and to establish their equivalence in a very strong sense: we will see that the flow event structure and the flow net interpretations agree in that they generate exactly the same *families of computations* for any CCS term. On the other hand their *domains of computations* are isomorphic – this is a looser correspondence – to the domain of computations (equivalence classes of sequences) given by the permutation semantics.

The connection between flow event structure and permutation semantics was already stated in [9], but the proof was not included. The essential elements of the proof are given here, while the complete proof is reported in [11]. We also include here the flow net semantics, and show its correspondence with the other two models. The general correlation of flow nets and flow event structures, as well as constructions between the two models generalising those of [43], are presented in [6].

We assume some familiarity with event structures and Petri nets, so we will not discuss these models here: of course they will be defined in the sections where they are used, and the paper is self-contained in this sense. On the other hand we would like to introduce briefly the *semantics by permutations*, which, although very close in spirit to Mazurkiewicz's theory of traces [38], come to us here from a different background. The notion of equivalence by permutations that we use here is rather general, and may be applied to various computational systems. This equivalence was first elaborated by Lévy for the λ-calculus [37], and then used for recursive program schemes in [3]. It was further extended to deterministic term rewriting systems by Huet and Lévy in [35], and to non-deterministic ones by Boudol in [5]. Let us shortly explain the idea.

A computational system evolves by elementary computations $s \longrightarrow s'$ from one state to the other. Examples of state changes are transitions of a machine, β-reductions of λ-terms and rewritings in a term rewriting system. To be able to reason about such transitions – e.g. to show a Church-Rosser property –, we need a concrete indication of *what* has been performed and *where* it has happened. We thus have to deal with *labelled* transitions $s \xrightarrow{w} s'$, where w denotes a specific *occurrence* of some action. Now if two transitions from a given state, $s \xrightarrow{u} s_0$ and $s \xrightarrow{v} s_1$, are *compatible*, or concurrent, it should be possible to perform them in any order without affecting the result. In other words, we should be able to define what remains of one move after the other, the *residual* of v by u, noted v/u, in such a way that $s_0 \xrightarrow{v/u} s'$ and $s_1 \xrightarrow{u/v} s'$, for some state s'. This is known as the *diamond property* for concurrent moves. This property induces an *equivalence on sequences* of transitions: two sequences are equivalent if they are the same up to permutation of compatible transitions, typically:

$$s \xrightarrow{u} s_0 \xrightarrow{v/u} s' \simeq s \xrightarrow{v} s_1 \xrightarrow{u/v} s'$$

This is the essence of Berry and Lévy's *equivalence by permutations* for sequences of (elementary) computations. In any case, this equivalence allows one to associate with each state a complete partial order of computations. These computations are equivalence classes of sequences of transitions, ordered by the prefix ordering modulo permutations.

The first semantics for CCS that we consider in this paper is a semantics by permutations. As we just saw, to be able to define such a semantics, we need a notion of *occurrence* of action. The usual operational semantics of CCS describes processes as performing transitions labelled by actions. These transitions are inferred using a system of structural rules. What we shall take here as the occurrence of action associated with a transition is the *proof* of that transition in the given system of rules. Each proof identifies uniquely one transition, and we use this information to define a relation of *concurrency* on (proved) transitions, and a notion of *residual* of a (proved) transition by a concurrent one. A diamond property for concurrent proved transitions may then be proved: this result is much simpler in CCS than in λ-calculus or term rewriting systems, since the proof of a transition cannot be duplicated or deleted by a concurrent one.

We may then move on to define the equivalence by permutations on sequences of proved transitions. The *computations* of a CCS term in this model are thus equivalence classes of sequences of proved transitions. Now any such computation may be represented as a one step transition, labelled by a *pomset* [48] of actions. We thus obtain a *partial order* semantics for CCS, which is directly derived from its usual operational semantics. Also, the permutation semantics given here may be seen as an extension of our semantics for "true concurrency" in [7,8], where communication (and restriction) were not considered.

As regards the semantics of concurrency, the idea of a computation as an equivalence class of sequences was first formalised by Mazurkiewicz in his theory of traces [38,39]. We recall that a *trace* is an equivalence class of sequences of actions up to commutation of concurrent actions. However *actions* in Mazurkiewicz's setting do not have the same meaning as in CCS (e.g. an action cannot be concurrent with itself, as it happens in the CCS process $a.\mathsf{nil} \parallel a.\mathsf{nil}$). In fact, actions in a trace are really *events*, and in this case the notion of residual is very simple: the residual of an action by a concurrent one is just the action itself. We shall see that this is not the case for our proved transitions: a proved transition may be modified by the occurrence of a concurrent one. Thus we need a more general notion of residual. Another difference between our approach and trace theory is that the concurrency relation is not given from the start here: instead, our starting point is the operational semantics, and we show how the concurrency relation may be *extracted from it* using the structure of labels.

Let us now briefly sketch how we establish the correspondence of our three models. The proved transition system generates at each step what we call *proofs* for a term p, which are *initial occurrences* of actions in p. This is a simple operational model, sufficient for the purpose of deriving a concurrency relation and a permutation semantics. On the other hand the two flow models – flow event structures and flow nets – give global representations of terms, modelling occurrences of actions as *events*, which are occurrences of arbitrary depth in a term.

Hence, in order to compare more easily the permutation semantics with the flow models, we generalize the proved transition system so that proofs can pass through actions – guards – thus giving rise to general events. The transition system thus obtained, a rather intensional one, is called the *event transition system* (or simply event system). Its transitions are labelled by *events* and its computations are *sets of events* labelling a transition sequence. The event system will act as an intermediate between the the flow models and the proved transition system. More precisely, we will show that, for any finite term p of CCS:

- the event system and the flow net associated with p are *isomorphic transition systems*: thus in particular they generate the same sets of labels – events – along their transition sequences.
- the event system and the flow event structure associated with p generate the same *sets of events* along their computations.

Thus the three event-based models – event system, flow nets, flow event structures, determine the *same families of computations*. On the other hand, we will prove that:

- the event system and the proved transition system associated with p yield *isomorphic domains of computations*.

This is indeed the most substantial part of our result: it involves defining a permutation equivalence on the event system itself, and we shall see that in this system equivalence classes of sequences are *trace computations* in the sense of [38,39].

In conclusion, we will have shown that the two flow models are *concretely* equivalent, while they are both *abstractly* equivalent to the permutation semantics.

As a matter of fact, the event system has an interest of its own. We mentioned that its computations are traces. In fact, it may be shown – and this is an interesting connection – that the event system is a *labelled asynchronous system* in the sense of [1,51], and it is known from [1,36] that such systems generate trace computations. Moreover our event system for CCS is an example of labelled asynchronous system determined by the *structure* of CCS terms, and thus gives a positive answer to a question raised by Kwiatkowska in her thesis [36, sec. 7.2].

A natural development of the work presented here will be the extension of our interpretations to recursive processes (in fact the first two semantics were already defined for infinite processes in [9]). However we should point out that our three models, being essentially operational descriptions of processes, will always give *infinite representations* for infinite behaviours.

We conclude this introduction with a brief outline of the paper. In section 2 we introduce the language (finite CCS) and present our *proved transition system* semantics for it. We show, in beginning of section 3, how this concrete description of processes may be used to derive a relation of concurrency between transitions, in a purely syntactic way. The remainder of section 3 is devoted to the permutation semantics: we give the diamond property for concurrent transitions and define the equivalence by permutations on sequences of transitions. In sections 4 and 5 we describe the flow event structure and flow net interpretations for CCS. Finally, in section 6, the various semantics are brought together, and we show how they relate to each other. This is also where the event system, our auxiliary model, is introduced and studied. In section 7 we give some references and comments on related work.

All results are stated without proof in this version of the paper, with the exception of the diamond lemma for proved transitions. However indications for proofs are often provided, and the main result – the equivalence of the three models – is described in its essential parts. For the remaining proofs the reader is referred to the complete version of the paper [11].

2. Finite CCS: terms and transitions

We start by introducing the syntax of finite CCS. We assume some familiarity with CCS, referring the reader to Milner's works [40,41,42] and to [33] for a general introduction to CCS and related algebraic languages.

As in [40], we let Δ be a fixed set of *names*. We use α, β,... to stand for names. We assume a set $\bar{\Delta}$ of *co-names* (complementary names), disjoint from Δ and in bijection with it: the co-name of α is $\bar{\alpha}$, while its name is $\mathsf{nm}(\bar{\alpha}) = \mathsf{nm}(\alpha) = \alpha$. Then $\Lambda = \Delta \cup \bar{\Delta}$ is the set of *labels*. We shall use λ to range over Λ, and extend the bijection so that $\bar{\bar{\lambda}} = \lambda$. As usual the set A of CCS *actions* is $A = \Lambda \cup \{\tau\}$, where τ is a new symbol, not in Λ; by convention the name of τ is τ. We use a, b, c,... to range over A.

In this paper we restrict ourselves to *finite* CCS terms, though the first semantics we describe – the permutation semantics – was originally presented for the whole language, in [9]. Also, we shall not consider the relabelling operator, although it would not introduce any difficulty. The set **T** of CCS terms we will study is then given by the grammar:

$$p \ ::= \ \mathsf{nil} \mid x \mid a.p \mid (p \parallel p') \mid (p + p') \mid p \backslash \alpha$$

We shall use p, q, $r, \ldots$ to range over terms. Terms of **T** may be viewed as finite *trees*, with parallel composition and sum as binary node constructors, action and restriction as unary ones (with a parameter in A and Δ respectively), and nil as a constant. For instance the term $r = (\alpha.\mathsf{nil} \parallel (\bar{\alpha}.\mathsf{nil} + \beta.\mathsf{nil}))\backslash\alpha$ may be identified with the syntactic tree:

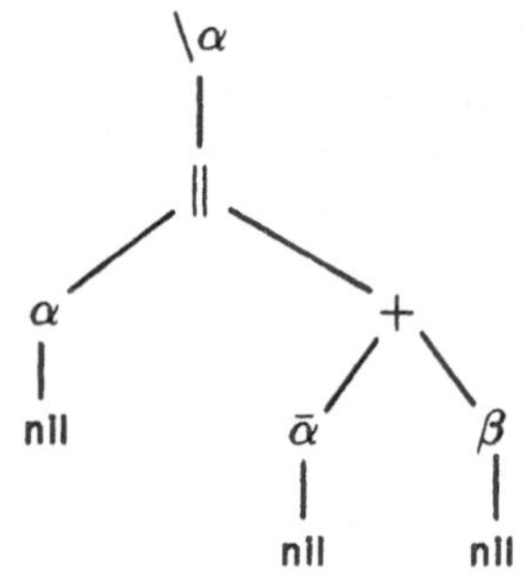

Our three semantics for CCS will be strongly based on such syntactic tree representation for terms. We recall first the standard operational semantics of CCS. This is given by means of *inference rules*, allowing one to prove *transitions* of the form $p \xrightarrow{a} p'$. The transitions of a term p are exactly those which can be proved in the following system of rules:

action	$\vdash \ a.p \xrightarrow{a} p$
parallel composition 1	$p \xrightarrow{a} p' \ \vdash \ (p \parallel q) \xrightarrow{a} (p' \parallel q)$
parallel composition 2	$q \xrightarrow{b} q' \ \vdash \ (p \parallel q) \xrightarrow{b} (p \parallel q')$
communication	$p \xrightarrow{\lambda} p' \ , \ q \xrightarrow{\bar{\lambda}} q' \ \vdash \ (p \parallel q) \xrightarrow{\tau} (p' \parallel q')$
sum 1	$p \xrightarrow{a} p' \ \vdash \ (p + q) \xrightarrow{a} p'$
sum 2	$q \xrightarrow{b} q' \ \vdash \ (p + q) \xrightarrow{b} q'$
restriction	$p \xrightarrow{a} p' \ , \ \mathsf{nm}(a) \neq \alpha \ \vdash \ (p\backslash\alpha) \xrightarrow{a} (p'\backslash\alpha)$

This set of rules is usually regarded as defining an *interleaving semantics* for CCS. Indeed, if we except the possibility of communication, the above rules for parallel composition describe $\parallel$ as an interleaving operator, allowing the components to move in any order, but not together. The reader is referred to [40,41] for a full account of CCS and the related interleaving theory.

Note that the semantics of a term – the set of transitions which can be inferred for it – contains no trace of the inference mechanism itself. We want now to show that, if we keep track of the *proofs* of transitions, we can extract much more information from the same set of rules. In particular, we will be able to derive a *non-interleaving semantics* for the language, without having to depart from its basic operational semantics.

2.1 The proved transition system

We shall now introduce our *proved transition system* for CCS, where transitions are labelled by their *proofs*. Let us first formalise the idea of *proof* in the inference system of CCS. In general, in an inference system one has rules of the form:

$$r: \frac{A_1, \ldots, A_n}{A} \tag{$*$}$$

to deduce an assertion from a finite set of assertions. Such rules generate proof trees of the form:

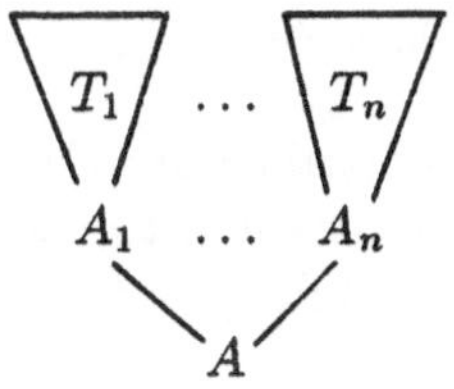

Here $T_1, \ldots, T_n$ are proof trees for $A_1, \ldots, A_n$, while the whole tree is a proof for A. Alternatively, one may represent the structure of a proof as a tree θ whose nodes are labelled by the *rules* which have been used in the derivation. It is not difficult to see that such a tree is isomorphic to the proof tree itself. For example, if $\theta_1, \ldots, \theta_n$ represent the (rule labelled) trees for $A_1, \ldots, A_n$ and the last step of derivation consists in applying rule r with premisses $A_1, \ldots, A_n$, the whole proof may be represented by the tree:

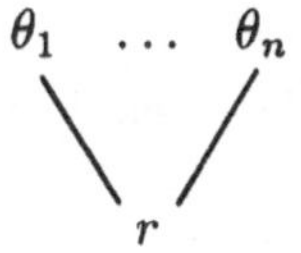

Since each rule has a fixed finite number of premisses, any tree of this kind may be denoted by a term $r(\theta_1, \ldots, \theta_n)$, what we call a *proof term* – or simply a *proof* – in the following. This is the kind of notation we will use for proofs of transitions in CCS.

Our next step will be to decorate assertions with their proofs, and consider *proved assertions* like $\theta : A$, where θ is a proof of A. To manipulate proved assertions, we will introduce, for each rule $(*)$ of the inference system, a decorated rule:

$$\frac{x_1 : A_1, \ldots, x_n : A_n}{r\,(x_1, \ldots, x_n) : A} \tag{$**$}$$

Such rules will build up proofs of assertions as the inference process goes on: whenever a rule is applied, the name r of the rule is recorded in the resulting proof term.

In the inference system of CCS, assertions are transitions of the form $p \xrightarrow{a} p'$. The proof terms θ will be built with the following symbols, one for each inference rule of CCS:

a	for the action rule (note that there is a separate rule for each action a)
$\|_0$	for the rule inferring a transition at the left of a parallel composition
$\|_1$	for the rule inferring a transition at the right of a parallel composition
$(,)$	for the communication rule
$+_0$	for the rule inferring a transition at the left of a sum
$+_1$	for the rule inferring a transition at the right of a sum
$\backslash_\alpha$	for the rule for restriction (one for each name α)

As we said, these rule names will be used as *proof constructors.* Each constructor takes as many parameters as are the hypotheses of the corresponding rule. For example the constructor a takes no parameters, while $(,)$ takes two.

The syntax for *proofs* of CCS transitions is thus given by the grammar, where $a \in Act$ and $\alpha \in \Delta$:

$$\theta ::= a \mid \ \|_0(\theta) \mid \|_1(\theta) \mid (\theta, \theta') \mid +_0(\theta) \mid +_1(\theta) \mid \backslash_\alpha(\theta)$$

Note that although we call them proof terms, the θ's do not always represent proper proofs; for instance $\backslash_\alpha(\alpha)$ and (α, β) do not correspond to any CCS transition. We give now the rules for building proper proof terms. Since any proper proof will contain the label (i.e. the action) of the corresponding transition, we define simultaneously the set of proper proof terms θ and their label $\ell(\theta)$. We will mostly use $\|_i\theta$, $+_i\theta$, $\backslash_\alpha\theta$ instead of $\|_i(\theta)$, $+_i(\theta)$, $\backslash_\alpha(\theta)$.

The set Θ of *proper proofs* and the *labelling* $\ell\colon \Theta \to Act$ are given by:

$$a \in Act \;\Rightarrow\; a \in \Theta \text{ and } \ell(a) = a$$
$$\theta \in \Theta \;\Rightarrow\; \|_i\theta \in \Theta \text{ and } \ell(\|_i\theta) = \ell(\theta)$$
$$\theta \in \Theta \;\Rightarrow\; +_i\theta \in \Theta \text{ and } \ell(+_i\theta) = \ell(\theta)$$
$$\theta, \theta' \in \Theta,\ \ell(\theta) = \overline{\ell(\theta)} \;\Rightarrow\; (\theta, \theta') \in \Theta \text{ and } \ell((\theta, \theta')) = \tau$$
$$\theta \in \Theta,\ \mathsf{nm}(\ell(\theta)) \neq \alpha \;\Rightarrow\; \backslash_\alpha\theta \in \Theta \text{ and } \ell(\backslash_\alpha\theta) = \ell(\theta)$$

We shall now bring together proofs and transitions. Usually one denotes by $\theta\colon A$ the fact that θ is a proof of the assertion A. Here we will use, instead of $\theta\colon p \xrightarrow{a} p'$, the notation $p \xrightarrow{a,\theta} p'$, which is more convenient to deal with sequences of transitions. Note that for such a transition $p \xrightarrow{a,\theta} p'$, we will always have $a = \ell(\theta)$ and thus we may omit the action a. We will then adopt the simpler notation $p \xrightarrow{\theta} p'$, to be interpreted as: θ is a proof of the fact that p performs the action $\ell(\theta)$ and becomes p' in doing so. We will call $p \xrightarrow{\theta} p'$ a *proved transition* for p.

Let us now give the rules for the new system of *proved transitions*:

A. $\vdash a.p \xrightarrow{a} p$

P0. $p \xrightarrow{\theta} p' \vdash (p \parallel q) \xrightarrow{\parallel_0 \theta} (p' \parallel q)$

P1. $q \xrightarrow{\theta} q' \vdash (p \parallel q) \xrightarrow{\parallel_1 \theta} (p \parallel q')$

C. $p \xrightarrow{\theta} p'\ ,\ q \xrightarrow{\theta'} q',\ \overline{\ell(\theta)} = \ell(\theta') \vdash (p \parallel q) \xrightarrow{(\theta, \theta')} (p' \parallel q')$

S0. $p \xrightarrow{\theta} p' \vdash (p + q) \xrightarrow{+_0 \theta} p'$

S1. $q \xrightarrow{\theta} q' \vdash (p + q) \xrightarrow{+_1 \theta} q'$

R. $p \xrightarrow{\theta} p'\ ,\ \mathsf{nm}(\ell(\theta)) \neq \alpha \vdash (p \backslash \alpha) \xrightarrow{\backslash_\alpha \theta} (p' \backslash \alpha)$

We shall call this new transition system the *proved transition system*. It should be clear that if we drop the proof terms – and retain their labels – we obtain the original rules of CCS. Hence the usual semantics of CCS is still explicitly present in the proved transition system.

Let us see an example. Take again the term $r = (\alpha.\mathsf{nil} \parallel (\bar{\alpha}.\mathsf{nil} + \beta.\mathsf{nil}))\backslash\alpha$. Let us write the proved transition corresponding to the communication on α, $\bar{\alpha}$. To illustrate our technique we picture the whole proof tree for the transition:

$$\dfrac{\dfrac{\dfrac{}{\alpha.\mathsf{nil} \xrightarrow{\alpha} \mathsf{nil}} \qquad \dfrac{\dfrac{}{\bar{\alpha}.\mathsf{nil} \xrightarrow{\bar{\alpha}} \mathsf{nil}}}{(\bar{\alpha}.\mathsf{nil} + \beta.\mathsf{nil}) \xrightarrow{+_0 \bar{\alpha}} \mathsf{nil}}}{(\alpha.\mathsf{nil} \parallel (\bar{\alpha}.\mathsf{nil} + \beta.\mathsf{nil})) \xrightarrow{(\alpha,\ +_0 \bar{\alpha})} (\mathsf{nil} \parallel \mathsf{nil})}}{(\alpha.\mathsf{nil} \parallel (\bar{\alpha}.\mathsf{nil} + \beta.\mathsf{nil}))\backslash\alpha \xrightarrow{\backslash_\alpha (\alpha,\ +_0 \bar{\alpha})} (\mathsf{nil} \parallel \mathsf{nil})\backslash\alpha}$$

Decorating the transitions with their proofs provides us with a "maximal" concrete information. As a matter of fact, our proof terms are closely related to syntactic trees. If we look back at the syntactic tree for the term r, we may notice that the proof θ of a transition specifies a *path* in the tree. In the simple case where $\ell(\theta) = a$, this path leads to the subterm $a.q$ which performs the action a. However, if the action is a communication as in the example above, the proof will be a path to a pair of complementary subterms $\lambda.q$ and $\bar{\lambda}.q'$.

To sum up, the proof of a transition $\xrightarrow{a}$ for a process p is an exact indication of how we get the action a from p. As a matter of fact, the proof of a transition identifies uniquely that transition: the new system of proved transitions is *deterministic*, that is:

$$p \xrightarrow{\theta} p' \text{ and } p \xrightarrow{\theta} p'' \quad \Rightarrow \quad p' = p''$$

Now the concrete information contained in proofs may be weakened in various ways to obtain more abstract semantics.

Here we shall use this concrete information to define a *concurrency relation* on transitions. This will enable us to define an equivalence by permutations on sequences of transitions, and thereby retrieve a *partial order semantics* for CCS.

A similar but somewhat dual approach was taken in [18] by Degano, De Nicola and Montanari, who use a concrete transition system for CCS to extract a *causality relation* on transitions: this allows them to reconstruct a partial order transition from any sequence of concrete transitions.

3. Permutation of transitions

We shall now introduce a notion of *concurrency* on proved transitions. Roughly speaking, two transitions are concurrent if they occur on different sides of a parallel composition, whereas they are in *conflict* (not concurrent) if they occur on different sides of a sum. However some complications arise from communication, which may introduce new conflicts. Typically, two communications will be in conflict if they share one component. Conversely, they will be concurrent if they are pairwise concurrent – i.e. they have concurrent components.

The relation of concurrency on proved transitions is induced from a relation of concurrency on proof terms, in notation $\theta \smile \theta'$, which we define now.

The *concurrency* relation $\smile$ on proof terms is the least symmetric relation that satisfies the following clauses (for any $\theta, \theta', \theta'' \in \Theta$):

(A1) $\|_0\theta \smile \|_1\theta'$

(A2) $\theta \smile \theta' \Rightarrow \begin{cases} \|_0\theta \smile (\theta', \theta'') \\ \|_1\theta \smile (\theta'', \theta') \end{cases}$

(A3) $\theta \smile \theta' \Rightarrow \begin{cases} \|_i\theta \smile \|_i\theta' \\ +_i\theta \smile +_i\theta' \\ \backslash_\alpha\,\theta \smile \backslash_\alpha\,\theta' \end{cases}$

(A4) $\theta_0 \smile \theta_0'$ and $\theta_1 \smile \theta_1' \Rightarrow (\theta_0, \theta_1) \smile (\theta_0', \theta_1')$

The essential rule is (A1). Rules (A3) and (A4) express the compatibility of $\smile$ with the various proof constructors. Rule (A2) also states a kind of compatibility of $\smile$ w.r.t. the constructors $\|_i$, since a proof (θ', θ'') stands for the co-occurrence of $\|_0(\theta')$ and $\|_1(\theta'')$.

We may now define the concurrency relation on proved transitions.

DEFINITION (CONCURRENT TRANSITIONS). *Let $t_0 = p \xrightarrow{\theta_0} p_0$ and $t_1 = p \xrightarrow{\theta_1} p_1$ be two proved transitions for the same* CCS *term p. The transitions are concurrent, in notation $t_0 \smile t_1$, if and only if $\theta_0 \smile \theta_1$.*

Note that by definition the concurrency relation between transitions is symmetric and irreflexive: it is easy to check that $\theta \smile \theta' \Rightarrow \theta \neq \theta'$.

To illustrate the application of clauses (A1)-(A4), we examine the relations between some transitions of the term $p = (\alpha \parallel \alpha) \parallel \bar{\alpha}$ (for simplicity we shall omit the trailing nil's in CCS terms). The two α-transitions are concurrent because $\|_0 \|_0 \alpha \smile \|_0 \|_1 \alpha$, by (A1) and (A3). The first α-transition and the communication on $\alpha, \bar{\alpha}$ of the remaining two components are also concurrent, because $\|_0 \|_0 \alpha \smile (\|_1 \alpha, \bar{\alpha})$ is an instance of (A2), with $\theta = \|_0 \alpha$ and $\theta' = \|_1 \alpha$. On the other hand $\|_0 \|_0 \alpha \not\smile (\|_0 \alpha, \bar{\alpha})$, since $\|_0 \alpha \not\smile \|_0 \alpha$ and thus (A2) does not apply.

The complementary relation of *conflict* could be formalized in a similar way (this will be done in the more general setting of event transitions, in section 6). For example we have a conflict between the two communications, since the two transitions

$$p \xrightarrow{(\|_0 \alpha, \bar{\alpha})} (\mathsf{nil} \parallel \alpha) \parallel \mathsf{nil} \quad , \quad p \xrightarrow{(\|_1 \alpha, \bar{\alpha})} (\alpha \parallel \mathsf{nil}) \parallel \mathsf{nil}$$

share the same "sub-transition" $\|_1 \bar{\alpha}$. Another case of conflict occurs in the term $r = (\alpha \parallel (\bar{\alpha} + \beta))\backslash\alpha$ considered earlier. Here the two transitions:

$$r \xrightarrow{\backslash_\alpha \|_1 +_1 \beta} (\alpha \parallel \mathsf{nil})\backslash\alpha \quad , \quad r \xrightarrow{\backslash_\alpha (\alpha,\, +_0 \bar{\alpha})} (\mathsf{nil} \parallel \mathsf{nil})\backslash\alpha$$

are in conflict because they made two different choices at the subterm $(\bar{\alpha} + \beta)$.

The intuition about concurrent transitions is that they are *compatible* and may be executed in any order without affecting the result. On the other hand the *proof* of a transition may be affected by the occurrence of a concurrent transition, because of nondeterministic choices: when a parallel composition is placed in a sum-context, the choice may be made by one of the parallel components, and does not have to be solved again by the other component (this point will be made clearer by an example below). Hence we need to define the *residual* t/t' of a proved transition t by a concurrent one t', namely what is left of the transition t after t'. We define first the *residual* θ/θ' of a proof term by a concurrent one.

For any concurrent proofs θ, θ', the *residual* of θ after θ', noted θ/θ', is defined by:

$$i \neq j \;\Rightarrow\; \|_i \theta \,/\, \|_j \theta' = \|_i \theta$$

$$\theta \smile \theta' \;\Rightarrow\; \begin{cases} \|_0 \theta \,/ (\theta', \theta'') = \|_0 (\theta/\theta') \text{ and } (\theta', \theta'')/\, \|_0 \theta = (\theta'/\theta, \theta'') \\ \|_1 \theta \,/ (\theta'', \theta') = \|_1 (\theta/\theta') \text{ and } (\theta'', \theta')/\, \|_1 \theta = (\theta'', \theta'/\theta) \end{cases}$$

$$\theta \smile \theta' \;\Rightarrow\; \begin{cases} \|_i \theta /\, \|_i \theta' = \|_i (\theta/\theta') \\ +_i \theta /\, +_i \theta' = \theta/\theta' \\ \backslash_\alpha \theta / \backslash_\alpha \theta' = \backslash_\alpha (\theta/\theta') \end{cases}$$

$$\theta_0 \smile \theta'_0 \text{ and } \theta_1 \smile \theta'_1 \;\Rightarrow\; (\theta_0, \theta_1)/(\theta'_0, \theta'_1) = (\theta_0/\theta'_0, \theta_1/\theta'_1)$$

Obviously the labels of proofs are preserved by residuals, that is to say $\ell(\theta) = \ell(\theta/\theta')$.

Let us look at an example, which shows how residuals are affected by choices. The term $p = ((a \parallel b) + c)$ has the following concurrent proved transitions:

$$p \xrightarrow{+_0 \parallel_0 a} (\mathsf{nil} \parallel b), \qquad p \xrightarrow{+_0 \parallel_1 b} (a \parallel \mathsf{nil})$$

Thus the proof of the b-transition from p is $+_0 \parallel_1 b$. On the other hand, once the a-transition has occurred, the proof of the b-transition becomes $+_0 \parallel_1 b / +_0 \parallel_0 a = \parallel_1 b$, i.e. we have:

$$p \xrightarrow{+_0 \parallel_0 a} (\mathsf{nil} \parallel b) \xrightarrow{\parallel_1 b} (\mathsf{nil} \parallel \mathsf{nil})$$

This shows a difference between our framework and Mazurkiewicz *theory of traces*. In a trace, two independent actions may always be commuted as they stand, since the residual of one action after the other is the action itself. Intuitively, this is because actions in a trace are essentially *events* (see later) rather than initial occurrences.

Note that it is indeed necessary to record choices in our proof terms: without the constructors $+_i$ we would not be able to define the concurrency relation on our proofs. For consider the term:

$$(a \parallel b) \; + \; (a \parallel c)$$

If we did not record the $+_i$ in our proofs, we would not be able to distinguish the two a-transitions and thus we would not know, by just looking at their proofs, which is concurrent with the b-transition and and which is concurrent with the c-transition.

We turn now to the main property of the concurrency relation. The following result, also known as the diamond property or the parallel moves property, states a "conditional Church-Rosser property", namely that whenever two transitions are concurrent then they are confluent. This result is much simpler in CCS than in λ-calculus or term rewriting systems, since here the proof of a transition cannot be duplicated or deleted by a concurrent one.

Lemma (The Diamond Lemma). *Let $t_0 = p \xrightarrow{\theta_0} p_0$ and $t_1 = p \xrightarrow{\theta_1} p_1$ be two proved transitions such that $\theta_0 \smile \theta_1$. Then there exists a unique term $\bar{p}$ such that $p_0 \xrightarrow{\theta_1/\theta_0} \bar{p}$ and $p_1 \xrightarrow{\theta_0/\theta_1} \bar{p}$.*

Proof: By induction on the definition of $\smile$. In all cases the uniqueness of $\bar{p}$ follows from the determinacy of the proved transition system, i.e. from the property: $(p \xrightarrow{\theta} p' \;\&\; p \xrightarrow{\theta} p'') \Rightarrow p' = p''$. We consider the most significant cases for $\theta_0 \smile \theta_1$, leaving the others to the reader.

1) *Basic case*: $\theta_0 = \parallel_0 \theta'_0$ and $\theta_1 = \parallel_1 \theta'_1$. In this case $p = q_0 \parallel q_1$ with $q_0 \xrightarrow{\theta'_0} q'_0$ and $q_1 \xrightarrow{\theta'_1} q'_1$, hence $p_0 = q'_0 \parallel q_1$ and $p_1 = q_0 \parallel q'_1$. Then applying rules $P1$ and $P0$ we obtain

$$p_0 \xrightarrow{\parallel_1 \theta'_1} q'_0 \parallel q'_1 \quad \text{and} \quad p_1 \xrightarrow{\parallel_0 \theta'_0} q'_0 \parallel q'_1$$

which are the required closing transitions since by definition of residual we have: $\theta_1/\theta_0 = \parallel_1 \theta'_1 / \parallel_0 \theta'_0 = \parallel_1 \theta'_1 = \theta_1$ and $\theta_0/\theta_1 = \parallel_0 \theta'_0 / \parallel_1 \theta'_1 = \parallel_0 \theta'_0 = \theta_0$.

2) $\theta_0 = \|_0\theta'_0$ and $\theta_1 = (\theta'_1, \theta''_1)$, with $\theta'_0 \smile \theta'_1$. Then $p = q_0 \parallel q_1$ with $q_0 \xrightarrow{\theta'_0} q'_0$, $q_0 \xrightarrow{\theta'_1} q''_0$, $q_1 \xrightarrow{\theta''_1} q'_1$, whence $p_0 = q'_0 \parallel q_1$ and $p_1 = q''_0 \parallel q'_1$. Now since $\theta'_0 \smile \theta'_1$, by induction there exists $\bar{q}_0$ such that $q'_0 \xrightarrow{\theta'_1/\theta'_0} \bar{q}_0$ and $q''_0 \xrightarrow{\theta'_0/\theta'_1} \bar{q}_0$. Then applying rules C and $P0$ we obtain

$$q'_0 \parallel q_1 \xrightarrow{(\theta'_1/\theta'_0, \theta''_1)} \bar{q}_0 \parallel q'_1 \quad \text{and} \quad q''_0 \parallel q'_1 \xrightarrow{\|_0(\theta'_0/\theta'_1)} \bar{q}_0 \parallel q'_1$$

which are the required transitions since the residuals are $\theta_1/\theta_0 = (\theta'_1, \theta''_1)/\ \|_0\ \theta'_0 = (\theta'_1/\theta'_0, \theta''_1)$ and $\theta_0/\theta_1 = \|_0\theta'_0/(\theta'_1, \theta''_1) = \|_0(\theta'_0/\theta'_1)$.

3) $\theta_0 = +_0\theta'_0$ and $\theta_1 = +_0\theta'_1$, with $\theta'_0 \smile \theta'_1$. Then $p = q_0 + q_1$ with $q_0 \xrightarrow{\theta'_0} q'_0$ and $q_0 \xrightarrow{\theta'_1} q''_0$, and thus $p_0 = q'_0$ and $p_1 = q''_0$. By induction we have for θ'_0, θ'_1 the transitions

$$q'_0 \xrightarrow{\theta'_1/\theta'_0} \bar{q}_0 \quad \text{and} \quad q''_0 \xrightarrow{\theta'_0/\theta'_1} \bar{q}_0$$

which are also closing transitions for θ_0, θ_1 since $\theta_1/\theta_0 = +_0\theta'_1/ +_0 \theta'_0 = \theta'_1/\theta'_0$ and $\theta_0/\theta_1 = +_0\theta'_0/ +_0 \theta'_1 = \theta'_0/\theta'_1$.

❑

This property is in fact much stronger than confluence: it says that any (proved) transition survives a concurrent one. We can then adopt the standard terminology of ([3,5,35,37]): the transition $p_0 \xrightarrow{\theta_1/\theta_0} \bar{p}$ (with the notations of the diamond lemma) is the *residual* of t_1 by t_0, denoted t_1/t_0, and similarly we have $t_0/t_1 = p_1 \xrightarrow{\theta_0/\theta_1} \bar{p}$.

We are now ready to define the equivalence by permutations (first defined by Lévy and Berry, see [37] and [3]) on sequences of transitions of CCS terms. Each term p determines a set $\mathcal{T}(p)$ of *sequences* of proved transitions of the form

$$p \xrightarrow{\theta_1} p_1 \ \cdots \ p_{n-1} \xrightarrow{\theta_n} p_n$$

which may equivalently be presented as sequences of steps:

$$t_1 \cdots t_n \quad \text{where} \quad t_i = p_{i-1} \xrightarrow{\theta_i} p_i, \ \ p_0 = p, \ \text{ and } 1 \leq i \leq n$$

Intuitively two sequences of proved transitions of $\mathcal{T}(p)$ are equivalent if they are the same up to permutations of concurrent steps. We give next the formal definition of permutation equivalence on $\mathcal{T}(p)$. Let ss' denote the concatenation of $s \in \mathcal{T}(p)$ and $s' \in \mathcal{T}(q)$, which is only defined if s ends at q.

DEFINITION (PERMUTATION EQUIVALENCE). *Let p be a CCS term. The equivalence by permutations on $\mathcal{T}(p)$ is the least equivalence $\simeq$ such that*

$$s_0 t_0 (t_1/t_0) s_1 \ \simeq \ s_0 t_1 (t_0/t_1) s_1$$

(provided that $t_0 \smile t_1$ and that concatenation is defined).

An example of equivalent sequences of transitions is:

$$(a.p \parallel b.q) + c.r \xrightarrow{+_0 \parallel_0 a} (p \parallel b.q) \xrightarrow{\parallel_1 b} (p \parallel q)$$

$$(a.p \parallel b.q) + c.r \xrightarrow{+_0 \parallel_1 b} (a.p \parallel q) \xrightarrow{\parallel_0 a} (p \parallel q)$$

Here one can commute the two steps. There is another kind of sequence of transitions where this is not possible, because a step is *caused*, or created, by a previous one. The typical example is obviously:

$$a.b \xrightarrow{a} b \xrightarrow{b} \mathsf{nil}$$

We may finally proceed to the definition of the partial order semantics. The equivalence class $[s]$ of a sequence

$$s = p \xrightarrow{\theta_1} \cdots \xrightarrow{\theta_n} p'$$

may be represented as a *one step transition* $p \xrightarrow{P} p'$ where P is a *pomset* (partially ordered multiset [48]) of actions of A, – that is an isomorphism class of posets labelled in A. Such pomset transitions were introduced in [7] for a subset of CCS. Let us formalize this idea: we shall write $s \sim_\zeta s'$ if s' results from s by the transposition of the steps i and $i+1$, and ζ is the corresponding transposition of $\{1, \ldots, n\}$, where n is the length of s (obviously $\simeq$ preserves the length of sequences). So $\zeta(i) = i + 1$ and $\zeta(i+1) = i$. It should be clear that $s' \simeq s$ if and only if there is a sequence $\zeta_1, \ldots, \zeta_k$ of such transpositions from s to s'. Let us denote this fact by $s \sim_{\zeta_1,\ldots,\zeta_k} s'$. Then the equivalence class of $s = p \xrightarrow{\theta_1} \cdots \xrightarrow{\theta_n} p'$ determines a transition $p \xrightarrow{P} p'$, where $P = (E, l, \leq)$ is the labelled poset defined (up to the naming of events) by:

$$\begin{cases} E = \{e_1, \ldots, e_n\} \\ l(e_i) = \ell(\theta_i) \\ e_i \leq e_j \;\Leftrightarrow\; \forall s' : \quad s' \sim_{\zeta_1,\ldots,\zeta_k} s \;\Rightarrow\; \eta(i) \leq \eta(j) \quad \text{where } \eta = \zeta_k \circ \cdots \circ \zeta_1 \end{cases}$$

Note that P is defined up to isomorphism, since the events e_i are taken arbitrarily. This construction is close to that of *dependency graph* corresponding to a trace – as defined by Mazurkiewicz in [38]. A similar definition is given in [24] for Petri nets.

Let us see an example. The equivalence class of the sequence

$$(a.p \parallel b.c.q) \xrightarrow{\parallel_0 a} (p \parallel b.c.q) \xrightarrow{\parallel_1 b} (p \parallel c.q) \xrightarrow{\parallel_1 c} (p \parallel q)$$

may be represented as a transition whose label is a pomset consisting of events e_1, e_2 and e_3 labelled a, b and c respectively, where e_2 precedes e_3 and e_1 is incomparable with e_2 and e_3, that is:

$$(a.p \parallel b.c.q) \xrightarrow{\left\{\begin{array}{cc} a & b \\ & | \\ & c \end{array}\right\}} (p \parallel q)$$

We define the set of *computations* of p to be the quotient $\mathcal{C} = \mathcal{T}/\simeq$. This is a partially ordered set – the ordering on equivalence classes (the prefix ordering up to permutations) will be denoted $\lesssim$. In section 6 we will show that the domain $\mathcal{D}_{\text{per}} = (\mathcal{T}/\simeq, \lesssim)$ is isomorphic both to the domain of configurations of an event structure and to the domain of computations of a Petri net. The first result was already stated in [9].

4. Flow event structure semantics

In this section we present an event structure semantics for finite CCS, which will be later related, in section 6, to the semantics by permutations. Terms of CCS will be interpreted as *flow event structures*: this semantics was first proposed in [9] and, in a slightly different form, in [16]. The flow event structure semantics may be seen as a variation of Winskel's interpretation of CCS by means of *stable* event structures [58], and agrees with it in a rather strong sense: it yields the same families of configurations for any term. We recall some general points about event structures, for the readers not familiar with this model.

Event structures (e.s.) were introduced by Nielsen, Plotkin and Winskel in [43] as a model for computational processes. These were first order structures, essentially sets of events with two binary relations of *causality* and *conflict* between them, satisfying particular constraints. These structures, also called *prime event structures*, were shown to be connected both with a class of Petri nets – called by the authors [43] *occurrence nets* – and with a class of domains: their spaces of computations (configurations) are *finitary prime algebraic coherent domains*. In fact prime event structures are just equivalent – if more concrete – representations for their domains of configurations. In particular they can be retrieved from such domains by picking up particular configurations – the *complete prime* elements of the domain.

Because they are essentially models of *computations*, i.e. unfoldings of processes, prime event structures are too rigid for interpreting in a simple way process operators like the parallel product or data type constructions like exponentiation. This is why in subsequent works [56,58,59] Winskel turned to a more general class of event structures, *stable event structures*, for which such constructions may be defined in a natural way – and coincide with categorical constructs.

However by stepping to more general structures one loses some of the suggestiveness of the model. Stable e.s. are described at a more abstract level than prime e.s.: the causality relation on events is replaced by a second order *enabling* relation for events, specifying when a set of events is a possible *set of causes* for a given event. As a consequence, one loses the graphical representation of processes as sets of events with two kinds of arcs between them, representing causality and conflict, which was a pleasant feature of prime event structures.

Flow event structures were proposed in [9] as an intermediate between prime event structures and stable event structures, allowing both a graphical representation and an easy definition of process operators. In fact, flow event structures are a direct generalisation of prime event structures, where the conflict relation is not inherited and the partial ordering of causality is replaced by a local *flow* relation on events, representing *immediate causality*. Moreover there is no requirement on the relation between flow and conflict. With these new structures it is fairly easy to interpret CCS terms in a "natural" way.

Let us be more precise about the meaning of "natural" here. We have somehow suggested that a semantics by means of stable or flow event structures may be more natural than one by prime event structures. On the other hand interpretations of CCS or related languages have been defined by means of prime e.s., by Goltz and Loogen [30], by Degano, De Nicola and Montanari [20], and more recently by Vaandrager [55].

Our point is that in Winskel's stable e.s. semantics, as well as in the flow e.s. semantics, *events* have a clear operational meaning: they are just *occurrences* of actions (or pairs of occurrences, for a communication) in the syntactic tree obtained by unfolding the CCS term. For instance in the term $(a\alpha \mid \bar{\alpha}b)$ the action b gives rise to a unique event, which can be caused in two incompatible ways, either by the action $\bar{\alpha}$ alone, or by the communication action. Stable and flow event structures account for such conflicting causes, while prime event structures – constrained by the principle of *conflict heredity* – require as many *copies* of an event as there are conflicting sets of causes for it. As a matter of fact, events in a prime event structure are *histories* of an occurrence in the syntactic tree. For example the prime event structure interpretation of $(a\alpha \mid \bar{\alpha}b)$ is:

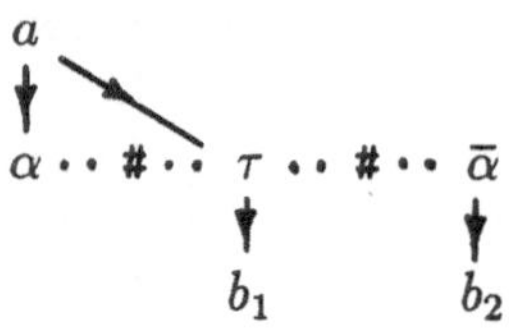

where there are two events b_1 and b_2 representing the two possible histories of the same occurrence b. Using prime event structures to interpret other simple terms may be quite laborious – try for instance $(\alpha a\beta \mid \bar{\beta}b\bar{\alpha})$ where causality cycles arise. Not surprisingly, the simplest – and most elegant – way to define an operation on prime e.s. is to define it first on the configurations (which are themselves histories), and then recover the corresponding prime e.s. (see [55], [58]).

This is the reason why, to our view, stable and flow e.s. are more suited than prime e.s. for modelling process operators. Flow e.s. are preferred here since they allow – just like prime e.s. – a graphical representation of processes. For instance, the flow event structure interpretation of the term $(a\alpha \mid \bar{\alpha}b)$ will be:

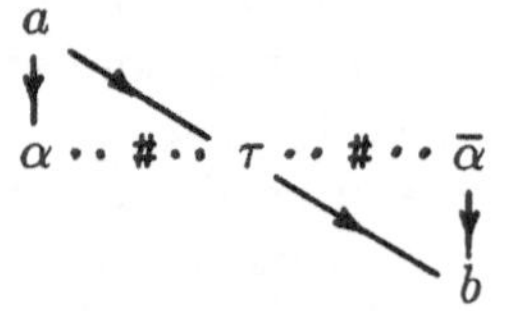

where the arrows represent now an immediate causality. Such causality is in general *not* transitive. Here for example a causes τ, and τ causes b, but a does *not* cause b: indeed a and b may occur independently, e.g. in the computation $\{a, \bar{\alpha}, b\}$ where the communication does not take place. We will see later in this section the flow e.s. interpretation of $(\alpha a\beta \mid \bar{\beta}b\bar{\alpha})$, together with various other examples.

Another advantage of flow event structures is their close correspondence with a class of Petri nets, the class of *flow nets* studied by one of the authors in [6].

Although the three classes of event structures – prime, flow, stable – have increasing expressive power for modelling families of configurations (see later), they are all "abstractly" equivalent in that they yield *isomorphic domains* of configurations.

In the rest of this section, we shall only be concerned with flow event structures. For more about prime and stable e.s. we refer the reader to [43] and to Winskel's papers [56,58,59]. We proceed now with the formal definitions. Although we will only use finite event structures in this paper, we give here the general definition.

DEFINITION (FLOW EVENT STRUCTURE). *A flow event structure is a structure* $S = (E,\ \#\ , \prec)$ *where*

- E *is a denumerable set of events*
- $\# \subseteq E \times E$ *is a symmetric relation, the conflict relation*
- $\prec \subseteq E \times E$ *is an irreflexive relation, the flow relation*

For those familiar with prime event structures, it will be clear that any prime event structure $S = (E,\ \#\ , \leq)$ is a flow event structure (with $\prec$ given by the strict ordering $<$ or by its covering relation). Note that the flow relation is not required to be transitive, nor its transitive closure $\prec^*$ to be acyclic. Intuitively, the flow relation represents a possible *immediate causality*. A simple way of understanding the flow relation is by analogy with Petri nets: a flow between two events in an event structure corresponds to the presence of a condition between the events in a net. This point is illustrated by the example below.

Note also that the conflict relation is not assumed to be irreflexive. This means that we allow *self-conflicting* or *inconsistent* events, that is events $e \in E$ such that $e \# e$. Such events will be used for defining the operation of *restriction* (and it may be shown that they are indeed convenient to obtain correct constructions on flow event structures, see [16]).

As we said, the first order flow event structures allow a graphical representation (with two kinds of arcs between events). In this representation we shall draw $e \prec e'$ as a directed arc $e \longrightarrow e'$, and $\#$ by a dotted line. Self-conflicts will be represented by dotted circles around events. The following is an example of flow event structure, together with a "corresponding" Petri net.

This example (which typically arises when modelling CCS communication) exhibits both a confluence after conflict, and a case where the flow $\prec$ is essentially *not* transitive: the events e_0 and e_3 are indeed causally related if e_1 occurs, but they are independent if e_2 occurs. In other words, e_0 and e_3 are in a different relation depending on the computation where they are considered.

We shall now formalise this notion of computation or *configuration* for flow event structures. A configuration is a set of events having occurred at some stage of evolution of a process. Since flow event structures are rather general, the definition of configuration is slightly more elaborated than for prime event structures. Let Cons_S be the set of conflict-free (consistent) sets of events: $X \in \mathit{Cons}_S$ iff $\forall e, e' \in X, \neg(e \# e')$. Obviously, an event e is inconsistent, i.e. $e \# e$, if and only if $e \notin X$ for any $X \in \mathit{Cons}_S$. For a subset X of E, let $\prec_X$ be the restriction of the flow relation to X and $\leq_X =_{def} \prec_X{}^*$ be the preordering generated by $\prec_X$. Again we give here the general definition of configuration (although condition iv) is obviously not needed for finite event structures).

Definition (Configurations). *Let $S = (E, \#, \prec)$ be a flow event structure. A configuration of S is a subset X of E such that:*

(i) *X is conflict-free: $X \in \mathit{Cons}_S$*

(ii) *X is left-closed up to conflicts: $e' \prec e \in X \;\&\; e' \notin X \;\Rightarrow\; \exists e'' \in X.\, e' \# e'' \prec e$*

(iii) *X has no causality cycles: the relation $\leq_X$ is an ordering*

(iv) *axiom of finite causes: for all $e \in X$ the set $\{e' \mid e' \in X \;\&\; e' \leq_X e\}$ is finite*

The first two conditions are essentially the same as for prime event structures: condition ii) is adapted to account for the more general – non-hereditary – conflict relation. It states that any event appears in a configuration with a "complete" set of causes. Condition iii) (and iv), in case of infinite configurations) ensure that any event in a configuration is actually reachable at some stage of computation. Note that an inconsistent event cannot appear in a configuration. So for example the structure:

has only the trivial configuration $\emptyset$. The set of configurations of a flow event structure S will be denoted by $\mathcal{F}(S)$, and its *domain of configurations*, the poset of these configurations ordered by inclusion, by $\mathcal{D}(S) =_{\text{def}} (\mathcal{F}(S), \subseteq)$. It is shown in [6] that for any flow e.s. S the poset $\mathcal{D}(S)$ is a coherent, prime algebraic and finitary domain (as for prime and stable event structures, see [43,56,59]).

We have seen that prime event structures are a subclass of flow event structures. In turn, any flow event structure $S = (E, \#, \prec)$ may be described as a stable event structure $G_S = (E, \#', \vdash_S)$ such that $\mathcal{F}(G_S) = \mathcal{F}(S)$, as explained in [6]. On the other hand there are stable event structures which cannot be represented as flow event structures (cf again [6]). To summarize, we have the following strict inclusion relations among the three classes of event structures (as regards their expressive power in modelling families of configurations):

$$\text{prime e.s.} \quad \subset \quad \text{flow e.s.} \quad \subset \quad \text{stable e.s.}$$

Let us turn now to the interpretation of CCS by means of flow event structures. Languages like CCS are parameterized on a set of actions A. To model processes in these languages one uses event structures *labelled* on the set of actions.

Definition (Labelled Flow Event Structures). *An A-labelled flow event structure is a structure $(E, \prec, \#, \ell)$ where*
(i) $(E, \prec, \#)$ is a flow event structure
(ii) $\ell : E \longrightarrow A$ is a labelling function over a set A of labels

We shall describe two ways of interpreting a CCS term as an event structure: in the first we directly define from the syntactical materials a structure $\mathcal{S}(p)$ for each term p, while in the second we define a construction on event structures for each CCS operator and interpret CCS by a morphism $\mathcal{I}$ into the event structure algebra. The constructions we use are adapted from those of Winskel [56,58].

4.1 Let us first define the "syntactic" interpretation $\mathcal{S}(p) = (\mathcal{E}(p), \prec, \#, \ell)$. We start by defining a global set of events $\mathcal{E}$, from which $\mathcal{E}(p)$ will be extracted. Events are occurrences of (possibly guarded) actions in a term: to specify them syntactically we just have to extend the syntax for proof terms (given in the previous section), so as to allow a proof to pass through a guard $a.p$. We will denote by $\widehat{a}.e$ the occurrence of e after a guard a. The set $\mathcal{E}$ of *events* has thus the following syntax:

$$e ::= a \mid \widehat{a}.e \mid \|_0 e \mid \|_1 e \mid (e, e') \mid +_0 e \mid +_1 e \mid \backslash_\alpha e$$

For instance the occurrence of the action b in $a.b.\mathsf{nil}$ will be $\widehat{a}.b$. The labelling is extended to events in the obvious way: $\ell(\widehat{a}.e) = \ell(e)$. Let us now define the notions of conflict and flow on events. The *conflict* relation $e \# e'$ is the least symmetric relation which satisfies the following, where we denote by $\sharp$ the reflexive closure of $\#$:

(B1) $\quad i \neq j \Rightarrow +_i e \# +_j e'$

(B2) $\quad e \sharp e' \Rightarrow \begin{cases} \|_0 e \# (e', e'') \\ \|_1 e \# (e'', e') \end{cases}$

(B3) $\quad e \# e' \Rightarrow \begin{cases} \|_i e \# \|_i e' \\ +_i e \# +_i e' \\ \backslash_\alpha e \# \backslash_\alpha e' \\ \widehat{a}.e \# \widehat{a}.e' \end{cases}$

(B4) $\quad \mathsf{nm}(\ell(e)) = \alpha \Rightarrow \backslash_\alpha e \# \backslash_\alpha e$

(B5) $\quad e_0 \sharp e_0'$ or $e_1 \sharp e_1'$ and $(e_0, e_1) \neq (e_0', e_1') \Rightarrow (e_0, e_1) \# (e_0', e_1')$
$\qquad e_0 \# e_0$ or $e_1 \# e_1 \Rightarrow (e_0, e_1) \# (e_0, e_1)$

Note the formal similarity with the definition of *concurrency* on proofs given in the previous section. In fact the concurrency relation could be defined on events too, by extending in the obvious way the definition for proofs (indeed concurrency on events will be considered later, in section 6).

We define now the *flow* relation on events. In the structure $\mathcal{S}(p)$, the flow represents a possible immediate precedence. Quite obviously the relation $e \prec e'$ is brought in by the action construct $a.p$ – loosely speaking $a \prec \widehat{a}.e$. More precisely $\prec$ is the least relation on $\mathcal{E}$ satisfying the following clauses:

(C1) $a \prec \widehat{a}.\theta$ where θ is any proof term

(C2) $e \prec e' \;\Rightarrow\; \begin{cases} (e,e'') \prec \|_0 e' \\ (e'',e) \prec \|_1 e' \end{cases}$ and $\begin{cases} \|_0 e \prec (e',e'') \\ \|_1 e \prec (e'',e') \end{cases}$

(C3) $e \prec e' \;\Rightarrow\; \begin{cases} (e,e_1) \prec (e',e_1') \\ (e_0,e) \prec (e_0',e') \end{cases}$

(C4) $e \prec e' \;\Rightarrow\; \begin{cases} \|_i e \prec \|_i e' \\ +_i e \prec +_i e' \\ \backslash_\alpha\, e \prec \backslash_\alpha\, e' \\ \widehat{a}.e \prec \widehat{a}.e' \end{cases}$

The relation $\prec$ is irreflexive; note on the other hand that it is not transitive: for instance if $e_0 \prec e_0'$ and $e_1 \prec e_1'$ then $\|_0 e_0 \prec (e_0', e_1)$ and $(e_0', e_1) \prec \|_1 e_1'$ but we do not have $\|_0 e_0 \prec \|_1 e_1'$. Let us see some examples: in the term $r = (\alpha.\alpha \parallel \bar{\alpha})$ we have

$$(\alpha, \bar{\alpha}) \prec (\widehat{\alpha}.\alpha, \bar{\alpha})$$
$$(\alpha, \bar{\alpha}) \;\#\; (\widehat{\alpha}.\alpha, \bar{\alpha})$$

This shows that # and $\prec$ are not necessarily disjoint. The following example shows that the transitive closure of $\prec$ is not disjoint from $\smile$ (extended to events in the obvious way, see section 6. for a formal definition): in the term $q = (a.\alpha \parallel \bar{\alpha}.b)$ we have

$$\|_0 a \prec (\widehat{a}.\alpha, \bar{\alpha}) \prec \|_1 \widehat{\bar{\alpha}}.b \quad \text{and} \quad \|_0\, a \smile \|_1 \widehat{\bar{\alpha}}.b$$

Note also that $\prec$ is not asymmetric; for instance in the term $(\alpha.\beta \parallel \bar{\beta}.\bar{\alpha})$ we have

$$(\alpha, \widehat{\bar{\beta}}\bar{\alpha}) \prec (\widehat{\alpha}\beta, \bar{\beta}) \prec (\alpha, \widehat{\bar{\beta}}\bar{\alpha})$$

To define the structure $\mathcal{S}(p)$ it just remains to define its set of events $\mathcal{E}(p) \subseteq \mathcal{E}$. Then the flow and conflict relations in $\mathcal{S}(p) = (\mathcal{E}(p), \prec, \#, \ell)$ will simply be the restrictions to $\mathcal{E}(p)$ of the corresponding relations on $\mathcal{E}$. The set $\mathcal{E}(p)$ of events of p is defined by induction on the structure of p as follows:

(E1) $a \in \mathcal{E}(a.p)$;
if $e \in \mathcal{E}(p)$ then $\widehat{a}.e \in \mathcal{E}(a.p)$;

(E2) if $e \in \mathcal{E}(p_i)$ then $\|_i e \in \mathcal{E}(p_0 \parallel p_1)$;
if $e \in \mathcal{E}(p_0)$ and $e' \in \mathcal{E}(p_1)$ and $\ell(e) = \overline{\ell(e')}$, then $(e,e') \in \mathcal{E}(p_0 \parallel p_1)$;

(E3) if $e \in \mathcal{E}(p_i)$ then $+_i e \in \mathcal{E}(p_0 + p_1)$;

(E4) if $e \in \mathcal{E}(p)$ then $\backslash_\alpha\, e \in \mathcal{E}(p \backslash \alpha)$;

For instance if $r = (a.\alpha \parallel \bar{\alpha}.b)\backslash\alpha$ then $\mathcal{S}(r)$ may be drawn

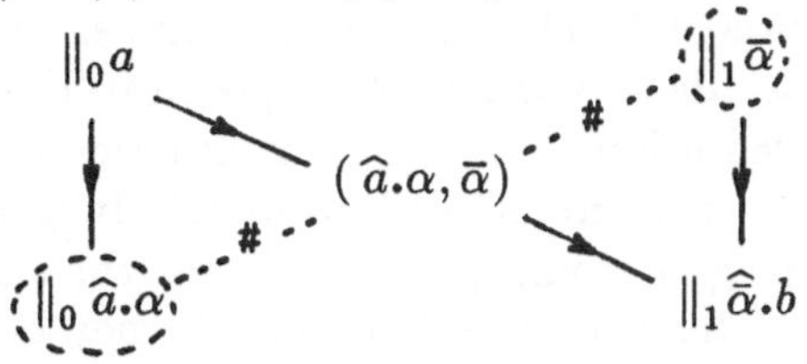

where the dotted circles around α and $\bar{\alpha}$ indicate that the corresponding events are self-conflicting. The flow $e \prec e'$ is represented by arrows $e \longrightarrow e'$. Clearly $\|_0\, \hat{a}.\alpha$ and $\|_1 \bar{\alpha}$ cannot occur in a configuration since they are inconsistent. From now on we will not write the full names of events in drawings, but only their labels. Then the structure $\mathcal{S}(r)$ will be drawn simply as

4.2 We give now the *constructions* on event structures corresponding to the operators of CCS. Let $\mathsf{Pred}(e) = \{e' \mid e' \prec e\}$. As in Winskel's semantics [58] we will use a dummy event $* \notin E$, with the convention that $\neg(*\, R\, x)$ for any $x \in E \cup \{*\}$ and $R \in \{\natural, \prec, \succ\}$. Then $(*, e)$ and $(e, *)$ represent the asynchronous occurrence of event e in the left, resp. the right, component of a parallel composition. The constructions are now as follows:

(i) nil is the empty event structure;

(ii) if $S = (E, \prec, \#, \ell)$ then $a.S = (\{\varepsilon\} \cup E, \prec', \#, \ell')$ where $\varepsilon \notin E$ and:
- $e \prec' e' \Leftrightarrow e \prec e'$ or $(e = \varepsilon$ and $\mathsf{Pred}(e') = \emptyset)$
- $\ell'(\varepsilon) = a$ and $\ell'(e) = \ell(e)$ for $e \in E$;

(iii) if $S_i = (E_i, \prec_i, \#_i, \ell_i)$ for $i = 0, 1$, then $S_0 \parallel S_1 = (E, \prec, \#, \ell)$ where:
- $E = (E_0 \times \{*\}) \cup (\{*\} \times E_1) \cup \{(e_0, e_1) \mid e_i \in E_i \;\&\; \ell(e_0) = \overline{\ell(e_1)}\}$
- $e \prec e' \Leftrightarrow e = (x, y)$, $e' = (x', y')$ and $x \prec_0 x'$ or $y \prec_1 y'$
- $e \# e' \Leftrightarrow \begin{cases} e = (x,y) \neq (x',y') = e' \text{ and } x \natural_0 x' \text{ or } y \natural_1 y', \text{ or} \\ e = (x,y) = e' \text{ and } x \#_0 x \text{ or } y \#_1 y \end{cases}$
- $\ell(e, *) = \ell_0(e)$, $\ell(*, e) = \ell_1(e)$ and $\ell(e_0, e_1) = \tau$

(iv) if $S_i = (E_i, \prec_i, \#_i, \ell_i)$ for $i = 0, 1$, then $S_0 + S_1 = (E, \prec, \#, \ell)$ where:
- $E = \{(i, e_i) \mid e_i \in E_i\}$
- $e \prec e' \Leftrightarrow e = (i, e_i)$, $e' = (i, e'_i)$ and $e_i \prec_i e'_i$
- $e \# e' \Leftrightarrow \begin{cases} e = (i, e_i),\ e' = (i, e'_i) \text{ and } e_i \#_i e'_i \quad \text{or} \\ e = (i, e_i),\ e' = (j, e'_j) \text{ and } i \neq j \end{cases}$
- $\ell(i, e) = \ell_i(e)$.

(v) if $S = (E, \prec, \#, \ell)$ then $S\backslash\alpha = (E, \prec, \#', \ell)$ where
- $e \#' e' \Leftrightarrow e \# e'$ or $(\, e = e'$ and $\mathsf{nm}(\ell(e)) = \alpha\,)$

The interpretation $\mathcal{I}(p)$ is then given by the unique morphism $\mathcal{I}$ from the free algebra of CCS trees to the algebra of labelled event structures. This second approach has been sometimes qualified as "denotational", as opposed to the more "operational" style of definition 4.1. In fact definition 4.2 is just a syntactic variant (where we use $(e,*)$ instead of $\|_0 e$, etc.) of the "operational" definition 4.1. In particular it should be clear that the two interpretations give isomorphic results for the same term p.
Let us see some examples. The structure $\mathcal{I}((\alpha.\beta \parallel \bar{\alpha}))$ may be drawn:

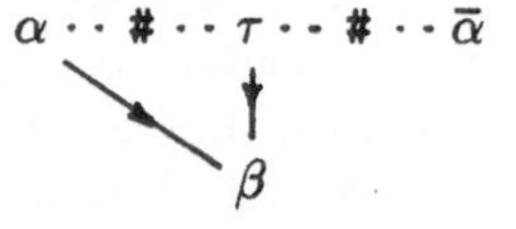

This example shows that $\mathcal{I}(p)$ may contain a substructure ∇' (see [7]). The interpretations of $(\alpha.a.\alpha \parallel \bar{\alpha})$ and $(a.\alpha \parallel \bar{\alpha}.b)$ may be drawn respectively

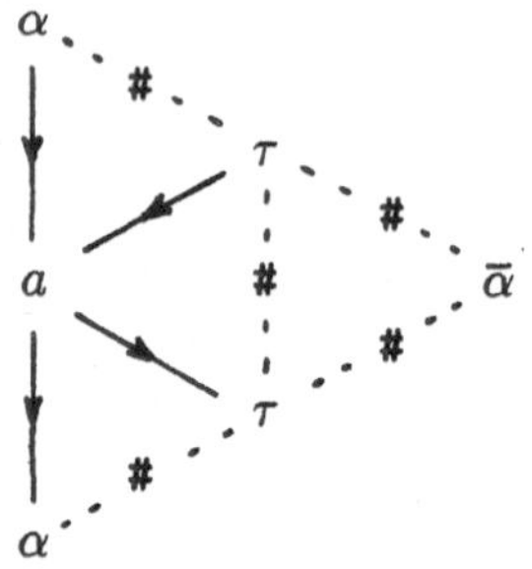

The second structure contains a substructure N and a substructure ∇, see [7]. An example, suggested by M. Nielsen, shows that $\prec^*$ is not an ordering: if we interpret $(\alpha.a.\beta \parallel \bar{\beta}.b.\bar{\alpha})$ we get

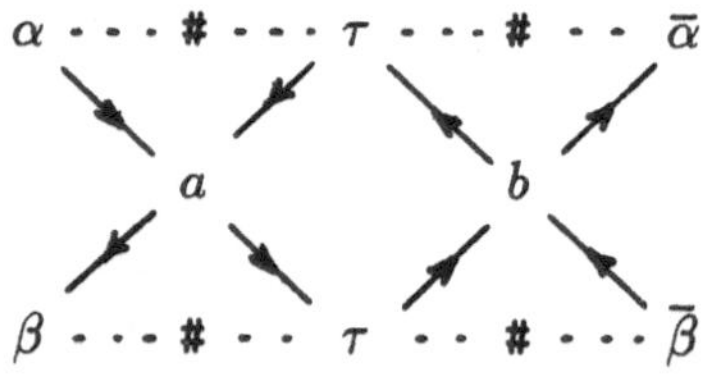

Note that if $r = (\alpha.a.\beta \| \bar{\beta}.b.\bar{\alpha})\backslash\alpha\backslash\beta$ then the structure $\mathcal{I}(r)$ has no proper configuration X (i.e. such that $X \neq \emptyset$). The same holds for the interpretation of $(\alpha.\beta \| \bar{\beta}.\bar{\alpha})\backslash\alpha\backslash\beta$. One can also see that in the interpretation of $((\alpha.\beta \parallel \bar{\alpha}) \parallel \alpha.\bar{\beta})\backslash\alpha\backslash\beta$, there is no configuration containing the β communication.

We will show that this flow event structure semantics of CCS has an *operational meaning*, in that it corresponds to the "truly concurrent" semantics defined in the previous section. More precisely, we will show that for any term p the domain of configurations of the event structure $(S(p))$, which we denote by $\mathcal{D}_{\mathsf{es}}(p) = \mathcal{D}(S(p))$, is *isomorphic* to the domain $\mathcal{D}_{\mathsf{per}}(p)$ of equivalence classes of proved transitions, as was defined in the previous section.

5. Flow Net semantics

In this section we give an interpretation of CCS terms as *safe flow nets*. We assume some elementary knowledge of Petri nets: the reader is referred to [23, 49] for a general introduction to nets.

Flow nets are a new class of nets introduced in [6], strictly more general than the *occurrence nets* considered in [43, 57, 29]: e.g. flow nets may have cycles in the flow relation. However they are still "semantically acyclic". It is shown in [6] that there is a very close correspondence between flow nets and flow event structures, the model we considered in the previous section. The reader may want to look at the definition of flow net in [6] (this volume), however this is not required for reading through this section: the flow net interpretation for CCS presented here is essentially the standard Petri net semantics (see [57,24,27,28,21,45,53]), with the particularity that events and places are defined themselves structurally, using the syntax of terms.

The idea of defining the places of a net syntactically is taken from [21]. Maintaining a syntax on events and states will allow us to compare more easily our flow net semantics with the other CCS semantics considered earlier on. We will use the following definition of (marked) net.

DEFINITION (NETS) *A net is a structure* $N = (B, E, \Phi, \mu)$, *where:*

- B *is the set of conditions (or places)*
- E *is the set of events, denumerable and disjoint from* B
- $\Phi \subseteq (B \times E) \cup (E \times B)$ *is the flow relation, satisfying the two conditions:*
  the set $\{b \mid \exists e, e'. \ (e, b) \in \Phi \ \& \ (b, e') \in \Phi\}$ *is denumerable*
  $\forall e \in E \ \exists b \in B. \ (b, e) \in \Phi$
- $\mu : B \rightarrow \mathbb{N}$ *is the initial marking.*

A place b is called *initial* if it is initially marked, that is $\mu(b) \geq 1$. It is often convenient to represent the flow relation as a mapping: $\phi : (B \times E) \cup (E \times B) \rightarrow \{0, 1\}$, where $\phi(x) = 1 \Leftrightarrow x \in \Phi$. We will use the notation $b \overset{e}{\longmapsto} b'$ to mean $\phi(b, e) = 1 = \phi(e, b')$, or also $b \overset{e}{\longmapsto} b'$ in Φ_N when we want to explicitly refer to the net N. The sets of *preconditions* and *postconditions* of an event e are given by:

$\mathsf{pre}(e) = \{b \mid \phi(b, e) = 1\}$
$\mathsf{post}(e) = \{b \mid \phi(e, b) = 1\}$

Similarly we may define the sets of pre-events and post-events of a place b, respectively $\mathsf{pre}(b)$ and $\mathsf{post}(b)$. We then say that a place b is a *precondition* if it has at least one post-event: $\mathsf{post}(b) \neq \emptyset$, and a *postcondition* if it has at least one pre-event: $\mathsf{pre}(b) \neq \emptyset$.

We shall now give an interpretation of CCS terms as (marked) nets. The nets thus obtained will be shown to be *one-safe*, as well as *flow nets* in the sense of [6]. When interpreting CCS (or similar algebraic languages), one may use the syntax of terms to specify places and events of the corresponding nets. We take the syntax of *events* to be the same as for flow event structures:

$$e \ ::= \ a \mid \widehat{a}.e \mid \|_0 e \mid \|_1 e \mid (e, e') \mid +_0 e \mid +_1 e \mid \backslash_\alpha e$$

In a similar style, the syntax of *places* is given by the grammar, where p is any CCS term:

$$b \ ::= \ \mathsf{nil} \mid a.p \mid \widehat{a}.b \mid \|_0 b \mid \|_1 b \mid (b + b') \mid +_0 b \mid +_1 b \mid \backslash_\alpha b$$

We shall comment in detail on the meaning of such events and places as we go along interpreting CCS terms. Let us just recall that events are built starting from an occurrence a (or two occurrences a and $\bar{a}$ in case of communication). Thus an event records an occurrence of an action a (or τ) together with its "past" (or pair of pasts). On the other hand, places - which are local states - record both past and "future". These points will be further illustrated by examples.

Note also that events and places are disjoint - as required by the definition of net - because the innermost component of a place is always nil. Therefore, in this section, although we will mostly omit the trailing nil's in CCS terms, we will avoid doing so in the names of places.

We now proceed to define the marked net $\mathcal{N}(p) = (B_p, E_p, \Phi_p, \mu_p)$ associated with a closed CCS term p. In the definition we will use the following conventions: since all events in $\mathcal{N}(p)$ will have at least one precondition and one postcondition, the flow relation Φ_p will be specified using the notation $b \overset{e}{\longmapsto} b'$ in Φ_p ; also, since in all constructions the initial marking will be safe (i.e. $\forall b.\ \mu_p(b) \leq 1$), we will specify μ_p as a subset of B_p.

The definition of $\mathcal{N}(p)$ is now given by structural induction on the term p.

(i) The net $\mathcal{N}(\mathsf{nil})$ consists of just one place nil, initially marked.

$$B_{\mathsf{nil}} = \mu_{\mathsf{nil}} = \{\mathsf{nil}\}$$
$$E_{\mathsf{nil}} = \Phi_{\mathsf{nil}} = \emptyset$$

(ii) Prefixing $\mathcal{N}(a.p)$ adds an event a with a precondition $a.p$ in front of net $\mathcal{N}(p)$, while shifting all the other events and conditions by $\widehat{a}.$. For a set X, we shall write $\widehat{a}.X$ for $\{\widehat{a}.x \mid x \in X\}$. Then $\mathcal{N}(a.p)$ is given by:

$$B_{a:p} = \{a.p\} \cup \widehat{a}.B_p$$
$$\mu_{a:p} = \{a.p\}$$
$$E_{a:p} = \{a\} \cup \widehat{a}.E_p$$

$\Phi_{a:p}$ is the least relation such that:

$$b \in \mu_p \Rightarrow a.p \overset{a}{\longmapsto} \widehat{a}.b \text{ in } \Phi_{a:p}$$
$$b \overset{e}{\longmapsto} b' \text{ in } \Phi_p \Rightarrow \widehat{a}.b \overset{\widehat{a}.e}{\longmapsto} \widehat{a}.b' \text{ in } \Phi_{a:p}$$

As for flow event structures, events not involving the constructors $\widehat{a}.$ - what we called *proof terms* earlier on - represent immediate occurrences of an action in a process, i.e. initial occurrences in its synchronisation tree; the constructor $\widehat{a}.$ allows one to pass a guard a and thus to specify events at any depth in the tree.

Similar remarks apply to places. A place of the form $a.p$ is an initial place (i.e. initially marked), more precisely the initial place of a guarded term; for a general term, we shall see that all places built without the constructors $\widehat{a}.$ are initial. Note that the initial event of $\mathcal{N}(a.p)$ is taken to be simply the label a. This is the only case where an event is confused with its label.

Example 1: the interpretation of the term $a.a.\text{nil}$ is the net

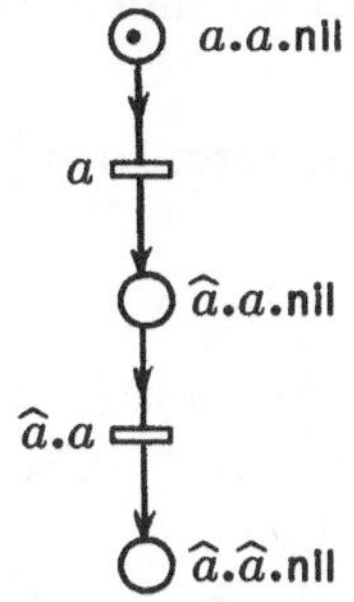

(iii) Parallel composition $\mathcal{N}(p \parallel q)$ puts side by side its components $\mathcal{N}(p)$ and $\mathcal{N}(q)$ while shifting their events and places by $\|_0$ and $\|_1$ respectively. It may also introduce communication events, which are built with the constructor (e, e'). On the other hand there are no special *place* constructors for communication, since the preconditions and postconditions of a communication are just those of its components. For a set X, we write $\|_i X$ for $\{\|_i x \mid x \in X\}$. Now $\mathcal{N}(p \parallel q)$ is given by:

$B_{p\|q} = \|_0 B_p \cup \|_1 B_q$

$\mu_{p\|q} = \|_0 \mu_p \cup \|_1 \mu_q$,

$E_{p\|q} = \|_0 E_p \cup \|_1 E_q \cup \{(e,e') \mid e \in E_p \ \&\ e' \in E_q \ \&\ \overline{\ell(e)} = \ell(e')\}$

$\Phi_{p\|q}$ is the least relation such that:

$b \overset{e}{\longmapsto} b' \text{ in } \Phi_p \Rightarrow \|_0 b \overset{\|_0 e}{\longmapsto} \|_0\, b' \text{ in } \Phi_{p\|q}$

$b \overset{e}{\longmapsto} b' \text{ in } \Phi_q \Rightarrow \|_1 b \overset{\|_1 e}{\longmapsto} \|_1\, b' \text{ in } \Phi_{p\|q}$

moreover for any $e \in E_p, e' \in E_q$ s.t. $\overline{\ell(e)} = \ell(e')$:

$b \overset{e}{\longmapsto} b' \text{ in } \Phi_p \Rightarrow \|_0 b \overset{(e,e')}{\longmapsto} \|_0\, b' \text{ in } \Phi_{p\|q}$

$b \overset{e'}{\longmapsto} b' \text{ in } \Phi_q \Rightarrow \|_1 b \overset{(e,e')}{\longmapsto} \|_1\, b' \text{ in } \Phi_{p\|q}$

Example 2: the interpretation of $(\alpha.\alpha \parallel \bar{\alpha})$ is, representing for simplicity the events by their labels:

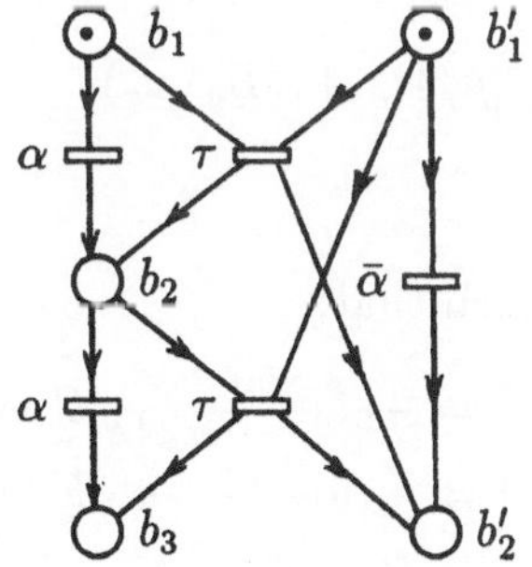

Here the places are: $b_1 = \|_0 \alpha.\alpha.\text{nil}$, $b_2 = \|_0 \widehat{\alpha}.\alpha.\text{nil}$, $b_3 = \|_0 \widehat{\alpha}.\widehat{\alpha}.\text{nil}$, $b'_1 = \|_1 \bar{\alpha}.\text{nil}$, $b'_2 = \|_1 \widehat{\bar{\alpha}}.\text{nil}$, while the events are: $\|_0 \alpha$, $\|_0 \widehat{\alpha}.\alpha$, $(\alpha, \bar{\alpha})$, $(\widehat{\alpha}.\alpha, \bar{\alpha})$, $\|_1 \bar{\alpha}$.

From now on we shall omit the names of places and events in the figures, showing only the labels of events – possibly with an index when the same label occurs more than once.

Example 3: the interpretation of the term $(\alpha.\beta \parallel \bar{\alpha}.\bar{\beta})$ will be drawn as:

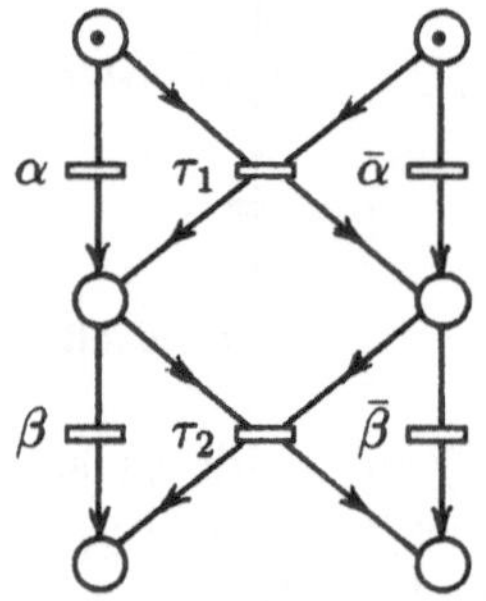

Here the places are:

$b_1 = \|_0\alpha.\beta.\mathsf{nil}$ $\quad b_2 = \|_0\widehat{\alpha}.\beta.\mathsf{nil}$ $\quad b_3 = \|_0\widehat{\alpha}.\widehat{\beta}.\mathsf{nil}$ and

$b'_1 = \|_1\bar{\alpha}.\bar{\beta}.\mathsf{nil}$ $\quad b'_2 = \|_1\widehat{\bar{\alpha}}.\bar{\beta}.\mathsf{nil}$ $\quad b'_3 = \|_1\widehat{\bar{\alpha}}.\widehat{\bar{\beta}}.\mathsf{nil}$.

and the communication events are:

$\tau_1 = (\alpha, \bar{\alpha})$ and

$\tau_2 = (\widehat{\alpha}.\beta, \widehat{\bar{\alpha}}.\bar{\beta})$.

Note that the "past" of τ_2 consists of the two events labelled α and $\bar{\alpha}$, regardless of the way these events have happened (independently or simultaneously as τ_1). In fact the past recorded in an event is its history projected on the local components, which is unique and statically determined, while in general an event may have different *execution* histories, due to communication.

(iv) Nondeterministic sum $\mathcal{N}(p+q)$ does not create new events. It shifts the names of events and non-initial places of its components respectively by $+_0$ and $+_1$. The constructor $(b + b')$ is used to build the cartesian product of the *initial* places of the two nets. Note that unlike (e, e') the constructor $(b + b')$ may be iterated any number of times. If X, Y are sets of places, we write $(X + Y)$ for $\{(b + b') \mid b \in X, b' \in Y\}$ and $+_iX$ for $\{+_ix \mid x \in X\}$. We recall that Θ is the set of initial events, built without the constructors $\widehat{a}.$.

$$B_{p+q} = (\mu_p + \mu_q) \cup +_0(B_p \backslash \mu_p) \cup +_1(B_q \backslash \mu_q)$$
$$\mu_{p+q} = (\mu_p + \mu_q)$$
$$E_{p+q} = +_0E_p \cup +_1E_q$$

Φ_{p+q} is the least relation such that:

$$b \overset{e}{\longmapsto} b' \text{ in } \Phi_p, \text{ with } e \notin \Theta \Rightarrow +_0b \overset{+_0e}{\longmapsto} +_0 b' \text{ in } \Phi_{p+q}$$
$$b \overset{e}{\longmapsto} b' \text{ in } \Phi_q, \text{ with } e \notin \Theta \Rightarrow +_1b \overset{+_1e}{\longmapsto} +_1 b' \text{ in } \Phi_{p+q}$$
$$b \overset{e}{\longmapsto} b' \text{ in } \Phi_p, \text{ with } e \in \Theta \Rightarrow (b + b'') \overset{+_0e}{\longmapsto} +_0 b' \text{ in } \Phi_{p+q}$$
$$b \overset{e}{\longmapsto} b' \text{ in } \Phi_q, \text{ with } e \in \Theta \Rightarrow (b'' + b) \overset{+_1e}{\longmapsto} +_1 b' \text{ in } \Phi_{p+q}$$

Example 4: (*symmetric confusion*) the interpretation of the term $(a \parallel b) + c$ is

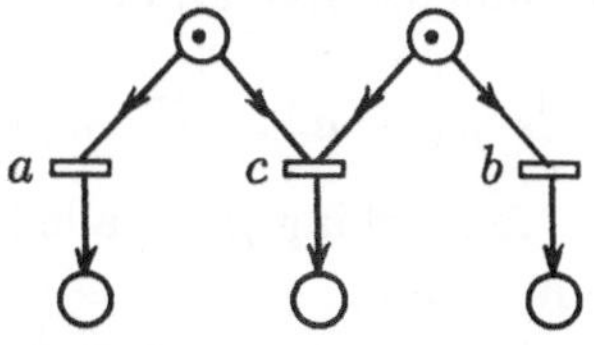

where the initial places are $(\|_0 a.\mathsf{nil} + c.\mathsf{nil})$ and $(\|_1 b.\mathsf{nil} + c.\mathsf{nil})$.

(iv) Restriction $\mathcal{N}(p\backslash\alpha)$ takes away from $\mathcal{N}(p)$ the subset of events bearing a given label α or its complement $\bar{\alpha}$, while maintaining places unchanged. All places and events are shifted by $\backslash_\alpha$.

$B_{p\backslash\alpha} = \backslash_\alpha B_p$

$\mu_{p\backslash\alpha} = \backslash_\alpha \mu_p$

$E_{p\backslash\alpha} = \backslash_\alpha (E_p \backslash E_\alpha)$, where $E_\alpha = \{e \in E_p \mid \mathsf{nm}(\ell(e)) = \alpha\}$

$\Phi_{p\backslash\alpha}$ is given by:

$$b \overset{e}{\longmapsto} b' \text{ in } \Phi_p, \text{ with } e \notin E_\alpha \Rightarrow \backslash_\alpha b \overset{\backslash_\alpha e}{\longmapsto} \backslash_\alpha b' \text{ in } \Phi_{p\backslash\alpha}$$

Recall that $b \overset{e}{\longmapsto} b'$ is a purely static relation, which should not be confused with the transition relation on markings describing the behaviour of the net – which is given below.

Example 5: (*asymmetric confusion*) the interpretation of the term $((a + \alpha) \parallel b.\bar{\alpha})\backslash\alpha$ is

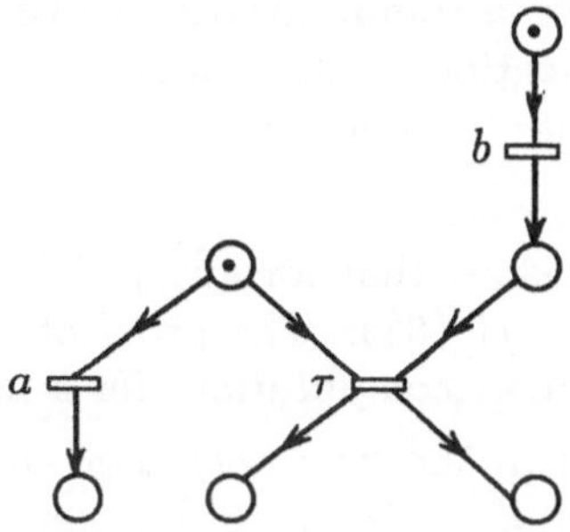

This concludes the definition of our net semantics for CCS. We shall now turn to the *behaviour* of such nets. It is well-known that a net determines a transition system on its markings. Let us briefly recall the definition.

A marking of the net $N = (B, E, \Phi, \mu_0)$ is any mapping $\mu : B \to \mathbb{N}$. If $\mu(b) > 0$ we say that the condition b holds at μ. A marking μ *enables* an event e if all the preconditions of e hold in μ, or more formally: $\forall b \in B : \ \phi(b, e) \leq \mu(b)$.

Then the *labelled transition system* on the markings of net N is defined as follows:

$$\mu \overset{e}{\longrightarrow} \mu' \Leftrightarrow_{\text{def}} \forall b \in B : \ \phi(b, e) \leq \mu(b) \text{ and } \mu'(b) = \mu(b) - \phi(b, e) + \phi(e, b)$$

It should be obvious that this transition system is deterministic: if μ enables e then the next marking μ' is uniquely determined. Given a net $N = (B, E, \Phi, \mu_0)$, a sequence of transitions:

$$\mu_0 \xrightarrow{e_1} \mu_1 \cdots \mu_{n-1} \xrightarrow{e_n} \mu_n \cdots$$

is called a *firing sequence* for N. A marking μ is called *safe* if $\forall b: \ \mu(b) \leq 1$. A net is *safe* if all its reachable markings are safe.

Now the nets $\mathcal{N}(p)$ obtained as interpretations of CCS terms may be shown to satisfy some simple structural properties. Let $\mathcal{N}(p) = (B_p, E_p, \Phi_p, \mu_p)$ be the net corresponding to some term p. Then it is easy to check that $\mathcal{N}(p)$ satisfies the following:

PROPERTY 5.1. *The initial marking μ_p is safe:* $\forall b \in B_p: \ \mu_p(b) \leq 1$.

PROPERTY 5.2. *There are no self-loops:* $e \in E_p \ \Rightarrow \ \mathsf{pre}(e) \cap \mathsf{post}(e) = \emptyset$.

PROPERTY 5.3. *A postcondition is not initially marked:*

$$\forall b \in B_p: \ \mathsf{pre}(b) \neq \emptyset \ \Rightarrow \ \mu_p(b) = 0$$

PROPERTY 5.4. *If two events share a postcondition they also share a precondition:*

$$\mathsf{post}(e) \cap \mathsf{post}(e') \neq \emptyset \quad \Rightarrow \quad \mathsf{pre}(e) \cap \mathsf{pre}(e') \neq \emptyset$$

Proof (informal). The only operator introducing backward branching for places is parallel composition, when it connects a communication to the postconditions of its components. But then the communication is also connected – in a symmetric way – to the preconditions of its components (by definition of $\mathcal{N}(p)$, any event has at least one precondition). ❑

These properties may be used to show that for any p the net $\mathcal{N}(p)$ is a *safe flow net* (flow nets are not necessarily safe, cf [6]). The proof of this result may be found in [11]. We define now what we take as *computations* for a net $\mathcal{N}(p)$.

DEFINITION 5.5. *(Computation in the flow net) For any CCS term p, a computation of $\mathcal{N}(p)$ is the set of events $X = \{e_1, \ldots e_n\}$ generated along a firing sequence $\mu_0 \xrightarrow{e_1} \mu_1 \cdots \mu_{n-1} \xrightarrow{e_n} \mu_n$ of $\mathcal{N}(p)$.*

Let $\mathcal{C}_{\text{net}}(p)$ be the set of computations of $\mathcal{N}(p)$. Then $\mathcal{D}_{\text{net}}(p) = (\mathcal{C}_{\text{net}}(p), \subseteq)$ is the poset of these computations, ordered by inclusion.

An important property of flow nets (as well as of the safe nets of [24]) is that for any firing sequence one can deduce a partial order of *causality* directly from the *structure* of the net: the (immediate) causality is given by the presence of a condition between two events (cf [6]). As a consequence, any computation may be regarded here, as in our previous semantics, as a *partially ordered* set of events.

We have thus established a third interpretation of CCS, by means of a simple class of Petri nets. In the next section we will study the relations between our three models for CCS.

6. Equivalence of the three semantics

In this section we undertake to compare our three interpretations for CCS. We will show that the three models – proved transition system, flow event structures and flow nets – are all *abstractly* equivalent, in that they yield *isomorphic domains* of computations for any CCS term. For the flow models – flow event structures and flow nets – we will establish a stronger equivalence result, namely that they determine the same *families of computations* for any term.

The reader may have noted the analogy between the two flow models: they both give *global* representations for terms, modelling occurrences of actions in a term as *events* – and using the same syntactic names for these events. Compared to them, the proved transition system stands a little aside: it appears as a purely operational model where terms are described step by step, as generating *initial occurrences* of actions.

In fact, although we know that in the three models computations may be seen as *posets* of occurrences, it is not immediately clear how to relate the proved transition system to the other two models, which appear somehow more "denotational".

Consider for example the flow net semantics. One simple way to relate it to the proved transition system would be to show a correspondence, for any term p, between the proved transitions of p and the transitions on markings in the net $\mathcal{N}(p)$. An immediate problem, detected by Degano de Nicola and Montanari [18] and Olderog [45], is that a reachable marking in the net is not necessarily the marking $\mu(p)$ determined by a term, the typical example being

$$\mu((a \parallel b) + c) \xrightarrow{+_0 \parallel_0 a} \{ +_0 \parallel_0 \hat{a}.\mathsf{nil},\ (\parallel_1 b.\mathsf{nil} + c.\mathsf{nil}) \}$$

Note that the resulting marking is somehow "mixed", since the part $+_0 \parallel_0 \hat{a}.\mathsf{nil}$ indicates that a choice has been passed, while in the part $(\parallel_1 b.\mathsf{nil} + c.\mathsf{nil})$ the choice is still present.

Here we will get over this problem by generalising the proved transition system so as to make it record the *history* of previous occurrences. We then obtain a very concrete transition system, which records CCS transitions while keeping track of the whole structure of a term. This system is called the *event transition system* (or simply the event system), because its labels are now occurrences with a "past" – and thus general events.

The event system for a term p may now be easily related to the transition system on markings of $\mathcal{N}(p)$: it turns out that the two transition systems are *isomorphic*. In particular they generate the same labels – i.e. the same events – along their transition sequences, and thus determine the same *families of computations*.

Similarly, the event system for p bears a direct correspondence to the flow event structure interpretation of p: the computations of the event system coincide, as sets of events, with the configurations of the event structure. Here again, the two models give rise to the same *families of computations*.

A consequence of these two results is that the three event-based models – flow event structures, flow nets and event system – give the same families of computations, and thus are *concretely equivalent*.

A more substantial task is showing that the event system is equivalent to the original proved transition system. We recall that computations in the proved transition system are equivalence classes of transition sequences, up to permutation of concurrent transitions. On the other hand computations in the event system are *sets of events* labelling a transition sequence.

We will start by giving a 1-1 correspondence between proved and event transition sequences. We shall then show that two proved transitions sequences are *permutation equivalent* if and only if the corresponding event transition sequences generate the *same sets of events*. As a result, we will know that the *domains of computations* have the "same elements". It is then easy to show that the domains also have the same orderings, and thus are *isomorphic*.

In other words, the proved transition system and the event system will be shown to be *abstractly equivalent*. As a consequence the proved system is also *abstractly equivalent* to the two flow models.

The situation may be summarized with a picture, where a simple line indicates a *concrete equivalence* and the double line represents *abstract equivalence*:

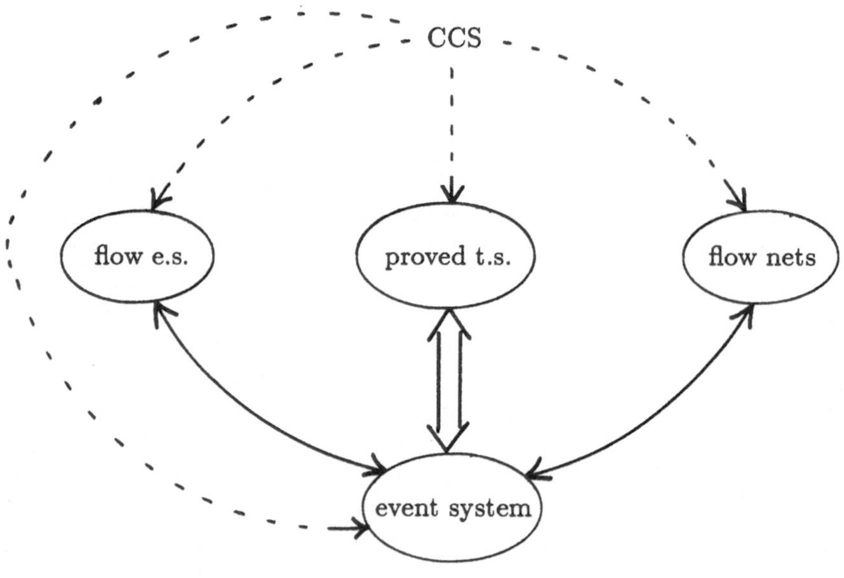

Table 1: Correspondence of models

6.1 Event system

The intermediate transition system is defined on a new set of terms representing partially executed CCS processes, which we shall call *marked terms*. The syntax of marked terms is as follows:

$$\xi \ ::= \ p \mid \widehat{a}.\xi \mid (\xi \parallel \xi') \mid (\xi \,\widehat{+}_0\, q) \mid (p \,\widehat{+}_1\, \xi) \mid \xi\backslash\alpha$$

where p, q are CCS terms. Marked terms keep track of the *dynamic* operators of a process as well as of the static ones: the construct $\widehat{a}.\xi$ means that a guard $a.p$ has been passed, while $(\xi \,\widehat{+}_0 q)$ and $(p \,\widehat{+}_1 \xi)$ mean that a choice has been made, respectively to the left and to the right of a sum. Thus marked terms keep *the whole structure* of a term while recording an execution. In particular it will always be possible, starting from a marked term, to reconstruct the CCS term from which it is derived.

We now define transitions of the form $\xi \overset{\eta}{\twoheadrightarrow} \xi'$ on marked terms. These transitions will be labelled by *events* (rather than simple proof terms), having exactly the same syntactic names as in flow event structures and flow nets. For this reason the corresponding transition system will be called *event transition system* – or simply *event system*. The inference rules for event transitions are given in Table 2. (where we also recall the rules for proved transitions, for an easy comparison).

The interesting rules for event transitions are $A0', S0', S1'$, which introduce the "past" constructors $\widehat{a}.$, $\widehat{+}_0$, $\widehat{+}_1$. Rules $A1', ST0', ST1'$ allow terms to move under these constructors, or, putting it another way, transmit the "past" to future occurrences. Note that some marked terms, like $(p\widehat{+}_0 q)$ or $(\widehat{a}.p)\backslash\alpha$, are never obtained as the target of some event transition. In what follows we shall always consider *proper* marked terms, i.e. marked terms that are generated via event transitions starting from some CCS term (these may be defined inductively, in the same way as we defined proper proof terms earlier on). Then (proper) marked terms represent CCS processes *at some state*, just like marked nets represent nets at some state. In fact, when we come to relate the event system to flow nets, we shall see that marked terms correspond to *markings* in a net: more precisely the event system will be shown to be the syntactic counterpart of flow nets, an event transition corresponding exactly to a transition between two markings in a net. The relation between event systems and flow nets will be established in section [asnets]. Let us see now some examples of event transitions.

Example 1 The term $p = (a.b) + c$ has the following event transition sequence:

$$(a.b) + c \xrightarrow{+_0 a}\!\!\!\!\twoheadrightarrow \widehat{a}.b \,\widehat{+}_0 c \xrightarrow{+_0 \widehat{a}.b}\!\!\!\!\twoheadrightarrow \widehat{a}.\widehat{b} \,\widehat{+}_0\, c$$

Note that no transition can be deduced at the right of the past operator $\widehat{+}_0$.

Example 2 The term $p = (a \parallel b) + c$ has the event transition sequence:

$$(a \parallel b) + c \xrightarrow{+_0 \parallel_0 a}\!\!\!\!\twoheadrightarrow (\widehat{a} \parallel b) \,\widehat{+}_0 c \xrightarrow{+_0 \parallel_1 b}\!\!\!\!\twoheadrightarrow (\widehat{a} \parallel \widehat{b}) \,\widehat{+}_0 c$$

Note that the two actions a and b give rise to symmetric events, even though action b occurs *after* the choice has been made.

RULES for proved transitions

A.	$\vdash a.p \xrightarrow{a} p$
P0.	$p \xrightarrow{\theta} p' \vdash (p \parallel q) \xrightarrow{\parallel_0 \theta} (p' \parallel q)$
P1.	$q \xrightarrow{\theta} q' \vdash (p \parallel q) \xrightarrow{\parallel_1 \theta} (p \parallel q')$
C.	$p \xrightarrow{\theta} p'\ ,\ q \xrightarrow{\theta'} q',\ \overline{\ell(\theta)} = \ell(\theta') \vdash (p \parallel q) \xrightarrow{(\theta, \theta')} (p' \parallel q')$
S0.	$p \xrightarrow{\theta} p' \vdash (p + q) \xrightarrow{+_0 \theta} p'$
S1.	$q \xrightarrow{\theta} q' \vdash (p + q) \xrightarrow{+_1 \theta} q'$
R.	$p \xrightarrow{\theta} p'\ ,\ \mathsf{nm}(\ell(\theta)) \neq \alpha \vdash (p \backslash \alpha) \xrightarrow{\backslash_\alpha \theta} (p' \backslash \alpha)$

RULES for event transitions

A0′.	$\vdash a.p \xrightarrow{a} \widehat{a}.p$
A1′.	$\xi \xrightarrow{\eta} \xi' \vdash \widehat{a}.\xi \xrightarrow{\widehat{a}.\eta} \widehat{a}.\xi'$
P0′.	$\xi \xrightarrow{\eta} \xi' \vdash (\xi \parallel \xi'') \xrightarrow{\parallel_0 \eta} (\xi' \parallel \xi'')$
P1′.	$\xi \xrightarrow{\eta} \xi' \vdash (\xi'' \parallel \xi) \xrightarrow{\parallel_1 \eta} (\xi'' \parallel \xi')$
C′.	$\xi_0 \xrightarrow{\eta} \xi_0'\ ,\ \xi_1 \xrightarrow{\eta'} \xi_1'\ ,\ \overline{\ell(\eta)} = \ell(\eta') \vdash (\xi_0 \parallel \xi_1) \xrightarrow{(\eta, \eta')} (\xi_0' \parallel \xi_1')$
S0′.	$p \xrightarrow{\eta} \xi \vdash (p + q) \xrightarrow{+_0 \eta} (\xi \widehat{+}_0 q)$
S1′.	$q \xrightarrow{\eta} \xi \vdash (p + q) \xrightarrow{+_1 \eta} (p \widehat{+}_1 \xi)$
ST0′.	$\xi \xrightarrow{\eta} \xi' \vdash (\xi \widehat{+}_0 q) \xrightarrow{+_0 \eta} (\xi' \widehat{+}_0 q)$
ST1′.	$\xi \xrightarrow{\eta} \xi' \vdash (p \widehat{+}_1 \xi) \xrightarrow{+_1 \eta} (p \widehat{+}_1 \xi')$
R′.	$\xi \xrightarrow{\eta} \xi', \mathsf{nm}(\ell(\eta)) \neq \alpha \vdash \xi \backslash \alpha \xrightarrow{\backslash_\alpha \eta} \xi' \backslash \alpha$

Table 2.

Indeed, this will be shown to be a fundamental property of the event system: by looking at the names of events only, one will never be able to tell which of two concurrent events has happened first. This is also an essential difference w.r.t. the proved transition system, where one could have different sets of labels (*proofs*) along equivalent sequences.

Now the reader should be easily convinced that the event system is *deterministic*, i.e.

$$\xi \xrightarrow{\eta}\!\!\!\!\rightarrow \xi' \text{ and } \xi \xrightarrow{\eta}\!\!\!\!\rightarrow \xi'' \quad \Rightarrow \quad \xi' = \xi''$$

The system has also the further property that two events generated in some event sequence for a term p have distinct names if and only if they correspond to different occurrences (or pairs of occurrences, for a communication) in the syntactic tree of p.

Example 3   Take the term $p = (\alpha.b \parallel \bar{\alpha})$. In the two event transition sequences for p:

$$(\alpha.b \parallel \bar{\alpha}) \xrightarrow{(\alpha, \bar{\alpha})}\!\!\!\!\rightarrow (\widehat{\alpha}.b \parallel \widehat{\bar{\alpha}}) \xrightarrow{\parallel_0 \widehat{\alpha}.b}\!\!\!\!\rightarrow (\widehat{\alpha}\,\widehat{b}. \parallel \widehat{\bar{\alpha}})$$

$$(\alpha.b \parallel \bar{\alpha}) \xrightarrow{\parallel_0 \alpha}\!\!\!\!\rightarrow (\widehat{\alpha}.b \parallel \bar{\alpha}) \xrightarrow{\parallel_0 \widehat{\alpha}.b}\!\!\!\!\rightarrow (\widehat{\alpha}\,\widehat{b}. \parallel \bar{\alpha})$$

the occurrence of b is represented by the same event $\parallel_0 \widehat{a}.b$, whether it follows the communication $(\alpha, \bar{\alpha})$ or the simple event $\parallel_0 \alpha$.

In fact events record the "syntactic history" of an occurrence, rather than a particular execution history. We shall see later that for any term p, the event system generates exactly the same events as the flow event structure and the flow net interpretations.

As we said, the event system is very intensional. From any proper state (marked term) ξ of the system one may trace back the original CCS term from which ξ arises, what we call the *ancestor* of ξ. The *ancestor* $\varrho(\xi)$ is defined on proper marked terms as follows:

$$\begin{aligned}
&\varrho(p) = p \quad \text{for any CCS term } p\\
&\varrho(\widehat{a}.\xi) = a.\varrho(\xi)\\
&\varrho(\xi \parallel \xi') = (\varrho(\xi) \parallel \varrho(\xi'))\\
&\varrho(\xi \,\widehat{+}_0 q) = (\varrho(\xi) + q)\\
&\varrho(p \,\widehat{+}_1 \xi) = (p + \varrho(\xi))\\
&\varrho(\xi \backslash \alpha) = \varrho(\xi) \backslash \alpha
\end{aligned}$$

It should be clear that ξ has ancestor $\varrho(\xi) = p$ if and only if ξ is the target of some event transition sequence starting from p.

We want now to show that the event transition system is *equivalent* to the proved transition system, in the sense that it yields the same domain of computations for any term p. We recall that the computations of a proved transition system are equivalence classes of sequences of transitions, ordered by the prefix ordering. (*cf* section [permut]). On the other hand a computation of a term p in the event transition system is taken to be the *set of events* occurring in some event transition sequence for p. Formally:

Definition 6.1. *(Computation in the event system)*
For any CCS term p, let $\mathcal{S}(p) = \{\sigma \mid \sigma = p \xrightarrow{\eta_1}\!\!\!\!\rightarrow \xi_1 \cdots \xi_{n-1} \xrightarrow{\eta_n}\!\!\!\!\rightarrow \xi_n\}$ be the set of event transition sequences starting from p. Then a computation of p in the event system is the set of events $\mathcal{E}_\sigma = \{\eta_i \mid i = 1,\ldots,n\}$ generated by some $\sigma \in \mathcal{S}(p)$, $\sigma = p \xrightarrow{\eta_1}\!\!\!\!\rightarrow \xi_1 \cdots \xi_{n-1} \xrightarrow{\eta_n}\!\!\!\!\rightarrow \xi_n$. We let $\mathcal{C}_{\rm ev}(p) = \{\mathcal{E}_\sigma \mid \sigma \in \mathcal{S}(p)\}$ be the set of computations of p, and $\mathcal{D}_{\rm ev}(p) = (\mathcal{C}_{\rm ev}(p), \subseteq)$ be the poset of these computations, ordered by inclusion.

Example 4 Consider the two event transition sequences for $p = (a \parallel b) + c$:

$$\sigma_1 = (a \parallel b) + c \xrightarrow{+_0 \parallel_0 a}\!\!\!\!\rightarrow (\widehat{a} \parallel b)\,\widehat{+}_0 c \xrightarrow{+_0 \parallel_1 b}\!\!\!\!\rightarrow (\widehat{a} \parallel \widehat{b})\,\widehat{+}_0 c$$

$$\sigma_2 = (a \parallel b) + c \xrightarrow{+_0 \parallel_1 b}\!\!\!\!\rightarrow (a \parallel \widehat{b})\,\widehat{+}_0 c \xrightarrow{+_0 \parallel_0 a}\!\!\!\!\rightarrow (\widehat{a} \parallel \widehat{b})\,\widehat{+}_0 c$$

Then the associated computations are equal: $\mathcal{E}(\sigma_1) = \mathcal{E}(\sigma_2) = \{+_0 \parallel_0 a,\ +_0 \parallel_1 b\}$.

6.2 Correspondence between event system and proved transition system

We show in this section that event and proved transition systems determine isomorphic domains of computations. We start by giving constructions between the two kinds of transition sequences. Looking at Table 2, it should be clear that event transitions $\xi \xrightarrow{\eta} \xi'$ contain in some sense the proved transitions $p \xrightarrow{\theta} p'$. We recall that in the proved system labels are *proofs*, that is events built without the constructors $\widehat{a}$.. Intuitively, it should be possible to reduce or "flatten" an event transition $\xi \xrightarrow{\eta}\!\!\!\!\rightarrow \xi'$ to a proved transition of the form $p \xrightarrow{\theta} p'$, by just forgetting the history information recorded in ξ, η, ξ'.

Let now formalise how an event transition $\xi \xrightarrow{\eta}\!\!\!\!\rightarrow \xi'$ may be *flattened* to a proved transition. First a proper marked term ξ may be reduced to a CCS term $\varphi(\xi)$ with the same "future", by just dropping the past operators in ξ. As we noted, a proper marked term ξ is the target of some event transition sequence of its ancestor $p = \varrho(\xi)$. Then $\varphi(\xi)$ should be exactly what we would have obtained by applying *ordinary* CCS transitions to the term p. We define $\varphi(\xi)$ inductively on proper marked terms as follows:

$\varphi(p) = p$ for any CCS term p
$\varphi(\widehat{a}.\xi) = \varphi(\xi)$
$\varphi(\xi \parallel \xi') = \varphi(\xi) \parallel \varphi(\xi')$
$\varphi(\xi \widehat{+}_0 q) = \varphi(\xi)$
$\varphi(p \widehat{+}_1 \xi) = \varphi(\xi)$
$\varphi(\xi \backslash \alpha) = \varphi(\xi) \backslash \alpha$

Looking back at the rules for event transitions, we may note that if $p \xrightarrow{\eta}\!\!\!\!\rightarrow \xi'$, where p is a CCS term, then η is a proof term (i.e. $\eta \in \Theta$). Then for an event transition of the form $p \xrightarrow{\theta}\!\!\!\!\rightarrow \xi'$ the flattening is straightforward:

Lemma 6.2. *For any CCS term p: $p \xrightarrow{\theta}\!\!\!\!\rightarrow \xi \ \Rightarrow\ p \xrightarrow{\theta} \varphi(\xi)$.*

For a general transition $\xi \overset{\eta}{\twoheadrightarrow} \xi'$ we need a second function ψ to reduce the event η to a proof term. However ψ cannot be simply a function of η, as shown by the example:

Example 5 We saw already that $p = (a \parallel b) + c$ has the event transition sequence:

$$p \xrightarrow{+_0 \parallel_0 a} (\widehat{a} \parallel b)\,\widehat{+}_0 c \xrightarrow{+_0 \parallel_1 b} (\widehat{a} \parallel \widehat{b})\,\widehat{+}_0 c$$

Now the corresponding proved sequence should be:

$$\sigma = p \xrightarrow{+_0 \parallel_0 a} (\mathsf{nil} \parallel b) \xrightarrow{\parallel_1 b} (\mathsf{nil} \parallel \mathsf{nil})$$

We can see that in order to obtain the proved sequence σ, we should retain the constructor $+_0$ when flattening the first event, whereas we should drop it in the second event. Intuitively, this is because in the first event the $+_0$ represents a choice occurring during the *current* transition, while in the second event the $+_0$ refers to a choice occurred sometime in the past and passed on by a term $(\xi \widehat{+}_0 q)$. Now, to be able to distinguish the two cases, we need to look at the structure of the marked term performing the event.

Hence ψ must be a function of ξ as well as η. We say that $\xi \overset{\eta}{\twoheadrightarrow} \xi'$ is a *proper* event transition whenever ξ is a proper marked term. Then for any proper transition $\xi \overset{\eta}{\twoheadrightarrow} \xi'$ we define the proof term $\psi(\xi, \eta)$ corresponding to the event η by:

$$\begin{aligned}
&\psi(a.p, a) = a\\
&\psi(\widehat{a}.\xi, \widehat{a}.\eta) = \psi(\xi, \eta)\\
&\psi(\xi_0 \parallel \xi_1, \parallel_i \eta) = \parallel_i \psi(\xi_i, \eta)\\
&\psi(\xi \parallel \xi', (\eta, \eta')) = (\psi(\xi, \eta), \psi(\xi', \eta'))\\
&\psi(p + q, +_i \eta) = +_i \eta\\
&\psi(\xi \widehat{+}_0 q, +_0 \eta) = \psi(\xi, \eta)\\
&\psi(p \widehat{+}_1 \xi, +_1 \eta) = \psi(\xi, \eta)\\
&\psi(\xi \backslash \alpha, \backslash_\alpha \eta) = \backslash_\alpha \psi(\xi, \eta)
\end{aligned}$$

REMARK: Note that if ξ is a CCS term p, we have $\eta = \theta \in \Theta$ and $\psi(p, \theta) = \theta$.

Using functions φ and ψ we may now define the *flattening* $t^\vee$ of an event transition t:

PROPOSITION 6.3. *(Transition flattening) If* $t = \xi \overset{\eta}{\twoheadrightarrow} \xi'$ *is a proper event transition then* $t^\vee = \varphi(\xi) \xrightarrow{\psi(\xi, \eta)} \varphi(\xi')$ *is a proved transition. We call* $t^\vee$ *the flattening of* t.

Hint for proof: Use induction on the proof of $\xi \overset{\eta}{\twoheadrightarrow} \xi'$. □

It is straightforward to extend this flattening to sequences of event transitions for p:

DEFINITION 6.4. *(Sequence flattening) Let* $\sigma = p \overset{\eta_1}{\twoheadrightarrow} \xi_1 \cdots \xi_{n-1} \overset{\eta_n}{\twoheadrightarrow} \xi_n$ *be an event transition sequence for p. Then* $\sigma^\vee = p \xrightarrow{\psi(p, \eta_1)} \varphi(\xi_1) \cdots \varphi(\xi_{n-1}) \xrightarrow{\psi(\xi_{n-1}, \eta_n)} \varphi(\xi_n)$ *is a proved sequence for p. We call* $\sigma^\vee$ *the flattening of* σ.

We want now to show the converse, namely that each proved sequence σ of a term p may be *lifted* to an event transition sequence $\sigma^\wedge$ for p. In fact, it will be convenient to define the lifting of a proved sequence of p starting from any ξ such that $\varphi(\xi) = p$. The first step is lifting a proved transition t to an event transition $t^\wedge$.

PROPOSITION 6.5. *(Transition lifting) Let p be a CCS term and $t = p \xrightarrow{\theta} p'$ a proved transition of p. Then for any proper marked term ξ such that $\varphi(\xi) = p$, there exists a unique event transition $t^\wedge(\xi) = \xi \xrightarrow{\eta}\!\!\rightarrow \xi'$ such that $\psi(\xi, \eta) = \theta$ and $\varphi(\xi') = p'$. We call $t^\wedge(\xi)$ the lifting of t from ξ. We call $t^\wedge =_{\text{def}} t^\wedge(p)$ the main lifting of t.*

Hint for proof. The event transition $t^\wedge(\xi)$ is built by induction on the structure of ξ. The uniqueness of $t^\wedge(\xi)$ follows from the determinacy of the event system. □

Lifting a proved sequence is slightly more involved than flattening an event transition sequence: the lifting of a step $p_i \xrightarrow{\eta_i} p_{i+1}$ of a proved transition sequence depends on the particular ξ_i obtained by lifting the segment $p_0 \xrightarrow{\theta_1} p_1 \cdots p_{i-1} \xrightarrow{\theta_i} p_i$ of the sequence.

COROLLARY 6.6. *(Sequence lifting) Let $\sigma = p_0 \xrightarrow{\theta_1} p_1 \cdots p_{n-1} \xrightarrow{\theta_n} p_n$ be a proved sequence for the term p_0, and ξ_0 be a proper marked term such that $\varphi(\xi_0) = p_0$. Then there exists a unique event transition sequence $\sigma^\wedge(\xi_0) = \xi_0 \xrightarrow{\eta_1}\!\!\rightarrow \xi_1 \cdots \xi_{n-1} \xrightarrow{\eta_n}\!\!\rightarrow \xi_n$ such that $\psi(\xi_{i-1}, \eta_i) = \theta_i$ and $\varphi(\xi_i) = p_i$ for $i = 1, \ldots, n$. The event transition sequence $\sigma^\wedge(\xi_0)$ is called the lifting of σ from ξ_0.*

Hint for proof: The sequence $\sigma^\wedge(\xi_0)$ is built by induction on the length n of σ. □

We will be mostly interested in the case $\xi_0 = p_0$, that is in lifting a sequence from a CCS term. We thus define the *main lifting* of a proved sequence σ of p to be $\sigma^\wedge =_{\text{def}} \sigma^\wedge(p)$.

Also, for any event sequence $\sigma = \xi_0 \xrightarrow{\eta_1}\!\!\rightarrow \xi_1 \cdots \xi_{n-1} \xrightarrow{\eta_n}\!\!\rightarrow \xi_n$, define the *target* of σ to be $\mathsf{tg}(\sigma) = \xi_n$ and the source of σ to be $\mathsf{sr}(\sigma) = \xi_0$.

We have thus given a 1–1 *correspondence* between proved transition sequences and event transition sequences for any term p: note that both flattening and lifting constructions determine uniquely the resulting sequence (for a given ξ, in the case of lifting). We want now to show that this correspondence extends to an *isomorphism* between the *domains of computations* associated with these sequences. This amounts to prove that for any pair of proved transition sequences σ_0 and σ_1 the following holds, where $\lesssim$ is the prefix ordering up to permutations:

$$\sigma_0 \lesssim \sigma_1 \Leftrightarrow \mathcal{E}(\sigma_0^\wedge) \subseteq \mathcal{E}(\sigma_1^\wedge)$$

The kernel of this result is showing that two proved sequences are equivalent exactly when the corresponding event transition sequences yield the same sets of events. Formally:

THEOREM 6.7. *Let σ_0, σ_1 be two proved sequences for a term p. Then:*

$$\sigma_0 \sim \sigma_1 \Leftrightarrow \mathcal{E}(\sigma_0^\wedge) = \mathcal{E}(\sigma_1^\wedge)$$

In order to prove this theorem, we need to define the notions of *concurrency* and *equivalence by permutations* on the event system itself. The equivalence on event sequences will also be denoted $\sim$. The statement of the theorem may then be divided in two steps. We show that for any term p:

LEMMA 6.8. *(The two permutation equivalences agree) If σ_0, σ_1 are proved transition sequences for p then:* $\sigma_0 \sim \sigma_1 \Leftrightarrow \sigma_0^\wedge \sim \sigma_1^\wedge$.

LEMMA 6.9. *(Equivalent event sequences generate equal events) If σ_0, σ_1 are event transition sequences for p then:* $\sigma_0 \sim \sigma_1 \Leftrightarrow \mathcal{E}(\sigma_0) = \mathcal{E}(\sigma_1)$.

Let us then proceed to show these lemmas. We first introduce the notions of concurrency and permutation equivalence on the event system. We start by defining the *concurrency* relation on events, noted as usual $\smile$. The relation $\smile$ on events is the least symmetric relation that satisfies the following clauses (for any $\eta, \eta', \eta'' \in \mathcal{E}$):

(A1) $\|_0\eta \smile \|_1\eta'$

(A2) $\eta \smile \eta' \Rightarrow \begin{cases} \|_0\eta \smile (\eta', \eta'') \\ \|_1\eta \smile (\eta'', \eta') \end{cases}$

(A3) $\eta \smile \eta' \Rightarrow \begin{cases} \|_i\eta \smile \|_i\eta' \\ +_i\eta \smile +_i\eta' \\ \backslash^\alpha\eta \smile \backslash^\alpha\eta' \end{cases}$

(A4) $\eta_0 \smile \eta_0'$ and $\eta_1 \smile \eta_1' \Rightarrow (\eta_0, \eta_1) \smile (\eta_0', \eta_1')$

(A5) $\eta \smile \eta' \Rightarrow \hat{a}.\eta \smile \hat{a}.\eta'$

The definition is thus formally identical to that of concurrency on proof terms, except for clause (A5) which allows concurrency to pass through a guard.

On the other hand the notion of *residual* is much simpler for events than for proofs, the residual of an event η by a concurrent event being just the event η itself. The diamond lemma for concurrent event transitions has then the following form:

LEMMA (DIAMOND LEMMA FOR EVENT TRANSITIONS). *Let $t_0 = \xi \xrightarrow{\eta_0}\!\!\!\!\rightarrow \xi_0$ and $t_1 = \xi \xrightarrow{\eta_1}\!\!\!\!\rightarrow \xi_1$ be two event transitions such that $\eta_0 \smile \eta_1$. Then there exists a unique term $\bar{\xi}$ such that $\xi_0 \xrightarrow{\eta_1}\!\!\!\!\rightarrow \bar{\xi}$ and $\xi_1 \xrightarrow{\eta_0}\!\!\!\!\rightarrow \bar{\xi}$.*

Proof: By induction on the definition of $\smile$. The proof is similar to that of the diamond lemma for proved transitions. □

We may now define the permutation equivalence on event sequences, in the same way as we did for proved transitions. We already defined $\mathcal{S}(p)$, the set of event sequences of p. In the same way we may define $\mathcal{S}(\xi)$, for any marked term ξ. Let $\sigma\sigma'$ denote the concatenation of $\sigma \in \mathcal{S}(\xi)$ and $\sigma' \in \mathcal{S}(\xi')$, which is only defined if $\mathsf{tg}(\sigma) = \xi'$. The permutation equivalence is as usual the *congruence* generated by the diamond lemma:

DEFINITION (PERMUTATION EQUIVALENCE ON EVENT SEQUENCES). *Let p be a CCS term. The equivalence by permutations on $\mathcal{S}(p)$ is the least equivalence $\simeq$ s.t.*

$$\sigma_0 t_0(t_1/t_0)\sigma_1 \;\simeq\; \sigma_0 t_1(t_0/t_1)\sigma_1$$

(provided that $t_0 \smile t_1$ and that concatenation is defined).

Note that there are events which are "syntactically" concurrent, according to our definition, and yet can never be permuted because there is no event transition sequence where they are adjacent. Let us see an example.

Example 6 In the term $r = (a.\alpha \parallel \bar{\alpha}.b)\backslash\alpha$ (see section 4 for its event structure representation), the events $\|_0 a$ and $\|_1 \widehat{\bar{\alpha}}.b$ are concurrent. However they can never be permuted since in the unique event sequence where they both occur they are not consecutive:

$$(a.\alpha \parallel \bar{\alpha}.b)\backslash\alpha \xrightarrow{\|_0 a} (\widehat{a}.\alpha \parallel \bar{\alpha}.b)\backslash\alpha \xrightarrow{(\widehat{a}.\alpha,\bar{\alpha})} (\widehat{a}.\alpha \parallel \widehat{\bar{\alpha}}.b)\backslash\alpha \xrightarrow{\|_1 \widehat{\bar{\alpha}}.b} (\widehat{a}.\alpha \parallel \widehat{\bar{\alpha}}\,\widehat{b}.)\backslash\alpha$$

Note that this is indeed desirable since the two events are intuitively *causally related* in this computation.

Now the proof of Lemma 6.8 – stating that the two permutation equivalences agree – is based on the following easy propositions:

PROPOSITION 6.10. *(Proof diamonds are lifted to event diamonds) Let p be a CCS term, and σ_0, σ_1 two-step proved transition sequences for p, such that $\sigma_0 \sim \sigma_1$. Then for any ξ such that $\varphi(\xi) = p$, the liftings $\sigma_0^{\wedge}(\xi)$, $\sigma_1^{\wedge}(\xi)$ are such that $\sigma_0^{\wedge}(\xi) \sim \sigma_1^{\wedge}(\xi)$.*

PROPOSITION 6.11. *(Event diamonds are flattened to proof diamonds) Let ξ be a proper marked term, and σ_0, σ_1 two-step event transition sequences for ξ, such that $\sigma_0 \sim \sigma_1$. Then their flattenings $\sigma_0^{\vee}$, $\sigma_1^{\vee}$ are such that $\sigma_0^{\vee} \sim \sigma_1^{\vee}$.*

Let us turn now to Lemma 6.9. It is an easy consequence of the above diamond lemma that the equivalence by permutation on event sequences preserves events:

COROLLARY 6.12. *(Equivalent event sequences generate equal events) Let σ_0, σ_1 be event transition sequences for a CCS term p. Then: $\sigma_0 \sim \sigma_1 \;\Rightarrow\; \mathcal{E}(\sigma_0) = \mathcal{E}(\sigma_1)$.*

This gives us one direction of the result. We want now to show the reverse implication, namely that equal events are always obtained through equivalent sequences transitions, that is, if σ_0, σ_1 are event transition sequences for a term p:

$$\mathcal{E}(\sigma_0) = \mathcal{E}(\sigma_1) \quad\Rightarrow\quad \sigma_0 \sim \sigma_1$$

We will only sketch the proof here. All we have to start with is a set of events $X = \mathcal{E}(\sigma_0) = \mathcal{E}(\sigma_1)$. It is clear that we have somehow to exploit the syntactic information contained in these events.

We shall proceed as follows. We define, for each event sequence σ, a *canonical ordering* $\preceq_X$ on the set of events $X = \mathcal{E}(\sigma)$, which uniquely depends on the syntax of the events of X. Intuitively, events will be ordered by increasing *causal depth* in X: events of lesser depth will precede events of greater depth, while events of equal depth are ordered according to some fixed global enumeration.

Now an event sequence where events occur in the canonical order is called a *canonical form*. The idea is to transform each event sequence σ into a canonical form $\mathsf{cf}(\sigma)$: then it is clear, since $\preceq_X$ only depends on X, that two event sequences σ_0, σ_1 with the same sets of events yield the same canonical form, that is:

$$\mathcal{E}(\sigma_0) = \mathcal{E}(\sigma_1) \Rightarrow \mathsf{cf}(\sigma_0) = \mathsf{cf}(\sigma_1)$$

Now the main point to prove is that an event sequence is brought into canonical form by just permuting *concurrent transitions*, namely that:

- Any event sequence σ is equivalent to its canonical form:

$$\forall\sigma : \sigma \sim \mathsf{cf}(\sigma)$$

The result will then follow since:

$$\mathsf{cf}(\sigma_0) = \mathsf{cf}(\sigma_1) \Rightarrow \sigma_0 \sim \sigma_1 \Rightarrow \sigma_0^{\vee} \sim \sigma_1^{\vee}$$

For the complete proofs we refer as usual to in [11].

6.3 Correspondence between event system and flow models

In this section we establish the *concrete equivalence* between the event system and the flow models. We start by considering the flow net model. We will show that for each CCS term p, the transition system on markings of the net $\mathcal{N}(p)$ is *isomorphic* to the event transition system generated by p. Then, since the transitions are labelled in both systems by events, it will follow that the two systems determine *equal computations*: we recall that in both cases computations are sets of events occurring in a transition sequence.

Recall the definition of *ancestor* $\varrho(\xi)$ from section 6. According to our intuition, if ξ has ancestor $\varrho(\xi) = p$, then ξ is a partially executed version of p. Then we expect ξ to correspond to some reachable marking in the net $\mathcal{N}(p)$. In fact, since a marked term ξ records both the original term – its ancestor $\varrho(\xi)$ – and a state of execution for it, it is rather straightforward to associate with ξ a marking in the net $\mathcal{N}(\varrho(\xi))$.

The marking $\mu(\xi)$ associated with marked terms is defined inductively starting from the marking $\mu(p) = \mu_p$ of CCS terms (μ_p is the initial marking of the net $\mathcal{N}(p)$ as given in the previous section). It will be convenient to distinguish two parts in the marking $\mu(\xi)$, which we note $\Gamma(\xi)$ and $\Delta(\xi)$. The set $\Gamma(\xi) =_{\mathsf{def}} \mu(\varrho(\xi)) \cap \mu(\xi)$ represents the part of the marking $\mu(\rho(\xi))$ which has not been affected by the execution reaching ξ, while $\Delta(\xi) =_{\mathsf{def}} \mu(\xi) - \mu(\varrho(\xi))$ is the part of the marking determined by this execution. This idea is somewhat similar to that of "concurrent residual" and "local residual" of [14]. Note that by definition we have $\Gamma(\xi) \cap \Delta(\xi) = \emptyset$ and $\mu(\xi) = \Gamma(\xi) \cup \Delta(\xi)$.

Now the marking $\mu(\xi)$ determined by a proper marked term ξ in the net $\mathcal{N}(\varrho(\xi))$ is defined as follows:

$$\mu(p) = \mu_p \quad \text{(the initial marking of } \mathcal{N}(p))$$
$$\mu(\widehat{a}.\xi) = \widehat{a}.\mu(\xi)$$
$$\mu(\xi \parallel \xi') = \|_0\mu(\xi) \cup \|_1\mu(\xi')$$
$$\mu(\xi \,\widehat{+}_0 q) = (\Gamma(\xi) + \mu(q)) \cup +_0\Delta(\xi)$$
$$\mu(p \,\widehat{+}_1 \xi) = (\mu(p) + \Gamma(\xi)) \cup +_1\Delta(\xi)$$
$$\mu(\xi \backslash \alpha) = \backslash^\alpha \mu(\xi)$$

We may now show that the transitions of a marked term ξ with ancestor p correspond exactly to the transitions from the marking $\mu(\xi)$ in the net $\mathcal{N}(p)$.

PROPOSITION 6.13. *For any proper marked term ξ, if $\xi \overset{\eta}{\twoheadrightarrow} \xi'$ then $\mu(\xi) \overset{\eta}{\longmapsto} \mu(\xi')$ in the net $\mathcal{N}(\varrho(\xi))$.*

Hint for proof: by induction on the proof of $\xi \overset{\eta}{\twoheadrightarrow} \xi'$. More precisely we show that

$$\xi \overset{\eta}{\twoheadrightarrow} \xi' \text{ with } p = \varrho(\xi) \quad \Rightarrow \quad \mathsf{pre}_p(\eta) \subseteq \mu(\xi) \text{ and } \mu(\xi') = \mu(\xi) - \mathsf{pre}_p(\eta) \cup \mathsf{post}_p(\eta)$$

The main point of the proof is to derive the precise expressions for $\mathsf{pre}_p(\eta)$ and $\mathsf{post}_p(\eta)$, depending on the structure of p. ❑

We want now to show the reverse correspondence, namely that any (reachable) marking M of $\mathcal{N}(p)$ is the marking of some marked term ξ such that $\varrho(\xi) = p$ and that the transitions from M induce corresponding transitions from ξ. Formally:

PROPOSITION 6.14. *For any proper marked term ξ, if η is firable at marking $\mu(\xi) \overset{\eta}{\longmapsto} \mu'$ in the net $\mathcal{N}(\varrho(\xi))$, then there exists ξ' such that $\xi \overset{\eta}{\twoheadrightarrow} \xi'$, with $\mu(\xi') = \mu'$.*

Hint for proof: By induction on the structure of the term ξ.

Putting together the two propositions we obtain the announced correspondence result:

COROLLARY 6.15. *For any proper marked term ξ such that $\varrho(\xi) = p$, we have $\xi \overset{\eta}{\twoheadrightarrow} \xi'$ in the event system if and only if $\mu(\xi) \overset{\eta}{\longmapsto} \mu(\xi')$ in the net $\mathcal{N}(p)$. Then also $p \overset{\eta_1}{\twoheadrightarrow} \xi_1 \cdots \xi_{n-1} \overset{\eta_n}{\twoheadrightarrow} \xi_n$ in the event system iff $\mu(p) \overset{\eta_1}{\longrightarrow} \mu(\xi_1) \cdots \mu(\xi)_{n-1} \overset{\eta_n}{\longrightarrow} \mu(\xi_n)$ in the net $\mathcal{N}(p)$.*

Note that since the both the event system and the transition system on markings are *deterministic*, the above corollary implies that they are *isomorphic* transition systems.

Another consequence of the corollary is that the sets of *computations* of the two systems are *equal*, namely: $\mathcal{C}_{\mathrm{ev}}(p) = \mathcal{C}_{\mathrm{net}}(p)$.

Let us turn now to the relation between the event system and the flow event structure interpretations for a term p. Again, the correspondence is a rather direct one: we may show that the *computations* of p in the event system are exactly the *configurations* of the flow event structure $S(p)$. To this end we shall use the following characterisation for configurations from [6]:

DEFINITION (PROVING SEQUENCES). *Given a flow event structure $S = (E, \# , \prec)$, a proving sequence in S is a sequence $e_1, \ldots, e_n, \ldots$ of distinct non-conflicting events (i.e. $i \neq j \Rightarrow e_i \neq e_j$ and $\neg(e_i \# e_j)$ for all i, j) satisfying:*

$$\forall i \forall e.\ e \prec e_i \Rightarrow \begin{cases} \exists j < i & e = e_j \quad \text{or} \\ \exists j < i & e \# e_j \prec e_i \end{cases}$$

PROPOSITION 6.16. *Given a flow event structure $S = (E, \# , \prec)$, a subset X of E is a configuration of S if and only if it can be enumerated as $\{e_1, \ldots, e_n, \ldots\}$, where $e_1, \ldots, e_n, \ldots$ is a proving sequence.*

Using this characterisation we may prove that:

THEOREM 6.17. *(Event sequences coincide with proving sequences) For any term p, there exists a sequence $p \xrightarrow{\eta_1} \xi_1 \cdots \xi_{n-1} \xrightarrow{\eta_n} \xi_n$ in the event system for p if and only if there is a proving sequence $\eta_1, \ldots, \eta_n$ in the flow event structure $S(p)$.*

Hint for proof: By induction on the structure of p.

Obviously this is enough to conclude that p has equal computations in the two models, namely that: $\mathcal{C}_{ev}(p) = \mathcal{C}(S(p))$.

7. Conclusions and related work

The idea of abstracting from the ordering of concurrent transitions was already applied to Petri nets by Nielsen, Plotkin and Winskel in [43]. More recently, Best and Devillers have established the correspondence between the equivalence by permutations for firing sequences and processes of Petri nets [4]. Also, the relation between trace semantics and a (prime) event structure semantics for a basic class of nets has been studied in a recent paper by Thiagarajan et al. [54].

Our idea of a proved transition system for CCS – where labels are *proofs* in the inference system of CCS – has been resumed by Montanari and Ferrari in [31,32], where a transition system similar to ours is used in a categorical framework. In these works the authors argue that in their setting, unlike in ours, they have an "algebraic framework where the commutativity of concurrent transitions is directly exploited to define equivalence classes of computations". However, we cannot agree with this criticism, since it is clear that our definition of the *equivalence* by permutations $\sim$ is equivalent to saying that $\sim$ is the least *congruence* on proved sequences such that:

$$t_0 t'_0 \sim t_1 t'_1$$

provided that: $t_0 \sim t_1$, $t'_0 = t_1/t_0$, and $t'_1 = t_0/t_1$.

REFERENCES

[1] M. A. BEDNARCZYK, *Categories of asynchronous systems*, Ph. D. Thesis, University of Sussex (1987).

[2] J. A. BERGSTRA, J. W. KLOP, *Algebra of communicating processes with abstraction*, TCS 37 (1985) 77-121.

[3] G. BERRY, J.-J. LÉVY, *minimal and optimal computations of recursive programs*, J. of ACM 26 (1979) 148-175.

[4] E. BEST, R. DEVILLERS, *Interleaving and partial orders in concurrency: a formal comparison*, in Formal Description of Programming Concepts III, North-Holland (1987) 299-321.

[5] G. BOUDOL, *Computational semantics of term rewriting systems*, in Algebraic Methods in Semantics (M. Nivat & J.C. Reynolds Eds), Cambridge University Press (1985) 169-236.

[6] G. BOUDOL, *Flow event structures and flow nets*, in this volume (1990).

[7] G. BOUDOL, I. CASTELLANI, *On the semantics of concurrency: partial orders and transition systems*, TAPSOFT 87, Lecture Notes in Comput. Sci. 249 (1987) 123-137.

[8] G. BOUDOL, I. CASTELLANI, *Concurrency and atomicity*, Theoretical Comput. Sci. 59 (1988) 25-84.

[9] G. BOUDOL, I. CASTELLANI, *Permutation of transitions: an event structure semantics for* CCS *and* SCCS, *in* Linear Time, Branching Time and Partial Orders in Logics and Models for Concurrency, Lecture Notes in Comput. Sci. 354 (1988) 411-427.

[10] G. BOUDOL, I. CASTELLANI, *A non-interleaving semantics for* CCS *based on proved transitions*, Fundamenta Informaticae XI (1988) 433-452.

[11] G. BOUDOL, I. CASTELLANI, *Computations of distributed systems, Part 2: three equivalent semantics for* CCS, full version of this paper, to appear as an INRIA report (1990).

[12] S. BROOKES, C. A. R. HOARE, A. ROSCOE, *A theory of communicating sequential processes*, JACM 31 (1984) 560-599.

[13] S. BROOKES, W. C. ROUNDS, *Behavioural equivalence relations induced by programming logics*, ICALP 83, Lecture Notes in Comput. Sci. 154 (1983) 97-108.

[14] I. CASTELLANI, M. HENNESSY, *Distributed Bisimulations*, JACM 36 (1989) 887-911.

[15] I. CASTELLANI, *Bisimulations for concurrency*, Ph. D. Thesis, University of Edinburgh, CST-51-88 (1988).

[16] I. CASTELLANI, G. Q. ZHANG, *Parallel product of event structures*, INRIA Res. Rep. 1078 and DAIMI Rep. PB-285, Aarhus University (1989).

[17] Ph. DARONDEAU, P. DEGANO, *Causal trees*, ICALP 89, Lecture Notes in Comput. Sci. 372 (1989) 234-248.

[18] P. DEGANO, R. DE NICOLA, U. MONTANARI, *Partial ordering derivations for* CCS, FCT 85, Lecture Notes in Comput. Sci. 199 (1985) 520-533.

[19] P. DEGANO, R. DE NICOLA, U. MONTANARI, *Concurrent histories: a basis for observing distributed systems,* J. of Computer and Systems Sciences 34 (1987) 422-461.

[20] P. DEGANO, R. DE NICOLA, U. MONTANARI, *On the consistency of "truly concurrent" operational and denotational semantics,* LICS 88 (1988) 133-141.

[21] P. DEGANO, R. DE NICOLA, U. MONTANARI, *A distributed operational semantics for CCS based on condition/event systems,* Acta Informatica 26 (1988) 59-91.

[22] R. DE NICOLA, *Extensional equivalences for transition systems,* Acta Informatica 24 (1987) 211-237.

[23] H.J. GENRICH, K. LAUTENBACH, P.S. THIAGARAJAN, *Elements of general net theory,* in Net Theory and Applications (W. Brauer, Ed.) Lecture Notes in Comput. Sci. 84 (1980) 21-163.

[24] R. van GLABBEEK, F. VAANDRAGER, *Petri net models for algebraic theories of concurrency,* Proceedings PARLE Conference, Eindhoven, Lecture Notes in Comput. Sci. 259 (1987) 224-242.

[25] R. van GLABBEEK, U. GOLTZ, *Equivalence notions for concurrent systems and refinement of actions,* MFCS 89, Lecture Notes in Comput. Sci. 379 (1989) 237-248.

[26] R. van GLABBEEK, U. GOLTZ, *Equivalence notions and refinement of actions for flow event structures,* Draft (*march*1990).

[27] U. GOLTZ, *Building structured Petri nets,* Arbeitspapiere der GMD 223 (1986).

[28] U. GOLTZ, *On representing CCS programs by finite Petri nets,* MFCS 88, Lecture Notes in Comput. Sci. 324 (1988) 339-350.

[29] U. GOLTZ, A. MYCROFT, *On the relationship of CCS and Petri nets,* ICALP 84, Lecture Notes in Comput. Sci. 172 (1984) 196-208.

[30] U. GOLTZ, R. LOOGEN, *A non-interleaving semantic model for nondeterministic concurrent processes,* Tech. Report 87-15, RWTH Aachen (1987).

[31] G.L. FERRARI, U. MONTANARI, *Towards the unification of models for concurrency,* to appear in Proc. CAAP90, Lecture Notes in Comput. Sci. 431 (1990).

[32] G.L. FERRARI, *Unifying models of concurrency,* Ph. D. Thesis, University of Pisa (1990).

[33] M. HENNESSY, *An Algebraic Theory of Processes,* MIT Press (1988).

[34] M. HENNESSY, *Observing processes, in* Linear Time, Branching Time and Partial Orders in Logics and Models for Concurrency, Lecture Notes in Comput. Sci. 354 (1988) 173-200.

[35] G. HUET, J.-J. LÉVY, *Call-by-need computations in non-ambiguous linear term rewriting systems,* IRIA-LABORIA Report 359 (1979).

[36] M.Z. KWIATKOWSKA, *Fairness for non-interleaving concurrency,* Ph. D. Thesis, Department of Computing Studies, University of Leicester, Techn. Rep. 22 (1989).

[37] J.-J. LÉVY, *Optimal reductions in the lambda calculus,* in To H.B. CURRY: Essays on Combinatory Logic, Lambda Calculus and Formalism (J.P. Seldin, J.R. Hindley, Eds), Academic Press (1980) 159-191.

[38] A. MAZURKIEWICZ, *Concurrent program schemes and their interpretations,* Aarhus Workshop on Verification of Parallel Programs, Daimi PB-78, Aarhus University (1977).

[39] A. MAZURKIEWICZ, *Basic notions of trace theory, in* Linear Time, Branching Time and Partial Orders in Logics and Models for Concurrency, Lecture Notes in Comput. Sci. 354 (1988) 285-363.

[40] R. MILNER, *A Calculus of Communicating Systems,* Lecture Notes in Comput. Sci. 92 (1980) reprinted in Report ECS-LFCS-86-7, Edinburgh University.

[41] R. MILNER, *Communication and Concurrency,* Prentice-Hall International Series in Computer Science (1989).

[42] R. MILNER, *Operational and algebraic semantics of concurrent processes,* LFCS Report ECS-LFCS-88-46, Edinburgh Univ. (1988).

[43] M. NIELSEN, G. PLOTKIN, G. WINSKEL, *Petri nets, event structures and domains,* Theoret. Comput. Sci. 13 (1981) 85-108.

[44] M. NIELSEN, G. ROZENBERG, P.S. THIAGARAJAN, *Elementary transition systems,* presented at the 2nd Workshop on Concurrency and Compositionality, S. Miniato (1990).

[45] E.-R. OLDEROG, *Operational Petri net semantics for* CCSP, Advances in Petri Nets 87, Lecture Notes in Comput. Sci. 266 (1987) 196-223.

[46] C.A. PETRI, *Non-sequential processes,* GMD-ISF Rep. 77-05 (1977).

[47] G. PLOTKIN, *A Structural approach to operational semantics,* Daimi FN-19, Aarhus University (1981).

[48] V.R. PRATT, *Modelling concurrency with partial orders,* Intern. J. of Parallel Programming 15 (1986) 33-71.

[49] W. REISIG, *Petri Nets: an Introduction,* EATCS monographs, Springer Verlag (1985).

[50] B. ROZOY, *On distributed languages and models for distributed computation,* presented at: 18ème Ecole de Printemps d'Informatique Théorique, La Roche-Posay (*april*1990).

[51] M.W. SHIELDS, *Deterministic asynchronous automata,* in: Formal Methods in Programming, North-Holland (1985).

[52] E.W. STARK, *Concurrent transition systems,* Theoret. Comput. Sci. 64 (1989) 221-269.

[53] D. TAUBNER, *Finite representations of* CCS *and* TCSP *programs by automata and Petri nets,* Lecture Notes in Comput. Sci. 369, Springer (1989).

[54] P.S. THIAGARAJAN, G. ROZENBERG, M. NIELSEN, *A relationship between the event structure and trace semantics of elementary net systems,* Draft (1988).

[55] F. VAANDRAGER, *A simple definition for parallel composition of prime event structures,* Tech. Rep. CS-R8903, CWI, Amsterdam (1989).

[56] G. WINSKEL, *Event structure semantics for* CCS *and related languages,* Daimi PB-159, Aarhus University (1983) s.a. 9th ICALP, Lecture Notes in Comput. Sci. 140 (1982) 561-576.

[57] G. WINSKEL, *Categories of models for concurrency,* Seminar on Concurrency, Lecture Notes in Comput. Sci. 197 (1985) 246-267.

[58] G. WINSKEL, *Event structures,* Advances in Petri Nets 86, Lecture Notes in Comput. Sci. 255 (1987) 325-392.

[59] G. WINSKEL, *An introduction to event structures, in* Linear Time, Branching Time and Partial Orders in Logics and Models for Concurrency, Lecture Notes in Comput. Sci. 354 (1988) 364-397.

Towards a Semantic Approach to SIMD Architectures and their Languages

Luc Bougé* Patrick Garda†

Abstract

We propose an abstract approach towards the fundamental concepts involved in SIMD architectures. Its specificity is to proceed by studying the abstract semantics of parallel languages designed to control those architectures in their various aspects. In this paper, we concentrate on the duality between the macroscopic view of SIMD architectures (a sequential processor operating on array variables), and the microscopic one (an array of parallel processors operating on private scalar variables). For this purpose, we define a simple language for each viewpoint, give their abstract operational semantics, set up a compilation function and prove it correct. In a second part, we consider more closely the macroscopic language. We study program equivalences and proofs, and we show how to use it to implement various routing strategies.

In the past recent years, much work has been done about the relationships between parallel architectures and the languages they implement. A large part of it focused on computational models where processors run asynchronously, access their private program and data, and exchange information using (usually point-to-point) communication links. These models are implemented in parallel machines like the Intel iPSC hypercube (with asynchronous communications) or the FPS-T hypercube (based on Transputers with synchronous communications). Those architectures are called MIMD (Multiple Instructions Multiple Data) in Flynn's taxonomy [5] because at any point in the computation, the processors (even if they are synchronized on a global clock) execute usually unrelated instructions on unrelated data. This work has eventually given rise to considerable advances in semantics, originated in Hoare's CSP and Milner's CCS languages.

But other kinds of parallel architectures are also competing to take the lead. A successful example is the Connection Machine [11] and a recent overview race can be

*LIENS, 45 rue d'Ulm, F-75230 Paris Cedex 05, France. Also affiliated with LIFO, University of Orléans, BP 6759, F-45067 Orléans Cedex 02, France. Email: bouge@ens.fr

†IEF, University Paris-Sud, Bât. 220, F-91405 Orsay, France.

found in [8]. In this case, all processors are synchronized on the same program operating on their private data. At each point of the computation, all processors execute then the same instruction. This kind of architecture is therefore called SIMD (Single Instruction Multiple Data) after Flynn's taxonomy. In contrast with the growing interest for SIMD architectures, little has still been said about the languages designed to control them and their semantics.

This paper is a step towards redressing this imbalance. In fact, we believe that studying those languages is an efficient method to catch the essentials of SIMD architectures, abstracting them from their technical details. In this paper, we illustrate this claim by studying the inherent duality between the macroscopic and the microscopic views of SIMD architectures. Section 1 presents a short survey about SIMD architectures and their languages. Section 2 describes a High Level language (called HL) the macroscopic view, and gives it operational semantics. So does section 3 for a Low Level language (called LL) for the microscopic view. Section 4 describes then a compilation function from HL to LL, and proves it correct, thereby proving the consistency between the two views. The HL language provides a rather low-level communication primitive, namely shifting an array in a given direction. We show in the last section that general communication primitives can be implemented in HL, based on various routing strategies.

1 A brief survey on SIMD architectures and their languages

The idea of using a 2-dimensional array of processors for array processing can be traced back as far as the early fifties. Such an architecture is specially suited for image processing (intuitively, store one pixel at each processor), numerical computations involving matrices and more generally all problems enjoying a spatial distribution of data. Since, technology has eventually made the idea a reality, and a number of massively parallel, processor array architectures have been proposed. We follow the survey of Fountain [7].

All those architectures enjoy a number of common features. They use "narrow" processors, often 1-bit large. They are comparatively weak processors. Each processor manages a private (usually small) memory. Thanks to their expected number (typically a few thousands) one can then easily obtain interesting speedups. The processors are controlled by an external *sequencer* which broadcasts at each point in the computation the instruction to be immediately executed by each of them on its own memory, *using the same address*. In each processor, an *inhibition flag* enables to inhibit instruction execution so that the memory is left unchanged. Such a facility is crucial to cope with conditional branching within a SIMD discipline.

The instructions fall in two classes. One finds first *local* (i.e. processor-wise) instructions, for instance usual arithmetics etc. There is no fundamental difference here with the sequential case, as far as we are concerned. Then, one finds *global instructions* which make processors communicate and cooperate. Communications occur usually along the square grid, in the same direction for all processors. Because the possible directions are usually referred to as North, East, West and South, those architectures are called NEWS architectures. Communications may be done by the processors themselves. It is however conceptually clearer to consider they are done (as in the Connection Machine) by additional specialized *routers* attached to processors. Finally, a *feed-back bus* passing to each processor in the array enables the sequencer to receive a global information from processors. This facility is crucial to cope with conditional iterations: the sequencer has to know that the exit condition is globally satisfied by *all* processors to stop broadcasting repeatedly the loop body and continue with the rest of the program.

One finds a great variety of communication patterns. Here are some typical examples. We follow the description of [9].

- ▷ In the MPP (Massively Parallel Processor, [2]) processors make their value available to their 4 neighbors in a special register. Then, processors are instructed to fetch the value broadcast by their neighbor along the given direction, the same direction for all processors, using an input multiplexer. The 3 other values are merely ignored.

- ▷ In the DAP (Distributed Array Processor, [12]), it is basically the same, but there is no special register. Processors are given a memory address, the same for all. Then, a multiplexer makes them use one of their neighbors' memory for fetching instead of their own one.

- ▷ In the CLIP4 machine (Cellular Logic Image Processor, [6]) each processor broadcasts to its 8 neighbors, and can receive the oring of a selected subset of the 8 values (input gating).

- ▷ In the GAPP (Geometric Arithmetic Parallel Processors, [13]) processors can simultaneously broadcast two different values along the North-South or the East-West directions. In GAPP as in CLIP4, no inhibition flag is provided.

- ▷ In the CM-1 Connection Machine (in the NEWS communication mode, [4]) a processor can selectively send a value to one of its four neighbors. Communications are not done by processors themselves, but by specialized routers attached to them.

In this paper, we will consider an architecture model similar to the Connection machine in its 2-dimensional NEWS mode. However, we will assume the grid is infinite in all directions. This avoids the problem of borders. Note the Connection Machine can be configured as a torus or by specifying that receiving from beyond the border yields an arbitrary value. The grid can then be identified with $\mathbf{Z}^2$ ($\mathbf{Z}$ is the set of signed integers). However, it should be clear that everything extends to higher dimensions and other topologies such as hypercubes. We consider only shift communications along some direction of the grid. Note there also exists SIMD architectures with programmable circuit-switching interconnection networks such as Opsila [1]. Yet, we will not consider them in this paper as a major difficulty in this case is to specify network configurations at the level of control languages.

A number of languages have been proposed and implemented to control SIMD architectures. Among them, we can cite Actus for Illiac IV [17], Parallel Pascal for MPP [18], DAP Fortran initially designed for the DAP, which inspired the Fortran 8X standard [19], *Lisp, an extension of Common Lisp for the Connection Machine [21], ParIS, the macro-assembler for the Connection Machine [16] and POMPC, an extension of C currently under design and implementation for Connection Machine-like architectures [15]. But, to our best knowledge, very little has been done about their semantics. We can divide the constructs proposed in those languages into four main classes: *control* constructs, that is sequencing, iterations etc.; *communication* constructs, that is sending, receiving, shifting data; constructs specifying the *interactions* with the host, either broadcasting a host scalar data to all processors or reducing an array of processor data to a single host scalar data; *additional* constructs, which can be seen as programming facilities. In this paper, we will only consider explicitly the first two classes. The third class will be implicitly taken into account by the form of our iteration construct. The forth class will appear as derived constructs and will not be directly addressed.

As pointed out by Steele and Hillis [20], it can be seen that those languages express in fact a mixture of two different views of SIMD architectures, leading thus to two different semantics.

- ▷ In the *macroscopic* view (see figure 1), one sees a sophisticated sequential processor with the capability of operating on arrays instead of scalars. Parallelism is thus on the level of data. Languages, or parts of them, expressing this view will thereafter be called *high level.*

- ▷ In the *microscopic* view (see figure 2), one sees an array of elementary sequential processors operating in parallel on their private scalar data. An external sequencer is in charge of synchronizing them. In our case, this is done by broadcasting successively the common instruction to be executed at the current step. Processors are connected together by a communication network. They interact with this network through specialized devices called routers, controlled by the sequencer. Parallelism is thus on the level of control. Languages expressing this view are called *low level.*

The next three sections will demonstrate how this duality can be expressed at an abstract level. Steele and Hillis actually proposed in [20] a quite elegant functional framework where this duality is caught by an algebraic relation between operators:

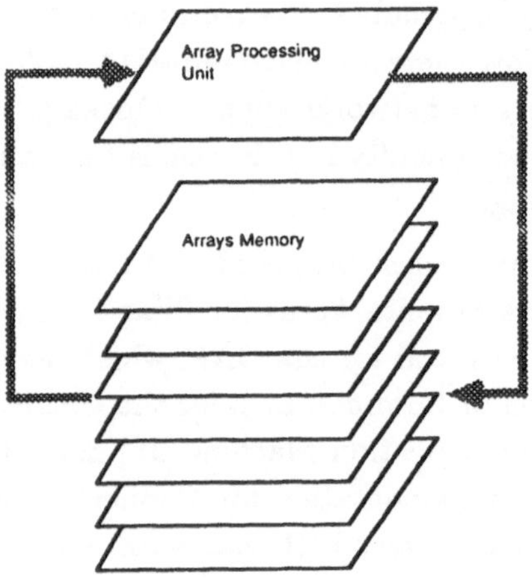

Figure 1: The macroscopic view: a processor of arrays

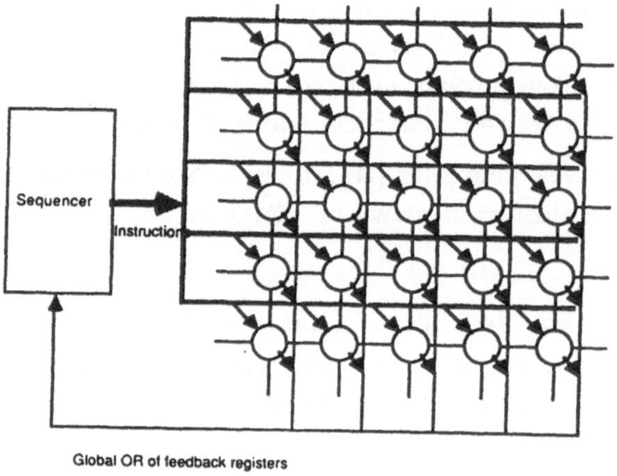

Figure 2: The microscopic view: an array of processors

$\bullet\alpha = \alpha\bullet =$ Identity. In this paper, we rather propose an operational approach, through the correctness proof of a compilation function from a high level language HL to a low level language LL. As it will be seen, this approach is much closer to "real" languages than the functional one, and it gives many interesting insights into them.

2 A High Level language and its semantics

2.1 The HL language

We describe below a simple High Level language HL to express the macroscopic view of SIMD architectures as described above. Uppercase letters X denote *global* objects, variables, values or whatever. Lowercase letters x denote *local* objects. Symbol u ranges on grid coordinates. The elementary processor located at coordinate u is called P_u. If X is an array, $X|_u$ is the array element of X located at coordinate u, or equivalently stored by processor P_u. Generally, x denotes the array element of X located at the current coordinate. Symbol d denotes directions N, E, W or S, and $\bar{d}$ denotes the opposite direction. Let $d(u)$ be the coordinate of the processor neighbor of P_u along direction d.

Language HL contains two kinds of instructions. We have first local assignments like for instance

$$\langle inst \rangle :: \; X := f(Y, Z)$$

which executes within each processor the sequential assignment $x := f(y, z)$. Observe that we write lowercase f to stress that f acts elementwise (think of matrix addition, as opposed to matrix multiplication). Observe that addressing a local array with a local offset value $X := Tab[K]$ is a special case of this construct. Also, *broadcasting* constant values from the host is implicitly contained in the case where f is a constant function.

We have then global communication instructions

$$\langle inst \rangle :: \texttt{shift}\ X\ \texttt{along}\ d$$

which stores into array element $X|_u$ the value of array element $X|_{\bar{d}(u)}$. Globally, array X is thus shifted one step along direction d. (Observe that would not hold if the grid had borders!) Note that d stands here for a syntactic constant, viz N, E, W or S, and *not* for a variable.

Finally, an instruction can be conditioned. It will then have its effect on a subset of the array elements.

$$\langle inst \rangle :: \texttt{where}\ B\ \texttt{then}\ \langle inst \rangle\ \texttt{end}$$

The intended semantics is as follows. Instruction $\langle inst \rangle$ is executed by all processors, but only those elements such that variable B is true locally record the resulting modifications. Observe that we *do* allow conditioned shifts and nested conditions. Yet, we *do not* allow conditioning more that one instruction at once.

A program in HL may be made of a sequence of 1 or more instructions:

$$\langle prog \rangle :: \ \langle inst \rangle | \langle prog \rangle ; \langle prog \rangle .$$

A program can be iterated up to a state where the control variable B is false *at each array element.*

$$\langle prog \rangle :: \texttt{while}\ B\ \textbf{do}\ \langle prog \rangle\ \textbf{done}\ .$$

Note that the global iteration is thus controlled by the oring of all the local values. This construct involves thus an implicit *reduction* of an array of values to a single value. The OR function is chosen here because of its practical importance, as its hardware implementation is almost trivial: a simple wire suffices! The reader may however wonder whether other global predicates $\phi(B)$ could be used to control loop iterations. The answer is yes, as the expressing power of HL makes it possible to concentrate all local values $B|_u$ into a single array element, and there compute (sequentially) predicate ϕ on those data. This is in general obviously unnatural and inefficient. Fortunately, most practical programs can be easily cast into the suitable OR exit condition, as it often expresses that *all* processes have simultaneously satisfied some local predicate, for instance they have completed their local task.

2.2 An example of program

The HL language is specially well fitted to image processing. As an example, consider the following problem. One is given a binary image A ($A|_u = 1$ if u belongs to the image, and 0 otherwise), and a coordinate u_0 identified with an image B with $B|_{u_0} = 1$ and $B|_u = 0$ otherwise. We want to determine the connected component (in the grid topology) of coordinate u_0 in A (it is empty if $u_0 \notin A$). We present a classical propagation algorithm. The connected component in A of u_0 is filled up by a wave originated from u_0. Image C contains the current state of the wave (see figure 3).

$$\begin{aligned}
F \equiv\ & C := A \wedge B; \\
& Old_C := 0; \\
& X := C \setminus Old_C; \\
& \texttt{while}\ X \\
& \textbf{do} \\
& \qquad Old_C := C; \\
& \qquad dil_4(Old_C, C); \\
& \qquad C := C \wedge A; \\
& \qquad X := C \setminus Old_C \\
& \textbf{done}
\end{aligned}$$

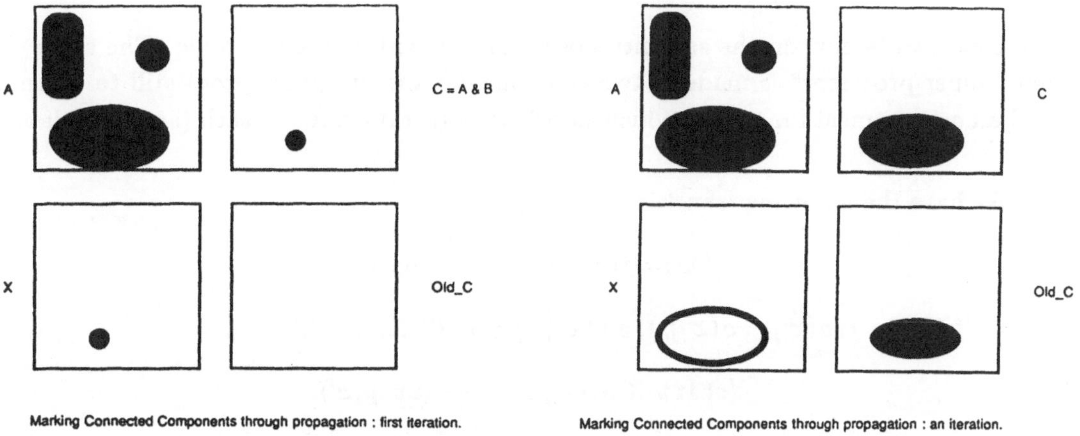

Figure 3: Finding the connected component of a point within an image

The dil_4 operator above "dilates" an image by 1 step in all 4 directions. The instruction $dil_4(C, D)$ is thus a shorthand for the following program.

$D := C;$

$Y := C;$
shift Y **along** N;
$D := D \vee Y;$

$Y := C;$
shift Y **along** E;
$D := D \vee Y;$

$Y := C;$
shift Y **along** W;
$D := D \vee Y;$

$Y := C;$
shift Y **along** S;
$D := D \vee Y$

2.3 Semantics

We concentrate now on the semantics of HL in the syntax-oriented style. The state of our "super-processor" is made of two components: the program $\langle prog\rangle$ still to be run and an environment function σ which associates a (array) value to each (array) variable X.

We have the following transitions:

$$\langle X := f(Y,Z),\sigma\rangle \longrightarrow \langle \mathtt{stop},\sigma'\rangle$$

with $\sigma'(X)|_u = f(\sigma(Y)|_u, \sigma(Z)|_u)$, and $\sigma'(T) = \sigma(T)$ for $T \neq X$;

$$\langle \mathtt{shift}\ X\ \mathtt{along}\ d,\sigma\rangle \longrightarrow \langle \mathtt{stop},\sigma'\rangle$$

with $\sigma'(X)|_u = \sigma(X)|_{\bar{d}(u)}$ and $\sigma'(T) = \sigma(T)$ for $T \neq X$.

The rules for sequencing and iteration are similar to the sequential case.

$$\frac{\langle\langle prog\rangle,\sigma\rangle \longrightarrow \langle\langle prog\rangle',\sigma'\rangle}{\langle\langle prog\rangle;\langle prog\rangle'',\sigma\rangle \longrightarrow \langle\langle prog\rangle';\langle prog\rangle'',\sigma'\rangle}$$

with the convention that $\mathtt{stop};\langle prog\rangle = \langle prog\rangle$;

$$\frac{\neg\bigvee_u \sigma(B)|_u}{\langle \mathtt{while}\ B\ \mathtt{do}\ \langle prog\rangle\ \mathtt{done},\sigma\rangle \longrightarrow \langle \mathtt{stop},\sigma\rangle}$$

and

$$\frac{\bigvee_u \sigma(B)|_u}{\langle \mathtt{while}\ B\ \mathtt{do}\ \langle prog\rangle\ \mathtt{done},\sigma\rangle \longrightarrow \langle\langle prog\rangle;\mathtt{while}\ B\ \mathtt{do}\ \langle prog\rangle\ \mathtt{done},\sigma\rangle}.$$

The rule for the where construct is more subtle.

$$\frac{\langle\langle inst\rangle,\sigma\rangle \longrightarrow \langle \mathtt{stop},\sigma'\rangle}{\langle \mathtt{where}\ B\ \mathtt{then}\ \langle inst\rangle\ \mathtt{end},\sigma\rangle \longrightarrow \langle \mathtt{stop},\sigma''\rangle}$$

with $\sigma''(T)|_u = \sigma'(T)|_u$ if $\sigma(B)|_u$ and $\sigma''(T)|_u = \sigma(T)|_u$ otherwise, for each variable T. In other words, the array element of T located at u is modified only if B evaluates to true at this location.

2.4 Program equivalence

The goal of this section is to derive a notion of program equivalence from the semantics of HL as described in section 2.3. The functional equivalence of Apt and Olderog will be convenient here [14]. Intuitively, programs P and Q are *equivalent* in this sense if, starting in similar environments, then either they both diverge, or they both terminate with similar environments. In some sense, they implement both the same function.

We now turn to the formal definition. Throughout this section, we fix an infinite set V of auxiliary variables. We say that two environments σ and σ' *agree* or are similar with respect to V if $\forall X \notin V\ \sigma(X) = \sigma'(X)$. We write then $\sigma \equiv_V \sigma'$.

Let $\stackrel{*}{\longrightarrow}$ be the reflexive transitive closure of the transition relation $\longrightarrow$. This means that $\langle P,\sigma\rangle \stackrel{*}{\longrightarrow} \langle Q,\sigma'\rangle$ iff one can go from the former to the latter by a finite (possibly null) number of $\longrightarrow$-steps. Let P be a program, that is a syntactical object of type $\langle prog\rangle$. We say that P *terminates* from environment σ with result σ' if there exists a sequence of transitions

$$\langle P,\sigma\rangle \stackrel{*}{\longrightarrow} \langle \texttt{stop},\sigma'\rangle.$$

Otherwise, we say that P diverges from σ.

Observe that language HL is deterministic: in a given environment, a program either diverges or terminates, and in this case its result is unique. In this sense, this language behaves pretty much like a sequential language, although it embodies parallel concepts.

Definition 1 *Two programs P and Q are equivalent with respect to V if, for any initial environment σ, P terminates from σ iff Q terminates from σ, and their results agree with respect to V. (And thus P diverges from σ iff Q diverges from σ.)*

We write then $P \equiv_V Q$. As an example, program $X := 0; X := X + 1$ is equivalent to $X := 1$. But can we replace the former by the latter within a larger program, and yet obtain equivalent programs? That is, can we use this equivalence as a basis for local program transformations and optimizations? For usual sequential languages, the answer is yes but for usual parallel MIMD languages, the answer is no. For instance,

$$X := 3 \parallel (X := 0; X := X + 1)$$

is *not* equivalent to

$$X := 3 \parallel X := 1$$

(as the former can terminate with $X = 4$ and not the latter) though their right parts are! But for the parallel SIMD language HL, the answer is yes.

To express this remarkable property, we need a notion of *syntactic* context $R[.]$. It is a program in HL with "holes" of type $\langle prog\rangle$. $R[P]$ is then the program obtained by filling those holes with P. We are now in a position to state the main *substitution property*.

Property 1 (substitution) *Assume $P \equiv_V Q$, and that no variable of V appears in syntactic context $R[.]$. Then $R[P] \equiv_V R[Q]$.*

Equivalence $\equiv_V$ is thus a congruence. Using this result, we can now show that it is possible to avoid conditioned **shift** in HL. Consider first the following example which illustrates the action of conditioned shifts as specified by the semantics. Let X be the following image:

$$X = \{(0,0),(0,1)\}.$$

Then **where** X **then shift** X **along** E **end** yields

$$X = \{(0,1)\}$$

which is a contraction along direction E. In full generality, consider now

$$P :: \texttt{where } B \texttt{ then shift } Y \texttt{ along } d \texttt{ end}$$

and

$$\begin{aligned} Q :: \quad & Aux := Y; \\ & \texttt{shift } Aux \texttt{ along } d; \\ & \texttt{where } B \texttt{ then } Y := Aux \texttt{ end} \end{aligned}$$

where Aux is an auxiliary variable. Then, starting from an environment σ, P terminates with result σ' defined by $\sigma'(Y)|_u = \sigma(Y)|_{\bar{d}(u)}$ if $\sigma(B)|_u$, and $\sigma'(Y)|_u = \sigma(Y)|_u$ otherwise. On its side, starting from σ, Q terminates with the same result for Y plus $\sigma'(Aux)|_u = \sigma(Y)|_{\bar{d}(u)}$. Programs P and Q are thus equivalent with respect to $\{Aux\}$, and can therefore be freely interchanged in all context where Aux does not appear. We have thus proved that conditioned shifts can be replaced by unconditioned ones.

We can also optimize nested conditions into one. More precisely, let

$$P :: \texttt{where } B \texttt{ then where } C \texttt{ then } I \texttt{ end end}$$

and

$$Q :: \quad Aux := (B \wedge C); \texttt{where } Aux \texttt{ then } I \texttt{ end}$$

with Aux being a new auxiliary variable. Then we can show that $P \equiv_{\{Aux\}} Q$. We can thus transform HL programs so as to eliminate all nested conditions.

The reader is referred to [3] for a detailed study of these program equivalences.

3 A Low Level language and its semantics

3.1 The LL language

We describe now a Low Level language LL to express the microscopic view. The precise view we have in mind is shown in figure 4. A processing element is made of 3 parts. The *processor* can be instructed by the external sequencer to perform an elementary operation on its local data. The *memory* stores the data. Writes in the memory are controlled by the *context register ct*. It is enabled only if the context is in the *active* state. By convention, the active state is the value true. The *router* manages the communication

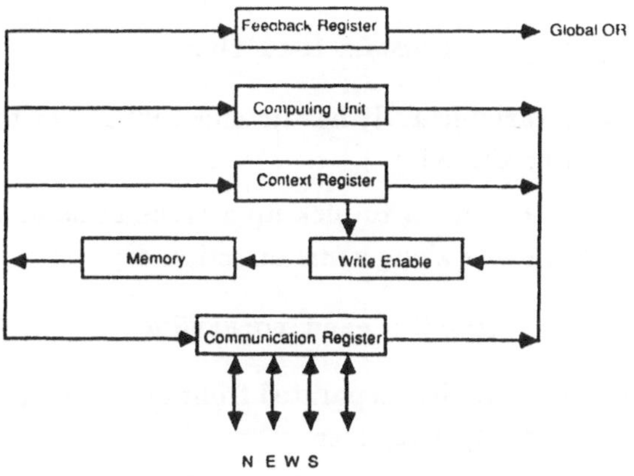

Figure 4: The architecture of a processing element

network. It exchanges data with the processor through the *communication register cm*. Finally, the processor is linked back to the sequencer through the *feedback register fb* to control loop iterations. We follow here the spirit of the Connection Machine implementation language ParIS (Parallel Instruction Set) [16].

The local instruction

$$\langle linst \rangle :: \; x := f(y, z)$$

stores into variable x the value $f(y, z)$ if *ct* is in the active state. Otherwise, it has no effect.

Register *ct* can be manipulated through load and store instructions:

$$\langle linst \rangle :: \texttt{load-ct}\ x$$

loads *ct* with the value of variable x, and

$$\langle linst \rangle :: \texttt{store-ct}\ x$$

stores the value of *ct* into variable x. Those instructions have always their effect whatever the state of *ct* is, as it is the only way of modifying it!

Register *cm* can be manipulated much in the same way.

$$\langle linst \rangle :: \texttt{load-cm}\ x$$

loads *cm* with the value of variable x. It has its effect whatever the state of *ct* is, as it always leaves the memory unaltered.

$$\langle linst \rangle :: \texttt{store-cm}\ x$$

stores the value of *cm* into variable *x*. It has its effect only if *ct* is in its active state.

Register *fb* only needs to be written.

$$\langle linst \rangle :: \texttt{load-fb}\ x$$

loads *fb* with the value of variable *x*. It has its effect whatever the state of *ct* is, as it always leaves the memory unaltered.

The only thing a router can do is to pick up a value at some *cm* register and then set it down at the neighbor's one along some direction *d*:

$$\langle rinst \rangle :: \texttt{send-to-NEWS}\ d.$$

As routers are (at least conceptually) separated from processors, this instruction is not affected by the value of the context register.

Finally, the sequencer is in charge of making the program run by broadcasting instructions to processors and routers.

$$\langle prog \rangle :: \ \langle linst \rangle | \langle rinst \rangle | \langle prog \rangle ; \langle prog \rangle .$$

It can also iterate some program up to the point where *all* feedback registers are false:

$$\langle prog \rangle :: \texttt{loop}\ \langle prog \rangle\ \texttt{end}\ .$$

Note that the sequencer is thus controlled by the oring of all the feedback registers. The same discussion as in section 2.1 applies here.

3.2 Semantics

We describe now a semantics for LL. It is split into two parts to reflect the local nature of processors and the global nature of the sequencer and routers.

At the local level, the state of a processor is simply a 4-uple $\langle \rho, ct, cm, fb \rangle$. Function ρ associates values to variables, and *ct*, *cm* and *fb* are the values of the corresponding registers.

Observe now that an elementary processor is essentially passive in a SIMD architecture. It receives an instruction and executes it. This behavior can thus be most accurately described by a function $\mathcal{L}$ which takes as input an instruction $\langle linst \rangle$ and a state $\langle \rho, ct, cm, fb \rangle$ and yields an output state. It is defined as follows:

▷

$$\mathcal{L}(x := f(y,z), \langle \rho, ct, cm, fb \rangle) = \langle \rho', ct, cm, fb \rangle$$

with $\rho'(x) = f(\rho(y), \rho(z))$ if *ct* is in its active state and $\rho'(x) = \rho(x)$ otherwise, and $\rho'(t) = \rho(t)$ for $t \neq x$;

▷

$$\mathcal{L}(\texttt{load-ct}\ x, \langle\rho, ct, cm, fb\rangle) = \langle\rho, \rho(x), cm, fb\rangle;$$

▷

$$\mathcal{L}(\texttt{store-ct}\ x, \langle\rho, ct, cm, fb\rangle) = \langle\rho', ct, cm, fb\rangle$$

with $\rho'(x) = ct$ and $\rho'(t) = \rho(t)$ for $t \neq x$;

▷

$$\mathcal{L}(\texttt{load-cm}\ x, \langle\rho, ct, cm, fb\rangle) = \langle\rho, ct, \rho(x), fb\rangle;$$

▷

$$\mathcal{L}(\texttt{store-cm}\ x, \langle\rho, ct, cm, fb\rangle) = \langle\rho', ct, cm, fb\rangle$$

with $\rho'(x) = cm$ if ct is in its active state and $\rho'(x) = \rho(x)$ otherwise, and $\rho'(t) = \rho(t)$ for $t \neq x$.

▷

$$\mathcal{L}(\texttt{load-fb}\ x, \langle\rho, ct, cm, fb\rangle) = \langle\rho, ct, cm, \rho(x)\rangle.$$

At the global level, a state of the sequencer is made of the program $\langle prog\rangle$ to be run and the states $\langle\rho_u, ct_u, cm_u, fb_u\rangle$ of each processor P_u. We denote $(x_u)_u$ the set of all variables x_u.

A local instruction broadcast by the sequencer acts processorwise:

$$\frac{\mathcal{L}(\langle inst\rangle, \langle\rho_u, ct_u, cm_u, fb_u\rangle) = \langle\rho'_u, ct'_u, cm'_u, fb'_u\rangle}{\langle\langle inst\rangle, (\langle\rho_u, ct_u, cm_u, fb_u\rangle)_u\rangle \longrightarrow \langle\texttt{stop}, (\langle\rho'_u, ct'_u, cm'_u, fb'_u\rangle)_u\rangle}.$$

A router instruction acts on communication registers only:

$$\langle\texttt{send-to-NEWS}\ d, (\langle\rho_u, ct_u, cm_u, fb_u\rangle)_u\rangle \longrightarrow \langle\texttt{stop}, (\langle\rho_u, ct_u, cm'_u, fb_u\rangle)_u\rangle$$

with $cm'_u = cm_{\overline{d}(u)}$.

Sequencing is defined by the usual rules. For the sake of readability, define $\tau = (\langle\rho_u, ct_u, cm_u, fb_u\rangle)_u$.

$$\frac{\langle\langle prog\rangle, \tau\rangle \longrightarrow \langle\langle prog\rangle', \tau'\rangle}{\langle\langle prog\rangle; \langle prog\rangle'', \tau\rangle \longrightarrow \langle\langle prog\rangle'; \langle prog\rangle'', \tau'\rangle}$$

with the convention $\texttt{stop}; \langle prog\rangle = \langle prog\rangle$.

$$\frac{\neg \bigvee_u fb_u}{\langle\texttt{loop}\ \langle prog\rangle\ \texttt{done}, \tau\rangle \longrightarrow \langle\texttt{stop}, \tau\rangle}$$

$$\frac{\bigvee_u fb_u}{\langle\texttt{loop}\ \langle prog\rangle\ \texttt{done}, \tau\rangle \longrightarrow \langle\langle prog\rangle; \texttt{loop}\ \langle prog\rangle\ \texttt{done}, \tau\rangle}$$

4 Implementing HL in LL

We make here precise the idea that the macroscopic view of SIMD architectures, as expressed by HL, is implemented by the microscopic view, as expressed by LL.

4.1 The compiling function

The first step is to define a compiling function C which translates programs in HL into programs in LL. We proceed by syntactic induction on the structure of HL programs. Let $V = \{v_0, v_1, \ldots\}$ be a fixed infinite set of new auxiliary variables of LL. We assume those variables cannot be accessed from HL: if X is a variable of HL, then the corresponding variable x of LL does not belong to V.

Local instructions carry over directly:

$$C[\![X := f(Y,Z)]\!] = x := f(y,z).$$

To compile a shift, we load the communication register with the value to shift, we instruct the router to send it in the specified direction and store the new value back:

$$\begin{aligned} C[\![\texttt{shift } X \texttt{ along } d]\!] = \; & \texttt{load-cm } x; \\ & \texttt{send-to-NEWS } d; \\ & \texttt{store-cm } x. \end{aligned}$$

Sequencing translates without change:

$$C[\![\langle prog\rangle; \langle prog\rangle']\!] = C[\![\langle prog\rangle]\!]; C[\![\langle prog\rangle']\!].$$

Iteration is translated by using the loop construct with suitable loadings of the feedback registers:

$$\begin{aligned} C[\![\texttt{while } B \texttt{ do } \langle prog\rangle \texttt{ done}]\!] = \; & \texttt{load-fb } b; \\ & \texttt{loop} \\ & \quad C[\![\langle prog\rangle]\!]; \\ & \quad \texttt{load-fb } b \\ & \texttt{end}. \end{aligned}$$

The **where** construct is implemented using the context register. Let *aux* be a fixed auxiliary variable of V. The current context is saved in a *new* auxiliary variable *save* of V left invariant by the body. The current context is then and-ed with the condition. The body is executed, and the initial context is then eventually restored. For well-definedness, let *save* be the variable of V with the least index which does not appear in the compilation of the body $C[\![\langle inst\rangle]\!]$ and different from *aux*. (Observe it exists as V

is infinite and the body is a finite program!).

$$
\begin{aligned}
\mathcal{C}[\![\texttt{where } B \texttt{ then } \langle inst \rangle \texttt{ end}]\!] = \; & \texttt{store-ct } save; \\
& aux := (save \wedge b); \\
& \texttt{load-ct } aux; \\
& \mathcal{C}[\![\langle inst \rangle]\!]; \\
& \texttt{load-ct } save
\end{aligned}
$$

For convenience, we also set $\mathcal{C}[\![\texttt{stop}]\!] = \texttt{stop}$.

4.2 Correctness of the implementation

The next step is to express the correctness of the compiling function $\mathcal{C}$ with respect to the semantics of HL and LL. For this purpose, we define an "adequation" relation $\mathcal{R}$ between states of HL and LL. Intuitively, two states are in relation $\mathcal{R}$ if they correspond to the "same machine state": the programs still to be run correspond via $\mathcal{C}$ and the corresponding variables have the same values. Say a HL environment σ and a LL environment $\tau = (\langle \rho_u, ct_u, cm_u, fb_u \rangle)_u$ *agree* if for all variable X of HL and for all position u, $\sigma(X)|_u = \rho_u(x)$ and $ct_u = true$.

Definition 2 *$\langle P, \sigma \rangle \; \mathcal{R} \; \langle Q, \tau \rangle$ if $Q = \mathcal{C}[\![P]\!]$ and σ and τ agree.*

Technically speaking, correctness is expressed by requiring $\mathcal{R}$ to be a *simulation.* Any step of $\langle P, \sigma \rangle$ can be "simulated" by a number of steps of $\langle Q, \rho \rangle$ so that the adequation relation $\mathcal{R}$ is preserved. Let $\xrightarrow{+}$ be the transitive closure of transition relation $\longrightarrow$: $\langle Q, \tau \rangle \xrightarrow{+} \langle Q', \tau' \rangle$ if one can go from the former to the latter by a sequence of *at least one* $\longrightarrow$-transitions.

Definition 3 *$\mathcal{C}$ is correct if for any states $\langle P, \sigma \rangle$ and $\langle Q, \tau \rangle$ the following holds.*

If $\langle P, \sigma \rangle \; \mathcal{R} \; \langle Q, \tau \rangle$ and $\langle P, \sigma \rangle \longrightarrow \langle P', \sigma' \rangle$ then there exists a state $\langle Q', \tau' \rangle$ such that $\langle P', \sigma' \rangle \; \mathcal{R} \; \langle Q', \tau' \rangle$ and $\langle Q, \tau \rangle \xrightarrow{+} \langle Q', \tau' \rangle$.

This cumbersome definition can be best understood by the following picture.

$$
\begin{array}{lccc}
\text{HL level} & \langle P, \sigma \rangle & \longrightarrow & \langle P', \sigma' \rangle \\
 & \updownarrow \mathcal{R} & & \updownarrow \mathcal{R} \\
\text{LL level} & \langle Q, \tau \rangle & \xrightarrow{+} & \langle Q', \tau' \rangle
\end{array}
$$

Property 2 *$\mathcal{C}$ is correct.*

We postpone the proof of this main property to section 4.5, and draw immediately two important consequences.

Property 3 *Let P be a* HL *program, σ a* HL *environment and τ a* LL *environment which agree together. If P terminates from σ with result σ', then $C[\![P]\!]$ terminates from τ with result τ', and σ' and τ' agree.*

This is easily proved using repeatedly the previous definition and $C[\![\texttt{stop}]\!] = \texttt{stop}$.

Property 4 *Let P be a* HL *program, σ a* HL *environment and τ a* LL *environment which agree together. If P diverges from σ then Q diverges from τ.*

This holds because Q must progress by at least one step ($\xrightarrow{+}!$) to simulate one step of P.

4.3 Alternative implementations of conditioning

Looking more closely at the compilation function, we can remark that variable *save* acts in fact as a stack. To reflect this fact, let us modify LL so as to make *ct* a stack of boolean registers instead of a single boolean register. The current state of *ct* is now the top element of this stack: it is active if the value at the top is true. (For well-definedness, say it is active if the stack is empty, too). In our compilation function, the context is explicitly accessed in the **where** instruction only. The sequence

$$\begin{array}{l}\texttt{store-ct}\ \mathit{save};\\ \mathit{aux} := (\mathit{save} \wedge b);\\ \texttt{load-ct}\ \mathit{aux}\end{array}$$

can thus be seen as a new LL instruction **push-ct-and** b which pushes on the top of the *ct* stack the and-ing of its top-value and b (cf. the ParIS instruction `logand-context`). (For well-definedness, say it merely pushes b on an empty stack). The sequence

$$\texttt{load-ct}\ \mathit{save}$$

can be seen as a new LL instruction `pop-ct` which pops the top value of the *ct* stack. (For well-definedness, say popping an empty stack leaves it unchanged). The compilation function becomes then

$$\begin{array}{rcl}C[\![\textbf{where}\ B\ \textbf{then}\ \langle inst\rangle\ \textbf{end}]\!] & = & \textbf{push-ct-and}\ b;\\ & & C[\![\langle inst\rangle]\!];\\ & & \texttt{pop-ct}\end{array}$$

and this is the only way a compiled HL programs accesses the context.

The implementation can even be further optimized as suggested by Paris in [15]. Observe that the pair **push-ct-and/pop-ct** enforces the following invariant property. The context stack is invariantly of the form

$$\text{(bottom) } T, T, T, \ldots, T, F, \ldots, F \text{ (top)}$$

where T denotes a true value (active state) and F a false value. Let n be the number of false values F. The context state is active if and only if $n = 0$. We want to show that it suffices in fact to manipulate n instead of the stack. Define

$$\text{incr}(n, b) = \begin{cases} 0 & \text{if } (n = 0) \wedge b \\ n + 1 & \text{otherwise} \end{cases}$$

and

$$\text{decr}(n) = \begin{cases} 0 & \text{if } n = 0 \\ n - 1 & \text{otherwise} \end{cases}$$

It is easy to check that the net effect of `push-ct-and` b is $n := \text{incr}(n, b)$, and the effect of `pop-ct` is $n := \text{decr}(n)$. We can thus modify LL so that to make *ct* a counter instead of a stack. This counter is accessed through two instructions:

`incr-ct` b

makes $ct := \text{incr}(ct, b)$, and

`decr-ct`

makes $ct := \text{decr}(ct)$ (both unconditionally, of course). The context is active iff $ct = 0$. The compilation function becomes then

$$\mathcal{C}[\![\texttt{where } B \texttt{ then } \langle inst \rangle \texttt{ end}]\!] = \texttt{incr-ct } b; \; \mathcal{C}[\![\langle inst \rangle]\!]; \; \texttt{decr-ct}$$

We can even go one step further and thereby close the loop. Observe that the context counter can be implemented by an ordinary variable, located in the memory, using a boolean context register as in the original LL. Say *counter* is a new fixed auxiliary variable not used elsewhere. We can replace the `incr-ct` b instruction by

`load-ct` *true*;
$aux := \neg((counter = 0) \wedge b)$;
`load-ct` *aux*;
$counter := counter + 1$;
`load-ct` *true*;
$aux := (counter = 0)$
`load-ct` *aux*

and the **decr-ct** instruction by

`load-ct` true;
$\mathit{aux} := \neg(\mathit{counter} = 0)$;
`load-ct` aux;
$\mathit{counter} := \mathit{counter} - 1$;
`load-ct` true;
$\mathit{aux} := (\mathit{counter} = 0)$;
`load-ct` aux.

Observe the following invariant is enforced: the context is active iff $\mathit{counter} = 0$.

4.4 Derived conditioning constructs

A derived construct of interest proposed in the POMPC language for instance is

where B **then** $\langle inst\rangle$ **else** $\langle inst\rangle'$ **end** .

We consider it as an abbreviation for

$C := \neg B$;
where B **then** $\langle inst\rangle$ **end**;
where C **then** $\langle inst\rangle'$ **end** .

with C being a *new* variable of `HL`. Its implementation through function $\mathcal{C}$ is as follows.

1 : $c := \neg b$;
2 : `incr-ct` b;
3 : $\mathcal{C}[\![\langle inst\rangle]\!]$;
4 : `decr-ct`;
5 : `incr-ct` c;
6 : $\mathcal{C}[\![\langle inst\rangle']\!]$;
7 : `decr-ct`

Our goal is to show that the middle pair `decr-ct; incr-ct` c can be replaced by a new optimized instruction `swap-ct`. For this purpose, consider the possible values of n, b and c at line 4. Let ν and β be the respective values of n and b at line 1.

$n = 0$, $c = \mathit{true}$ Because C is a new variable of `HL`, it does not appear between line 2 and line 5. At line 4, it has thus its original value $\neg\beta$. We infer thus β is false. Variable b is thus false at line 2. Hence $n \geq 1$ at line 3 by the semantics of `incr-ct`. Line 3 leaves n unchanged and $n \geq 1$ at line 4. A contradiction.

$n = 0$, $c = \mathit{false}$ Line 4 leaves n unchanged and line 5 increases it to 1.

$n = 1$, $c = \textit{true}$ Line 4 sets n to 0 and line 5 leaves it unchanged.

$n = 1$, $c = \textit{false}$ By reasoning as in the first case, we get β is true. If $\nu = 0$, then lines 1 and 2 leave n unchanged and $n = 0$ at line 4. A contradiction. If $\nu \geq 1$, then line 2 increases n by 1 and $n \geq 2$ at line 4. A contradiction again.

$n \geq 2$ Line 4 decreases n by 1 so that $n \geq 1$ at line 5. Line 5 increases then it by 1 so that it gets its original value back.

The value of n at line 6 depends thus on its value at line 4 only, and *not* on the values of b and c! Define

$$\text{swap}(n) = \begin{cases} 1 & \text{if } n = 0 \\ 0 & \text{if } n = 1 \\ n & \text{otherwise} \end{cases}$$

and define a new instruction `swap-ct` whose net effect is $n := \text{swap}(n)$. The compilation function becomes then

$$\begin{array}{l} \texttt{incr-ct}\ b; \\ \mathcal{C}[\![\langle inst \rangle]\!]; \\ \texttt{swap-ct}; \\ \mathcal{C}[\![\langle inst \rangle']\!]; \\ \texttt{decr-ct}\ . \end{array}$$

Observe that c does not appear any more.

4.5 Proof of correctness

We turn now to the correctness proof of the compiling function. We proceed by induction on the syntactic structure of the HL program P.

Atomic instructions

We start with atomic instructions. Let

$$P :: \texttt{where}\ B_1\ \texttt{then} \ldots \texttt{where}\ B_n\ \texttt{then}\ I\ \texttt{end} \ldots \texttt{end}$$

where I is either an assignment or a shift, and $n \geq 0$. Observe the case $n = 0$ corresponds to an unconditioned instruction. Let

$$\beta_u = (\sigma(B_1)|_u \wedge (\sigma(B_2)|_u \wedge (\ldots \sigma(B_n)|_u)))$$

By an easy induction on n, we show that

$$\frac{\langle I, \sigma \rangle \longrightarrow \langle \texttt{stop}, \sigma' \rangle}{\langle P, \sigma \rangle \longrightarrow \langle \texttt{stop}, \sigma'' \rangle}$$

with $\sigma''(T)|_u = \sigma'(T)|_u$ if β_u, and $\sigma''(T)|_u = \sigma(T)|_u$ otherwise. Consider $Q = \mathcal{C}[\![P]\!]$ and τ agreeing with σ. An easy induction on n shows that

$$
\begin{aligned}
Q :: \ & \texttt{store-ct}\ save_1; aux := save_1 \wedge b_1; \texttt{load-ct}\ aux;\\
& \ldots\\
& \texttt{store-ct}\ save_n; aux := save_n \wedge b_n; \texttt{load-ct}\ aux;\\
& \mathcal{C}[\![I]\!];\\
& \texttt{load-ct}\ save_n;\\
& \ldots\\
& \texttt{load-ct}\ save_1.
\end{aligned}
$$

Let τ' be the environment such that $\langle Q, \tau\rangle \xrightarrow{+} \langle \texttt{stop}, \tau'\rangle$. Let us check that σ'' and τ' agree together as soon as σ and τ do so. Observe that, by the condition on V, all variables b_i, $save_i$ and aux are distinct. Hence variables b_i keep their initial values up to $\mathcal{C}[\![I]\!]$ at least, that is $\rho_u(b_i)$. An easy induction on n shows then that, as $ct_u = true$ initially,

$$ct_u = (((\rho_u(b_1) \wedge \rho_u(b_2)) \wedge \ldots) \wedge \rho_u(b_n))$$

just before $\mathcal{C}[\![I]\!]$. But σ and ρ agree, and thus $\rho_u(b_i) = \sigma(B_i)|_u$. Hence, ct_u is true at this point iff β_u is true. We consider the two possible cases separately.

Assignment $I :: \ X := f(Y, Z)$. Then

$$J = \mathcal{C}[\![I]\!] :: \ x := f(y, z).$$

Again by the condition on V, variable y and z still have their initial values at this point, that is $\rho_u(y) = \sigma(Y)|_u$ and $\rho_u(z) = \sigma(Z)|_u$. After executing J, the new value of x is thus $f(\rho_u(y), \rho_u(z))$ if β_u and $\rho_u(x)$ otherwise, that is namely $\sigma''(X)|_u$ as σ and τ agree.

Communication $I ::$ **shift** X **along** d. Then

$$J = \mathcal{C}[\![I]\!] :: \texttt{load-cm}\ x; \texttt{send-to-NEWS}\ d; \texttt{store-cm}\ x.$$

After the `load-cm`, cm_u gets value $\rho_u(x)$. After the `send-to-NEWS`, it gets $\rho_{\vec{d}(u)}(x)$. After the `store-cm`, x gets value $\rho_{\vec{d}(u)}(x)$ if β_u and $\rho_u(x)$ otherwise, that is namely $\sigma''(X)|_u$ as σ and τ agree.

Finally, by the condition on *save* in the definition of the compiling function, variable $save_1$ does not appear between the first and the last instructions. It keeps thus its value all the way long, which was namely $ct_u = true$. We have thus $ct'_u = true$ as wanted. This shows that σ'' and τ' agree, as wanted.

Observe the context restoring instructions have no effect but the last one. This is a well-known phenomenon in compiling tail-recursive functions. Observe also that the proof uses crucially that the `load-cm`, `load-ct` and `store-ct` instructions are unconditional.

Sequencing

Consider now the case $P :: R; S$. A step of P is a step of R, and so for the corresponding steps of

$$\mathcal{C}[\![P]\!] = \mathcal{C}[\![R]\!]; \mathcal{C}[\![S]\!].$$

The result follows by the induction hypothesis.

Iteration

Consider finally the case P :: **while** B **do** R **done**. A step of P is either an unfolding to $R; P$ if $\bigvee_u \sigma(B)|_u$, or to **stop** otherwise. In both cases, the environment remains unchanged. We have

$$Q = \mathcal{C}[\![P]\!] :: \texttt{load-fb}\ b; \texttt{loop}\ \mathcal{C}[\![R]\!]; \texttt{load-fb}\ b\ \texttt{end}\ .$$

After the first step of Q, fb_u has value $\rho_u(b) = \sigma(B)|_u$ as σ and τ agree, and the loop unfolds either to $Q' :: \mathcal{C}[\![R]\!]; Q$, that is $\mathcal{C}[\![R; P]\!]$ if $\bigvee_u \rho_u(b) = \bigvee_u \sigma(B)|_u$ or to **stop** otherwise. Thus $Q' = \mathcal{C}[\![P']\!]$, $\tau' = \tau$, $\sigma' = \sigma$ and τ' and σ' agree as wanted. This concludes the proof.

5 General addressing and routing

In the HL language, we have considered a restricted form of communication, namely shifting: the relative address of the recipient is a syntactic constant, the same for all processors, restricted to be the address of some neighbor. This is an accurate model for specialized image processing processor arrays like MPP, DAP or GAPP, and for the Connection Machine in its NEWS mode. But general purpose processor arrays like the Connection Machine offer also more general forms of communication, where the recipient address is computed locally by each processor and may be arbitrary. In this section, we extend HL with the general **get** and **send** communication primitives. Our goal is to show that classical routing algorithms can be conveniently expressed and studied in our framework, and that such algorithms do not require any advanced programming or architecture feature.

5.1 Extending HL with general communication primitives

We define an extension of HL called $\mathtt{HL}^G$ (for HL with General communications) by adding to it the two instructions below. First comes the get instruction

$$\langle inst \rangle :: \texttt{get}\ X\ \texttt{from}\ A$$

where X is the variable to access and A the (locally computed) *absolute* address to get it from. Each processor P_u evaluates first the address $A|_u$. Let v be the local result. Then, the (local) variable $X|_u$ of P_u is loaded with the value of (remote) variable $X|_v$ of P_v.

The dual send instruction is a bit more complex, as we have to consider the case where several processors send to a single one. Some way of combining the incoming values has to be provided. Observe also that a given value can be sent by several processors. Let $\oplus$ be a commutative, associative combining function with a neutral element e. (Non-commutative or non-associative operators would yield non-deterministic communications which could also be of interest in some cases.) Typical examples found in the Connection Machine are add, max, min etc. Then $\oplus$ extends to an n-ary operator $\oplus_u x_u$, which is e if the index set is empty, and $x_{u_1} \oplus x_{u_2} \oplus \ldots$ otherwise. The send instruction is then

$$\langle inst \rangle :: \texttt{send } X \texttt{ to } A \texttt{ with } \oplus$$

where X is the variable to access, A is the (locally) computed *absolute* address to send it to, and $\oplus$ the function to used to merge incoming values. Each processor P_u evaluates first $A|_u$, yielding say v. It then sends to P_v the value of (local) P_u's variable $X|_u$. It collects then the values sent to him, combines them with $\oplus$ and stores the result into $X|_u$. Observe that the general case

$$\texttt{send } X \texttt{ to } A \texttt{ into } Y \texttt{ with } \oplus$$

is obtained using an auxiliary variable Aux by

$$Aux := X; \texttt{send } Aux \texttt{ to } A \texttt{ with } \oplus; Y := Aux.$$

We can easily describe the semantics of $\texttt{HL}^G$ by adding the following rules to the semantics of HL.

▷

$$\langle \texttt{get } X \texttt{ from } A, \sigma \rangle \longrightarrow \langle \texttt{stop}, \sigma' \rangle$$

with, for each array position u, $v = \sigma(A)|_u$ and $\sigma'(X)|_u = \sigma(X)|_v$ and $\sigma'(T)|_u = \sigma(T)|_u$ for $T \neq X$.

▷

$$\langle \texttt{send } X \texttt{ to } A \texttt{ with } \oplus, \sigma \rangle \longrightarrow \langle \texttt{stop}, \sigma' \rangle$$

with $S = \{v \mid u = \sigma(A)|_v\}$ (S is the set of all those processors P_v which send to P_u) and $\sigma'(X)|_u = \oplus_{v \in S} \sigma(X)|_v$, and $\sigma'(T)|_u = \sigma(T)|_u$ for $T \neq X$.

Observe that the intuitive duality between **send** and **get** communications is hidden in the mathematical semantics because a **get** is a one-to-one function when considered locally though it is many-to-one globally, whereas the **send** remains a many-to-one function even when considered locally.

As for HL in section 2.4, a substitution property for $\mathtt{HL}^G$ programs can be defined, and it can be checked that it is satisfied. As a consequence, a number of program optimizations can be derived from the semantics. We assume thereafter that a special array variable *This* is available which contains the coordinates of its elements: $This|_u = u$. For instance, it is right to optimize

$$A := This + (0,1); \mathbf{get}\ X\ \mathbf{from}\ A$$

by

$$\mathbf{shift}\ X\ \mathbf{along}\ W$$

and

$$A := This + (1,0); \mathbf{send}\ X\ \mathbf{to}\ A\ \mathbf{with}\ \oplus$$

by

$$\mathbf{shift}\ X\ \mathbf{along}\ E$$

whatever $\oplus$ is. Also, one can merge two successive **get** instructions with constant relative addresses into a single one. For instance, the program

$$\begin{array}{l} A := This + (\alpha,\beta); \mathbf{get}\ X\ \mathbf{from}\ A; \\ A := This + (\alpha',\beta'); \mathbf{get}\ X\ \mathbf{from}\ A \end{array}$$

is equivalent to

$$A := This + (\alpha+\alpha',\beta+\beta'); \mathbf{get}\ X\ \mathbf{from}\ A$$

and both can be freely interchanged.

As for **shift** in section 2, conditioned **get** and **send** can be reduced to unconditioned ones using an auxiliary variable. Finally, observe that our semantics even gives a well-defined meaning to such strange constructs as **get** X **from** X.

5.2 Implementing $\mathtt{HL}^G$ in HL : routing

Implementing $\mathtt{HL}^G$ in HL consists in reducing the general **get** and **send** instructions of $\mathtt{HL}^G$ into a combination of instructions of GL, including in particular **shift** communications. This is thus exactly what is usually called *routing*. The correctness of the routing algorithm is then namely the correctness of the implementation it specifies, as defined in section 4.2.

In this paper, we will consider two paradigms for routing general communications using shift communications. They can be probably best explained using the following story. Consider a sand grain lying on the bottom of the Ocean among all his colleagues, somewhere nearby North-America. Well, this sand grain looks forward visiting Europe... but how?

A first choice (see figure 5) is to jump into the Gulf Stream and to remain suspended in it as long as needed. Eventually, the sand grain says, the stream will make me hug the right shore and I will just drop down! In our terminology, this is called *passive* routing as the sand grain basically waits and sees within the global stream. Observe that the stream may carry many such grains at the same time, some to France, other to England.

A second choice (see figure 6) is to define beforehand the direct route the grain wants to follow through the Ocean. A each step, the sand grain says, I will wait and hitch-hike for a wave in the right direction. It will eventually come, I will jump into it for the length of the step and quickly drop down, waiting for a wave in the next direction. In our terminology, this is called *active* routing as the sand grain chooses the adequate waves to jump into according its own route.

All the algorithms below are described through three basic procedures.

Procedure *Init*: It makes all necessary initializations: the sand grain jumps into the Gulf Stream. It involves local computation only.

Procedure *Deliver*: It tests whether the message has reached its destination, and delivers it if so: the sand grain hugs the shore and jumps down. It involves local computation only.

Procedure *Step*(d): A general shift is proposed along direction d: the Gulf Stream proceeds one step in the direction, or a casual wave in this direction occurs. It contains an instruction **shift** ... **along** d, and this is the only place where a communication instruction occurs.

Variable *Routing*: It indicates that the message is still in transit. The routing has terminated when all elements of the array *Routing* are false.

The algorithms are then all built on the same skeleton. For each kind of routing, an infinite sequence of directions $(d_i)_i$ is given, with a generating local function $direction(i) = d_i$. The skeleton is then

```
I := 0;
Init;
Deliver;
while Routing
do
      I := I + 1;
      D := direction(I);
      Step(D);
      Deliver
done
```

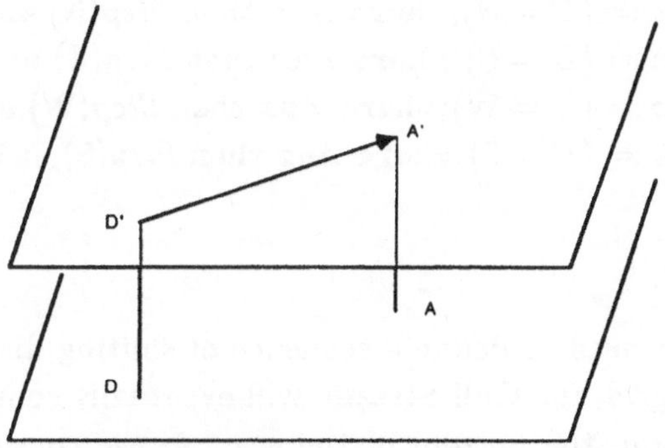

Figure 5: Passive routing

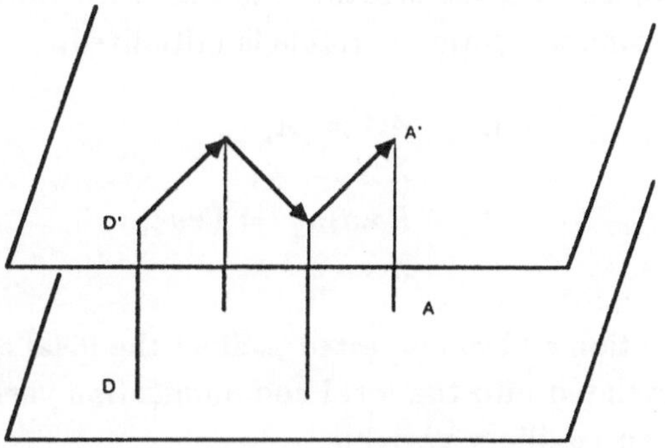

Figure 6: Active routing

Here, $Step(D)$ where D is a variable, is a shorthand for

$$\begin{array}{l} Aux := (D = \mathrm{N}); \texttt{where } Aux \textbf{ then } Step(\mathrm{N}) \textbf{ end}; \\ Aux := (D = \mathrm{E}); \texttt{where } Aux \textbf{ then } Step(\mathrm{E}) \textbf{ end}; \\ Aux := (D = \mathrm{W}); \texttt{where } Aux \textbf{ then } Step(\mathrm{W}) \textbf{ end}; \\ Aux := (D = \mathrm{S}); \texttt{where } Aux \textbf{ then } Step(\mathrm{S}) \textbf{ end} . \end{array}$$

5.2.1 Passive routing

For passive routing, we need to define a sequence of shifting directions such that each element of the shifted grid, the Gulf Stream, will eventually come in contact with each element of the fixed grid, the bottom of the sea. As we consider a two-dimensional infinite grid here, a spiral is a convenient choice. The first terms are N, E, S, S, W, W, N, N, N, E, E, E etc. It should be clear that function $direction(i)$ can be easily defined by simple arithmetics.

Consider now the send instruction `send` X `to` A `with` $\oplus$. In the initialization, the values to be sent are copied into the stream, together with their delivery address and their routing flag. The communication variable is initialized.

$$\begin{array}{ll} Init :: & AA := A; \\ & XX := X; \\ & Routing := True; \\ & X := e \end{array}$$

At each step, the destination address is tested against the local address. If they match, then the value is accumulated into the local communication variable, and the *Routing* flag is set. Let *Aux* be an auxiliary variable.

$$\begin{array}{ll} Deliver :: & Aux := (AA = This); \\ & \texttt{where } Aux \textbf{ then } X := X \oplus XX \textbf{ end}; \\ & \texttt{where } Aux \textbf{ then } Routing := False \textbf{ end} \end{array}$$

The stream proceeds one step ahead by shifting AA, XX, and *Routing*.

$$\begin{array}{ll} Step(d) :: & \texttt{shift } AA \textbf{ along } d; \\ & \texttt{shift } XX \textbf{ along } d; \\ & \texttt{shift } Routing \textbf{ along } d \end{array}$$

It is easy to check that this routing program terminates if and only if the relative destination addresses, that is $A - This$, are bounded, as it is always the case with a finite grid, of course.

Consider now the instruction `get` X `from` A. It is fortunately possible to avoid using successive waves of sending. The trick is to exchange the respective rôles of the moving and the fixed values A and $This$. This possibility illustrates probably best the intuitive duality between the send and the communication constructs, which is hidden in their semantics. The moving variable AA is now initialized to $This$, now the moving value.

$$\begin{aligned} \mathit{Init} ::\ & AA := \mathit{This}; \\ & XX := X; \\ & \mathit{Routing} := \mathit{True} \end{aligned}$$

It is now tested against A, the new fixed value.

$$\begin{aligned} \mathit{Deliver} ::\ & \mathit{Aux} := (AA = A); \\ & \texttt{where } \mathit{Aux} \textbf{ then } X := XX \textbf{ end}; \\ & \texttt{where } \mathit{Aux} \textbf{ then } \mathit{Routing} := \mathit{False} \textbf{ end} \end{aligned}$$

Variable *Routing* is now fixed.

$$\begin{aligned} \mathit{Step}(d) ::\ & \texttt{shift } AA \textbf{ along } d; \\ & \texttt{shift } XX \textbf{ along } d \end{aligned}$$

The same remark concerning termination holds here, as with the send instruction.

5.2.2 Active routing

For active routing, we need to define a sequence of shift directions (the waves) such that each direction is used infinitely many times (this is usually called a *fair* sequence). A round robin sequence N, E, S, W, N etc. can for instance be used, but it could be interesting in practical cases to have privileged directions occurring more often than others: N, E, N, S, N, W, N, N, N, E etc. It should be clear how to define the $\mathit{direction}(i)$ function. The description below is strongly influenced by the description of the routing strategy used in the Connection Machine, as found in [11]. In particular, procedure $\mathit{Step}(d)$ corresponds more or less to a part of a *dimension-cycle*.

Instead of considering global streams of addresses and values, we build individual messages made of a single address and a single value. Here, a message m is a pair $\langle \mathit{address}, \mathit{value} \rangle$. The fields are accessed by the notation $m.a$ and $m.x$. For simplicity, we use also a special message called *no_message*, with fields *no_address* and *no_value*, distinct from all other fields values. Each processor maintains a (unbound) heap of "hitch-hiking" messages waiting for a wave in the convenient direction to move ahead. The local function $m = \mathit{extract}(\mathit{heap}, d)$ extracts from the heap a message willing to move along direction d, or the special message *no_message* if none is found. The local function $\mathit{append}(m, \mathit{heap})$ adds a message to the heap, or does nothing if $m = \mathit{no\_message}$. Finally, $\mathit{reset}(\mathit{heap})$ initializes the heap, and $\mathit{empty}(\mathit{heap})$ tests it for emptyness. Observe that we do *not* make any hypothesis on the implementation of functions *extract* and *append* apart those mentioned above. In particular, it may be the case that the *extract*/*append* strategy is not FIFO.

We consider first the instruction **send** X **to** A **with** $\oplus$. In the initialization phase, messages are formed. The recipient variable is initialized.

$$\begin{aligned} \mathit{Init} ::\ & \mathit{reset}(\mathit{Heap}); \\ & M := \langle A, X\rangle; \\ & \mathit{Routing} := \mathit{True}; \\ & X := e \end{aligned}$$

At each step, a message is extracted. Its address is tested against the local address. If they match, it is accumulated into the recipient variable and the message is deleted (that is transformed into *no_message*). Otherwise, it is added to the heap of waiting messages.

$$\begin{aligned} \mathit{Deliver} ::\ & \mathit{Aux} := (M.a = \mathit{This}); \\ & \textbf{where } \mathit{Aux} \textbf{ then } X := X \oplus M.x \textbf{ end}; \\ & \textbf{where } \mathit{Aux} \textbf{ then } M := \mathit{No\_message} \textbf{ end}; \\ & \mathit{append}(M, \mathit{Heap}); \\ & \mathit{Routing} := \neg \mathit{empty}(\mathit{Heap}) \end{aligned}$$

Finally, a wave is proposed along some direction d. Extracted messages are shifted, waiting for their delivery.

$$\begin{aligned} \mathit{Step}(d) ::\ & M := \mathit{extract}(\mathit{Heap}, d); \\ & \textbf{shift } M \textbf{ along } d \end{aligned}$$

We cannot guarantee that this routing algorithm terminates without any extra hypothesis. Assume therefore that we have a measure δ to evaluate the distance between two positions in the grid, and that *extract* respects it, that is to say a message is extracted only if a move along the given direction strictly decreases the distance from its goal. This can be expressed by stating that, in each processor P_u,

$$m = \mathit{extract}(\mathit{heap}, d) \text{ implies } (\delta(u, m.a) > \delta(d(u), m.a)).$$

Then the usual termination property holds. If relative addresses (that is $A - \mathit{This}$) are bounded, then the program terminates.

Consider now the instruction **get** X **from** A. We implement it by a request/answer pair of send communications. A naive idea would be to make those waves proceed sequentially one after the other. Fortunately, we can even make those waves overlap. In counterpart, we have to tag all messages as "request" or "answer" according to the wave they belong to. Messages are now triples $\langle \mathit{address}, \mathit{tag}, \mathit{value}\rangle$. Fields are accessed as above by $m.a$, $m.t$ and $m.x$. Again, we define a special message *no_message* with address *no_address*, tag *no_tag* and value *no_value*, each distinct from all other field values. In the initialization phase, each processor builds a message with the address of the remote processor whose value is requested, tag "request" and as value its own address. Yet, a subtle synchronization problem may occur, due to the overlapping of the request and answer waves. A processor may receive the answer to its own request and set its variable X *before* answering to the request of other processors addressed to it. In consequence, each processor saves into an auxiliary variable *Xbis* the contents of its variable X to be sent to requesting processors.

$$\begin{aligned} \mathit{Init} ::\ & \mathit{reset}(\mathit{Heap}); \\ & M := \langle A, \text{“request”}, \mathit{This}\rangle; \\ & \mathit{Routing} := \mathit{True}; \\ & \mathit{Xbis} := X \end{aligned}$$

On receiving a message, two cases can occur. If it is a request message, then the processor deletes this message and creates a new one with address the value of the requesting message, tag "answer" and value the requested value saved in variable *Xbis* as explained above. If it is an answer message, then it and stores its value into its variable X and deletes it.

$$\begin{aligned} \mathit{Deliver} ::\ & \mathit{Aux} := ((M.a = \mathit{This}) \wedge (M.t = \text{“request”})); \\ & \texttt{where } \mathit{Aux} \texttt{ then } M := \langle M.x, \text{“answer”}, \mathit{Xbis}\rangle \texttt{ end}; \\ & \mathit{Aux} := ((M.a = \mathit{This}) \wedge (M.t = \text{“answer”})); \\ & \texttt{where } \mathit{Aux} \texttt{ then } X := M.x \texttt{ end}; \\ & \texttt{where } \mathit{Aux} \texttt{ then } M := \mathit{No\_message} \texttt{ end}; \\ & \mathit{append}(M, \mathit{Heap}); \\ & \mathit{Routing} := \neg \mathit{empty}(\mathit{Heap}) \end{aligned}$$

Finally, a wave is proposed along some direction d. Extracted messages are shifted and wait there for their delivery.

$$\begin{aligned} \mathit{Step}(d) ::\ & M := \mathit{extract}(\mathit{Heap}, d); \\ & \texttt{shift } M \texttt{ along } d \end{aligned}$$

The same remarks as above hold here.

Observe that we have up to now considered unbounded heaps only. If bounded heap are considered instead, as it is the case in practice, then the *append* of the *Deliver* phase may fail. One has thus to guarantee that at least one slot is still empty in the heap at the beginning of the *Deliver* phase. [11] proposes the following solution. When the heap gets almost full, one of the waiting message is mandatorily forwarded at the next step, even though the proposed direction may move it away from its goal. This can be easily guaranteed by modifying the semantics of *extract*(*heap*, d). If the heap is full and no message is willing to move along the proposed direction, then one of the waiting messages is arbitrarily extracted. Otherwise, it behaves as before. Note that the hypothesis about distances is then invalidated, an termination is no more guaranteed.

5.2.3 Remarks

A first remark is that passive routing is much simpler to describe in HL than active routing. It is in some sense much more "SIMD-like" in its spirit, as active routing involves some form of competition between messages. Also, we have not described in details house-keeping functions *append*, *extract*, *reset* and *empty*. Yet, it should be clear that they can be implemented in HL. Again, the only property needed for the correctness of the active routing algorithms is that the heap data structure is a multiset. We do not assume any FIFO hypothesis. Observe that an explicit coding of these functions will probably involve indirect addressing with local offset $Tab[K]$. This causes no semantic problem, as this possibility is implicitly contained in the instruction pattern $X := f(Y, Z)$. Another remark is that our routing algorithms can be adapted to handle the case where processors send or get several messages at a time. It suffices in fact to change the initialization phase only. This occurs in the Connection Machine for instance, when several virtual processors are emulated by a single one.

6 Conclusion

We are basically interested in the relationships between parallel architectures and the languages designed to control them. In the case of the MIMD architectures, for a long time there has been a considerable effort to develop both architectures and languages in mutual symbiosis. This effort has been extremely fruitful, as shown by the recent advent of the Transputer architecture and the Occam language. The situation is quite different in the case of SIMD architectures. There, it seems that the effort has been put on stretching the performances as far as possible, without regards to the languages and their semantics. (Number) Crunchers have already too much in their mouth to pay attention to their language...

A notable exception is the Connection Machine. Its hardware design supports a control language embodying minimal and orthogonal semantic concepts, and yet enjoying an adequate expressive power. This makes large scale structured programming *really* possible. Without simple and well-defined semantic concepts, the brute-force of the machine gets simply lost, as it is impossible for the programmer to design safely large and complex programs!

In this paper, we have proposed a minimal language HL with such properties.

- ▷ As far as we can see, many desirable language constructs found in "real" high level SIMD languages like *Lisp or POMPC can be expressed in HL.
- ▷ The conceptual simplicity of HL enables giving its formal semantics and studying program equivalences and transformations. In particular, we can give a precise

semantics for the **where** construct and show the correctness of its implementation through context registers.

- ▷ The two fundamental concepts of *conditioning* (**where**) and *communication* (**shift**) are rendered by two specific constructs in HL. The possibility of transforming a conditioned **shift** into an unconditioned one, as show in section 2.4, is the mathematical expression of the orthogonality of those two concepts.

- ▷ Nevertheless, the expressive power of HL enables expressing complex algorithms, including routing algorithms with various strategies, in an elegant way.

Yet, the design of HL raises a number of semantic difficulty common to all SIMD languages, but up to now left hidden in most cases.

- ▷ Those languages involve in fact two forms of communication: *internal* communication, as expressed by the **shift** instruction of HL, and *external* communication with the host by broadcast/reduce, as expressed by the **while** construct. The relationships between those two worlds are subtle and complex.

- ▷ There is a trade-off between communicating and conditioning. *The more you mix them arbitrarily, the less holds the substitution property.* In some sense, SIMD languages fall half the way between sequential languages and usual (we mean MIMD) parallel languages. Conditioning corresponds there to asynchrony. SIMD languages enjoy *both* the substitution property of sequential languages and some form of communication and asynchrony as found in parallel languages. The trade-off between conditioning and communicating in the language enables to adjust this balance. Language HL appears a bit restrictive in this respect, as asynchrony (conditioning) is limited to one atomic instruction only. It is possible to make it more liberal, as shown in [3]: asynchrony may involve arbitrary programs without communication, neither internal (shifts) nor external (while loops). This trade-off sounds actually very close to the SPMD (Single Program Multiple Data) principle, as found in Opsila for instance [1].

Here are some important future research directions.

- ▷ Our compiling function C extends to the liberal version of HLwithout problems. Yet, the proof does not extend at all to this case. The reason is that one has to handle context explicitly in the induction, whereas it could (admittingly with some effort) be left implicit in HL. In fact, the heart of the correctness proof is to go from a *syntactic* specification of context in HL trough the **where** B **then** ... **end** construct, to a *semantic* one in LL through values ct_u.

- ▷ In spite of the (implicit) parallelism, Hoare's proof methods ([10]) based on pre- and post-assertions may be applied to HL. In fact, the problem is *not* with communications, which are handled as special cases of assignments, but with asynchrony.

At this moment, we can derive formally a correctness proof for the program of section 2.2, which contains no `where`. But we do not know how to handle the `where` constructs properly in this framework.

▷ The problem of communicating beyond the borders of the grid has been left aside in this work. In fact, it is left unspecified by most SIMD languages. No specific semantic construct is given, and it is up to the programmer to find ad-hoc tricks to avoid unwanted effects. The simplicity of HL makes it possible to tackle this problem at the right level of semantic abstraction.

▷ In the design of HL, we have stuck to array variables. In real SIMD languages, one can manipulate *both* scalar variables and array variables. The interactions between those two worlds deserve further studies. For instance, how can one understand the well-known trick consisting in simulating a scalar variable by an array variable having its value as the common value of all its elements? Also, how can one take into account the scalar reduction functions in the language?

We believe this paper provides a convenient framework to tackle these problems at the right level of abstraction.

Acknowledgments

This work originates in the seminar "Architectures and Algorithms for Parallel Image Processing" held at LIENS in 1988. The first author thanks Philippe Clermont, Philippe Matherat and Nicolas Paris for having introduced him to the world of SIMD architectures. We thank the CNRS project C^3 for its support.

References

[1] Auguin, M., Boeri, F. The Opsila Computer. In: Parallel Algorithms and Architectures, Cosnard, M. et al. (Eds), Elsevier Science Publishers, 1986, pp. 143–153.

[2] Batcher, K. The design of a Massively Parallel Processor. IEEE Trans. on Computers C-29, 9, 1979, pp. 836–840.

[3] Bougé, L. On the semantics of languages for massively parallel SIMD architectures. Rept. No. 90-13, LIENS, Paris, 1990.

[4] Connection Machine Model CM-2 Technical Summary. Techn. Rept. HA 87-4, Thinking Machine Corp., 1987.

[5] Flynn, M.J. Some Computer Organizations and Their Effectiveness. IEEE Trans. on Computers C-21, 9, 1972, pp. 948–960.

[6] Fountain, T.J. CLIP4: A Progress Report. In: Languages and Architectures for Image Processing, Duff, M.J.B., Levialdi, S. (Eds), Academic Press, 1981, pp. 283–291.

[7] Fountain, T.J. A Survey of Bit-Serial Array Processor Circuit. In: Computing Structures for Image Processing, Duff, M.J.B. (Ed), Academic Press, 1983, pp. 1–14.

[8] Frenkel, K. Evaluating two massively parallel machines. Comm. ACM 29, 8, 1986, pp. 752–758.

[9] Gerritsen, F.A. A comparison of the CLIP4, DAP and MPP processor-array implementations. In: Computing Structures for Image Processing, Duff, M.J.B. (Ed), Academic Press, 1983, pp. 15–30.

[10] Hoare, C.A.R. An axiomatic basis for computer programming. Comm. ACM 12, 10, 1969, pp. 576–580, 583.

[11] Hillis, W.D. The Connection Machine. MIT Press, Cambridge, Mass., 1985.

[12] Hunt, D.J. The ICL DAP and its application to image processing. In: Languages and Architectures for Image Processing, Duff, M.J.B., Levialdi, S. (Eds), Academic Press, 1981, pp. 275–282.

[13] Lua, K.T., Wong, W.F. Geometric Arithmetic Parallel Processor — An Evaluation. Proc. Interdepartment Seminar on Supercomputers and Applications, Publ. TRIO/87, Dept. Information Systems and Comp. Science, Nat. Univ. Singapore, 1987, pp. 44–61.

[14] Olderog, E.-R., Apt, K. Fairness in parallel programs: the transformational approach. ACM Trans. on Progr. Lang. and Systems 10, 3, 1988, pp. 420–455.

[15] Paris, N. Définition de POMPC. Typescript, LIENS, Paris, 1989.

[16] ParIS: The C Interface. Reference Manual. Thinking Machine Corporation, 1987.

[17] Perrott, R.H. A language for array and vector processors. ACM Trans. Progr. Lang. 1, 2, 1979, pp. 177–195.

[18] Reeves, R.W. Parallel Pascal and the Massively Parallel Processor. In: The Massively Parallel Processor, Potter, J.L. (Ed), MIT Press, 1985, pp. 230–260.

[19] Hockney, R.W., Jesshope, C.R. Parallel Computers 2: Architectures, Programming and Algorithms. IOP Publishing Ltd, 1988.

[20] Steele, G.H., Hillis, W.D. Connection Machine Lisp : Fine-Grain Parallel Symbolic Processing. Proc. 1986 ACM Conf. on Lisp and Funct. Progr., Cambridge, MA, 1986, pp. 279–297.

[21] *Lisp Language Reference Manual. Thinking Machine Corporation, 1988.

Concerning the size of clocks

Bernadette Charron-Bost
I.N.T., 9 rue C. Fourier, 91011 Evry
L.R.I. Université Paris XI, 91405 Orsay
France

1 Introduction

Distributed systems with no known bounds on relative processor speed and transmission delay are called *asynchronous*. In such a system coordination and synchronization between processes are difficult to achieve. So the design and the proof of distributed algorithms for asynchronous systems are much subtle than for a classical centralized environment.

These difficulties vanish if the processes have a common time base, *i.e.* have access to perfectly synchronized clocks. But in asynchronous systems, such common clock cannot be achieved.

In [8] Lamport shows how to simulate a global clock by a clock that just captures causality. Such clocks are called *logical clocks* and are sufficient for instance to solve the mutual exclusion problem or for achieving a snapshot.

However with a logical clock we loose some informations about the causality relation which are crucial for implementing causal ordering (*cf.* [4]), debugging distributed systems (*cf.* [5]) or for assessing concurrency (*cf.* [1]). In [6] and [9] Fidge and Mattern independently improve Lamport's virtual time with a clock that entirely reflects the partial order defined by the causality relation. The dates assigned to the events are vectors of $\mathbf{R}^n$ where n is the number of processes and the use of such vectors may seem very heavy as soon as one is concerned with a distributed system on a large number of processes.

In this paper by constructing an appropriate distributed computation we prove that smaller clocks do not work if one wants to characterize causality. Then we use classical theorems of the theory of partially ordered sets to give a mathematical interpretation of this result.

2 Description of the model

Let us briefly describe the formal model of distributed systems and their computations we use in the sequel.

2.1 Model of a distributed system

A distributed system consists of a finite set of *processes* $\{P_1, \cdots, P_n\}$. A process P_i is characterized by a set of finite sequences C_i of *events*. This set is prefix closed. An event of C_i is either an internal event or the sending of a message to another process P_j or the receipt of a message which is sent to P_i. Notice that the processes are sequential since they are defined by sequences.

We assume that all the messages and all the events are different. Multiple occurrences of the same message or the same event could be distinguished by affixing subscripts to them. Every message sent by P_i to P_j contains the two names P_i and P_j. So a message cannot be sent (resp. received) by two different processes.

2.2 Computation of a distributed system

Let $\{P_1, \cdots, P_n\}$ be a distributed system and, for any i, let C_i be one of the sequences which define P_i. We define the relation $\prec$ on the set of events of $C_1 \cup \cdots \cup C_n$ as the smallest transitive relation satisfying the following conditions: (1) if a and b occur in the same process and if a comes before b then $a \prec b$; (2) if a is the sending of a message m and if b is the receipt of m, then $a \prec b$.

Definition 1 *A n-tuple $C = (C_1, \cdots, C_n)$ is a computation of $\{P_1, \cdots, P_n\}$ if it satisfies the following two properties: (1) $(C, \prec)$ contains no cycle; (2) for every receipt of the message m, there is a single sending of m.*

Thus in this model, the communications are asynchronous and point to point. Moreover the messages may be received in a different order than sent.

From (1), it follows that the events of C are partially ordered by the relation $\prec$ which is called the *causality* relation. We define the relation $\preceq$ by: $a \preceq b$ iff $a \prec b$ or $a = b$. We shall say that two events a and b of a distributed computation are *concurrent* (and we shall denote a co b) iff we have $\neg(a \preceq b)$ and $\neg(b \preceq a)$.

It is helpful to use the space-time diagrams introduced by Lamport in [8] to picture computations (see Figure 2). In these diagrams, the vertical lines denote processes; a send event and its corresponding receipt are joined together by a directed line. Such a diagram entirely defines a computation.

3 Clocks

As mentioned in Introduction, the design of efficient or simpler algorithms may require to have a tool to decide whether two events are causally dependent or concurrent. A natural way to detect causality is the "dating" of events: one assigns a timestamp to every event and one establishes that two events are concurrent by comparing their dates. Every procedure that allots a date to each event in a computation will be called *a clock*.

3.1 Logical clocks

In this section, if a is an event of a distributed computation equipped with a clock, we shall denote $\chi(a)$ its date according to this clock. In [8] Lamport dates the events by integers and distinguishes the clocks that satisfy the following condition:

$$(*) \quad a \prec b \Longrightarrow \chi(a) < \chi(b).$$

These clocks preserve the causality relation and are called *logical clocks*. In his paper Lamport explains how to construct such clocks by stamping the messages.

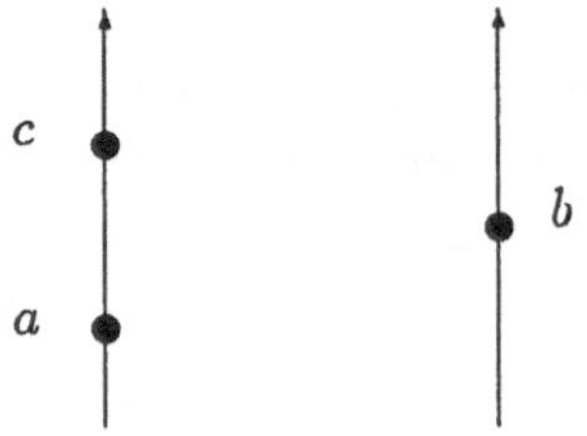

Figure 1

Let us observe that the implication converse of (*) cannot hold because that would imply $\chi(a) = \chi(b)$ if a and b are concurrent; but it is easy to build an example of computation where this equality cannot be true. For instance, in the computation C defined by Figure 1 we would get $\chi(a) = \chi(c) = \chi(b)$. This would contradict (*).

Logical clocks are sufficient for designing some efficient distributed algorithms. For instance, in [8] the use of a virtual time implemented by logical clocks provides a distributed solution for the mutual exclusion problem. However for implementing causal ordering (*cf.* [4]) or for assessing concurrency (*cf.* [1]), it is crucial to design a clock that not only preserves but also *characterizes concurrency*, *i.e.* satisfies (*) and the converse of (*).

Fidge and Mattern have independently constructed a clock that characterizes concurrency (see [6] and [9]); the dates which are assigned by this clock are not numbers but vectors. We now recall the construction and the main properties of this clock.

3.2 Vector clock

Let us introduce some notations. If v is a vector in $\mathbf{R}^n$ then the i-th component of v will be denoted by $v[i]$. The set $\mathbf{R}^n$ is naturally ordered by the relation $\leq$ defined by: $u \leq v$ iff $u[i] \leq v[i]$ for any index i. If u and v are two vectors of $\mathbf{R}^n$ we shall denote $w = \sup(u, v)$ the vector of $\mathbf{R}^n$ the i-th component of which is $\max(u[i], v[i])$.

Now we describe the construction of a clock for the distributed computations with n processes following [6] and [9]. The dates assigned by this clock will belong to $\mathbf{N}^n$; such a clock will be called a *vector clock of size n*.

Each process P_i is equipped with a clock Θ_i with values in $\mathbf{N}^n$. The initial value of Θ_i is $[0, \cdots, 0]$ and after each event on P_i the i-th component of Θ_i is incremented by 1 before any other event occurs on P_i. As in Lamport's scheme, every message m coming from P_i contains a timestamp that is equal to the value of Θ_i when m has been sent (timestamps are vectors). Upon receiving a message timestamped by t, a process adapts its clock by $\Theta_i := \sup(\Theta_i, t)$. Finally to any event a we assign its vector date $\Theta(a) = \Theta_i(a)$ if a occurs in C_i. Figure 2 shows an example of the time propagation scheme.

3.3 Properties of the clock Θ

The clock Θ satisfies the following property as a direct consequence of its definition.

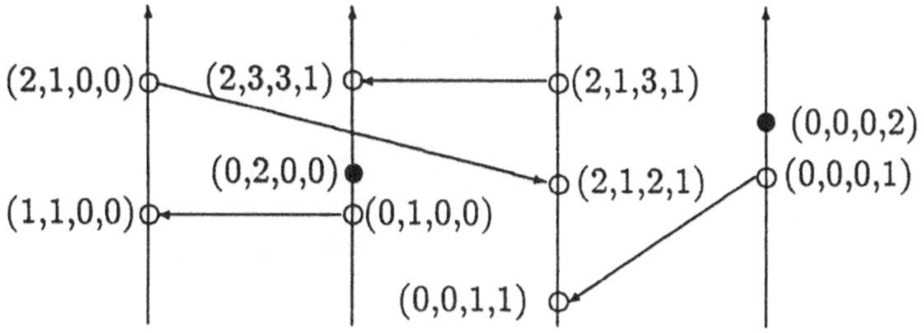

Figure 2

Proposition 1 *For any event a, $\Theta(a)[i]$ equals the number of the events of P_i which belong to the past of a:*

$$\Theta(a)[i] = |C_i \cap (\downarrow a)|.$$

This basic property allows to prove that Θ characterizes concurrency.

Theorem 1 *For any events a and b of a distributed computation, we have*

$$a \prec b \Longleftrightarrow \Theta(a) < \Theta(b).$$

Observe that the implication $\Longrightarrow$ is a direct consequence of Proposition 1. For a complete proof of Theorem 1, see [1].

4 The size n is necessary

Theorem 1 proves that it is possible to design a clock that characterizes concurrency by using vectors of size the number of processes. The use of such vectors may seem very heavy, for instance if one is concerned with a distributed computation on a large number of processes.

The object of this section is to build a computation C distributed over n processes such that any vector clock which characterizes concurrency among the events of C has a size at least equal to n. This will prove that we cannot reduce the size of the clocks characterizing concurrency if we just know the number of processes.

4.1 Description of a computation C

Let C_i be the sequence

$$C_i = [e_i^{i+1}, e_i^{i+2}, \cdots, e_i^n, e_i^1, \cdots, e_i^{i-2}, r_i^{i-1}, r_i^{i-2}, \cdots, r_i^1, r_i^n, \cdots, r_i^{i+2}]$$

where e_i^j denotes the sending of a message from the process P_i to the process P_j and r_i^j the receipt of a message coming from P_j by P_i (see Figure 3). Clearly $C = (C_1, \cdots, C_n)$ is a distributed computation, in the sense of the definition of Section 2.2.

Let $a_i = r_i^{i+2}$ and $b_{i-1} = e_i^{i+1}$. Then we have:

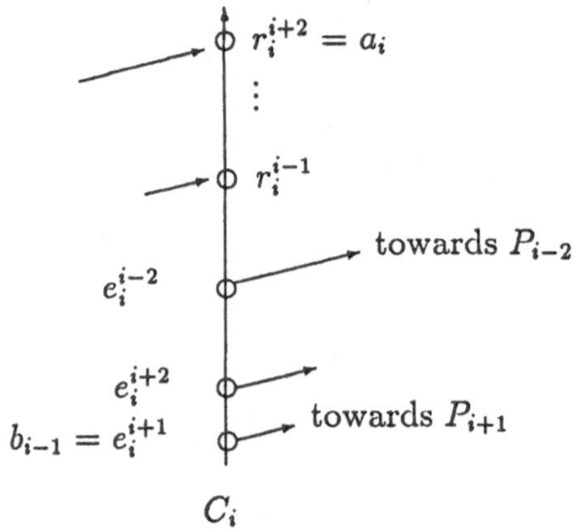

Figure 3

P1 $\forall (i,j) \in \{1,\cdots,n\}^2, \quad i \neq j \Longrightarrow b_i \prec a_j.$

Indeed if $i = j-1$ then a_j and b_i occur on the same process and $b_i = b_{j-1} \prec a_j$; else $b_i = e_{i+1}^{i+2} \preceq e_{i+1}^{j} \prec r_j^{i+1} \preceq r_j^{j+2} = a_j$.

Moreover, by using the fact that the future of any receipt or the past of any sending consists of events on the same process and that there is no message from P_{i+1} to P_i, one easily checks the following property:

P2 $\forall i \in \{1,\cdots,n\}, \quad a_i \operatorname{co} b_i.$

4.2 The computation C needs vector clocks of size n

The following theorem is a formal consequence of the properties P1 and P2.

Theorem 2 *If* $\Theta : C \longrightarrow \mathbf{R}^m$ *is a vector clock that characterizes concurrency then*

$$m \geq n.$$

Proof As Θ characterizes concurrency, it follows from P2 that for any index $i \in \{1,\cdots,n\}$ there exists $k \in \{1,\cdots,m\}$ such that

$$\Theta(a_i)[k] < \Theta(b_i)[k].$$

Let us choose one of these indices k and denote it by $\phi(i)$. In that way, we define a map $\phi : \{1,\cdots,n\} \longrightarrow \{1,\cdots,m\}$.

In order to establish Theorem 2, it is enough to prove that ϕ is injective. Assume the contrary, *i.e.* that there exist three indices i,j,k such that

$$\phi(i) = \phi(j) = k \quad \text{and} \quad i \neq j.$$

Then according to the definition of ϕ we have

$$\Theta(a_i)[k] < \Theta(b_i)[k]$$

and

$$\Theta(a_j)[k] < \Theta(b_j)[k].$$

From P1, it follows

$$\Theta(b_i)[k] < \Theta(a_j)[k].$$

Therefore

$$\Theta(a_i)[k] < \Theta(b_j)[k].$$

As Θ characterizes causality, this inequality contradicts P1. □

Remarks

1) Consider the total algorithm D described by Tel in [12] for a network such that

$$\forall i \in \{1, \cdots, n\},\ \forall j \in \{1, \cdots, n\} \setminus \{i-1, i\}, P_j \text{ is a neighbour of } P_i.$$

Then the computation C corresponds to anyone of the two phases of D.
2) Theorem 2 shows that if we just know that a computation is distributed over n processes, we need a vector clock of size n for characterizing concurrency. If we have informations about the partial order $(C, \prec)$, it is possible to reduce this size.

For instance, if a distributed computation $C = (C_1, \cdots, C_n)$ is entirely concurrent (*i.e.* contains no receipt, *cf.* [1]), and if we know the cardinality of each C_i equals q_i then we easily check that the vector clock of size 2 which assigns the couple

$$(q_1 + \cdots + q_{i-1} + |C_i \cap (\downarrow a)|, |C_i \cap (\downarrow a)| + q_{i+1} + \cdots + q_n) \in \mathbf{N}^2$$

to $a \in C_i$ characterizes concurrency.

5 Mathematical interpretation

The aim of this section is to give a mathematical discussion of Theorem 1 and Theorem 2 using classical notions of combinatorics.

First let us recall some basic definitions and results.

Let X be a nonempty set with a partial order P. A *linear extension* of (X, P) is a total order (X, L) such that

$$\forall (x, y) \in X^2,\quad xPy \Longrightarrow xLy.$$

Szpilrajn has proved the following theorem in [11].

Theorem 3 (Szpilrajn) *Every partial ordering P of a set X has a linear extension and the intersection of all the linear extensions of P is P itself.*

Generally, one doesn't need all the linear extensions for determining a partial order. A *realizer* of P is any collection of linear extensions the intersection of which is the order P. In order to analyze the "complexity" of P, one considers the minimum cardinality of a realizer of P. This number is called the *dimension* of (X, P) and is denoted by $\dim(X, P)$ (*cf.* [3]).

By extension, we shall call *dimension of a distributed computation* $C = (C_1, \cdots, C_n)$ the dimension of the partial order $(\cup_{i=1}^n C_i, \prec)$.

Clearly, this number equals 1 iff C is sequential, *i.e.* the causality relation defines a total order (*cf.* [1]). By considering the two linear extensions[1]

$$L = [C_1; \cdots; C_n] \quad \text{and} \quad L' = [C_n; \cdots; C_1]$$

we check that if C is entirely concurrent, its dimension is 2.

Let us recall another definition from the theory of partially ordered set. A partial order (X, P) is said *to be embedded* in a partial order (Y, Q) if there exists a map $\Phi : X \longrightarrow Y$ such that

$$\forall (x, y) \in X^2 \quad xPy \Longleftrightarrow \Phi(x) Q \Phi(y).$$

Thus Theorem 1 shows that every distributed computation over n processes (or more exactly the partial order $(\cup_{i=1}^n C_i, \prec)$) is embedded in $(\mathbf{R}^n, <)$.

In [10] Ore gives a characterization of the dimension of a partially ordered set in terms of embedding in $(\mathbf{R}^n, <)$.

Theorem 4 (Ore) *A finite partially ordered set (X, P) can be embedded in $(\mathbf{R}^k, <)$ if and only if*

$$k \geq dim(X, P).$$

It follows that the minimal size of a vector clock that characterizes concurrency among the events of a distributed computation equals its dimension.

Finally, let us recall that an *antichain* of a partially ordered set (X, P) is a subset A of X such that for any two distinct elements a, b of A we have neither aPb nor bPa.

In [7] Hiragushi connects the size of the antichains of (X, P) with its dimension.

Theorem 5 (Hiragushi) *If the size of the largest antichain of the finite partially ordered set (X, P) is m then*

$$dim(X, P) \leq m.$$

From this result we deduce that the dimension of a computation distributed over n processes is less than n since any set of events of cardinality strictly greater than n cannot be an antichain because it contains two events that occur on the same process. Combining this result with Ore's Theorem, we obtain that there exists a vector clock of size n characterizing concurrency.

Let us again consider the computation defined in Section 4.1. Combining Ore's Theorem and Theorem 2, we get that the dimension of this computation distributed over n processes equals n. We straightforwardly rediscover this result by translating the proof of Theorem 2 in terms of linear extension (see [2], page 24).

Thus classical theorems of combinatorics provide a direct proof of the existence of vector clocks characterizing concurrency of size the number of processes. Of course this was already known by the results of Fidge and Mattern who moreover give an explicit algorithm for defining such a clock. Yet the combinatorial interpretation also gives an explanation of the occurrence of the number n of processes in the size of clocks: this number is the upper bound of the dimensions of the computations distributed over n processes.

---

[1] The semicolon denotes concatenation.

6 Conclusion

By Fidge and Mattern's algorithm, it was already known that it is sufficient to use n-tuple as timestamps of events for a system distributed over n processes if causal independence is to be characterized. In this paper we have shown that smaller clocks do not work if we just know the number of processes. Then using theorems about the dimension of partially ordered sets we have given a mathematical interpretation of this result.

Finally we would like to mention that these combinatorial notions allow to rephrase our result about the "necessity of size n" in a way which does not give any special role to the partially ordered sets $(\mathbf{R}^n, <)$ or $(\mathbf{N}^n, <)$.

Indeed, causality can be characterized by using other reference partially ordered sets than these ones. For instance we can allot $q_1, \cdots, q_n$ to the processes $P_1, \cdots, P_n$ and we can use the numbers $\Pi_{i=1}^{n} q_i^{u[i]}$ instead of the vectors $u = \Theta(a) \in \mathbf{R}^n$ ("Gödel coding"). Then the causality between the events a is detected by the divisibility of these numbers.

However, whatever reference partial order is used to define a clock, the example of Section 4 shows that its dimension must be at least n if this clock has to characterize concurrency of systems distributed over n processes.

References

[1] B. Charron-Bost. Combinatorics and geometry of consistent cuts. In *Third International Workshop on Distributed Algorithms*, pages 48–61, LNCS,Springer Verlag, 1989.

[2] B. Charron-Bost. *Mesures de la Concurrence et du Parallélisme des calculs répartis.* PhD thesis, Université Paris 7, Septembre 1989.

[3] R.P. Dilworth. A decomposition theorem for partially ordered sets. *Annals of Mathematics*, 51:161–166, 1948.

[4] J. Eggli, A. Sandoz, and A. Schiper. A new algorithm to implement causal ordering. In *Third International Workshop on Distributed Algorithms*, pages 219–232, LNCS,Springer Verlag, 1989.

[5] J. Fidge. Partial orders for parallel debugging. In *Proc. ACM/SIGPLAN/SIGOPS Workshop on Parallel and Distributed Debugging*, pages 183–194, 1988.

[6] J. Fidge. Timestamps in message passing systems that preserve the partial ordering. In *Proc. 11th. Australian Computer Science Conference*, pages 55–66, 1988.

[7] T. Hiraguchi. *On the dimension of orders.* Technical Report, University of Kanazawa, 1955.

[8] L. Lamport. Time, clocks and the orderings of events in a distributed system. *Comm. of ACM*, 21,7:558–564, 1978.

[9] F. Mattern. Virtual time and global states of distributed systems. In *Parallel and Distributed Algorithms*, pages 215–226, North-Holland, 1988.

[10] O. Ore. Theory of graphs. In *Math. Soc. Colloq. Publ. 38*, Providence R.I., 1962.

[11] E. Szpilrajn. Sur l'extension de l'ordre partiel. *Fund. Math.*, 16:386–389, 1930.

[12] G. Tel. Total algorithms. In *Parallel and Distributed Algorithms*, pages 187–198, North-Holland, 1988.

Transition Systems with Algebraic Structure as Models of Computations*

Andrea Corradini, Gian Luigi Ferrari and Ugo Montanari

Università di Pisa
Dipartimento di Informatica
Corso Italia 40
I - 56125, Pisa, Italy

Abstract. This paper is a tutorial introduction to a general methodology, consisting of categorical constructions, for the definition of new algebraic semantics for transition-based formalisms. The methodology individuates three levels of semantic description: programs, structured transition systems, and models. The various formalisms differ for the structure on states and transitions, with respect to which all the categorical constructions of the methodology are parametric. These constructions generate in an automatic way the induced transition system and the free model of a program. One characterizing issue of the methodology is that structured transition systems have a (usually algebraic) structure on *both* the states and the transitions, while for example in Plotkin's SOS approach just the structure of states is relevant. The advantage of considering transition systems with an algebraic structure on transitions, too, resides in the fact that often the same structure can be automatically extended to the computations of the system. This yields to categories whose arrows are not simple sequences of elementary transitions, but are instead abstract computations, equipped with a rich algebraic structure. The methodology generalizes the algebraic treatment of Petri nets proposed in [MM88], and includes the main ideas of the algebraic semantics for Horn Clause Logic presented in [Co90, CM90], and of the algebraic treatment of Milner's CCS, reported in [Fe90, FM90].

Table of Contents

---

* Research partially supported by Esprit Basic Research Action Program, Project n. 3011 CEDISYS, and by Progetto Finalizzato Sistemi Informatici e Calcolo Parallelo, Project LAMBRUSCO.

1 Introduction

A considerable number of different approaches to the description of the semantics of computational systems have been proposed, ranging from logical to algebraic and from operational to denotational. Thus, one of the challenging problems in Theoretical Computer Science is to unify the different approaches to semantics. In this paper, we approach this problem by defining a general mathematical framework for the uniform description of the semantics of computational systems, based on (structured) transition systems.

The technical approach has been inspired by a joint work of the third author with J. Meseguer [MM88], where a new algebraic definition for Place/Transition Petri nets [Rei85] has been proposed in terms of graphs with a commutative monoidal structure on states and transitions. In this paper we generalize the approach introduced in [MM88] by developing a methodology for defining an algebraic semantics for a wide class of formalisms. We show the generality and the expressiveness of the methodology by providing with a new algebraic semantics both Logic Programs [Ll87], and Process Description Languages (e.g. Milner's Calculus of Communicating Systems (CCS) [Mi89]).

It is widely recognized that *transition systems* [Ke76] are a rather universal model of computations. Almost every computational system, either sequential or parallel, can be equipped with operational definitions in terms of transition systems. It is sufficient to identify the collection of *states* or *configurations* of the system, and then to describe how the system evolves from one configuration to another.

Often, transition systems are endowed with an algebraic structure on states, i.e. states are terms of an algebra. Transitions are then defined by axioms and inference rules driven by the syntactic structure of states. According to this techniques, called *Structured Operational Semantics* [Pl81], to show that a transition exists in the transition system means to prove that the transition is a theorem of a deductive system.

Transition systems are well suited to handle computational systems characterized by their on-going behaviour, e.g. concurrent and distributed systems. Properties of the behaviour of these systems cannot be described by resorting to a function from initial to final states, but the intermediate states of the computations the system may perform should be also taken into account. Computations based semantics permit to deal with properties like deadlock, fairness, and so on, which could not be captured within an initial/final state (or input/output) semantics.

However, the computations of a transition system are usually defined as *sequences* of elementary transitions. This simple notion of computation fails in capturing many relevant properties of computations of systems which manifest, for example, some aspects of spatial distribution or concurrency. For instance, computations which differ just for the order of independent transitions cannot be identified because, within a classical transition system semantics, there is no way of expressing the notion of independence between transitions. This limitation has led to extend the notion of transition system by enriching either the structure of states [DM87, DDM88a, DDM88b, DDM89], or the structure of transitions [St89, BC89]. Identifying different concrete computations yields to consider abstract computations, i.e. equivalence classes of concrete computations. In other words, an abstract computation is an equivalence class of computations which have the same specifications or properties, but which are implemented in different ways.

One characterizing issue of our proposal is to consider transition systems which have algebraic structure *both* on states and transitions, namely ***structured transition systems***. As pointed out in [Co90], often a computational system (for example logic programs, Petri nets, and grammars are considered there: let us call them 'programs' for short) is endowed with a natural notion of states and transitions. However, such programs cannot be considered, as they are, as true transition systems. In fact, while in the case of transition systems a transition t: u → v can be applied only to state u, usually a more permissive *matching rule* is either implicitly or explicitly associated to such programs, stating when and how a transition can be applied to a state, and which the resulting new state is. For example, in the case of a Petri net a transition can be fired at a marking (i.e. at a global state) if its preconditions are included in the marking itself; in the case of a logic program, a clause can be applied to a goal if its head unifies with an atomic formula of that goal.

Although those programs are not transition systems, often it is the case that a *structured* transition system can be defined, which, incorporating the matching rule into the structure of transitions, is able to suitably model the behaviour of the original program. This will be called the *induced transition system* of the program. For Petri nets, for example, the induced transition system of a net is its marking graph. As we will see, if certain conditions are satisfied, the induced transition system can be automatically generated from the program it simulates via a free construction which lifts the algebraic structure of states to transitions. It should be stressed that in the case of CCS, unlike logic programs and Petri nets, a structured transition system can be directly defined, without the need of a free construction like the one just mentioned.

The fundamental advantage of considering transition systems with an algebraic structure on transitions, too, resides in the fact that often the same structure can be automatically and consistently extended to the set of computations of the system, through a free construction which generalizes the well-known generation of the free category of a graph. Thus every program can be associated (through this two step construction) with a *structured* category (called its *free model*) whose arrows are not simple sequences of elementary transitions, but are instead *abstract* computations, equipped with an algebraic structure. For Petri nets, the abstract computations obtained this way are shown to be isomorphic to *Petri Non Sequential Processes* [DMM89].

The above constructions associate to each system a single, free model. However, often it is useful to consider a collection of models for a system, where each model describes the computations of the system at a different level of abstraction. Thus we will define a class of *acceptable models* for a system, and a relationship among them representing a notion of simplification. This class has the free model as its 'initial' object, while the most reduced model (the one that cannot be reduced anymore) corresponds to the most abstract semantics.

The way the notions of acceptable models and of simplification among them are defined heavily depends on the specific formalism one considers. For example, for CCS this is the level where the notion of *weak observational equivalence* can be dealt with, and while simplifying a model its observable behaviour is required to be preserved (cf. Section 5). On the contrary, in the case of Petri nets and logic programs, since no observational mechanism has to be taken into account, a model can be simplified (i.e. made more abstract) by identifying (some of) the distinct computations between each pair of states.

Let us summarize the steps of the general methodology we just outlined, whose purpose is equipping the programs of a given formalism with a class of acceptable models.

i) Define a collection of graphs with an algebraic structure on states, which 'statically' represent the programs of the given formalism.

ii) Define a collection of transition systems with algebraic structure both on states and transitions, which are able to simulate the dynamic behaviour of the programs of level i). Show how to associate to each program, through a free construction, its *induced transition system.* Typically, this construction 'lifts' the algebraic structure of states to the transitions.

iii) Add an associative sequentialization operation on the transitions, equipped with suitable axioms which describe how to extend the algebraic structure of transitions to computations. This free construction associates to each structured transition system of level ii) its *free model*, whose arrows are equivalence classes of computations, i.e. *abstract computations.*

iv) Define the collection of *acceptable models* of a transition system, and a relation among them expressing a notion of simplification between models. This collection has the free model as its initial element, while the most reduced model (if it exists) defines the most abstract semantics of the program. Other models, corresponding to different semantics at various levels of abstraction, can be individuated via suitable techniques, for example by imposing suitable equations explicitly stating which computations have to be identified.

In this paper, the methodology is applied first (in Section 2) to Place/Transition Petri Nets, essentially following the algebraic presentation of [MM88]. Then, taking the treatment of Petri Nets as running example, the methodology is discussed again in Section 3, this time in a more formal way, using tools and techniques of category theory. The three levels of description mentioned above (namely programs, structured transition systems, and models) are defined as three categories of 'internal' structures in a suitable 'universe' category, while the free constructions generating the induced transition system and the free model of a program are rephrased in the categorical language as 'free adjunctions' between the corresponding categories.

The 'universe' category is actually the parameter of the methodology (see [Co90] for a deeper discussion of this point). Taking category **Set** as universe, one gets the classic (unstructured) transition systems; **CMon** (the category of commutative monoids) is the right universe for the treatment of Petri Nets; **Mon** (that of non-commutative monoids) serves for Phrase Structured Grammars (which are not discussed here, see [Co90]); and finally **SCart** (the category of (small, strict) cartesian categories) is shown to be the right universe for the treatment of logic programs, as discussed in Section 4 (see also [CM89-90]).

In Section 4, indeed, the methodology is applied to logic programs, for which a new algebraic semantics is proposed, corresponding to the free model of a program. This model includes a representation of all the (abstract) computations of a program, equipped with a rich algebraic structure. On the other hand, the final acceptable model of a program is sufficient to recover the classical semantics of Horn Clause Logic: this point is just hinted here, and is discussed more in detail in [Co90, CM90].

In Section 5, we define a new algebraic semantics for Process Description Languages (see [FM90, Fe90] for the details). The algebraic treatment of these languages involves the definition of structures (structured transition systems, models) which include a notion of observable behaviour, i.e. an observation mechanism on transitions. Therefore, in this case the methodology will be taken mainly as a guideline, and the actual steps will be modified to deal with the characterizing issues of process description languages. As a yardstick of the approach, we model the semantics of Milner's Calculus of Communicating Systems (CCS) [Mi80, Mi89], in both its interleaving and its true concurrency versions. We will define a class of CCS transition systems, and a class of corresponding CCS models (or categories). Observations are defined, in both levels of description, using comma category constructions; this allows us to characterize the interleaving observational congruences as terminal objects in appropriate categories. In particular, while the *strong* observational congruence can be captured at the level of CCS transition systems (intuitively, it is sufficient to consider elementary transitions and their observations), for the *weak* observational congruence one has to consider CCS models (i.e. observations over entire computations). The last point is just hinted here, but is completely developed in [Fe90]. Instead, we characterize a model of CCS which faithfully represents its truly concurrent semantics as defined in [Wi82].

The relevance and the practical usefulness of category theory to theoretical computer science has been emphasized by several authors. Among the others we mention [Go89] where some guidelines for the correct use of a number of categorical concepts in theoretical computer science have been suggestively discussed. The basic definitions of category theory used along the paper are reported in the Appendix. For a comprehensive introduction to category theory we refer to [ML71, AL89].

2 Petri Nets as Graphs with Monoidal Structure

Petri Nets [Pe62] are the first and maybe the most popular formalism for specifying and modelling distributed activities. In this section we briefly discuss Place/Transition Petri nets (nets for short) [Rei85], focusing on their algebraic presentation, first proposed in [MM88]. As the title *Petri Nets are Monoids* suggests, the algebraic structure which in some sense 'characterizes' the nets is that of commutative monoids.

We think it is instructive to introduce first the classical definitions of nets and of their dynamic behaviour, following [Rei85], and then the algebraic presentation of [MM88], in order to show how a small change of perspective in the basic definitions can facilitate the definition of the derived structures, characterizing them through free constructions. In particular, we want to stress the different nature of the definition of the *marking graph* of a net in the two mentioned approaches: unlike the classic presentation, the algebraic approach makes explicit the monoidal structure of the arcs of the marking graph. The main consequence of this fact is that while the computations of a net (regarded as paths in the marking graph) are just *step sequences* in the classical case (i.e. total orderings of multisets of elementary transitions), in the algebraic case they can be naturally equipped with a monoidal operation, and correspond to the more abstract notion of *nonsequential processes* as defined in [BD87].

Let us now start with the basic definitions. A Petri Net is classically defined as a set of places which can contain tokens, a set of transitions, and a flow relation connecting places and transitions. In the following we just consider finite nets.

2.1 Definition *(Place/Transition Petri Nets)*

A Petri Net N is a quadruple $\langle S, T, F, M_0\rangle$ where:

- S is a non empty, finite set of places;
- T is a finite set of transitions, $S \cap T = \varnothing$;
- F is a multiset relation over $(S \times T) \cup (T \times S)$ called the *flow relation*;
- M_0 is a non-empty multiset of places, called the *initial marking*. ♦

The flow relation (also called *causal dependency relation*) can be represented as a function from $(S \times T) \cup (T \times S)$ to the set $\mathbb{N}$ of natural numbers. Also a marking M can be interpreted as a function $M: S \to \mathbb{N}$; since S is finite, M can be written as $M = \{n_1 s_1, \ldots, n_p s_p\}$ where the natural number $n_i > 0$ indicates the number of the occurrences (*tokens*) of the place s_i in M, that is $n_i = M(s_i)$. For any transition $t \in T$ its *preset* is defined as the multiset over S pre(t), defined as pre(t)(s) = F(s, t). Similarly, the *postset* of t is defined as post(t)(s) = F(t, s).

2.2 Example (*A Place Transition Petri Net*)

Petri nets are graphically represented as in the following picture. Places (resp. transitions) are represented by circles (resp. boxes). The dots inside the places represent the tokens. The numbers associated to the arcs, called *weights*, describe the flow relation. The net shown below has a set of places S = {A, B, C, D, E} and a set of transitions T = {t, t', t"}. The initial marking is M = {2A, 3B}.

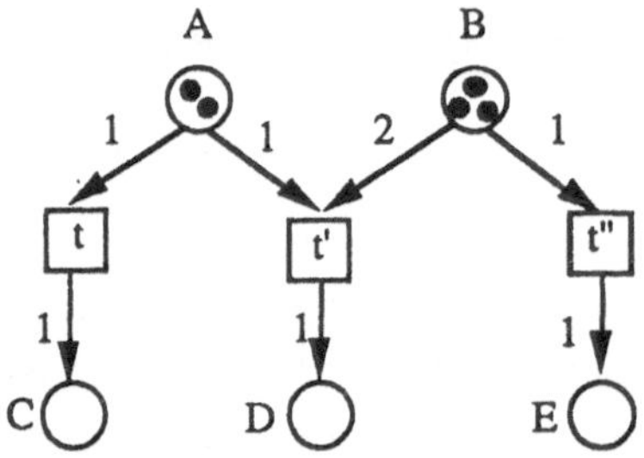

♦

The dynamic behaviour of P/T Nets is defined by the *token game*. The occurrence (*firing* in the standard Petri net terminology) of each enabled transition moves tokens from the places connected to it by the in-coming arcs to the places connected to it by the out-going arcs, respecting the weights on the arcs.

2.3 Definition (*Enabling*)

Let N be a net, and M be a marking of N; then

- A transition t is *enabled at M* if and only if for every place s, $pre(t)(s) \leq M(s)$.
- A multiset $T: T \to \mathbb{N}$ of transitions is *enabled* at M if and only if for every place s

$$\left(\Sigma_{t \in T}\, T(t) * pre(t)(s)\right) \leq M(s)$$ ♦

Based on the notions of enabling, two firing rules (transition rules) can be defined on nets. These rules specify how a net evolves from one marking to another.

2.4 Definition (*Firing Rules*)

Let $N = \langle S, T, F, M_0 \rangle$ be a net, M and M' be markings of N, and t be a transition. Then

- M evolves to M' under the *firing* of t, written M [t > M', if and only if
  - i) t is enabled at M;
  - ii) $M'(s) = M(s) - pre(t)(s) + post(t)(s)$, for each $s \in S$.

Let T: T → ℕ be a multiset of transitions, then

- M evolves to M' under the *concurrent firing* of T, written M [T >M', if and only if
  - i) T is enabled at M;
  - ii) $M'(s) = M(s) - \left(\Sigma_{t\in T}\ T(t) * pre(t)(s)\right) + \left(\Sigma_{t\in T}\ T(t) * post(t)(s)\right)$, for each $s \in S$. ♦

The concurrent firing of a set of transitions is usually called a *step*. Each firing rule gives rise to a different notion of computation for nets.

2.5 Definition *(Net Computations: Firing and Step Sequences)*

Let N be a net, and let M_0 be the initial marking of N. Then

- A *firing sequence* from M_0 to M_n is a sequence of markings and transitions such that
  $M_0[t_1> M_1 \ldots [t_n > M_n$.
- A *step sequence* from M_0 to M_n is a sequence of markings and steps such that
  $M_0[T_1> M_1 \ldots [T_n> M_n$. ♦

2.6 Example *(Firing and Step)*

Let us consider again the net of Example 2.2 with the initial marking M = {2A, 3B}. The net on the left, below, describes the result of the firing at M of the transition t', while the net on the right describes the marking M' = {C, D, E} reached after the concurrent firing of the transitions t, t' and t", i.e. after the step M [{t, t', t"}>M'.

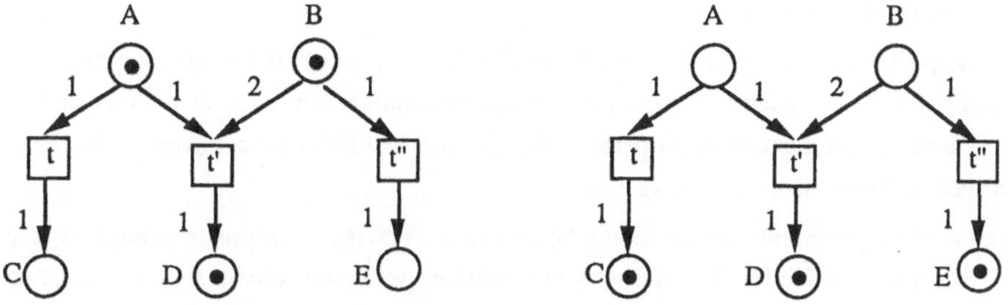

♦

The steps of a net N can be considered as the arcs of the so called *marking graph* of N.

2.7 Definition *(The Marking Graph of a Net)*

If N is a net, its *marking graph* is a graph (see Definition A.1) $\langle \mathbf{M}(N), \mathbf{T}(N), \partial_0, \partial_1 \rangle$, where $\mathbf{M}(N)$ is the set of all the markings of N, $\mathbf{T}(N)$ is the set of all steps of N, and $\partial_0, \partial_1: \mathbf{T}(N) \to \mathbf{M}(N)$ are defined as $\partial_0(M[T>M') = M$, and $\partial_1(M[T>M') = M'$ ♦

With the last definition, the step sequences of a net N are simply the finite paths of the marking graph of N starting from the initial marking M_0. Clearly, neither the firing sequences nor the step sequences are completely satisfactory as notions of net computations, since they do not express the causal dependencies among transitions: in other words, a *truly concurrent* semantics for Petri nets cannot be based on these concepts. Thus in [GR83] the *nonsequential processes* of a net are introduced, which constitute a more abstract notion of computation, giving also an account of the causal dependencies among transitions.

In the rest of this section we show that structures similar to the nonsequential processes naturally arises as 'paths' of the marking graph of a net, if one just makes explicit the algebraic structure of the arcs of that graph, and extends that structure to the entire computations.

We now briefly report the algebraic approach to Petri nets proposed in [MM88]. The basic idea is to regard the finite multisets of places (i.e. the markings) as the elements of the free commutative monoid generated by the set of places. Moreover, a transition t is considered as an arc between two multisets of places. In other words, a Petri net is simply a graph whose set of nodes is the free commutative monoid of places. For simplicity we consider just nets without initial marking.

2.8 Definition *(Petri Nets as Graphs with a Monoidal Structure on Nodes)*

A Petri net is a graph $N = \langle S^{\otimes}, T, \partial_0, \partial_1\rangle$, where $S^{\otimes}$ is the free commutative monoid generated by the set of places S, T is a set of transitions, and $\partial_0, \partial_1: T \to S^{\otimes}$ are functions associating to each transition its preset and its postset, respectively. ♦

If t is a transition, we write $t: u \to v$ to say that $\partial_0(t) = u$ and $\partial_1(t) = v$. As an example, the net of Example 2.2 is a graph having as nodes the free commutative monoid generated by {A, B, C, D, E}, and as transitions the arcs $t: A \to C$, $t': A\otimes 2B \to D$ and $t'': B \to E$.

Considering nets as structured graphs, it is natural to define *net morphisms* as graph morphisms which preserve the monoidal structure of states. As a consequence, a category of nets can be defined.

2.9 Definition *(Category Petri)*

A *Petri net morphism* h from $N = \langle S^{\otimes}, T, \partial_0, \partial_1\rangle$ to $N = \langle S'^{\otimes}, T', \partial'_0, \partial'_1\rangle$ is a graph morphism $\langle f, g\rangle$, with $f: T \to T'$ and $g: S^{\otimes} \to S'^{\otimes}$, such that g is a monoid homomorphism (i.e. g leaves the unit of the monoid fixed, and commutes with the monoidal operation $\otimes$). We will call **Petri** the category having Petri nets as objects, and Petri net morphisms as arrows. ♦

The description of nets as graphs with a monoidal structure on nodes corresponds to the first level of the methodology outlined in Section 1. Following that outline, we should obtain the structured transition system induced by a net by generating (in a free way) a commutative monoidal structure on transitions, too. It turns out that this free construction generates exactly the marking graph of a net.

2.10 Definition *(From a Net to its Marking Graph)*

Let $N = \langle S^{\otimes}, T, \partial_0, \partial_1\rangle$ be a net. Its *marking graph* $C[N] = \langle S^{\otimes}, T', \partial'_0, \partial'_1, id\rangle$ is the reflexive graph (cf. Definition A.1) obtained by the following inference rules and equations:

ID) $$\frac{u \in S^{\otimes}}{id_u : u \to u \text{ in } C[N]}$$

INC) $$\frac{t: u \to v \text{ in } N}{t: u \to v \text{ in } C[N]}$$

OP) $$\frac{t: u \to v \text{ and } t': u' \to v' \text{ in } C[N]}{t\otimes t' : u\otimes u' \to v\otimes v' \text{ in } C[N]}$$

IDOP) $id_{u\otimes v} = id_u \otimes id_v$

UNIT) $t \otimes id_0 = t$, where 0 is the unit of $S^{\otimes}$

ASSOC) $(t_1 \otimes t_2) \otimes t_3 = t_1 \otimes (t_2 \otimes t_3)$

COMM) $t \otimes t' = t' \otimes t$ ♦

From the above rules it is clear that C[N] has a commutative monoidal structure not only on the nodes $S^{\otimes}$, but also on the transitions T' (by rule OP and equations UNIT, ASSOC, and COMM). Moreover, this structure is preserved by the identity function id: $S^{\otimes} \rightarrow T'$ (by IDOP and UNIT), and by the source and target functions (implicitly defined by ID and OP): ∂_0, ∂_1 and id are indeed monoid homomorphisms. Clearly, if w is a marking, the identity transition id_w models the fact that the corresponding tokens remain idle.

It is easy to check that this definition of marking graph is essentially equivalent to the one of Definition 2.7, except for the fact that we keep explicit the monoidal structure of the transitions. The importance of this fact is fully exploited in the following construction, where we show how to generate all the abstract computations of a net, and how to extend the monoidal operation to entire computations, too, in a way that is consistent with the sequentialization operation. This free construction generates the free model of a Petri net, corresponding to the third level of the methodology sketched in Section 1.

2.11 Definition *(The Petri Category of a Net)*

Given a net $N = \langle S^{\otimes}, T, \partial_0, \partial_1 \rangle$, its *free Petri category* $T[N] = \langle S^{\otimes}, T'', \partial''_0, \partial''_1, id, ; \rangle$ is generated from the marking graph $C[N] = \langle S^{\otimes}, T', \partial'_0, \partial'_1, id \rangle$ via the following inference rules and equations:

$$\text{INC1)}\quad \frac{t: u \rightarrow v \text{ in } C[N]}{t: u \rightarrow v \text{ in } T[N]} \qquad\qquad \text{COMP)}\quad \frac{t: u \rightarrow v \text{ and } t': v \rightarrow w \text{ in } T[N]}{t\,;\,t' : u \rightarrow w \text{ in } T[N]}$$

UNIT') $id_u ; t = t$ and $t ; id_v = t$, if $t: u \rightarrow v$

ASSOC') $(t_1 ; t_2) ; t_3 = t_1 ; (t_2 ; t_3)$

EXCH) $(t_1 ; t_2) \otimes (t_3 ; t_4) = (t_1 \otimes t_3) ; (t_2 \otimes t_4))$

and moreover OP, UNIT, ASSOC, and COMM as for Definition 2.10, with T[N] in place of C[N]. ♦

In practice, T[N] is the free category generated by the reflexive graph C[N], obtained by closing the transitions of C[N] under a partial sequentialization operation _;_, which satisfies the axioms for categories (by ASSOC' and UNIT'). Clearly, the arrows of T[N] are just the computations of the transition system C[N]. Moreover, the commutative monoidal operation ⊗ is extended to arrows in T'' (by OP, UNIT, ASSOC and COMM), and has the intuitive meaning of *parallel composition* of computations.

The most interesting axiom is EXCH, which states a relationship between the sequential and parallel composition of transitions: if all the compositions are defined, it says that the parallel composition of two sequences of transitions can be regarded as the sequence of the parallel compositions of their elementary steps. As anticipated above, it turns out that the arrows in the Petri category T[N] are related to the nonsequential processes of N, and in particular they coincide with the processes defined in [BD87]. We refer to [DMM89] for an analysis of these relationships.

Before closing this section, let us anticipate some concepts which will become clear after the formal definitions of the next section. It should be stressed that the algebraic presentation of nets naturally yields to the definition of *categories* of nets and of related structures. In Definition 2.9 we already introduced the category **Petri** of Petri nets, whose objects are graphs with a free commutative monoidal structure on nodes. Similarly, a category including all marking graphs can be defined: this category is called **CMonRPetri** in [MM88], and has as objects all the reflexive graphs with a commutative monoidal structure on both nodes and arcs, such that the monoid of nodes is free, and such that the source, target, and identity mappings are monoid homomorphisms. Moreover, the arrows of the category **CMonRPetri** are reflexive graph morphisms which in addition preserve the monoidal structure on both nodes and arcs.

The advantage of defining these categories resides in the fact that the free construction of the marking graph of a net, presented in Definition 2.10, can elegantly be characterized in categorical terms as the *free adjoint functor* C[_]: **Petri** → **CMonRPetri**, i.e. the left adjoint to the obvious forgetful functor U[_]: **CMonRPetri** → **Petri**, which forgets the reflexive structure of the argument graph, and the monoidal structure of its arcs. This construction will be regarded in the next section as a particular instantiation of the first step of our general methodology, i.e. the one which associates to a program its induced structured transition system.

Similarly, a category called **CatPetri** is defined in [MM88] which includes as objects, among others, the Petri categories of all nets. Again, the free construction generating the free Petri category T[N] can be characterized as the free adjoint functor T[_]: **Petri** → **CatPetri**, i.e. the left adjoint to the obvious forgetful functor **CatPetri** → **Petri**. T[_] is actually the composition of functor C[_] and another left adjoint functor S[_]: **CMonRPetri** → **CatPetri**, which, in the terminology of the next section, associates to the structured transition system induced by a program its *free model* of abstract computations. Functor S[_] is defined by the rules and equations of Definition 2.11.

3 Formalizing the Methodology in the Categorical Setting

In this section we introduce in a more formal way the general methodology for the analysis of computational models. As hinted at the end of the last section, the basic idea is to define suitable categories for each of the levels of description of a system (i.e. programs, structured transition systems, and models), and to relate these categories with free adjoint functors, which generate from a given program its induced transition system and its free model of computations. Moreover, in general a class of acceptable models, a subcategory of all possible models, can be associated to a given program; the free model is initial among them, and sometimes a final (most abstract) model can be determined, too. Other models, describing the behaviour of a program at different levels of abstractions, can be characterized via suitable techniques. Fot instance some equations stating which computations should be identified could be imposed.

The generality of our methodology comes from the fact that all the definitions and results are parametric with respect to the algebraic structure of states and transitions: for example we will show that the algebraic treatment of Petri nets discussed in the last section can be obtained as an instantiation of the methodology, if we choose *commutative monoids* as the structure of states and transitions. Indeed, Petri nets will be used as a running example in the rest of this section.

In the following subsection we introduce the main definitions and results of category theory needed to formalize the methodology, which is then defined in Section 3.2.

3.1 Categories of Internal Structures: Definitions and Results

The technique we use to abstract from the actual structure of the states and transitions of a system is that of *internalization*. A simple example will explain the basic rationale. A (directed) *graph* (see also Definitions A.1-2) is a tuple $G = \langle V, T, \partial_0, \partial_1 \rangle$, where V is a set of *nodes*, T is a set of *arcs*, ∂_0 and ∂_1: T → V are the *source* and *target* functions, respectively. A *graph morphism* f: $\langle V, T, \partial_0, \partial_1 \rangle \rightarrow \langle V', T', \partial'_0, \partial'_1 \rangle$ is a pair

$\langle f_0, f_1\rangle$ of functions, with f_0: $V \to V'$, f_1: $T \to T'$, and such that $\partial'_i(f_1(t)) = f_0(\partial_i(t))$ $\forall t \in T$, $i = 0,1$. The category having all (small) graphs as objects, and graph morphisms as arrows, is called **Graph**.

Presented in this way, a graph can be considered as described *internally* to the category **Set**, which has *sets* as objects and *total functions* as arrows. In fact, T and V are both objects of **Set**, while ∂_0 and ∂_1 are arrows of **Set**: thus a graph is just a diagram with the following shape in **Set**:

Moreover, graph morphisms are pairs of arrows of **Set** which commute in the right way with the source and target arrows.

Let us consider now *structured graphs*, i.e. graphs whose collections of arcs and nodes have a structure richer than a simple set. In many situations, arcs and nodes have a similar algebraic structure, and the source and target mappings are required to preserve that structure. If C is the category of those algebraic structures, then the structured graph can be regarded as a diagram having the same shape as above, but this time in the category C. This yields to the definition of *internal* graphs.

3.1 Definition *(Internal Graphs)*

Let C be a category. An *internal graph of C* is a tuple $G = \langle c_0, c_1, \partial_0, \partial_1\rangle$, where:

- $c_0, c_1 \in |C|$
- ∂_0, ∂_1: $c_1 \to c_0$ are arrows in C.

Let $G = \langle c_0, c_1, \partial_0, \partial_1\rangle$ and $G' = \langle c'_0, c'_1, \partial'_0, \partial'_1\rangle$ be two internal graphs of C. Then an *internal graph morphism* f: $G \to G'$ is a pair $\langle f_0, f_1\rangle$ of arrows of C (f_0: $c_0 \to c'_0$, f_1: $c_1 \to c'_1$), such that the following diagrams commute:

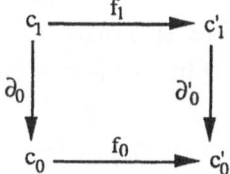

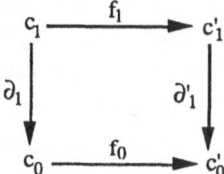

Graph(C) is the category having internal graphs of C as objects, and internal graph morphisms as arrows. ♦

Analogously, the notions of *reflexive graph* and of *category* (Definition A.1) can be generalized to their corresponding *internal* versions, too (see Definitions A.4-5).

As an example, calling **CMon** the category of commutative monoids, the marking graph of a net (Definition 2.10) is an object of category **RGraph(CMon)**, i.e. it is an internal reflexive graph of **CMon**. Similarly, a Petri category is an object of **Cat(CMon)**, i.e. an internal category of **CMon**.

Like for Petri nets, in the general case we want to define the structured transition systems associated to the programs as internal (reflexive) graphs of a suitable universe category C, and the categories of computations of the programs (i.e. the models) as internal categories of the same universe C, since we want to extend the same algebraic structure of transitions to computations. Moreover, we require that the category of computations of a program be uniquely determined through a free construction; in categorical terms we are looking for an *adjunction* [ML71] between the categories [R]**Graph(C)** and **Cat(C)**.

In the case of unstructured graphs (i.e. graphs internal to **Set**) it is well known that between the categories **Graph**, **RGraph**, and **Cat** (Definition A.2) there exist the obvious forgetful functors **Cat** → **RGraph** and **RGraph** → **Graph**, with their free adjoints R: **Graph** → **RGraph** and C: **RGraph** → **Cat**. Informally, if G is a graph, R[G] is obtained by adding one reflexive arc to each node of G. On the other hand, C[G] is obtained by adding to G a new arc $t_1; \ldots; t_n: \partial_0(t_1) \rightarrow \partial_1(t_n)$ for each sequence $\langle t_1, \ldots, t_n \rangle$ of 'composable' arcs of G (i.e. such that $\partial_1(t_i) = \partial_0(t_{i+1})$).

In the case of structured graphs, it is natural to ask under which conditions these free constructions can be generalized. More precisely, we want to point out which properties a category **C** must satisfy, in order to guarantee the existence of the free adjoints for the obvious forgetful functors **Cat(C)** → **RGraph(C)** and **RGraph(C)** → **Graph(C)**. Let us summarize the results that will be used in the following. The proofs can be found in [Co90].

3.2 Theorem *(From Internal Graphs to Internal Reflexive Graphs and Categories)*

a) If **C** is a category with binary coproducts (Definition A.3), then the forgetful functor **RGraph(C)** → **Graph(C)** has a free adjoint R_C: **Graph(C)** → **RGraph(C)**. If G ∈ |**Graph(C)**|, then $R_C[G]$ has as arcs the coproduct of the arcs and the nodes of G.

b) If **C** is the category of models in **Set** of a left-exact sketch, then the obvious forgetful functor **Cat(C)** → **RGraph(C)** has a free adjoint C_C: **RGraph(C)** → **Cat(C)**. ♦

The definition of *left-exact sketches* and of their models goes beyond the scope of the paper: we refer to [BW85] for an introduction of these notions. For the goals of this paper, it is sufficient to notice that many interesting categories can be characterized as categories of models of a left-exact sketch. For example, many categories of algebras (like rings, groups, (commutative) monoids, etc.) enjoy this property, and also **Graph**, **RGraph**, **Cat**, **PreOrd** (the category of preorders), **PO** (the category of partial orders), and **Cart** (the category of small cartesian categories).

We can apply the last result to the case of Petri nets: since **CMon** satisfies the hypotheses of Theorem 3.2b, there exists a free adjoint functor C_{CMon}: **RGraph(CMon)** → **Cat(CMon)**. This is essentially the functor S[_], introduced at the end of Section 2, which generates the category of computations from a marking graph. More precisely, it is easy to show that category **CMonRPetri** (resp. **CatPetri**) is the full subcategory of **RGraph(CMon)** (resp. of **Cat(CMon)**) including the reflexive graphs (resp. categories) with a *free* monoid as nodes. Therefore S[_] is exactly the restriction of C_{CMon} to **CMonRPetri**.

3.1.1 Heterogeneous Graphs

Although internal graphs are a good formalization of the notion of structured transition systems, in many situations we have to consider graphs where the structure of nodes is richer than the structure of arcs. A typical example is a Petri net, which, by Definition 2.8, has a free commutative monoid as nodes, but just a *set* as transitions. We will call this kind of graphs *heterogeneous graphs*.

3.3 Definition *(Heterogeneous Graphs)*

Let **C** and **B** be two categories, such that a forgetful functor U: **C** → **B** exists. Then G = ‹c, b, ∂_0, ∂_1› is an *heterogeneous graph with arcs in B and nodes in C* iff c ∈ |**C**|, b ∈ |**B**|, and ∂_0, ∂_1: b → U[c] are arrows of **B**. A *heterogeneous graph morphism* f: ‹c, b, ∂_0, ∂_1› → ‹c', b', ∂'_0, ∂'_1› is a pair ‹f_0, f_1› where f_1: b → b' is an arrow in **B**, f_0: c → c' is an arrow in **C**, such that $f_1;\partial'_0 = \partial_0;U[f_0]$ and $f_1;\partial'_1 = \partial_1;U[f_0]$. **Graph(B, C)** is the category having heterogeneous graphs with arcs in **B** and nodes in **C** as objects, and heterogeneous graph morphisms as arrows. ♦

Basically, an heterogeneous graph ‹c, b, ∂_0, ∂_1› ∈ |**Graph(B, C)**| can be considered as an internal graph ‹U[c], b, ∂_0, ∂_1› ∈ |**Graph(B)**|, but the morphisms are required to preserve the richer structure of nodes. As an example, **Petri** (Definition 2.8) is a category of heterogeneous graphs which, in our terminology, is called **Graph(Set, FCMon)**, **FCMon** being the category of free commutative monoids.

The following result shows that if the forgetful functor U: **C** → **B** has a free adjoint, then one can safely enrich the structure of arcs of an heterogeneous graph in order to get an internal graph of the more structured category.

3.4 Proposition *(Enriching the Arcs of a Heterogeneous Graph)*

Let C and **B** be two categories, such that there exists a forgetful functor U: **C** → **B** with free adjoint F: **B** → **C**. Then the forgetful functor U': **Graph(C)** → **Graph(B, C)**, obviously induced by U (i.e. U'[‹c_0, c_1, ∂_0, ∂_1›] = ‹c_0, U[c_1], U[∂_0], U[∂_1]› on objects, and U'[‹f_0, f_1›] = ‹f_0, U[f_1]› on arrows), has a free adjoint F'. ♦

Considering again our running example of Petri nets, the functor C: **Petri** → **CMonRPetri** described in Definition 2.10 is the restriction to **Petri** of the functor R_{CMon}∘F': **Graph(Set,CMon)** → **RGraph(CMon)**, where R_{CMon} is as in Theorem 3.2a, while F': **Graph(Set,CMon)** → **Graph(CMon)** exists thanks to the last proposition, since there exists a free adjoint functor F: **Set** → **CMon**, mapping each set to its free commutative monoid.

It is worth noting that the definition of heterogeneous graphs given here uses the notion of 'forgetful functor', which is not formally defined. Actually, the definition could be given for an arbitrary functor G: C → **B**, and the proposition still holds for an arbitrary adjunction ‹K, G, θ›. Nevertheless, we prefer to stress the informal interpretation that will be given, in the rest of the paper, to the application of Proposition 3.4, that is the lifting of the richer structure of nodes to the arcs.

3.2 Defining the Methodology

Putting together all the above definitions and results, we can define in a more formal way the methodology. For a given formalism, the methodology recognizes the existence of three levels (programs, structured transition systems, and models) which correspond to three different categories of internal structures, related by adjunctions. An additional, fourth level is often necessary to focus the attention on the acceptable models of a program, i.e. on a suitable subcategory of all possible models. In a simplified but quite general situation, the methodology can be summarized as follows.

3.5 Definition *(Guidelines for the Methodology)*

Suppose we have a class of 'programs' **Prog**. The following steps define a methodology which associates to each program in **Prog** with a class of models.

1) Determine the 'natural' structure of the states and of the transitions of programs in **Prog**, and what the morphisms among systems in **Prog** are, in order to regard **Prog** as a category. This category has the form **Graph(B, C)**, i.e. it is a category of heterogeneous graphs with states in **C** and transitions in **B**. We assume that **C** is more structured than **B**, thus there exists a forgetful functor U^C_B: **C** → **B**. In order to apply the next steps, one has to look for its free adjoint F^B_C: **B** → **C**.
2) Define a category of *transition systems* which describe the dynamic behaviour of the programs of **Prog**. This category usually has the form **RGraph(C)**, i.e. it is the category of reflexive internal graphs having both transitions and states in **C**. If **C** has binary coproducts, by Theorem 3.2a and Proposition 3.4 the forgetful functor U: **RGraph(C)** → **Graph(B,C)** has a free adjoint F: **Graph(B,C)** → **RGraph(C)**, which associates to a system its *induced transition system.*
3) Define a category of *models* for transition systems. This category usually has the form **Cat(C)**, i.e. it includes internal categories of **C**. If **C** satisfies the hypotheses of Theorem 3.2b, the forgetful functor **Cat(C)** → **RGraph(C)** has a free adjoint C_C, which associates to each transition system its *free model.*
4) Define the category of *acceptable models* for a program P ∈ **Prog**, i.e. a suitable subcategory of **Cat(C)**, rooted at the free model of P. The final object of this subcategory, if it exists, is the most abstract model of P. Other models, which describe the behaviour of P at different levels of abstraction, can be characterized via suitable categorical techniques. ♦

The relevance and the practical usefulness of category theory in theoretical computer science has been emphasized by several authors. This methodology can be considered as an excellent example of the way category theory provides guidelines for formulating definitions, as stressed in [Go89]. Having characterized the constructions as left adjoint functors, the generation of the free models for the programs belonging to a given formalism simply reduces to the definition of the category mentioned in point 1) above, i.e. to the choice of the right structure for states (**C**) and transitions (**B**). In fact, if category **C** satisfies the hypotheses of Theorem 3.2, everything else is uniquely determined, thanks to the uniqueness of left adjoints.

Another immediate, relevant consequence of the use of category theory in the definition of the methodology is that the proposed semantics is *compositional* in a strong sense: in fact, any composition operation defined in terms of *colimits* in the category of programs is automatically preserved by the free constructions, since they correspond to left (free) adjoint functors. Moreover, as argued in [Me89, Me90], the categorical setting allows to encompass the traditional distinction between *operational* and *declarative* semantics: the same construction can be operationally defined through inference rules and equations, or can be declaratively characterized by a universal property.

For what concerns the fourth point of the methodology, it should be stressed that the actual definition of the class of acceptable models of a system heavily depends on the considered formalism. As we will see in Section 5, in the case of CCS this is the level where the notion of *observational equivalence* can be dealt with, yielding to a nice characterization of the terminal model. In the case of Petri nets, since the transitions are not labelled and therefore no observation mechanism has to be taken into account, the class of the models associated to a net N can be defined as the subcategory of **Cat(CMon)** including all the internal categories M such that there exists a functor f: T[N] → M, which is surjective and preserves the states. With this definition, the terminal model of N is a preorder P[N], which is the *reachability relation* among markings, i.e. M $\leq_{P[N]}$ M' iff there exists a step (or firing) sequence from M to M'.

As the last point, it should be stressed that in many real situations the steps of the methodology defined above cannot be directly applied, and some 'ad hoc' solutions have to be found. Nevertheless, the methodology summarized above still remains a useful guideline. In particular, in order to satisfy the requirements on category C, often one has to choose a category which is bigger than the one which, at a first glance, could seem natural to consider. In the case of Petri nets, for example, we saw that category **Petri** is exactly **Graph(Set, FCMon)**: thus one could be tempted to take **FCMon** as the universe category where the internal structures have to be defined. But **FCMon** cannot be characterized as the category of models of a left-exact sketch, thus the existence of the free model cannot be guaranteed. This is the reason why we always considered category **CMon**, which does enjoy that property, and includes **FCMon** as a full subcategory. The following fact ensures that widening the category of the structures of states we do not go into troubles, since the states are preserved by the construction of the free model.

3.6 Proposition *(Generation of the Free Category Preserves the States)*

Let C be a category with all pullbacks, and G be an internal graph of C. Then the free internal category of C generated by G, if it exists, has exactly the nodes of G as objects. ♦

4 An Algebraic Semantics for Horn Clause Logic

In this section we apply our methodology to logic programs [Ll87]. This will equip logic programs with a new algebraic semantics, which associates a category of models to each program. The final model of a program corresponds, roughly speaking, to its classic semantics, while the initial one has a much richer structure, since, as expected, it includes all the (abstract) computations as arrows. The full treatment of this topic can be found in [Co90], while partial results are reported in [CM89, CM90]. In the following we try to summarize the basic ideas, without describing the details of the constructions: all proofs are omitted.

4.1 Logic Programming: Syntax and Operational Semantics

We introduce here the basic definitions about the syntax of logic programs and their operational semantics. The definitions essentially follow [Ll87], but some of them are suitably adapted in order to fit better into our categorical approach.

4.1 Definition *(Terms, Formulas and Substitutions)*

Let Σ be a ranked set of function symbols ($\Sigma = \cup_n \Sigma_n$), and Π be a ranked set of predicate symbols ($\Pi = \cup_n \Pi_n$).

- The pair ‹Σ, Π› is called a *logic program (*or *lp-) signature*, and is a special kind of two-sorted signature, since the sort of predicates cannot appear in the arity of any operator. In the following we will denote by 'T' (for 'terms') the sort of the operators in Σ, and by 'P' (for 'predicates') that of the operators in Π. If **P** is a program, the lp-signature including its function and predicate symbols is denoted by Σ_P.

- Let $T^n \equiv \langle x_1, \ldots, x_n \rangle$ be a *canonical tuple* of distinct variables, uniquely determined by its length; a *term (over T^n)* is an element of $T_\Sigma(T^n)$, that is an element of the free Σ-algebra generated by T^n. Notice that we consider terms (resp. formulas, substitutions) over *tuples* (instead of *sets*) of variables.
- $p(t_1, \ldots, t_n)$ is an *atomic formula over* T^n, iff p is a predicate symbol, $p \in \Pi_n$, and $t_1, \ldots, t_n$ are terms over T^n. A *(conjunctive) formula* is simply a tuple of atomic formulas.
- If T^n and T^m are canonical tuples of variables, a *substitution from T^m to T^n* is a function $\sigma: T^n \rightarrow T_\Sigma(T^m)$, also represented as $\langle x_1/\sigma(x_1), \ldots, x_n/\sigma(x_n)\rangle$. Since the names of the variables are inessential (they are individuated by the position in the tuple), σ can also be written as $\langle\sigma(x_1), \ldots, \sigma(x_n)\rangle$; thus a substitution is simply a tuple of terms.
- If t is a term (resp. a formula) over T^n, and σ is a substitution from T^m to T^n, *the application of σ to t*, written $t \circ \sigma$, is the term (resp. formula) over T^m obtained by simultaneously substituting in t all the occurrences of the variables in T^n with their image through σ. The term (resp. formula) $t \circ \sigma$ is also called an *instantiation* of t.
- Finally, if σ is a substitution from T^m to T^n, and σ' is a substitution from T^i to T^m, its *composition* is the substitution $\sigma \circ \sigma'$ from T^i to T^n, defined as $\sigma \circ \sigma' \equiv \langle \sigma(x_1) \circ \sigma', \ldots, \sigma(x_n) \circ \sigma' \rangle$. Given two substitutions σ and σ', σ is said to be *more general* than σ' if there exists a substitution θ such that $\sigma \circ \theta = \sigma'$. ♦

It must be noted that, as usual in a categorical framework [Go88] (but unlike the classical set-theoretical treatment of [Ll87]), in this paper substitution composition and application are considered as partial functions. For example, $\sigma' \circ \sigma$ is defined iff σ is from T^m to T^n, σ' is from T^i to T^j, and $m = j$.

4.2 Definition *(Definite Clauses, Goals and Logic Programs)*

- A *definite clause c* is an expression of the form

  $$H :- B_1, \ldots, B_n \qquad (n \geq 0)$$

  where ':-' means logic implication (right to left), ',' means logical conjunction, and H, B_i are atomic formulas.
- A *goal G* is an expression of the form

  $$:- A_1, \ldots, A_m \qquad (m > 0)$$

  where each A_i is an atomic formula.
- A *logic* (or *HCL*) *program P* is a finite set of definite clauses. ♦

A logic program can be interpreted in many different but equivalent ways (see [Ll87] for a formal treatment of all of them). As a first order theory, its semantics is defined in a model-theoretic way as its *least Herbrand model*. Under the operational reading, instead, a *resolution rule* states how to transform a goal into another. The operational semantics is then defined as the set of all (ground) atomic formulas which can be transformed into the empty goal through a sequence of resolution steps. The equivalence between the operational and model-theoretic semantics of a program is proved by showing that the resolution inference rule is both sound and complete for definite clauses. In this paper we focus on the operational behaviour of a program, which will be simulated by its induced transition system.

4.3 Definition *(Unification, Resolution Steps, and Refutations)*

- Two atomic formulas A and B *unify* if there exists a substitution θ such that $A \circ \theta = B \circ \theta$. In this case θ is called a *unifier* of A and B. The set of unifiers of any two atomic formulas is either empty, or it has a most general element (up to variable renaming) called the *most general unifier* (*mgu*).
- Given a clause $c = (H :- B_1, \ldots, B_n)$ and a goal $G = (:- G_1, \ldots, G_m)$, a *resolution step* involves the selection of an atomic goal G_i and the construction of the most general unifier (if any) θ between H and G_i. The result of such a step is the new goal $G' = (:- G_1, \ldots, G_{i-1}, B_1, \ldots, B_n, G_{i+1}, \ldots, G_m) \circ \theta$. In this case we will say that there is a *resolution step from G to G' via c and θ.*
- A *refutation* of a goal G is a finite sequence of resolution steps which starts with G and ends with the empty goal. If the refutation has length n, where step i uses clause c_i and the mgu θ_i, then the substitution $\theta = (\theta_1 \circ \ldots \circ \theta_n)|_{Var(G)}$ (i.e. the restriction of $\theta_1 \circ \ldots \circ \theta_n$ to the variables appearing in G), is called a *computed answer substitution* for G. In this case we say that there is a *refutation of G via* $c_1, \ldots, c_n$ *and* $\theta = (\theta_1 \circ \ldots \circ \theta_n)_{Var(G)}$. Finally, a *correct answer substitution* is any instantiation of a *computed* answer substitution. ♦

4.2 Applying the Methodology to Logic Programs

As stressed in Section 3.2, the main point in the application of our methodology to a class of programs is the choice of the right structure for the states and the transitions, in order to regard a program as a heterogeneous graph. A logic program can be represented in a natural way as a graph, where the arcs represent the program clauses, and the nodes are *goals*, regarded as tuples of atomic formulas. For example, the clause $c = (A :- B_1, \ldots, B_n)$ is represented as an arc $c: \langle B_1, \ldots, B_n \rangle \rightarrow \langle A \rangle$.

The nodes of a logic program, regarded as a graph, have a quite rich structure: the main (possibly partial) operations we can define over tuples of formulas (goals) are indeed:

- *projections,* to extract atomic formulas out of a tuple,
- *tupling,* to build a tuple from its component atomic formulas,
- *application* of a term substitution to a formula,
- *unification* of two formulas.

Moreover, since also substitutions are involved, we have to consider *substitution composition,* too. Formulas and substitutions constructed over a given logic program signature $\langle \Sigma, \Pi \rangle$ can be faithfully represented as the arrows of a suitable *(strict) cartesian category,* in such a way that all the above operations directly correspond to basic categorical constructions.

A *cartesian category* C is a category with a terminal object $\mathbf{1} \in |C|$, and with a product diagram for every pair of objects $X, Y \in |C|$ (Definition A.3). A cartesian category is *strict* if its objects form a monoid with the product as monoidal operation, and the terminal object as unit. The product diagrams induce a tupling operation on the arrows with the same source which, by strictness, is associative.

Given a logic program signature $\langle \Sigma, \Pi \rangle$, it is possible to build a strict cartesian category $SCC(\langle \Sigma, \Pi \rangle)$, called the *category of formulas and substitutions of* $\langle \Sigma, \Pi \rangle$, having as arrows all terms, formulas, and substitutions built over $\langle \Sigma, \Pi \rangle$. In particular, the objects of the category represent canonical tuples of variables, the tupling operation allows us to construct substitutions (i.e. tuples of terms) and goals (tuples of formulas); arrow composition models both the application of substitutions to terms (or goals), and the composition of substitutions (thus they are naturally partial); and finally, the unification of two formulas is the pullback of the corresponding arrows, if it exists. Similar categories have been introduced for example in [AM89] and [Go88], following the ideas of Lawvere's Thesis [La63].

4.4 Example *(Formulas and Terms as Arrows of a Category)*

As a running example, let us consider the following simple program for the *append* predicate

c_1 = append(x_1, [], x_1).

c_2 = append(x_1, [x_2|x_3], [x_2|x_4]) :- append(x_1, x_3, x_4).

For this program we have $\Sigma_0 = \{[]\}$, $\Sigma_2 = \{[\_|\_]\}$, $\Pi_3 = \{append\}$, and all others Σ_i, Π_j are empty: we call Σ_{AP} this logic program signature.

The following picture shows some arrows of category **SCC**(Σ_{AP}). For example, the formula *append(x_1, [x_2/x_3], [x_2/x_4])* is represented as an arrow from T^4 (representing the canonical tuple ‹x_1, ..., x_4›) to P. That formula is obtained as the application of substitution *‹x_1, [x_2/x_3], [x_2/x_4]›* to the formula *append(x_1, x_2, x_3)*. On the other hand, *‹x_1, [x_2/x_3], [x_2/x_4]›* is the tupling of three distinct arrows from T^4 to T. The projections faithfully correspond to variables [AM89]: for example x_i: $T^n \rightarrow T$ is a shorthand for the composition of projections $snd_{T^{i-1},T} \circ fst_{T^i,T^{n-i}}$: $T^n \rightarrow T$ which extracts the i-th component of the canonical tuple of variables T^n.

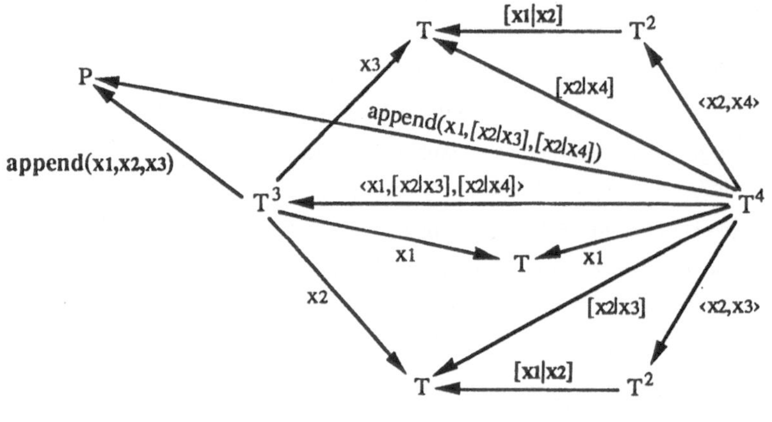

In the above diagram, some objects are represented with many occurrences, to avoid unnecessary confusion. The arrows whose name is in bold type are the operators of signature Σ_{AP}, and can be considered as the *generators* of category **SCC**(Σ_{AP}). ♦

Since the algebraic structure of the 'states' of a logic programs (i.e. the goals) naturally corresponds to the structure of the arrows of a strict cartesian category, we take **SCart**, the category of all such categories, as the universe which corresponds to category **C** in the outline of the methodology (Definition 3.5).

In order to represent logic programs as heterogeneous graphs we still have to look for a suitable representation of program clauses. To this aim, we must observe that every clause of a program cannot be regarded simply as a pair of independent formulas (its head and its body), since it also carries an additional information, namely which are the variables shared by the head and the body. To take this fact into account, we will represent the clauses of a logic program essentially as if they were distinct operators of a many-sorted signature: each clause has a distinct sort, and its arity is the number of the distinct variables appearing in it. The signature of the clauses of a logic program **P** will be denoted by $\Sigma_{Cl(\mathbf{P})}$.

Regarding the clause of a program in this way, it is easy to represent them as objects of a category. In fact, the operators of a many sorted signature can be represented as the arcs of a (heterogeneous) graph, having as nodes the free monoid generated by the sorts. An operation f with n arguments of types (sorts) $s_1, \ldots, s_n$, and returning a value of sort s, is simply an arc $f: s_1 \cdot \ldots \cdot s_n \rightarrow s$. Therefore a many sorted signature is a heterogeneous graph of **Graph(Set, FMon)** (where **FMon** is the category of free monoids).

4.5 Example *(A Signature as Heterogeneous Graph)*

Let us show how the lp-signature $\Sigma_{\mathbf{AP}}$ of Example 4.4 is represented as a heterogeneous graph. Since $\Sigma_{\mathbf{AP}}$ is two-sorted, its nodes form the free monoid $\{T, P\}^*$. Thus $\Sigma_{\mathbf{AP}}$ is the graph $\langle \{T, P\}^*, \{append, [\_|\_], []\}, ary, typ\rangle$ where the source and target functions (*ary* and *typ*, respectively) are as in follows picture:

$$P \xleftarrow{\;append\;} T \cdot T \cdot T \qquad\qquad T \cdot T \xrightarrow{\;[\_|\_]\;} T \xleftarrow{\;[]\;} 0$$

On the other hand, since the program for the *append* predicate includes two clauses, with one and four distinct variables respectively, its *signature of clauses* $\Sigma_{Cl(\mathbf{AP})}$ is

$$\Sigma_{Cl(\mathbf{AP})} = \langle \{T, C_1, C_2\}^*, \{c_1, c_2\}, ary', typ'\rangle,$$

where $c_1: T \rightarrow C_1$, and $c_2: T^4 \rightarrow C_2$. ♦

For technical reasons, it is convenient to consider as the universe from which the structures of arcs of logic programs can be taken, the larger category **Graph(Set, Mon)** (shortly **MGraph**) instead of **Graph(Set, FMon)**. In fact, it is easy to check that there exists a forgetful functor U: **SCart** → **MGraph**, which is exactly the functor we need for defining a logic program as a heterogeneous graph (by Definition 3.3). Thus **MGraph** will play the role of category **B** of Definition 3.5. The representation of a program **P** as graph has the category of formulas and substitutions of its signature, $\mathbf{SCC}(\Sigma_{\mathbf{P}})$, as nodes, and the signature of its clauses, $\Sigma_{Cl(\mathbf{P})}$, as arcs. The source morphism maps a clause to the arrow of $\mathbf{SCC}(\Sigma_{\mathbf{P}})$ which represents its body, while the target maps each clause to the arrow representing its head.

4.6 Example *(The Program for* ***append*** *as a Heterogeneous Graph)*

Let us consider again the program for the *append* predicate of Example 4.4. It can be represented as the following heterogeneous graph of **Graph(MGraph, SCart)**, where $\Sigma_{\mathbf{AP}}$ and $\Sigma_{Cl(\mathbf{AP})}$ are as in Example 4.5:

$$\mathbf{AP} = \langle \mathbf{SCC}(\Sigma_{\mathbf{AP}}), \Sigma_{Cl(\mathbf{AP})}, src, trg\rangle$$

Graphically, we have the following situation, where the higher part of the diagram shows the arcs of $\Sigma_{Cl(\mathbf{AP})}$, while the lower part includes the relevant arrows of $\mathbf{SCC}(\Sigma_{\mathbf{AP}})$. The dashed arrows labelled *src* and *trg* are sufficient to uniquely determine the graph morphisms src, trg: $\Sigma_{Cl(\mathbf{AP})} \rightarrow U[\mathbf{SCC}(\Sigma_{\mathbf{AP}})]$.

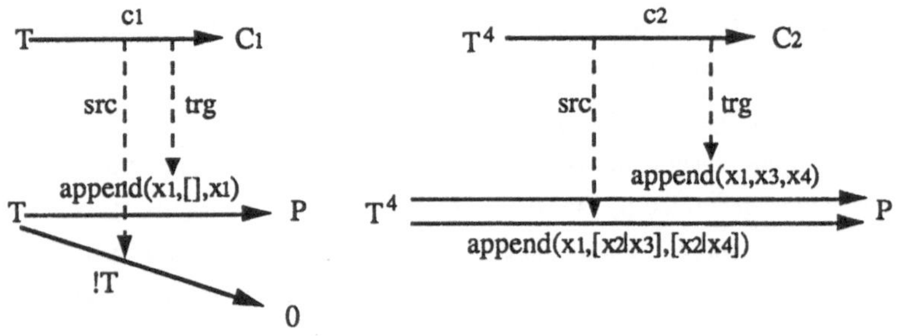

The source of clause c_1 is arrow !T: T $\rightarrow$ 0, i.e. the unique arrow to the terminal object in SCC(Σ_{AP}), representing the empty formula. ♦

Following the outline of our methodology, till now we have just defined the first level of structures (that of 'programs'). The next step is to define the category of structured transition systems for logic programs. As for Petri nets, also in the case of logic programs the transition system induced by a program will be a reflexive graph having the same structure (this time a strict cartesian category) on both states and transitions. Intuitively, by extending the tupling operation to clauses, one gets transitions that correspond to the concurrent application of many clauses to the same goal (similar to the multi-head clauses proposed by [FLP84]); by adding substitutions and their application to the clauses all the possible instantiations of clauses are obtained as transitions; and the identity transitions can be used to indicate that some atomic goals stay idle during a resolution step. We refer to [Co90, CM90] for a deeper discussion of this point.

The immediate consequence of this fact is that the category of structured transition systems we are looking for is **RGraph(SCart)**, i.e. the category of internal reflexive graphs of **SCart**. Now the question arises whether the induced transition system of a logic program can be freely generated by the program itself. Since it can be proved that functor U: **SCart** $\rightarrow$ **MGraph** has a left adjoint SCC: **MGraph** $\rightarrow$ **SCart**, by Proposition 3.4 there exists a free adjoint functor F: **Graph(MGraph, SCart)** $\rightarrow$ **Graph(SCart)**. Incidentally, it is worth stressing that the category of formulas and substitutions of a logic program signature SCC(‹Σ, Π›) is exactly the free strict cartesian category generated by the representation of signature ‹Σ, Π› as a graph of **MGraph**.

If **P** is a logic program (represented as a heterogeneous graph), the internal graph of **SCart** F[**P**] has the same structure of nodes as **P** (i.e. the category SCC(Σ_P)), while its arcs are the free strict cartesian category generated by the signature of clauses, that is SCC($\Sigma_{CL(P)}$). To complete the construction, we still have to make graph F[**P**] reflexive. Since **SCart** has binary products, by Theorem 3.2a the free reflexive graph of F[**P**] exists, and is obtained by taking as arcs the coproduct of the nodes and the arcs of F[**P**] itself. However, it is shown in [CM89] that the resulting reflexive graph, when regarded as a transition system, does not simulates program P correctly: intuitively, the problem is that the sort T of terms, occurring in both categories SCC(Σ_P) and SCC($\Sigma_{CL(P)}$), originates two distinct sorts in their coproducts. On the contrary, the two occurrences of T should be identified. In order to force this identification, we can take as induced transition system the free internal reflexive graph, but in the subcategory of **SCart** where the functors are required to preserve sort T.

4.7 Definition *(The Transition System Induced by a Logic Program)*

Let $P = \langle SCC(\Sigma_P), \Sigma_{Cl(P)}, \partial_0, \partial_1 \rangle$ be the graph representing a logic program, and $F[P] = \langle SCC(\Sigma_P), SCC(\Sigma_{Cl(P)}), \partial'_0, \partial'_1 \rangle$ be its free internal graph of **SCart**. Moreover, let $\mathbf{SCart_T}$ be the subcategory of **SCart** including as objects all the strict cartesian categories with an object T, and as arrows the functors which preserve T. Since $\mathbf{SCart_T}$ has binary coproducts, by Theorem 3.2a there exists a free functor R_{SCartT}, mapping each internal graph to its free reflexive graph of $\mathbf{SCart_T}$. Then the *induced transition system of P* is defined as $TS[P] \equiv R_{SCartT}[F[P]]$. ♦

TS[P] has category $SCC(\Sigma_P)$ as nodes, and (by Theorem 3.2a) category $SCC(\Sigma_P) +_T SCC(\Sigma_{Cl(P)})$ as arcs, where '$+_T$' denotes the coproduct in $\mathbf{SCart_T}$. Since $\mathbf{RGraph(SCart_T)}$ is a subcategory of **RGraph(SCart)**, in the following we consider TS[P] as a internal reflexive graph of **SCart**.

Following the guidelines of the methodology, after defining the structured transition system induced by a program, we have to look for the existence of its free model, and to define the category of acceptable models for a logic program. A model of a logic program will be an internal category in **SCart**, accordingly to the requirement that the algebraic structure of the transitions should be extended to the entire computations. Since **SCart** is the category of models in **Set** of a left exact sketch [Co90], by Theorem 3.2b there exists a free adjoint functor C_{SCart}: **RGraph(SCart)** $\rightarrow$ **Cat(SCart)**, which maps each structured transition system of **RGraph(SCart)** to its free model of computations.

In the following, we denote by $[\![P]\!]_F$ the free model of a logic program P, i.e. $[\![P]\!]_F \equiv C_{SCart}[TS[P]]$. Let us shortly analyze the structure of $[\![P]\!]_F$. Since it is an internal category of **SCart**, having the same states as P (by Proposition 3.6), it must have a structure like

$$[\![P]\!]_F = \langle SCC(\Sigma_P), X, dom, cod, id, \_;\_ \rangle,$$

where X is the strict cartesian category of the computations of the transition system TS[P]. Moreover, by the definition of internal category, dom and cod: $X \rightarrow SCC(\Sigma_P)$, id: $SCC(\Sigma_P) \rightarrow X$ and $\_;\_$: $X \times_0 X \rightarrow X$, are arrows of **SCart**.

The rich structure of category X provides some interesting operators on computations, i.e. on sequences of composable transitions of TS[P]. For example, arrow composition in X models the application of substitutions to computations, and two computations involving the same variables can be tupled in a sort of parallel composition. The behaviour of these operations is regulated by some axioms, enforced by the structure, which provide a rich, modular proof system, where (pieces of) computations can be managed exactly as if they were original clauses of the program. For a deeper discussion of this topic we refer to [Co90]; we only want to stress here that the abstract computations of the free model of a program automatically turn to be *partial ordering*, since, for example, two computations differing just for the order in which two clauses are applied to two independent goals are identified. This could provide the basis for a 'truly concurrent' semantics of AND-parallelism.

For what concerns the definition of the category of *acceptable models* for a logic program P, more abstract models can be obtained by identifying some of the computations of $[\![P]\!]_F$. Since the classical semantics of a logic program (i.e. its least Herbrand model [Ll87]) can be rephrased in our framework as a suitable subset of the global states (i.e. goals) which are reachable through a computation starting from the empty goal, it seems natural to require that the structure of states be the same in all the models for **P**. This yields to the following definition.

4.8 Definition *(The Acceptable Models of a Logic Program)*

Let **P** be a logic programs and $[\![\mathbf{P}]\!]_F$ be its free model. An *acceptable model* of **P** is a pair ‹h, C› where C ∈ |**Cat(SCart)**|, and h: $[\![\mathbf{P}]\!]_F \rightarrow$ C is an internal functor of **SCart**, which is an isomorphism of objects, and an epimorphism on arrows.

The *category of acceptable models of P*, called **Mod(P)**, is the category having acceptable models of **P** as objects, and such that f: ‹h, C› → ‹h', C'› is an arrow of **Mod(P)** if f is an internal functor of **SCart**, and h' = h;f. ♦

Mod(P) has obviously an initial object, which is $\langle id_{[\![P]\!]_F}, [\![\mathbf{P}]\!]_F\rangle$; moreover, it also has a terminal object, denoted by $\langle po, [\![\mathbf{P}]\!]_{IO}\rangle$, which is the most abstract model of **P** [Co90]. $[\![\mathbf{P}]\!]_{IO}$ (also called the *input/output model*) is actually an *internal preorder* of **SCart**, thus it can be essentially regarded as representing a reachability relation among goals: this implies that all the refutations for the same goal are identified.

Since the classical semantics of a logic program **P** if defined as the set of (ground, atomic) goals which have a refutation in **P**, and thus does not distinguish among two different refutations of the same goal, it turns out that the terminal model of **P** is sufficient to recover its classic semantics, and also some extensions of it. Since we are mainly interested in showing the rationale which lies behind the application of our methodology to a concrete, complex case, we refer to [CM90, Co90] for a more detailed discussion of the relationships among the algebraic semantics just presented and the classical semantics of logic programs. In particular, although we focused on the operational behaviour of programs, in [CM90] it is shown (in a more set-theoretic setting) that also their declarative semantics (i.e. the model-theoretic and the fixpoint ones) can be defined for arbitrary transition systems. Thus, analyzing the behaviour of logic programs through their induced transition systems, one is able to preserve the existence of three distinct but equivalent semantics.

5 Towards an Algebraic Theory of Concurrency

We can distinguish two approaches to the semantics of concurrency: the *interleaving* approach and the *partial order* or *true concurrency* one. Interleaving models (among others [Mi89, Ho85, Pnu77, BK84]) describe the possible behaviours of a system as total orderings of actions, and, as a consequence, concurrency is reduced to non-determinism. In fact two concurrent actions may occur in any order in the possible behaviours of the system. On the contrary, true concurrency models (among others [Rei85, NPW81, Pra86, BC88, DM87]) describe concurrent computations by means of partial orders, where the ordering relation describes the causal dependencies among actions: concurrency is represented by absence of ordering. This section aims at defining a new algebraic semantics to *process description languages* in terms of categories of graphs with algebraic structure, and at providing a general mathematical framework in which the different approaches can be unified. As a test case we will consider Milner's CCS.

The algebraic treatment of the semantics of process description languages requires the definition of suitable mathematical techniques to deal with the observation mechanisms which are usually used in the description of the semantics of those languages. Indeed, the definition of a semantics for a process description language can be reduced to the problem of defining the equivalence classes of its computations with respect to a suitable notion of observation. The distinction between interleaving and true concurrency models regards the 'power' of the observation function: interleaving observation functions are able to observe just sequences of actions, while true concurrency observation functions are able to record the causal dependencies among the actions performed in a computation.

The methodology described in Section 3 does not include any technique for dealing with the sophisticated observation mechanisms which can be defined on the computations of *labelled* transition systems, like the ones which define the operational behaviour of process description languages. In fact, as stressed in the concluding section, the methodology has been conceived mainly for *unlabelled* systems. Therefore, in the case of process description languages the methodology will be taken mainly as a guideline, and the actual steps will be modified to deal with the characterizing issues of those languages. For example, a labeling technique will be developed to describe the observation function on computations: every computation will be labelled with its observation. The full treatment of this topic can be found in [FM90, Fe90].

The operational semantics of CCS is defined in terms of a labelled transition system, where states are CCS agents and transitions are defined by axioms and inference rules driven by the syntactic structure of agents. This construction defines the transition system which corresponds to the interpreter (the abstract machine) of the language. The behaviour of a particular CCS agent is then the subpart of the transition system reachable from the state corresponding to that agent.

According to Milner's definition, in presenting the algebraic semantics of CCS we do not consider the level of description of programs (i.e. point 1) of Definition 3.5), but we start directly from the level of structured transition systems. Milner's transition system (forgetting the labels on transitions) can be regarded as having algebraic structure on both states and transitions: the operations on states are those of the syntax of CCS agents, while each inference rule of the operational semantics corresponds to one operation on transitions. Once the algebraic structure of states and transitions has been determined, this naturally yields to the definition of a category of (unlabelled) CCS transition systems, called **CCS**, which includes as objects all graphs with those structures on nodes and arcs, and as arrows graph morphisms preserving the structure.

CCS transition systems are not necessarily free: nonfreeness may reflect a particular interpretation of the operations. This allows us to individuate in the category **CCS** an object L, called *the transition system of labels*, where the operations on transitions are interpreted in a way which embodies the standard CCS notion of observable behaviour. This object can be used to label the transitions of the CCS transition systems: a *labelled CCS transition system* is a pair ‹G, h›, where G is an object of **CCS**, and h: G $\rightarrow$ L is a morphism of **CCS**. Therefore an observation function on the transitions of G is simply a morphism from G to L.

The labelling construction defines a category, called **LCCS**, where the objects are labelled CCS transition systems and where the arrows are **CCS** morphisms which respect the labels. Certain objects of category **LCCS** capture the properties of CCS interleaving derivations. As an example, the traditional labelled transition system of CCS coincides with an object called Standard Model, which is obtained by identifying all the transitions with the same source and target nodes, and with the same labels.

In the standard interleaving semantics of CCS, congruences among agents are defined by means of various types of bisimulation [Pa81]. In our approach, the interleaving observational congruences are characterized in terms of final universal properties. For example, by restricting the arrows of **LCCS** to those morphisms which express a notion of simplification and preserve the observable behaviours, one gets a minimal realization as terminal object, i.e. a minimal abstract CCS machine. The unique mapping from the initial to that final object induces a congruence on CCS agents which coincides with the strong observational congruence.

Following the guideline of the methodology, we can define the category of models of CCS, **CatCCS**, whose objects are small categories. Since the forgetful functor **CatCCS** $\rightarrow$ **CCS** has a left adjoint, each CCS transition system can be associated with a free model, much in the spirit of step 3) of the methodology of Definition 3.5. Also in the case of **CatCCS**, the observation function on computations can be handled by a labelling construction, yielding to the definition of a category of *labelled CCS models*, **CatLCCS**. The details of these constructions can be found in [Fe90].

By extending the techniques mentioned above to characterize the strong congruence, the third author in a joint paper with V. Sassone [MS90] has shown that the subcategory of **CatLCCS** which consists of all the objects reachable via simplification mappings which preserve the computations outgoing from any state, has a terminal element which characterizes the coarsest equivalence which is both a congruence and a weak bisimulation: this is called the *dynamic* bisimulation. It should be remarked that also the *weak observational congruence* can be characterized by a universal property of finality in a suitable category of CCS models. The details of this rather complex construction can be found in [Fe90].

Within our algebraic framework (see [MY89] for an alternative solution) a truly concurrent model can be obtained by imposing, on the computations of the free CCS model, certain equations stating that parallel independent transitions can commute. As a result of the construction, we obtain a CCS model where the arrows (abstract computations) which differ just for the order of independent parallel transitions are identified. The resulting CCS model is *truly concurrent* in a very precise sense. In fact, if we select a state (i.e. a CCS agent) and we consider the outgoing morphisms ordered by prefix with respect to morphism composition, we obtain the domain of configurations of an *event structure* [Wi87, Wi89]. The construction above is straightforward, being the usual way of unfolding a transition system, and event structures are the most accepted semantic domain for true concurrency. Moreover, by adding the information on labels we show that our truly concurrent semantics coincides with that proposed by Winskel [Wi82].

5.1 CCS and its Interleaving Semantics

In this section we give an overview of Milner's Calculus of Communicating Systems (CCS) [Mi80, Mi89] and its interleaving semantics. Let $\Delta = \{\alpha, \beta, \gamma, \dots\}$ be a fixed set of actions, and let $\bar{\Delta} = \{\bar{\alpha} \mid \alpha \in \Delta\}$ be the set of complementary actions (being $^{-}$ the operation of complementation). Set $\Lambda = \Delta \cup \bar{\Delta}$ (ranged over by λ) is the set of *visible actions*. Finally, let $\tau \notin \Lambda$ be the *invisible action*, $\Lambda \cup \{\tau\}$ is ranged over by μ.

5.1 Definition *(CCS Expressions and Agents)*

The syntax of *CCS Expressions* is defined as follows:

$$E ::= x \mid nil \mid \mu.E \mid E\backslash\alpha \mid E[\Phi] \mid E + E \mid E|E \mid rec\ x.\ E$$

where x is a variable, and Φ is a permutation of $\Lambda \cup \{\tau\}$ which preserves τ and the operation $\bar{}$ of complementation. A CCS agent is a CCS expression with no free variables. ♦

The operational semantics of CCS is defined in terms of structured rules given in the Plotkin's style [Pl81]. The essence of this approach is to formalize what means for a CCS agent to evolve, by introducing a deductive system whose theorems are the transitions the agents may perform.

5.2 Definition *(CCS Transition Relation)*

The transition relation $\xrightarrow{\mu}$ is defined by the following axioms and inference rules.

$$\mu.E \xrightarrow{\mu} E$$

$$\frac{E_1 \xrightarrow{\mu} E_2}{E_1\backslash\alpha \xrightarrow{\mu} E_2\backslash\alpha} \text{ if } \mu \notin \{\alpha, \bar{\alpha}\} \qquad \frac{E_1 \xrightarrow{\mu} E_2}{E_1[\Phi] \xrightarrow{\Phi(\mu)} E_2[\Phi]}$$

$$\frac{E_1 \xrightarrow{\mu} E_2}{E_1{+}E \xrightarrow{\mu} E_2 \text{ and } E{+}E_1 \xrightarrow{\mu} E_2} \qquad \frac{E_1 \xrightarrow{\mu} E_2}{E_1 \mid E \xrightarrow{\mu} E_2 \mid E \text{ and } E \mid E_1 \xrightarrow{\mu} E \mid E_2}$$

$$\frac{E_1 \xrightarrow{\lambda} F_1 \text{ and } E_2 \xrightarrow{\bar{\lambda}} F_2}{E_1 \mid E_1 \xrightarrow{\tau} F_1 \mid F_2} \qquad \frac{E_1[\text{rec } x.\ E_1/x] \xrightarrow{\mu} E_2}{\text{rec } x.\ E_1 \xrightarrow{\mu} E_2}$$

♦

A transition $E \xrightarrow{\mu} F$ expresses the fact that the agent E may evolve to become the agent F through the action μ, being μ either a stimulus from the environment, or the internal action τ, which is independent from the environment. Park's notion of *bisimulation* [Pa81] is almost the standard device for defining behavioural equivalences for process algebras.

5.3 Definition *(Strong Observational Equivalence)*

If R is a relation over CCS agents, then Ψ, a function from relations to relations, is defined as follows:

$\langle E_1, E_2\rangle \in \Psi(R)$ if and only if $\forall\, \mu \in \Lambda \cup \{\tau\}$:

- whenever $E_1 \xrightarrow{\mu} F_1$ there exists F_2 such that $E_2 \xrightarrow{\mu} F_2$ and $\langle F_1, F_2\rangle \in R$
- whenever $E_2 \xrightarrow{\mu} F_2$ there exists F_1 such that $E_1 \xrightarrow{\mu} F_1$ and $\langle F_1, F_2\rangle \in R$

A relation R is called *Strong Bisimulation* iff $R \subseteq \Psi(R)$. The relation $\sim\ = \cup\{R \mid R \subseteq \Psi(R)\}$ is called *Strong Observational Equivalence.* ♦

It is a well known fact that the strong observational equivalence is a congruence on CCS agents, i.e. it is preserved by all the operations on agents. However, Definition 5.3 does not consider τ-actions as special actions representing the occurrence of invisible internal moves. If we take into account the special status of τ-actions, agents are weakly equivalent if they could perform the same sequences of visible actions, and then reach weakly equivalent states. The notion of Weak Observational Equivalence takes care of this kind of abstraction.

5.2 A Category of Structured Transition Systems for CCS

In this section we introduce a category of structured transition systems for CCS. The starting point is to understand what is the algebraic structure on states and transitions. On states, the operations are directly given by the syntax of agents, while the operations on transitions correspond to the inference rules of the operational semantics.

5.4 Definition *(CCS Transition Systems)*

A *CCS transition system* is a graph $G = \langle V, T, \partial_0, \partial_1 \rangle$, where V and T are equipped with an algebraic structure. The operations that yield states are given by the following syntax:

$$u ::= x \mid nil \mid \mu.u \mid u\backslash\alpha \mid u[\Phi] \mid u + u \mid u|u \mid rec\ x.\ u$$

where x is a variable. On the elements of the algebra of states the usual operation of substitution $u[u'/x]$ must be defined. The algebra of states is subjected to the following axiom:

$$rec\ x.\ u = u\ [rec\ x.\ u\ /\ x]$$

The operations that return transitions are given by the following syntax:

$$t ::= [\mu, u> \mid t\backslash\alpha \mid t[\Phi] \mid t <\!+\ u \mid u +\!> t \mid t \rfloor u \mid u \lfloor t \mid t|t.$$

Moreover, the following axioms define ∂_0 and ∂_1, stating that corresponding operations on states and transitions commute with the source and target functions.

$$[\mu, u> : \mu.u \to u$$

$$\frac{t: u \to v}{t\backslash\alpha : u\backslash\alpha \to v\backslash\alpha} \qquad \frac{t: u \to v}{t[\Phi] : u[\Phi] \to v[\Phi]}$$

$$\frac{t: u \to v}{t <\!+\ w: u + w \to v} \qquad \frac{t: u \to v}{w +\!> t: w + u \to v}$$

$$\frac{t: u \to v}{t \rfloor w: u \mid w \to v \mid w} \qquad \frac{t: u \to v}{w \lfloor t: w \mid u \to w \mid v}$$

$$\frac{t: u \to v \text{ and } t': w \to z}{t \mid t' : u \mid w \to v \mid z}$$

♦

Notice that there is no operation for handling recursion because, in this algebraic framework, recursion is handled by imposing on states the equation above. Basically, the operations of the algebra of states are those of CCS; agents are sometimes used to denote the state [E] they evaluate to, when the operations are interpreted in a particular algebra of states.

Clearly, a CCS transition system can be essentially considered as a heterogeneous graph (Definition 3.3), but with the structure of transitions richer than the one of states. This yields to the definition of category CCS.

5.5 Definition *(The Category of CCS Transition System, CCS)*

A *CCS morphism* $f: G \to G'$ is a graph morphism $\langle f_0, f_1 \rangle$, where f_0 (resp. f_1) is required to preserve the algebraic structure of the nodes (resp. transitions). **CCS** is the category having CCS transition systems as objects, and CCS morphisms as arrows. ♦

It is easy to check that the obvious forgetful functor U: **CCS** $\to$ **Graph** (which forgets the algebraic structure of both states and transitions) has a left adjoint. Since left adjoints preserve colimits, applying this functor to the initial object of **Graph** (i.e. the empty graph), one gets the initial object of **CCS**, denoted by $\mathfrak{S}$. $\mathfrak{S}$ has as algebra of nodes the free algebra generated by the syntax of CCS agents modulo the equation on recursion, while its transitions are freely generated by the operations on transitions.

Transitions in the initial object $\mathfrak{I}$ are proofs of operational derivations. For instance, both transitions $[\alpha, nil> <+ \alpha.nil$ and $\alpha.nil +> [\alpha, nil>$ correspond to the same CCS derivation $\alpha.nil + \alpha.nil \xrightarrow{\alpha} nil$. Moreover, the synchronization mechanism is completely free: there exist transitions for every possible term of the corresponding algebra. For example, the transition $[\alpha, u_1> \mid [\beta, u_2>$ belongs to $\mathfrak{I}$ even if the actions α and β cannot synchronize in accordance with the CCS synchronization laws. Furthermore, also transitions like $[\alpha, nil>\backslash\alpha$ are allowed.

A possible solution to this problem is to label the transitions of a CCS transition system: erroneous transitions like $[\alpha,u_1> \mid [\beta, u_2>$ will get a special label denoting the occurrence of an error. The idea is to represent the labels as a specific object of the category, where the operations of the algebra of states and transitions are suitably interpreted to embody the standard CCS laws. Of course, other notions of labelling can be defined by giving a different interpretation to the operations of the algebra of transitions, i.e. resorting to a different calculus of actions.

We now introduce the CCS transition system of labels, which correctly represents the standard calculus of actions of CCS. Transitions are labelled by α, β, ... , or by their complementary labels $\bar{\alpha}$, $\bar{\beta}$, ... Moreover, only two transitions with complementary labels may synchronize yielding the action τ. The special label $*$, $* \notin \Lambda \cup \{\tau\}$, will be used to indicate the occurrence of an error.

5.6 Definition *(CCS Transition System of Labels)*

The CCS Transition System of Labels $L = (\partial_0, \partial_1\colon \mathrm{Synchr} \to \mathbf{1})$ is an object of the category CCS, where **1** is the one state algebra, transitions are α, β, ..., $\bar{\alpha}$, $\bar{\beta}$, ... The operations on states always yield the state **1** while the interpretation of the operations on transitions is defined as follows:

$$[\mu, \mathbf{1}> = \mu, \quad t\backslash\alpha = \textbf{if } t \in \{\alpha, \bar{\alpha}\} \textbf{ then } * \textbf{ else } t, \quad t[\Phi] = \textbf{if } t = * \textbf{ then } * \textbf{ else } \Phi(t),$$
$$t <+ \mathbf{1} = t, \quad \mathbf{1} +> t = t, \quad \mathbf{1} \lfloor t = t, \quad t \rfloor \mathbf{1} = t, \quad t \mid t' = \textbf{if } t' = \bar{t} \textbf{ then } \tau \textbf{ else } *$$ ♦

5.7 Definition *(The Category LCCS)*

The objects of **LCCS** are pairs $\langle G, l\colon G \to L\rangle$ where:

- G is a CCS transition system,
- L is the CCS transition system of labels,
- $l = \langle l_T, l_V\rangle$ is a **CCS** morphism.

Pair $\langle f,g\rangle$ is a **LCCS** morphism from $\langle G,l\rangle$ to $\langle G',l'\rangle$ if and only if $\langle f,g\rangle$ is a **CCS** morphism from G to G' and $l = \langle f, g\rangle ; l'$. ♦

It is easy to check that if $\langle G, l_G\rangle$ is an object of **LCCS**, then l_G is a labelling of the transitions of G with labels taken from L. In fact, since l_G is a **CCS** morphism, it respects the algebraic structure on states and transitions. As an example, we have:

$$l_G([\mu, u>) = \mu$$
$$l_G(t\backslash\alpha) = l_G(t)\backslash\alpha = \textbf{if } l_T(t) \in \{\alpha, \bar{\alpha}\} \textbf{ then } * \textbf{ else } l_G(t)$$
$$l_G(t \mid t') = \textbf{if } l_G(t') = l_G(\bar{t}) \textbf{ then } \tau \textbf{ else } *.$$

The construction of the category **LCCS** is a standard categorical construction called comma category [ML71]. It is easy to prove that $\langle \mathfrak{I}, l_{\mathfrak{I}}\colon \mathfrak{I} \to L\rangle$ is the initial object of **LCCS**.

5.3 Algebraic Characterization of Strong Observational Congruence

In this section, we relate the traditional operational semantics of CCS with a particular object of **LCCS**: the Standard Model. Moreover, we show that the Strong Observational equivalence is characterized by a universal property of finality.

5.8 Definition *(Standard Model)*

Let $\equiv$ be the congruence over the transitions of a labelled CCS transition system defined as follows: $t_1 \equiv t_2$ if and only if $l(t_1) = l(t_2)$, $\partial_0(t_1) = \partial_0(t_2)$ and $\partial_1(t_1) = \partial_1(t_2)$.

Let M be the CCS transition system obtained by applying to $\mathfrak{S}$ the congruence above. M together with its obvious mapping $l_M : M \to \boldsymbol{L}$ is an object of **LCCS**. It is called the *Standard CCS Model.* ♦

5.9 Theorem *(Correspondence with the Interleaving Derivations)*

a) If $E \xrightarrow{\mu} E'$ is a derivation, then there is a unique transition t: $[E] \to [E']$ in M and $l_M(t) = \mu$.

b) If t: $[E] \to v$ is a transition of M with $l_M(t) = \mu$, then there is a derivation $E \xrightarrow{\mu} E'$ with $v = [E']$. ♦

We show now that the Strong Observational Congruence is characterized by a reduction mapping, and by a canonical object of **LCCS** which includes all the information about the congruent states, i.e. it is characterized by a final universal property in the appropriate connected component of **LCCS**.

5.10 Definition *(Transition Preserving Homomorphism)*

A **LCCS** morphism $\langle f, g\rangle$: $(G, l_G) \to (G', l_{G'})$ is called a *transition preserving homomorphism*, tp-homomorphism for short, if and only if:

- f: $T \to T'$ is a surjective homomorphism,
- g: $V \to V'$ is a surjective homomorphism,
- $t' \in T'$, $l_{G'}(t') \neq *$, t': $g(u) \to v'$ implies $\exists\, t \in T$, t: $u \to v$ with $f(t) = t'$. ♦

Intuitively, tp-homomorphisms are simplification mappings which preserve the correct behaviours.

5.11 Example

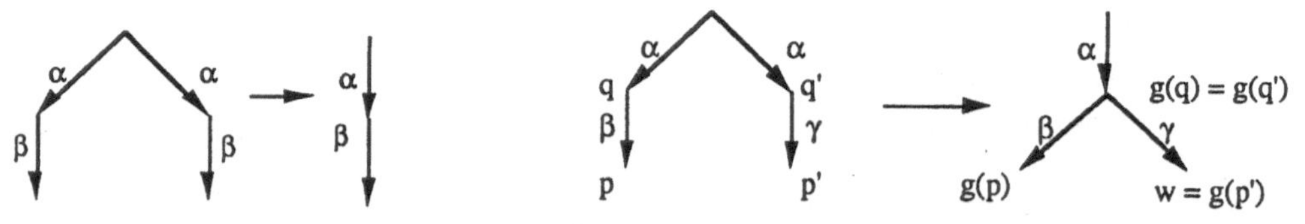

The first example illustrates a mapping which is a tp-homomorphisms. The example on the right illustrates a mapping which is not a tp-homomorphism; in fact if we take the transition t' : $g(q) \to w$ with label γ we cannot find any transition t with label γ such that t : $q \to q''$ and $f(t) = t'$ ♦

5.12 Theorem *(tp-homomorphisms $\leftrightarrow$ Strong Bisimulation Congruences)*

a) Let $\langle f,g\rangle$: $(\mathfrak{S}, l_{\mathfrak{S}}) \to (G, l_G)$ be a tp-homomorphism. Then, the relation $R_{\langle f,g\rangle}$ defined as $E_1\, R_{\langle f,g\rangle}\, E_2$ if and only if $g([E_1]) = g([E_2])$ is a strong bisimulation congruence.

b) Let R be a strong bisimulation congruence. Then there exists a labelled CCS transition system (G, l_G) such that the unique morphism ‹f,g›: ($\mathfrak{I}$, $l_{\mathfrak{I}}$) → (G, l_G) is a tp-homomorphism, and g([E_1]) = g([E_2]) if and only if E_1 R E_2. ♦

5.13 Theorem *(The Characterization Theorem)*

a) The subcategory of **LCCS**, which consists of all the objects reachable from ($\mathfrak{I}$, $l_{\mathfrak{I}}$) via tp-homomorphisms, and whose morphisms are tp-homomorphisms, has a terminal object.

b) $E_1 \sim E_2$ if and only if $g_\sim(E_1) = g_\sim(E_2)$, being ‹$f_\sim$,$g_\sim$› the canonical tp-homomorphism from ($\mathfrak{I}$, $l_{\mathfrak{I}}$) to the terminal object. ♦

Following the guidelines of the methodology (i.e. adding the identity transitions, and an operation of sequential composition of transitions), we can introduce the category of CCS models whose objects (CCS Models) are small categories: the arrows of these small categories represent computations. The transitions (computations) of each CCS model are more complex than the standard CCS computations (multistep derivations) which are obtained by concatenating the single derivations. In fact, the operations on transitions can be applied to sequences of transitions (computations), e.g.(t_1 ; t_2)\α, or (t_1 ; t_2) | t'. This feature can be suitably exploited to provide a semantic understanding of *refinement of actions* where a transition t can be refined into a sequence of transitions at lower level, i.e. a computation [GMM90].

In order to obtain the correspondence with the standard notion of CCS computations (the arrow $\overset{s}{\Rightarrow}$ of Milner's semantics), the CCS model of observable behaviours can be thought of as the monoid freely generated by the alphabet of actions Λ with the addition of the special symbol * (acting as absorbing element). To obtain the right notion of behaviour the τ invisible action will be identified with the empty sequence, i.e. the identity of the CCS model of observable behaviours. The CCS model of observable behaviours associates the value * to transitions like (t_1 ; t_2) | t'.

As far as the weak congruence is concerned, we cannot directly apply the constructions and techniques used to characterize the strong congruence. The reason is that the weak observational congruence is not a bisimulation, and the definition of tp-homomorphism implies that, from congruent states, corresponding transitions lead to congruent states. This is not the case for the weak congruence. As an example, consider the states (agents) α.τ.β.nil and α.β.nil. In fact, they are weakly congruent, but after the transition [α, τ.β.nil >: α.τ.β.nil → τ.β.nil, we end up in the state τ.β.nil which is not congruent to β.nil. Therefore, the weak observational congruence cannot be directly characterized by tp-homomorphisms in the appropriate sub-category of the category of CCS models. The third author in a joint paper with V. Sassone [MS90] has shown that the subcategory of the category of CCS models which consists of all the objects reachable via tp-homomorphisms has a terminal element which characterizes the coarsest equivalence which is both a congruence and a weak bisimulation. This behavioural equivalence is called Dynamic Bisimulation. However, also the weak congruence may be characterized by a universal property of finality in a suitable category which is constructed from the category of CCS models. The details of this construction can be found in [Fe90].

5.4 A Truly Concurrent Semantics

In this section, we define a truly concurrent semantics for CCS by taking fully advantage of the algebraic structure on transitions. We consider the initial object of CCS, the CCS transition system $\mathfrak{S}$, and we define the *concurrency relation* χ which relates parallel independent transitions. Then, we consider the CCS model which identifies computations which are obtained one from the other by permuting independent parallel transitions. This relation extends within our algebraic framework a similar proposal by Boudol and Castellani [BC89].

5.14 Definition *(The Concurrency Relation)*

Let _ **then** _ χ _ **then** _ be a quaternary relation on transitions of the CCS transition system $\mathfrak{S}$ defined by the following clauses ($t: u \to v$ and $t_i: u_i \to v_i$, for each $i \in \{1, \ldots 4\}$):

$$t_1 \textbf{ then } t_2 \;\chi\; t_3 \textbf{ then } t_4 \quad \textbf{iff} \quad t_3 \textbf{ then } t_4 \;\chi\; t_1 \textbf{ then } t_2$$

$$t_1 \rfloor u_2 \textbf{ then } v_1 \lfloor t_2 \;\chi\; u_1 \lfloor t_2 \textbf{ then } t_1 \rfloor v_2$$

$$\frac{t_1 \textbf{ then } t_2 \;\chi\; t_3 \textbf{ then } t_4}{t_1\backslash\alpha \textbf{ then } t_2\backslash\alpha \;\chi\; t_3\backslash\alpha \textbf{ then } t_4\backslash\alpha} \qquad \frac{t_1 \textbf{ then } t_2 \;\chi\; t_3 \textbf{ then } t_4}{t_1[\Phi] \textbf{ then } t_2[\Phi] \;\chi\; t_3[\Phi] \textbf{ then } t_4[\Phi]}$$

$$\frac{t_1 \textbf{ then } t_2 \;\chi\; t_3 \textbf{ then } t_4}{t_1\texttt{<+}w \textbf{ then } t_2 \;\chi\; t_3\texttt{<+}w \textbf{ then } t_4} \qquad \frac{t_1 \textbf{ then } t_2 \;\chi\; t_3 \textbf{ then } t_4}{w\texttt{+>}t_1 \textbf{ then } t_2 \;\chi\; w\texttt{+>}t_3 \textbf{ then } t_4}$$

$$\frac{t_1 \textbf{ then } t_2 \;\chi\; t_3 \textbf{ then } t_4}{t_1\rfloor w \textbf{ then } t_2\rfloor w \;\chi\; t_3\rfloor w \textbf{ then } t_4\rfloor w} \qquad \frac{t_1 \textbf{ then } t_2 \;\chi\; t_3 \textbf{ then } t_4}{w\lfloor t_1 \textbf{ then } w\lfloor t_2 \;\chi\; w\lfloor t_3 \textbf{ then } w\lfloor t_4}$$

$$\frac{t_1 \textbf{ then } t_2 \;\chi\; t_3 \textbf{ then } t_4 \text{ and } t: u \to v}{t_1 \mid t \textbf{ then } t_2\rfloor v \;\chi\; t_3\rfloor u \textbf{ then } t_4 \mid t} \qquad \frac{t_1 \textbf{ then } t_2 \;\chi\; t_3 \textbf{ then } t_4 \text{ and } t: u \to v}{t \mid t_1 \textbf{ then } v\lfloor t_2 \;\chi\; u\lfloor t_3 \textbf{ then } t \mid t_4}$$

$$\frac{t_1 \textbf{ then } t_2 \;\chi\; t_3 \textbf{ then } t_4 \text{ and } t'_1 \textbf{ then } t'_2 \;\chi\; t'_3 \textbf{ then } t'_4}{t_1 \mid t'_1 \textbf{ then } t_2 \mid t'_2 \;\chi\; t_3 \mid t'_3 \textbf{ then } t_4 \mid t'_4}$$ ♦

The first axiom states that χ is a symmetric relation between terms of the form t **then** t'. The second axiom expresses the commutativity between parallel independent transitions, i.e. executing the transition of the first process while the second stays idle, and then executing the transition of the second process, while the first stays idle, is the same as performing the two transitions in the reverse order. The concurrency relation is compatible with the other operators of the algebra of transitions. The last inference rule expresses the commutativity of independent transitions with respect to communications.

5.15 Definition *(Concurrent CCS Model)*

Given the CCS transition system $\mathfrak{S}$, the Concurrent CCS Models $\mathbf{C}[\mathfrak{S}]$ is the category generated by $\mathfrak{S}$ (where _ ; _ denotes the composition of arrows, and idle(u) denotes the identity on state u), defined by the following generating rules

$$\frac{u \text{ in } \mathfrak{S}}{\text{idle}(u) \text{ in } \mathbf{C}[\mathfrak{S}]} \qquad \frac{t: u \to v \text{ in } \mathfrak{S}}{t: u \to v \text{ in } \mathbf{C}[\mathfrak{S}]} \qquad \frac{t: u \to v \text{ and } t': v \to z \text{ in } \mathbf{C}[\mathfrak{S}]}{t\,;\,t' : u \to z \text{ in } \mathbf{C}[\mathfrak{S}]}$$

and subject to the following equations

$$idle(u) \,;\, t = t = t \,;\, idle(v)$$

$$t_1 \,;\, (t_2 \,;\, t_3) = (t_1 \,;\, t_2) \,;\, t_3$$

$$\frac{t_1 \ \mathbf{then}\ t_2 \ \chi\ t_3 \ \mathbf{then}\ t_4}{t_1 \,;\, t_2 = t_3 \,;\, t_4} \qquad \blacklozenge$$

For instance, in $\mathbf{C}[\mathfrak{S}]$ the following transitions are identified:

$[\alpha, nil\rangle \rfloor \beta.nil \,;\, nil \lfloor [\beta, nil\rangle : \alpha.nil \mid \beta.nil \rightarrow nil,$

$\alpha.nil \lfloor [\beta.nil\rangle \,;\, [\alpha, nil\rangle \rfloor nil : \alpha.nil \mid \beta.nil \rightarrow nil.$

Let E be the CCS agent $(\alpha.nil \mid \gamma.nil) \mid (\bar{\alpha}.nil \mid \bar{\gamma}.nil)$. From

$([\alpha, nil\rangle \rfloor \gamma.nil)$ **then** $(nil \lfloor [\gamma, nil\rangle)\ \chi\ (\alpha.nil \lfloor [\gamma, nil\rangle)$ **then** $([\alpha, nil\rangle \rfloor nil)$ and

$([\bar{\alpha}, nil\rangle \rfloor \bar{\gamma}.nil)$ **then** $(nil \lfloor [\bar{\gamma}, nil\rangle)\ \chi\ (\bar{\alpha}.nil \lfloor [\bar{\gamma}, nil\rangle)$ **then** $([\bar{\alpha}, nil\rangle \rfloor nil)$

we can infer the following equality

$([\alpha, nil\rangle \rfloor \gamma.nil) \mid ([\bar{\alpha}, nil\rangle \rfloor \bar{\gamma}.nil) \,;\, (nil \lfloor [\gamma, nil\rangle) \mid (nil \lfloor [\bar{\gamma}, nil\rangle) =$

$(\alpha.nil \lfloor [\gamma, nil\rangle) \mid (\bar{\alpha}.nil \lfloor [\bar{\gamma}, nil\rangle) \,;\, ([\alpha, nil\rangle \rfloor nil) \mid ([\bar{\alpha}, nil\rangle \rfloor nil).$

Since $\mathbf{C}[\mathfrak{S}]$ is a small category, we can apply standard categorical constructions. In the following will play an important role the comma category $([E]\!\downarrow\!\mathbf{C}[\mathfrak{S}])$, being E a CCS agent. The objects of this category are all the transitions, t_i: $[E] \rightarrow v_i$: they are all the computations starting from agent E. $([E]\!\downarrow\!\mathbf{C}[\mathfrak{S}])$ has the structure of a partially ordered set, where the order relation is defined as follows. Let t_1: $[E] \rightarrow v_1$, and t_2: $[E] \rightarrow v_2$, $t_1 \leq t_2$ if and only if there is t: $v_1 \rightarrow v_2$ such that $t_1 \,;\, t = t_2$. The partial order $([E]\!\downarrow\!\mathbf{C}[\mathfrak{S}], \leq)$ represents the *finite* computations, ordered by prefix, starting from the CCS agent E. Indeed, $([E]\!\downarrow\!\mathbf{C}[\mathfrak{S}], \leq)$ does not have limit points; it is not a domain, i.e. a complete partial order. However, limit points can be added by taking the *completion by ideals*. We indicate with $(\mathbf{C}^{\infty}_{E}, \leq)$ the completion of $([E]\!\downarrow\!\mathbf{C}[\mathfrak{S}], \leq)$.

Our semantics of CCS based on $(\mathbf{C}^{\infty}_{E}, \leq)$ is compatible with the classical Labelled Event Structure semantics. It is possible to prove that the partial order $(\mathbf{C}^{\infty}_{E}, \leq)$ is isomorphic to the domain of configurations of an event structure [NPW81, Wi87, Wi89]. Then, by introducing a suitable notion of labelling, it can be proved that our semantics coincides with Winskel's denotational semantics of CCS [Wi82]. The detailed treatment of this topic can be found in [FM90, Fe90].

5.16 Example

Let E be the CCS agent $E = ((\alpha.nil \mid \beta.nil) + \gamma.nil)$. The figures below illustrate the relevant part of $\mathfrak{S}$ (on the left) and the relevant part of $\mathbf{C}[\mathfrak{S}]$ except identities (on the right).

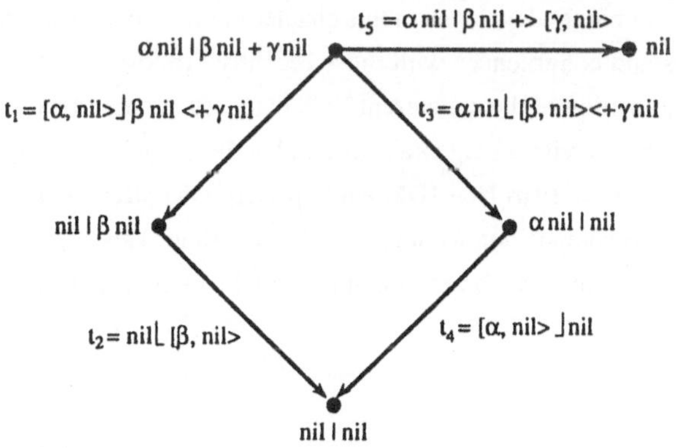

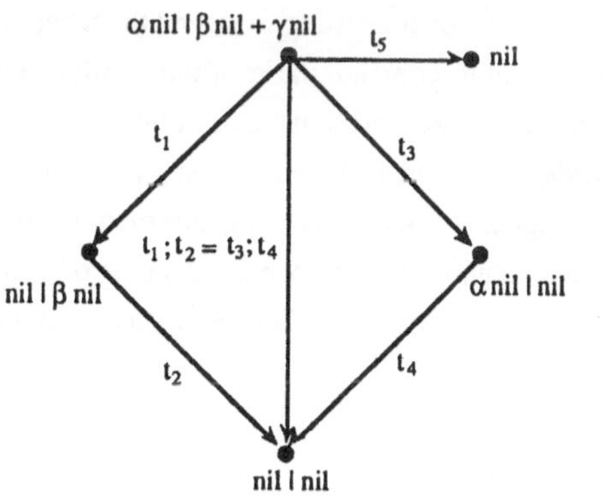

The next two figures show the relevant part of $(\mathbf{C}^{\infty}_{E}, \leq)$ (growing downwards) and the corresponding labelled event structure.

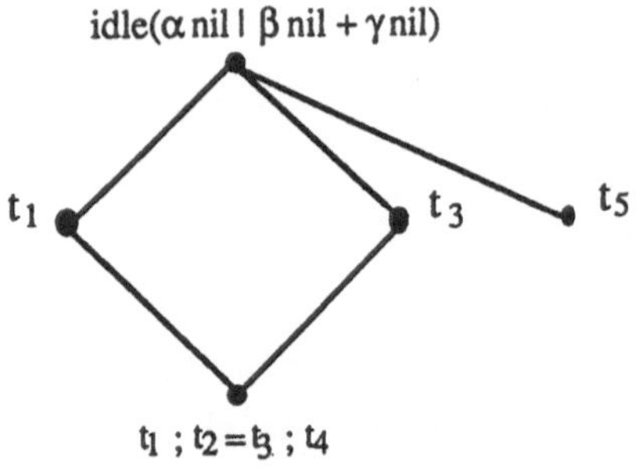

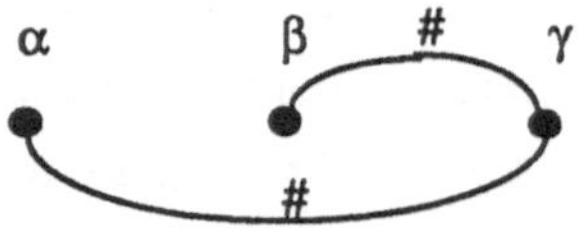

♦

5.5 Related Works

Categories with enough structure to support the labelling have been also employed by [CCMP89] in the context of enriched categories over a monoidal category. Due to the expressive power of the framework, they are able to define several notions of labelled structures (e.g. labelled partial orders, labelled metric spaces, etc.) by varying the base monoidal category and by using special forgetful functors for the labelling operation. In our approach the functorial labelling is more direct: it is an internal operation because the model of the labels is an object of the category.

It has been shown in [BB88] that CCS defines certain automata and that CCS strong and weak equivalences define certain classes of equivalent automata with a unique minimal representing automata. Our approach has some similarities with [BB88], but it is more informative since it models more aspects of the language.

We have already remarked that the approach by Boudol and Castellani based on permutations of transitions [BC89] is the most similar to what is described in this chapter. They introduce a language to represent proofs of operational derivations but they still remain at the level of classical transition system, not exploiting an algebraic framework to represent the commutativity of parallel independent transitions. Indeed, they decorate transitions with their proofs and then induce relations on transitions from the relations of their proofs. In our approach, relations on transitions are used to impose equational constraints on the transitions, i.e. on the morphisms of the category.

It will also be interesting to extend the labelling techniques developed in this chapter to the truly concurrent case and to compare the resulting equivalences and congruences with those recently proposed for truly concurrent semantics of CCS. In this respect, a transition of the concurrent CCS category denotes a partial order, and thus the labelling construction requires to devise an algebraic way to handle partial orders, i.e. an algebra of partial ordering observations. In the case of Petri Nets [DMM89], partial order structure have been equipped with a general operation of sequential composition within an algebraic setting. This approach has been extended in [FMM90] to deal with more complex algebraic structures than the monoidal structure of Petri Nets.

6 Conclusions and Future Work

In this paper we have introduced a general algebraic framework for the semantic analysis of computational systems. Two are the main contributions: the definition of a methodology, completely described in categorical terms, and its application to well known formalisms like Petri Nets and Logic Programming; and the algebraic characterization of both the interleaving and the truly concurrent semantics of the process description language CCS.

A relevant aspect of the proposed methodology is the fact that once the algebraic structure of states and transitions of a class of programs has been singled out, all the constructions which associate to such programs their induced transition systems and their models are almost completely automatic, thanks to the expressive power of the categorical language. Moreover, the methodology provides a unifying categorical framework where the specific aspects of several different formalisms can be analyzed, compared, extended, and possibly exported to other formalisms.

However, an intrinsic limitation of the methodology is that it can be satisfactorily applied only to a class of formalisms which has been called *state oriented* in [Co90], namely formalisms where the states include most of the semantic information. Informally, this characteristic implies that the transitions of those systems are not labelled, and thus no sophisticated observational mechanism can be defined on them. This class includes many interesting formalisms, like Petri Nets, Horn Clause Logic, Phrase Structure Grammars, and Term Rewriting Systems. However, process description languages do not fall in this class, because most of the semantic information is associated to their transitions, to which suitable labels are associated. The labels are the basis of the definition of complex observational mechanisms, which allow to identify states (i.e. agents in the CCS case) whose observational behaviours are 'equivalent' (under a suitable definition of 'equivalence'). This is the main reason why the methodology could not be applied directly to CCS, and was used mainly as a guideline in Section 5.

We plan to use the internal labelling operation via a comma category construction introduced in Section 5 within the general methodology of Section 3 to deal with *labelled* transition systems and their associated observational mechanisms. This will allow us to better integrate the results about concurrency in the methodology, possibly providing some general techniques which could be applied, for example, for providing a truly concurrent semantics to concurrent logic programming languages.

Recently a similar approach has been proposed by Meseguer [Me90], which considers *concurrent rewriting systems* as a unified model of concurrency. Also this work moves from a generalization of the algebraic approach of [MM88], but in a somewhat different perspective. It is shown that the programs of a wide class of paradigms (including functional, logical, and object oriented programming, Petri Nets, Turing Machines, Chemical Abstract Machines, and much more) can be represented as concurrent rewriting systems, i.e. transition systems having as states the elements of $T_{\Sigma,E}(X)$ (i.e. the free algebra generated by signature $\langle\Sigma, E\rangle$, where E is a set of equations which depends on the specific formalism), and as transitions the rewriting rules (implicitly regarded as operators, as we did for program clauses). Such systems can also be regarded as *theories* of the so called *directed equational logic*. Then a notion of *model* for such systems is proposed, which is essentially a structured category having a similar algebraic structure on both states and arrows. The initial model is generated by a free construction, which defines a left adjoint functor.

Although the two approaches are strictly related, it seems that our proposal is more general, since we do not require the states of our systems to be terms of an algebra: using the notion of *internal* structures of a universe category, we allow the collection of states (and that of transitions) to be objects of an (almost) arbitrary category. For example, in our treatment of Horn Clause Logic, the states are the arrows of a (small) category: it is not clear how an analogous treatment could be done in the framework proposed in [Me90]. Nevertheless, the analysis of the precise relationships between our approach and that of [Me90] requires further investigation.

7 References

[AL89] Asperti, A., Longo, G., *Applied Category Theory,* Technical Report TR-18/89, Dipartimento di Informatica, Università di Pisa, 1989. Forthcoming by MIT Press, 1990.

[AM89] Asperti, A., Martini, S., *Projections instead of variables: A category theoretic interpretation of logic programs*, Proc. 6th Int. Conf. on Logic Programming, Lisboa, Portugal, 1989, pp. 337-352.

[BB88] Benson, D., Ben-Shachar O., *Bisimulations of Automata*, Information and Computation, **79**, 1988, pp. 60-83.

[BC88] Boudol, G., Castellani, I., *Concurrency and Atomicity*, Theoretical Computer Science **59**, 1988, pp. 25-84.

[BC89] Boudol, G., Castellani, I., *Permutation of Transition: an Event Structure Semantics for CCS and SCCS*, in Linear Time, Branching Time and Partial Order in Logics and Models for Concurrency, LNCS 354, 1989.

[BD87] Best E., Devillers R., *Sequential and Concurrent Behaviour in Petri Net Theory*, Theoretical Computer Science, **55** (1), 1987, pp. 87-136.

[BK84] Bergstra, J., Klop, W., *Process Algebra for Syncronous Communication*, Information and Control, **60**, 1984, pp. 109-137.

[BW85] Barr, M., Wells, C., *Toposes, Triples and Theories*, Grundlehren der mathematischen Wissenschaften 278, Springer Verlag, 1985.

[CCMP89] Casley, R., Crew, R., Meseguer, J., Pratt, W., *Temporal Structures*, in in Third Symposium on Category Theory and Computer Science, LNCS 389, 1989, to appear in Mathematical Structures in Computer Science.

[CM89] Corradini, A., Montanari, U., *An Algebraic Representation of Logic Program Computations*, Technical Report TR-36/89, Dipartimento di Informatica, Università di Pisa, Dec. 1989. Also in Lassez, J., Editor, *Festschrift in Honor of J. A. Robinson*, to appear.

[CM90] Corradini, A., Montanari, U., *Towards a Process Semantics in the Logic Programming Style*, in Proc. 7th Symposium on Theoretical Aspects of Computer Science, STACS '90, LNCS 415, 1990, pp. 95-108.

[Co90] Corradini, A., *An Algebraic Semantics for Transition Systems and Logic Programming*, Ph.D. Thesis TD-8/90, Dipartimento di Informatica, Università di Pisa, March '90.

[DDM88a] Degano, P., De Nicola, R. Montanari, U., *A Distributed Operational Semantics for CCS based on Condition/Event Systems*, Acta Informatica, **26**, 1988, pp. 59-92.

[DDM88b] Degano, P., De Nicola, R. Montanari, U. *A Partial Ordering Semantics for CCS*, Technical Report TR-3/88, Dipartimento di Informatica, Università di Pisa, 1988 (To appear on Theoretical Computer Science)

[DDM89] Degano, P., De Nicola, R., Montanari, U., *Partial Ordering Descriptions and Observations of Nondeterministic Concurrent Processes*, in Linear Time, Branching Time and Partial Order in Logics and Models for Concurrency, LNCS 354, 1989, pp.438-466.

[DM87] Degano, P., Montanari, U., *Concurrent Histories, A Basis for Observing Concurrency*, Journal of Computer and System Science, **34**, 1987, pp.422-461.

[DMM89] Degano, P., Meseguer, J., Montanari, U., *Axiomatizing Net Computations and Processes*, in Proc. 4th Annual Symposium on Logic in Computer Science, Asilomar, CA, USA, 1989, pp.175-185.

[Fe90] Ferrari, G., *Unifying Models of Concurrency*, Ph.D. Thesis TD-4/90, Dipartimento di Informatica, Università di Pisa, March '90.

[FLP84] Falaschi, M., Levi, G., Palamidessi, C., *A Synchronization Logic: Axiomatics and Formal Semantics of Generalized Horn Clauses*, in Inf. and Control, **60** (1-3), Academic Press, 1984, pp. 36-69.

[FM90] Ferrari, G., Montanari, U., *Towards the Unification of Models for Concurrency*, in Proc. CAAP 1990, LNCS 431, pp.162-176.

[FMM90] Ferrari, G., Montanari, U., Mowbray, M., *On Causality Observed Incrementally, Finally*, Submitted for pubblication.

[GMM90] Gorrieri, R., Marchetti, S., Montanari, U. *A^2CCS: Atomic Actions for CCS*, Theoretical Computer Science, **72**, 1990, pp.203-223.

[Go88] Goguen, J.A., *What is Unification? A Categorical View of Substitution, Equation and Solution*, SRI Research Report SRI-CSL-88-2R2, SRI International, Menlo Park, California, 1988.

[Go89] Goguen, J.A., *A Categorical Manifesto*, Technical Monograph PRG-72, Oxford University Computing Laboratory, Programming Research Group, March 1989, to appear in Mathematical Structures in Computer Science.

[GR83] Goltz U., Reisig W., *The Non Sequential Behaviour of Petri Nets*, Information and Computation, **57**, 1983, pp. 125-147.

[Hoa85] Hoare, C.A.R., *Communicating Sequential Processes*, Prentice Hall, 1985.

[Ke76] Keller, R., *Formal Verification of Parallel Programs*, Com. ACM, **7**, 1976, pp. 371-384.

[La63] Lawvere, F.W., *Functorial Semantics of Algebraic Theories*, PhD Thesis, Columbia University.

[Ll87] Lloyd, J.W., *Foundations of Logic Programming*, Springer Verlag, 1984, (Second Edition 1987).

[Me89] Meseguer, J., *General Logics*, in Proc. Logic Colloquium '87, H.-D. Ebbinghaus et al. (eds), North-Holland, 1989, pp. 275-329.

[Me90] Meseguer, J., *Rewriting as a Unified Model of Concurrency*, Technical Report SRI-CSL-90-02, SRI International, February '90, to appear in Proc. CONCUR '90.

[Mi80] Milner, R., *A Calculus of Communicating Systems*. LNCS 92, 1980.

[Mi89] Milner, R., *Concurrency and communication*, Prentice Hall, 1989.

[ML71] Mac Lane, S., *Categories for the Working Mathematician*, Springer Verlag, New York, 1971.

[MM88] Meseguer, J., Montanari, U., *Petri Nets are Monoids: A New Algebraic Foundation for Net Theory*. Proc. Logics In Computer Science, Edinburgh, 1988, pp. 155-164. Also SRI-CSL-88-3, Jan. 88, to appear in *Info and Co.*

[MS90] Montanari, U., Sassone, V., *Dynamic Bisimulation*, Technical Report TR-13/90, Dipartimento di Informatica, Università di Pisa, 1990.

[MY89] Montanari, U., Yankelevich, D., *An Algebraic View of Interleaving and Distributed Operational Semantics*, in Third Symposium on Category Theory and Computer Science, LNCS 389, 1989, pp. 5-20.

[NPW81] Nielsen, M., Plotkin G., Winskel G,. *Petri Nets, Event Structures and Domains*, Part1. Theoretical Computer Science, **13**, 1981, pp. 85-108.

[Pa81] Park, D., *Concurrency and Automata on Infinite Sequences*, in Proc. GI, LNCS 104, 1981, pp. 167-183.

[Pe62] Petri, C.A., *Kommunication mit Automaten*, Schriften des Institutes für Instrumentelle Mathematik, Bonn 1962.

[Pl81] Plotkin, G., *A Structural Approach to Operational Semantics*, Technical Report DAIMI FN-19, Aarhus University, Department of Computer Science, Aarhus, 1981.

[Pnu77] Pnueli, A., *The Temporal Logic of Programs*, in 18-th Symp. on Foundations of Computer Science, 1977.

[Pra86] Pratt, V., *Modelling Concurrency with Partial Orders*, Int. Journal of Parallel Programming, **15**, 1986, pp.33-71.

[Rei85] Reisig, W., *Petri Nets: An Introduction*, EACTS Monographs on Theoretical Computer Science, Springer-Verlag, 1985.

[St89] Stark, E.W., *Concurrent Transition Systems*, Theo. Comp. Scie., **64**, 1989 , pp. 221-269.

[Wi82] Winskel, G., *Event Structures for CCS and Related Languages*, Proc. 9th ICALP, LNCS 140, 1982, pp. 561-576.

[Wi87] Winskel, G., *Event Structures* Invited lecture for the Advanced Course on Petri Nets, LNCS 255, 1987, pp. 393-415.

[Wi89] Winskel, G., *An Introduction to Event Structures*, in Linear Time, Branching Time and Partial Order in Logics and Models for Concurrency, LNCS 354, 1989.

Appendix

Definition A.1 *(graphs, reflexive graphs, and categories)*

i) A *(directed) graph* is 4-tuple $G = \langle V, T, \partial_0, \partial_1\rangle$, where V is a set of *nodes*, T is a set of *arcs*, ∂_0 and ∂_1: $T \to V$ are the *source* and *target* functions, respectively.

ii) A *reflexive graph* $R = \langle V, T, \partial_0, \partial_1, id\rangle$ is a graph $\langle T, V, \partial_0, \partial_1\rangle$, equipped with a function id: $V \to T$ such that for each $v \in V$, $\partial_0(id(v)) = \partial_1(id(v)) = v$.

ii) A *category* $C = \langle V, T, \partial_0, \partial_1, id, ;\rangle$ is a reflexive graph equipped with a partial binary operation _;_ on arcs (*arrow composition*). If $t, t' \in T$, then $t ; t'$ is defined iff $\partial_1(t) = \partial_0(t')$. In this case, $\partial_0(t ; t') = \partial_0(t)$, and $\partial_1(t ; t') = \partial_1(t')$. Moreover the following axioms must be satisfied for all arrows t, t' and t'' in T:

Associativity: $(t ; t') ; t'' = t ; (t' ; t'')$

Identity: $t ; id(\partial_1(t)) = t$ and $id(\partial_0(t)) ; t = t$

In a category $C = \langle V, T, \partial_0, \partial_1, id, ;\rangle$, V are the *objects* (usually denoted by $|C|$), and T are the *arrows*, sometimes denoted by Mor_C. The set of arrows of C between objects a and b is denoted by C(a,b).

iii) Category $C' = \langle V', T', \partial'_0, \partial'_1, id', ;'\rangle$ is a *subcategory* of $C = \langle V, T, \partial_0, \partial_1, id, ;\rangle$ iff $V' \subseteq V$, $T' \subseteq T$, ∂'_0, ∂'_1 and ;' are the restrictions of ∂_0, ∂_1, and ; to T', and id' is the restriction of id to V'. C' is *full* iff $C'(a,b) = C(a,b)$ for each $a,b \in V'$. ♦

Definition A.2 *(categories **Graph**, **RGraph** and **Cat**)*

A *graph morphism* f: $\langle V, T, \partial_0, \partial_1\rangle \to \langle V', T', \partial'_0, \partial'_1\rangle$ is a pair $\langle f_0, f_1\rangle$ of mappings, with f_0: $V \to V'$, f_1: $T \to T'$, and such that $\partial'_i(f_1(t)) = f_0(\partial_i(t))$ $\forall t \in T$, $i = 0,1$. The category having all (small) graphs as objects, and graph morphisms as arrows is called **Graph**.

A *reflexive graph morphism* f: $\langle V, T, \partial_0, \partial_1, id\rangle \to \langle V', T', \partial'_0, \partial'_1, id'\rangle$ is a graph morphism $\langle f_0, f_1\rangle$ such that moreover $id'(f_0(a)) = f_1(id(a))$. **RGraph** is the category having (small) reflexive graphs as objects, and reflexive graphs morphisms as arrows.

If C and D are two categories, a (covariant) *functor* f: $C \to D$ is a reflexive graph morphism $f = \langle f_0, f_1\rangle$ which preserves sequential composition, i.e. such that $f_1(t;t') = f_1(t);f_1(t')$. **Cat** is the category having (small) categories as objects, and functors as arrows. ♦

Definition A.3 *(some limits and colimits)*

In the following definitions, let C be a category.

i) t is a *terminal object* in C iff for each object $a \in |C|$ there exists exactly one arrow $!_a$: $a \to t$.

ii) The (categorical) *product* of two objects a, b ∈ |C| is an object a × b ∈ |C| with two arrows (projections), $fst_{a,b} : a \times b \to a$ and $snd_{a,b} : a \times b \to b$ such that for every pair of arrows f: c → a, g: c → b, there exists a unique arrow ‹f, g›: c → a × b such that diagram PROD below commutes:

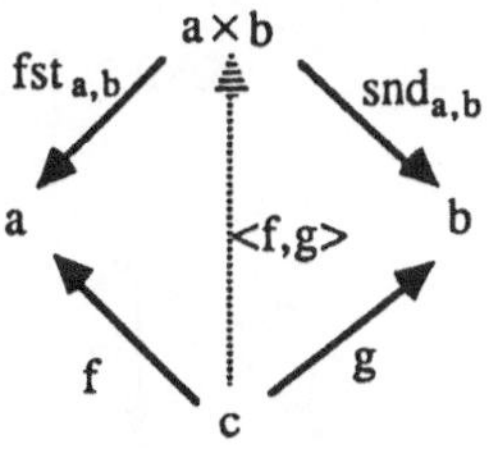

PROD

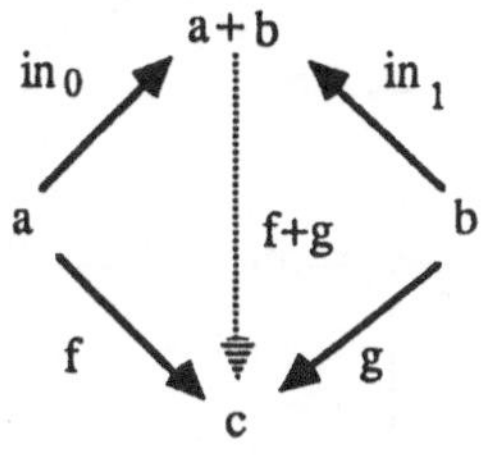

COPROD

iii) The *coproduct* of two objects a, b ∈ |C| is an object a+b ∈ |C| with two arrows (injections), $in_0 : a \to a+b$ and $in_1 : b \to a+b$ such that for every pair of arrows f: a → c, g: b → c, there exists a unique arrow f+g : a+b → c such that diagram COPROD above commutes. ♦

Definition A.4 *(internal reflexive graphs)*

Let C be a category. G is an *internal reflexive graph* of C (G ∈ **RGraph**(C)) iff G = $\langle c_0, c_1, \partial_0, \partial_1, id\rangle$, where $\langle c_0, c_1, \partial_0, \partial_1\rangle$ is an internal graph of C (Def. 2.5), and id: $c_0 \to c_1$ is an arrow in C such that $id;\partial_0 = id;\partial_1 = id_{c_0}$.

An *internal reflexive graph morphism* h: $\langle c_0, c_1, \partial_0, \partial_1, id\rangle \to \langle c'_0, c'_1, \partial'_0, \partial'_1, id'\rangle$ is an internal graph morphism h = ‹f, g› : $\langle c_0, c_1, \partial_0, \partial_1\rangle \to \langle c'_0, c'_1, \partial'_0, \partial'_1\rangle$ such that the following diagram commutes:

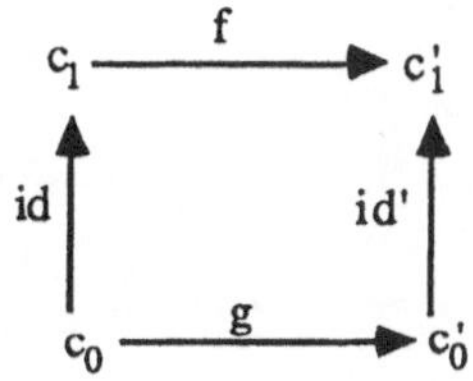

RGraph(C) is the category of internal reflexive graphs of C with internal reflexive graph morphisms as arrows. ♦

Definition A.5 *(internal categories)*

Internal categories of a category C can be defined as internal reflexive graphs including one additional arrow of C which represents arrow composition. This is possible by considering arrow composition as a *total* function (i.e. an arrow of **Set**) having as domain the set $\{\langle t, t'\rangle \mid \partial_1(t) = \partial_0(t')\}$, which can be characterized as a suitable *pullback object* [ML71] of **Set**. This yields to the following definition.

B is an *internal category of C* if B = $\langle c_0, c_1, \partial_0, \partial_1, id, comp\rangle$, where $\langle c_0, c_1, \partial_0, \partial_1, id\rangle$ ∈ |**RGraph**(C)|, and comp: $c_1 \times_0 c_1 \to c_1$ is an arrow in C, $\langle \pi_0, \pi_1\rangle: c_1 \times_0 c_1 \to c_1$ being the pullback of $\partial_1, \partial_0: c_1 \to c_0$. Moreover the following diagrams must commute in C;

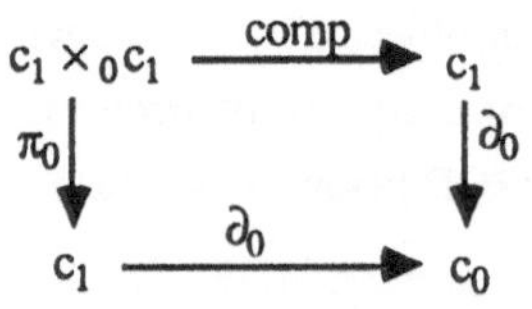

COMP1

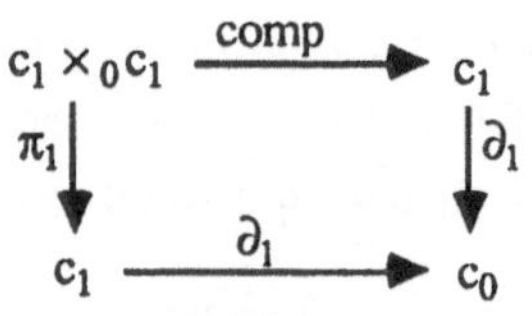

COMP2

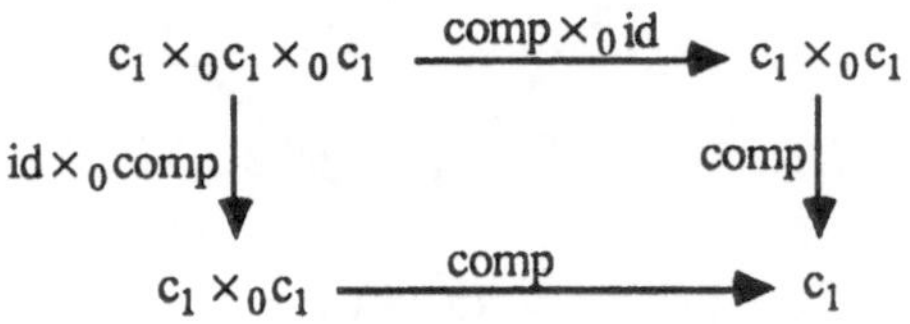

ASSOC

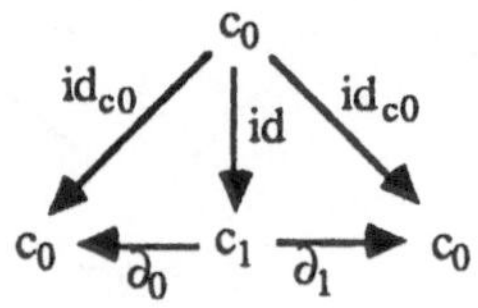

IDENT

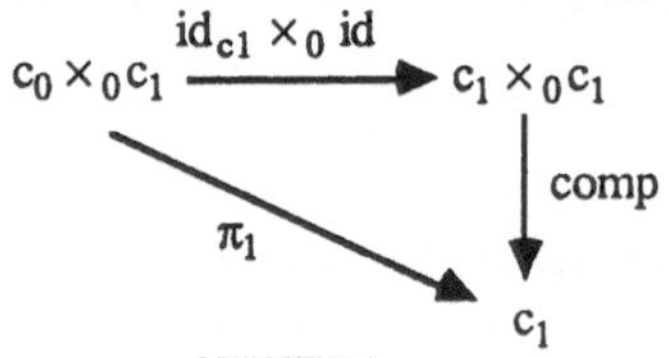

NEUTR1

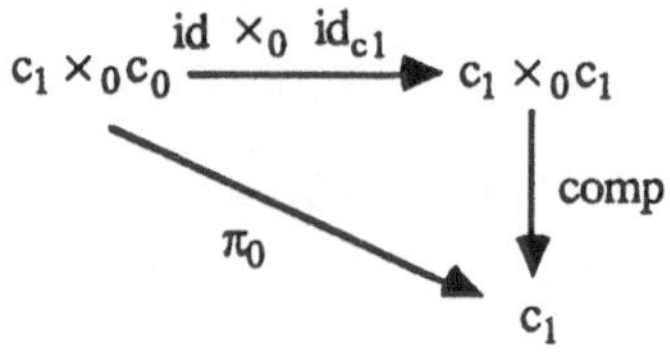

NEUTR2

An *internal functor* h: B → B' is an internal reflexive graph morphism which preserves arrow composition. Cat(C) is the category of internal categories of C, with internal functors as arrows. ♦

Concurrency and Computability

Ph.Darondeau

IRISA Campus de Beaulieu
F35042 Rennes-cedex

Abstract *This paper surveys some computability aspects in structural operational specifications, fairness concepts and testing equivalences, with special emphasis on infinite behaviours.*

I. Introduction

In the domain of functional programming, termination is a must and infinite computations are symptomatic of partial undefinedness. A diametrically opposed view is taken for communicating systems. There, termination may be thought of as a failure to maintain the service due to the environment. At first sight and on pragmatical grounds, it is insane to conceive of everlasting computing agents. Nevertheless, in the present state of art, idealized systems with unbounded lifetime lend themselves more readily to theoretical models, because we have no helpful theory dealing jointly with concurrency and scalar time. And of course, if no upper bound is imposed on the length of computations, infinite computations arise as natural limits of increasing sequences of partial computations.

Computations defined as sequences of steps may bear two different interpretations, depending on the synchronous or asynchronous approach. In synchronous models such as SCCS [Milner 1], a concurrent system is ruled by a global clock on which all agents synchronize by acting simultaneously at each tick. Regrettably, this assumption is unrealistic outside the realm of finite state and hardware systems, and for other fields of application, the rigid synchronization must be alleviated by idling operators which entail the loss of determinism and raise the issue of fairness. In asynchronous models such as CCS [Milner 2], computations are formed by interweaving concurrent threads in a single sequence of atomic actions, and the consequences are the same as regards non-determinism and fairness. To sum up, the behaviour of a concurrent and communicating system is a set of finite or infinite sequences of actions labelling transitions between states. To complicate things, that set is not necessarily closed in the natural topology on words: this is false as soon as fairness constraints are imposed on the race between concurrent agents, and this is false if on top of it some invisible action is abstracted from.

The well-known Church thesis claims that any general language for functional programming is just a set of notations for the partial recursive functions. There are two reasons why no comparable thesis applies to programming languages for concurrent and communicating systems. The first reason lies in the variety of the *basic* equivalences already defined on communicating systems within the tight limits of uniform concurrency, which sets all actions on a par by assigning them the free interpretation [de Bakker, Meyer, Olderog]. The second reason lies in the number of the different interpretations which may be defined for actions, thus inducing an equal number of *abstract* versions for the basic equivalences (and quotient models). Among those basic equivalences, one may distinguish between testing equivalences and bisimulation equivalences, that account for behavioural properties expressed respectively in linear time logics and in branching time logics [Pnueli], or between finitary equivalences and infinitary equivalences, that account respectively for properties of finite and infinite behaviours. One may further distinguish between extensional equivalences that ignore causality, and intensional equivalences that capture causal dependencies between actions.

The different equivalences and models may nevertheless be examined and compared in the light of logical complexity. The complexity analysis applies both to the equivalences which induce the models and to the objects which represent behaviours in those models. That analysis is insensitive to appearances, hence the intrinsic role of the different parameters will be shown by correlative variations in complexity. Because most models of concurrency are highly ineffective, their complexity will be scored in Kleene's arithmetical and analytical hierarchies of sets of numbers/functions, where all decidable relations are uniformly assigned the minimal score. By now, our comparative analysis of models is far from complete, even for the undecidable. We have thoroughly analysed models of linear behaviour, but we have only a few results for models of branching behaviour, and no result at all for intensional models. For instance, we have no characterization for sets of fair computations in partially ordered models, nor any characterization of trees definable in CCS up to observational congruence. A different theme of research which deserves further attention is the analysis of the complexity of semantic operators induced by contexts, interpreted in recursively presented metric spaces defined by domain equations [Yoccoz 1].

The relevance of the program outlined above is stressed by the following: the logical complexity of an equivalence measures the cost of the associated proof system. Finite or infinite proofs are in principle recursive objects, thus coded by natural numbers. The cost of a proof system measures the difficulty of that coding and it increases with the degree of sophistication of the proof rules. We will see that the β-rule, which is a sophisticated rule of transfinite induction in second order logic, is necessary for proving process equivalences induced by infinitary tests.

The remaining sections are organized as follows. Section II recalls the basics about the arithmetical and analytical hierarchies. Section III analyses at length structural operational specifications. Section IV analyses briefly the issue of fairness in recursively enumerable transition graphs. The grounds of uniform concurrency are finally left in section V, where we analyse various testing equivalences.

This note does not present original results. It is intended as a survey of papers written by Gérard Boudol, Robert De Simone, and by the author in collaboration with Doris Nolte, Lutz Priese and especially Serge Yoccoz.

II. The arithmetical and analytical hierarchies

This presentation is inspired from [Rogers]. In the sequel, ω is the set of natural numbers, variables i to n and x to z range over numbers ($\in \omega$), and variables f, g, h range over functions ($\in \omega^\omega$).

A set of numbers $A \subseteq \omega$ (resp. a set of functions $F \subseteq \omega^\omega$) is *arithmetical* if it may be expressed as $\{x \mid Q(y_1 \ldots y_n).\ R(x, y_1 \ldots y_n)\}$ for some relation R recursive in n+1 number variables (resp. if it may be expressed as $\{f \mid Q(y_1 \ldots y_n).\ R(f, y_1 \ldots y_n)\}$ for some relation R recursive in one function variable and n number variables) where $Q(y_1 \ldots y_n)$ is an alternated sequence of n first order quantifiers $\exists y_1\ \forall y_2 \ldots$ or $\forall y_1\ \exists y_2 \ldots$. The set A (resp.F) is in Σ^0_n- form if the leading quantifier is existential, in Π^0_n- form if the leading quantifier is universal. So, the recursive sets of numbers are both Σ^0_0 and Π^0_0 and the recursively enumerable sets of numbers are the Σ^0_1 sets, whence a set of numbers is recursive iff it is both Σ^0_1 and Π^0_1.

A set of numbers $A \subseteq \omega$ (resp. a set of functions $F \subseteq \omega^\omega$) is *analytical* if it may be expressed as $\{x \mid Q(g_1 \ldots g_n, y).\ R(x, g_1 \ldots g_n, y)\}$ for some relation R recursive in n function variables and two number variables (respectively if it may be expressed as $\{f \mid Q(g_1 \ldots g_n, y).\ R(f, g_1 \ldots g_n, y)\}$ for some relation R recursive in n+1 function variables and one number variable) where $Q(g_1 \ldots g_n, y)$ is an alternated sequence of n second order quantifiers followed by a unique first order quantifier, thus of one of the forms $(\exists g_1\ \forall g_2 \ldots \exists g_n\ \forall y)$ or $(\forall g_1\ \exists g_2 \ldots \forall g_n\ \exists y)$ if n is odd, and of one of the forms $(\exists g_1\ \forall g_2 \ldots \forall g_n\ \exists y)$ or $(\forall g_1\ \exists g_2 \ldots \exists g_n\ \forall y)$ if n is even. The set A (resp.F) is in Σ^1_n - form if the leading quantifier is existential, in Π^1_n - form if the leading quantifier is universal.

Thus in Σ^i_n or Π^i_n, the superscript $i=1$ shows the presence of second order quantifiers, whereas $i=0$ indicates their absence. The definitions carry to arithmetical and analytical relations in arbitrary products $\omega^k \times (\omega^\omega)^l$. In any case, a relation is Σ^i_n if and only if the complementary relation is Π^i_n, and the inclusion $(\Sigma^i_n \cup \Pi^i_n) \subseteq (\Sigma^i_{n+1} \cap \Pi^i_{n+1})$ shows the existence of a hierarchy which does not collapse in view of the theorem stating that $\Sigma^i_{n+1} \neq \Pi^i_{n+1}$. Let $\Delta^i_n = \Sigma^i_n \cap \Pi^i_n$, whence rec $= \Delta^0_0 = \Delta^0_1$ and $\Sigma^0_n \cup \Pi^0_n \subseteq \Delta^1_1$, then we have the following diagram of strict inclusions for any $n \geqslant 0$ and $i \in \{0,1\}$, with the exception that $\Sigma^0_0 = \Delta^0_1 = \Pi^0_0$:

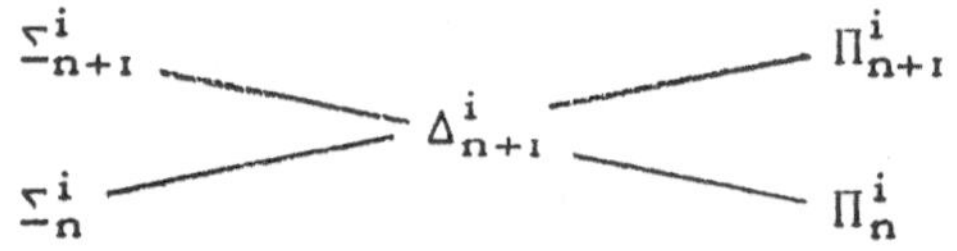

Arithmetical or analytical sets and relations may also be defined (from recursive relations) by logical forms in which first or second order quantifiers and logical connectives are used in free combinations not allowed in the Σ^i_n or Π^i_n forms defined above. The corresponding expressions may always be transformed into equivalent expressions with a single sequence of quantifiers Q (in leading position), by repetitively using the duality rules and the rule $Q'\varphi \;\&\; Q''\psi \to Q'Q''(\varphi \,\&\, \psi)$. The location in the hierarchy may then be determined by simple computations, known as Tarski-Kuratowski's computations, which allow to convert arbitrary sequences of quantifiers to standard alternations. The rules for the conversion are the following ($\exists^0$ and $\forall^0$ represent first order quantifiers, $\exists^1$ and $\forall^1$ represent second order quantifiers, and the dots stand for quantification sequences).

$$
\begin{array}{rcl}
\ldots \forall^0 \forall^0 \ldots & \to & \ldots \forall^0 \ldots \\
\ldots \exists^0 \exists^0 \ldots & \to & \ldots \exists^0 \ldots \\
\ldots \forall^1 \forall^1 \ldots & \to & \ldots \forall^1 \ldots \\
\ldots \exists^1 \exists^1 \ldots & \to & \ldots \exists^1 \ldots \\
\ldots \forall^0 \ldots & \to & \ldots \forall^1 \ldots \\
\ldots \exists^0 \ldots & \to & \ldots \exists^1 \ldots \\
\ldots \forall^0 \exists^1 \ldots & \to & \ldots \exists^1 \forall^0 \ldots \\
\ldots \exists^0 \forall^1 \ldots & \to & \ldots \forall^1 \exists^0 \ldots \\
\ldots \exists^1 & \to & \ldots \exists^0 \\
\ldots \forall^1 & \to & \ldots \forall^0
\end{array}
$$

The above rules may for instance be used to prove that Σ^i_n relations (resp. Π^i_n relations) are closed under finite union or intersection, and also under recursive denumerable union (resp. intersection). Moreover, there exists a procedure which, given a Tarski-Kuratowski computation, converts arithmetical or analytical relations to the form indicated by that computation. But beware: the equivalence of two Σ^i_n or Π^i_n forms is definitely not effective (even for $n=0$).

III. Structural operational semantics (SOS)

Given a signature Σ and a set of variables X, identified with recursive sets of numbers, let $T(\Sigma,X)$ be the recursive set of terms over X defined by the BNF syntax

$$t ::= x \mid \sigma_k(t_1,\ldots,t_k) \mid \underline{rec}\, x.\, t$$

where $x \in X$, σ_k is an operator of arity k, and $\underline{rec}\,x$ is the usual binding operator. Following the approach of structural operational semantics proposed in [Plotkin], an algebraic system of labelled transitions between terms is specified by a finite family of (schemes of) axioms and (schemes of) conditional rules of inference for transitions $t \xrightarrow{\lambda} t'$, where λ ranges over some recursive set of actions Λ (possibly equipped with recursive operations such as product of actions). Needless to say, all rules are finitary.

Structural operational specifications are more or less reminiscent of Gentzen's style of natural deduction, but elimination rules have no useful counterpart and different forms of introduction rules are possible (we shall examine that topic in a few lines). Transitions are proved by well-founded trees whose nodes represent logical inferences. Since all rules are finitary, those trees are finitely branching and therefore finite. And because schemes of rules induce procedures deciding whether rules are instances of schemes, the set of proof trees is recursive and the set of transitions is at most recursively enumerable (Σ^0_1) as a subset of ω^3.

In order to obtain finer results, let us introduce a precise form of rules. Let W be a new alphabet of meta-variables ($u, v \in W$). We will focus on rules (called axioms when k=o) which conform to the following pattern:

$$\frac{u_{i_1} \xrightarrow{\lambda_1} v_{i_1}\,,\ \ldots\,,\ u_{i_k} \xrightarrow{\lambda_k} v_{i_k}}{\sigma_n(u_1 \ldots u_n) \xrightarrow{\lambda} t}\quad R(\lambda,\lambda_1 \ldots \lambda_k)$$

where:

- $\sigma_n \in \Sigma$,
- $u_1 \ldots u_n$, $v_{i_1} \ldots v_{i_k}$ are different variables ($\in W$), $u_{i_1} \ldots u_{i_k}$ are different variables and $\{u_{i_1} \ldots u_{i_k}\} \subseteq \{u_1 \ldots u_n\}$,
- let $v'_j = v_{i_m}$ if $j = i_m$ for some m and $v'_j = u_j$ otherwise, then
- t is a Σ-term over $\{v'_1 \ldots v'_n\}$ and each variable v'_j occurs at most once in t,
- the side condition $R(\lambda,\lambda_1 \ldots \lambda_k)$ is a recursive predicate of n+1 variables.

The above format of SOS rules, known as De Simone's format [De Simone], allows neither duplication of arguments $u_1 \dots u_n$ nor lookahead into their structure. Hence the specified operators σ_n just synchronize the moves of their arguments. We will examine the power of De Simone's rules used in conjunction with two alternative rules for rec, namely the following:

$$\frac{u \xrightarrow{\lambda} v}{\text{rec}\, x.\, u \xrightarrow{\lambda} v\,[\text{rec}\, x.\, u\,/\,x\,]} \quad \text{REC I}$$

$$\frac{u\,[\text{rec}\, x.u\,/\,x\,] \xrightarrow{\lambda} v}{\text{rec}\, x.\, u \xrightarrow{\lambda} v} \quad \text{REC II}$$

We say that a *recursive* term rec x. t is guarded if any free occurence of x in t is inside at least one subterm $\sigma_n(t_1 \dots t_n)$ which cannot be unified with the left member of the consequence of any rule different from an axiom. Such well-guarded terms form a recursive set. It may be then shown that REC I is equivalent to REC II in the absence of unguarded recursion [Badouel, Darondeau].

Let us assume that De Simone's format of rules is used in conjunction with REC I. Suppose moreover that for each term t, actions labelling transitions from t are taken from a finite subset of Λ defined effectively from t. The induced transition system is then finitely branching and even recursive: for any t, $\{ <\lambda,t'> \mid t \xrightarrow{\lambda} t' \}$ is finite, and $\{ <t,\lambda,t'> \mid t \xrightarrow{\lambda} t' \}$ is recursive as a subset of ω^3. As a matter of fact, for each fixed consequence, there is only a finite number of possible applications of rules deriving that consequence, and for each possible application of a rule, the left members of the premisses are strict subterms of the left member of the consequence. Those conditions are precisely met in CCS.

When combined with REC II, De Simone's rules permit to define (up to strong bisimulation) any recursively enumerable set of transitions $T \subseteq Q \times \Lambda \times Q$ where Λ and Q are (identified with) recursive sets of numbers [De Simone][Boudol]. As a matter of fact, any recursively enumerable transition system may be realized in MEIJE (up to strong bisimulation), and MEIJE is specified by rules in De Simone's format and the rule REC II for unguarded recursion (even though the exact syntax for recursive terms is different). Since any process calculus specified by rules in De Simone's format is a subcalculus of MEIJE [ibidem], strong bisimulation $\sim$ is preserved by all operators defined in that format. The natural semantics of a process calculus specified in that way is thus the quotient $(T/\!\sim)$ of a recursively enumerable transition systems $T \subseteq Q \times \Lambda \times Q$ by the strong *T*-bisimulation.

Let us recall that a bisimulation over T is any symmetric binary relation $R \subseteq Q \times Q$ which satisfies the universal implication:

$$q_1 R q_2 \Rightarrow \left((q_1 \xrightarrow{\lambda} q'_1) \Rightarrow \exists q'_2 . (q_2 \xrightarrow{\lambda} q'_2) \,\&\, (q'_1 R q'_2) \right)$$

The collection of all bisimulation relations over T forms a complete lattice whose top element is the strong T-bisimulation [Park]. The labelled transition system $(T/\!\sim)$ is then the subset of $(Q/\!\sim) \times \Lambda \times (Q/\!\sim)$ defined by the quotient transition rules:

$$([q_1]_\sim \xrightarrow{\lambda} [q_2]_\sim) \quad \textit{iff} \quad \exists q'_1 . \exists q'_2 . \left((q'_1 \xrightarrow{\lambda} q'_2) \,\&\, q_1 \sim q'_1 \,\&\, q_2 \sim q'_2 \right).$$

Let us analyse the logical complexity of $(T/\!\sim)$. When T is recursive and $\sim$ is decidable, $T/\!\sim$ is recursively enumerable, because each equivalence class $[q]_\sim$ may be represented effectively by its least element (taken as a number) and then any enumeration of T induces a recursive enumeration of $(T/\!\sim)$. Nevertheless, $T/\!\sim$ is not recursively enumerable in the general case. A simple example, shown in [Darondeau 1], is the following system $T \subseteq Q \times \Lambda \times Q$ where $\Lambda = Q = (\omega \cup \{-1\})$. For each $z \in \omega$, T has one transition $(-1) \xrightarrow{z} z$, and it has one reverse transition $z \xrightarrow{-1} (-1)$ if and only if $\varphi_z(z)$ converges, i.e. if z belongs to the domain of the partial recursive function φ_z with index z. If $T/\!\sim$ was an effective transition system, the recursive enumeration of transitions would afford a recursive procedure deciding whether $\varphi_z(z)$ converges, but such a procedure does not exist [Rogers, p.25].

Upper bounds may be set easily on the logical complexity of $\sim$ and $T/\!\sim$. It is patent from the definition of a bisimulation that the collection Bis(T) of bisimulation relations over a recursively enumerable transition system T is Π^0_2. As $\sim$ is the greatest bisimulation, $q \sim q'$ in T if and only if $\exists R. (R \in \mathrm{Bis}(T) \,\&\, q R q')$. Hence $\sim$ is a Σ^1_1- subset of $Q \times Q$, and $(T/\!\sim)$ is then a Π^1_1-transition system. Whether the indicated bounds are optimal is an open question.

When a process calculus is specified by rules in De Simone's format used in conjunction with REC I, the algebraic transition system $(T/\!\sim)$ may be ineffective but the format guarantees the automatic construction of a standard denotational version of that model, where terms are represented by synchronisation trees obtained by unravelling $(T/\!\sim)$ from the corresponding nodes. The original construction was given in [Badouel], following preliminary work in [Darondeau-Gamatié 1]. A variant construction for a larger format of rules enabling to copy parameters was given in [Rutten]. The avoidance of lookahead in the premisses of rules is crucial in all the above references.

Nevertheless, different formats of rules with lookahead exist in the litterature, and the question of what formats define computable finitely branching transition systems is not closed. In [Groote-Vaandrager], strong bisimulation is proved to be a congruence for an extended format of rules enabling lookahead and parameter copy. Transition systems specified in the extended format are still recursively enumerable. Now, as noted in [Van Glabbeek], strong bisimulation coincides with Milner's observational equivalence if one adds the τ-rules:

$$\frac{u \xrightarrow{\lambda} v \ , \ v \xrightarrow{\tau} w}{u \xrightarrow{\lambda} w} \qquad\qquad \frac{u \xrightarrow{\tau} v \ , \ v \xrightarrow{\lambda} w}{u \xrightarrow{\lambda} w}$$

and this shows by the way that observational congruence is a Σ^1_1-relation.

Rules with negative premisses have been dealt with in [Bloom, Istrail, Meyer], and more recently in [Groote], where it is proved that strong bisimulation is the largest equivalence of *completed traces* which is preserved by a family of operators specified by rules enabling lookahead into parameters, parameter copy, and (stratified) negation in premisses. We have not analysed the logical complexity of those negative rules. Groote's result is important, for it tells us in what circumstances strong bisimulation may be considered as a testing equivalence without disrupting the symmetry between testors and testees.

A much simpler format which deserves attention is the *finite state* format. There, transitions are defined by rules in De Simone's format, but their consequences $\sigma_n(u_1 \ldots u_n) \xrightarrow{\lambda} t$ are restricted to terms t with at most one operator symbol. Moreover, the formation of open terms is subject to constraints depending on the rules. Namely, one bans any non closed term $\sigma_n(t_1 \ldots t_n)$ such that

$$\frac{u_{i_1} \xrightarrow{\lambda_1} v_{i_1} \ , \ \ldots \ , \ u_{i_k} \xrightarrow{\lambda_k} v_{i_k}}{\sigma_n(u_1 \ldots u_n) \xrightarrow{\lambda} t} \quad R(\lambda, \lambda_1 \ldots \lambda_k)$$

where $k>0$, and some variable u_j occurs in t. If this restriction is enforced, the closed terms which are left are always the roots of finite graphs in $(T/\sim)$, hence strong bisimulation, observational congruence, and other testing equivalences are decidable. Fully abstract models for those equivalences may be constructed in simple domains of regular trees or (vectors of) regular (or ω-regular) languages. This idyllic situation extends even to the case where fairness is taken into account [Darondeau-Kott]. Because there exists a complete system of <u>axioms</u> for the equivalence of ω-regular expressions [Wagner], induction is never needed for proving equivalences on finite state programs, hence the presence of induction rules in proof systems for such equivalences is at least inelegant. The case of finite state programs will not be considered any more in this paper.

IV. Fairness and distances

The following is an abstract from [Darondeau, Nolte, Priese, Yoccoz]

In interleaved models of concurrency, agents compete for engaging themselves in the flow of computation even though they are logically independent, and abnormal ω-behaviours arise therefrom. Those anomalies may be discarded by regulating the race between concurrent agents, which is precisely the purpose of fairness. The most popular forms of fairness are weak fairness and strong fairness [Francez]. In a weakly (resp. strongly) fair computation, an agent which is almost always (resp. infinitely often) enabled to act, acts infinitely often. For an unbounded set of agents, weak fairness is expressed by a Π^0_2- predicate on ω-computations, whereas strong fairness is expressed by a Π^0_3- predicate. In fact, f is fair if and only if:

$\forall a. \big((\exists l. \forall k \geqslant l.\ a\ \underline{\text{enabled}}\ \underline{\text{at}}\ f[k]) \Rightarrow (\forall n. \exists m \geqslant n.\ a\ \underline{\text{active}}\ \underline{\text{at}}\ f[m])\big)$ ***weak form***

$\forall a. \big((\forall l. \exists k \geqslant l.\ a\ \underline{\text{enabled}}\ \underline{\text{at}}\ f[k]) \Rightarrow (\forall n. \exists m \geqslant n.\ a\ \underline{\text{active}}\ \underline{\text{at}}\ f[m])\big)$ ***strong form***

and the following reductions are correct:

$$\forall^0(\forall^0\exists^0 \vee \forall^0\exists^0) \rightarrow \forall^0(\forall^0(\forall^0\exists^0 \vee \exists^0)) \rightarrow \forall^0(\forall^0(\forall^0\exists^0\exists^0)) \rightarrow \forall^0\exists^0,$$

$$\forall^0(\exists^0\forall^0 \vee \forall^0\exists^0) \rightarrow \forall^0(\forall^0(\exists^0\forall^0 \vee \exists^0)) \rightarrow \forall^0(\forall^0(\exists^0\exists^0\forall^0)) \rightarrow \forall^0\exists^0\forall^0.$$

Not surprisingly, the family of fair computations is more complex than the family of arbitrary ω-computations, which is Π^0_1 for recursive transition graphs and Π^0_2 for recursively enumerable transition graphs. In fact, given a transition graph $\mathcal{T} = (T, S, \sigma_0, \sigma_1)$ where T, S are sets of numbers representing transitions resp. states and σ_0, σ_1 are recursive mappings from T to S indicating the source resp. target of transitions, the set Inf($\mathcal{T}$) of ω-computations in $\mathcal{T}$ may be represented in the form:

$$\text{Inf}(\mathcal{T}) = \{f \mid \forall i. \,(f(i) \in T \ \&\ \sigma_1(f(i)) = \sigma_0(f(i+1)))\},$$

and that form is Π^0_1 if T is recursive, Π^0_2 if T is recursively enumerable i.e. Σ^0_1. (The present definition of transition graphs is recursively equivalent to the variant definition given in section III).

Moreover Inf($\mathcal{T}$) is the derived set (i.e. set of cluster points) w.r.t. the natural Baire metric of the set of finite computations in $\mathcal{T}$ which may be represented as:

$$\text{Fin}(\mathcal{T}) = \{\tau^* <x_1 \dots x_k> \mid (\forall i \leqslant k.\ x_i \in T) \ \&\ (\forall i < k.\ \sigma_1(f(i)) = \sigma_0(f(i+1)))\},$$

using the standard one-one function τ^* [Rogers, p.71] which maps ω^* onto ω.

Suppose T is recursively enumerable and let enabled(at) and active(at) be recursive predicates of two number variables representing respectively the number of an agent and an initial segment of computation. For both weak and strong fairness, the set of fair computations in T is still the derived set of $\mathrm{Fin}(T)$ in a metric topology which refines the natural topology, meaning that the associated distance d is greater than the Baire distance δ. This central property, shown first for weak fairness in the context of a special programming language [Degano-Montanari], was established later on for strong fairness in CCS [Costa]. An interesting question is to determine what sets of functions may be characterized as sets of fair computations for variant definitions of fairness.

We prove in our paper that any Π^0_3-subset of ω^ω is the derived set of ω for some Π^0_1-metric representing a concept of effective fairness. A concept of effective fairness is entirely determined by a recursive predicate enabled(at) $\subseteq \omega^2$. Intuitively, (i enabled at f[k]) means that agent number i is enabled at the kth step in computation f. A *fair* computation is then an ω-computation in which no agent is enabled infinitely often. In formulas:

$$f \text{ is fair} \Leftrightarrow \forall i. \neg \overset{\omega}{\exists} k. (i \text{ enabled at } f[k]) \Leftrightarrow \forall i. \overset{\omega}{\forall} k. \neg (i \text{ enabled at } f[k]).$$

Since no agent is infinitely often enabled, no agent may be infinitely often active, and this explains why the predicate active(at) has been dropped. The non persistent agents considered here may for instance proceed from the decomposition of persistent agents into sequences of atomic actions. A complete presentation of the results and proofs is given in this volume by Lutz Priese.

Because those proofs are constructive, we are justified to claim that fairness conditions are closed under conjunction, disjunction and recursive ω-conjunction (recall that Π^0_3-sets are closed under the corresponding operations). Our results also show that the so-called metric approach to uniform concurrency [de Bakker], developped hitherto around the Baire metric, is not incompatible with fairness.

V. *Testing equivalences*

In the present section, we leave the grounds of uniform concurrency, and analyse the logical complexity of several equivalences which account for the abstract behaviour of communicating systems observed on line (i.e. in linear time). Our analysis applies validly to any programming language which fulfills the following requirements:

- the language defines a recursive and finitely branching transition system T,
- there are one invisible action (τ) and at least four visible actions ($a, \bar{a}, b, \bar{b} \in \Lambda$),
- up to observational equivalence, any (rooted) recursively enumerable transition system T' labelled on Λ is realized as the subsystem reachable from some corresponding node t' in T, determined effectively from T',
- there is an asynchronous composition operator $|$ defined by the following rules where $\lambda \in \Lambda$ and $\mu \in \Lambda \cup \{\tau\}$:

$$\frac{u \xrightarrow{\mu} u'}{u|v \xrightarrow{\mu} u'|v} \qquad \frac{v \xrightarrow{\mu} v'}{u|v \xrightarrow{\mu} u|v'} \qquad \frac{u \xrightarrow{\lambda} u' \qquad v \xrightarrow{\bar{\lambda}} v'}{u|v \xrightarrow{\tau} u'|v' \qquad v|u \xrightarrow{\tau} v'|u'}$$

The above conditions are satisfied in CCS, and they may be enforced in any general programming language by just adding rules for non deterministic selection and asynchronous composition.

Clearly any maximal sequence of silent transitions $((p_i|q_i) \xrightarrow{\tau} (p_{i+1}|q_{i+1}))_{i<\alpha}$ where $\alpha \in (\omega \cup \{\omega\})$ is necessarily inferred from two concurrent computations $(p_{i_n} -\mu_{i_n}\!\!\to p_{i_{n+1}})_{i<\beta}$ and $(q_{j_n} - \nu_{j_n}\!\!\to q_{j_{n+1}})_{j<\gamma}$ originating respectively from $p_{i_0}=p_0$ and $q_{j_0}=q_0$. When $q(=q_0)$ is considered as a test on $p(=p_0)$, the result of the test may be defined in various ways, leading to different equivalences on programs. Among others are equivalences based on finitary tests with binary results [De Nicola-Hennessy], and equivalences based on infinitary tests with infinitary results [Darondeau-Gamatie 2]. We conjectured long ago that the largest congruences included in the respective testing equivalences were the same [Darondeau 2], but disproved the conjecture later on [Darondeau 3]. The reasons of the divergence are explained below.

<u>The following is an abstract from [Darondeau-Yoccoz]</u>

For any program t, let $L^\omega(t)$ be the set of infinite words $w = \mu_0\mu_1 \dots$ labelling infinite computations from t in the transition system T. Let $\approx^\omega$ denote the equivalence on ω-words defined as $w \approx^\omega w'$ if and only if there exist infinite factorizations $w = w_0 w_1 \dots$ and $w' = w'_0 w'_1 \dots$ such that $w_i \approx w'_i$ for all i, letting $\approx$ be the least congruence on words induced by the axioms $\lambda \approx \lambda\tau$ and $\lambda \approx \tau\lambda$ for any $\lambda \in \Lambda$. Up to the equivalence $\approx^\omega$, $L^\omega(t)$ may be normalized into the representation $[L^\omega(t)] = \{w \in (\Lambda^\omega \cup \Lambda^* \tau^\omega) \mid \exists w' \in L^\omega(t).\ w \approx^\omega w'\}$. Then we have the following.

Theorem To any Σ^1_1-subset $P\ (\subseteq \Lambda^\omega)$ corresponds a program $p\ (\in T)$ determined effectively from P such that $[L^\omega(p)] = (P \cup \Lambda^* \tau^\omega)$.

proof We recall from [Rogers, p.377] that a Σ^1_1-set $P\ (\subseteq \omega^\omega)$ can always be represented in the normal form:
$P = \{f \mid \exists g.\ \forall i.\ R(<f(0),\ldots,f(i)>, <g(0),\ldots,g(i)>)\}$,
where R is a recursive relation. Hence there suffices to select from T an automaton which approximates f (and g) by successive guesses at f(i) (and g(i)), checks at each step the recursive relation R, and diverges in case of failure. An adequate program exists always by the assumptions on T.

Since a set which is closed w.r.t. the natural metric δ is Π^0_1, the visible behaviours of programs are not always closed. Thus different ω-behaviours are in general not finitely distinguished, but the situation is still worse as we show now. Let *indiscernibility* be the equivalence on Σ^1_1-sets of functions defined as follows:

$$P \equiv_\Sigma Q \iff \forall R \in \Sigma^1_1.\ (P \cap R = \emptyset) \iff (Q \cap R = \emptyset).$$

There exist Σ^1_1-subsets P and Q of $\{0,1\}^\omega$ which are different but indiscernible. In the case of CCS, this implies the existence of corresponding programs p and q which have different ω-behaviours but which cannot be distinguished in any context by any kind of binary tests (finite or infinite, fair or unfair...), see [Darondeau 3].

In order to clarify things we recast the various definitions of testing in a common framework and compare the logical complexity of the induced equivalences.

Notations

- for any program p, let [p] resp. $[p]^*$ resp. $[p]^\omega$ be the set of computations $(p_{i_n} -\mu_{i_n}\!\!\to p_{i_{n+1}})_{i<\alpha}$ in T, where $\alpha \leq \infty$ resp. $\alpha \in \omega$ resp. $\alpha = \infty$,
- for any program p, let $\equiv$ (resp. $\equiv^\omega$) be the equivalence on [p] (resp. $[p]^\omega$) such that $\rho \equiv \rho'$ (resp. $\rho \equiv^\omega \rho'$) iff computations ρ and ρ' have identical traces on $\Lambda^* \cup \Lambda^\omega$ (resp. have identical traces on Λ^ω or both have finite visible traces, not necessarily identical),
- for any programs p and q, let Twin (resp. Twin* resp. Twin^ω) be the subset of $[p]\times[q]$ (resp. $[p]^* \times [q]^*$ resp. $[p]^\omega \times [q]^\omega$) that contains, for each maximal (resp. finite resp. infinite) sequence ρ of silent transitions from $(p|q)$, the minimal pairs of computations (ρ_p, ρ_q) from which ρ may be inferred by the rules of parallel composition (pairs are compared according to the componentwise extension of the order prefix).

De Nicola and Hennessy's equivalences

Those equivalences are based on finitary tests with finitary results [De Nicola, Hennessy]. They are three in number, linked by the relation $\approx_1 = \approx_2 \cap \approx_3$. The equivalence $\approx_2$ (the must part of $\approx_1$) compares programs according to the properties they satisfy in the inevitable mode, and concerns finite as well as infinite sequences of transitions. The equivalence $\approx_3$ (the may part of $\approx_1$) compares programs according to the properties they satisfy in the optional mode, and concerns exclusively the finite sequences of transitions.

For i=2,3 the equivalences $\approx_i$ are defined as $\leqslant_i \cap \leqslant_i^{-1}$ where preorders $\leqslant_i$ depend on two recursive sets of terms in *T*, namely the set of winning respectively diverging program states, both of which are recursive. Let Success*(ρ) be the Σ_1^0 predicate of one number variable expressing that some winning configuration is reached in course of the finite computation ρ. Let Success(ρ,ρ') be the Σ_1^0-predicate of two function variables ρ,ρ' meaning that ρ reaches a winning configuration before any of ρ,ρ' reaches a diverging configuration in any parallel run of computations ρ and ρ', finite or not, synchronized on their complementary actions. Preorders $\leqslant_2$, $\leqslant_3$ may then be specified as:

$p \leqslant_2 q$ iff $\forall t.\ (p$ must $t \Rightarrow q$ must $t)$

$p \leqslant_3 q$ iff $\forall t.\ (p$ may $t \Rightarrow q$ may $t)$

where may and must are the following binary relations on programs:

p must t iff $\forall f. \forall f'. (f \in [p]\ \&\ f' \in [t]\ \&\ \mathrm{Twin}(f,f') \Rightarrow \mathrm{Success}(f,f'))$

p may t iff $\exists n. \exists n'. (n \in [p]^*\ \&\ n' \in [t]^*\ \&\ \mathrm{Twin}^*(n,n')\ \&\ \mathrm{Success}^*(n))$.

It is patent that p may t is a Σ_1^0-predicate in p and t, whence $\leqslant_3$ and $\approx_3$ are in Π_2^0. It is slightly more difficult to reckon that p must t is a Σ_1^0-predicate in p and t, whence $\leqslant_2$ and $\approx_2$ are also in Π_2^0, as claimed in [Phillips]. This depends strongly on the assumption of a recursive and finitely branching transition system *T*.

Because program contexts C[.] may be enumerated by a recursive procedure, the largest congruences included in the respective testing equivalences $\approx_i$ (i=1,2,3) are Π_2^0 as recursive intersections of Π_2^0 relations. Similar remarks will be omitted from now on. The considered equivalences and congruences have therefore complete systems of recursive ω-proofs in the language of second order Peano arithmetic PA^2. We recall from [Girard 1] that recursive ω-proofs, given by recursive ω-branching trees whose nodes represent applications of ω-rules such as Scott's rule of induction are logically complete for Π_1^1-formulas. There emerges from recent work presented in [Yoccoz 1] that complete proof systems based on Scott induction in the natural language of programs and order relations remain logically complete when they are restricted to recursive proofs. This applies in particular to the complete proof systems given in [De Nicola-Hennessy].

Infinitary tests with infinitary results

Two programs may be equivalent w.r.t. De Nicola and Hennessy's tests but nevertheless differ by their respective sets of infinite computation traces (on Λ). This may be corrected by the introduction of infinitary tests, inducing a testing preorder $\leqslant$ as follows (we let t range over tests, i.e. over programs):

$$p \leqslant q \quad \text{iff} \quad \forall t.\ \forall f.\ \forall g.\ \Big((f \in [p]\ \&\ g \in [t]\ \&\ \mathrm{Twin}(f,g)) \Rightarrow \exists f'.\ \exists g'.\ (f' \in [q]\ \&\ g' \in [t]\ \&\ \mathrm{Twin}(f',g')\ \&\ g \equiv g') \Big)$$

Let $\sim\ =\ \leqslant \cap \leqslant^{-1}$, thus two programs are $\sim$ equivalent iff they have identical sets of finite or infinite computation traces (on Λ). Clearly, $\leqslant$ is Π^1_2 and the same holds for the infinitary testing equivalence $\sim$. Relying on the tight similarity between linear behaviours of non-deterministic programs and Σ^1_1-sets, we prove in our paper that $\sim$ is Π^1_2-complete, which means that for any Π^1_2-set of numbers A, there exists a recursive one-one function f mapping numbers to pairs of programs such that $i \in A$ iff f(i) is a pair of equivalent programs. An important consequence is the following. Because recursive ω-proofs are Π^1_1-complete, there cannot exist any complete system of recursive ω-proofs for equivalence $\sim$: a general rule of ordinal induction inducing non denumerably branching trees, such as the β-rule, is needed. The power of recursive β-proofs in second order arithmetic PA^2 is indeed required, see [Girard 2]. The equivalence $\sim$ has therefore no model in which operators are continuous extensions of recursive operators. We conjecture that it has no inductive model at all, and this may explain the problems encountered in [Darondeau-Gamatié 2], where we nevertheless construct a model for $\sim$.

Infinitary tests with binary results

Infinitary tests with binary results are an attempt to fill in the gap in logical complexity between the finitary testing equivalences $\sim_i$ (Π^0_2) and the infinitary testing equivalence $\approx$ (Π^1_2). The idea is to extend De Nicola and Hennessy's testing apparatus by adding just enough to allow the distinction between programs with discernible sets of infinite traces. Corresponding definitions follow.

Let $\text{Success}^{\omega}(\rho)$ be the Π_2^0 – predicate of one function variable expressing that an infinite number of non–τ actions are performed in course of computation ρ. Let $\approx_4$ be the equivalence on programs defined as $\approx_4 = \leqslant_4 \cap \leqslant_4^{-1}$ where $\leqslant_4$ is the testing preorder introduced as follows:

$p \leqslant_4 q$ iff $\forall t. \,(p \ \underline{\text{may}}^{\omega}\ t \Rightarrow q\ \underline{\text{may}}^{\omega}\ t)$,

$p\ \underline{\text{may}}^{\omega}\ t$ iff $\exists f. \exists g. \,(f \in [p]^{\omega}\ \&\ g \in [t]^{\omega}\ \&\ \text{Twin}^{\omega}(f,g)\ \&\ \text{Success}^{\omega}(g)$.

Then $p \approx_4 q$ if and only if $[p]^{\omega}$ and $[q]^{\omega}$ are indiscernible (i.e. $[p]^{\omega} \equiv_{\leq} [q]^{\omega}$). Since $p\ \underline{\text{may}}^{\omega}\ t$ is Σ_1^1, relations $\leqslant_4$ and $\approx_4$ are denumerable recursive intersections of relations in the boolean closure of Π_1^1. We prove in the full paper that $\approx_4$ is not Π_1^1. A similar claim applies to $\approx_{\cup} = \approx_2 \cap \approx_3 \cap \approx_4$, a possible alternative to $\approx_1$. Hence $\approx_4$ has no complete system of recursive ω–proofs, but complete proof systems exist of course in β–logic.

References

[Badouel] E. Badouel. Une construction systématique de modèles à partir de spécifications opérationnelles structurelles, INRIA–RR 764, 1987

[Badouel, Darondeau] E. Badouel, Ph. Darondeau. A Note on Guarded Recursion, IRISA–PI 535, 1990

[de Bakker, Meyer, Olderog] J.W. de Bakker, J.J.Ch. Meyer, E.R. Olderog. Infinite streams and finite observations in the semantics of uniform concurrency, *TCS* **49**, pp.87–112, 1987

[Bloom, Istrail, Meyer] B. Bloom, S. Istrail, A.R. Meyer. Bisimulation can't be traced: preliminary report, 15th ACM–POPL, pp.229–239, 1988

[Boudol] G. Boudol. Notes on algebraic calculi of processes, in: Logics and Models of Concurrent Systems (Apt ed.), Springer Verlag NATO–ASI series, 1985

[Darondeau 1] Ph. Darondeau. Bisimulation and effectiveness, *IPL* **30**, pp. 19–20, 1989

[Darondeau 2] Ph. Darondeau. Quelques problèmes relatifs à la composition parallèle, Congrès AFCET (Gif sur Yvette), Editions Hommes et Techniques, 1981

[Darondeau 3] Ph. Darondeau. Une critique de la notion de test de processus fondée sur la non séparabilité de certaines classes de langages, *Informatique théorique et applications* **20**(3), pp.291–317, 1986

[Darondeau, Gamatié 1] Ph. Darondeau, B. Gamatié. Modelling infinitary behaviours of communicating systems, INRIA–RR 749, 1987

[Darondeau, Gamatié 2] Ph. Darondeau, B. Gamatié. Infinitary behaviours and infinitary observations (to appear in *Fundamenta Informaticae*)

[Darondeau, Kott] Ph. Darondeau, L. Kott. On the observational semantics of fair parallelism, 10th ICALP, LNCS 154, pp. 147–159, 1983

[Darondeau, Nolte, Priese, Yoccoz] Ph. Darondeau, D. Nolte, L. Priese, S. Yoccoz. Fairness, distances and degrees. INRIA-RR 1199, 1990

[Darondeau, Yoccoz] Ph. Darondeau, S. Yoccoz. Proof systems for infinite behaviours (to appear in *Information and Computation*)

[Degano, Montanari] P. Degano, U. Montanari. Liveness properties as convergence in metric spaces, STOC, pp.31-38, 1984

[De Nicola, Hennessy] R. De Nicola, M. Hennessy. Testing equivalences for processes, *TCS* **34**, pp.83-113, 1984

[De Simone] R. De Simone. Calculabilité et expressivité dans l'algèbre de processus MEIJE, thèse de 3ème cycle, Paris VII, 1984

[Dugundji] J. Dugundji. *Topology*, Allyn and Bacon, 1966

[Francez] N. Francez. *Fairness*, Sringer Verlag, 1986

[Girard 1] J.Y. Girard. *Proof theory and logical complexity* (vol.1) Bibliopolis (Napoli), 1987

[Girard 2] J.Y. Girard. Π^1_2 logic, part 1: dilators, *Annals of Mathematical Logic* **21**, pp.75-219, 1981

[van Glabbeek] R. van Glabbeek. Bounded nondeterminism and the approximation induction principle in process algebras, STACS , LNCS 247, pp.336-347, 1987

[Groote] J.F. Groote. Transition system specifications with negative premisses, CWI, CS- R8950, 1989

[Groote, Vaandrager] J.F. Groote, F. Vaandrager. Structured operational semantics and bisimulation as a congruence, 16th ICALP, LNCS 372, pp.423-438, 1989

[Milner 1] R. Milner. Calculi for synchrony and asynchrony, *TCS* **25**, pp.267-310, 1983

[Milner 2] R. Miner. *A calculus of communicating systems*, LNCS 92, 1980

[Park] D. Park. Concurrency and automata on infinite sequences, 5th GI - Conf. LNCS 104, pp.167-183, 1981

[Pnueli] A. Pnueli. Linear and branching structures in the semantics and logics of reactive systems, 12th ICALP, LNCS 194, pp.15-32, 1985

[Plotkin] G. Plotkin. A structural approach to operational semantics, DAIMI FN-19 Aarhus Univ., 1981

[Rogers] H. Rogers. *Theory of recursive functions and effective computability*, Mc Graw Hill, 1967

[Rutten] J. Rutten. Deriving metric models for bisimulation from transition system specifications, Int. Workshop and Tutorial on formal models of concurrent computations, Telavi, Georgia, USSR, 1989

[Wagner] K. Wagner. Eine Axiomatisierung der Theorie der regulären Folgenmengen, *EIK* **12**, pp.337-354, 1976

[Yoccoz 1] S. Yoccoz. Effective solutions to domain equations: an approach to effective denotational semantics. To appear in CONCUR, Amsterdam, 1990

[Yoccoz 2] S. Yoccoz. Recursive omega-rule for proof systems. *IPL* **31**, pp. 291-294, 1989

CAUSAL TREES
Interleaving + Causality

Philippe Darondeau
IRISA
Campus Universitaire de Beaulieu
F-35042 RENNES (France)

Pierpaolo Degano [1]
Dipartimento di Informatica
Corso Italia, 40
I-56100 PISA (Italy)

Abstract. Causal Trees are a variant of Milner's Synchronization Trees with enriched action labels which supply indication of the observable causes of observable actions, thus providing us with an interleaving description of concurrent systems which faithfully expresses causality. This model borrows from the interleaving models most of their mathematical simplicity and enhances their descriptive power. Actually, Labelled Event Structures can be easily translated to Causal Trees, maintaining all the causal structure the former express. Moreover, various notions of equivalences are defined on Causal Trees, among which those based on causal strong and weak bisimulation, and axiomatized. Also, history preserving bisimulation on Labelled Event Structures coincides with causal strong bisimulation, and a notion of weak history preserving bisimulation is induced by causal weak bisimulation.

1987 CR Categories: D.1.3, D.3.1, D.3.3, F.1.2, F.1.3, F.3.2

Key word and phrases: concurrency, non-determinism, bisimulation, causality

I Introduction

The models used to describe concurrent systems, or processes, mainly differ on the way they give meaning to computations, particularly on how they represent the occurrence of concurrent actions. A first group of models, often called *interleaving* models (among the others [Mil80, AB84, BHR84, BK85, DG87, Niv82]) take as a basic principle that concurrent actions can occur in any temporal ordering, thus reducing concurrency to interleaving and non-determinism. The followers of the second group (among the others [Maz77, Pet80, Wink80, NPW81, Pra86, Win87, DM87, BC88, DDM88a and b, GG89, REX89]) claim that their models are *truly concurrent*, because they faithfully treat causal dependencies and carefully avoid confusion between concurrency and independence.

---

[1] Partially supported by ESPRIT Basic Research Action n° 3011 CEDISYS

The interleaving approach has its main advantage in the simplicity of the underlying mathematics which permits quite an elegant representation of processes as trees, called *synchronization trees* [Mil80] (or sometimes as graphs [BK89]). Synchronization trees are labelled by the actions a concurrent system may perform, and their branching structure naturally reflects the structure of non-deterministic choices a process may have. They can be equipped with operations, thus giving to this semantic domain an algebraic structure. Moreover, equivalence relations can be easily defined on them, even when some particular invisible actions have to be ignored. This is done *via* bisimulations which have a differential definition. The essence of these definitions, which relate nodes, is that two nodes are bisimilar if whenever there is an arc outgoing from the first node, there is an arc with the same label outgoing from the second node, such that both arcs have bisimilar targets; then, two trees are equivalent if their roots are bisimilar. It is worth noting that these equivalences can be axiomatized, when some weak and rather reasonable conditions are put over the trees. A further nice feature of interleaving models is that terms of process description languages originate synchronization trees *via* labelled transition systems. In turn, these transition systems are defined in the so-called Structural Operational Semantics [Plo81] (SOS) approach, by inducing on the syntactic structure of the terms of the language in a merely compositional way, according to a set of axioms and inference rules. Hopefully, links can be established between the operational and the denotational semantics proving the latter fully abstract. However, Synchronization Trees lack discriminating power, because they do not distinguish interleaving of sequential non-deterministic actions from their concurrent execution. The most popular example is given by the following two processes (written according to CCS syntax) $\alpha.\beta.\mathrm{nil} + \beta.\alpha.\mathrm{nil}$ and $\alpha.\mathrm{nil} \mid \beta.\mathrm{nil}$, which both originate the same synchronization tree.

On the contrary, the truly concurrent models directly express when two actions are causally related and when they are independent, instead. This goal is achieved by representing computations as partial orderings (of labelled events) in which the absence of ordering is interpreted as concurrency, with the further advantage of a clear and understandable graphical representation. Within this approach, Labelled Event Structures [Win87] are maybe the most studied model from a theoretical point of view. The structure of non-deterministic choices of a process is here represented by an additional relation over the events, called conflict relation, which relates those events which cannot occur in the same computation. The theory of Event Structures is mainly a categorical one. Actually, they form a category, and the operations on them are categorical constructions, although also operational ones have been proposed [DDM88c]. Through these operations, a semantics can be given to Process Description Language which has a denotational flavour. Mainly because there is no immediate representation of Labelled Event Structures as terms, the definitions of equivalence relations are given in terms of homomorphisms over them [C87], and only recently bisimulations have been defined between them [DDM89, GG89], in which actually all the labels are visible. All these bisimulations have an integral definition, i.e., in order to determine whether two processes will behave similarly from one point of their computation onwards, it is necessary to explicitly resort also to the whole past computations that lead to that point; a longer discussion on this issue is at the end of Section III. Although it is not difficult to define bisimulations which abstract from invisible actions, it is quite hard to obtain through them equivalences that are preserved under the usual operators of Process Description Languages. We do not know any simple congruence induced from such definitions of bisimulation on algebras of Labelled Event Structures. Moreover, no axiomatization of the existing equivalences on algebras of Labelled Event Structures is presently known, except for the one by [BC88], where, however, no communication is allowed. A similar situation arises also in those models which reflect the non-deterministic choices of processes through node-labelled trees like NMS [DDM87] or similar structures [TR88]. Finally, only recently it has been shown by [DDM88a and b, Old87] how a truly concurrent, compositional SOS semantics can be defined for Process Description Languages. As a matter of fact, a new equivalence on the interleaving domain of Synchronization Trees, called distributed bisimulation, has recently been proposed [CH89, KI90], that permits to take causality into account. It resorts to information about the spatial location of processes (e.g., the CCS processes at the end of the last paragraph wil be distinguished) and is incomparable with the partial ordering based relations. Notably, the congruence induced by distributed bisimulation has been axiomatized for CCS without the restriction operator.

We aim at reconciling the above antagonist views of semantics in a synthesis which keeps the tree-like structure of the former and the descriptive power of the latter. We achieve this goal by enriching the labels of the arcs with indication of their causes. More precisely, a label will be a pair consisting of an action, and of a set of backwards pointers to those arcs which caused it. When the action is intended to be invisible, then the causes are not present. This model, called *Causal Trees*, has been originally presented in [DD89a]. In order to give an intuitive idea of how they look like, we have drawn in Figure 1.1 those corresponding to the above considered CCS terms $\alpha.\beta.nil + \beta.\alpha.nil$ (in part a) and $\alpha.nil \mid \beta.nil$ (in part b). For the sake of presentation, we have numbered the arcs, and we have omitted the brackets when the causes form a singleton. Let us shortly comment the labelling. Arc 1 has label $\langle\alpha, \emptyset\rangle$, thus it has no cause in the tree (just as for arcs 2, 5 and 6). More interesting, the same is true for arcs 7 and 8: since they have the empty set as their indicated cause, the corresponding events do not depend on their immediate predecessors. On the contrary, arcs 3 and 4 do depend on 1 and 2, respectively, since they point back to them. Thus, the different causal relations originated by the above processes are completely reflected in the corresponding causal trees.

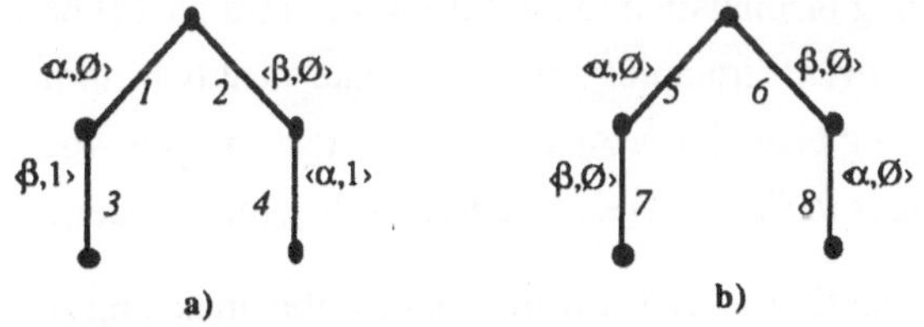

Figure 1.1 Two causal trees, originated by the CCS terms $\alpha.\beta.nil + \beta.\alpha.nil$ (a) and $\alpha.nil \mid \beta.nil$ (b).

A further example is in Figure 1.2 that shows a causal tree which can be generated from the TCSP-like term $(\alpha\gamma\delta \parallel_{\{\delta\}} \beta\delta) + \alpha\beta$. The label of arc 1 contains the empty set, so indicating that it has no causes. Now, consider arc 4: its cause points back to the previous arc, labelled by α, which is also referred to by arc 9. Actually, the cause of arc 9 is 2, for it is independent of arc 5 and occurs immediately thereafter. Arc 8 has again no cause, correctly reflecting that action β is independent of both actions α and γ; arcs 11, 12 and 13 have backwards pointers to both actions β and γ which cause δ. Finally, note that while arc 5 is independent of arc 1, the back-pointer 1 of arc 7 expresses the causal dependency of that action β on the previous action α.

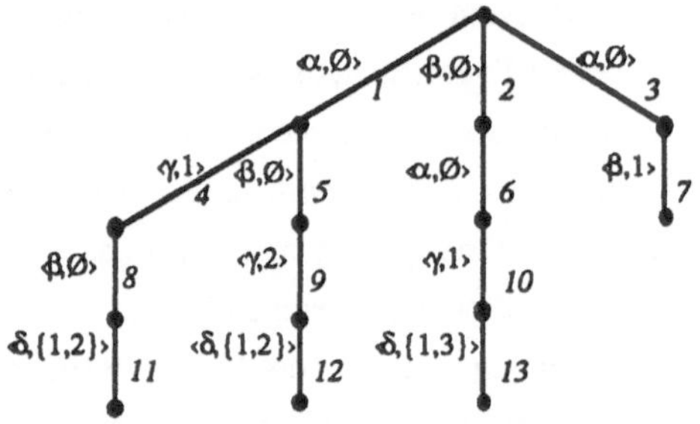

Figure 1.2 A causal tree for the TCSP term $(\alpha\gamma\delta \parallel_{\{\delta\}} \beta\delta) + \alpha\beta$

Causal Trees are simply a variant of Synchronization Trees, with a richer labelling, which permits to borrow from the latter most of the definitions and the results we may wish. In particular, we will give differential definitions of causal bisimulation, even ignoring a specific invisible action, which are adaptations of the analogous definitions in the interleaving case, and such will be the axiomatizations of the induced equivalences. Of course, these notions are more discriminating than those given in the interleaving approach, yet they coincide when there is no causal independence at all.

Our claim is that Causal Trees are a basic, convenient semantic domain for true concurrency. In order to support our claim, we will show how Labelled Event Structures can be easily given a semantics in terms of Causal Trees. More precisely, an event structure evaluates to a causal tree, which basically corresponds to the tree obtained by unfolding the family of configurations of the event structure ordered by inclusion, and by labelling it in the obvious way. A further interesting fact is that two event structures E and E' are history preserving bisimilar [DDM89, GG89] if and only if the causal trees they originate are causal strong bisimilar. Therefore, Causal Trees have at least the same expressive power as Event Structures, but form a more tractable semantic domain, due to the above considerations: essentially, the former can be represented as terms of a suitable language because of their tree-like structure. An example of two history preserving bisimilar event structures that happen to generate the *same* causal tree is reported in Figure 1.3. Also, the above result suggests us to extend the notion of history preserving bisimulation to the case when the alphabet of actions contains a distinguished invisible one: two event structures which originate weakly bisimilar causal trees will be called weakly history preserving bisimilar [2]. As a matter of fact, our previously sketched mapping from Labelled Event Structures to Causal Trees will need only a minor extension to work in this case.

We have just averred that Causal Trees, which express the branching structure and causality of concurrent systems in the interleaving approach through a rich labelling of trees, have at least the same descriptive power as Event Structures, which express these aspects through the relations of conflict and partial ordering. Actually, Causal Trees form much broader a model, mainly because they may express also temporal constraints between *causally independent* actions. In other words, systems can

[2] The name ***weak history preserving*** bisimulation is presently in use [GG89] with a completely different meaning. We overload it here to denote a history preserving bisimulation that abstracts from internal actions in analogy with the weak bisimulation of [Mil80].

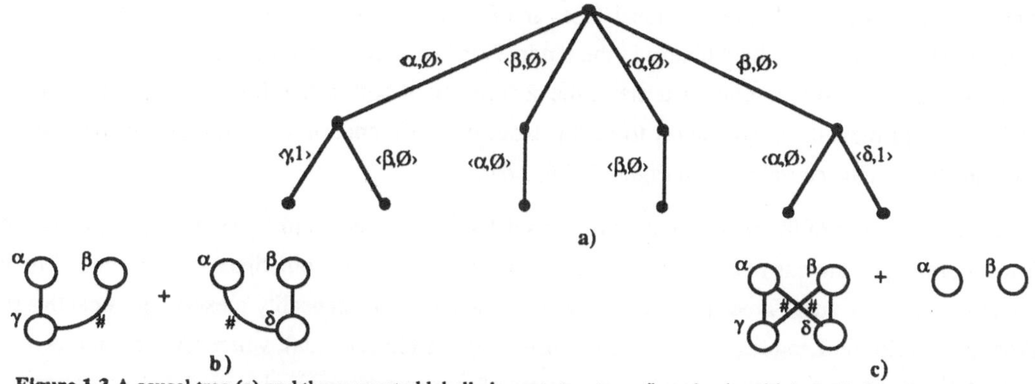

Figure 1.3 A causal tree (a) and the generated labelled event structures (b and c, in which the "+" means conflict).

be described for which the causal independence and the temporal ordering between the occurrence of actions may not coincide. Instead, in any operational setting of Event Structures, two causally independent events would be enabled to occur either one before the other or *viceversa*. However, in the real world it might happen that two events are indeed causally independent, but they may occur in a given, fixed ordering only. This is the case with Easter that always precedes Pesah, but does not cause it, albeit they may have a common cause in a vernal pagan festival. More computer-oriented examples can be found in Petri nets with confusion or contacts; a detailed discussion is in [DM87]. An example is in Figure 1.4.a that shows a causal tree in which the topmost α must *always* occur before the β, although the two are causally unrelated: this is typical in Petri Condition/Event systems when there are contacts. Also, this tree represents the left-merge $\alpha \lfloor\!\lfloor \beta$ of α and β [BK85]. Instead, the asynchronous composition of α and β will originate the tree of Figure 1.1.b: it has two branches with labels expressing that the two actions may occur in any temporal ordering.

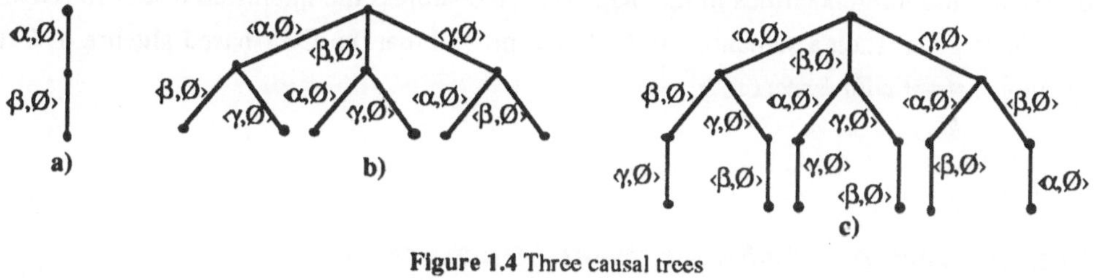

Figure 1.4 Three causal trees

A further example, due to E. Best, is again in Petri Nets, supplied this time with a notion of priority on transitions. Consider the Place/Transition net depicted in Figure 1.5.a, and let transition γ have priority over β. The causal tree describing this situation is reported in Figure 1.5.b; note that the right branch has two causally independent, but temporally related arcs, namely $\langle \beta,\emptyset \rangle$ and $\langle \alpha,\emptyset \rangle$.

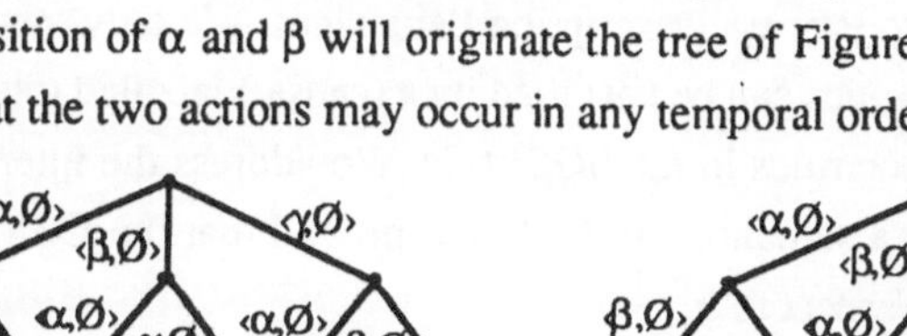

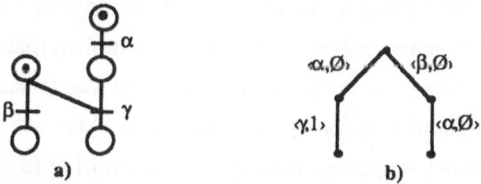

Figure 1.5 A P/T net in which γ has priority over β (a) and the corresponding causal tree (b)

Another basic difference between Causal Trees and Event Structures has to do with the conflict relation, which is usually assumed binary in the latter. This is not the case here, and Figure 1.4.d shows a tree where the conflict relation is ternary: the occurrence of both α and β (of both α and γ, or of both β and γ) prevents γ (β, or α) to occur. Note the difference in the structure of the conflict relation between the causal trees in Figure 1.4.b and c.

A nice consequence of the representation of Causal Trees as terms (up to causal strong bisimulation) is that defining operations over them in an inductive way is easy, yet sometimes cumbersome. Therefore, we can give Causal Trees an algebraic structure and obtain a causality preserving semantics for Process Description Languages. This line has been followed in [DD89a], where CCS operators have been defined that respect the causal counterparts of strong and weak observational congruences. Other operators have also been considered, like the sequential composition, and two versions of refinement. More precisely, in [DD89b] we have considered refinement as substitution of a causal tree for an arc, while in [DD90] refinement is more "syntactic", in that the arcs of the refining tree can be interleaved with those of the refined one. Remarkably enough, both refinement operations respect the causal version of (rooted) branching bisimulation [GW89]. Lack of space prevents us to give here a detailed account of how these semantic operations are defined, and we will only present two of them, namely prefixing and parallel composition. The interesting fact is that the latter offers a surprising causality preserving expansion law: parallel composition is reduced to nondeterminism plus interleaving, but causality is faithfully expressed!

Because of space limitations again, we will not show here how operational semantics in terms of Causal Trees can be given to Process Description Languages. We only mention that such a causality preserving operational semantics can be specified by a (causal) labelled transition system defined *via* a set of axioms and inference rules in the SOS style. We address the interested reader to [DD89a], where we have given such a semantics to CCS and proved that the CCS-based algebra of Causal Trees is fully abstract with respect to it.

II Causal Trees and Labelled Event Structures

One of the starting points of our work has been the fact that Synchronization Trees [Mil80] do not convey enough information to express the causal relations among the actions of a concurrent system. Causal Trees, originally presented in [DD89a], are a variant of Synchronization Trees which overcome this problem, because their labels carry also information about causes. Actually, a label will be a pair consisting of an action, and a set of backwards pointers to those arcs which caused it. Our claim is that this representation of concurrent systems is more economical than those based on partial orderings of events which are more common in the framework of true concurrency, although the latter have nicer and more understandable graphical representation. Also, we will define a bisimulation relation over Causal Trees which respects causality, thus permitting to write them as terms; moreover, we will axiomatize this causality preserving bisimulation in the finitary case.

Definition 2.1 (*causal trees*)

We assume as given a fixed set of actions Λ, ranged over by λ, and we let K range over the sets of non-zero natural numbers $\wp(N)$.

A *causal tree* over Λ is a tree ‹N, A, f›, where

- N is a (possibly infinite) set of *nodes*;
- $A \subseteq N \times N$ is the set of *arcs*;
- $f : A \to \Lambda \times \wp(N)$, is a *labelling function.*

Given a label ‹λ, K›, we will sometimes call K the *causes* of λ.

We will now justify our claim that Causal Trees are more economical a representation of true concurrency and nondeterministic branching than trees labelled by partial orderings, like NMS [DDM87a] and such. We first informally show how a partial ordering of events can be derived from a path of a causal tree. An event *a*, labelled by λ, will be generated in correspondence to every arc a of the given path, labelled by ‹λ, K›, and set greater than all the events corresponding to arcs pointed back by K. As an example, consider the causal tree of Figure 1.2 and its path made of arcs 1, 4, 8, 11. It originates four events, *1, 4, 8, 11*, labelled by α, γ, β, δ, partially ordered by (the reflexive and transitive closure of) $1 \leq 4$ (because $f(4) = \langle\gamma, 1\rangle$ and arc 1 immediately precedes 4 in the given path), and $4, 8 \leq 11$ (because $f(11) = \langle\delta, \{1,2\}\rangle$, and cause 1 and 2 point back to 8 and to 4, respectively).

A tree with arcs (or nodes) labelled by partial orderings can thus be immediately recovered from a causal tree. However, such a tree would provide us with an integral description of a concurrent system, while a causal tree gives a differential one, hence more economic. Indeed, we can see an arc as representing the occurrence of an event *e*, and say that its label contains exactly the information needed to correctly grow the partial ordering of events set up so far with *e* itself. Moreover, our differential approach permits to define truly concurrent bisimulations much in the standard way, thus improving over the "integral" bisimulation of [DDM87], refined in [TR88], and adapted to Labelled Event Structures in [DDM89] and [GG89, Vaa89]. In order to have a meaningful notion of equivalence, we put over Causal Trees a "normalization" constraint. More in detail, we will consider a causal tree to be closed if all the causes of an arc are present in its label and are within the tree, be them direct or hereditary. Therefore, given a label ‹λ, K› of an arc at depth i, K cannot contain any digit greater than i; moreover, if K contains a pointer to an arc labelled by ‹λ', K'›, then all the causes in K', properly updated, are to be contained in K, as well.

Definition 2.2 (*closed Causal Trees*)

A causal tree T is *closed* if, for every path with label $\langle\lambda_i, K_i\rangle\cdot\langle\lambda_{i-1}, K_{i-1}\rangle\ldots\langle\lambda_1, K_1\rangle\cdot\langle\lambda, K\rangle$, the set K is such that for every $j \in K$, $j \leq i$ and $\{j+k \mid k \in K_j\} \subseteq K$.

We now introduce a first notion of equivalence, rather of congruence over Causal Trees, following [Par81] and [Mil80 and 85].

Definition 2.3 (*causal strong bisimulation*)

Two causal trees T and T' are *causally strongly bisimilar* if and only if there exists a relation ~ on the nodes of T and T' such that

i) if r and r' are the roots of T and T', then r ~ r';

ii) if n ~ m and ‹n, n'› is an arc of T labelled by ‹λ, K›, then there exists an arc ‹m, m'› of T' labelled by ‹λ, K› and n' ~ m';

iii) symmetric of (ii).

As usual, we will consider the maximal causal strong bisimulation only, also denoted by ~.

Congruence ~ can by axiomatized for finite causal trees, adapting Hennessy' and Milner's [HM85].

Theorem 2.1

Causal strong bisimulation ~ on finite causal trees is exactly the congruence induced by the following four axioms

(A1) $x + (y + z) = (x + y) + z$ (A2) $x + y = y + x$

(A3) $x + x = x$ (A4) $x + NIL = x$, where $NIL = \Sigma_{i \in \emptyset} T_i$

As already pointed out, causal strong bisimulation makes less identifications than the interleaving strong bisimulation defined, e.g., by Milner in [Mil80]. Actually, the two notions coincide when the considered trees represent only sequential non-deterministic processes.

Theorem 2.2

Causal strong bisimulation is finer than interleaving strong bisimulation.

Remarks

If we consider causal trees up to causal strong bisimulation, we can denote them as terms of a language with operations ‹λ, K› of prefixing · and + of non-deterministic choice, with neutral element NIL. Thus, we obtain normal sum-forms for causal trees, which will have the following pattern $T = \Sigma_{i \in I} \langle\lambda_i, K_i\rangle T_i$. For example, Figure 1.2.a shows $\langle\alpha, \emptyset\rangle \cdot \langle\beta, 1\rangle \cdot NIL + \langle\beta, \emptyset\rangle \cdot \langle\alpha, 1\rangle \cdot NIL$.

Strong bisimulation coincides with causal strong bisimulation when the considered trees represent purely sequential processes. Indeed, in absence of concurrency, the causes of all arcs will be the empty set, thence can be removed with no harm.

Event Structures [Win80, MS80, NPW81, Win87] are a suggestive well-known domain for describing true concurrency. In their oldest and simplest version [NPW81] which we call Conflict Event Structures concurrent processes are represented via sets of event occurrences equipped with two relations which describe how events are causally related and when the occurrences of certain events exclude others. When events are labelled by actions, we get the model we use here: Conflict Labelled Event Structures. We first recall some basic notions.

Definition 2.4 (*Conflict Labelled Event Structures*)

A(n hereditary) conflict labelled event structure is a quadruple

$L = \langle E, \leq, \#, l\rangle$, where:

i) ‹E, ≤› is a partial ordering of events, such that for all $e \in E$, the set $\{e' \in E \mid e' \leq e\}$ of its predecessors is finite (i.e., ≤, the causal relation, is *finitely preceded*);

ii) #, the conflict relation, is a symmetrical, irreflexive relation on E.
is hereditary, i.e., e # e' and $e' \leq e''$ implies e # e''.

iii) $l: E \rightarrow \Lambda$ is a labelling function from events to a given set of actions Λ.

As an abbreviation, we let co = $(E \times E) - \leq - \geq - \#$.

If $e \neq e'$, we have that these two events are in either relation:

- $e \leq e'$, i.e., e *causes* e';
- $e' \leq e$, i.e., e' *causes* e;
- e # e', i.e., e and e' are *mutually exclusive*;
- e co e', i.e., e and e' are *concurrent.*

A subset E' of E is

- *left closed* if $e \in E'$ and $e' \leq e$ implies e' in E'.
- *conflict free* if for every e, $e' \in E'$ either e=e' or $e \leq e'$ or $e' \leq e$ or e co e'.
- *configuration* if it is left closed and conflict free. $C(L)$ will denote the set of configurations of L.

Figure 2.1 shows a conflict labelled event structure following the standard graphical conventions, that we have already used in Figure 1.3.

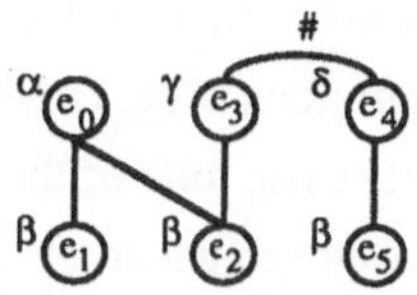

Figure 2.1 A conflict labelled event structure

In the following we will deal only with event structures which are finitely enabling, in the sense made precise by the following definition. Roughly, the set of events which are enabled to fire at a given computation step is always finite.

Definition 2.5

Given a conflict labelled event structure $L = \langle E, \leq, \#, l \rangle$, let $E' \in C(L)$, $E'' = E - (E' \cup \{e \in E \mid \exists e' \in E'.\ e \# e'\})$, and $L\text{-}E' = \langle E'', \leq|_{E''}, \#|_{E''}, l|_{E''} \rangle$ (where $\cdot|_{E''}$ stands for restriction to E'').
L is *finitely enabling* if, for every configuration $E' \subseteq E$ of L, $\min_{\leq}(L\text{-}E')$ is finite.

The next definition introduces a natural notion of sequential computation of Conflict Labelled Event Structures, together with its length.

Definition 2.6

A *trace* of a conflict labelled event structure $L = \langle E, \leq, \#, l \rangle$ is a configuration E' of L, equipped with a total ordering compatible with $\leq$ (i.e. including $\leq$). A trace may be represented as a word $\underline{\sigma} \in (E')^*$ with no letter $e_i \in E'$ occurring twice. Furthermore, let

- $\max(\underline{\sigma}) = \max_{\leq}(e \in E')$;
- $|\underline{\sigma}| = \begin{cases} 0 & \text{if } \underline{\sigma} = \varepsilon \\ 1 + |\underline{\sigma}'| & \text{if } \underline{\sigma} = e\underline{\sigma}'. \end{cases}$

Let us now recall a bisimulation relation on (Conflict) Labelled Event Structures originally introduced by [TR88] and [DDM89] and studied by [GG89] who called it history preserving bisimulation; we use here a version of the former. The reader may check that the event structures of Figure 1.3 are indeed history preserving bisimilar.

Definition 2.7 (*history preserving bisimulation*)
Let L = ‹E, ≤, #, l› and L' = ‹E', ≤', #', l'› be two labelled event structures, and write $E_1 \rightarrow_L E_2$ (resp. $E_1 \rightarrow_{L'} E_2$) whenever $E_1, E_2 \in C(L)$ (resp. $C(L')$) and $E_1 \subseteq E_2$.
L and L' are *history preserving bisimilar*, in symbols $L \leftrightarrows L'$, if they are related by the maximal relation $\mathfrak{R} \subseteq C(L) \times C(L) \times \wp(E \times E')$ such that

- $\langle \emptyset, \emptyset, \emptyset \rangle \in \mathfrak{R}$
- whenever $(E_0, E'_0, \phi) \in \mathfrak{R}$ then
  i) $\phi: E_0 \rightarrow E'_0$ is a bijection;
  ii) $E_0 \rightarrow_L E_1$ implies that $\exists\, E'_1 \in C(L')$ and $\phi' \in \wp(E \times E')$ such that $E'_0 \rightarrow_{L'} E'_1$, $\phi'|_{\langle E_0 \times E'_0 \rangle} = \phi$ and $\langle E_1, E'_1, \phi' \rangle \in \mathfrak{R}$;
  iii) symmetric of (ii).

Our claim is that the above definition has an integral shape, and all the others related to it have, as well. This is because the *whole* configuration E_0 (and E'_0) must actually appear in the second condition when defining how the computation may proceed ($E_0 \rightarrow_L E_1$). Such an observation might seem irrelevant, since bisimulations are global notions *in se*. However, their definitions in the interleaving approach, and also our Definition 2.3, make use *only* of the labels of the transitions, and there is no need of watching inside the computation states to get an observation of them. Hence, the interleaving based definitions are more incremental.

Now, we give an interpretation of Conflict Labelled Event Structures in terms of Causal Trees.

Definition 2.8 (*from a conflict labelled event structure to a causal tree*)
The interpretation of a given conflict labelled event structure L = ‹E, ≤, #, l› is the causal tree
$\mathcal{L}(L)$ = ‹N, A, f›, where

- $N = \{\underline{\sigma} \in E^* \mid \underline{\sigma} \text{ is a trace of } L\}$;
- $A \subseteq N \times N$, $A = \{\langle \underline{\sigma}, \underline{\sigma}e \rangle \mid \underline{\sigma}, \underline{\sigma}e \in N\}$;
- $f: A \rightarrow \Lambda \times \wp(N)$, $f(\langle \underline{\sigma}, \underline{\sigma}e \rangle) = \langle l(e), K \rangle$, with

$$K = \{k \in K \mid k = \begin{cases} \emptyset & \text{if } \forall e' \in \underline{\sigma}.\ e' \text{ co } e \\ |\underline{\sigma}'|+1 & \text{if } \exists e' \leq e \text{ such that } \underline{\sigma} = \underline{\sigma}'' e' \underline{\sigma}' . \end{cases}$$

Figure 2.2 reports the causal tree generated by the labelled event structure of Figure 2.1, according to the mapping $\mathcal{L}$ above.

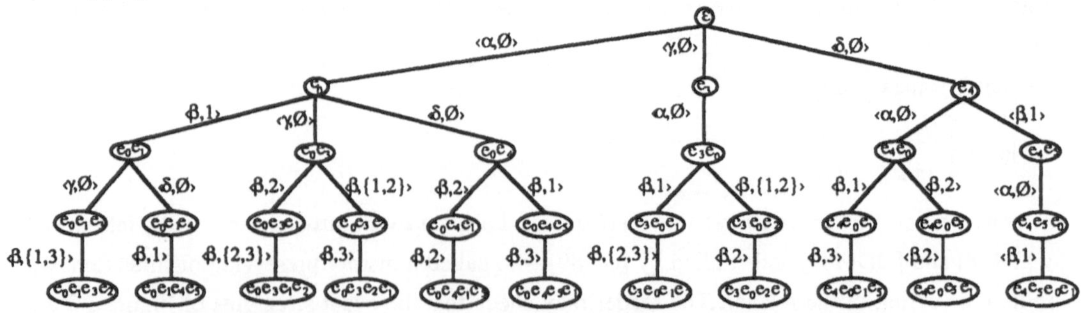

Figure 2.2 The causal tree generated by the labelled event structure of Figure 2.1.

We can now state the main theorem, proved by F. Vaandrager, that relates strong causal bisimulation and history preserving bisimulation.

Theorem 2.1

Given two finitely enabling conflict labelled event structure L and L',

$L \leftrightarrows L'$ if and only if $\mathcal{L}(L) \sim \mathcal{L}(L')$.

An important feature of a model for concurrent languages is its ability in abstracting from unwanted details. To this aim, we introduce a distinguished event label, called τ, which will be considered as recording an internal action, thus invisible to an external observer. Here, we differ a little from more traditional approaches in that an arc of a causal tree corresponding to an internal action will be labelled by τ only, bearing no causes at all. So to speak, the abstraction is defined *ab ovo*, and we followed this line since we will see that the definition of causal weak bisimulation will have exactly the same pattern as Milner's. Of course, we could attach causes to τ as well, but in such a case defining causal weak bisimulation would be considerably more intricated. In order to cope with τ, only some trivial extensions are needed.

Definition 2.9

Let $\tau \notin \Lambda$; let $\Delta = \Lambda \cup \{\tau\}$; and let the set of labels $(\Lambda \times \wp(N)) \cup \{\tau\}$ be ranged over by μ.

Changes to Definitions 2.2, 2.6, 2.8

(*trace*)

Modify in Definition 2.6 the length of a trace as follows

- $|\underline{\sigma}| = \begin{cases} 0 & \text{if } \underline{\sigma} = \varepsilon \\ 1+|\underline{\sigma}'| & \text{if } \underline{\sigma} = e\underline{\sigma}' \text{ and } l(e) \neq \tau \\ |\underline{\sigma}'| & \text{if } \underline{\sigma} = e\underline{\sigma}' \text{ and } l(e) = \tau. \end{cases}$

(*closed Causal Trees*)

A causal tree T is *closed* if, for every path σ, with label $\mu_i \cdot \mu_{i-1} \ldots \mu_1 \cdot \mu$, μ is either τ or $\langle \lambda, K \rangle$ with K such that for every $j \in K$, $j \leq |\sigma|$ and $\mu_j = \langle \lambda_j, K_j \rangle$ implies $\{|\mu_j \ldots \mu_1| + k \mid k \in K_j\} \subseteq K$.

(*from a conflict labelled event structure to a causal tree*)

The labelling function of Definition 2.8 becomes

- $f : A \rightarrow (\Lambda \times \wp(N)) \cup \{\tau\}$

$$f(\langle \underline{\sigma}, \underline{\sigma}e \rangle) = \begin{cases} \langle l(e), K \rangle \text{ if } l(e) \neq \tau, \text{ where } K = \{k \in N \mid k = \begin{cases} \emptyset & \text{if } \forall e' \in \underline{\sigma}.\ e' \text{ co } e \\ |\underline{\sigma}'|+1 & \text{if } \exists e' \leq e \text{ such that } \underline{\sigma} = \underline{\sigma}'' e' \underline{\sigma}' \end{cases}\}; \\ \tau \qquad \text{otherwise.} \end{cases}$$

Also the definition of causal weak bisimulation has the same shapc as Milner's weak bisimulation [Mil85], as it was the case for the strong one. Then, we shall need a notation for sequences of internal actions.

Notation (*sequence of internal actions*)

Given a causal tree T, we will write $n_0 \Rightarrow n_k$ if $\langle n_0, n_1 \rangle \cdot \langle n_1, n_2 \rangle \cdot \ldots \cdot \langle n_{k-1}, n_k \rangle$ is a path of T such that $f(\langle n_i, n_{i+1} \rangle) = \tau$, $0 \leq i \leq k-1$. Also, $n{=}\mu{\Rightarrow}m$ will denote $n \Rightarrow p \langle p, q \rangle q \Rightarrow m$, with $f(\langle p,q \rangle) = \mu$. Finally, $n{=}s{\Rightarrow}m$, with $s = \lambda_1.\lambda_2 \cdot \ldots \cdot \lambda_k$, $0 \leq k$, will denote $n{=}\lambda_1{\Rightarrow}n_1{=}\lambda_2{\Rightarrow}n_2 \ldots {=}\mu_k{\Rightarrow}m$.

Definition 2.10 (*causal weak bisimulation*)

Two causal trees T and T' are *causally weakly bisimilar* if and only if there exists a symmetric relation $\approx$ on the nodes of T and T' such that

i) if r and r' are the roots of T and T', then $r \approx r'$;

ii) if $n \approx m$ and $n = s \Rightarrow n'$ then $m = s \Rightarrow m'$ and $n' \approx m'$;

iii) symmetric of (ii).

As usual, we will consider the maximal causal weak bisimulation only, also denoted by $\approx$.

Weak bisimulation induces an equivalence relation which is not a congruence, because it is not preserved under summation. As in [Mil85], we will strengthen it to a congruence.

Definition 2.11 (*causal weak congruence*)

Two causal trees T and T' are *causally weakly congruent* if and only if there exists a symmetric relation $\approx^c$ on the nodes of T and T' such that

i) if r and r' are the roots of T and T', then $r \approx^c r'$;

ii) if $n \approx m$ and $\langle n, n' \rangle$ is an arc of T with $f(\langle n, n' \rangle) = \mu$, then there exists a path in T' such that $m{=}\mu{\Rightarrow}m'$ and $n' \approx m'$;

iii) symmetric of (ii).

Also congruence $\approx^c$ can easily by axiomatized for finite causal trees as done in the previous section, following Hennessy' and Milner's [HM85].

Theorem 2.4

Causal weak bisimulation $\approx^c$ on finite synchronization trees is exactly the congruence induced by the following seven axioms

(A1)	$x + (y + z) = (x + y) + z$	(A2)	$x + y = y + x$
(A3)	$x + x = x$	(A4)	$x + NIL = x$
(A5)	$\mu\tau x = \mu x$	(A6)	$\tau x = \tau x + x$
(A7)	$\mu(x + \tau y) = \mu(x + \tau y) + \mu y$.		

Again it is worth noting that weak causal congruence is finer than Milner's weak observational congruence and that it coincides with it when the considered trees represent sequential processes.

Theorem 2.5

Causal weak congruence is finer than weak observational congruence.

The reader may immediately transfer other definitions of bisimulation on Causal Trees, e.g., branching bisimulation [GW89], or dynamic bisimulation [MS90], which both induce directly a congruence. As for their logic characterization, besides laws (A1-A4), the former is completely axiomatized by law $\mu(\tau(x + y) + x) = \mu(x + y)$, while the latter by axioms (A6) and (A7), again mimicking their interleaving counterparts.

We end this section by defining a notion of weak bisimulation and congruence on Conflict Labelled Event Structures. The former notion refines history preserving bisimulation in that invisible actions are ignored, and the latter has the nice feature of being preserved under most of the operators used in the current Process Description Languages, e.g., under those of CCS. To the best of our knowledge, no definition of such equivalences has been given, yet. We will consider as weakly bisimilar (congruent, resp.) any two events structures which originate causally weakly bisimilar (congruent, resp.) causal trees. For example, the conflict labelled event structures of Figure 2.3 are causally weakly congruent.

Definition 2.12 (*weak history preserving bisimulation and congruence*)
Two labelled event structure L and L' are

- *weakly history preserving bisimilar*, $L \underline{\leftrightarrow} L'$, if and only if $\mathcal{L}(L) \approx \mathcal{L}(L')$;
- *weakly history preserving congruent*, $L \underline{\leftrightarrow} L'$, if and only if $\mathcal{L}(L) \approx^c \mathcal{L}(L')$.

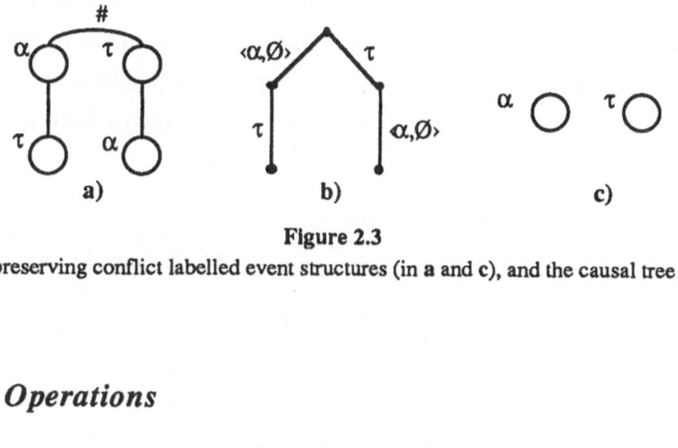

Figure 2.3
Two weakly history preserving conflict labelled event structures (in **a** and **c**), and the causal tree they generate (in **b**).

III Semantic Operations

In this section we will present some algebraic operations over Causal Trees suitable for giving semantics to Process Description Languages. Space limitations force us to focus only on prefixing trees by actions and on parallel composition of trees. In particular, we will use the TCSP parallel operator $\|_A$, the intuition of which is that all the actions not belonging to the communication set A may be performed asynchronously, and that synchronous communication is enforced on those belonging to A. Other important operations, like sequential composition, non-deterministic choice, restriction, relabelling, hiding, refinement, and so on, can be found in some other paper of ours (see References). We will see that all the operations on Causal Trees have the same shape as the usual counterparts on Synchronization Trees, the only difference being in the way causes are dealt with (sometimes in quite an admitted heavy manner, see, e.g., the treatment of causes with CCS communication [DD89a]). The nice, surprising fact we want to stress is that concurrency is reduced to non-determinism plus a sort of *causality preserving* interleaving. For simplicity sake, we will consider trees without the invisible action τ, and we leave to the reader the extensions to the following definitions needed to cope with this case.

Before giving the inductive definitions of the semantic operations of prefixing and parallel composition, let us briefly describe them intuitively. Prefixing an arc to a tree T is quite a simple operation, and so turns out to be also updating its causes. Indeed, all the arcs of T will be caused by the newly added one. Therefore, the causes K of an arc at depth n (in T) will be augmented with a pointer to the new arc resulting in $K \cup \{n\}$. The auxiliary operator *«n»* will take care of such an updating of causes. The parallel composition of two trees is a bit more involved. As for the expansion law on Synchronization Trees, it can be divided in three parts: the first (the second, respectively) when an arc from the first (the second, respectively) tree is taken, the third when a communication occurs. The structure of the resulting causal tree is again easy to define, but updating the causes requires attention. In the first case, the second tree has "lost one tick", therefore 1 has to be added to its causes. (Similarly for the second case.) However, not all the pointers must be incremented, but only those that point to arcs already "consumed in the inductive steps"; the causes "inside" the tree must instead be left untouched. As an example, take an arc at depth n: its causes greater than or equal to n will become n+1 for they refer to arcs belonging to the prefix of the result, while the other remain as they are for they point to arcs in the residual part of the tree. This is the task of the auxiliary operator *[n]*. In the third case, a communication occurs, thus its causes are the union of the causes of both the communicating arcs, say *a* and *b*. Recursively, all the arcs depending on either *a* or *b*, should contain the causes of both. The auxiliary operator *{K/n}* implements such a cross inheritance of causes.

Definition 3.1 (*prefixing and parallel composition*)
Let in the following $T = \Sigma_i \langle\lambda_i, K_i\rangle \cdot T_i$, and $U = \Sigma_j \langle\nu_j, K_j\rangle \cdot U_j$ be causal trees.

The operation $\circ$ of prefixing the causal tree $\langle\lambda, \emptyset\rangle$ to T is

$$\langle\lambda, \emptyset\rangle \circ T = \langle\lambda, \emptyset\rangle \cdot «1» T,$$

where the auxiliary operator *«n»* is defined hereafter.

The parallel composition of T and U is inductively defined as follows

$$T \parallel_A U = \Sigma\lambda_{i \notin A} \langle\lambda_i, K_i\rangle \cdot (T_i \parallel_A [1]U) + \Sigma\nu_{j \notin A} \langle\nu_j, K_j\rangle \cdot ([1]T \parallel_A U_j) +$$
$$\Sigma\lambda_i{=}\nu_{j \in A} \langle\lambda_i, K_i \cup K_j\rangle \cdot (\{1{+}K_j/1\}T_i \parallel_A \{1{+}K_i/1\}U_j)$$

where $1{+}K = \{1{+}k \mid k \in K\}$ and the auxiliary operators *[n]* and *{K/n}* are defined hereafter.

Definition 3.2 (*auxiliary cause-updating operators*)
The families of auxiliary operators (indexed over non-zero natural numbers) *«n»*, *[n]* and *{K/n}* are inductively defined by cases as follows.

$$«n» NIL = NIL$$
$$«n» \Sigma_i \langle\lambda_i, K_i\rangle \cdot T_i = \Sigma_i \langle\lambda_i, K_i \cup \{n\}\rangle \cdot «n{+}1» T_i$$

$$[n]\ NIL = NIL$$
$$[n]\ \Sigma_i \langle\lambda_i, K_i\rangle \cdot T_i = \Sigma_i \langle\lambda_i, [n]\ K_i\rangle \cdot [n{+}1]\ T_i$$

where

$[n]K = \{[n]k \mid k \in K\}$

$$[n]k = \begin{cases} k+1 & \text{if } k \geq n \\ k & \text{otherwise.} \end{cases}$$

$\{K/n\}NIL = NIL$

$\{K/n\}\Sigma_i \langle\mu_i, K_i\rangle\cdot T_i = \Sigma_i \langle\mu_i, \{K/n\}K_i\rangle\cdot\{1+K/n+1\}T_i$

$$\{K/n\}H = \begin{cases} K\cup H & \text{if } n\in H \\ H & \text{otherwise.} \end{cases}$$

Example 3.1

Let us consider the two trees depicted in Figure 3.1 a and b, namely

$T = \langle\alpha,\emptyset\rangle\cdot\langle\beta,1\rangle\cdot\langle\gamma,\{1,2\}\rangle\cdot NIL$ and $U = \langle\delta,\emptyset\rangle\cdot(\langle\beta,1\rangle\cdot NIL + \langle\rho, 1\rangle\cdot\langle\sigma,\{1,2\}\rangle\cdot NIL)$,

and let us compute a few steps of their parallel composition $T \|_\beta U$; actually, this will be the semantics of the TCSP-like term $\alpha\beta\gamma \|_\beta \delta(\beta + \rho\sigma)$. Let us consider only the addend obtained by taking the first action from U, which leads to the intermediate stage

$\langle\delta,\emptyset\rangle\cdot$ ($(\langle\alpha,\emptyset\rangle\cdot\langle\beta,1\rangle\cdot\langle\gamma,\{1,2\}\rangle\cdot NIL) \|_\beta(\langle\beta,1\rangle\cdot NIL + \langle\rho,1\rangle\cdot\langle\sigma,\{1,2\}\rangle\cdot NIL)$),

where T has been left untouched, for all its causes point inside itself. We now proceed with an action from T, obtaining the following partially evaluated tree, shown in Figure 3.1.c,

$\langle\delta,\emptyset\rangle\cdot\langle\alpha,\emptyset\rangle$ ($(\langle\beta,1\rangle\cdot\langle\gamma,\{1,2\}\rangle\cdot NIL) \|_\beta(\langle\beta,2\rangle\cdot NIL + \langle\rho,2\rangle\cdot\langle\sigma,\{1,3\}\rangle\cdot NIL)$)

for

$[1](\langle\beta,1\rangle\cdot NIL + \langle\rho,1\rangle\cdot\langle\sigma,\{1,2\}\rangle\cdot NIL) = [1]\langle\beta,1\rangle\cdot NIL + [1]\langle\rho,1\rangle\cdot\langle\sigma,\{1,2\}\rangle\cdot NIL =$
$(\langle\beta,2\rangle\cdot NIL + \langle\rho,2\rangle\cdot[2]\langle\sigma,\{1,2\}\rangle\cdot NIL) = \langle\beta,2\rangle\cdot NIL + \langle\rho,2\rangle\cdot\langle\sigma,\{1,3\}\rangle\cdot NIL.$

Note that only the pointer 2 of σ is incremented, while 1 is not, because it points inside the tree. Let us now proceed with the synchronization, yielding the tree of Figure 3.1.d,

$\langle\delta,\emptyset\rangle\cdot\langle\alpha,\emptyset\rangle\cdot\langle\beta,\{1,2\}\rangle\cdot$($\langle\gamma,\{1,2,3\}\rangle\cdot NIL \|_\beta NIL$),

where γ inherits the causes of both the synchronization actions β. Indeed,

$\{1+\{2\}/1\}\langle\gamma,\{1,2\}\rangle\cdot NIL = \langle\gamma, \{3/1\}\{1,2\}\rangle\cdot NIL = \langle\gamma,\{1,2, 3\}\rangle\cdot NIL$

Eventually, the branch resulting from the above is $\langle\delta,\emptyset\rangle\cdot\langle\alpha,\emptyset\rangle\cdot\langle\beta,\{1,2\}\rangle\cdot\langle\gamma,\{1,2,3\}\rangle\cdot NIL$. Drawing the whole tree should now be easy.

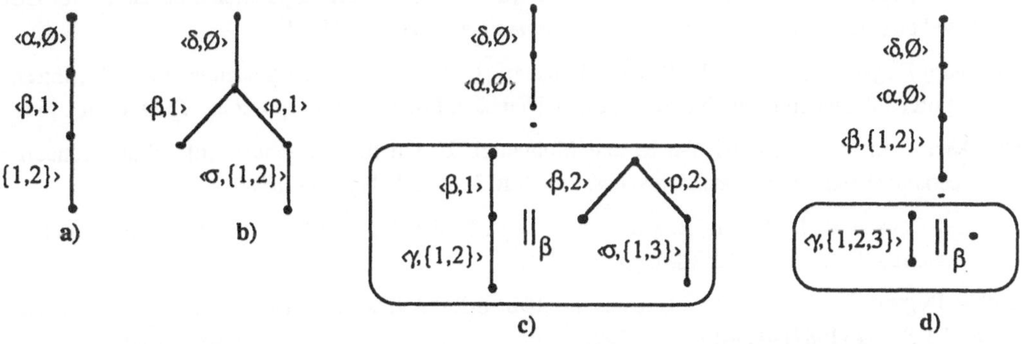

Figure 3.1 The causal trees of the TCSP-like processes $\alpha\beta\gamma$ (in **a**) and of $\delta(\beta + \rho\sigma)$ (in **b**). Two snapshots in evaluating a branch of their parallel composition with communication on β, (in **c** and **d**)

Acknowledgements. We wish to thank Roberto Gorrieri and Frits Vaandrager for unvaluable comments and suggestions. The second author acknowledges Jaco de Bakker for making it possible to enjoy the friendly and quiet atmosphere at CWI, where large portions of this paper have been written.

References

[AB84] Austry, D. and Boudol, G. Algébre de Processus et Synchronization, *Theoret. Compt. Sci. 30* , 1 (1984), 91-131.

[BC88] Boudol, G. and Castellani, I. Concurrency and Atomicity, *Theoret. Comput. Sci. 59*, 1-2 (1988), 25-84.

[BHR84] Brookes, S.D., Hoare C.A.R. and Roscoe A.D. A Theory of Communicating Sequential Processes, *Journal of A.C.M.* , 31, 3 (1984), 560-599.

[BK84] Bergstra, J.A. and Klop, J.W. Process Algebra for SynchronousCommunication, *Info. and Control 61* (1984) 109-137.

[BK89] Bergstra, J.A. and Klop, J.W. Process TheoryBased on Bisimulation Semantics, in: [REX89], pp. 50-122.

[C87] Castellani, I. Bisimulation and Abstraction Homomorphisms, *J.C.S.S.*, 34 (1987)

[CH89] Castellani, I. and Hennessy, M. Distributed Bisimulations, *J. of A.C.M.*, 36, 4 (1989) 887-911.

[DD89a] Darondeau, Ph. and Degano, P. Causal Trees, Proc. 16th ICALP (G. Ausiello, M. Dezani-Ciancaglini and S. Ronchi Della Rocca Eds), Stresa, 11-15 July 1989, Springer-Verlag L.N.C.S. (1989) pp. 234-248.

[DD89b] Darondeau, Ph. and Degano, P. About semantic action refinement, *Fundamenta Informaticae*, to appear.

[DD90] Darondeau, Ph. and Degano, P. Causal Trees, Event Structures and Refinement , to appear in Proc. 15th Symp. on Math. Foundations of Computer Science, Banskà Bystrica (CS) 1990.

[DG87] Darondeau, Ph. and Gamatié, B. Modelling Infinitary Behaviours of Communicating Systems, INRIA-Rennes, Research Report 749 (1987).

[DDM87] Degano, P., De Nicola, R. and Montanari, U. Observational Equivalences for Concurrency Models, in *Formal Description of Programming Concepts III* (M. Wirsing ed.), North-Holland (1987), pp. 105-132.

[DDM88a] Degano, P., De Nicola, R. and Montanari, U. A Distributed Operational Semantics for CCS based on Condition/Events Systems, *Acta Informatica 26* (1988), 59-91.

[DDM88b] Degano, P. De Nicola, R. and Montanari, U. Partial Ordering Semantics for CCS, Internal Report 88-3, Dipartimento di Informatica, Università di Pisa (1988), to appear in *Theo. Comp. Sci.*

[DDM88c] Degano, P., De Nicola, R. and Montanari, U. On the Consistency of Truly Concurrent Operational and Denotational Semantics, Proc. LICS '88, Edinburgh (1988).

[DDM89] Degano, P., De Nicola, R. and Montanari, U. Partial Ordering Description of Nondeterministic Concurrent Systems, in [REX88], pp. 438-466.

[DM87] Degano, P. and Montanari, U. Concurrent Histories: A Basis for Observing Distributed Systems, *J.C.S.S., 34* (1987) 442-461.

[GG89] van Glabbeek, R. and Goltz, U. Equivalence Notions for Concurrent Systems and Refinement of Actions, Proc. MFCS 89 (A. Kreczmar and G. Mirkowska Eds), Springer LNCS (1989) pp. 237-248.

[GW89] van Glabbeek, R. and Weijland, W.P. Branching Time and Abstraction in Bisimulation Semantics, Proc. *IFIP Congress '89*, (1989).

[HM85] Hennessy, M. and Milner, R. Algebraic Laws for Nondeterminism and Concurrency, *Journal of A.C.M.*, 32 (1985), 137-161.

[KI90] Kiehn, A. Distributed Bisimulation for Finite CCS, Proc. 2 nd Workshop on Concurrency and Compositionality, S. Miniato, 1990, pp. 45-47.

[Maz77] Mazurkiewicz, A. Concurrent Program Schemas and their Interpretation, Proc. Aarhus Workshop on Verification of Parallel Programs (1977).

[Mil80] Milner, R. *A Calculus of Communicating Systems*, Springer-Verlag L.N.C.S. 92 (1980).

[Mil85] Milner, R. Notes on a Calculus for Communicating Systems, in: *Control Flow and Data Flow: Concepts of Distributed Programming* (M. Broy Ed.), NATO ASI Series F: Vol. 14, (Springer-Verlag, Heidelberg, 1984), 205-228.

[MS80] Montanari, U. and Simonelli, C. On Distinguishing between Concurrency and Nondeterminism, Proc. Ecole de Printemps on Concurrency and Petri Nets, Colleville sur mer (1980).

[MS90] Montanari, U. and Sassone, V. Dynamic Bisimulation, Università di Pisa, Dipartimento di Informatica, Technical Report TR 13/90, 1990.

[NPW81] Nielesn, M., Plotkin, G. and Winskel, G. Petri Nets, Event Structures and Domains, Part 1, *Theoret. Comput. Sci. 13* (1981) 85-108.

[Niv82] Nivat, M. Behaviours of Processes and Synchronized Systems of Processes, in: *Theoretical Foundations of Programming Methodology* Dordrecht Reidel (1982), pp. 473-550.

[Old87] Olderog, E.R. Operational Petri Net Semantics for CCSP, in: *Advances in Petri Nets* 1987, Springer-Verlag L.N.C.S. 266 (1987), pp. 196-223.

[Pet80] Petri, C.A. Concurency, in: *Net Theory and Applications* , Springer-Verlag L.N.C.S. 84 (1980), pp. 1-19.

[Pra86] Pratt V.R. Modelling Concurrency with Partial Orders, *International Journal of Parallel Programming 15* (1986) 33-71.

[Plo81] Plotkin, G. A Structural Approach to Operational Semantics, DAIMI Report FN-19, Department of Computer Science, Aarhus (1981).

[REX89] Proc. REX School/Workshop on *Linear Time, Branching Time and Partial Order in Logics and Models for Concurrency* (J. de Bakker, W. de Roever, and G. Rozenberg Eds), 1988, Springer-Verlag L.N.C.S. 354 (1989).

[TR88] Trakhtenbrot, B. and Rabinovich, A. Nets of Processes, *Fundamenta Informaticae XI* (1988), 357-404.

[Vaa89] Vaandrager, F. An Explicit Representation of Equivalence Classes of the History Preserving Bisimulation, Unpublished Manuscript, June 1989.

[Wink80] Winkowski, J. Behaviours of Concurrent Systems, *Theor. Comp. Sci. 12* (1980) 39-60.

[Win80] Winskel, G. Events in Computations, Ph.D. Thesis, University of Edinburgh, CST-10-80 (1980).

[Win87a] Winskel, G. Petri Nets, Algebras, Morphisms and Compositionality, *Info. and Co.*, **72**, (1987), 197-238.

PARTIALLY COMMUTATIVE FORMAL POWER SERIES

G. DUCHAMP D. KROB

Laboratoire d'Informatique de Rouen (LITP) and CNRS
Université de Rouen - 76134 Mont Saint Aignan - Cedex

INTRODUCTION

Let $\mathcal{C}$ be a category of sets (this means that every object of $\mathcal{C}$ is a set and that every arrow is a mapping). We will say that $\mathcal{C}$ is equipped with a *notion of commutation* iff for every object X in $\mathcal{C}$, there is given on X a reflexive and symmetrical binary relation C_X .For the following classical categories, we have the commutation relations :

Categories	$(a,b) \in C_X$
Monoid Group K-algebra	$ab = ba$
Lie algebra	$[a,b] = 0$

Fig. 1

Observe that in these cases, all the corresponding morphisms φ "respect the commutations" in the sense that :

$$(a,b) \in C_X \quad \Longrightarrow \quad (\varphi(a),\varphi(b)) \in C_X$$

Of course, the smallest commutation structure we can imagine on the set X is the couple (X,ϑ) where ϑ is a symmetrical and irreflexive (i.e. $(x,x) \notin \vartheta$ for every $x \in X$) relation. These couples form a category, the corresponding commutation relation $C_{(X,\vartheta)}$ being $\vartheta \cup \Delta_X$ where $\Delta_X = \{ (x,x), x \in X \}$ is the diagonal of X. The arrows φ from (X,ϑ_X) into (Y,ϑ_Y) are the mappings from X to Y that satisfy to the following property :

$$(x,y) \in \vartheta_X \quad \Longrightarrow \quad (\varphi(x),\varphi(y)) \in \vartheta_Y \cup \Delta_Y$$

The objects (X,ϑ) are called *dependence alphabets* and their category will be denoted by **DA**. If $\mathcal{C}$ is a category equipped with a notion of commutation, we then get a forgetful functor F from $\mathcal{C}$ into **DA** defined by :

$$F(X) = (X, C_X - \Delta_X) \qquad \text{for every X in } \mathcal{C}$$

This gives rise and sense to the problem of the right adjoint functor of F. Roughly speaking, for a given category $\mathcal{C}$ with a notion of commutation and for (X,ϑ) belonging to **DA**, does it exist $\mathcal{C}(X,\vartheta)$ in $\mathcal{C}$ and an arrow i from (X,ϑ) into $\mathcal{C}(X,\vartheta)$ which respects the commutations such that the following universal property holds : for every $\mathcal{A}$ in $\mathcal{C}$ and for every mapping f from X into $\mathcal{A}$ that respects the commutations, there exists an unique arrow $\bar{f}$ that maps $\mathcal{C}(X,\vartheta)$ on $\mathcal{A}$, such that the following diagram is commutative :

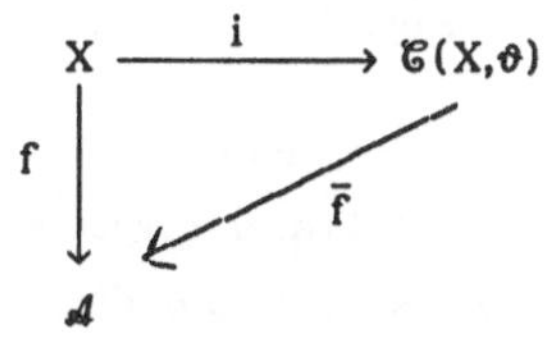

Fig. 2

This problem has well represented solutions for the four categories that were considered in Fig. 1, that is :

- *Monoids* : here, $\mathcal{C}(A,\vartheta)$ is the *free partially commutative monoid* $M(A,\vartheta)$ associated with a dependence alphabet (A,ϑ). It has been viewed as a model for parallel computing (see [Mz]) and widely studied as well as its subsets (called since trace languages) (cf [Ch], [Db], [Me], [Pe], [Zi] ....)

- *Groups* : the free object is here called *free partially commutative group*. It is defined by the group presentation $\langle A;\ ab = ba \text{ for } (a,b) \in \vartheta \rangle$ and denoted $F(A,\vartheta)$. It was considered in [Di], [Db] and also in [Dc], [Dr]. The latter proved that if $F(A,\vartheta_A)$ was isomorphic to $F(B,\vartheta_B)$, then the two graphs (A,ϑ_A) and (B,ϑ_B) are isomorphic (see also below).

- *K-algebras* : the associated free object is the K-algebra of $M(A,\vartheta)$. It was considered by [KMNR] who proved that if $K\langle A,\vartheta_A\rangle$ is isomorphic to $K\langle B,\vartheta_B\rangle$, then the corresponding graphs are isomorphic (1).

(1) The results of [Dr] and [KMNR] are closely related (see the remark ending Droms' paper). They take place in the same movement of studies, the objects being then called "graph groups" and "graph algebras".

- *Lie K-algebras* : the corresponding free object is denoted $L_K(A,\theta)$. As in the free case, it turns that $L_K(A,\theta)$ is the least Lie subalgebra of $K\langle A,\theta\rangle$ generated by the letters (cf [Du], [DK.1-2]). It has combinatorial bases that can be computed from a generalized Lazard's elimination process (cf [DK.1]).

We now have to say a little about the relations which exist between these different categories :

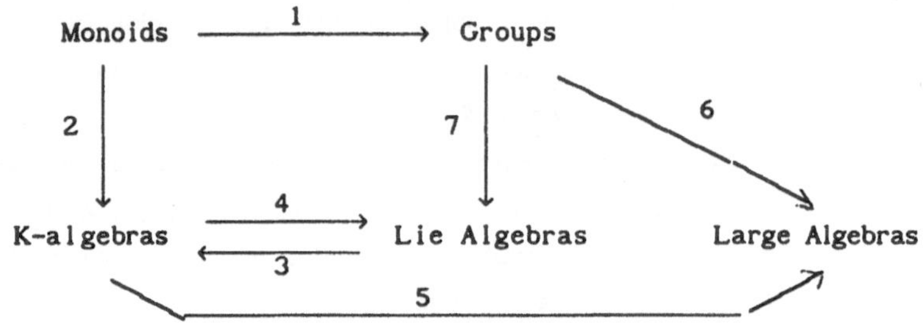

Fig. 3

1) *From monoids to groups* : the natural mapping from A into $F(A,\theta)$ that maps every letter $a \in A$ onto $a \in F(A,\theta)$ respects the commutations and hence extends to a morphism j_{GM} from $M(A,\theta)$ into $F(A,\theta)$. Moreover this morphism is in fact an embedding (see [Ch], [Db]) : hence, $M(A,\theta)$ is cancellative.

2-3-4) *From monoids and Lie algebras to K-algebras* : $K\langle A,\theta\rangle$ is the algebra of $M(A,\theta)$ (see [DK.1]), but also the envelopping algebra of $L_K(A,\theta)$. If M is a quotient monoid of A^*, the kernel of the natural "projection morphism" from $K\langle A\rangle$ into $K\langle M\rangle$ is a two-sided ideal of $K\langle A\rangle$ called *monoidal*. If $\mathfrak{G}$ is a Lie algebra quotient of the free Lie algebra L(A), then the kernel of the natural "projection morphism" from $K\langle A\rangle = \mathcal{U}(L(A))$ into $\mathcal{U}(\mathfrak{G})$ is again a two-sided ideal of $K\langle A\rangle$, called "of *Lie type*". When K is a ring of characteristic 0, it can be shown that, if a two-sided ideal I of $K\langle A\rangle$ is both monoidal and of Lie type, there exists a unique equivalence relation λ on A and a partial commutation relation θ on A/λ such that :

$$K\langle A\rangle/I \simeq K\langle A/\lambda;\theta\rangle$$

(see [DK.2] for more details). Hence the partial commutations relations are, roughly speaking, the only and maximal frame in which the two correspondances number 2 and 3 can be obtained. Observe also that, since $K\langle A,\theta\rangle$ is in fact an envelopping bialgebra (see [Bo.3] II. § 1), $L_K(A,\theta)$ is (when char. K = 0) the Lie algebra of the primitive elements of $K\langle A,\theta\rangle$: this gives, when we have the extra data of comultiplication, the correspondance 4 in Fig. 3.

5-6) *Large K-algebras* : we can construct the algebra $K\langle\langle A,\theta\rangle\rangle$ of partially commutative formal series (see below) and the correspondance 5 becomes then a topological completion. The augmentation ideal of $K\langle\langle A,\vartheta\rangle\rangle$:

$$\mathfrak{M} = \{ S = \sum_{w\in M(A,\vartheta)} (S|w)\, w \ , \ \ (S|1) = 0 \}$$

has the property that $1+\mathfrak{M}$ is a group, called the Magnus group (see [Bo.3] or [MKS]). Then the mapping from A into $1+\mathfrak{M}$ which maps every letter a in A onto 1+a respects the commutations and hence extends to a group morphism, denoted μ, from $F(A,\vartheta)$ into $1+\mathfrak{M}$. This morphism turns to be an embedding (see [DK.3]), called the partially commutative Magnus transformation. Hence, we get also the correspondance number 6 of Fig.3 .

7) *From groups to Lie algebras* : For every group G, we can construct the lower central series $(G_n)_{n\geq 1}$ of G as follows :

$$G_1 \quad \text{and} \quad G_{n+1} = (G_n,G) \quad \text{for every } n \geq 1$$

where (G_n,G) is the subgroup generated by the commutators $xyx^{-1}y^{-1}$ with x in G_n and y in G. It occurs that, if we denote by $(F_n(A,\vartheta))_{n\geq 1}$ the lower central series of $F(A,\vartheta)$, then $\mu(F_n(A,\vartheta)) \subset 1+\mathfrak{M}^n$ for every $n \geq 1$ and hence :

$$\bigcap_{n\geq 1} F_n(A,\vartheta) = \{1\}$$

Such a group is called residually nilpotent and is canonically associated with a structure of Lie ring on the graded $\mathbb{Z}$-module (see [Lz], [MKS]) :

$$gr(F(A,\vartheta)) = \bigoplus_{n\geq 1} F_n(A,\vartheta)/F_{n+1}(A,\vartheta)$$

Here we have again as in the free case : $gr(F(A,\vartheta)) \simeq L_{\mathbb{Z}}(A,\vartheta)$. Hence our last connexion 7 is established.

Let us end this introduction with giving the structure of our paper. In what follows, we will study the notion of series over an arbitrary monoid and also different classes of "small" series, especially the recognizable and the rational ones. We will show decision results and give several tools for working with these series (pull back, reconstruction, Möbius funtion, ...)

0. PRELIMINARIES

1) The free partially commutative monoid

The *free partially commutative monoid* $M(A,\vartheta)$ is the free object that solves the universal problem of Fig. 2 for the category of monoids (i.e. $\mathcal{C}$ = Mon). A dependence alphabet (A,ϑ) being given, it can easily be shown that $M(A,\vartheta)$ can be defined by the following monoid presentation :

$$M(A,\vartheta) = \langle\, A \ ; \ ab = ba \ \text{ for } (a,b) \in \vartheta \,\rangle_{Mon}$$

This monoid can also be geometrically realized as a monoid of heaps ([Vi]).

2) The free partially commutative K-algebra

Let K be a semiring. Then the *free partially commutative* K-*algebra* is the K-algebra of the free partially monoid $M(A,\theta)$. It is straighforward to see that it solves the universal problem of Fig.2 for the category of K-algebras. Note that it can also be defined by the following K-algebra presentation :

$$K\langle A,\theta\rangle = \langle\ A\ ;\ ab = ba \quad \text{for } (a,b) \in \theta\ \rangle_{Alg}$$

(see [DK.1], [KMNR] or [DT] for more details).

Example $K\langle A,\theta\rangle$ occurs naturally as an algebra of operators. Let us consider for instance the operators of the $\mathbb{R}$-algebra $\mathcal{C}^{\infty}(\mathbb{R},\mathbb{R})$ that are defined by :

$$c : f \longrightarrow (\ x \longrightarrow f(x^2)\ )$$

$$\sigma_t : f \longrightarrow (\ x \longrightarrow f(x+t)\ ) \qquad \text{for } t \in \mathbb{R}$$

It can be shown that if $(t_i)_{i\in I}$ is $\mathbb{Q}$-free in $\mathbb{R}$, the family $\mathcal{O}p = ((\sigma_{ti})_{i\in I}\ ,c)$ is algebraically free "up to some commutations", that is to say that :

$$\mathbb{R}\langle (X_i)_{i\in I}, Y;\ \theta\rangle \simeq \langle\ (\sigma_{ti})_{i\in I}, c\ \rangle$$

where the right above member denotes the $\mathbb{R}$-subalgebra of $\mathcal{C}^{\infty}(\mathbb{R},\mathbb{R})$ generated by $\mathcal{O}p$ and where θ is defined by :

$$X_i \ \text{———}\ X_j \quad \text{for every } i,j \in I$$

c

Moreover, $\mathcal{C}^{\infty}(\mathbb{R},\mathbb{R})$ can be in fact replaced by $\mathbb{R}[X]$ in what preceeds.

3) Graduations

Let us recall that we can define in A^* the following notion of degree :

- *total degree* : $|w|$ is just the length of $w \in A^*$.
- *multidegree* : $|w|_A = (|w|_a)_{a\in A} \in \mathbb{N}^{(A)}$ where $|w|_a$ is the number of a in w.

A congruence $\equiv$ on A^* is said to be *homogeneous* (resp. *multihomogeneous*) iff it is compatible with the previous degree functions, i.e. :

$$u \equiv v \Longrightarrow |u| = |v| \quad (\text{resp. } |u|_A = |v|_A)$$

In the corresponding cases, the degree functions previously defined, make sense in $M(A;\equiv) = A^*/\equiv$ itself. Therefore we can also define :

$$M_\alpha = \{\ m \in M(A;\equiv),\ |m|_A = \alpha\ \} \quad \text{when } \equiv \text{ is multihomogeneous}$$

$$M_n = \{\ m \in M(A;\equiv),\ |m| = n\ \} \quad \text{when } \equiv \text{ is homogeneous}$$

for every $n \in \mathbb{N}$ and $\alpha \in \mathbb{N}^{(A)}$. Obviously we have the formulas :

$$M_\alpha M_\beta \subset M_{\alpha+\beta} \quad \text{and} \quad M_n M_m \subset M_{n+m}$$

for every $n,m \in \mathbb{N}$ and $\alpha,\beta \in \mathbb{N}^{(A)}$. This permits to equip $K\langle A;\equiv\rangle = K[M(A;\equiv)]$ with the corresponding graduations :

$$K_\alpha = \mathrm{span}(M_\alpha) \quad \text{and} \quad K_n = \mathrm{span}(M_n)$$

Note finally that any partially commutative congruence is multihomogeneous. Therefore the previous results can be applied in this case.

4) Formal power series over an arbitrary monoid

Let K be a non necessarily commutative semiring and let M be a monoid. Then we will denote by K[[M]] the K-module of the mappings from M into K. Every mapping $S \in K[[M]]$ can be written under the form of a formal power series :

$$S = \sum_{m \in M} (S|m)\ m$$

in an obvious way. It explains why K[[M]] is called the K-module of *formal power series* over M with coefficients in K. We also denote by K[M] the sub K-module of K[[M]] which consists of the *polynomials* over M with coefficients in K, i.e. of the formal power series in K[[M]] with only finitely many non zero coefficients. In order to equip K[[M]] with some extra structures, let us now introduce the following kinds of monoids :

a) Finite decomposition monoids

DEFINITION 0.1 A monoid M is said to be a *finite decomposition monoid* iff it satisfies to the following condition [(2)] :

$$\text{(FD)} \qquad \forall\ m \in M,\ |\{\ (u,v) \in M\times M,\ m = uv\ \}| < +\infty$$

When M is a finite decomposition, K[[M]] can be equipped with the Cauchy or convolution product which is defined by :

$$S.T = \sum_{m \in M} \Big(\sum_{uv=m} (S|u)(T|v) \Big)\ m$$

Therefore, K[[M]] becomes a K-algebra in this case.

b) Locally finite monoids

DEFINITION 0.2 A monoid M is said to be *locally finite* (cf [Eil]) iff it

(2) This property is the (D)-condition of [Bo.1] III. §2 N° 10 or the finite factorization property of [HW].

satisfies the following condition :

$$\text{(LF)} \quad \forall\, m \in M,\ \left|\{\, (n,u_1,\dots,u_n),\ m = u_1 \dots u_n \quad \text{where } u_i \neq 1 \,\}\right| < +\infty$$

A locally finite monoid is obviously a finite decomposition monoid, but the converse is false since every non trivial finite group satisfies (FD) for instance, but is not locally finite since it has torsion.

When M is locally finite, we can equip the K-algebra K[[M]] with a star operation defined for every proper series S (i.e. such that $(S|1) = 0$) by :

$$S^* = \sum_{m \in M} \Big(\sum_{u_1 \dots u_n = m} (S|u_1) \dots (S|u_n) \Big)\, m$$

(i.e. by $S^* = \sum S^n$) (see also [Eil], [BeRe]). In this frame, we can define the *rational series* : it consists of the smallest class, denoted KRat(M), of formal power series of K[[M]] containing the series m for every m in M and stable by the K-algebras operations and for the star (when it makes sense). Observe that KRat(M) is also the smallest "full" (i.e. closed by inverse when this operation makes sense) K-subalgebra of K[[M]] which contains K[M] (see [Bo.4] I. §1 N°4 def. 3).

c) Möbius monoids

DEFINITION 0.3 A monoid M is said to be **Z**-*Möbius* (resp. **Q**-*Möbius*) iff it is a finite decomposition monoid such that the characteristic series $\underline{M}$ of M :

$$\underline{M} = \sum_{m \in M} m \ \in \mathbb{N}[[M]]$$

is invertible in $\mathbb{Z}[[M]]$ (resp. in $\mathbb{Q}[[M]]$).

Remark According to the previous definition, a monoid M is **Z**-Möbius (resp. **Q**-Möbius) iff there exists a series (the *Möbius series*) :

$$\mu_M = \sum_{m \in M} \mu(m)\, m \ \in \mathbb{Z}[[M]] \quad (\text{resp. } \in \mathbb{Q}[[M]])$$

such that the following identity holds in $\mathbb{Z}[[M]]$ (resp. in $\mathbb{Q}[[M]]$) :

$$\mu_M\, \underline{M} = \underline{M}\, \mu_M = 1_M$$

In order to state further results concerning Möbius monoids, we will need the following important property of a **Q**-Möbius monoid :

PROPOSITION 0.1 Let M be a **Q**-Möbius monoid. Then, the set $M^+ = M-\{1\}$ is a subsemigroup of M.

Proof First, let us introduce the group Inv(M) consisting of all invertible elements of M, i.e. which is defined by :

$$Inv(M) = \{ m \in M, \exists n \in M, nm = mn = 1 \}$$

Let us now consider the submonoids of M, denoted $Inv_l(M)$ and $Inv_r(M)$, that consists respectively of the left and right invertible elements of M :

$$Inv_l(M) = \{ m \in M, \exists n \in M, nm = 1 \}$$

$$Inv_r(M) = \{ m \in M, \exists n \in M, mn = 1 \}$$

Let us first prove the following lemma :

LEMMA 0.2 Let M be a finite decomposition monoid. Then, the group Inv(M) is finite. Moreover, we have the following relations :

$$Inv_l(M) = Inv_r(M) = Inv(M)$$

Proof of the lemma Since M is a finite decomposition monoid, there are only a finite number of couples $(n,m) \in M \times M$ such that : $nm = 1$. It follows clearly that $Inv_l(M)$ is a finite submonoid of M. Hence, to prove our lemma, it will suffice by symmetry to show that the following relation holds :

$$Inv_l(M) = Inv(M) \quad (0)$$

Let now $m \in Inv_l(M)$: since $Inv_l(M)$ is a monoid, m^n belongs to $Inv_l(M)$ for every $n \geq 0$. Therefore, since $Inv_l(M)$ is finite, there exists necessarily two integers $p \geq 0$ and $q \geq 1$ such that : $m^p = m^{p+q}$ (1). But, m has by definition a left inverse n. Therefore, multiplying relation (1) at the left by n^p, it follows immediately that : $m^q = 1$ (2). Hence, since $q \geq 1$, m is invertible in M. Thus, we showed that : $Inv_l(M) \subset Inv(M)$. Since the converse inclusion is obvious, relation (0) follows. Our lemma is now proved. ■

Since every Q-Möbius is a finite decomposition monoid, we can apply the previous lemma. Hence, Inv(M) is a finite group and we have the property :

$$x.y \in Inv(M) \Longrightarrow x \in Inv(M) \text{ and } y \in Inv(M) \qquad (*)$$

which is equivalent to the fact that : $Inv_l(M) = Inv_r(M) = Inv(M)$ as it can be easily checked. Let us now associate with every series S in $\mathbb{Q}[[M]]$ the series $\sigma(S)$ which is defined as follows :

$$\sigma(S) = \sum_{m \in Inv(M)} (S|m)\, m \quad \in \mathbb{Q}[Inv(M))]$$

Then, it follows immediately from property (*) that the mapping σ is in fact a Q-algebra morphism from $\mathbb{Q}[[M]]$ into $\mathbb{Q}[Inv(M)]$. On the other hand, since M is Q-Möbius, there exists a series μ in $\mathbb{Q}[[M]]$ such that we have :

$$\mu_M \underline{M} = \underline{M}\, \mu_M = 1_M$$

in $\mathbb{Q}[[M]]$. Applying σ to this relation, we obtain immediately the identity :

$$\sigma(\mu_M)\ \underline{\mathrm{Inv}(M)} = \underline{\mathrm{Inv}(M)}\ \sigma(\mu_M) = 1_M$$

that holds in $\mathbb{Q}[\mathrm{Inv}(M)]$. Hence, we proved that the group Inv(M) is $\mathbb{Q}$-Möbius. But we have the following lemma :

<u>LEMMA 0.3</u> Let G be a group. Then, G is $\mathbb{Q}$-Möbius iff $G = \{1\}$.

<u>Proof</u> Let G be a group which is $\mathbb{Q}$-Möbius. Therefore, there exists a series μ_G in $\mathbb{Q}[[G]]$ such that we have :

$$\mu_G\ \underline{G} = 1_G \qquad (1)$$

When we develop relation (1) relatively to 1_G ,we obtain :

$$1 = \sum_{gh=1} \mu_G(g) \qquad \Longleftrightarrow \qquad 1 = \sum_{g\in G} \mu_G(g) \qquad (2)$$

since G is a group. Let us suppose now that G is non trivial. Hence, let $q \neq 1$ be in G. Then, if we develop relation (1) relatively to q, we obtain :

$$0 = \sum_{gh=q} \mu_G(g) \qquad \Longleftrightarrow \qquad 0 = \sum_{g\in G} \mu_G(g) \qquad (3)$$

since G is a group. But, relation (3) contradicts relation (2). Hence, G must be trivial. Thus, our lemma is now proved. ■

It follows now clearly from this last lemma that : $\mathrm{Inv}(M) = \{1\}$. Therefore, according to lemma 0.2, we have the identities :

$$\mathrm{Inv}_l(M) = \mathrm{Inv}_r(M) = \mathrm{Inv}(M) = \{1\}$$

which are exactly equivalent to the fact that $M^+ = M - \{1\}$ is a subsemigroup of M. Thus, our proof is now complete. ■

<u>Remark</u> The previous proposition claims equivalently that a $\mathbb{Q}$-Möbius monoid M satisfies to the following property :

$$\forall\ m,n \in M,\quad m.n = 1 \quad\Longrightarrow\quad m = n = 1$$

which is also equivalent to the fact that 1_M is the only left (resp. right) invertible element in a $\mathbb{Q}$-Möbius monoid M.

<u>COROLLARY 0.4</u> Let M be a $\mathbb{Q}$-Möbius monoid. Then, we have : $\mu_M(1) = 1$.

<u>Proof</u> Let μ_M be the Möbius series of M which satisfies by definition to the relation : $\mu_M\ \underline{M} = 1_M$ .If we develop this relation on 1_M, we obtain :

$$1 = \sum_{mn=1} \mu_G(m)$$

Hence, the corollary follows now immediately from the above remark. ∎

As shows the following proposition, the class of $\mathbb{Z}$-Möbius monoids is only significant for infinite monoids :

PROPOSITION 0.5 Let M be a non trivial $\mathbb{Z}$-Möbius monoid. Then M is infinite.

Proof Let us suppose that M is a finite $\mathbb{Z}$-Möbius monoid. Since M is finite, we can consider the $\mathbb{Z}$-algebra morphism χ from $\mathbb{Z}[[M]] = \mathbb{Z}[M]$ into $\mathbb{Z}$ which is defined for every polynomial S in $\mathbb{Z}[M]$ by :

$$\chi(S) = \sum_{m \in M} (S|m)$$

But, since M is $\mathbb{Z}$-Möbius, we can write : $\mu_M \, \underline{M} = 1_M$ in $\mathbb{Z}[M]$. Then, if we apply χ to this relation, we obtain :

$$\chi(\mu_M)\, \chi(\underline{M}) = 1 \quad \Longleftrightarrow \quad (\sum_{m \in M} \mu_M(m)).|M| = 1$$

Since this last relation holds in $\mathbb{Z}$, it follows now immediately that $|M|$ is equal to 1, i.e. that M is the trivial monoid {1}. ∎

Note It follows also from the proof of the previous proposition that in a finite $\mathbb{Q}$-Möbius monoid M, we always have :

$$\sum_{m \in M} \mu_M(m) = \frac{1}{|M|}$$

Let us now study the relations that exist between the different classes of monoids we introduced. At first, there exists finite decomposition monoids that are not $\mathbb{Q}$-Möbius : for instance, every finite monoid which has a non trivial group of invertible elements, is a finite decomposition monoid (since it is finite) which cannot be $\mathbb{Q}$-Möbius according to prop. 0.1. Observe also that there exists monoids which are $\mathbb{Q}$-Möbius, but not $\mathbb{Z}$-Möbius as $\mathcal{B} = \{0,1\}$ with $1+1 = 1$. Finally, it should be noticed that every locally finite monoid M is $\mathbb{Z}$-Möbius. Indeed, we can then write :

$$\underline{M} = 1 + \underline{M^+} = 1 - (-\underline{M^+}) \quad \text{where } \underline{M^+} = \sum_{m \neq 1} m$$

Therefore we have :

$$\underline{M}\, (-\underline{M^+})^* = (-\underline{M^+})^*\, \underline{M} = 1$$

It follows that :

$$(-\underline{M^+})^* = \sum_{n \geq 0} (\underline{M^+})^{2n} - \sum_{n \geq 0} (\underline{M^+})^{2n+1} = \sum_{m \in M} \mu(m)\, m \in \mathbb{Z}[[M]]$$

is the inverse of $\underline{M}$. Moreover, $\mu_M(m)$ can be interpreted as the difference between the number of odd and even decompositions of m (this is the classical definition of the Möbius function of a locally finite monoid (see [CaFo] or [Lal])). We can now summarize our study by the following inclusions :

$$\text{locally finite} \subset \mathbb{Z}\text{-Möbius} \not\subset \mathbb{Q}\text{-Möbius} \not\subset \text{finite decomposition}$$

Although it seems quite probable, we do not know if there exist $\mathbb{Z}$-Möbius monoids that are not locally finite. Note also that any partially commutative monoid $M(A,\vartheta)$ is $\mathbb{Z}$-Möbius with the following Möbius series :

$$\mu_{M(A,\vartheta)} = \sum_{w \in M(A,\vartheta)} \mu_{M(A,\vartheta)}(w)\ w$$

where we have :

$$\mu_{M(A,\vartheta)}(w) = \begin{cases} (-1)^{|w|} & \text{if } w = \prod_{a \in \rho} a \text{ where } \rho \text{ a clique of } \vartheta \\ 0 & \text{if not} \end{cases}$$

(see [CaFo], [Lal] or below for the proof).

As an example, the multiplicative monoid of strictly positive integers $\mathbb{N}^*$ can be viewed as the free totally commutative monoid on the infinite alphabet of prime integers. In view of the above formula, $(\mathbb{N}^*,\times)$ has a Möbius function which is exactly the usual arithmetical one.

I. SUFFIX CONDITIONS FOR PARTIALLY COMMUTATIVE WORDS

1) Terminal alphabet

Let (A,ϑ) be a dependence alphabet. Then, a subalphabet $B \subset A$ is said to be *commutative* (resp. *non commutative*) iff we have :

$$\vartheta_B = \vartheta \cap B^2 = B^2 - \Delta_B \quad (\text{resp. } \vartheta_B = \emptyset)$$

It will be useful to have the following notion (which is also called "maximal letters" in [CMZ]) :

DEFINITION I.1 For every word $w \in M(A,\vartheta)$, the *terminal alphabet* of w is the set denoted TA(w) and defined as follows :

$$TA(w) = \{\ a \in A,\ w \in M(A,\vartheta).a\ \}$$

PROPOSITION I.1 For every $w \in M(A,\vartheta)$, TA(w) is a commutative subset of A.

Proof The proposition follows immediately from the following lemma :

LEMMA I.2 For every $a,b \in A$ and for every $w \in M(A,\vartheta)$, we have :

$$(a,b) \in \vartheta \Longrightarrow M(A,\vartheta).a \cap M(A,\vartheta).b = M(A,\vartheta).ab$$

$$(a,b) \notin \vartheta \Longrightarrow M(A,\vartheta).a \cap M(A,\vartheta).b = \emptyset$$

whose proof is easy and is left to the reader. ■

2) Applications

a) Reconstruction lemma and Möbius function

Let M be a monoid, let K be a semiring and let S be a series in K[[M]]. We can now give the following classical formulas which define the two coadjoint representations of M on K[[M]] :

$$(*)\quad \begin{cases} n^{-1}S = \sum_{m\in M} (S|nm)\, m \\ Sn^{-1} = \sum_{m\in M} (S|mn)\, m \end{cases} \quad \text{for every } n \text{ in } M$$

Note When M is the free monoid A^*, the previous formulas are exactly the relations that define classically the left and right quotients of a formal power series S in $K\langle\langle A^*\rangle\rangle$ (see [BeRe]). Note also that we have in this case the reconstruction lemma which claims that the following identity :

$$S = (S|1) + \sum_{a\in A} a\, .\, a^{-1}S$$

holds for every series S in $K\langle\langle A^*\rangle\rangle$. Observe that the above relation makes sense whenever A is infinite, since the family $(a.a^{-1}S)_{a\in A}$ is always *locally finite* (see [BeRe] or [Eil] for more details).

We have in fact the following proposition for every Möbius monoid :

PROPOSITION I.3 Let K be a ring (resp. a field of characteristic 0), let M be a $\mathbb{Z}$-Möbius (resp. $\mathbb{Q}$-Möbius) monoid, let μ_M be the Möbius series of M and let S be a series of K[[M]]. Then, the family $(\mu_M(m)\ m.m^{-1}S)_{m\in M}$ is locally finite and we have the relation :

$$S = (S|1) - \sum_{m\neq 1} \mu_M(m)\ m\, .\, m^{-1}S$$

Proof According to cor. 0.4, we have : $\mu_M(1) = 1$. Hence, it is now easy to see that the relation to prove is in fact equivalent to the following one :

$$(S|1) = \sum_{m\in M} \mu_M(m)\ m\, .\, m^{-1}S$$

which is also equivalent to the following relations :

$$1 = \sum_{xy=1} \mu_M(x) \quad \text{and} \quad 0 = \sum_{xy=m} \mu_M(x) \quad \text{for } m \neq 1$$

as it can be easily checked. Since these relations are exactly the defining relations of μ_M ,the proposition follows immediately. ■

Note In fact, the above formula is equivalent to the defining relation of the Möbius function of M (take S = $\underline{M}$ in it).

Hence, when M is a free partially commutative monoid, we have :

COROLLARY I.4 Let (A,ϑ) be a dependence alphabet, let K be a ring and let S be a series of K<<A,ϑ>>. Then, we have :

$$S = (S|1) + \sum_{w \text{ clique}} (-1)^{|w|-1} \, w. \, w^{-1}S$$

Note This last reconstruction result can also be established directly by an inclusion/exclusion argument based on lemma I.2.

Example Let us consider the commutation relation ϑ defined by the graph :

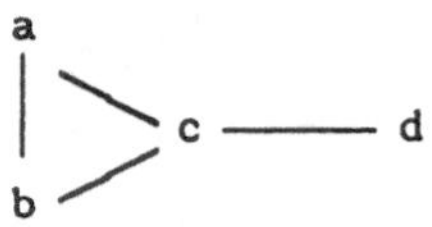

Then, cor. I.4 claims that we have for every S ∈ K<<A,ϑ>> when K is a ring :

$$S = (S|1) + a. \, (a^{-1}S) + \ldots + d. \, (d^{-1}S)$$
$$- ab. \, (ab^{-1}S) - \ldots - cd. \, (cd^{-1}S) + abc. \, (abc^{-1}S)$$

Note A specialization of the previous formula permits us to enumerate the sets M_α and M_n (when $|A| < +\infty$) for every free partially commutative monoid M(A,ϑ) (see [DK.1]). For instance, in the previous example, we have :

$$\sum_{n\geq 0} |M_n| \, X^n = (1 - 4X + 4X^2 + X^3)^{-1}$$

b) Lazard's elimination (Z-codes)

Let (A,ϑ) be a dependence alphabet, let Z be a *non commutative* subalphabet of A and let B = A−Z. Then, we define :

$$C_Z = \{ \, wz, \; w \in \langle B \rangle, \; TA(wz) = \{z\} \, \}$$

Example If we consider the commutation relation ϑ defined by :

a ——— b ——— c

we will obviously have :

$$C_{\{b\}} = \{b\}, \quad C_{\{a,c\}} = \{a,c\} \quad \text{and} \quad C_{\{a\}} = c^*a$$

Then, we have the following result whose proof can be found in [DK.2] :

<u>THEOREM I.5</u> Every element w of $M(A,\vartheta)$ can be written in a unique way under the following form :

$$w = c_1 \ldots c_n\, d \quad \text{where } c_i \in C_Z \text{ and } d \in \langle B\rangle$$

<u>Note</u> This factorization can be computed both sequentially in linear time and as well by a parallel algorithm.

<u>Consequence</u> It follows that C_Z^* is a free monoid of base C_Z which is hence a code, called Z-code. Note also that, using characteristic series in $\mathbb{N}\langle\langle A,\vartheta\rangle\rangle$, the previous theorem is equivalent to the fact that :

$$\underline{M(A,\vartheta)} = \underline{C_Z^*}\ \underline{M(B,\vartheta_B)} \qquad (\mathcal{F}act)$$

Applying the same decomposition to $M(B,\vartheta_B)$ and so on, it follows easily that, when A is finite, $M(A,\vartheta)$ can be factorized in the following way :

$$\underline{M(A,\vartheta)} = \underline{C_{Z_1}^*} \ldots\ldots \underline{C_{Z_n}^*}$$

where the monoids $C_{Z_i}^*$ are all free monoids.

<u>Examples</u> 1) When $\vartheta = \emptyset$, every subset of A is non commutative. Therefore the previous theorem gives us the classical Lazard's bisection :

$$\underline{A^*} = \underline{(B^*(A-B))^*}\ \underline{B^*}$$

2) When $\vartheta = A^2 - \Delta_A$, the only non commutative subsets of A are the letters. It follows that th. I.5 reduces to giving the classical factorization :

$$\underline{A^\oplus} = \underline{a^*}\ \underline{(A-\{a\})^\oplus} \qquad \text{with } a \in A$$

3) Let us consider again the commutation relation ϑ defined in the example that follows cor. I.4. Then we can take $Z_1=\{a,d\}$, $Z_2=\{b\}$ and $Z_3=\{c\}$ in order to apply our result which gives us the following factorization :

$$\underline{M(\{a,b,c,d\},\vartheta)} = \underline{C_{Z_1}^*}\ \underline{C_{Z_2}^*}\ \underline{C_{Z_3}^*}$$

<u>Remark</u> Taking the inverse of relation $(\mathcal{F}act)$ in $\mathbb{Z}\langle\langle A,\vartheta\rangle\rangle$, we obtain :

$$\mu_{M(A,\vartheta)} = \mu_{M(B,\vartheta_B)}(1-C_Z)$$

with the corresponding Möbius series. Therefore, using the euclidian division algorithm in $\mathbb{Z}\langle\langle A,\vartheta\rangle\rangle$ (see [DT]), we can compute C_Z by the relation :

$$C_Z = 1 - \mu_{M(A,\vartheta)}\,(\mu_{M(B,\vartheta_B)})^{-1}$$

It follows now immediately from this last identity that we have :

<u>COROLLARY I.6</u> Let K be a ring, let A be a finite alphabet equipped with a

partial commutation relation ϑ and let Z be a non commutative subalphabet of A. Then, the Z-code C_Z is in KRat(A,ϑ).

II. SMALL SERIES

1) Recognizable series

When K is a field, the recognizable series are exactly the "finite vectors" of the coadjoint representations. In fact, we have the theorem whose proof can be easily adapted from the corresponding result of [BeRe] for $M = A^*$:

THEOREM II.1 Let K be a field, let M be a monoid and let S be a series in K[[M]]. Then the following conditions are equivalent :

i) $(m^{-1}S)_{m\in M}$ (resp. $(Sm^{-1})_{m\in M}$; resp. $(m^{-1}Sn^{-1})_{m,n\in M}$) is of finite rank.

ii) The Hankel matrix $((S|mn))_{m,n\in M\times M}$ is of finite rank.

iii) There exists n in $\mathbb{N}$, two vectors α,β of K^n and a morphism ρ from M into $\mathcal{M}_n(K)$ such that :

$$(S|m) = \alpha\ \rho(m)\ \beta \quad \text{for every } m \in M$$

Notes 1) The equivalence between the three conditions given in i) remains valid when K is just a principal domain.

2) When K is a finite semiring, conditions i) and ii) may be reformulated replacing "of finite rank" by "finite" : then, the different above properties are again equivalent.

We are then led to the following definition :

DEFINITION II.1 Let K be a semiring and let M be a monoid. Then a series S of K[[M]] is said to be *recognizable* iff it satisfies to the relation iii) of the previous theorem. Their set is a submodule of K[[M]], denoted KRec(M).

Note When K is a field, the ranks in question in the two first assertions of i) are both equal to the rank of the minimal representation of iii).

We have now the following result :

THEOREM II.2 Let K be a ring (resp. a field of characteristic 0) and let M be a $\mathbb{Z}$-Möbius (resp. $\mathbb{Q}$-Möbius) monoid such that its associated Möbius series μ_M is $\mathbb{Z}$-rational (resp. $\mathbb{Q}$-rational). Then, we have :

$$KRec(M) \subset KRat(M)$$

Proof First, observe that we can associate with every representation of a monoid M into a matrix semiring $\mathcal{M}_n(K)$ the following representation :

$$\hat{\rho} : M \longrightarrow \mathcal{M}_n(K[[M]])$$
$$m \longrightarrow \rho(m).m$$

Moreover, if M is a finite decomposition monoid, $\hat{\rho}$ can be naturally extended to a K-algebra morphism from K[[M]] into $\mathcal{M}_n(K[[M]])$ by defining :

$$\forall\ S \in K[[M]], \quad \hat{\rho}(S) = \sum_{m \in M} (S|m)\ \hat{\rho}(m)\ m \quad \in \mathcal{M}_n(K[[M]])$$

Let us now come to the proof of our result : we will only argue when K is a ring, since the other case is completely similar. Then, let now K be a ring and let M be a $\mathbb{Z}$-Möbius monoid. Therefore, if S is a recognizable series of K[[M]] and if (α,ρ,β) are as in iii) of th. II.1, we can write :

$$S = \alpha\ (\ \sum_{m \in M} \rho(m)\ m\ )\ \beta = \alpha\ \hat{\rho}(\underline{M})\ \beta = \alpha\ \hat{\rho}(\mu_M^{-1})\ \beta = \alpha\ \hat{\rho}(\mu_M)^{-1}\ \beta$$

Observe that, if μ_M is $\mathbb{Z}$-rational, μ_M is also clearly K-rational. Hence, our result follows now easily from the lemma :

LEMMA II.3 Let K be a ring and let N be a matrix in $\mathcal{M}_n(KRat(M))$ such that $(N|1)$ is invertible. Then, N is invertible and N^{-1} is also in $\mathcal{M}_n(KRat(M))$.

whose proof is an easy adaptation of the corresponding classical proof in the free case (see [BeRe] lemma I.6.2 p. 23). ■

Notes 1) When K is a ring, we clearly have for every $\mathbb{Q}$-Möbius monoid M :

$$\mu_M \in KRat(M) \iff \underline{M} \in KRat(M)$$

2) In particular, the previous result holds for $M = M(A,\vartheta)$.

3) The inclusion of th. II.2 is strict in general as shows the example of the series $S = (ab)^*$ in the case of $M = \langle a,b \rangle^{\oplus}$.

2) Pull back of a series

Let M be a monoid, let K be a semiring and let Γ be a generating set of M. Then, we can consider the unique monoid morphism π from the free monoid Γ^* into M such that we have :

$$\forall\ \gamma \in \Gamma, \quad \pi(\gamma) = \gamma$$

For every series $S \in K[[M]]$, we will denote by S_* the *pull back* of S : it is the series of $K\langle\langle\Gamma^*\rangle\rangle$ defined by :

$$\forall\ w \in \Gamma^*,\ (S_*|w) = (S|\pi(w))$$

One can characterize the image and kernel of the mapping β_* that associates with every series $S \in K[[M]]$ its pullback S_* :

PROPOSITION II.4 The mapping β_* is into and its image is given by :

$$S \in \mathrm{Im}\,\beta_* \iff (S|u) = (S|v) \text{ for every } u,v \in \Gamma^* \text{ such that } \pi(u) = \pi(v)$$

Proof The proof is easy and is left to the reader. ∎

Note also that we have the formula for every series S in K[[M]] :

$$\forall\, w \in \Gamma^*,\ w^{-1}S_* = [(\pi(w)^{-1}S]_* \qquad (\mathcal{F})$$

The connexion between recognizable series in Γ^* and in M is now enlighten by the following result :

PROPOSITION II.5 Let K be a (non necessarily commutative) field or a finite semiring. Then, we have for every series $S \in K[[M]]$:

$$S_* \in \mathrm{KRec}(M) \iff S \in \mathrm{KRec}(M)$$

Moreover, when K is a field, we have for every recognizable series S :

$$\mathrm{rank}(S) = \mathrm{rank}(S_*)$$

Proof According to th. II.1 and to the remarks that follow it, our result is an easy consequence of relation $(\mathcal{F})$ and of the injectivity of β_*. ∎

Let us now give the following result :

THEOREM II.6 Let K be a (non necessarily commutative) field and let M be a monoid generated by Γ. Then, if S is in KRec(M), we have :

$$\forall\, m \in \Gamma^{\mathrm{rank}(S)},\ (S|m) = 0 \implies S = 0$$

Proof Indeed, the previous condition implies that we have :

$$\forall\, w \in \Gamma^*,\ |w| \le \mathrm{rank}(S) \implies (S_*|w) = 0$$

Hence, according to prop. II.5 and to the equality theorem of [Eil] p. 143, we obtain that : $S_* = 0$. Our result follows now clearly from prop. II.4. ∎

The following corollary follows now immediately :

COROLLARY II.7 Let K be a (non necessarily commutative) field and let M be a finitely generated monoid. Then, it is decidable if two recognizable series of K[[M]] are equal.

<u>Note</u> The previous corollary applies especially for $M = M(A,\vartheta)$ with a finite alphabet A.

<u>3) Recognizability of a product</u>

Let K be a semiring and let M be a monoid. Then the K-module K[[M]] can be always equipped with the *Hadamard product* defined for every $S,T \in K[[M]]$ by :

$$S \odot T = \sum_{m \in M} (S|m)\,(T|m)\,m$$

<u>PROPOSITION II.8</u> Let (A,ϑ) be a dependence alphabet, let $B \subset A$, let $\chi_{<B>}$ be the characteristic mapping of $<B>$ into $\{0,1\}$, let K be an arbitrary semiring and let S be a series in $K<<A,\vartheta>>$. Then, we have for every w in $M(A,\vartheta)$:

$$w^{-1}(S \odot \underline{<B>}) = \chi_{<B>}(w)\ (\ w^{-1}S \odot \underline{<B>})$$

<u>Proof</u> Let u be a word in $M(A,\vartheta)$. Then we have :

$$\begin{aligned}(w^{-1}(S \odot \underline{<B>})|u) &= (S \odot \underline{<B>})|wu) = (S|wu)\ (\underline{<B>}|wu) \\ &= (w^{-1}S|u)\ \chi_{<B>}(w)\ (\underline{<B>}|u) = \chi_{<B>}(w)\ (w^{-1}S \odot \underline{<B>}|u)\end{aligned}$$

The proposition follows now easily. ■

<u>THEOREM II.9</u> Let (A,ϑ) be a dependence alphabet, let K be a semiring, let S,T be in $K<<A,\vartheta>>$, let $a \in A$ and let $\vartheta(a)$ be the set of the letters distinct from a which commute with a. Then, we have :

$$a^{-1}(ST) = (a^{-1}S)T + (S \odot \underline{<\vartheta(a)>})\ a^{-1}T$$

<u>Proof</u> Let w be an element of $M(A,\vartheta)$. Then, we can clearly write :

$$\begin{aligned}(a^{-1}ST|w) &= (ST|aw) = \sum_{uv=aw} (S|u)(T|v) \\ &= \sum_{\substack{uv=aw \\ u \in aM(A,\vartheta)}} (S|u)(T|v) + \sum_{\substack{uv=aw \\ u \notin aM(A,\vartheta) \\ ua=au}} (S|u)(T|v) + \sum_{\substack{uv=aw \\ u \notin aM(A,\vartheta) \\ ua \neq au}} (S|u)(T|v) \\ &= \sum_{xv=w} (S|ax)(T|v) + \sum_{\substack{ux=w \\ u \in <\vartheta(a)>}} (S|u)(T|ax) + 0 \\ &= ((a^{-1}S)T|w) + ((S \odot \underline{<\vartheta(a)>})(a^{-1}T)|w)\end{aligned}$$

The theorem follows now immediately. ■

<u>Note</u> When $\vartheta = \emptyset$, we have $\vartheta(a) = \emptyset$. Hence : $S \odot \underline{<\vartheta(a)>} = S \odot \underline{\{1\}} = (S|1)$. Then, it follows that we obtain from th. II.9 the classical corresponding formula.

COROLLARY II.10 Let (A,θ) be a dependence alphabet, let K be a field or a finite semiring and let S,T be two recognizable series in $K\langle\langle A,\theta\rangle\rangle$. Then, ST is recognizable. Moreover, when K is a field, ranks are related by :

$$\text{rank}(ST) \le \text{rank}(S).\text{rank}(T).2^{|A|}$$

Proof It follows easily from ths. II.8, II.9 and prop. II.8. ■

4) Around the formula

$$\sum (S|w)\ w \in K?(A,\theta) \longrightarrow \sum (S|w)\ |w|\ w \in K?(A,\theta)$$

This formula is here an occasion to develop operations stabilizing KRat and KRec over $M(A,\theta)$ when K is an arbitrary semiring :

- $KRec(A,\theta)$: Using the classical technique of taking the tensor product of two representations, it is easy to see that the Hadamard product of two recognizable series of K[[M]] is recognizable (for every monoid M) (cf [SaSo] p. 31-33 for more details). Hence since :

$$\sum |w|\ w \in KRec(A,\theta)$$

(it is an easy adaptation of the example given in [BeRe] p. 22), it follows that the previous formula holds when ? = Rec.

- $KRat(A,\theta)$: Observe that the mapping δ defined by : $\delta(S)= \sum (S|w)|w|\ w$ is a derivation of the K-algebra $K\langle\langle A,\theta\rangle\rangle$, i.e. satisfies to :

$$\delta(ST) = \delta(S)\ T + S\ \delta(T)$$

The derivation is rational in the sense that for every letter a in A, $\delta(a)$ is in $KRat(A,\theta)$. Hence, by induction on the star-heigth and from the fact that $\delta(S^{-1}) = - S^{-1}\delta(S)S^{-1}$, it follows that $\delta(S)$ belongs to $KRat(A,\theta)$ (see also [Kr]). Hence, the above formula holds for ? = Rat. Observe finally that this result is also a consequence of th.4.5 p. 32 of [SaSo].

III. CONCLUSION

As a way of concluding this paper, let us give some further research directions which can be interesting :

- As far as rationality is concerned, it would be instructive to control the ranks of the Magnus transformation of the elements of $F(A,\theta)$ since we have $\mu(g) \in ZRat(A,\theta)$ for every g in $F(A,\theta)$.

- On the other hand, every automorphism of the graph of θ induces in a natural way an automorphism on each partially commutative structure. It would be interesting to explore the case when the commutation graph is rich in symmetries. Let us give an example : let us take $A = \{ x_{i,j}\ ,\ (i,j) \in \mathbb{Z}/n\mathbb{Z} \}$ which is an alphabet with n^2 letters equipped with ϑ defined by :

$$(x_{i,j}, x_{i\pm 1, j\pm 1}) \notin \vartheta \qquad \text{for every } i,j \in \mathbb{Z}/n\mathbb{Z}$$

The automorphism group of this graph consists in the automorphisms :

$$x_{i,j} \longrightarrow x_{j,i} \qquad x_{i,j} \longrightarrow x_{-i,j}$$

$$x_{i,j} \longrightarrow x_{i+1,j} \qquad x_{i,j} \longrightarrow x_{i,j+1}$$

It is a $8.n^2$ group that was already considered for other purposes ([Co]).

REFERENCES

[BeRe] BERSTEL J., REUTENAUER C., *Les séries rationnelles et leurs langages*, Masson, 1984

[Bo.1] BOURBAKI N., *Algèbre*, Chap. 1 à 3, CCLS, 1970

[Bo.2] BOURBAKI N., *Algèbres et Groupes de Lie*, Chap. 1, CCLS, 1971

[Bo.3] BOURBAKI N., *Algèbres et Groupes de Lie*, Chap. 2 et 3, CCLS, 1972

[Bo.4] BOURBAKI N., *Théories spectrales*, Chap. 1 et 2, Hermann, 1967

[CaFo] CARTIER P., FOATA D., *Problèmes combinatoires de commutation et de réarangements*, Lect. Notes in Math., 85, Springer Verlag, 1969

[Ch] CHOFFRUT C., *Free partially commutative monoids*, LITP Report N°86-20, Paris, 1986

[CMZ] CORI R., METIVIER Y., ZIELONKA W., *Asynchronous mappings and asynchronous cellular automata*, LABRI Report N°89-97, Bordeaux, 1990

[Co] COMMON H., *Magic and diabolic squares* (Private communication)

[Dc] DICKS W., *An exact sequence for rings of polynomials in partly commuting indeterminates*, Journal of Pure and Applied Algebra, 22, pp. 215-228, 1980

[Di] DIECKERT V., *Some mathematical aspects of trace theory*, Preprint, 1990

[Dr] DROMS C., *Isomorphisms of graph groups*, Proc. Amer. Math. Soc., 100, N°3, pp. 407-408, 1987

[Db] DUBOC C., *Commutations dans les monoïdes libres : un cadre théorique pour l'étude du parallélisme*, Thèse d'Université, University of Rouen, LITP Report N°86-25, Paris, 1986

[Du] DUCHAMP G., *On the free partially commutative Lie algebra*, LITP Report, N°89-74, Paris, 1989

[DK.1] DUCHAMP G., KROB D., *The free partially commutative Lie algebra : bases and ranks*, LITP Report N°89-93, To appear in Adv. in Math.

[DK.2] DUCHAMP G., KROB D., *Partially commutative structures*, LITP Report, Paris, 1990 (Submitted)

[DK.3] DUCHAMP G., KROB D., *Partially commutative Magnus transformations*, LITP Report, Paris, 1990

[DT] DUCHAMP G., THIBON J.I., *Théorèmes de transfert pour les polynômes partiellement commutatifs*, Theor. Comp. Sci., 57, pp. 239-249, 1988

[Eil] EILENBERG S., *Automata, Languages and Machines*, Volume A, Academic Press, 1974

[HW] HEBISCH U., WEINERT H.J., *Generalized semigroup semirings which are zero divisor free or multiplicatively left cancellative* (preprint)

[KMNR] KI HANG KIM, MAKAR-LIMANOV L., NEGGERS J., ROUSH F.W., *Graph algebras*, Journal of Algebra, 64, pp. 46-51, 1980

[Kr] KROB D., *Expressions K-rationnelles*, Thèse d'Université, University Paris 7, LITP Report N°88-23, Paris, 1988

[Lal] LALLEMENT G., *Semigroups and combinatorial applications*, Wiley, 1979

[Lz] LAZARD M., *Groupes, anneaux de Lie et problème de Burnside*, Inst. Mat. dell. Universita Roma, 1960

[MKS] MAGNUS W., KHARASS A., SOLITAR D., *Combinatorial group theory*, Dover, 1976

[Mz] MAZURKIEVITCH A., *Concurrent program schemes and their interpretations* DAIMI Report, PB 78, Aarhus University, 1977

[Me] METIVIER Y., *Contribution à l'étude des monoïdes de commutation*, Thèse University Bordeaux I, 1987

[Pe] PERRIN D., *Commutations partielles*, Lect. Notes in Comput. Sci., **372**, pp. 637-651, Springer Verlag, 1989

[SaSo] SALOMAA A., SOITTOLA M., *Automata theoretic aspects of formal power power series*, Springer Verlag, 1978

[Vi] VIENNOT G.X., *Heaps of pieces, I : basic definitions and combinatorial lemmas*, Proc. of "Colloque de Combinatoire Enumérative", UQUAM, Lect. Notes in Math., **1234**, pp. 321-350, Springer Verlag, 1986

[Zi] ZIELONKA W., *Notes on finite asynchronous automata and trace languages* RAIRO Inf. Theor., 21, pp. 99-135, 1987

INFINITE TRACES*

Paul GASTIN

LITP
Université Paris 6
4, Place Jussieu
75252 PARIS CEDEX 05
FRANCE

Abstract: Trace languages are used in computer science to provide a description of the behaviours of concurrent systems. If we are interested in systems which never stop then we have to consider languages of infinite traces. In this paper, we generalize to infinite traces three well known points of view about finite traces: equivalence class of words, projections on the dependence cliques and dependence graphs. These approaches are complementary and, depending on the problem we deal with, each of them can prove to be more appropriate than the others. In this way, we obtain an infinitary trace monoid and extend Levi's lemma and the Foata normal form. Next, we prove that the infinitary trace monoid is a completely coherent PoSet. We also define an ultrametric distance and prove that it is a complete metric space. Therefore, either the PoSet or the topological framework can be used to solve fix-point equations and then to provide semantics of recursive constructs. Finally, we introduce recognizable languages of finite and infinite traces. We prove that they are characterized by a syntactic congruence and that the family of recognizable languages is closed by concatenation and by the Boolean operations: union, intersection and complement.

Introduction

The theory of traces was introduced in 1977 by Mazurkiewiez [Ma 77]. The aim of this theory is to provide a mathematical description of concurrent systems behaviours. When we deal with sequential systems, the theory of word (string languages has been proved to be of great importance. In this case any behaviour of the system is exactly abstracted by a sequence of events (a word). We can also use sequential observations to describe a concurrent system behaviour. But now some actions a and b may be independent and may occur concurrently in a behaviour. Thus these actions may occur in a different order in two observations of the same behaviour. Therefore a trace will be an equivalence class of observations (words) and will abstract a concurrent system behaviour. In fact, two observations are equivalent iff they differ by commutations of independent actions. This is precisely the theory of partially commutative monoids which were first introduced by Cartier and Foata in order to study problems of rearrangements of strings [CF 69]. Trace theory has been extensively studied in the past years and we refer the reader to [Ch 86], [Ma 86], [AR 88] and [Pe 89] for recent overviews.

* *This work has been supported by the* ESPRIT Basic Research Actions No. 3166 (ASMICS) and No. 3148 (DEMON).

In the classical trace theory, one considers only finite traces. However, in order to describe concurrent systems that are not supposed to eventually stop, such as distributed operating systems, one has to extend this theory to infinite traces. This is precisely the aim of this paper. The theory of infinite words is recognized to be fundamental in the study of infinite behaviours of sequential systems [Ei 74], [Pe 84], [HR 86], [PP 90]. We believe that it will be the same for the theory of infinite traces with respect to concurrent systems. Infinite traces were first introduced in [Ga 88] and their connections with event structures were settled in [GR 90]. Independently, they were also introduced in [Kw 89].
There are three well known points of view about finite traces: equivalence class of words, projections on the dependence cliques and dependence graphs. These approaches are complementary and, depending on the problem we deal with, each of them can prove to be more appropriate than the others. That's why the first part of this paper (Section 2) generalizes these three points of view to infinite traces and proves their equivalence. Thus we obtain an infinitary trace monoid. The Foata normal form is another canonical representation of finite traces which is extended to infinite traces. The existence of a Foata normal form for infinite traces was also proved in [BMP 89] using a quite different method.
Next, we investigate in Section 3 some properties of the partial order set (PoSet) of infinitary traces. Since we have a monoid, the partial order is naturally the prefix order on traces. Mainly, we prove that the set of traces is a completely coherent PoSet. Therefore it is possible to use least upper bounds to solve fix-point equations and then to provide semantics of recursive constructs. On the other hand, using least upper bounds and greatest common prefixes, we will generalize Levi's lemma to infinite traces.
In Section 4, we investigate infinitary traces from the topological point of view. We define an ultrametric distance and prove that the infinitary trace monoid is a complete metric space which admits as dense subset the finitary trace monoid. Therefore, one can also use the topological framework to solve fix-point equations. This framework is even more general than the partial order one since we prove that every increasing sequence admits its least upper bound as limit. In fact, there are several non equivalent way to define a distance which makes $M(A^{\infty},I)$ a complete metric space. One could find in [BMP 89] another metric which is based on the Foata normal form of a trace. However for this metric, the concatenation of traces is not continuous.
Finally, we study in Section 5 recognizable languages of finite and infinite traces. The theory of recognizable languages has been extensively studied for (finite or infinite) words as well as for finite traces. In this paper, we define the recognizability as for infinite words [PP 90] by means of morphisms in finite monoids. Then we define the syntactic congruence of a language of infinite traces and prove that its recognizability is characterized by some properties of its syntactic congruence (this result was proved for words in [Ar 85]). Finally, we establish that the family of recognizable languages is closed by concatenation and by the Boolean operations: union intersection and complement.
Section 6 concludes this paper. We give some alternatives to the construction of infinitary trace monoids and we mention some research directions concerning recognizable languages.

1. Finite traces

We consider a finite alphabet A and a binary irreflexive and symmetric relation I over A called the independence relation. The letters of A can be viewed as events in a distributed system and two events are independent iff they are related by I. According to the relation I, we define an equivalence relation $\sim_I$ or simply $\sim$ on sequences of events. As usual, A^* denotes the free monoid over A and the relation $\sim$ over A^* is the transitive closure of the relation $\{(uabv,ubav), u,v \in A^*, (a,b) \in I\}$. The relation $\sim$ is indeed a congruence over A^* and the quotient monoid is denoted $A^*/\sim$ or $M(A^*,I)$. The members of $M(A^*,I)$ are called traces and φ will denote the canonical morphism from A^* to $M(A^*,I)$.

For any subset B of the alphabet A, Π_B will be the morphism from A^* to B^* that erases occurrences of non-members of B. Let $D = A \times A \setminus I$ be the dependence relation over A and let $\mathscr{C}$ be a covering of A by cliques of D.

For instance, let $A = \{a,b,c,d,e\}$ and $I = \{(a,c),(a,d),(a,e),(b,e),(c,a),(c,e),(d,a),(d,e),(e,a),(e,b),(e,c),(e,d)\}$, $\mathscr{C} = \{\{a,b\},\{b,c\},\{c,d\},\{d,b\},\{e\}\}$ and $\mathscr{C}' = \{\{a,b\},\{b,c,d\},\{e\}\}$ are covering of D by cliques.

We give now a fundamental characterization of the relation $\sim$ using the projections on the cliques [CP 85].

Proposition 1.1. $\forall\, u,v \in A^*,\ u \sim v \Leftrightarrow \forall\, C \in \mathscr{C},\ \Pi_C(u) = \Pi_C(v)$.

We will now define the prefix relation on traces and the preorder[1] relation on words, called I-prefix, associated to this prefix order on traces. The I-prefix relation on words is basic in the definition of the equivalence on infinite words that we will define later.

Definition 1.2.

i) Let $r,s \in M(A^*,I)$, r is a prefix of s, denoted $r < s$ iff $\exists\, t \in M(A^*,I)$, such that $s = r.t$.

ii) Let $u,v \in A^*$, u is an I-prefix of v, denoted $u <_I v$ iff $\varphi(u) < \varphi(v)$ ($\exists\, w \in A^*, v \sim_I u.w$).

For instance, if we consider $A = \{a,b,c\}$ and $I = \{(a,c),(c,a)\}$ we get abca $<_I$ abccaa. It is easy to check that $(A^*/\sim, <)$ is a Partial Order Set and that the preorder on A^* is weaker than the usual prefix order. Now, we generalize Proposition 1.1 to the preorder $<_I$.

Proposition 1.3. $\forall\, u,v \in A^*,\ u <_I v \Leftrightarrow \forall\, C \in \mathscr{C},\ \Pi_C(u) < \Pi_C(v)$.

Proof. Let u,v be in A^*, $u <_I v \;\Rightarrow\; \exists\, w \in A^*, v \sim uw$

$\Rightarrow\; \exists\, w \in A^*, \forall\, C \in \mathscr{C}, \Pi_C(v) = \Pi_C(u)\Pi_C(w)$

$\Rightarrow\; \forall\, C \in \mathscr{C}, \Pi_C(u) < \Pi_C(v)$

Conversely, we use an induction on the length of u. First assume that $|u| = 0$, then $u = \varepsilon$ and $v \sim uv$ thus $u <_I v$. Now suppose that $|u| > 0$, then $u = au'$ with $a \in A$. For all $C \in \mathscr{C}$ such that

[1] a preorder is a reflexive and transitive relation.

$a \in C$, we have $\Pi_C(u) = a\Pi_C(u') < \Pi_C(v)$ thus $v = v'av''$ with $C \cap alph(v')$[1] $= \emptyset$. Hence we have $v \sim av'v''$.

Now $\forall\, C \in \mathscr{C}$, $a \in C \Rightarrow \Pi_C(u) = a\Pi_C(u') < \Pi_C(v) = a\Pi_C(v'v'') \Rightarrow \Pi_C(u') < \Pi_C(v'v'')$ and
$a \notin C \Rightarrow \Pi_C(u) = \Pi_C(u') < \Pi_C(v) = \Pi_C(v'v'')$.

By induction, we get $u' <_I v'v''$.

Hence there exists w such that $v'v'' \sim u'w$ and we have $v \sim av'v'' \sim au'w = uw$. Thus $u <_I v$. ◊

2. Infinite traces

In this section, we want to give three points of view about infinite traces. First we define them using a generalization to infinite words of the I-prefix and the equivalence relations introduced in section 1. Thus a trace will be an equivalence class of words. Next, we extend to infinite words the characterization of these relations, using projections on the cliques. This gives rise to an embedding of the set of infinite traces into a direct product of free monoids, which is the second point of view. As for finite traces, this embedding is not onto and we give a characterization of traces in this direct product of free monoids. Lastly, we define dependence graphs and introduce a mapping Γ from words to dependence graphs. We prove that Γ is onto and that two words are equivalent iff they are mapped to the same dependence graph. Therefore dependence graphs represent exactly infinite traces. The Foata normal form is another canonical representation of finite traces which is extended to infinite traces. Finally, we define the concatenation on infinite traces using dependence graphs and prove that the set of traces is a cancellative monoid.

Let us first recall some classical definitions and notations about infinite words (see [Ei 74], [HR 86] and [PP 90] for more details). An infinite word u is simply a countable infinite sequence of events $u = u(1)u(2)\ldots$ We denotes A^{ω} the set of infinite words over A and $A^{\infty} = A^* \cup A^{\omega}$ the infinitary free monoid with the usual concatenation: $\forall\, u,v \in A^{\omega} \times A^{\infty}$, $u.v = u$ and $\forall\, u,v \in A^* \times A^{\infty}$, $u.v = u(1)u(2)\ldots u(n)v(1)v(2)\ldots$ where $u = u(1)u(2)\ldots u(n)$ and $v = v(1)v(2)\ldots$ As for finite words, a prefix order may be derived from this concatenation: $u < v$ iff $\exists\, w \in A^{\infty}$ such that $v = u.w$. For u in A^{∞}, $|u|$ denotes the length of u and $u[n]$ denotes the prefix of u of length $\min(n,|u|)$.

We turn now to the definition of the equivalence between infinite sequences of events which is generated by the independence relation I. The first natural idea is to consider again the transitive closure of the relation $\{(uabv,ubav),\ u,v \in A^{\infty},\ (a,b) \in I\}$. This is not satisfactory since if we assume that $(a,c) \in I$, we will expect that $(ac)^{\omega} \sim (ca)^{\omega}$ which is not the case with the transitive closure since it allows only finitely many commutations.

In fact, we will rather use the following observation in order to generalize to infinite words the equivalence relation. From Propositions 1.1 and 1.3 we can clearly deduce that for finite words, $u \sim v$ iff $u <_I v$ and $v <_I u$. Therefore we first generalize the I-prefix relation to infinite words and then use it to define the equivalence.

---

[1] alph(u) is the set of letters which occur in u.

Definition 2.1. Let $u,v \in A^\infty$,

i) u is an I-prefix of v, denoted for the time being $u \ll_I v$, iff $\forall\, n \in \mathbb{N}, \exists\, p \in \mathbb{N}$ such that $u[n] <_I v[p]$.

ii) u and v are I-equivalent, denoted for the time being $u \approx_I v$, iff $u \ll_I v$ and $v \ll_I u$.

For instance, let $A = \{a,b,c\}$ and $I = \{(a,c),(c,a)\}$, we get $u = a^\omega \ll_I v = (ac)^\omega$ since $\forall\, n \in \mathbb{N}$, $u[n] <_I v[2n]$. In the same way, $v = (ac)^\omega \ll_I w = (ca)^\omega$ since $\forall\, n \in \mathbb{N}$, $v[n] <_I w[n+1]$. Then we get $v \approx_I w$ but not $u \approx_I v$.

The use of finite prefixes to define the I-prefix relation for infinite words is quite natural since we often approximate an infinite word by means of its finite prefixes. More precisely, in the PoSet $(A^\infty,<)$ any word u (finite or infinite) is the least upper bound of its finite prefixes: $u = \sqcup\{u[n],\, n \in \mathbb{N}\}$[1].

We generalize now the results of Propositions 1.1 and 1.3 to infinite words. For any subset B of A, Π_B denotes again the projection from A^∞ onto B^∞ which erases non-members of B. Note that with infinite words Π_B is not a morphism. Nevertheless it has the following properties which allow us to use it efficiently with infinite words:

i) Let $u \in A^*$, $v \in A^\infty$ then $\Pi_B(u.v) = \Pi_B(u).\Pi_B(v)$.

ii) Π_B is an increasing continuous mapping from $(A^\infty,<)$ to $(B^\infty,<)$ that is if we assume that $(u_n)_{n\in \mathbb{N}}$ is an increasing sequence of A^∞, then $\Pi_B(\sqcup\{u_n, n\in \mathbb{N}\}) = \sqcup\{\Pi_B(u_n), n\in \mathbb{N}\}$.

Proposition 2.2. Let $u,v \in A^\infty$, we have:

i) $u \ll_I v \Leftrightarrow \forall\, C \in \mathscr{C}, \Pi_C(u) < \Pi_C(v)$.

ii) $u \approx_I v \Leftrightarrow \forall\, C \in \mathscr{C}, \Pi_C(u) = \Pi_C(v)$.

Therefore $\ll_I$ is a preorder relation on A^∞ and $\approx_I$ is an equivalence relation on A^∞.

Proof.

i) Let $C \in \mathscr{C}$, $\Pi_C(u) = \Pi_C(\sqcup\{u[n], n\in \mathbb{N}\}) = \sqcup\{\Pi_C(u[n]), n\in \mathbb{N}\}$

but $\forall\, n \in \mathbb{N}, \exists\, m \in \mathbb{N}$, $u[n] <_I v[m]$, thus $\Pi_C(u[n]) < \Pi_C(v[m]) < \Pi_C(v)$ (Proposition 1.3). Hence $\Pi_C(u) < \Pi_C(v)$.

Conversely, let us fix $n \in \mathbb{N}$. $\forall\, C \in \mathscr{C}$, $\Pi_C(u[n]) < \Pi_C(u) < \Pi_C(v) = \sqcup\{\Pi_C(v[m]), m\in \mathbb{N}\}$. Since $\mathscr{C}$ is finite and $\forall\, C \in \mathscr{C}$, $\Pi_C(u[n])$ is also finite there exists $m \in \mathbb{N}$ such that $\forall\, C \in \mathscr{C}$, $\Pi_C(u[n]) < \Pi_C(v[m])$, thus $u[n] <_I v[m]$ (Proposition 1.3).

The other facts are direct consequences of i). ◊

This proposition shows clearly that for finite words the relation $<_I$ and $\ll_I$ are identical and so are $\sim_I$ and $\approx_I$. This explains why we used the same terminology (I-prefix and I-equivalent) and why we will now use the simpler notation $u <_I v$ instead of $u \ll_I v$ and $u \sim_I v$ or simply $u \sim v$ instead of $u \approx_I v$ for both finite and infinite words.

[1] $\sqcup\{u_n, n\in \mathbb{N}\}$ denotes the least upper bound of the increasing sequence $(u_n)_{n\in \mathbb{N}}$.

Proposition 2.2 allows us to define the set of finite and infinite traces as the quotient $A^{\infty}/\sim$. Moreover, it is possible to extend to traces the projections on the cliques of $\mathcal{C}$ and to define a prefix order on traces.

Definition 2.3.

i) The set of finite and infinite traces is the quotient $A^{\infty}/\sim$ also denoted $M(A^{\infty},I)$. Again φ will denote the canonical mapping from A^{∞} onto $A^{\infty}/\sim$.

ii) $\forall C \in \mathcal{C}, \Pi_C: A^{\infty}/\sim \to C^{\infty}$ is defined by $\Pi_C(r) = \Pi_C(u)$ where $r = \varphi(u)$.

iii) $\forall r,s \in A^{\infty}/\sim, r < s$ iff $\forall C \in \mathcal{C}, \Pi_C(r) < \Pi_C(s)$.

Note that the prefix order relation on traces derives directly from the I-prefix preorder on words: $\forall u,v \in A^{\infty}, u <_I v \Leftrightarrow \varphi(u) < \varphi(v)$. Remark also that at present the set $A^{\infty}/\sim$ is not a monoid. We will discuss later the definition of the concatenation. Let us show now that, as for finite traces [CP 85], [Pe 89] the PoSet $(A^{\infty}/\sim,<)$ can be embedded in a cartesian product of free monoids.

In the following, m will denote the number of cliques in the covering $\mathcal{C}$ and $C_1,C_2,\ldots,C_m$ the members of $\mathcal{C}$. As usually, [m] will denote the set of integer $\{1,2,\ldots,m\}$. We will write Π_i instead of Π_{C_i} in order to lighten the notations. $\vec{C} = C_1^{\infty} \times \ldots \times C_m^{\infty}$ is the cartesian product of the free monoids over the cliques of $\mathcal{C}$. A member of $\vec{C}$ will be denoted by $\vec{u} = (u_1,u_2,\ldots,u_m)$. We will use the canonical concatenation and prefix relation on $\vec{C}$: $\forall\ \vec{u},\vec{v} \in \vec{C}$, $\vec{u}.\vec{v} = (u_1v_1,u_2v_2,\ldots,u_mv_m)$ and $\vec{u} < \vec{v} \Leftrightarrow \forall\ i \in [m],\ u_i < v_i$. $\vec{\Pi} : A^{\infty} \to \vec{C}$ is defined by $\forall\ u \in A^{\infty}, \vec{\Pi}(u) = (\Pi_1(u),\ldots,\Pi_m(u))$. $\vec{\Pi}$ denotes also the mapping from $A^{\infty}/\sim$ to $\vec{C}$ defined by $\forall r \in A^{\infty}/\sim, \vec{\Pi}(r) = (\Pi_1(r),\ldots,\Pi_m(r))$.

Proposition 2.4. $\vec{\Pi}$ is an increasing injective mapping from $(A^{\infty}/\sim,<)$ to $(\vec{C},<)$.

Proof. Follows easily from previous definitions and Proposition 2.2. ◊

It is easy to see that $\vec{\Pi}$ is not onto. Let $A = \{a,b,c,d\}$ and $I = \{(a,c),(c,a),(b,d),(d,b)\}$. $C_1 = \{a,b\}$, $C_2 = \{b,c\}$, $C_3 = \{c,d\}$, $C_4 = \{d,a\}$ is a covering of D by cliques. Firstly, $\vec{u} = (bb,b,\varepsilon,\varepsilon)$ has no antecedent by $\vec{\Pi}$ because u_1 and u_2 have not the same number of b. Secondly, $\vec{v} = (ab,bc,cd,da)$ has no antecedent by $\vec{\Pi}$ but for a different reason. Assume that there exists $u \in A^{\infty}$ such that $\vec{\Pi}(u) = \vec{v}$, then u will have exactly one occurrence of a, b, c and d. $\Pi_1(u) = v_1 = ab$ implies that a occurs before b in u. Similarly b occurs before c, c occurs before d, and d occurs before a, which is contradictory. In the following, we will characterize the subset $\vec{\Pi}(A^{\infty}/\sim)$ of $\vec{C}$. This characterization is important and could be used to define the concatenation and to prove main properties about infinite traces. In the examples above we have exhibited the only two reasons why $\vec{\Pi}$ is not onto. The second reason is the existence of a causal cycle induced by $\vec{v}$. This causal cycle can easily be formalized with the help of dependence graphs. Therefore, we will introduce them first and then we will characterize traces in $\vec{C}$.

A dependence graph or occurrence graph is known as a fundamental representation for finite traces [Du 86], [AR 88]. They are a very good support for the intuition on traces and can be used to present conveniently a lot of properties about traces [AR 88]. We will generalize this notion to infinite traces. Formally, a dependence graph is a labelled acyclic graph or rather an isomorphism[1] class of a labelled acyclic graph.

Definition 2.5. A dependence graph is a labelled acyclic graph (V,E,λ) with V a countable set of vertices, $E \subset V \times V$ a set of edges and $\lambda: V \to A$ a labelling function which satisfies:

(γ_1) $\forall$ x,y $\in$ V, $(\lambda(x),\lambda(y)) \in D \Leftrightarrow (x,y) \in E$ or $(y,x) \in E$

(γ_2) $\forall$ x $\in$ V, {y $\in$ V, there exists a path from y to x} is finite.

The set of dependence graphs will be denoted $\mathcal{G}(A,D)$.

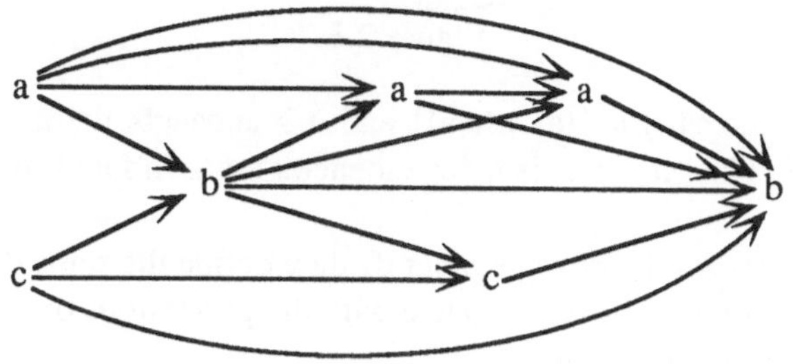

figure 2.1

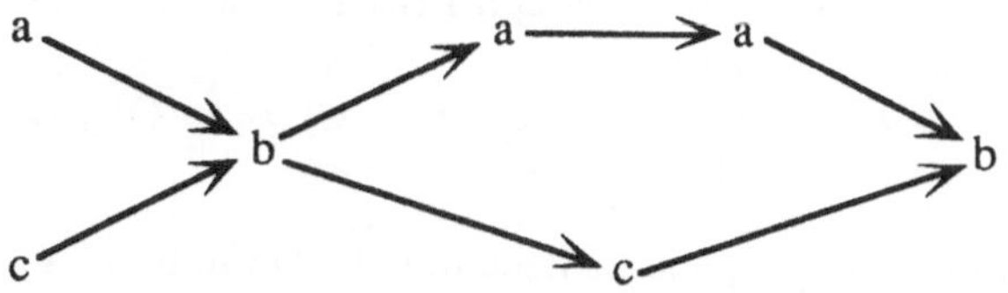

Figure 2.2

For instance, let A = {a,b,c} and I = {(a,c),(c,a)}. A dependence graph is presented in figure 2.1. Since we are only interested in the isomorphism class of the graph, we only write the labelling of a vertex. Note that this graph is not transitive since there is no edge between the first a and the second c. In fact, the important relation that we will consider in these graphs is the causal relation that is the existence of a path from a vertex to another one. With respect to this relation, some edges have not to be drawn, thus we will only draw the minimal representation of this relation (the Hasse diagram) in the following figures. The previous graph will thus be simply pictured as in figure 2.2.

Dependence graphs are well known and intuitive representation of finite traces. In other words, two finite words are equivalent iff they define the same dependence graph. In order to generalize this result to infinite traces we will associate a dependence graph to each word.

---

1 An isomorphism of graphs is a bijection between the vertices of two graphs which preserves the edges and the labelling.

Definition 2.6. Let $u \in A^{\infty}$, the graph $\Gamma(u) = (V,E,\lambda)$ is defined by:

$V = \{ (a,j),\ a \in A, 1 \leq j \leq |u|_a \}$

$E = \{ (a,j) \rightarrow (b,k),\ (a,b) \in D$ and the jth a occurs before the kth b in u $\}$

$\lambda((a,j)) = a$.

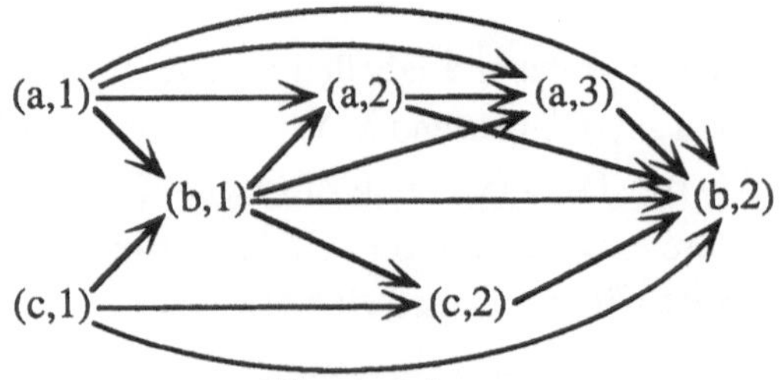

Figure 2.3

For instance, let $A = \{a,b,c\}$, $I = \{(a,c),(c,a)\}$ and u = acbaacb, the graph associated to u is presented in figure 2.3. Note that this is a dependence graph. In fact it is the same graph as in figure 2.1.

In order to prove that two words are equivalent iff they define the same dependence graph, we will use the characterization of the equivalence with the projections on the cliques. Therefore, we first define graphs for members of $\vec{C}$.

Definition 2.7. Let $\vec{u} \in \vec{C}$, we define the graph $\vec{\Gamma}(\vec{u})$ associated to $\vec{u}$ as follows:

$$\vec{\Gamma}(\vec{u}) = \bigcup_{i=1}^{m} \Gamma(u_i) = \left(\bigcup_{i=1}^{m} V_i \,,\, \bigcup_{i=1}^{m} E_i \,,\, \bigcup_{i=1}^{m} \lambda_i \right) = (\vec{V}, \vec{E}, \vec{\lambda})$$

where $\Gamma(u_i) = (V_i\,, E_i\,, \lambda_i)$ is the graph associated to u_i by Definition 2.6, that is

$V_i\,(u_i) = \{(a,j),\ a \in C_i,\ 1 \leq j \leq |u_i|_a\},\ \lambda_i((a,j)) = a$

$E_i\,(u_i) = \{(a,j) \rightarrow (b,k)$, the jth a occurs before the kth b in $u_i\}$.

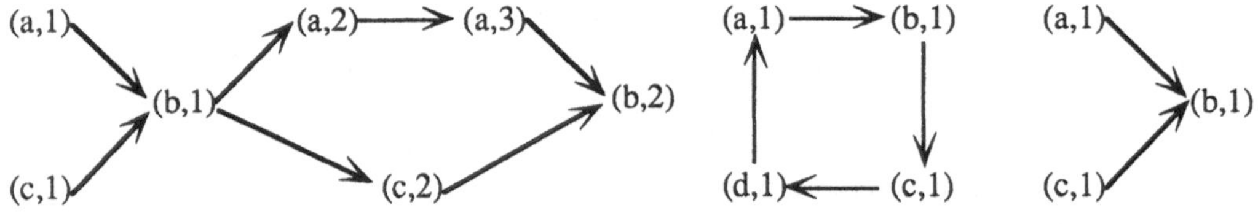

(a) (b) (c)

Figure 2.4

For instance, let $A = \{a,b,c,d\}$ and $I = \{(a,c),(c,a),(b,d),(d,b)\}$. Let $\vec{u}$ = (abaab,cbcb,cc,aaa), using again the Hasse diagram, the graph $\vec{\Gamma}(\vec{u})$ is given in figure 2.4.a. In the same way, let $\vec{v}$ = (ab,bc,cd,da) and $\vec{w} = (ab,cb,\varepsilon,\varepsilon)$, $\vec{\Gamma}(\vec{v})$ and $\vec{\Gamma}(\vec{w})$ are given in figure 2.4.b and 2.4.c.

Let us now define the depth of a vertex in a graph.

Definition 2.8. Let $G = (V,E)$ be a graph and let $x \in V$, we define the depth of x in G by:

$$\delta(x) = \sup\{\text{length}(p) \text{ where p is any path from any vertex y to x}\}.$$

For instance, let G be the graph of figure 2.3, we have $\delta(a,1) = 0$, $\delta(a,2) = 2$, $\delta(b,2) = 4$. Now if we consider the graph of figure 2.4.b, we have $\delta(a,1) = \delta(b,1) = \delta(c,1) = \delta(d,1) = \infty$, since we have arbitrarily long path ending in any vertex of G.

We are now able to prove that traces are represented by dependence graphs.

Proposition 2.9.

i) Let $u \in A^\infty$, then $\Gamma(u)$ is a dependence graph.

ii) Let $u \in A^\infty$, set $\vec{u} = \vec{\Pi}(u)$; then $\Gamma(u) = \vec{\Gamma}(\vec{u})$.

iii) Let $u,v \in A^\infty$, then $u \sim v \Leftrightarrow \Gamma(u) = \Gamma(v)$.

iv) Γ is a surjective mapping from A^∞ onto $\mathcal{G}(A,D)$.

Therefore Γ is a bijection between $A^\infty/\sim$ and $\mathcal{G}(A,D)$.

Proof. i) Obvious.

ii) $V = \{(a,j),\ a \in A,\ 1 \le j \le |u|_a\}$ and $V_i = \{(a,j),\ a \in C_i,\ 1 \le j \le |u_i|_a\} = \{(a,j),\ a \in A,\ 1 \le j \le |u_i|_a\}$

thus $\vec{V} = \bigcup_{i=1}^{m} \{(a,j),\ a \in A,\ 1 \le j \le |u_i|_a\} = \{(a,j),\ a \in A,\ 1 \le j \le \max\{|u_i|_a,\ 1 \le i \le m\}\}$,

but $\forall\, i \in [m]$, $a \in C_i \Rightarrow |u_i|_a = |u|_a$, and $a \notin C_i \Rightarrow |u_i|_a = 0$. Thus, $\max\{|u_i|_a,\ 1 \le i \le m\} = |u|_a$. Therefore $V = \vec{V}$. It is obvious that $\lambda = \vec{\lambda}$ and it remains to prove that $E = \vec{E}$.

$(a,j) \to (b,k) \in E \Leftrightarrow (a,b) \in D$ and the jth a occurs before the kth b in u

$\Leftrightarrow \exists\, i \in [m]$ s.t. $(a,b) \in C_i$ and the jth a occurs before the kth b in u

$\Leftrightarrow \exists\, i \in [m]$ s.t. $(a,b) \in C_i$ and the jth a occurs before the kth b in $u_i = \Pi_i(u)$

$\Leftrightarrow \exists\, i \in [m]$ s.t. $(a,j) \to (b,k) \in E_i$

$\Leftrightarrow (a,j) \to (b,k) \in \vec{E}$

iii) Let $u,v \in A^\infty$, set $\vec{u} = \vec{\Pi}(u)$ and $\vec{v} = \vec{\Pi}(v)$, $u \sim v \Leftrightarrow \vec{u} = \vec{v} \Rightarrow \Gamma(\vec{u}) = \Gamma(\vec{v}) \Leftrightarrow \Gamma(u) = \Gamma(v)$.

Conversely, let us assume that $\Gamma(u) = \Gamma(v)$. $E(u) = E(v)$ thus u and v have the same occurrences of letters and then so have u_i and v_i, $\forall\, i \in [m]$. Hence if $u_i \neq v_i$, there exists two occurrences (a,j) and (b,k) such that (a,j) occurs before (b,k) in u_i and (b,k) occurs before (a,j) in v_i. But in this case we have the edges $(a,j) \to (b,k)$ in $\Gamma(u)$ and $(b,k) \to (a,j)$ in $\Gamma(v)$ which is contradictory since $\Gamma(u) = \Gamma(v)$ and is acyclic. Thus $\forall\, i \in [m]$, $u_i = v_i$ and $u \sim v$.

iv) Let $G = (V,E,\lambda) \in \mathcal{G}(A,D)$. Since G is acyclic and satisfies (γ_2), the depth of any vertex of G is finite. Now from (γ_1) we can easily deduce that $\forall\, x,y \in V$, $\delta(x) = \delta(y) \Rightarrow x = y$ or $(\lambda(x),\lambda(y)) \in D$. Let us now construct an antecedent to G. For all integer k, let w_k be the word formed with the letters of depth k in G. For instance, if G is the graph of figure 2.1, we get $w_0 = ac$, $w_1 = b$, $w_2 = ac$, $w_3 = a$, $w_4 = b$. Previous remark shows that each word w_k is composed of independent letters which explains why we have not fixed any order on the letters

in w_k. Let $v = w_0w_1w_2\ldots$, we will prove that $\Gamma(v) = (V',E',\lambda')$ is isomorphic to G. We define the mapping $g: V \to V'$ by $g(x) = (\lambda(x),k(x))$ where $k(x) = |w_0\ldots w_{\delta(x)}|_{\lambda(x)}$. The mapping g is clearly injective since $g(x) = g(y) \Rightarrow (\lambda(x) = \lambda(y)$ and $\delta(x) = \delta(y)) \Rightarrow x = y$.
Now g is also surjective: let $(a,k) \in V'$, there exists n such that (a,k) comes from w_n. Hence, there exists $x \in V$ such that $\delta(x) = n$ and $\lambda(x) = a$ and we obtain $g(x) = (a,k)$.
It remains to verify that the bijection g preserves the edges and the labelling. For the labelling, it is trivial. For the edges we have:

$(x,y) \in E \Leftrightarrow \delta(x) < \delta(y)$ and $(\lambda(x),\lambda(y)) \in D$

$\Leftrightarrow$ the $k(x)^{th}$ $\lambda(x)$ is before the $k(y)^{th}$ $\lambda(y)$ in v and $(\lambda(x),\lambda(y)) \in D$

$\Leftrightarrow (g(x),g(y)) \in V'$

Finally we have proved that $\Gamma(v) = G$ and Γ is surjective. ◊

The first consequence of the previous proposition, more precisely of its proof, is the extension to infinite traces of the Foata normal form [CF 69], [Pe 89]. The existence of a Foata normal form for infinite traces was also proved in [BMP 89] using a quite different method.

Definition 2.10. Let $t \in A^\infty/\sim$. A Foata normal form of t is a factorization $t = t_0t_1t_2\ldots$ such that:

i) $\forall\, i \geq 0$, the actions of t_i are distinct and independent.

ii) $\forall\, i \geq 1$, $\forall\, a \in alph(t_i)$, $\exists\, b \in alph(t_{i-1})$ such that $(a,b) \in D$.

For instance, (ac)(b)(ac)(a)(b) is a Foata normal form of the trace presented in figure 2.1. The following result is a generalization of the similar one for finite traces [CF 69].

Proposition 2.11. Any trace $t \in A^\infty/\sim$ has an unique Foata normal form.

Proof. The existence of a Foata normal form is in fact proved in Proposition 2.9 iv) Let $t \in A^\infty/\sim$ and let G be the dependence graph $\Gamma(t)$. Let $v = w_0w_1w_2\ldots$ be the word constructed in the proof of Proposition 2.9 iv). We already saw that $\forall\, i \geq 0$, the actions of w_i are distinct and independent. Now let $i \geq 1$ and $a \in alph(w_i)$, this occurrence of a has depth i in G hence it has at least one immediate predecessor, say an occurrence of b, which has depth i-1. Therefore $b \in alph(w_{i-1})$ and $(a,b) \in D$. This proves that $\varphi(w_0).\varphi(w_1).\varphi(w_2)\ldots$ is a Foata normal form of t.
The uniqueness follows from the next property which can easily be proved by induction.
Let $t_0t_1t_2\ldots$ be a Foata normal form of t, then for all i, the occurrences of letters of t_i have depth i and therefore $t_i = \varphi(w_i)$. ◊

We come back now to the characterization of $\vec{\Pi}(A^\infty/\sim)$ in $\vec{C}$. The members of $\vec{\Pi}(A^\infty/\sim)$ are called reconstructible, this notion has been introduced for finite traces in [CM 85]. The first idea is to postulate that $\vec{u} \in \vec{C}$ is reconstructible iff $\vec{\Gamma}(\vec{u})$ is a dependence graph. This turns to be false since the graph presented in figure 2.4.c is a dependence graph whereas $\vec{w} = (ab,cb,\varepsilon,\varepsilon)$ is not reconstructible. In fact, the characterization of reconstructible t-uples is the following.

Proposition 2.12. Let $\vec{u} \in \vec{C}$ then $\vec{u}$ is reconstructible iff $\vec{u}$ satisfies (ρ_1) and (ρ_2).

(ρ_1) $\forall$ i,j $\in$ [m], $\Pi_i(u_j) = \Pi_j(u_i)$.

(ρ_2) $\vec{\Gamma}(\vec{u})$ is acyclic.

Proof. Let $\vec{u} \in \vec{C}$ be reconstructible, there exists $v \in A^\infty$ such that $\vec{\Pi}(v) = \vec{u}$.
$\forall$ i,j $\in$ [m], $\Pi_i(u_j) = \Pi_i(\Pi_j(v)) = \Pi_{C_i \cap C_j}(v) = \Pi_j(\Pi_i(v)) = \Pi_j(u_i)$.
On the other hand $\vec{\Gamma}(\vec{u}) = \Gamma(v)$ is acyclic.
The converse is not so easy to prove. We first establish some facts. Let $\vec{u} \in \vec{C}$ and set $\vec{G} = \vec{\Gamma}(\vec{u}) = (\vec{V}, \vec{E}, \vec{\lambda})$.

Fact 1: if $\vec{u}$ satisfies (ρ_1) then $\forall$ i $\in$ [m], $\forall$ a $\in C_i$, $|u_i|_a = |\vec{G}|_a$ (where $|\vec{G}|_a = |\vec{\lambda}^{-1}(a)|$).
Let i $\in$ [m], a $\in C_i$ and k $\in \mathbb{N}^*$. If $|u_i|_a \geq k$ then $(a,k) \in V_i \subset \vec{V}$. Hence $|u_i|_a \leq |\vec{G}|_a$. Conversely, if $(a,k) \in \vec{V}$ then there exists j $\in$ [m] such that $|u_j|_a \geq k$. Now, $\Pi_j(u_i) = \Pi_i(u_j)$ and $a \in C_i$, thus $|\Pi_j(u_i)|_a = |\Pi_i(u_j)|_a \geq k$, therefore $|u_i|_a \geq k$ and then $|u_i|_a \geq |\vec{G}|_a$.

Fact 2: $\vec{G}$ is acyclic iff $\forall$ x $\in \vec{V}$, $\delta(x) < \infty$.
As we have seen in the graph of figure 2.4.b, as soon as there exists a cycle in $\vec{G}$, all the vertices of this cycle have an infinite depth. Conversely, let us assume that there exist infinite depth vertices in $\vec{G}$. Let (b,k) be such a vertex, let C_{i_1} be a clique such that b $\in C_{i_1}$ and let (a_1,j_1) be the first occurrence of infinite depth in u_{i_1}. (a_1,j_1) has at most m immediate predecessors in $\vec{G}$ (one on each clique C_k such that $a_1 \in C_k$). Thus one of them has an infinite depth, let i_2 be its component and let (a_2,j_2) be the first occurrence of infinite depth in u_{i_2}. (a_2,j_2) occurs before (a_1,j_1) in u_{i_2} thus we have the edge $(a_2,j_2) \to (a_1,j_1)$ in $\vec{G}$. We go on this way until we obtain $i_k \in \{i_1,i_2,\ldots,i_{k-1}\}$. Without loss of generality we may assume that $i_k = i_1$, we have exhibited the following cycle in $\vec{G}$:
$(a_1,j_1) = (a_k,j_k) \to (a_{k-1},j_{k-1}) \to \ldots \to (a_2,j_2) \to (a_1,j_1)$.

Fact 3: if $\vec{u}$ satisfies (ρ_1) and (ρ_2) then $\vec{G}$ is a dependence graph.
$\vec{G}$ is a labelled acyclic graph which clearly satisfies (γ_2) (Fact 2). Let us see that $\vec{G}$ also satisfies (γ_1). $(a,j) \to (b,k) \in \vec{E} \Leftrightarrow \exists$ i $\in$ [m], (a,j) occurs before (b,k) in $u_i \Rightarrow (a,b) \in D$. Conversely, let $(a,j),(b,k) \in \vec{V}$ be such that $(a,b) \in D$. $\exists$ i $\in$ [m] such that a,b $\in C_i$ and by Fact 1, $|u_i|_a \geq j$ and $|u_i|_b \geq k$. For instance we have (a,j) occurs before (b,k) in u_i and then $(a,j) \to (b,k) \in \vec{E}$.

Now let $v \in A^\infty$ be such that $\Gamma(v) = \vec{G}$, we will prove that $\vec{\Pi}(v) = \vec{u}$. Let $v_i = \Pi_i(v)$, by Fact 1 we get $|v_i|_a = |v|_a = |\vec{G}|_a = |u_i|_a$. Hence it remains to prove that the letters occur in the same order in u_i and v_i. Let (a,j) and (b,k) be two occurrences in v_i (and thus in u_i): (a,j) occurs before (b,k) in v_i iff (a,j) occurs before (b,k) in v iff $(a,j) \to (b,k)$ in $\Gamma(v) = \vec{G}$ iff (a,j) occurs before (b,k) in u_i. Therefore $u_i = v_i$ and $\vec{\Pi}(v) = \vec{u}$. ◊

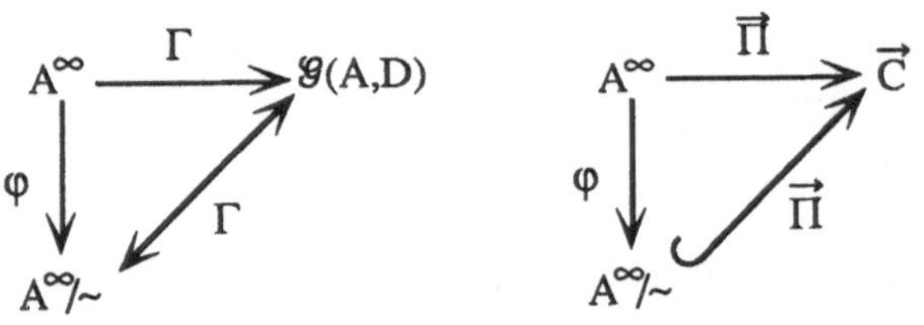

Figure 2.5

We turn now to the definition of the concatenation on infinite traces. We have introduced three points of view about traces. The set of traces is either the quotient of the free monoid by an equivalence relation or the set of dependence graphs or a subset of a direct product of free monoids (figure 2.5). Each of these points of view can be used to define the concatenation on infinite traces.

First, let us consider the quotient of the free monoid. Despite the fact that the projections are no more morphisms in the infinite case, we can use them to prove that $\sim$ is a congruence over A^∞. Thus, there is a classical way to define a concatenation on the quotient $A^\infty/\!\sim$. But we will see that this definition is not satisfactory. In the sequential case, (A^∞,d)[1] is the completion of (A^*,d) and the concatenation defined on A^∞ is the unique continuous extension of the concatenation on A^*. A good concatenation over $A^\infty/\!\sim$ would have to satisfy the same property. For any reasonable topology on $A^\infty/\!\sim$, one should have $\lim \varphi(a^n) = \varphi(a^\omega)$. Now suppose that a concatenation is continuous, then we will have $\lim \varphi(c)\varphi(a^n) = \varphi(c)\varphi(a^\omega)$ and $\lim \varphi(a^n)\varphi(c) = \varphi(a^\omega)\varphi(c)$; but if $(a,c) \in I$ we have $a^n c \sim c a^n$, thus a continuous concatenation will verify $\varphi(a^\omega)\varphi(c) = \varphi(c)\varphi(a^\omega)$. This equality is not satisfied by the concatenation mentioned above since $a^\omega.c = a^\omega \not\sim c.a^\omega$.

Another possibility is based on the embedding of $A^\infty/\!\sim$ in $\vec{C}$. Let $r,s \in A^\infty/\!\sim$ and set $\vec{u} = \vec{\Pi}(r)$ and $\vec{v} = \vec{\Pi}(s)$. The idea is then to define $r.s = \vec{\Pi}^{-1}(\vec{u}.\vec{v})$. For instance, let $A = \{a,b,c\}$ and $I = \{(a,c),(c,a)\}$. Let $r = \varphi(a^\omega)$ and $s = \varphi(c)$, we get $\vec{u}.\vec{v} = (a^\omega,\varepsilon).(\varepsilon,c) = (a^\omega,c) = \vec{v}.\vec{u}$ and then we obtain $r.s = s.r$ as expected above. But unfortunately the product $\vec{u}.\vec{v}$ is not always reconstructible. Let $t = \varphi(b)$ and $\vec{w} = \vec{\Pi}(t) = (b,b)$, we get $\vec{u}.\vec{w} = (a^\omega,b)$ which is not reconstructible. Therefore, this approach yields a concatenation which is only partially defined. What is more problematic is that this definition depends on the covering $\mathscr{C}$ chosen and worse, yields a non associative law.

Therefore we will rather use the dependence graphs to define the concatenation.

Definition 2.13. Let $G_1 = (V_1,E_1,\lambda_1)$ and $G_2 = (V_2,E_2,\lambda_2)$ be dependence graphs with $V_1 \cap V_2 = \varnothing$, their concatenation is defined by:

$$G_1.G_2 = (V_1 \cup V_2\,,\, E_1 \cup E_2 \cup \{(x,y) \in V_1 \times V_2\,,\, (\lambda_1(x)\,,\, \lambda_2(y)) \in D\}\,,\, \lambda_1 \cup \lambda_2)$$

Clearly, $G_1.G_2$ is a labelled acyclic graph with a countable set of vertices and satisfies (γ_1). Now it verifies (γ_2) iff $\mathrm{alphinf}(G_1) \times \mathrm{alph}(G_2) \subset I$, where $\mathrm{alph}(G) = \lambda(V)$ and

[1] d is the usual distance on words whose definition will be given in the topological section.

alphinf(G) = $\{a \in A, |\lambda^{-1}(a)| = \infty\}$. Therefore the concatenation is only partially defined on dependence graphs. In order to get a monoid, we add a new element: $\perp$ which means error and will be the result of $G_1.G_2$ when this graph does not satisfy (γ_2). We will denote $\mathcal{A}$ the set $A^\infty/\!\sim \cup \{\perp\}$.

Definition 2.14. The concatenation on $\mathcal{A}$ is defined as follows: let $r,s \in A^\infty/\!\sim$, $G_1 = \Gamma(r)$ and $G_2 = \Gamma(s)$. We set $r.s = \Gamma^{-1}(G_1.G_2)$ if $\text{alphinf}(r) \times \text{alph}(s) \subset I$ and $r.s = \perp$ otherwise. And $\forall\, r \in \mathcal{A}$, $r.\perp = \perp.r = \perp$ ($\perp$ is a zero).

One can simply consider $\perp$ as an easy way to denote that the concatenation is not defined but the following remark[1] gives a justification of this notation. Let $\mathcal{G}'$ be the set of dependence graphs which don't necessarily satisfy (γ_2). With the concatenation of Definition 2.13, $\mathcal{G}'$ is clearly a monoid. Now, let $\mathcal{R} = \{G \in \mathcal{G}'$ such that G does not satisfy $(\gamma_2)\}$, it is easy to see that $\mathcal{R}$ is an ideal of $\mathcal{G}'$. Therefore $(\mathcal{A},.)$ is exactly the Rees quotient of $(\mathcal{G}',.)$.
Let us see an example. Let $A = \{a,b,c,d\}$, $I = \{(a,c),(c,a),(b,d),(d,b)\}$, let $r = \varphi(acbdca^\omega)$, $s = \varphi(cc)$ and $t = \varphi(cbc)$. We get $r.s = \varphi(acbdccca^\omega)$ and $r.t = \perp$. We would like to emphasize on the following fact: if the first trace is finite, then this concatenation coincide with the *natural* one obtained from the quotient of the free monoid, that is, if $r = \varphi(u)$ is finite and $s = \varphi(v)$ then $r.s = \varphi(u.v)$. In fact, this partial case is often all we need.
We will now state some properties of this concatenation. Mainly, $(\mathcal{A},.)$ is a cancellative monoid and the concatenation is related to the direct product of free monoids and to the partial order.

Proposition 2.15.

i) $(\mathcal{A},.)$ is a monoid.
ii) $\forall\, r,s \in A^\infty/\!\sim$, $r.s \neq \perp \Rightarrow \vec{\Pi}(r.s) = \vec{\Pi}(r).\vec{\Pi}(s)$
iii) $\forall\, r,s \in A^\infty/\!\sim$, $r < s \Leftrightarrow \exists\, t \in A^\infty/\!\sim$ such that $s = r.t$
iv) $\forall\, r,s,t \in A^\infty/\!\sim$, $r.s = r.t \neq \perp \Rightarrow s = t$
v) $\forall\, r \in A^*/\!\sim$, $\forall\, s,t \in A^\infty/\!\sim$, $s.r = t.r \neq \perp \Rightarrow s = t$

Proof.
i) ε is clearly a neutral element. Let $r,s,t \subset \mathcal{A}$, the associativity is clear if one of them is equal to $\perp$, hence we assume that $r,s,t \in A^\infty/\!\sim$.

$$\begin{aligned}(r.s).t = \perp \quad &\Leftrightarrow \quad \text{alphinf}(r) \times \text{alph}(s) \not\subset I \text{ or } (\text{alphinf}(r) \cup \text{alphinf}(s)) \times \text{alph}(t) \not\subset I\\ &\Leftrightarrow \quad \text{alphinf}(r) \times (\text{alph}(s) \cup \text{alph}(t)) \not\subset I \text{ or } \text{alphinf}(s) \times \text{alph}(t) \not\subset I\\ &\Leftrightarrow \quad r.(s.t) = \perp\end{aligned}$$

Finally, when $(r.s).t \neq \perp$, the problem reduces to the associativity of the graph concatenation (Definition 2.13) which is obvious.
ii) Let $r,s \in A^\infty/\!\sim$ be such that $r.s \neq \perp$. Let $\vec{u} = \vec{\Pi}(r)$ and $\vec{v} = \vec{\Pi}(s)$, we will prove that $\vec{u}.\vec{v}$ is reconstructible. We can easily verify that $\vec{\Gamma}(\vec{u}).\vec{\Gamma}(\vec{v}) = \vec{\Gamma}(\vec{u}.\vec{v})$. Therefore $\vec{u}.\vec{v}$ satisfies (ρ_2).

---

[1] This remark is due to V. Diekert.

Now let $i \in [m]$ be such that $|u_i| = \infty$ and let $a \in C_i$ be such that $|u_i|_a = \infty$. We have $a \in alphinf(r)$, then we get $alph(s) \cap C_i = \emptyset$. Therefore we have proved that $\forall i \in [m]$, $|u_i| = \infty \Rightarrow v_i = \varepsilon$. From this, we deduce easily that $\vec{u}.\vec{v}$ satisfies (ρ_1).
Let t be such that $\vec{\Pi}(t) = \vec{u}.\vec{v}$, we have $\Gamma(t) = \vec{\Gamma}(\vec{u}.\vec{v}) = \vec{\Gamma}(\vec{u}).\vec{\Gamma}(\vec{v}) = \Gamma(r).\Gamma(s)$. Therefore $t = r.s$ and $\vec{\Pi}(r.s) = \vec{\Pi}(r).\vec{\Pi}(s)$.
iii) Let $r,s \in A^{\infty}/\sim$ be such that $r < s$ and set $\vec{u} = \vec{\Pi}(r)$, $\vec{v} = \vec{\Pi}(s)$. Since $r < s$ we have $\forall i \in [m]$, $u_i < v_i$, then set $w_i = \varepsilon$ if $|u_i| = \infty$ and w_i defined by $v_i = u_i.w_i$ otherwise. Using the characterization of Proposition 2.12, let us see that $\vec{w}$ is recontructible.
$\forall i,j \in [m]$, $\Pi_i(u_jw_j) = \Pi_i(v_j) = \Pi_j(v_i) = \Pi_j(u_iw_i)$. Since $\Pi_i(u_j) = \Pi_j(u_i)$ and $\forall k \in [m]$, $|u_k| = \infty \Rightarrow w_k = \varepsilon$, we easily infer that $\vec{w}$ satisfies (ρ_1). Now, $\vec{w}$ clearly satisfies (ρ_2) since $\vec{\Gamma}(\vec{w})$ is a subgraph of $\vec{\Gamma}(\vec{v})$ which is acyclic. Therefore $\vec{w}$ is reconstructible. Let $t = \vec{\Pi}^{-1}(\vec{w})$, we get $s = r.t$. The converse is trivial.
iv) Let $r,s,t \in A^{\infty}/\sim$ be such that $r.s = r.t \neq \perp$ and set $\vec{u} = \vec{\Pi}(r)$, $\vec{v} = \vec{\Pi}(s)$ and $\vec{w} = \vec{\Pi}(t)$. We get $\forall i \in [m]$, $u_i.v_i = u_i.w_i$ and $\forall i \in [m]$, $|u_i| = \infty \Rightarrow v_i = w_i = \varepsilon$. Since the free monoid is left cancellative by finite words, we get $\forall i \in [m]$, $|u_i| < \infty \Rightarrow v_i = w_i$. Therefore, $\vec{v} = \vec{w}$ and $s = t$.
v) As above, using this time that the free monoid is right cancellative by finite words. ◊

3. Partial Order Set

In this section, we investigate some properties of the PoSet (Partial Order Set) $(A^{\infty}/\sim,<)$. Again, all the results presented here are generalization of properties of the PoSet $(A^{\infty},<)$. The PoSet properties of $(A^{\infty}/\sim,<)$ have been deeply studied in [GR 90]. Some of the results presented here were already stated in [GR 90]. They are needed in next sections and we prove them here for completeness.
We prove that $(A^{\infty}/\sim,<)$ is a completely coherent PoSet and consequently, it is a CPO (Complete Partial Order); any bounded subset admits a least upper bound; any increasing sequence admits a least upper bound and any non empty set admits a greatest lower bound. On the other hand, we prove that any (infinite) trace can be approximate with (is the least upper bound of) an increasing sequence of finite traces. This approximation which generalizes the sequential case is really helpful because it allows us to deal with finite traces and then to infer results to infinite traces. Finally, we generalize Levi's lemma to infinite traces (see [CP 85], [Du 86] for finite traces).
The following proposition states some results on the PoSet $(A^{\infty},<)$. We first need to give some definitions. A subset X of a PoSet $(Z,<)$ is pairwise bounded if any pair $\{x,y\} \subset X$ admits a bound in Z. The PoSet $(Z,<)$ is a completely coherent PoSet if any pairwise bounded subset of Z admits a least upper bound.

Proposition 3.1.

i) Any increasing sequence $(u_n)_{n\in \mathbf{N}} \subset A^{\infty}$ admits a least upper bound.

ii) A^{∞} is a completely coherent PoSet.

Moreover, let L be a subset of A^{∞} which admits a least upper bound, then

iii) There exists an increasing sequence $(u_n)_{n\in \mathbf{N}} \subset L$ such that $\sqcup L = \sqcup\{u_n, n \in \mathbf{N}\}$[1].

iv) $\forall v \in A^*, v < \sqcup L \Rightarrow \exists u \in L$ such that $v < u$.

Proof.

i) Let $u \in A^{\infty}$ be defined by $|u| = \sup\{|u_n|, n \in \mathbf{N}\}$ and $\forall n \in \mathbf{N}, u[|u_n|] = u_n$[2]. We can easily verify that $u = \sqcup\{u_n, n \in \mathbf{N}\}$.

ii) We use the following remark: $\forall u,v,w \in A^{\infty}, (u < w \text{ and } v < w) \Rightarrow (u < v \text{ or } v < u)$.

Let L be a pair-wise bounded subset of A^{∞}. Using the previous remark, we easily infer that L is totally ordered. Now, either $L \subset A^*$ or $L \cap A^{\omega} \neq \emptyset$. In the first case, we can enumerate the members of L in an increasing sequence, hence $\sqcup L$ exists.

In the second case, let $u \in L \cap A^{\omega}$, since L is totally ordered we easily get $u = \sqcup L$.

iii) Since L is bounded by $\sqcup L$, it is totally ordered. If $L \subset A^*$, we take the increasing sequence defined in ii), otherwise $L \cap A^{\omega} = \{u\}$ and we take the constant sequence $u_n = u \ \forall n \in \mathbf{N}$.

iv) Let $(u_n)_{n\in \mathbf{N}}$ be the increasing sequence defined in iii). Let v be a finite word such that $v < \sqcup L$. Since $|\sqcup L| = \sup\{|u_n|, n \in \mathbf{N}\}$, there exists $n \in \mathbf{N}$ such that $|v| \leq |u_n|$. Now, v and u_n are both prefixes of $\sqcup L$ and then v is a prefix of u_n. ◊

Now, we turn to the study of the PoSet $(A^{\infty}/\sim,<)$. Most of the proofs lay on the embedding of $(A^{\infty}/\sim,<)$ in the direct product of free monoid $(\vec{C},<)$ (Proposition 2.4). The following proposition gives the relationship between the least upper bound of a trace subset T and the least upper bounds of its projections on the cliques.

Proposition 3.2. Let T be a subset of $A^{\infty}/\sim$, $\forall i \in [m]$, let $T_i = \{\Pi_i(s), s \in T\} \subset C_i^{\infty}$, then

$$\sqcup T \text{ exists in } A^{\infty}/\sim \Leftrightarrow \forall i \in [m], \sqcup T_i \text{ exists in } C_i^{\infty}.$$

Moreover in this case we have $\forall i \in [m], \Pi_i(\sqcup T) = \sqcup T_i$.

Proof. Let us assume that $t = \sqcup T$ exists in $A^{\infty}/\sim$. Clearly $\forall s \in T, \forall i \in [m], \Pi_i(s) < \Pi_i(t)$ that is T_i is bounded by $\Pi_i(t)$. Therefore $\sqcup T_i$ exists in C_i^{∞} (Proposition 3.1). Conversely, let us assume that $\forall i \in [m], u_i = \sqcup T_i$ exists in C_i^{∞} and set $\vec{u} = (u_1,\ldots,u_m)$. We will prove that $\vec{u}$ is reconstructible.

• Let us fix $i \in [m]$, since $u_i = \sqcup T_i$ there exists a sequence $(s_n)_{n\in \mathbf{N}} \subset T$ such that $(\Pi_i(s_n))$ is an increasing sequence and $u_i = \sqcup\{\Pi_i(s_n), n \in \mathbf{N}\}$ (Proposition 3.1).

$\forall n \in \mathbf{N}, \forall j \in [m]$, we have $\Pi_j(\Pi_i(s_n)) = \Pi_i(\Pi_j(s_n)) < \Pi_i(u_j)$.

---

[1] $\sqcup L$ denotes the least upper bound of L.

[2] We recall that u[k] denotes the prefix of u of length inf(|u|,k).

Hence $\Pi_j(u_i) = \Pi_j(\sqcup\{\Pi_i(s_n), n \in \mathbf{N}\}) = \sqcup\{\Pi_j(\Pi_i(s_n)), n \in \mathbf{N}\} < \Pi_i(u_j)$. In the same way we get $\Pi_i(u_j) < \Pi_j(u_i)$ and then $\vec{u}$ satisfies (ρ_1).

• Let us assume that $\vec{\Gamma}(\vec{u})$ has a cycle. Then we have:

$$v_{i_1} = \ldots(a_k,j_k)\ldots(a_1,j_1) < u_{i_1}$$
$$v_{i_2} = \ldots(a_1,j_1)\ldots(a_2,j_2) < u_{i_2}$$
$$\ldots$$
$$v_{i_k} = \ldots(a_{k-1},j_{k-1})\ldots(a_k,j_k) < u_{i_k}$$

where (a_p,j_p) denotes the $j_p{}^{th}$ occurrence of a_p in u_{i_p} and $u_{i_{p+1}}$. Now, v_{i_k} is finite thus there exists $s \in T$ such that $v_{i_k} < \Pi_{i_k}(s)$ (Proposition 3.1). Let us see that $\forall\ p \in [k]$, $v_{i_p} < s_{i_p}$. Remark that both v_{i_p} and s_{i_p} are prefixes of u_{i_p} thus one is a prefix of the other and it is enough to prove that $|s_{i_p}|_{a_p} \geq j_p$. Now v_{i_k} is a prefix of s_{i_k} hence $|s_{i_{k-1}}|_{a_{k-1}} = |s|_{a_{k-1}} = |s_{i_k}|_{a_{k-1}} \geq j_{k-1}$ and then $v_{i_{k-1}} < s_{i_{k-1}}$. In the same way we obtain $\forall\ p \in [k]$, $v_{i_p} < s_{i_p}$. Therefore this is a cycle of $\vec{\Gamma}(\vec{s}) = \Gamma(s)$ which is contradictory since the dependence graph of a trace is acyclic. Hence $\vec{u}$ satisfies (ρ_2) and is then reconstructible. Let $t = \vec{\Pi}^{-1}(\vec{u})$, we will prove that $t = \sqcup T$.

$\forall\ s \in T$, $\forall\ i \in [m]$, we have $\Pi_i(s) < \sqcup T_i = u_i = \Pi_i(t)$, that is $s < t$. Hence t is an upper bound of T. Now, let r be any upper bound of T. $\forall\ s \in T$, $\forall\ i \in [m]$, we have $\Pi_i(s) < \Pi_i(r)$. Therefore $\Pi_i(t) = u_i = \sqcup T_i < \Pi_i(r)$, that is $t < r$. Consequently we get $t = \sqcup T$ which achieves the proof. ◊

From previous results we can infer that $A^\infty/\!\sim$ is a completely coherent PoSet.

Theorem 3.3. $A^\infty/\!\sim$ is a completely coherent PoSet

Proof. Let T be a pair-wise bounded subset of $A^\infty/\!\sim$. We easily deduce that $\forall\ i \in [m]$, $T_i = \Pi_i(T)$ is a pair-wise bounded subset of C_i^∞. Thus, by Proposition 3.1, $\sqcup T_i$ exists which implies that $\sqcup T$ exists by Proposition 3.2. ◊

Many results can be deduced from the previous theorem and some of them are stated in the following corollary. Let us first recall that a subset X of a PoSet (Z,<) is directed if any pair $\{x,y\} \subset X$ admits an upper bound ***in*** X. The PoSet (Z,<) is a CPO (Complete Partial Order) if it admits a least element and if any directed subset admits a least upper bound.

Corollary 3.4.

i) $A^\infty/\!\sim$ is a bounded complete PoSet that is any bounded subset admits a least upper bound.
ii) $A^\infty/\!\sim$ is a CPO.
iii) Any increasing sequence in $A^\infty/\!\sim$ admits a least upper bound.

Proof. These results are direct consequences of Theorem 3.3 since a bounded subset, a directed subset and an increasing sequence are all pairwise bounded subsets. Moreover the least element of $A^\infty/\!\sim$ is indeed the empty trace. ◊

Now we prove that any trace is the least upper bound of an increasing sequence of *finite* traces. Therefore, in some cases, from properties of finite traces we can infer analogous properties of infinite traces. We also use this result in the next section to prove that $A^*/\sim$ is dense in $A^\infty/\sim$.

Proposition 3.5. Let $s \in A^\infty/\sim$,

i) s is the least upper bound of an increasing sequence of finite prefixes of s.

ii) $s = \sqcup\{r \in A^*/\sim, r < s\}$

Proof.

i) We use the notation of the proof of Proposition 2.9. Let $G = \Gamma(s)$, $v = w_0 \ldots w_n \ldots$ and $v_n = w_0 \ldots w_n$. $(v_n)_{n \in \mathbf{N}}$ is clearly an increasing sequence in A^∞ and $v = \sqcup\{v_n, n \in \mathbf{N}\}$. By Proposition 2.12, we get $\forall i \in [m]$, $\Pi_i(s) = \Pi_i(v)$, therefore $\Pi_i(s) = \sqcup\{\Pi_i(v_n), n \in \mathbf{N}\}$.
Now let $s_n = \varphi(v_n)$ be the trace generated by v_n, $(s_n)_{n \in \mathbf{N}}$ is an increasing sequence of finite prefixes of s. Since $\forall i \in [m]$, $\Pi_i(s_n) = \Pi_i(v_n)$, we get $\Pi_i(s) = \sqcup\{\Pi_i(s_n), n \in \mathbf{N}\}$. Therefore by Proposition 3.2 we obtain $s = \sqcup\{s_n, n \in \mathbf{N}\}$.
ii) Now let $T = \{r \in A^*/\sim, r < s\}$, T is bounded by s thus $\sqcup T$ exists and $\sqcup T < s$. On the other hand, $\{s_n, n \in \mathbf{N}\} \subset T$ thus $s = \sqcup\{s_n, n \in \mathbf{N}\} < \sqcup T$. Therefore $s = \sqcup T$. ◊

Now we study greatest lower bounds. We first prove that any non empty set T admits a greatest lower bound in $A^\infty/\sim$ denoted $\sqcap T$. Moreover if T is bounded in $A^\infty/\sim$ we can characterize $\sqcap T$ with the projections on the cliques as in Proposition 3.2.

Proposition 3.6. Any non empty set $T \subset A^\infty/\sim$ admits a greatest lower bound $\sqcap T$ in $A^\infty/\sim$. Moreover if T is bounded we get $\forall i \in [m]$, $\Pi_i(\sqcap T) = \sqcap T_i$ where $T_i = \{\Pi_i(t), t \in T\}$.

Proof. Let T be a non empty set of $A^\infty/\sim$ and set $S = \{s \in A^\infty/\sim, \forall t \in T, s < t\}$. S is a non empty ($\varepsilon \in S$) bounded set, hence it admits a least upper bound which is clearly a greatest lower bound of T. Remark that this result holds for words as well.
Now let us assume that T is bounded. $\forall i \in [m]$, let $r_i = \sqcap T_i \in C_i^\infty$. We will prove that $\vec{r} = (r_1, \ldots, r_m)$ is reconstructible.
• Let $i,j \in [m]$. Since T is bounded so is T_i. Hence T_i is totally ordered and there exists $t \in T$ such that $r_i = t_i$. Then we get $\Pi_i(r_j) < \Pi_i(t_j) = \Pi_j(t_i) = \Pi_j(r_i)$. In the same way we get $\Pi_j(r_i) < \Pi_i(r_j)$ and then $\vec{r}$ satisfies (ρ_1).
• Let $t \in T$, $\forall i \in [m]$, $r_i < t_i$ therefore $\vec{\Gamma}(\vec{r})$ is a subgraph of $\vec{\Gamma}(\vec{t}) = \Gamma(t)$ which is acyclic. Then $\vec{r}$ satisfies (ρ_2).
Now let $r = \vec{\Pi}^{-1}(\vec{r})$, we will prove that $r = \sqcap T$. $\forall t \in T$, $\forall i \in [m]$, we have $r_i < t_i$ thus $r < t$, that is r is a lower bound of T. Conversely, let s be a lower bound of T, $\forall t \in T$, $\forall i \in [m]$, we have $s_i < t_i$. Thus $s_i < \sqcap T_i = r_i$ and then $s < r$. ◊

The last proposition of this section generalizes Levi's lemma to infinite traces. The same result is proved for finite traces in [CP 85].

Proposition 3.7. Let $x,y,z,t \in A^\infty/\sim$ then

$$xy = zt \neq \bot \quad \Leftrightarrow \quad \exists\, u,v,r,s \in A^\infty/\sim \text{ such that } x = u.v,\ y = r.s,\ z = u.r,\ t = v.s,$$
$$\text{alph}(v) \times \text{alph}(r) \subset I \text{ and } xy \neq \bot.$$

Proof. Let us assume that $xy = zt \neq \bot$, then x and z are bounded by $xy = zt$. Hence $\forall\, i \in [m]$, x_i and z_i are bounded by $x_iy_i = z_it_i$ and then either $x_i < z_i$ or $z_i < x_i$. Now by Proposition 3.6, $u = x \sqcap z$ exists in $A^\infty/\sim$ and $\forall\, i \in [m]$, $u_i = x_i$ or $u_i = z_i$. By Proposition 2.15, there exist $v,r \in A^\infty/\sim$ such that $x = u.v$ and $z = u.r$. Since $x = uv \neq \bot$ and $\forall\, i \in [m]$, $u_i = x_i$ or $u_i = z_i$, we get $v_i \neq \varepsilon \Rightarrow x_i \neq u_i \Rightarrow z_i = u_i \Rightarrow r_i = \varepsilon$. In the same way we get $r_i \neq \varepsilon \Rightarrow v_i = \varepsilon$. Therefore we have $\text{alph}(v) \times \text{alph}(r) \subset I$.
Now it also holds that $\forall\, i \in [m]$, $x_i \sqcup z_i = u_ir_iv_i = u_iv_ir_i$. Hence by Proposition 3.2, we get $w = x \sqcup z = urv = uvr$. Now $w < xy = zt$ then there exists $s \in A^\infty/\sim$ such that $ws = xy = zt$ (Proposition 2.15). Therefore $ws = uvrs = xy = uvy$ and then $y = rs$ (Proposition 2.15). In the same way we get $t = vs$ which achieves this part of the proof.
The converse is trivial. Note that if we don't assume that $xy \neq \bot$, we will get $xy = zt$ as well. ◊

Finally, let us mention that other important results have been proved in [GR 90] as for instance the following ones: $(A^\infty/\sim,<)$ is a Scott-Domain and is Prime Algebraic.

4. Topology

In this section, we will investigate the set of infinitary traces from the topological point of view. There are two main reasons for this study.
On one hand, we want to prove that the set of infinitary traces is the natural completion of the set of finitary traces in order to legitimize previous definitions. Such a step is followed in [PP 90] for words. For the usual distance on words, they prove that A^∞ is the completion of A^* and that the usual concatenation on A^∞ is the unique continuous extension of the concatenation on A^*. We pursue here similar aims. We will define an ultrametric distance which makes $\mathcal{A}$ a complete metric space. Then we prove that with this topology, $M(A^*,I)$ is dense in $M(A^\infty,I)$ and that the concatenation on $\mathcal{A}$ is continuous in (r,s) as soon as r.s is not "error". These results are quite satisfactory in our framework since the concatenation is only partially defined on $A^\infty/\sim$ and it is continuous whenever it is defined.
In fact, there are several non equivalent way to define a distance which makes $M(A^\infty,I)$ a complete metric space. One could find in [BMP 89] another metric which is based on the Foata normal form of a trace. With this metric, $M(A^\infty,I)$ is also a complete metric space. However this metric is not equivalent to the one we will define and it appears that there is no continuous extension of the concatenation for the topology induced. For instance, let $A = \{a,b,c\}$ and $I = \{(a,c), (c,a)\}$ and let $r_n = a^n$, $s_n = a^nc$, $t_n = a^nb$ and $u_n = a^nbc$. With the metric defined in [BMP 89] we get $\lim_{n\to\infty} r_n = a^\omega$, $\lim_{n\to\infty} s_n = ca^\omega$ and $\lim_{n\to\infty} t_n = \lim_{n\to\infty} u_n = a^\omega$. Now if the

concatenation were continuous, we would obtain $a^{\omega}c = ca^{\omega}$, $a^{\omega}b = a^{\omega}$ and $a^{\omega}(bc) = a^{\omega}$ which is clearly a non associative law.
On the other hand, we would like to make $\mathcal{A}$ a good semantical framework. Usually, one uses fix-point operators to give semantics of recursive constructs. These fix-point operators require either a cpo or a topological framework. The partial order structure of $\mathcal{A}$ has been overviewed in previous section and extensively studied in [GR 90]. In the following, we will define an ultrametric distance and prove that $\mathcal{A}$ is a complete metric space. Thus, one could freely use fix-point operators for contracting functions on $\mathcal{A}$. The topological framework is even more general than the partial order one since we prove that every increasing sequence admits its least upper bound as limit.
First, we will recall some results about topology on words. We refer the reader to [HR 86] and [PP 90] for details.

Definition 4.1. Let u,v be in A^{∞}, we set $d(u,v) = 2^{-n}$ with $n = \sqcup\{k \in \mathbb{N}, u[k] = v[k]\} \in \overline{\mathbb{N}}$ with the usual convention $2^{-\infty} = 0$.

For instance, we have $d(abaab,ababba) = 2^{-3}$, $d(abab,(ab)^{\omega}) = 2^{-4}$, $d(aba,aba) = 0$, $d((ab)^{\omega},(ab)^{\omega}) = 0$. d is an ultrametric distance and induces on A^{∞} a canonical topology: the topology induced by d on A and A^* is the discrete one and the topology induced by d on $A^{\omega} = A^{\mathbb{N}}$ is the product topology induced by the discrete topology on A. Moreover, this distance legitimizes the definition of infinite words in the following way.

Proposition 4.2.

i) Let $(v_n)_{n \in \mathbb{N}}$ be an increasing sequence in A^{∞}, then it admits a limit which is its least upper bound.
ii) (A^{∞},d) is a complete metric space and (A^*,d) is dense in (A^{∞},d). In other words, (A^{∞},d) is the completion of (A^*,d).
iii) The concatenation on A^* is uniformly continuous, therefore, it admits a unique continuous extension to A^{∞} which is the usual one.

There are many other results about the topology on A^{∞}, but we focus ourselves on the ones mentioned above because our aim is to generalize them to the partially commutative case. The first idea is to use the embedding of $M(A^{\infty}, I)$ in $\vec{C}$ and the canonical topology on $\vec{C}$.

Definition 4.3. Let $\vec{u},\vec{v} \in \vec{C}$, we set $\vec{d}(\vec{u},\vec{v}) = \max\{d(u_i,v_i), i \in \{1,\dots,m\}\}$

The topology induced by $\vec{d}$ on $\vec{C}$ is the product topology induced by the canonical topology on the sets C_i^{∞}. The following proposition is then a consequence of general topology results.

Proposition 4.4.

i) $\vec{d}$ is an ultrametric distance on $\vec{C}$.
ii) $\vec{C}$ is the completion of $C_1^* \times \dots \times C_m^*$.

We will now give an example which shows why the topology induced by $\vec{C}$ on $M(A^\infty,I)$ is not satisfactory. Let $A = \{a,b,c\}$ and $I = \{(a,c),(c,a)\}$, the two cliques are $C_1 = \{a,b\}$ and $C_2 = \{b,c\}$. Let us consider the sequences of finite traces (r_n) and (s_n) defined by $r_n = a^n b$ and $s_n = c^n b$. For the topology induced by $\vec{C}$ on $M(A^\infty,I)$, (r_n) and (s_n) are Cauchy sequences: $\vec{u}_n = \vec{\Pi}(r_n) = (a^n b,b)$, $\vec{v}_n = \vec{\Pi}(s_n) = (c^n b,b)$ and for $n > p$, $\vec{d}(\vec{u}_n,\vec{u}_p) = \vec{d}(\vec{v}_n,\vec{v}_p) = 2^{-p}$. The sequences $(\vec{u}_n)$ and $(\vec{v}_n)$ converge to $\vec{u} = (a^\omega,b)$ and $\vec{v} = (c^\omega,b)$ respectively which are not reconstructible. Therefore, for this topology, the Cauchy sequences (r_n) and (s_n) admit no limit in $M(A^\infty,I)$ which is then not complete. Now, if we want $\mathcal{A}$ to be a complete metric space we have to set both $\lim_{n\to\infty} r_n = \perp$ and $\lim_{n\to\infty} s_n = \perp$ which is impossible since for $n > 0$, $\vec{d}(\vec{u}_n,\vec{v}_n) = 1$. Hence, we have to find another topology. For this purpose, we will use $\vec{d}$ in a more sophisticated way.

Definition 4.5. Let $r,s \in M(A^\infty, I)$, let $\vec{u} = \vec{\Pi}(r)$, $\vec{v} = \vec{\Pi}(s)$ and $\vec{w} = \vec{\Pi}(r \sqcap s)$[1], we set

$$\delta(r,s) = \max(\vec{d}(\vec{u},\vec{w}), \vec{d}(\vec{v},\vec{w}))$$
$$\delta(r,\perp) = \delta(\perp,r) = 1$$

For instance, let $A = \{a,b,c\}$ and $I = \{(a,c),(c,a)\}$. We consider the traces $r = acbaabc$ and $s = acbaacb$, their greatest common prefix is $t = r \sqcap s = acbaa$. With the same notations as in the previous definition, we have $\vec{u} = (abaab,cbbc)$, $\vec{v} = (abaab,cbcb)$ and $\vec{w} = (abaa,cb)$, then we have $\delta(r,s) = \vec{d}(\vec{u},\vec{w}) = \vec{d}(\vec{v},\vec{w}) = 2^{-2}$. Note that in this case, $\delta(r,s) = \vec{d}(\vec{u},\vec{v})$ but the following example will exhibit the differences between these metrics. Let (r_n) be the sequence of finite traces defined by $r_n = a^n b$.
For $n > p$ we have $t_p = r_n \sqcap r_p = a^p$ and then $\delta(r_n,r_p) = \vec{d}(\vec{r}_n,\vec{t}_p) = \vec{d}(\vec{r}_p,\vec{t}_p) = 1$ whereas $\vec{d}(\vec{r}_n,\vec{r}_p) = 2^{-p}$. Therefore, with the metric δ, (r_n) is no more a Cauchy sequence.

Proposition 4.6. δ is an ultrametric distance on $\mathcal{A}$.

Proof.
- The symmetricity is clear.
- $\delta(r,s) = 0 \Leftrightarrow \vec{d}(\vec{r},\overrightarrow{r \sqcap s}) = \vec{d}(\vec{s},\overrightarrow{r \sqcap s}) = 0 \Leftrightarrow \vec{r} = \overrightarrow{r \sqcap s} = \vec{s} \Leftrightarrow r = r \sqcap s = s$.
- Let $r,s,t \in \mathcal{A}$. First we assume that $r,s,t \in M(A^\infty,I)$.

For instance, we have $\delta(r,t) = \vec{d}(\vec{r},\overrightarrow{r \sqcap t})$. Since $\vec{d}$ is an ultrametric distance we get
$\delta(r,t) \leq \max(\vec{d}(\vec{r},\overrightarrow{r \sqcap s}),\vec{d}(\overrightarrow{r \sqcap s},\vec{s}),\vec{d}(\vec{s},\overrightarrow{s \sqcap t}),\vec{d}(\overrightarrow{s \sqcap t},\vec{t}), \vec{d}(\vec{t},\overrightarrow{r \sqcap t}))$
then, since we have assumed that $\vec{d}(\vec{t},\overrightarrow{r \sqcap t}) \leq \vec{d}(\vec{r},\overrightarrow{r \sqcap t})$ we get
$\delta(r,t) \leq \max(\vec{d}(\vec{r},\overrightarrow{r \sqcap s}),\vec{d}(\overrightarrow{r \sqcap s},\vec{s}),\vec{d}(\vec{s},\overrightarrow{s \sqcap t}),\vec{d}(\overrightarrow{s \sqcap t},\vec{t})) = \max(\delta(r,s),\delta(s,t))$.
The inequality is clear if we suppose that $r = s = t = \perp$ and in the other case (at least one but not all of them are $\perp$) we get $\delta(r,t) \leq 1 = \max(\delta(r,s), \delta(s,t))$. ◊

[1] We recall that $r \sqcap s$ denotes the greatest common prefix of r and s.

We will see that the metric δ is satisfactory for our purpose. Nevertheless the topology induced by δ depends on the covering by cliques chosen even if we restrict ourselves to coverings by maximal cliques. For instance, let A = {a,b,c,d,e,f}, I = {(a,d),(d,a),(b,e),(e,b),(c,f),(f,c)}, there exist two different coverings by maximal cliques:

$$\mathcal{C}_1 = \{\{a,b,c\},\{b,d,f\},\{c,d,e\},\{a,e,f\}\}$$

$$\mathcal{C}_2 = \{\{b,c,d\},\{a,c,e\},\{a,b,f\},\{d,e,f\}\}.$$

Let δ_1 and δ_2 be the metrics associated to $\mathcal{C}_1$ and $\mathcal{C}_2$. We consider two sequences of traces $r_n = \varphi((abc)^n)$ and $s_n = \varphi((abc)^n d)$ and the infinite trace $r = \varphi((abc)^\omega)$. We can easily verify that $\delta_1(r_n,r) = \delta_1(s_n,r) = 2^{-n}$ and $\delta_2(r_n,r) = 2^{-2n}$, $\delta_2(s_n,r) = 1$. Therefore the topologies induced by δ_1 and δ_2 are not equivalent.

Let us see now, that this is not a serious problem since there is a canonical way to choose the covering, namely a covering which contains the letters.

Proposition 4.7. Let $\mathcal{C}_1$ and $\mathcal{C}_2$ be two coverings by cliques and let δ_1 and δ_2 be the associated metrics. If $\mathcal{C}_1$ contains the letters ($\forall a \in A$, $\{a\} \in \mathcal{C}_1$) then $\delta_2 \le \delta_1$.

Proof. Let $r,s \in M(A^\infty,I)$ and set $t = r \sqcap s$. Let us assume that $\delta_2(r,s) = \vec{d}_2(r,t) = 2^{-(n-1)}$. There exists $C \in \mathcal{C}_2$ such that $\Pi_C(r)[n] \neq \Pi_C(t)[n]$. Since $t < r$, we get $\Pi_C(r)[n] = \Pi_C(t)au$, for some letter a and some word u. Hence $|t|_a < n$ and $|t|_a < |r|_a$.
Therefore $\Pi_a(t)[n] \neq \Pi_a(r)[n]$ and $\delta_1(r,s) \ge \vec{d}_1(r,t) \ge 2^{-(n-1)} = \delta_2(r,s)$. ◊

This result proves that the topology induced by a covering which contains the letters is finer than the topology induced by any other covering. This remark provides a canonical choice of the metric. However, the following results of this section are valid whatever covering one chooses.

Now we will investigate some properties of this metric. First we will prove that the notion of limit induced by this topology generalizes the least upper bound operator in $A^\infty/\sim$. This result is then an extension of the similar one in the non commutative case (Proposition 4.2).

Proposition 4.8. Let $(s_n)_{n\in \mathbb{N}}$ be an increasing sequence in $A^\infty/\sim$, then it admits a limit which is its least upper bound.

Proof. By Corollary 3.4, the increasing sequence $(s_n)_{n\in \mathbb{N}}$ admits a least upper bound s which verifies: $\forall i \in [m]$, $\Pi_i(s) = \sqcup \{\Pi_i(s_n), n \in \mathbb{N}\}$. Now, by Proposition 4.2, we get $\lim_{n\to\infty} \Pi_i(s_n) = \Pi_i(s)$ in C_i^∞, and therefore $\lim_{n\to\infty} \vec{s_n} = \vec{s}$ in $\vec{C}$. Now, $\forall n \in \mathbb{N}$, $s_n < s$ which implies $\delta(s_n,s) = \vec{d}(\vec{s_n}, \vec{s})$. Thus the sequence $(s_n)_{n\in \mathbb{N}}$ converges to s in $A^\infty/\sim$. ◊

As a corollary, we will prove that $A^*/\sim$ is dense in $A^\infty/\sim$ for the topology induced by the metric δ.

Corollary 4.9. $(A^*/\sim,\delta)$ is dense in $(A^\infty/\sim,\delta)$.

Proof. Let $s \in A^\infty/\sim$, by Proposition 3.5, there exists an increasing sequence $(s_n)_{n\in \mathbf{N}}$ of finite prefixes of s such that $s = \sqcup \{s_n, n \in \mathbf{N}\}$. Now, by Proposition 4.8, the sequence $(s_n)_{n\in \mathbf{N}}$ converges to s. ◊

Now, we will prove that with this topology, the set of infinitary traces is a complete metric space. Together with the previous corollary, this will imply that $A^\infty/\sim$ is a completion of $A^*/\sim$. But first we establish two lemmas. The first one states the relationship between the distances of three traces when they are ordered by the prefix order.

Lemma 4.10. Let $r,s,t \in \mathcal{A}$ such that $r < s < t$. Then $\delta(r,s) \leq \delta(r,t)$ and $\delta(s,t) \leq \delta(r,t)$.

Proof. We first prove the same result in A^∞ and in $\vec{C}$.

- Let $u,v,w \in A^\infty$ such that $u < v < w$.
  - if $u = v$ then $d(u,v) = 0 \leq d(u,w)$ and $d(v,w) = d(u,w)$
  - if $v = w$ then $d(u,v) = d(u,w)$ and $d(v,w) = 0 \leq d(u,w)$
  - if $u \neq v \neq w$ then $d(u,v) = 2^{-|u|} = d(u,w)$ and $d(v,w) = 2^{-|v|} < 2^{-|u|} = d(u,w)$
- Let $\vec{u}, \vec{v}, \vec{w}, \in \vec{C}$ such that $\vec{u} < \vec{v} < \vec{w}$
  - Let $i \in [m]$ be such that $\vec{d}(\vec{u},\vec{v}) = d(u_i,v_i)$.
  - We get $\vec{d}(\vec{u},\vec{v}) = d(u_i,v_i) \leq d(u_i,w_i) \leq \vec{d}(\vec{u},\vec{w})$.
  - The other inequality is proved in the same way.
- Let $r,s,t \in \mathcal{A}$ such that $r < s < t$.
  - if $r = \perp$ then $r = s = t = \perp$ and it is clear.
  - if $r \neq \perp$ and $t = \perp$ then $\delta(r,s) \leq 1 = \delta(r,t)$ and $\delta(s,t) \leq 1 = \delta(r,t)$
  - if $t \neq \perp$ then $r,s,t \in A^\infty/\sim$, since $r < s < t$, we get $\delta(r,s) = \vec{d}(\vec{r},\vec{s})$, $\delta(s,t) = \vec{d}(\vec{s},\vec{t})$, $\delta(r,t) = \vec{d}(\vec{r},\vec{t})$ and $\vec{r} < \vec{s} < \vec{t}$. Then the conclusion follows from the result in $\vec{C}$. ◊

Lemma 4.11. Let $r \in A^\infty/\sim$ and $S = \{ s \in A^\infty/\sim, \delta(s,r) \leq 2^{-n} \}$, then $\sqcap S \in S$.

Proof. Let $T = \{ s \in S, s < r \}$, we will first prove that $t = \sqcap T \in T$. Let $T_i = \Pi_i(T)$, by Proposition 3.6 we get: $\forall i \in [m]$, $t_i = \Pi_i(t) = \sqcap T_i$. Clearly, $t < r$. Now, $\forall s \in T$ we have $s < r$ thus $\delta(r,s) = \vec{d}(\vec{r},\vec{s}) \leq 2^{-n}$ which implies that $\forall i \in [m]$, $s_i[n] = r_i[n]$. Therefore $\forall i \in [m]$ we have $t_i[n] = r_i[n]$ and $\delta(t,r) = \vec{d}(\vec{t},\vec{r}) \leq 2^{-n}$. Hence $t \in T$.

Now let us prove that $\sqcap S = \sqcap T$. Since $T \subset S$, we get $\sqcap S < \sqcap T$. Conversely, let $s \in S$, $\delta(r,s) = \max(\vec{d}(\vec{r},\overrightarrow{r \sqcap s}), \vec{d}(\overrightarrow{r \sqcap s},\vec{s})) \leq 2^{-n}$. Hence, $\delta(r \sqcap s,r) = \vec{d}(\overrightarrow{r \sqcap s},\vec{r}) \leq 2^{-n}$. Then $r \sqcap s \in T$ and $\sqcap T < r \sqcap s < s$. Therefore we get $\sqcap T < \sqcap S$.

Then we obtain $\sqcap S = \sqcap T \in T \subset S$. ◊

Now, we are able to prove the main result of this section.

Theorem 4.12. $(A^{\infty}/\sim,\delta)$ and $(\mathcal{A},\delta)$ are complete metric spaces and $A^{*}/\sim$ is a dense subset of $A^{\infty}/\sim$.

Proof.
• Let $(s_n)_{n\in\mathbf{N}}$ be a Cauchy sequence in $A^{\infty}/\sim$. We set $r_n = \sqcap\{s_p, p \geq n\}$, then $(r_n)_{n\in\mathbf{N}}$ is clearly an increasing sequence which converges to its least upper bound $r = \sqcup\{r_n, n \in \mathbf{N}\}$ (Proposition 4.8). We will prove that the two sequences $(s_n)_{n\in\mathbf{N}}$ and $(r_n)_{n\in\mathbf{N}}$ are adjacent. Let $n \in \mathbf{N}$ and let N be such that $\forall\, p,q \geq N$, $\delta(s_p,s_q) \leq 2^{-n}$. We set $S = \{s \in A^{\infty}/\sim, \delta(s,s_N) \leq 2^{-n}\}$ and $t = \sqcap S$. Now, $\forall\, p \geq N$, we have $s_p \in S$ and then $t = \sqcap S < \sqcap\{s_q, q \geq p\} = r_p$. Hence $t < r_p < s_p$ and by Lemma 4.10 we get $\delta(s_p,r_p) \leq \delta(t,s_p)$. Now by Lemma 4.11 we get $t \in S$ and then $\delta(t,s_p) \leq \max(\delta(t,s_N),\delta(s_N,s_p)) \leq 2^{-n}$. Therefore, the sequences $(s_n)_{n\in\mathbf{N}}$ and $(r_n)_{n\in\mathbf{N}}$ are adjacent. Now, since $(r_n)_{n\in\mathbf{N}}$ converges to r, so does $(s_n)_{n\in\mathbf{N}}$ and we have proved that $(A^{\infty}/\sim,\delta)$ is a complete metric space.
• The case of $(\mathcal{A},\delta)$ follows now directly since $\mathcal{A} = A^{\infty}/\sim \cup \{\perp\}$ and $\perp$ is an isolated point for this topology. ◊

To conclude this section, it remains to deal with the continuity of the concatenation. Unfortunately, this point is not as satisfactory as the previous ones because the concatenation is not uniformly continuous on $A^{*}/\sim$. For instance, we consider again $A = \{a,b,c\}$ and $I = \{(a,c),(c,a)\}$, let $r_n = a^n$ and $s = b$. For $n > p$, we have $r_n.s \sqcap r_p.s = a^p$ and then $\delta(r_n.s,r_p.s) = 1$, but, $\max(\delta(r_n,r_p),\delta(s,s)) = \delta(r_n,r_p) = 2^{-p}$. This example proves that the concatenation is not uniformly continuous on $A^{*}/\sim$ and then there is no canonical way to extend it to the set of infinitary traces. Nevertheless we will prove that the concatenation is continuous on $A^{\infty}/\sim$ as soon as it is well defined, that is the result is not $\perp$. Thus the topology induced by the metric δ is as consistent as possible with our concatenation.

Proposition 4.13. Let $r,r' \in \mathcal{A}$ such that $r.r' \neq \perp$ then the concatenation is continuous in (r,r'). More precisely, $\exists\, C > 0$ such that $\forall\, s,s' \in \mathcal{A}$,

$$\delta(r,s) \leq C \text{ and } \delta(r',s') \leq 1/2 \Rightarrow \delta(rr',ss') \leq \max(\delta(r,s), \delta(r',s')).$$

Proof. The result is obvious if $\max(\delta(r,s),\delta(r',s')) = 0$. Therefore, in the following, we assume that $\max(\delta(r,s),\delta(r',s')) \neq 0$. Let $J = \{i \in [m], |r_i| < \infty\}$, let $M = 1 + \max\{|r_i|, i \in J\}$ and $C = 2^{-M}$. Let $s,s' \in \mathcal{A}$ such that $\delta(r,s) \leq C$ and $\delta(r',s') \leq 1/2$.
Fact 1: $\forall\, i \in J$, $r_i = s_i$ and $\forall\, i \notin J$, $r'_i = s'_i = \varepsilon$. Therefore $s.s' \neq \perp$.
$\vec{d}(\vec{r},\vec{s}) \leq \delta(r,s) \leq 2^{-M}$ that is $\forall\, i \in [m]$, $r_i[M] = s_i[M]$. Now, $\forall\, i \in J$, $|r_i| < M$ hence $\forall\, i \in J$, $r_i = s_i$. In the same way, $\vec{d}(\vec{r'},\vec{s'}) \leq \delta(r',s') \leq 1/2$ that is $\forall\, i \in [m]$, $r'_i[1] = s'_i[1]$. Now, $r.r' \neq \perp$ hence $\forall\, i \notin J$, $r'_i = \varepsilon$, and then $r'_i = s'_i = \varepsilon$.
Fact 2: Let $t = r \sqcap s$ and $t' = r' \sqcap s'$, we have $tt' < rr'$ and $tt' < ss'$.
• Let $S = \{x \in A^{\infty}/\sim, \delta(x,r) \leq 2^{-M}\}$, by Lemma 4.11 we get $y = \sqcap S \in S$. Since $\delta(r,s) \leq 2^{-M}$ we get $r,s \in S$ and then $y < t < r$. Hence by Lemma 4.10, we obtain $\delta(t,r) \leq \delta(y,r) \leq 2^{-M}$. By

Fact 1, this implies that $\forall\ i \in J$, $r_i = s_i = t_i$. Moreover $t'_i \le r'_i$ and $t'_i \le s'_i$ then we get $t_it'_i \le r_ir'_i$ and $t_it'_i \le s_is'_i$.

• $\delta(r',s') \le 1/2$ hence $\forall\ i \notin J$, $r'_i = s'_i = t'_i = \varepsilon$, moreover $t_i \le r_i$ and $t_i \le s_i$ therefore $t_it'_i \le r_ir'_i$ and $t_it'_i \le s_is'_i$.

Finally, let n be such that max ($\delta(r,s)$, $\delta(r',s')$) = 2^{-n}, we have:

$\forall\ i \in J$, $r_i = t_i$ and $r'_i[n] = t'_i[n]$ then $(r_ir'_i)[n] = (t_it'_i)[n]$.

$\forall\ i \notin J$, $r_i[n] = t_i[n]$ and $r'_i = t'_i = \varepsilon$ then $(r_ir'_i)[n] = (t_it'_i)[n]$.

Therefore $\delta(rr',tt') = \vec{d}(\overrightarrow{rr'},\overrightarrow{tt'}) \le 2^{-n}$. In the same way we get $\delta(ss',tt') \le 2^{-n}$. Then since δ is ultrametric we get $\delta(rr',ss') \le 2^{-n}$. ◊

5. Recognizable languages

In this section, we will study recognizable languages of infinitary traces. But first, we recall some results concerning the recognizability in the non commutative case or in the finitary partially commutative case.

The case of the free monoid A^*, is well known [Lo 83], [Ei 74]. There are several equivalent ways to define the recognizability: one can use a saturating morphism in a finite monoid, the syntactic congruence, a finite automaton, etc....

In the finitary partially commutative monoid, we can also define recognizable languages equivalently by means of a saturating morphism in a finite monoid, the syntactic congruence or a special kind of automata namely asynchronous automata [Zi 87].

Now, if we consider infinite words, some difficulties will occur. The notion of recognizability is not defined as above for general monoids. It is possible to define a recognizable language of infinite words by means of a saturating morphism in a finite monoid [PP 90], but the range of this morphism is A^* and not A^∞ as it would be with the general definition in some monoids. A. Arnold has introduced a special kind of syntactic congruence which characterizes the recognizable languages in A^ω [Ar 85], but again this congruence is defined on A^* and not on A^∞. Finally, it is also possible to define recognizable languages by means of special automata, namely Büchi or Muller automata [Bu 62], [Mu 63], [Ei 74], [PP 90].

The theory of recognizable languages has been extensively studied. We just want to recall some closure properties of the family of recognizable languages which hold in the three monoids A^*, A^∞ and M(A,I). It is closed by concatenation and by Boolean operations: union, intersection and complement.

The aim of this section is then to generalize to infinitary traces some of the results mentioned above. First we define the recognizability as for infinite words by means of morphisms or rather by means of congruences which is practically the same. Then we define the syntactic congruence of a language of infinite traces and again, as for infinite words, we prove that the recognizability is characterized by some properties of the syntactic congruence. finally, we generalize the closure properties mentioned above to the family of recognizable languages of finite and infinite traces.

In order to define the recognizability by means of congruences, we first need to define the infinite concatenation of a sequence of traces and then the infinite iteration of a trace language.

Definition 5.1. Let $(s_i)_{i \in \mathbf{N}}$ be a sequence of traces, the infinite product of this sequence is the least upper bound of its partial products, that is $s_0s_1s_2\ldots = \sqcup\{ s_0s_1\ldots s_n, n \in \mathbf{N} \}$.

Note that either the partial products are equal ultimately to $\bot$ and the infinite product is equal to $\bot$, or the partial products form an increasing sequence of traces and by Corollary 3.4 the infinite product is a trace. Note also that as soon as we use more than $|A|$ infinite traces then the infinite product is inevitably equal to $\bot$ and then an infinite product is eventually a product of finite traces. In the restricted case of finite traces we can relate the infinite product of traces to the infinite product of words. More precisely, let $(u_i)_{i \in \mathbf{N}}$ be a sequence of finite words then it is easy to verify that $\varphi(u_0)\varphi(u_1)\varphi(u_2)\ldots = \varphi(u_0u_1u_2\ldots)$.
We are now able to define the infinite concatenation of trace languages and therefore the infinite iteration of a trace language.

Definition 5.2.
i) $\forall i \in \mathbf{N}$, let $T_i \subset M(A^\infty,I)$ then we set $T_0.T_1.T_2\ldots = \{t_0t_1t_2\ldots \ / \forall i \in \mathbf{N}, t_i \in T_i\}$
ii) Let $T \subset M(A^\infty,I)$, we set $T^\omega = (T \setminus \{\varepsilon\}).(T \setminus \{\varepsilon\}).(T \setminus \{\varepsilon\})\ldots$

Now we turn to the definition of recognizable languages. As mentioned above, we will give this definition by means of congruences rather than morphisms. These two approaches are indeed equivalent but the first one gives a more uniform framework for us, since we will also deal with the syntactic congruence of infinite trace languages.

Definition 5.3. Let $\approx$ be a congruence over $M(A^*,I)$ and $T \subset M(A^\omega,I)$, for a finite trace t we denote by $[t]_\approx$ the $\approx$-class of t. We say that $\approx$ saturates T iff $\forall t \in T$

$$t = t_0t_1t_2\ldots \text{ with } t_i \in M(A^+,I) \Rightarrow [t_0]_\approx[t_1]_\approx[t_2]_\approx\ldots \subset T$$

We would like to point out that if we replace "traces" by "words" in the definition above, we obtain exactly the definition of a saturating congruence for words ([PP 90] in terms of morphisms). On the other hand, the definition of a saturating congruence given in [Ar 85] looks rather different at first glance (this definition is the translation for words of proposition 5.4 ii)). In fact, using Ramsey's theorem [Gr 81], we prove in the following proposition that both definitions are equivalent if we consider only finite[1] congruences. In [PP 90] we find a word version of this result with a direct proof which does not use Ramsey's theorem.

Proposition 5.4. Let $\approx$ be a finite congruence over $M(A^*,I)$ and $T \subset M(A^\omega,I)$. Then the following assertions are equivalent:
i) $\approx$ saturates T .
ii) $\forall r,s \in M(A^*,I)$, $[r]_\approx[s]_\approx^\omega \cap T \neq \emptyset \Rightarrow [r]_\approx[s]_\approx^\omega \subset T$
iii) $\forall r,s \in M(A^*,I)$ with $r.s \approx r$ and $s.s \approx s$, we have $[r]_\approx[s]_\approx^\omega \cap T \neq \emptyset \Rightarrow [r]_\approx[s]_\approx^\omega \subset T$

[1] A finite congruence is a congruence with a finite number of classes.

Proof.
i) $\Rightarrow$ ii) Let r,s $\in$ M(A*,I) be such that $[r]_{\approx}[s]_{\approx}^{\omega} \cap T \neq \emptyset$. Chose $(t_i)_{i \in \mathbb{N}} \subset M(A^*,I)$ such that $t_0 \approx r$, $\forall\, i \geq 1\ t_i \approx s$ and $t = t_0t_1t_2\ldots \in T$. We have $[r]_{\approx}[s]_{\approx}^{\omega} = [t_0]_{\approx}[t_1]_{\approx}[t_2]_{\approx}\ldots \subset T$.
ii) $\Rightarrow$ iii) Obvious.
iii) $\Rightarrow$ i) Let $t = t_0t_1t_2\ldots \in T$ with $t_i \in M(A^*,I)\ \forall\, i \in \mathbb{N}$. Let χ be the mapping from the pairs of $\mathbb{N}$ to $M(A^*,I)/\approx$ defined by $\chi(\{i,j\}) = [t_i\ldots t_{j-1}]_{\approx}$ if $i < j$ (according to Ramsey's terminology, χ will be called a coloring). Since the index of $\approx$ is finite, this coloring uses finitely many colors and we can apply Ramsey's theorem [Gr 81]: there exists an infinite subset of $\mathbb{N}$, say J, such that all pairs in J have the same color. Let $i_0 < i_1 < i_2\ldots$ be an enumeration of J, let $[r]_{\approx} = [t_0\ldots t_{i_1-1}]_{\approx}$ and let $[s]_{\approx}$ be the color of the pairs of J. We have:

$$s \approx t_{i_0}\ldots t_{i_1-1} \approx t_{i_1}\ldots t_{i_2-1} \approx t_{i_0}\ldots t_{i_2-1} \approx s.s$$
$$r \approx t_0\ldots t_{i_0-1}.t_{i_0}\ldots t_{i_1-1} \approx t_0\ldots t_{i_0-1}s \approx t_0\ldots t_{i_0-1}s.s \approx r.s$$
$$[t_0]_{\approx}[t_1]_{\approx}[t_2]_{\approx}\ldots = [t_0\ldots t_{i_1-1}]_{\approx}[t_{i_1}\ldots t_{i_2-1}]_{\approx}[t_{i_2}\ldots t_{i_3-1}]_{\approx}\ldots = [r]_{\approx}[s]_{\approx}^{\omega}.$$

Now, $t \in [r]_{\approx}[s]_{\approx}^{\omega} \cap T$, then $[t_0]_{\approx}[t_1]_{\approx}[t_2]_{\approx}\ldots = [r]_{\approx}[s]_{\approx}^{\omega} \subset T$. ◊

It has been proved that the recognizability of a language L of infinite words is characterized by the existence of a finite congruence which saturates L [Bu 62], [Ar 85], [PP 90]. This fact legitimizes the following definition of a recognizable language of infinite traces.

Definition 5.5. Let us denote $Rec(A^*,I)$, $Rec(A^{\omega},I)$ and $Rec(A^{\infty},I)$ the recognizable languages of $M(A^*,I)$, $M(A^{\omega},I)$ and $M(A^{\infty},I)$ respectively which are defined by:

i) $T \in Rec(A^*,I)$ iff there exists a finite congruence $\approx$ such that $[T]_{\approx} = T$.
ii) $T \in Rec(A^{\omega},I)$ iff there exists a finite congruence which saturates T.
iii) $T \in Rec(A^{\infty},I)$ iff $T = T_{fin} \cup T_{inf}$ with $T_{fin} \in Rec(A^*,I)$ and $T_{inf} \in Rec(A^{\omega},I)$.

Now we define the syntactic congruence of an infinite trace language in the same way as A. Arnold did for words in [Ar 85].

Definition 5.6. Let $T \subset M(A^{\omega},I)$ and $t,s \in M(A^*,I)$, we define the syntactic congruence of T by:

$$t \approx_T s \text{ iff } \forall\, u,v,w \in M(A^*,I), \begin{cases}(utv)w^{\omega} \in T \Leftrightarrow (usv)w^{\omega} \in T \\ u(vtw)^{\omega} \in T \Leftrightarrow u(vsw)^{\omega} \in T\end{cases}$$

Clearly, $\approx_T$ is a congruence. Moreover, we will prove that it is the coarsest congruence which saturates T, which justifies its name.

Proposition 5.7. Let $T \subset M(A^{\omega},I)$ then $\approx_T$ is the coarsest congruence which saturates T.

Proof. Let $\approx$ be a congruence which saturates T and let $t,s \in M(A^*,I)$ such that $t \approx s$.
$\forall\, u,v,w \in M(A^*,I)$, we have

$$(utv)w^{\omega} \in T \Rightarrow [utv]_{\approx}[w]_{\approx}^{\omega} \cap T \neq \emptyset \Rightarrow [utv]_{\approx}[w]_{\approx}^{\omega} \subset T \Rightarrow (usv)w^{\omega} \in T$$

and in the same way $u(vtw)^{\omega} \in T \Rightarrow u(vsw)^{\omega} \in T$. Therefore $t \approx_T s$ and $\approx_T$ is coarser than $\approx$.

◊

Now we give two characterizations of recognizable languages. The first one generalizes a well known result for finite traces and the second one generalizes the case of infinite words [Ar 85].

Theorem 5.8. Let $T \subset M(A^{\omega},I)$, the following properties are equivalent

i) $T \in Rec(A^{\omega},I)$

ii) $\varphi^{-1}(T) \in Rec(A^{\omega})$

iii) $\approx_T$ recognizes T (i.e. is finite and saturates T).

Proof. Let $\approx$ be a congruence over $M(A^*,I)$, we define the relation $\doteqdot$ on A^* in the following way:

$$\forall\, u,v \in A^*,\; u \doteqdot v \Leftrightarrow \varphi(u) \approx \varphi(v)$$

Clearly $\doteqdot$ is a congruence over A^* and $\sim_I$ is finer than $\doteqdot$. Let $T \subset M(A^*,I)$, we will denote $[T]_{\approx} = \{t \in M(A^*,I), \exists\, s \in T, s \approx t\}$ the closure of T under $\approx$. First we will investigate the relationship between $\approx$ and $\doteqdot$.

Fact 1: $\forall\, L \subset A^*$, $[\varphi(L)]_{\approx} = \varphi([L]_{\doteqdot})$.

Let $t \in M(A^*,I)$ and $v \in \varphi^{-1}(t)$, we have the following:

$t \in [\varphi(L)]_{\approx} \Leftrightarrow \exists s \in \varphi(L), s \approx t \Leftrightarrow \exists u \in L, \varphi(u) \approx t \Leftrightarrow \exists u \in L, u \doteqdot v \Leftrightarrow v \in [L]_{\doteqdot} \Leftrightarrow t \in \varphi([L]_{\doteqdot})$

Fact 2: $\approx$ and $\doteqdot$ have the same index.

Let $C = \{L \subset A^*$ such that $\varphi^{-1} \circ \varphi(L) = L\}$. The mapping $\varphi : C \to \mathcal{P}(M(A^*,I))$ is clearly a bijection with φ^{-1} as inverse: by definition of C we have $\varphi^{-1} \circ \varphi(L) = L$ for all L in C and the surjectivity of $\varphi : A^* \to M(A^*,I)$ implies that $\forall\, T \subset M(A^*,I)$, $\varphi \circ \varphi^{-1}(T) = T$.

Now, for all u in A^* we have $[u]_{\doteqdot} \in C$ (since $\sim_I$ is finer than $\doteqdot$) and $\varphi([u]_{\doteqdot}) = [\varphi(u)]_{\approx}$. Therefore φ: $A^*/\doteqdot \to M(A^*,I)/\approx$ is an injective mapping. It remains to prove that it is onto which is easy: let $t \in M(A^*,I)$ and let $u \in \varphi^{-1}(t)$, we have:

$$\varphi^{-1}([t]_{\approx}) = \varphi^{-1}([\varphi(u)]_{\approx}) = \varphi^{-1}(\varphi([u]_{\doteqdot})) = [u]_{\doteqdot}.$$

Hence φ: $A^*/\doteqdot \to M(A^*,I)/\approx$ is a bijection which proves that $\approx$ and $\doteqdot$ have the same index.

Fact 3: Let $T \subset M(A^{\omega},I)$ then $\approx$ saturates $T \Leftrightarrow \doteqdot$ saturates $\varphi^{-1}(T)$.

Let $u,v \in A^*$ and set $t = \varphi(u)$ and $s = \varphi(v)$, we have $[t]_{\approx}[s]_{\approx}{}^{\omega} = [\varphi(u)]_{\approx}[\varphi(v)]_{\approx}{}^{\omega} = \varphi([u]_{\doteqdot})\varphi([v]_{\doteqdot})^{\omega} = \varphi([u]_{\doteqdot}[v]_{\doteqdot}{}^{\omega})$ (the last equality follows easily from definitions 5.1 and 5.2).

Now, fact 3 follows from the two following points:

- $[t]_{\approx}[s]_{\approx}{}^{\omega} \cap T \neq \varnothing \Leftrightarrow \varphi([u]_{\doteqdot}[v]_{\doteqdot}{}^{\omega}) \cap T \neq \varnothing \Leftrightarrow [u]_{\doteqdot}[v]_{\doteqdot}{}^{\omega} \cap \varphi^{-1}(T) \neq \varnothing$
- $[t]_{\approx}[s]_{\approx}{}^{\omega} \subset T \Leftrightarrow \varphi([u]_{\doteqdot}[v]_{\doteqdot}{}^{\omega}) \subset T \Leftrightarrow [u]_{\doteqdot}[v]_{\doteqdot}{}^{\omega} \subset \varphi^{-1}(T)$

Fact 4: Let $T \subset M(A^{\omega},I)$ and $L = \varphi^{-1}(T)$, we have $\sim_L = \dot{\approx}_T$.

Let $x,y,u,v,w \in A^*$ and set $x' = \varphi(x)$, $y' = \varphi(y)$, $u' = \varphi(u)$, $v' = \varphi(v)$, $w' = \varphi(w)$, we have:

- $(uxv)w^{\omega} \in L \quad \Leftrightarrow \quad \varphi((uxv)w^{\omega}) \in T \quad \Leftrightarrow \quad (u'x'v')w'^{\omega} \in T$, and

• $u(vxw)^{\omega} \in L \iff \varphi(u(vxw)^{\omega}) \in T \iff u'(v'x'w')^{\omega} \in T$

Therefore we get

$$x \approx_L y \iff \forall\, u,v,w \in A^*, \begin{cases} (uxv)w^{\omega} \in L \iff (uyv)w^{\omega} \in L \\ u(vxw)^{\omega} \in L \iff u(vyw)^{\omega} \in L \end{cases}$$

$$\iff \forall\, u',v',w' \in M(A^*,I), \begin{cases} (u'x'v')w'^{\omega} \in T \iff (u'y'v')w'^{\omega} \in T \\ u'(v'x'w')^{\omega} \in T \iff u'(v'y'w')^{\omega} \in T \end{cases}$$

$$\iff x' \approx_T y'$$

$$\iff x \mathrel{\dot{\approx}_T} y$$

We are now able to prove the theorem

i) $\Rightarrow$ ii) Let T be in $Rec(A^{\omega},I)$ and let $\approx$ be a finite congruence which saturates T then $\dot{\approx}$ is a finite congruence which saturates $\varphi^{-1}(T)$ hence $\varphi^{-1}(T) \in Rec(A^{\omega})$.

ii) $\Rightarrow$ iii) Let $T \subset M(A^{\omega},I)$ such that $L = \varphi^{-1}(T) \in Rec(A^{\omega})$ then $\approx_L = \dot{\approx}_T$ is finite and saturates L ([Ar 85]) therefore $\approx_T$ is finite and saturates T.

iii) $\Rightarrow$ i) is clear ◊

An important consequence of the first characterization of $Rec(A^{\omega},I)$ is the following.

Corollary 5.9.

i) $T \in Rec(A^{\infty},I) \iff \varphi^{-1}(T) \in Rec(A^{\infty})$

ii) $Rec(A^{\omega},I)$ and $Rec(A^{\infty},I)$ are closed under the Boolean operations: union, intersection and complement.

Proof. This result follows from

1) $T \in Rec(A^*, I) \iff \varphi^{-1}(T) \in Rec(A^*)$ [CP 85]

2) $T \in Rec(A^{\omega}, I) \iff \varphi^{-1}(T) \in Rec(A^{\omega})$ (Theorem 5.8)

3) $Rec(A^{\omega})$ is closed by union, intersection and complement [Bu 62], [PP 90].

4) $\varphi^{-1}(T \cup S) = \varphi^{-1}(T) \cup \varphi^{-1}(S)$; $\varphi^{-1}(T \cap S) = \varphi^{-1}(T) \cap \varphi^{-1}(S)$; $\varphi^{-1}(T^c) = (\varphi^{-1}(T))^c$ ◊

Finally, we prove that $Rec(A^{\infty},I)$ is closed by concatenation. In the restricted case of finite traces, this result was proved in [CP 85] and [Oc 85].

Proposition 5.10. Let $R,S \in Rec(A^{\infty},I)$ then $T = (R\,.\,S) \setminus \{\bot\} \in Rec(A^{\infty},I)$.

Proof. We will prove that $L = \varphi^{-1}(T)$ is a recognizable language of A^{∞}. Let A_1 and A_2 be two disjoint copies of A and let $B = A_1 \cup A_2$, we will use the following morphisms:

$$\sigma_1 : A^{\infty} \to A_1{}^{\infty};\ a \mapsto a_1 \qquad \sigma_2 : A^{\infty} \to A_2{}^{\infty};\ a \mapsto a_2 \qquad \sigma : B^{\infty} \to A^{\infty};\ a_i \mapsto a$$

Let $M = \sigma_1(\varphi^{-1}(R))$, $N = \sigma_2(\varphi^{-1}(S))$, $K = B^{\infty} \setminus \bigcup_{(a,b) \in D} B^*\sigma_2(b)B^*\sigma_1(a)B^{\infty}$

and $L' = (M \sqcup\!\sqcup N) \cap K$.[1]

Using some classical results on words[2], we can state that M, N, K and L' are recognizable languages of B^∞, therefore $\sigma(L')$ is a recognizable language of A^∞. Now, it remains to prove that $\sigma(L') = L$.

• Let $w' \in L'$, there exist $r \in R$, $s \in S$, $u' \in \sigma_1(\varphi^{-1}(r))$, $v' \in \sigma_2(\varphi^{-1}(s))$ such that $w' \in u' \sqcup\!\sqcup v'$. First let us see that r.s is well defined. Let $a \in$ alphinf(r) and $b \in$ alph(s), $|w'|_{a_1} = |u'|_{a_1} = |r|_a = \infty$ and $|w'|_{b_2} = |v'|_{b_2} = |s|_b > 0$, hence since $w' \in K$ we get $(a,b) \notin D$. Therefore alphinf(r) $\times$ alph(s) $\subset I$ and $r.s \neq \perp$.

Now, let us show that $w = \sigma(w') \in \varphi^{-1}(r.s) \subset L$. Recall that $C_1, C_2, \ldots C_m$ is a covering by cliques of (A,D). $\forall i \in [m]$, we denote Π'_i the projection from B^∞ onto $(\sigma_1(C_i) \cup \sigma_2(C_i))^\infty$. Since $w' \in K$, we get $\Pi'_i(w') = \Pi'_i(u').\Pi'_i(v')$. Then $\Pi_i(w) = \sigma(\Pi'_i(w')) = \sigma(\Pi'_i(u')).\sigma(\Pi'_i(v')) = \Pi_i(\sigma(u')).\Pi_i(\sigma(v')) = \Pi_i(r).\Pi_i(s) = \Pi_i(r.s)$. Therefore $w \in \varphi^{-1}(r.s)$.

• Conversely, let $w \in L$ and let $r \in R$, $s \in S$ be such that $w \in \varphi^{-1}(r.s)$.

Note that $\forall a \in A$, $|r|_a = \infty \Rightarrow |s|_a = 0$ ($r.s \neq \perp$) and $|w|_a = |r.s|_a = |r|_a + |s|_a$. Let w' be the word obtained from w in the following way: $\forall a \in A$, we replace in w the first $|r|_a$ occurrences of a by a_1 and the next $|s|_a$ occurrences of a by a_2. It is clear that $\sigma(w') = w$, now let us prove that $w' \in L'$.

- Let $(a,b) \in D$ and let C_i be a clique such that $a,b \in C_i$.

Since $w \in \varphi^{-1}(r.s)$ we have $\Pi_i(w) = \Pi_i(r.s) = \Pi_i(r).\Pi_i(s)$. Now, by definition of w' we get $\Pi'_i(w') = \sigma_1(\Pi_i(r)).\sigma_2(\Pi_i(s))$. Hence $w' \notin B^*\sigma_2(b)B^*\sigma_1(a)B^\infty$ and then $w' \in K$.

- Let u' and v' be the projections of w' on A_1^∞ and A_2^∞. By definition we have $w' \in u' \sqcup\!\sqcup v'$ and it remains to prove that $u' \in M$ and $v' \in N$.

$\forall i \in [m]$, we have $\Pi'_i(w') \in \Pi'_i(u') \sqcup\!\sqcup \Pi'_i(v')$ and we have just proved that $\Pi'_i(w') = \sigma_1(\Pi_i(r)).\sigma_2(\Pi_i(s))$. Therefore $\Pi'_i(u') = \sigma_1(\Pi_i(r))$ and $\Pi'_i(v') = \sigma_2(\Pi_i(s))$ that is $\sigma(u') \in \varphi^{-1}(r)$ and $\sigma(v') \in \varphi^{-1}(s)$. Then we get $u' \in M$ and $v' \in N$. ◊

6 Conclusion

Finally, we would like to give some alternative to the construction of the infinitary trace monoid. The main criticism we could formulate against the choice presented here, is that the concatenation is only partially defined. However, we think that this is the best definition we can find within the set of infinitary traces exhibited here. Therefore, in order to have a concatenation fully defined, one has probably to consider much more traces. Intuitively, one has to keep in some traces actions with an infinite past, for instance if the actions a and b are dependent, then the action b in $a^\omega b$ has an infinite past. It is possible to make such an attempt using as

---

[1] $M \sqcup\!\sqcup N$ denotes the shuffle of M and N, that is the set of words w such that the projection on A_1^∞ (resp. A_2^∞) is a member of M (resp. N).

[2] For words, we have $Rat(A^\infty) = Rec(A^\infty)$ and this family is closed by complement, intersection, shuffle and morphism.

sequential set something like $(A^{\infty})^{\infty}$ but we have rejected this attempt mainly because it is complex and because we do not see what could be its interpretation.

The topological approach gives another alternative. One has to find a metric on $A^*/\sim$ such that the concatenation is uniformly continuous. Then we would consider the completion of $A^*/\sim$ as the set of infinitary traces and the concatenation would admit a unique continuous extension to this completion. A very recent work by V. Diekert follows this way successfully [Di 90].

Secondly, we would like to mention some research direction concerning the recognizability. First, it is easy to define the family of rational languages of finite and infinite traces: it is the least family which contains the empty set, the sets $\{a\}$, $a \in A$ and which is closed by concatenation, union, iteration and infinite iteration. In the free monoids A^* and A^{∞}, Kleene's theorem states that a language is recognizable iff it is rational. This is false in the finitary trace monoid, it only holds that any recognizable language is rational. This result can probably be extended to infinite traces. Since the family of recognizable languages is closed by union and concatenation, the failure of Kleene's theorem for traces is due to the iteration. A good deal of work has been done to find sufficient conditions on a recognizable language to ensure that its iteration is still recognizable [CM 85], [Me 86], [Ro 87]. On the other hand E. Ochmanski has defined in [Oc 85] a variant of the iteration, namely the concurrent iteration and has proved that a trace language is recognizable iff it is co-rational where the family of co-rational languages is defined as the family of rational languages with the concurrent iteration instead of the iteration. An interesting problem is then to generalize these results to infinite traces. This problem is probably non trivial since the methods used to prove these results do not generalize to infinite traces.

Another direction is to introduce automata on infinite traces. For infinite words, two acceptance conditions are known: Büchi's one and Muller's one [Bu 62], [Mu 63], [Ei 74], [PP 90]. For finite traces, we know that a language is recognizable iff it is recognized with an asynchronous automaton [Zi 87] or with an asynchronous cellular automaton [Zi 89], [CMZ 89]. An interesting problem is then to generalize Büchi's and Muller's acceptance conditions to asynchronous automata in order to characterize the recognizable languages of infinite traces.

7. References

[Ar 85] A. ARNOLD, "A syntactic congruence for rational ω-languages", Theoretical Computer Science 39, p. 333-335, 1985.

[AR 88] I.J. AALBERSBERG and G. ROZENBERG, "Theory of traces", Theoretical Computer Science 60, p. 1-82, 1988.

[AW 86] I.J. AALBERSBERG and E. WELZL, "Traces languages defined by regular string languages", RAIRO Theoretical Informatics and Applications 20, p. 103-119, 1986.

[BMS 89] A. BERTONI, G. MAURI and N. SABADINI, "Membership problem for regular and context-free trace languages", Information and Computation 82, p. 135-150, 1989.

[BMP 89] P. BONIZZONI, G. MAURI and G. PIGHIZZINI, "About infinite traces", Proceedings of the ASMICS Workshop on Partially Commutative Monoids, Tech. Rep. TUM-I 9002, Technische Universität München, 1989.

[Bü 62] J.R. BUCHI, "On a decision method in restricted second order arithmetic", Proc. Internat. Congress on Logic, Methodology and Philosophy (Standford University Press), p. 1-11, 1962.

[CF 69] P. CARTIER and D. FOATA, "Problèmes combinatoires de commutation et réarrangements", Lecture Notes in Math. 85, 1969.

[Ch 86] C. CHOFFRUT, "Free partially commutative monoids", Tech. Rep. 86-20, LITP, Université Paris 6, France, 1986.

[CM 85] R. CORI and Y. METIVIER, "Recognizable subsets of some partially abelian monoids", Theoretical Computer Science 35, p. 179-189, 1985.

[CMZ 89] R. CORI, Y. METIVIER and W. ZIELONKA, "Asynchronous mappings and asynchronous cellular automata", Tech. Rep. 89-97, LaBRI, Université de Bordeaux, France, 1990.

[CP 85] R. CORI and D. PERRIN, "Automates et commutations partielles", RAIRO Theoretical Informatics and Applications 19, p. 21-32, 1985.

[Di 90] V. DIEKERT, "Combinatorics on traces", to appear in Lecture Notes in Computer Science.

[Di 90] V. DIEKERT, "On the concatenation of infinite traces", Tech. Rep. TUM, Technische Universität München, 1990.

[Du 86] C. DUBOC, "Commutations dans les monoïdes libres: un cadre théorique pour l'étude du parallélisme", Thèse, Université de Rouen, France, 1986.

[Du 86] C. DUBOC, "Mixed product and asynchronous automata", Theoretical Computer Science 48, p. 183-199, 1986.

[Ei 74] S. EILENBERG, "Automata, Languages and Machines", Academic Press, New York, 1974.

[Ga 87] P. GASTIN, "Un modèle distribué", Thèse, LITP, Université Paris 7, France, 1987.

[Ga 88] P. GASTIN, "Un modèle asynchrone pour les systèmes distribués", Tech. Rep. 88-59, LITP, Université Paris 6, France, 1988, to appear in T.C.S.

[Ga 89] P. GASTIN, "Infinite traces - Recognizable sets of infinite traces", Proceedings of the ASMICS Workshop on Partially Commutative Monoids, Tech. Rep. TUM-I 9002, Technische Universität München, 1989.

[Gr 81] R. L. GRAHAM, "Rudiments of Ramsey theory ", Regional conference series in mathematics 45, 1981.

[GR 90] P. GASTIN and B.ROZOY, "The Poset of infinitary traces", Tech. Rep. 90-24, LITP, Université Paris 6, France, 1990.

[HR 86] H.J. HOOGEBOOM and G. ROZENBERG, "Infinitary languages: basic theory and applications to concurrent systems", Lecture Notes in Computer Science 224, p. 266-342, 1986.

[Kw 89] M.Z. KWIATKOWSKA, "On infinitary trace languages", Tech. Rep. 31, University of Leicester, England, 1989.

[Lo 83] M. LOTHAIRE, "Combinatorics on words", Addison Wesley, 1983.

[Ma 77] A. MAZURKIEWICZ, "Concurrent program Schemes and their interpretations", Aarhus University, DAIMI Rep. PB 78, 1977.

[Ma 84] A. MAZURKIEWICZ, "Trace, histories, graphs: instances of a process monoid", Lecture Notes in Computer Science 176, p. 115-133, 1984.

[Ma 86] A. MAZURKIEWICZ, "Trace theory", Advanced Course on Petri Nets, Lecture Notes in Computer Science 255, p. 279-324, 1986.

[Me 86] Y. METIVIER, "Une condition suffisante de reconnaissabilité dans un monoïde partiellement commutatif", RAIRO Theoretical Informatics and Applications 20, p. 121-127, 1986.

[Me 86] Y. METIVIER, "On recognizable subsets in free partially commutative monoids", ICALP 1986, Lecture Notes in Computer Science 226, p. 254-264, 1986.

[Mu 63] D.E. MULLER, "Infinite sequences and finite machines", Proc. 4th IEEE Ann. Symp. on Switching Circuit Theory and Logical Design, p. 3-16, 1963.

[Oc 85] E. OCHMANSKI, "Regular behaviour of concurrent systems", Bulletin of EATCS 27, p. 56-67, October 1985.

[Pe 84] D. PERRIN, "Recent results on automata and infinite words", Lecture Notes in Computer Science 176, p. 134-148, 1984.

[Pe 89] D. PERRIN, "Partial commutations", ICALP 89, Lecture Notes in Computer Science 372, p. 637-651, 1989.

[PP 90] D.PERRIN and J.E. PIN, "Mots Infinis", Tech. Rep., LITP, Université Paris 6, France, 1990. Book to appear.

[Ro 86] G. ROZENBERG, "Behaviour of elementary net systems", Advanced Course on Petri Nets, Lecture Notes in Computer Science 254, p. 60-94, 1986.

[Ro 87] B. ROZOY, "On the recognizability of X^* in trace monoids", Tech. Rep. 87-34, LITP, Université Paris 6, France, 1987.

[RT 87] B. ROZOY and P.S. THIAGARAJAN, "Trace monoids and event structures", Tech. Rep. 87-47, LITP, Université Paris 6, France, 1987, to appear in Theoretical Computer Science.

[Sa 87] J. SAKAROVITCH, "On regular trace languages", Theoretical Computer Science 52, p. 59-75, 1987.

[Th 88] W. THOMAS, "Automata on infinite objects", to appear in Handbook of Theoretical Computer Science (J.V. Leeuwen, Ed.), North-Holland, Amsterdam.

[Zi 87] W. ZIELONKA, "Notes on finite asynchronous automata and trace languages", RAIRO Theoretical Informatics and Applications 21, p. 99-135, 1987.

[Zi 89] W. ZIELONKA, "Safe execution of recognizable trace languages by asynchronous automata", Lecture Notes in Computer Science 363, p. 278-289, 1989.

Equivalences and Refinement

Rob J. van Glabbeek
Institut für Informatik der TU München
Postfach 20 24 20, D-8000 München 2

Ursula Goltz
Gesellschaft für Mathematik und Datenverarbeitung
Postfach 1240, D-5205 Sankt Augustin 1

Abstract

We investigate equivalence notions for concurrent systems. We consider "linear time" approaches where the system behaviour is characterised as the set of possible runs as well as "branching time" approaches where the conflict structure of systems is taken into account. We show that the usual interleaving equivalences, and also the equivalences based on *steps* (multisets of concurrently executed actions) are not preserved by refinement of actions. We prove that "linear time" partial order semantics, where causality in runs is explicit, is invariant under refinement. Finally, we consider various bisimulation equivalences based on partial orders and show that the strongest one of them is preserved by refinement whereas the others are not.

Notes This is an extended and updated version of our paper [GG a]. The extension consists of considering equivalences and refinement for the domain of flow event structures — instead of the subdomain of prime event structures — and allowing also infinite refinements and refinements with conflicts. This more general refinement operation was introduced in [GG b], however equivalences were not considered there. The results of this paper are also contained in [van Glabbeek b]. The work presented here has partly been carried out within the Esprit Basic Research Action 3148 (DEMON) and the Sonderforschungsbereich 342 of the TU München.

1 Introduction

A large body of research is devoted to equivalence notions for concurrent systems. Most of the equivalence notions currently being considered are based on a semantics where concurrency is modelled by arbitrary interleaving of atomic actions. In [Pratt] and in [CDP] it is pointed out that this approach has a severe drawback. It leads to complications when changing the level of atomicity of events; "...we would like a theory of processes to be just as usable for events having a duration or structure, where a single event can be atomic from one point of view and compound from another" ([Pratt]). In [CDP], an example is given, showing that the usual interleaving equivalences are not invariant under refinement of actions when this is simply modelled by textual replacement. Both [Pratt] and [CDP] claim that modelling concurrency by expressing causal dependencies explicitly using partial orders [Petri] could help to solve this problem. [CDP] sketches a proof of this claim that is valid for "linear time" partial order semantics, where the set of all possible executions of a system is considered, without taking into account where conflicts are resolved. This is also the model considered by Pratt.

In this paper, we will consider various equivalence notions based on interleaving of actions, interleaving of steps (multisets of concurrently executable actions), and on partial orders. We will discuss "linear time" semantics, but we will also take the conflict structure of systems into account by considering various forms of bisimulation ("branching time" semantics). We will show that the known equivalences based on steps are not invariant under action refinement. We will rephrase in our framework the proof–sketch of [CDP], showing that "linear time" partial order semantics is indeed robust against changing the level of atomicity. Then we consider several equivalence notions based on "branching time" partial order semantics. We give examples, showing that pomset bisimulation equivalence [BC a] and the NMS partial ordering equivalence suggested in [DDM a] are not preserved by refinement of atomic actions. We also show that NMS partial ordering equivalence does not imply pomset bisimulation and vice versa; these notions are incomparable. Finally we show that a stronger equivalence notion, first suggested in [TRH] under the name BS-bisimulation, is indeed preserved by refinement. [DDM c] shows that this equivalence fits smoothly in their NMS framework; [Vaandrager] shows that this equivalence coincides with bisimulation equivalence on causal trees [DD a].

We do not intend to advocate any particular equivalence notion here, the purpose of this investigation is to find out about the consequences of the different approaches. There will certainly be a tradeoff between simplicity and distinguishing power. We just want to illustrate that the appropriate notion has to be chosen carefully with regard to the questions considered.

2 Refinement of actions in prime event structures

In this paper we consider systems that are capable of performing actions from a given set *Act* of action names. By an action we understand any activity which is considered as a conceptual entity on a chosen level of abstraction. As our model for this kind of systems we have chosen labelled event structures here; we could have chosen other models like Petri nets or behaviour structures [TRH], but in these models it would be more cumbersome to define the desired refinement operation. We will not distinguish external and internal actions here; we do not consider abstraction by hiding of actions.

In this section, we show how to refine actions in the most simple form of event structures, prime event structures with a binary conflict relation [NPW]. Furthermore, we motivate our move to more general structures in the next section because of the limitations of this approach.

We will frequently give process algebra terms for our examples, to make them easier to understand: + will denote choice (as in CCS), | will denote parallel composition (without communication), $a, b, \ldots \in Act$ denote actions, and ; denotes a general sequential composition operator. Semicolons in expressions $a; P$ will be omitted. However, this notation is only used for intuition; formally our results are established for event structures.

2.1 Definition

A *(labelled) prime event structure (over an alphabet Act)* is a 4–tuple $\mathcal{E} = (E, \leq, \#, l)$ where

- E is a set of *events*,
- $\leq \subseteq E \times E$ is a partial order (the *causality relation*) satisfying the *principle of finite causes:*

$$\forall e \in E : \{d \in E | d \leq e\} \text{ is finite,}$$

- $\# \subseteq E \times E$ is an irreflexive, symmetric relation (the *conflict relation*) satisfying the *principle of conflict heredity:*

$$\forall d, e, f \in E : d \leq e \wedge d \# f \Rightarrow e \# f,$$

- $l : E \rightarrow Act$ is a *labelling function.*

The components of a prime event structure $\mathcal{E}$ will be denoted by $E_\mathcal{E}, \leq_\mathcal{E}, \#_\mathcal{E}$ and $l_\mathcal{E}$. If clear from the context, the index $\mathcal{E}$ will be omitted. As usual, we write $d < e$ for $d \leq e \wedge d \neq e$, etc.

A prime event structure represents a concurrent system in the following way: action names $a \in Act$ represent actions the system might perform, an event $e \in E$ labelled with a represents an occurrence of a during a possible run of the system, $d < e$ means that d is a prerequisite for e and $d\#e$ means that d and e cannot happen both in the same run.

Causal independence (*concurrency*) of events is expressed by the derived relation $co \subseteq E \times E$: $d \; co \; e$ iff $\neg(d < e \vee e < d \vee d\#e)$. By definition, $<, >, \#$ and co form a partition of $E \times E$.

Throughout the paper, we assume a fixed set Act of action names as labelling set. Let $\mathbb{E}_{prime}$ denote the domain of prime event structures labelled over Act.

A prime event structure $\mathcal{E}$ is *finite* if $E_\mathcal{E}$ is finite; $\mathcal{E}$ is *conflict-free* if $\#_\mathcal{E} = \emptyset$. O denotes the empty event structure $(\emptyset, \emptyset, \emptyset, \emptyset)$.

For $X \subseteq E_\mathcal{E}$, the *restriction of $\mathcal{E}$ to X* is defined as

$$\mathcal{E}\lceil X = (X, \leq \cap (X \times X), \# \cap (X \times X), l\lceil X).$$

Two prime event structures $\mathcal{E}$ and $\mathcal{F}$ are *isomorphic* ($\mathcal{E} \cong \mathcal{F}$) iff there exists a bijection between their sets of events preserving $\leq, \#$ and labelling. Generally, we will not distinguish isomorphic event structures.

Isomorphism classes of conflict-free prime event structures are called *pomsets* [Pratt]. Pomsets generated by certain subsets of events may be considered as possible "executions" of the system represented by the event structure. The partial order between action occurrences then represents causal dependencies in the execution. Subsets of events representing executions (called *configurations*) have to be conflict-free; furthermore they must be left-closed with respect to $\leq$ (all prerequisites for any event occurring in the "execution" must also occur). It is assumed that in a finite period only finitely many actions are performed. We will consider only finite executions when describing the behaviour of systems. So, unlike [Winskel], we require configurations to be finite. This does not cause a loss of expressiveness, since the infinite configurations of an event structure are completely determined by the finite ones.

2.2 Definition

i. A subset $X \subseteq E$ of events in a prime event structure $\mathcal{E}$ is *left-closed* in $\mathcal{E}$ iff, for all $d, e \in E$, $e \in X \wedge d \leq e \Rightarrow d \in X$.
   X is *conflict-free in* $\mathcal{E}$ iff $\mathcal{E}\lceil X$ is conflict-free.

ii. A subset $X \subseteq E$ will be called a *(finite) configuration* of a prime event structure $\mathcal{E}$ iff X is finite, left-closed and conflict-free in $\mathcal{E}$. $Conf(\mathcal{E})$ denotes the set of all configurations of $\mathcal{E}$. A configuration $X \in Conf(\mathcal{E})$ is called *complete* iff $\forall d \in E : d \notin X \Rightarrow \exists e \in X$ with $d\#e$.

Configurations may be considered as possible states of the system; they determine the remaining behaviour of the system as being the set of all events which have not yet occurred and are not excluded because of conflicts. Note that a configuration X is complete iff it is maximal, i.e. $X \subseteq Y \in Conf(\mathcal{E})$ implies $X = Y$.

2.3 Example

Let us consider the event structure $\mathcal{E}$ corresponding to the expression $a|b + ab$.

In graphical representations, only immediate conflicts — not the inherited conflicts — are indicated. The $<$-relation is represented by arcs, omitting those derivable by transitivity. Furthermore, instead of events only their labels are displayed; if a label occurs twice it represents two different events. Thus these pictures determine event structures only up to isomorphism.

Following these conventions, $\mathcal{E}$ is represented as

$$\begin{array}{l} a \\ \# \\ a \rightarrow b \\ \# \\ b \end{array} \qquad .$$

The possible executions of $\mathcal{E}$ are represented by the pomsets

$$\emptyset,\ a,\ b,\ \begin{smallmatrix} a \\ b \end{smallmatrix} \text{ and } a \longrightarrow b.$$

$\begin{smallmatrix} a \\ b \end{smallmatrix}$ and $a \longrightarrow b$ correspond to complete configurations.

We will now define a refinement operation substituting actions by finite, conflict-free, non-empty event structures. We will later explain why we have to restrict to finite and conflict-free refinements of actions, and why we exclude empty refinements.

A refinement function will be a function *ref* specifiying, for each action a, an event structure $ref(a)$ which is to be substituted for a. Interesting refinements (and also the refinements in our examples) will mostly refine only certain actions, hence replace most actions by themselves. However, for uniformity (and for simplicity in proofs) we consider all actions to be refined.

Given an event structure $\mathcal{E}$ and a refinement function *ref*, we construct the refined event structure $ref(\mathcal{E})$ as follows. Each event e labelled by a is replaced by a disjoint copy, $\mathcal{E}_e$, of $ref(a)$. The causality and conflict structure is inherited from $\mathcal{E}$: every event which was causally before e will be causally before all events of $\mathcal{E}_e$, all events which causally followed e will causally follow all the events of $\mathcal{E}_e$, and all events in conflict with e will be in conflict with all the events of $\mathcal{E}_e$.

Graphically, the idea may be sketched as follows.

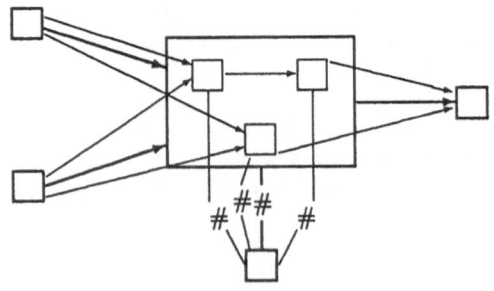

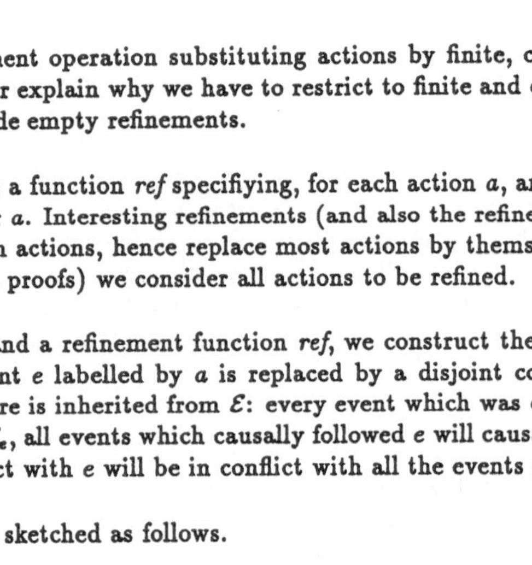

2.4 Definition

(i) A function $ref: Act \rightarrow \boldsymbol{E}_{prime} - \{O\}$ is called a *refinement function (for prime event structures)* if $\forall a \in Act$: $ref(a)$ is finite and conflict–free.

(ii) Let $\mathcal{E} \in \boldsymbol{E}_{prime}$ and let ref be a refinement function.
Then $ref(\mathcal{E})$ is the prime event structure defined by
- $E_{ref(\mathcal{E})} = \{(e,e') | e \in E_{\mathcal{E}}, e' \in E_{ref(l_{\mathcal{E}}(e))}\}$,
- $(d,d') \leq_{ref(\mathcal{E})} (e,e')$ iff $d <_{\mathcal{E}} e$ or $(d = e \wedge d' \leq_{ref(l_{\mathcal{E}}(d))} e')$,
- $(d,d') \#_{ref(\mathcal{E})} (e,e')$ iff $d \#_{\mathcal{E}} e$,
- $l_{ref(\mathcal{E})}(e,e') = l_{ref(l_{\mathcal{E}}(e))}(e')$.

We show that refinement is a well–defined operation on prime event structures, even when isomorphic prime event structures are identified.

2.5 Proposition

(i) If $\mathcal{E} \in \boldsymbol{E}_{prime}$ and ref is a refinement function then $ref(\mathcal{E})$ is a prime event structure indeed.

(ii) If $\mathcal{E} \in \boldsymbol{E}_{prime}$ and ref, ref' are refinement functions with $ref(a) \cong ref'(a)$ for all $a \in Act$ then $ref(\mathcal{E}) \cong ref'(\mathcal{E})$.

(iii) If $\mathcal{E}, \mathcal{F} \in \boldsymbol{E}_{prime}$, ref is a refinement function and $\mathcal{E} \cong \mathcal{F}$ then $ref(\mathcal{E}) \cong ref(\mathcal{F})$.

Proof Straightforward. ■

2.6 Example

Consider the design of a sender which reads data and sends them to a receiver. For simplicity, we assume that the sender sends only once. (For representing infinite behaviours we need event structures with infinite sets of events.)

A first description of the system is given below.

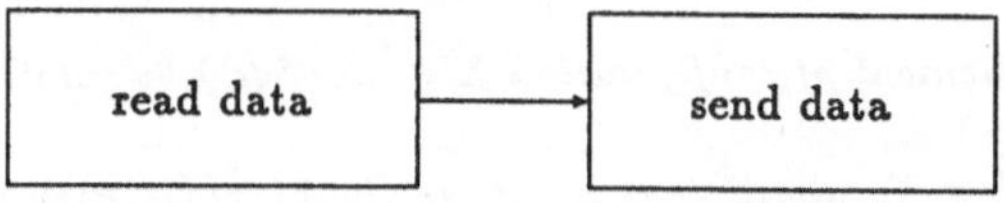

On a slightly less abstract description level the action "send data" might turn out to consist of two parts "prepare sending" and "carry out sending", to be executed sequentially.

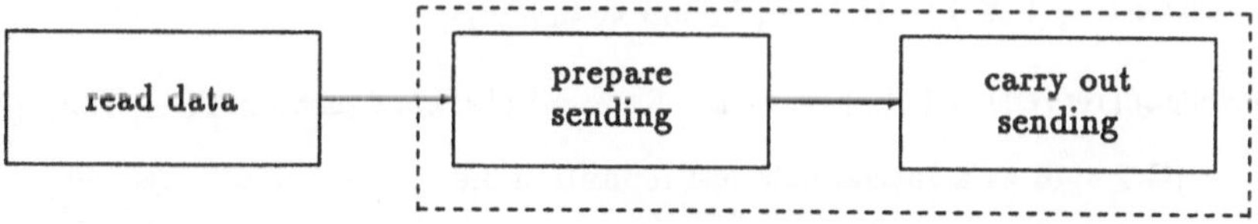

Then the action "prepare sending" may be decomposed in two independent activities "prepare data for transmission" and "get permission to send", to be executed on different processors.

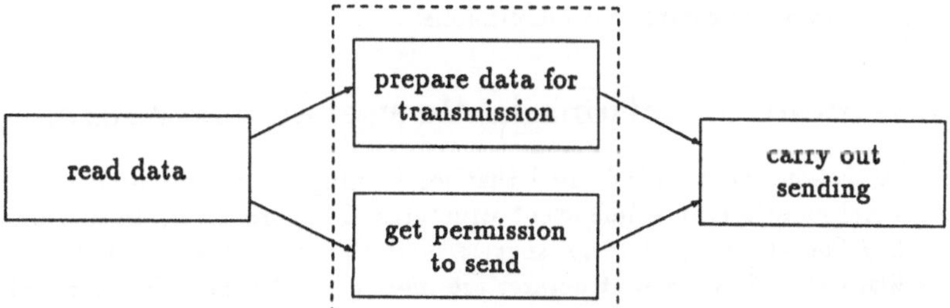

Now assume that in the next refinement step we would allow data to be received from two alternative channels. This would require to refine the action "read data" by two alternative actions, to be represented by two conflicting events. This is not possible in our framework up to now.

The reason that we can only refine actions by conflict–free event structures is the axiom of conflict heredity and the notion of configuration in prime event structures. They imply that any event will always occur with a unique history (in terms of its causal predecessors).

Consider e.g. $\mathcal{E} = \begin{matrix} a \\ \downarrow \\ b \end{matrix}$ Replacing a by $c\#d$ would require to duplicate the event labelled by b in some way, since b should then occur either caused by c or by d. Since this would lead to a complicated definition, we will consider a more general form of event structures that does not require duplication in Section 3.

The restriction to refinement of actions by finite event structures is necessary to ensure that the resulting event structure will obey the axiom of finite causes. In the more general model we will consider later, we will not assume this axiom, and this will allow also refinements by infinite behaviours.

The restriction to non–empty refinements is motivated by conceptual reasons rather than technical ones. As argued in [GG b], refinements where actions are replaced by the empty event structure (forgetful refinements) can drastically change the behaviour of concurrent systems; they can not be explained by a change in the level of abstraction at which systems are regarded.

Finally, we show how the behaviour of the refined event structure $ref(\mathcal{E})$ is determined by the behaviour of $\mathcal{E}$ and by the behaviour of the event structures which are substituted for actions.

2.7 Proposition

Let $\mathcal{E} \in \boldsymbol{E}_{prime}$, let ref be a refinement function.

We call $\tilde{X}$ *a refinement of configuration* $X \in Conf(\mathcal{E})$ *by* ref iff

- $\tilde{X} = \bigcup_{e \in X} \{e\} \times X_e$ where $\forall e \in X : X_e \in Conf(ref(l_{\mathcal{E}}(e))) - \{\emptyset\}$,

- $e \in busy(\tilde{X}) \Longrightarrow e$ maximal in X with respect to $\leq_{\mathcal{E}}$
  where $busy(\tilde{X}) := \{e \in X \mid X_e \text{ not complete}\}$.

Then $Conf(ref(\mathcal{E})) = \{\tilde{X} \mid \tilde{X}$ is a refinement of a configuration $X \in Conf(\mathcal{E})\}$.

Proof [GG a] or as a special case of Proposition 3.9. ■

Hence the configurations of $ref(\mathcal{E})$ are exactly those configurations which are refinements of configurations of $\mathcal{E}$. A refinement of a configuration X of $\mathcal{E}$ is obtained by replacing each event e in X by a non–empty configuration X_e of $ref(l_{\mathcal{E}}(e))$. Events which are causally necessary for other events in X may only be replaced by complete configurations.

3 Refinement of actions in flow event strucures

In the previous section, we have indicated that for refining actions by event structures with conflicts more general models than prime event structures are appropriate. In [BC b] a form of event structures, called *flow event structures*, is suggested which is particularly suited for giving semantics to languages like CCS. Flow event structures are more general than prime event structures in the following sense: they do not assume conflict heredity and the axiom of finite causes, they allow inconsistent (self-conflicting) events and the causality relation is not required to be transitive and may even contain (syntactic) cycles. This makes it very easy to define operations like parallel composition and restriction, and we will show here that they are also well suited to deal with refinement of actions.

For defining a general refinement operator also other generalisations of prime event structures are being considered; we will discuss these approaches in the conclusion.

3.1 Definition

A *(labelled) flow event structure (over an alphabet Act)* is a 4-tuple $\mathcal{E} = (E, \prec, \#, l)$ where

- E is a set of *events*,
- $\prec \subseteq E \times E$ is an irreflexive relation, the *flow relation*,
- $\# \subseteq E \times E$ is a symmetric relation, the *conflict relation*,
- $l : E \rightarrow Act$ is the *labelling function*.

Let $\boldsymbol{E}$ denote the domain of flow event structures labelled over Act. The components of $\mathcal{E} \in \boldsymbol{E}$ will be denoted by $E_{\mathcal{E}}, \prec_{\mathcal{E}}, \#_{\mathcal{E}}$ and $l_{\mathcal{E}}$. The index $\mathcal{E}$ will be omitted if clear from the context. $\mathcal{E}$ is *conflict-free* if $\#_{\mathcal{E}} = \emptyset$. For $X \subseteq E_{\mathcal{E}}$, $\mathcal{E}\lceil X = (X, \prec_{\mathcal{E}} \lceil X, \#_{\mathcal{E}}\lceil X, l_{\mathcal{E}}\lceil X)$ is the *restriction of $\mathcal{E}$ to X*.

Two flow event structures $\mathcal{E}$ and $\mathcal{F}$ are *isomorphic* ($\mathcal{E} \cong \mathcal{F}$) iff there exists a bijection between their sets of events preserving $\prec, \#$ and labelling.

The interpretation of the conflict and the flow relation is formalised by defining configurations of flow event structures. Configurations must be conflict free; in particular, self-conflicting events will never occur in any configuration. $d \prec e$ will mean that d is a *possible immediate cause* for e. For an event to occur it is necessary that a *complete* non-conflicting set of its causes has occurred. Here a set of causes is complete if for any cause which is not contained there is a conflicting event which is contained. Finally, no cycles with respect to causal dependence may occur.

3.2 Definition Let $\mathcal{E} \in \boldsymbol{E}$.

(i) $X \subseteq E$ is *left-closed in $\mathcal{E}$ up to conflicts* iff $\forall d, e \in E$: if $e \in X, d \prec e$ and $d \notin X$ then there exists an $f \in X$ with $f \prec e$ and $d\#f$.
$X \subseteq E$ is *conflict-free* iff $\mathcal{E} \lceil X$ is conflict-free.

(ii) $X \subseteq E$ is a *(finite) configuration* of $\mathcal{E}$ iff X is finite, left-closed up to conflicts and conflict-free and does not contain a causality cycle: $\leq_X := (\prec \cap (X \times X))^*$ is an ordering. A configuration X is called *maximal* iff $X \subseteq Y \in Conf(\mathcal{E})$ implies $X = Y$. A configuration X is called *complete* iff $\forall d \in E : d \notin X \Rightarrow \exists e \in X$ with $d\#e$. $Conf(\mathcal{E})$ denotes the set of all configurations of $\mathcal{E}$.

The causal dependence between action occurrences in a configuration may again, as for prime event structures, be represented by a pomset; for $X \in Conf(\mathcal{E})$, we take the isomorphism class of $(X, \leq_X, l_{\mathcal{E}}\lceil X)$. Concurrency is now defined relative to a configuration, as the derived relation $co_X \subseteq X \times X$: $d \; co_X \; e$ iff $\neg(d <_X e \vee e <_X d)$, where $d <_X e$ means $d \leq_X e \wedge d \neq e$.

3.3 Example

The system $((a + b) \mid c); d$ may be represented by the flow event structure

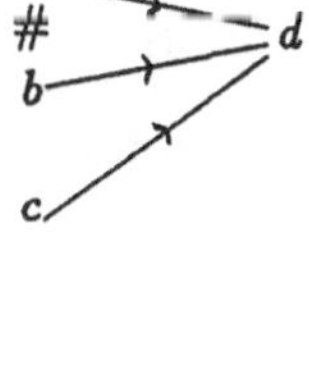

(in graphical representations we omit names of events and represent $\prec$ by arcs of the form $\longrightarrow\!\!\!\!\!\!\!+$).

The pomsets 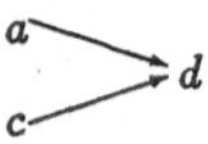

and 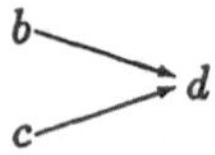

correspond to complete configurations.

Note that prime event structures are special flow event structures defining $d \prec e$ iff $d < e$; the definition of configuration then coincides, and in each configuration X, $\leq_X$ equals $\leq$.

However, in contrast to prime event structures, not all maximal configurations are complete. Partly this is due to the fact that, in flow event structures, syntactic and semantic conflict not necessarily coincide (two events are in *semantic conflict* if there is no configuration containing them both). Flow event structures where syntactic and semantic conflict coincide are called *faithful* in [Boudol b]. However, also in faithful flow event structures maximal configurations are not necessarly complete, either due to inconsistent events, but also in flow event structures without inconsistent events, as shown by the following example.

3.4 Example

Let $\mathcal{E}$ =

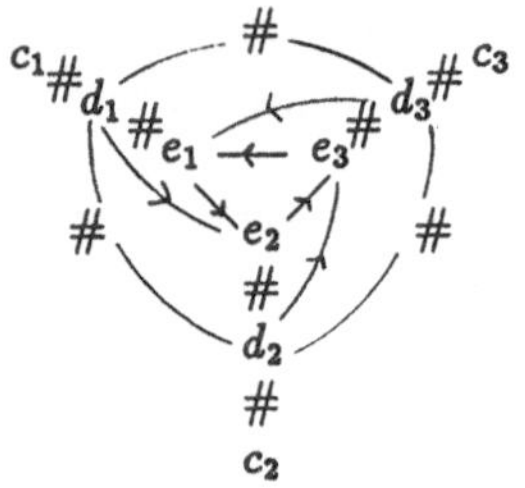

The configuration $\{c_1, c_2, c_3\}$ is maximal but not complete.

Maximal but incomplete configurations may be interpreted as deadlocking behaviours. Assume that a semantic sequential composition is defined for flow event structures by putting all events in the first component in $\prec$-relation with the events of the second component. Any incomplete maximal configuration of the first component would then disable the second component. Thus, in flow event structures, deadlock and termination may be distinguished.

3.5 Definition

A flow event structure $\mathcal{E}$ is *deadlock-free* iff every maximal configuration of $\mathcal{E}$ is complete.

Refinement of actions in flow event structures may now be defined as follows. We assume a refinement function $ref: Act \to \mathbb{E} - \{O\}$ (where O denotes the empty flow event structure) and replace each event labelled by a by a disjoint copy of $ref(a)$. The conflict and causality structure will just be inherited.

Hence, we may replace actions also by behaviours with conflicts and by infinite behaviours.

3.6 Definition

(i) A function $ref: Act \to \mathbb{E} - \{O\}$ is called a *refinement function (for flow event structures)*.

(ii) Let $\mathcal{E} \in \mathbb{E}$ and let *ref* be a refinement function.
Then the *refinement of* $\mathcal{E}$ *by ref*, $ref(\mathcal{E})$, is the flow event structure defined by
- $E_{ref(\mathcal{E})} = \{(e, e') | e \in E_{\mathcal{E}}, e' \in E_{ref(l_{\mathcal{E}}(e))}\}$,
- $(d, d') \prec_{ref(\mathcal{E})} (e, e')$ iff $d \prec e$ or $(d = e \wedge d' \prec_{ref(l_{\mathcal{E}}(d))} e')$,
- $(d, d') \#_{ref(\mathcal{E})} (e, e')$ iff $d \#_{\mathcal{E}} e$ or $(d = e \wedge d' \#_{ref(l_{\mathcal{E}}(d))} e')$,
- $l_{ref(\mathcal{E})}(e, e') = l_{ref(l_{\mathcal{E}}(e))}(e')$.

As for prime event structures, we verify that *ref*($\mathcal{E}$) is well-defined, even when isomorphic flow event structures are identified.

3.7 Proposition

(i) If $\mathcal{E} \in \boldsymbol{E}$ and *ref* is a refinement function then *ref*($\mathcal{E}$) is a flow event structure indeed.

(ii) If $\mathcal{E} \in \boldsymbol{E}$ and *ref*, *ref'* are refinement functions with $ref(a) \cong ref'(a)$ for all $a \in Act$ then $ref(\mathcal{E}) \cong ref'(\mathcal{E})$.

(iii) If $\mathcal{E}, \mathcal{F} \in \boldsymbol{E}$, *ref* is a refinement function and $\mathcal{E} \cong \mathcal{F}$ then $ref(\mathcal{E}) \cong ref(\mathcal{F})$.

Proof Straightforward. ■

3.8 Example

Now Example 2.6 can be completed. Refining the action "read data" by a conflicting event structure yields a flow event structure that is not prime.

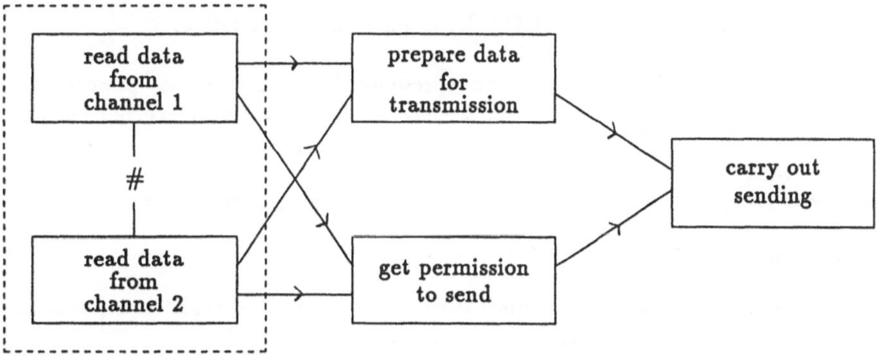

Finally, we show that, analogously to prime event structures, the behaviour of a refined flow event structure *ref*($\mathcal{E}$) may be deduced compositionally from the behaviour of $\mathcal{E}$ and the behaviour of the refinements of actions.

3.9 Proposition

Let $\mathcal{E} \in \boldsymbol{E}$, let *ref* be a refinement function for flow event structures.

We call $\tilde{X}$ *a refinement of configuration* $X \in Conf(\mathcal{E})$ *by ref* iff

- $\tilde{X} = \bigcup_{e \in X} \{e\} \times X_e$ where $\forall e \in X : X_e \in Conf(ref(l_{\mathcal{E}}(e))) - \{\emptyset\}$,
- $e \in busy(\tilde{X}) \Longrightarrow e$ maximal in X with respect to $\leq_X$
  where $busy(\tilde{X}) := \{e \in X \mid X_e \text{ not complete}\}$.

Then $Conf(ref(\mathcal{E})) = \{\, \tilde{X} \mid \tilde{X}$ is a refinement of a configuration $X \in Conf(\mathcal{E})\}$.

Proof [GG b]. ■

4 Interleaving semantics

In this section we define two interleaving equivalences (a "linear time" and a "branching time" variant) and recall the example of [CDP], showing that they are not preserved under refinement. In the remaining sections we will consider step equivalences and partial order equivalences. All definitions and theorems that follow apply to the domain of flow event structures — and thus to the subdomain of prime event structures as well —; however all event structures figuring in counterexamples are prime.

In the previous section it is explained how configurations model the states of a concurrent system. We may now ask which actions may occur in a configuration and which configuration is then obtained.

4.1 Definition Let $\mathcal{E} \in \boldsymbol{E}$.

i. $X \longrightarrow_{\mathcal{E}} X'$ if $X, X' \in Conf(\mathcal{E})$ and $X \subseteq X'$.

ii. $X \xrightarrow{a} X'$ iff $a \in Act$, $X \longrightarrow_{\mathcal{E}} X'$ and $X' \setminus X = \{e\}$ with $l(e) = a$.

Note that $X \longrightarrow_{\mathcal{E}} X'$ implies that $\mathcal{E}\lceil(X' \setminus X)$ is finite and conflict–free.

Here $X \xrightarrow{a} X'$ says that if $\mathcal{E}$ is in the state represented by X, then it may perform an action a and reach a state represented by X'. Likewise, $X \longrightarrow_{\mathcal{E}} X'$ says that $\mathcal{E}$ may evolve from X to X'.

Considering transitions $X \xrightarrow{a} X'$ only, one can define the usual *interleaving semantics*. The simplest form is that of comparing just the possible sequences of action occurrences.

4.2 Definition

$w = a_1 \cdots a_n \in Act^*$ is a *(sequential) trace* of $\mathcal{E} \in \boldsymbol{E}$ iff there exist configurations $X_o, \cdots, X_n$ of $\mathcal{E}$ such that $X_o = \emptyset$ and $X_{i-1} \xrightarrow{a_i} X_i$ $(i = 1, \cdots, n)$.
SeqTraces $(\mathcal{E})$ denotes the set of all sequential traces of $\mathcal{E} \in \boldsymbol{E}$.
$\mathcal{E}, \mathcal{F} \in \boldsymbol{E}$ are called *interleaving trace equivalent* $(\mathcal{E} \approx_{it} \mathcal{F})$ iff *SeqTraces* $(\mathcal{E})$ = *SeqTraces* $(\mathcal{F})$.

With the concept of labelled transition systems, we obtain a stronger equivalence notion based on the idea of bisimulation [Park, Milner a] For example, the systems $a(b+c)$ and $ab+ac$ have the same traces but are distinguished by bisimulation equivalence.

4.3 Definition Let $\mathcal{E}, \mathcal{F} \in \boldsymbol{E}$.

A relation $R \subseteq Conf(\mathcal{E}) \times Conf(\mathcal{F})$ is called an *interleaving bisimulation between $\mathcal{E}$ and $\mathcal{F}$* iff $(\emptyset, \emptyset) \in R$ and if $(X, Y) \in R$ then

- $X \xrightarrow{a} X' \Rightarrow \exists Y'$ with $Y \xrightarrow{a} Y'$ and $(X', Y') \in R$,
- $X \xrightarrow{a} Y' \Rightarrow \exists X'$ with $X \xrightarrow{a} X'$ and $(X', Y') \in R$.

$\mathcal{E}$ and $\mathcal{F}$ are *interleaving bisimulation equivalent* $(\mathcal{E} \approx_{ib} \mathcal{F})$ iff there exists an interleaving bisimulation between $\mathcal{E}$ and $\mathcal{F}$.

Clearly, $\mathcal{E} \approx_{ib} \mathcal{F}$ implies $\mathcal{E} \approx_{it} \mathcal{F}$.

4.4 Example

We now recall the example of [CDP], showing that both $\approx_{it}$ and $\approx_{ib}$ are not preserved by refinement. They considered the two systems $P = a|b$ and $Q = ab + ba$, representable by the following event structures.

$$\mathcal{E}_P = \begin{array}{cc} a & b \end{array} \;,\quad \mathcal{E}_Q = \begin{array}{ccc} a & \# & b \\ \downarrow & & \downarrow \\ b & & a \end{array}$$

In all known interleaving semantics, P and Q are considered equivalent, we have $\mathcal{E}_P \approx_{ib} \mathcal{E}_Q$. However, if we allow to refine the action a into the pomset $a_1 \rightarrow a_2$, this gives rise to the two systems

$$\mathcal{E}_{P'} = \begin{array}{cc} a_1 & b \\ \downarrow & \\ a_2 & \end{array} \;,\quad \mathcal{E}_{Q'} = \begin{array}{ccc} a_1 & \# & b \\ \downarrow & & \downarrow \\ a_2 & & a_1 \\ \downarrow & & \downarrow \\ b & & a_2 \end{array}$$

and they are not interleaving equivalent; indeed they are not even interleaving trace equivalent: $\mathcal{E}_{P'}$ allows for the sequence $a_1\,b\,a_2$ whereas $\mathcal{E}_{Q'}$ doesn't.

This shows that both interleaving trace equivalence and interleaving bisimulation equivalence are not preserved by action refinement. Even more, the same can be said for all equivalences identifying P and Q and respecting interleaving trace equivalence, e.g. failure equivalence [BHR], testing equivalence [DH].

As an event structure equivalence which is indeed preserved by refinement one could consider event structure isomorphism (Proposition 3.7 (iii)). However, the main purpose of introducing an equivalence notion is to abstract from certain details in a system representation. For example, we would like to express that the processes a and $a+a$ exhibit the same behaviour. Furthermore, we would like to identify processes like $(a|(b+c))+(a|b)+((a+c)|b)$ and $(a|(b+c))+((a+c)|b)$ (absorption law, see [BC a]). This is not possible when using event structure isomorphism. Hence, in the sequel we will consider various equivalence notions in between these two extremes (interleaving trace equivalence and event structure isomorphism), taking into account the concurrency and the conflict structure ("branching-time" semantics) in more and more detail.

5 Step semantics

A more discriminating view of concurrent systems than that offered by interleaving semantics is obtained by modelling concurrency as either arbitrary interleaving or simultaneous execution. This view is taken in calculi like SCCS [Milner b], CIRCAL [Milne] and MEIJE [AB]. In [TV], this idea is applied to give a non-interleaving semantics to theoretical CSP, called *step failure semantics*. The word *step* originates from Petri net theory where it denotes a set (or multiset) of concurrently executable transitions. Recently, a step semantics for CCS has been defined [DDM b], inspired by [AB]. Step semantics give a more precise account of concurrency than interleaving semantics, e.g. the systems $a|b$ and $ab+ba$ are distinguished. This means that Example 4.4 constitutes an argument against interleaving semantics but not against step semantics. We will formalise some step equivalence notions and then discuss examples which show that even these equivalences are not preserved by refinement.

Step semantics are defined by generalising the single action transitions $X \xrightarrow{a} X'$ from Section 4 to transitions of the form $X \xrightarrow{A} X'$ where A is a multiset over *Act*, representing actions occurring concurrently. In particular, we allow actions to occur concurrently with themselves ("autoconcurrency"). Using this new kind of transitions, *step trace equivalence* and *step bisimulation equivalence* are straightforward generalisations of the corresponding interleaving equivalences, see e.g. [Pomello].

5.1 Definition Let $\mathcal{E} \in \boldsymbol{E}$.

$X \xrightarrow{A} X'$ iff $A \in \mathbb{N}^{Act}$ (A is a multiset over Act), $X \longrightarrow_{\mathcal{E}} X'$ and $X' \setminus X = G$ such that $\forall d, e \in G \;\; d \; co_{X'} \; e$ and $l(G) = A$ where $l(G)(a) = |\{e \in G | l(e) = a\}|$.

5.2 Definition

$W = A_1 \cdots A_n$ where $A_i \in \mathbb{N}^{Act}$ $(i = 1, \cdots, n)$ is a *step trace* of $\mathcal{E} \in \boldsymbol{E}$ iff there exist configurations $X_o, \cdots, X_n$ of $\mathcal{E}$ such that $X_o = \emptyset$ and $X_{i-1} \xrightarrow{A_i} X_i$ $(i = 1, \cdots, n)$.
StepTraces $(\mathcal{E})$ denotes the set of all step traces of $\mathcal{E} \in \boldsymbol{E}$.
$\mathcal{E}, \mathcal{F} \in \boldsymbol{E}$ are called *step trace equivalent* $(\mathcal{E} \approx_{st} \mathcal{F})$ iff *StepTraces* $(\mathcal{E}) =$ *StepTraces* $(\mathcal{F})$.

5.3 Definition Let $\mathcal{E}, \mathcal{F} \in \boldsymbol{E}$.

A relation $R \subseteq Conf(\mathcal{E}) \times Conf(\mathcal{F})$ is called a *step bisimulation between $\mathcal{E}$ and $\mathcal{F}$* iff $(\emptyset, \emptyset) \in R$ and if $(X, Y) \in R$ then

- $X \xrightarrow{A} X' \Longrightarrow \exists Y'$ with $Y \xrightarrow{A} Y'$ and $(X, Y) \in R$,
- $Y \xrightarrow{A} Y' \Longrightarrow \exists X'$ with $X \xrightarrow{A} X'$ and $(X, Y) \in R$.

$\mathcal{E}$ and $\mathcal{F}$ are *step bisimulation equivalent* $(\mathcal{E} \approx_{sb} \mathcal{F})$ iff there exists a step bisimulation between $\mathcal{E}$ and $\mathcal{F}$.

Clearly the two event structures $\mathcal{E}_P$ and $\mathcal{E}_Q$ in Example 4.4 are not equivalent in step semantics. The step $\{a, b\}$ is possible in $\mathcal{E}_P$ but not in $\mathcal{E}_Q$.

As for interleaving, $\mathcal{E} \approx_{sb} \mathcal{F}$ implies $\mathcal{E} \approx_{st} \mathcal{F}$. Moreover (as far as we know) all other interesting step equivalence notions are positioned somewhere in between (recall that we do not consider abstraction from internal actions).

Next we give examples showing that both $\approx_{st}$ and $\approx_{sb}$ are not invariant under refinement of actions, as well as all equivalences included between them, e.g. step failure equivalence.

The following example shows that step trace semantics is in general not invariant under refinement.

5.4 Example

We consider the two systems

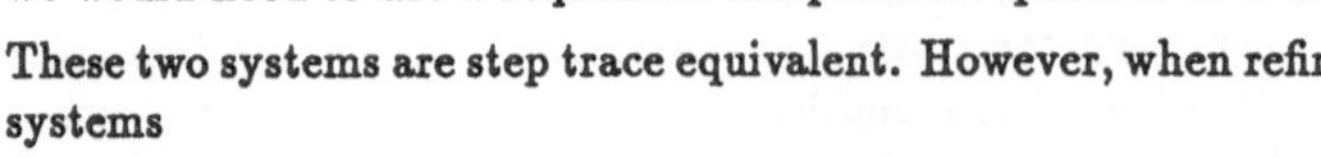

$\mathcal{E}$ performs a followed by b, and c in parallel with this, whereas $\mathcal{F}$ either performs a and c in parallel and then b, or first a and then b and c in parallel. The +-sign may easily be "implemented" by indicating that all events in the first component are in conflict with all events in the second component and vice versa. (For representing the whole system as a term, we would need to use a sequential composition operator or a TCSP-like parallel composition.)

These two systems are step trace equivalent. However, when refining c into $c_1 \rightarrow c_2$, the resulting systems

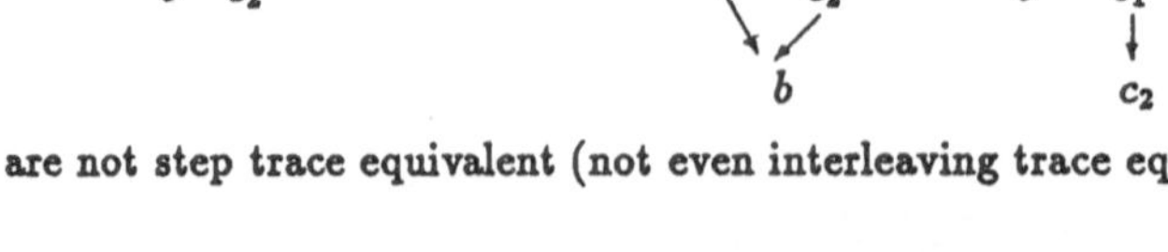

are not step trace equivalent (not even interleaving trace equivalent).

This example shows that $\approx_{st}$ is not preserved by refinement. However, the example is not adequate for step bisimulation equivalence since $\mathcal{E}$ and $\mathcal{F}$ are not step bisimulation equivalent (after performing a, the b is always possible in $\mathcal{E}$ but not always in $\mathcal{F}$). The next example shows that also $\approx_{sb}$ is not preserved by refinement.

5.5 Example

Consider $P = a|b$ and $Q = (a|b) + ab$,

$$\mathcal{E}_P = a \quad b \quad , \quad \mathcal{E}_Q = \begin{array}{ccccc} a & \# & a & \# & b \\ & & \downarrow & & \\ & & b & & \end{array} .$$

It is easy to verify that $\mathcal{E}_P \approx_{sb} \mathcal{E}_Q$. However, refining a into $a_1 \rightarrow a_2$ yields

$$\mathcal{E}_{P'} = \begin{array}{cc} a_1 & \\ \downarrow & b \\ a_2 & \end{array} \quad , \quad \mathcal{E}_{Q'} = \begin{array}{ccccc} a_1 & \# & a_1 & \# & b \\ \downarrow & & \downarrow & & \\ a_2 & & a_2 & & \\ & & \downarrow & & \\ & & b & & \end{array}$$

After the step $\{a_1\}$, the step $\{b\}$ is always possible in $\mathcal{E}_{P'}$. However, in $\mathcal{E}_{Q'}$, it may be the case that the step $\{b\}$ is impossible after executing a_1 (choosing the branch $a_1 \rightarrow a_2 \rightarrow b$). Hence $\mathcal{E}_{P'}$ and $\mathcal{E}_{Q'}$ are not step bisimulation equivalent (not even interleaving bisimulation equivalent).

However, this example is still not suitable for disqualifying the whole range of equivalence notions included between $\approx_{st}$ and $\approx_{sb}$, as Example 4.4 does in the interleaving case, since the refined systems $\mathcal{E}_{P'}$ and $\mathcal{E}_{Q'}$ turn out to be step trace equivalent. A slightly more complicated example may be given, disqualifying all equivalence notions between $\approx_{sb}$ and $\approx_{st}$.

5.6 Example

First consider the following three systems:

$$\mathcal{E}_1 = \begin{array}{ccc} & a & \\ \swarrow & & \searrow \\ b & & c \end{array} \quad , \quad \mathcal{E}_2 = \begin{array}{ccc} a & & c \\ & \searrow \; \swarrow & \\ & b & \end{array} \quad , \quad \mathcal{E}_3 = \begin{array}{cc} a & \\ \downarrow & c \\ b & \end{array} .$$

Now we consider the two composed systems

$$\mathcal{E} = \mathcal{E}_1 + \mathcal{E}_2, \qquad \mathcal{F} = \mathcal{E}_1 + \mathcal{E}_2 + \mathcal{E}_3.$$

We have $\mathcal{E} \approx_{sb} \mathcal{F}$ [GV]. However, when refining c into $c_1 \rightarrow c_2$ only the refinement of $\mathcal{F}$ may perform the sequence of actions $c_1\ a\ b\ c_2$. The resulting systems $\mathcal{E}'$ and $\mathcal{F}'$ are not even interleaving trace equivalent.
So let $\approx$ be an equivalence included between $\approx_{st}$ and $\approx_{sb}$, then also $\mathcal{E} \approx \mathcal{F}$, but $\mathcal{E}' \not\approx \mathcal{F}'$.

Thus we have shown that all the currently known versions of step equivalence are not preserved by refinement.

6 "Linear time" partial order semantics

In [CDP] it was claimed that equivalence based on considering partially ordered executions is preserved by refinement. In this section we will make this claim more precise. We will show that this is indeed true when considering the set of all possible executions of systems (*traces*), formalising the proof sketch from [CDP] in terms of event structures. However, in the next section, we will consider equivalence notions taking account of the timing of choices, based on the idea of bisimulation, and we will show that in this case this claim is not so obvious.

In Sections 2 and 3, we discussed that the possible executions of a system may be represented as isomorphism classes of labelled partial orders (*pomsets*), thus taking full account of the causality relation for event occurrences.

6.1 Definition

(i) Let $X = (X, \leq_X, l_X)$ and $Y = (Y, \leq_Y, l_Y)$ be partial orders which are labelled over *Act*. X and Y are *isomorphic* ($X \cong Y$) iff there exists a bijection between X and Y respecting the ordering and the labelling. The isomorphism class of a partial order labelled over *Act* is called a *pomset over Act*.

(ii) Let $\mathcal{E} \in \boldsymbol{E}$.
$Pomsets\,(\mathcal{E}) := \{\, [(X, \leq_X, l_\mathcal{E} \lceil X)]_\cong \mid X \in Conf(\mathcal{E})\}$.

(iii) $\mathcal{E},\ \mathcal{F} \in \boldsymbol{E}$ are *pomset trace equivalent* ($\mathcal{E} \approx_{pt} \mathcal{F}$) iff $Pomsets\,(\mathcal{E}) = Pomsets\,(\mathcal{F})$.

Clearly, pomset trace equivalence implies step trace equivalence. Example 5.4 shows that pomset trace equivalence is strictly stronger than step trace equivalence. On the other hand, pomset trace equivalence and step bisimulation equivalence (or interleaving bisimulation equivalence) are incomparable: $a(b+c) \underset{\not\approx_{sb}}{\overset{\approx_{pt}}{}} ab + ac$ and for $\mathcal{E}_P$ and $\mathcal{E}_Q$ of Example 5.5, $\mathcal{E}_P \approx_{sb} \mathcal{E}_Q$ but $\mathcal{E}_P \not\approx_{pt} \mathcal{E}_Q$.

The following theorem shows that pomset trace equivalence is preserved under refinement.

6.2 Theorem Let $\mathcal{E}, \mathcal{F} \in \boldsymbol{E}$.

Then $\mathcal{E} \approx_{pt} \mathcal{F}$ implies $ref(\mathcal{E}) \approx_{pt} ref(\mathcal{F})$ for any refinement function *ref*.

Proof
Let $\mathcal{E} \approx_{pt} \mathcal{F}$ and let *ref* be a refinement function. We have to show

$$Pomsets\,(ref(\mathcal{E})) = Pomsets\,(ref(\mathcal{F})).$$

"$\subseteq$" Let $u \in Pomsets\,(ref(\mathcal{E}))$.
Then $u = [(\tilde{X}, \leq_{\tilde{X}}, l_{ref(\mathcal{E})} \lceil \tilde{X})]_\cong$ where $\tilde{X} \in Conf(ref(\mathcal{E}))$.

With Proposition 3.9 we have that $\tilde{X}$ is a refinement of some configuration X of $\mathcal{E}$. Since $Pomsets\,(\mathcal{E}) = Pomsets\,(\mathcal{F})$, there exists $Y \in Conf(\mathcal{F})$ such that $(X, \leq_X, l_\mathcal{E} \lceil X)$ and $(Y, \leq_Y, l_\mathcal{F} \lceil Y)$ are isomorphic. Since isomorphism preserves labelling, we can refine Y to a configuration $\tilde{Y}$ (by choosing identical refinements for corresponding events) such that

$$(\tilde{X}, \leq_{\tilde{X}}, l_{ref(\mathcal{E})} \lceil \tilde{X}) \cong (\tilde{Y}, \leq_{\tilde{Y}}, l_{ref(\mathcal{F})} \lceil \tilde{Y}),$$

hence $u \in Pomsets\,(ref(\mathcal{F}))$.

"$\supseteq$" by symmetry. ■

7 "Branching time" partial order semantics

In this section, we discuss several suggestions to define equivalence notions based on partial orders and recording where choices are made. We show that most of these fail in general to be preserved by refinement. Finally we show that the last and strongest notion is indeed invariant with respect to refinement.

7.1 Pomset bisimulation equivalence

In [BC a] it was suggested to generalise the idea of bisimulation by considering transitions labelled by pomsets. So we consider now transitions $X \xrightarrow{u} X'$ where u is a pomset over Act.

7.1 Definition Let $\mathcal{E} \in \boldsymbol{E}$.

$X \xrightarrow{u} X'$ iff $X \longrightarrow_{\mathcal{E}} X'$ and u is the isomorphism class of $\mathcal{E}\lceil(X' \setminus X)$.

7.2 Definition Let $\mathcal{E}, \mathcal{F} \in \boldsymbol{E}$.

A relation $R \subseteq Conf(\mathcal{E}) \times Conf(\mathcal{F})$ is called a *pomset bisimulation between $\mathcal{E}$ and $\mathcal{F}$* iff $(\emptyset, \emptyset) \in R$ and if $(X, Y) \in R$ then

- $X \xrightarrow{u} X' \Rightarrow \exists Y'$ with $Y \xrightarrow{u} Y'$ and $(X', Y') \in R$,
- $Y \xrightarrow{u} Y' \Rightarrow \exists X'$ with $X \xrightarrow{u} X'$ and $(X', Y') \in R$.

$\mathcal{E}$ and $\mathcal{F}$ are *pomset bisimulation equivalent* ($\mathcal{E} \approx_{pb} \mathcal{F}$) iff there exists a pomset bisimulation between $\mathcal{E}$ and $\mathcal{F}$.

This equivalence notion is clearly stronger than both step bisimulation equivalence and pomset trace equivalence: $\mathcal{E} \approx_{pb} \mathcal{F}$ implies $\mathcal{E} \approx_{sb} \mathcal{F}$ and $\mathcal{E} \approx_{pt} \mathcal{F}$; moreover, the processes $a|b$ and $(a|b) + ab$ considered in Example 5.5 are *sb*–equivalent but not *pb*–equivalent; $a(b+c)$ and $ab + ac$ are pomset trace equivalent but not *pb*–equivalent.

However, *pb*–equivalence is not preserved by refinement.

7.3 Example

Consider $a(b+c) + (a|b)$ and $a(b+c) + (a|b) + ab$. We have $P \approx_{pb} Q$. However, when refining a into $a_1 \twoheadrightarrow a_2$ and executing a_1, we may arrive in a situation in the second system where a_2 and b may be only executed sequentially and where c is excluded. This is not possible in the first system.

In [GV], pomset bisimulation was critisized for violating "the real combination of causality and branching time". The criticism is that only the first system of Example 7.3 has the property that any action a that is causally preceeding b is also preceeding the choice between b and c. Therefore they suggested a generalised pomset bisimulation equivalence, that is finer then pomset bisimulation equivalence, does not identify the two systems of Example 7.3, and still satisfies $a = a + a$ and the absorption law of Section 4.

However, generalised pomset bisimulation equivalence is also not preserved by refinement.

7.4 Example

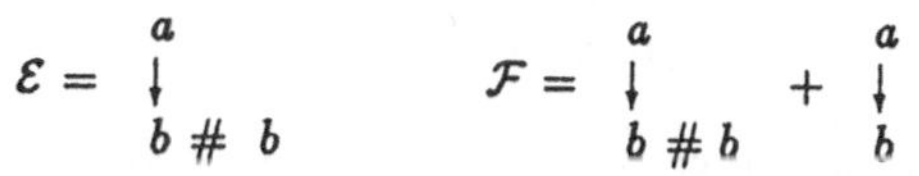

These two systems are generalised pomset bisimulation equivalent [GV]. However, when refining a into $a_1 \twoheadrightarrow a_2$, the resulting systems

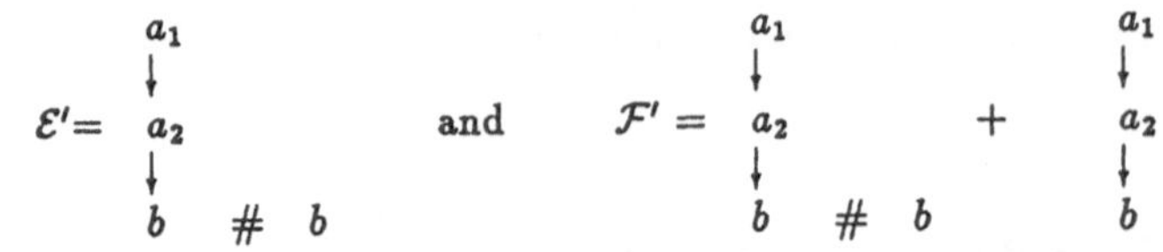

are not even interleaving bisimulation equivalent. After the action a_1 the action b is always possible in $\mathcal{E}'$. However in $\mathcal{F}'$ it may be the case that b is impossible after executing a_1 (choosing the branch $a_1 \to a_2 \to b$).

7.2 History preserving bisimulation

In [DDM a] another generalisation of the idea of bisimulation was proposed by considering *states* labelled by pomsets. The idea is to relate two states only if they have the same causal history. Their *NMS partial order equivalence* was defined on so-called *Nondeterministic Measurement Systems*. We rephrase the definition here in terms of event structures as follows.

7.5 Definition Let $\mathcal{E}, \mathcal{F} \in \mathbf{E}$.

A relation $R \subseteq Conf(\mathcal{E}) \times Conf(\mathcal{F})$ is called a *weak history preserving bisimulation between $\mathcal{E}$ and $\mathcal{F}$* iff $(\emptyset, \emptyset) \in R$ and if $(X, Y) \in R$ then

- there is an isomorphism between $(X, \leq_X, l_{\mathcal{E}}\lceil X)$ and $(Y, \leq_Y, l_{\mathcal{F}}\lceil Y)$,
- $X \longrightarrow_{\mathcal{E}} X' \Rightarrow \exists Y'$ with $Y \longrightarrow_{\mathcal{F}} Y'$ and $(X', Y') \in R$,
- $Y \longrightarrow_{\mathcal{F}} Y' \Rightarrow \exists X'$ with $X \longrightarrow_{\mathcal{E}} X'$ and $(X', Y') \in R$.

$\mathcal{E}$ and $\mathcal{F}$ are *weakly history preserving equivalent* ($\mathcal{E} \approx_{wh} \mathcal{F}$) iff there exists a weak history preserving bisimulation between $\mathcal{E}$ and $\mathcal{F}$.

Note that the isomorphism requirement guarantees that the labels of the events in $X' \setminus X$ and $Y' \setminus Y$ correspond as well.

In fact it is sufficient to consider only those transitions $X \longrightarrow_{\mathcal{E}} X'$ (resp. $Y \longrightarrow_{\mathcal{F}} Y'$) where $X'(Y')$ is obtained from $X(Y)$ by executing exactly one event.

The two systems considered in Example 7.3 are pomset bisimulation equivalent but not weakly history preserving equivalent. However, *wh*-equivalence is not stronger than pomset bisimulation, as shown by the following example; the two notions are in general incomparable. We will show later that *wh*-equivalence does respect pomset bisimulation for systems without autoconcurrency.

The following example will also show that *wh*-equivalence is in general not preserved by refinement. This example was suggested to us by Rabinovich. He used it for showing that $\approx_{wh}$ is not a congruence with respect to a TCSP-like parallel composition.

7.6 Example

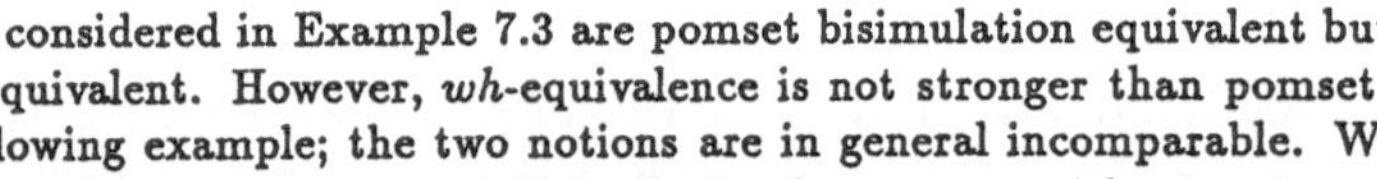

It is straightforward to check that $\mathcal{E} \approx_{wh} \mathcal{F}$. However, $\mathcal{E}$ and $\mathcal{F}$ are not pomset bisimulation equivalent. After executing a, it is alway possible to execute $a \to b$ in $\mathcal{E}$, in $\mathcal{F}$ it may be impossible to execute $a \to b$ after a. When refining a into $a_1 \to a_2$, the resulting systems are no longer *wh*-equivalent, not even interleaving bisimulation equivalent. This can be proven by providing a formula in Hennessy–Milner logic [HM] that is satisfied by the refinement of $\mathcal{F}$, but not by the refinement of $\mathcal{E}$. Such a formula is:

$$\langle a_1\rangle \langle a_2\rangle (\langle b\rangle T \wedge \langle a_1\rangle \neg \langle b\rangle T).$$

An equivalence respecting both pomset bisimulation and wh–equivalence may be considered by extending the definition of pomset bisimulation with the requirement that, for any $(X,Y) \in \mathcal{R}$, $(X, \leq_X, l_\mathcal{E}\lceil X)$ and $(Y, \leq_Y, l_\mathcal{E}\lceil Y)$ should be isomorphic. However, the following example shows that also this equivalence would not preserve refinement.

7.7 Example

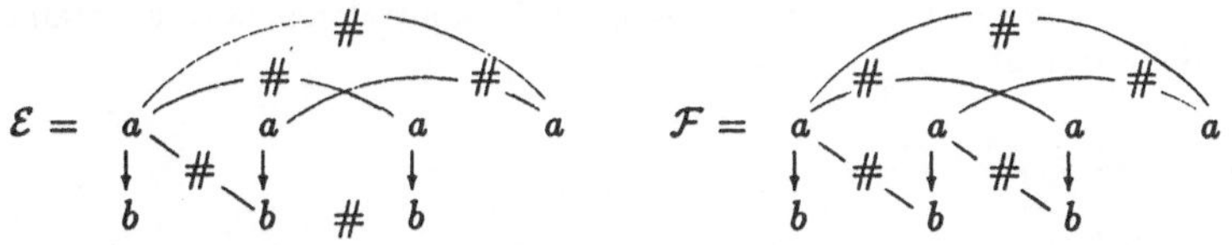

As is quite difficult to check, $\mathcal{E}$ and $\mathcal{F}$ are equivalent according to the equivalence notion proposed above, but after refining a into $a_1 \to a_2$ they are not even bisimulation equivalent.

The formula $\langle a_1\rangle \langle a_1\rangle [a_2] \langle b\rangle T$ is satisfied by the refinement of $\mathcal{E}$, but not by the refinement of $\mathcal{F}$.

We finally define a stronger version of history perserving equivalence which will respect pomset bisimulation. This notion was first suggested in [TRH] in terms of behaviour structures. We will show that this equivalence is preserved by refinement. For systems without autoconcurrency, this equivalence coincides with $\approx_{wh}$. This will imply the result that $\approx_{wh}$ is invariant against refinement for systems without autoconcurrency.

7.8 Definition Let $\mathcal{E}, \mathcal{F} \in \boldsymbol{E}$.

A relation $R \subseteq Conf(\mathcal{E}) \times Conf(\mathcal{F}) \times \mathcal{P}(E_\mathcal{E} \times E_\mathcal{F})$ is called a *history preserving bisimulation between $\mathcal{E}$ and $\mathcal{F}$* if $(\emptyset, \emptyset, \emptyset) \in R$ and whenever $(X, Y, f) \in R$ then

- f is an isomorphism between $(X, \leq_X, l_\mathcal{E}\lceil X)$ and $(Y, \leq_Y, l_\mathcal{E}\lceil Y)$,
- $X \longrightarrow_\mathcal{E} X' \Rightarrow \exists Y', f'$ with $Y \longrightarrow_\mathcal{F} Y'$, $(X', Y', f') \in R$ and $f'\lceil X = f$,
- $Y \longrightarrow_\mathcal{F} Y' \Rightarrow \exists X', f'$ with $X \longrightarrow_\mathcal{E} X'$, $(X', Y', f') \in R$ and $f'\lceil X = f$.

$\mathcal{E}$ and $\mathcal{F}$ are *history preserving equivalent* ($\mathcal{E} \approx_h \mathcal{F}$) iff there exists a history preserving bisimulation between $\mathcal{E}$ and $\mathcal{F}$.

Clearly, we have $\mathcal{E} \approx_h \mathcal{F} \Rightarrow \mathcal{E} \approx_{wh} \mathcal{F}$. However the two systems of Example 7.7 are not h–equivalent.

7.9 Proposition Let $\mathcal{E}, \mathcal{F} \in \boldsymbol{E}$.

Then $\mathcal{E} \approx_h \mathcal{F} \Rightarrow \mathcal{E} \approx_{pb} \mathcal{F}$.

Proof

We show that any history preserving bisimulation between $\mathcal{E}$ and $\mathcal{F}$ is also a pomset bisimulation between $\mathcal{E}$ and $\mathcal{F}$ (after leaving out the isomorphism component). Let R be a h–bisimulation, and suppose $(X, Y, f) \in R$ and $X \xrightarrow{u} X'$. Then $X \longrightarrow_\mathcal{E} X'$, thus $\exists Y', f'$ with $Y \longrightarrow_\mathcal{F} Y', (X', Y', f') \in R$

and $f'\lceil X = f$. Since f' is an isomorphism and $f'\lceil X = f$, *range* $(f'\lceil(X' \setminus X)) =$ *range* $(f')\setminus$ *range* $(f) = Y' \setminus Y$, so $f'\lceil(X' \setminus X)$ is an isomorphism between $X' \setminus X$ and $Y' \setminus Y$. Hence $Y \xrightarrow{u} Y'$, so R satisfies the first clause of a pomset bisimulation. The second clause follows by symmetry. ■

From this proof we learn that h-bisimulation not only respects pomset bisimulation but even the previous proposal combining weak history preserving equivalence and pomset bisimulation. Thus $\approx_h$ is the strongest equivalence considered so far (except for event structure isomorphism of course). Nevertheless it is possible to abstract from certain details in a system representation: we have $a \approx_h a+a$ and $(a|(b+c)) + (a|b) + ((a+c)|b) \approx_h (a|(b+c)) + ((a+c)|b)$ (absorption law).

We now show that considering only those transitions $X \longrightarrow_{\mathcal{E}} X', Y \longrightarrow_{\mathcal{F}} Y'$, respectively, where $X'(Y')$ is obtained from $X(Y)$ by executing exactly one event yields the same equivalence. We write $X \triangleright_{\mathcal{E}} X'$ for $X \rightarrow_{\mathcal{E}} X'$ and $|X' \setminus X| = 1$. Let $\approx_{oh}$ be the equivalence notion obtained by replacing $\longrightarrow$ by $\triangleright$ in the definition of $\approx_h$.

7.10 Proposition Let $\mathcal{E}, \mathcal{F} \in \mathbb{E}$.

Then $\mathcal{E} \approx_h \mathcal{F}$ iff $\mathcal{E} \approx_{oh} \mathcal{F}$.

Proof
The implication $\mathcal{E} \approx_h \mathcal{F} \Rightarrow \mathcal{E} \approx_{oh} \mathcal{F}$ is trivial. The implication $\mathcal{E} \approx_{oh} \mathcal{F} \Rightarrow \mathcal{E} \approx_h \mathcal{F}$ immediately follows from the observation that whenever $X \longrightarrow_{\mathcal{E}} X'$, there exist configurations $X_0, \ldots, X_n$ $(n \in \mathbb{N})$ such that $X = X_0 \triangleright_{\mathcal{E}} \ldots \triangleright_{\mathcal{E}} X_n = X'$. ■

Next we show that $\approx_h$ is preserved by refinement.

7.11 Theorem Let $\mathcal{E}, \mathcal{F} \in \mathbb{E}$ and let *ref* be a refinement function.

Then $\mathcal{E} \approx_h \mathcal{F} \Longrightarrow ref(\mathcal{E}) \approx_h ref(\mathcal{F})$.

Proof
Let $R \subseteq Conf(\mathcal{E}) \times Conf(\mathcal{F}) \times \mathcal{P}(E_{\mathcal{E}} \times E_{\mathcal{F}})$ be a history preserving bisimulation between $\mathcal{E}$ and $\mathcal{F}$. Define the relation $\tilde{R}$ by:

$\tilde{R} = \{(\tilde{X}, \tilde{Y}, \tilde{f}) \in Conf(ref(\mathcal{E})) \times Conf(ref(\mathcal{F})) \times \mathcal{P}(E_{ref(\mathcal{E})} \times E_{ref(\mathcal{F})}) \mid$
$\exists (X, Y, f) \in R$ such that

- $\tilde{X}$ is a refinement of X,
- $\tilde{Y}$ is a refinement of Y
- and $\tilde{f}: \tilde{X} \rightarrow \tilde{Y}$ is a bijection, satisfying $\tilde{f}(e, e') = (f(e), e')\}$.

We show that $\tilde{R}$ is a history preserving bisimulation between $ref(\mathcal{E})$ and $ref(\mathcal{F})$.

i. $(\emptyset, \emptyset, \emptyset) \in \tilde{R}$ since $(\emptyset, \emptyset, \emptyset) \in R$.

ii. Suppose $(\tilde{X}, \tilde{Y}, \tilde{f}) \in \tilde{R}$. Take $(X, Y, f) \in R$ such that
- $\tilde{X}$ is a refinement of X,
- $\tilde{Y}$ is a refinement of Y
- and $\tilde{f}: \tilde{X} \rightarrow \tilde{Y}$ is bijection, satisfying $\tilde{f}(e, e') = (f(e), e')$.

Now three things have to be established:

1. $\tilde{f}$ satisfies $(d,d') \leq_{\tilde{X}} (e,e') \Longleftrightarrow \tilde{f}\,(d,d') \leq_{\tilde{Y}} \tilde{f}\,(e,e')$ and $l_{ref(\mathcal{F})}(\tilde{f}\,(e,e')) = l_{ref(\mathcal{E})}(e,e')$.
2. $\tilde{X} \longrightarrow_{ref(\mathcal{E})} \tilde{X}' \Longrightarrow \exists\, \tilde{Y}', \tilde{f}'$ such that $\tilde{Y} \longrightarrow_{ref(\mathcal{F})} \tilde{Y}', \tilde{f}' \lceil \tilde{X} = \tilde{f}$ and $(\tilde{X}', \tilde{Y}', \tilde{f}') \in \tilde{R}$.
3. $\tilde{Y} \longrightarrow_{ref(\mathcal{F})} \tilde{Y}' \Longrightarrow \exists\, \tilde{X}', \tilde{f}'$ such that $\tilde{X} \longrightarrow_{ref(\mathcal{E})} \tilde{X}', \tilde{f}' \lceil \tilde{X} = \tilde{f}$ and $(\tilde{X}', \tilde{Y}', \tilde{f}') \in \tilde{R}$.

ad 1. Straightforward.

ad 2.

Suppose $\tilde{X} \longrightarrow_{ref(\mathcal{E})} \tilde{X}'$, i.e. $\tilde{X}' \in Conf(ref(\mathcal{E}))$ and $\tilde{X} \subseteq \tilde{X}'$.
We have $\tilde{X}' = \bigcup_{e \in X'} \{e\} \times X'_e$ where $X' \in Conf(\mathcal{E})$ and $\forall e \in X' : X'_e \in Conf(ref(l_{\mathcal{E}}(e))) - \{\emptyset\}$.
Then $X = pr_1(\tilde{X})$ and $X' = pr_1(\tilde{X}')$, so $X \longrightarrow_{\mathcal{E}} X'$.

Since R is a history preserving bisimulation, $\exists Y', f'$ with $Y \longrightarrow_{\mathcal{F}} Y', f' \lceil X = f$ and $(X', Y', f') \in R$.
Let $\tilde{Y}' = \{(f'(e), e') | (e,e') \in \tilde{X}\}$
and $\tilde{f}' = \{((e,e'), (f'(e), e')) | (e,e') \in \tilde{X}'\}$.
It now suffices to show that $\tilde{Y}'$ is a refinement of Y', since then it follows immediately with Proposition 3.9 that $\tilde{Y}' \in Conf(ref(\mathcal{F}))$, $\tilde{Y} \longrightarrow_{ref(\mathcal{F})} \tilde{Y}'$ (using that $f' \lceil X = f$), $\tilde{f}' \lceil X = \tilde{f}$ (likewise) and $(\tilde{X}', \tilde{Y}', \tilde{f}') \in \tilde{R}$.

- By construction $\tilde{Y}' = \bigcup_{e \in X'} \{f'(e)\} \times X'_e = \bigcup_{e \in Y'} \{e\} \times Y'_e$ where
  $\forall e \in Y' : Y'_e = X'_{f'^{-1}(e)} \in Conf(ref(l_{\mathcal{E}}(f'^{-1}(e)))) - \{\emptyset\} = Conf(ref(l_{\mathcal{F}}(e))) - \{\emptyset\}$.
- $e \in busy(\tilde{Y}') = \{e \in Y' | Y'_e \text{ not complete }\} \Longleftrightarrow$
  $f'^{-1}(e) \in busy(\tilde{X}') = \{e \in X' | X'_e \text{ not complete }\}$ by construction.
  Furthermore, e maximal in $Y' \Longleftrightarrow f'^{-1}(e)$ maximal in X', since f' is an isomorphism.
  Hence $e \in busy(\tilde{Y}')$ implies e maximal in Y', since $\tilde{X}'$ is a refinement of X'.

From this it follows that $\tilde{Y}'$ is a refinement of Y'.

ad 3. By symmetry. ■

Finally we show that $\approx_{wh}$ and $\approx_h$ coincide for event structures where concurrent events may not carry the same label. As a corrollary we then have that also $\approx_{wh}$ is preserved by refinement in this case and respects pomset bisimulation.

7.12 Definition $\mathcal{E} \in \boldsymbol{E}$ is *without autoconcurrency* iff

$$\forall X \in Conf(\mathcal{E}),\ \forall d, e \in X : d \ co_X\ e \text{ and } l(d) = l(e) \Rightarrow d = e.$$

7.13 Theorem Let $\mathcal{E}, \mathcal{F} \in \boldsymbol{E}$ be without autoconcurrency.

Then $\mathcal{E} \approx_{wh} \mathcal{F} \Leftrightarrow \mathcal{E} \approx_h \mathcal{F}$.

Proof
First note that a *wh*-bisimulation can be regarded as a *h*-bisimulation without the requirements that $f' \lceil X = f$. The isomorphisms that are required to exist anyway are then included as a third component in the bisimulation.

Now "$\Leftarrow$" is trivial.
In order to establish "$\Rightarrow$" we first make two observations.

1. Let $\mathcal{E} \in \mathbf{E}$, $X, X' \in \mathit{Conf}(\mathcal{E}), X \longrightarrow_{\mathcal{E}} X'$ and $e \in X$. Then there exists no $d \in X' \backslash X$ with $d \prec_{\mathcal{E}} e$. For if such a d would exist then there would be an $f \in X$ with $f \prec_{\mathcal{E}} e$ and $f \#_{\mathcal{E}} d$, contradicting the conflict-freeness of X'. Hence

$$(d \in X' \wedge d \leq_{X'} e) \Longleftrightarrow (d \in X \wedge d \leq_X e)\,.$$

2. If g is an isomorphism between two labelled partial orders $(X, \leq_X, l_X)$ and $(Y, \leq_Y, l_Y)$, and $e \in X$ then

$$|\{d \in X \mid d \leq_X e\}| = |\{d \in Y \mid d \leq_Y g(e)\}|\,.$$

Now suppose $\mathcal{E} \approx_{wh} \mathcal{F}$. Let R be a h–bisimulation between $\mathcal{E}$ and $\mathcal{F}$ without the requirements $f' \lceil X = f$. We proof that these requirements are met nevertheless. Assume that $(X, Y, f) \in R$ and $X \longrightarrow_{\mathcal{E}} X'$. Then there exists $(X', Y', f') \in R$ with $Y \longrightarrow_{\mathcal{F}} Y'$. Suppose $f' \lceil X \neq f$. Then there exists an $e \in X$ with $f'(e) \neq f(e)$. With the observations above it follows that

$$|\{d \in Y' \mid d \leq_{Y'} f(e)\}| = |\{d \in Y \mid d \leq_Y f(e)\}| =$$
$$|\{d \in X \mid d \leq_X e\}| = |\{d \in X' \mid d \leq_{X'} e\}| = |\{d \in Y' \mid d \leq_{Y'} f'(e)\}|\,.$$

Hence we cannot have $f'(e) <_{Y'} f(e)$ or $f(e) <_{Y'} f'(e)$. Thus $f'(e)\ co_{Y'}\ f(e)$.
Moreover, f' and f preserve labelling, so $l_{\mathcal{F}}(f'(e)) = l_{\mathcal{E}}(e) = l_{\mathcal{F}}(f(e))$.
This is a contradiction since $\mathcal{F}$ was assumed to have no autoconcurrency. ■

7.14 Corollary Let $\mathcal{E}, \mathcal{F} \in \mathbf{E}$ be without autoconcurrency and let *ref* be a refinement function.

Then $\mathcal{E} \approx_{wh} \mathcal{F} \Rightarrow \mathit{ref}(\mathcal{E}) \approx_{wh} \mathit{ref}(\mathcal{F})$.

Conclusion

In this paper we have shown that equivalences based on interleaving of atomic actions or of steps (multisets of concurrently executable actions) are not preserved when changing the level of atomicity of actions. However, we could show that certain equivalences based on modelling causal relations explicitly by partial orders are indeed preserved by refinement of actions. We considered "linear time" approaches, where the behaviour of a system is equated to the set of possible runs, and "branching time" approaches, where the conflict structure of systems is taken into account. We could show the negative results about the interleaving approaches regardless of the level of detail in modelling the conflict behaviour. However, for the positive results about the partial order approaches, the conflict structure turned out to be crucial. An interesting topic for further research would be to investigate testing equivalences based on partial orders, taking the conflict structure in a weaker form into account. However, since the systems $\mathcal{E}'$ and $\mathcal{F}'$ of Example 7.4 are not even interleaving failure equivalent, no equivalence that is included between interleaving failure and pomset bisimulation equivalence, such as the partial order equivalence of [ADF], can be preserved under action refinement. For an overview consider the following diagram:

runs / conflict structure	sequences of actions	sequences of steps	pomsets
paths	$\approx_{it}$	$\approx_{st}$	$\approx_{pt}$
⋮ e.g. testing			?
bisimulation	$\approx_{ib}$	$\approx_{sb}$	$\approx_{pb}$ $\approx_{wh}$ comb. of $\approx_{pb}$ and $\approx_{wh}$ $\approx_{h}$

//// means: not preserved by refinement

This diagram is not at all complete. A naturally arising question is to what extent it is actually necessary to move to partial order semantics to achieve invariance of equivalence under refinement (here we have only shown that steps are not sufficient). In [van Glabbeek a] it is proved that also ST-bisimulation [GV] is preserved by refinement. ST-bisimulation does not respect pomset trace equivalence. Thus it is not necessary to use the full distinguishing power of partial order semantics. Which part of it is needed is determined in [van Glabbeek a] and [Vogler a].

Furthermore we would like to adress the question whether history preserving bisimulation as defined here is the coarsest equivalence respecting pomset bisimulation and being preserved by refinement. We conjectured in [GG a] that this is not the case, in particular, that for

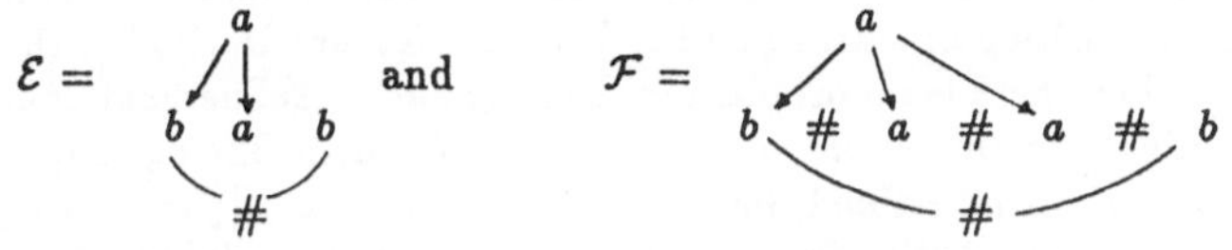

$\mathcal{E} \not\approx_h \mathcal{F}$, but for any refinement *ref*, $ref(\mathcal{E}) \approx_{pb} ref(\mathcal{F})$. This conjecture has in the meantime been proven in [Vogler b], using an equivalence that combines ST-bisimulation and pomset-bisimulation.

Nevertheless, if it is required to model the interplay of causality and branching in full detail, history preserving bisimulation seems to be the coarsest suitable equivalence.

In [GG a] we had established these results for conflict-free refinements using prime event structures as our system model. In this paper we have extended them to refinements with conflicts and with possibly infinite behaviours.

For this it was convenient to use a more expressive model. We have chosen here *flow event structures* which are also very suited for giving semantics to CCS-like languages. We could have used simpler forms of event structures where just the axiom of finite causes is dropped, and the axiom of conflict heredity is dropped [BC a] or weakened [DD b]. These forms of event structures may be seen — like prime event structures — as special cases of flow event structures. [DD b] also states a refinement theorem for history preserving bisimulation and the same class of refinements as considered here.

A problem which we have not adressed in detail in this paper is the treatment of deadlocks in flow event structures. Since the notion of configuration does not distinguish deadlock and termination and the equivalences considered here are based on this notion, these equivalences will not be congruences for sequential composition and for refinement. For example, we may have $\forall a \in Act : ref(a) \approx_h ref'(a)$, however $ref(\mathcal{E}) \not\approx_h ref'(\mathcal{E})$.

We could also have used more general models than flow event structures. In [GG b] we have considered refinement for *configuration structures* (closely resembling *families of configurations* [Winskel]), a more general and abstract model where a system is represented by its set of configurations. This provides a general framework to investigate refinement independently of a particular representation.

Refinement of actions has also been considered in the theory of Petri nets by investigating several constructions for refining transitions in nets (for an overview see [BGV]). We have slightly extended one type of these approaches in [GG b]. A refinement theorem for history preserving bisimulation and a restricted class of refinements is proved in [BDKP]. In [Devillers], this result has been generalised to a setting with internal moves.

The refinement operation we have considered was defined directly on a semantic domain for concurrent systems. An alternative would be to introduce refinement as syntactic substitution, for example in a CCS–like language (*syntactic action refinement*).

In principle there are two ways to treat syntactic action refinement in languages like CCS. One of them is to use the CCS–actions for modelling the refinable actions of this paper. In the absence of communication (or synchronisation) refinement can simply be defined as syntactic substitution of an action by a process expression. This approach has been taken in [AH] and [NEL]. In [AH] also an equivalence which is invariant under refinement is proposed, but for a more restricted class of systems. In the presence of communication defining such a refinement operator is much more difficult.

An alternative is to use the actions of CCS for modelling "atomic" actions that cannot be refined, and representing our refinable actions by means of variables or *parameters*. This approach requires a general sequential composition operator and has been carried out in [BT] in the setting of ACP. In particular [BT] shows that there is no problem in defining such a refinement operator while working in interleaving semantics: atomic actions a, b cannot be refined, so the equation $a \mid b = a;b + b;a$ is harmless; parameters x, y can be refined, but there is no equation $x \mid y = x;y + y;x$. Note that the refinement operator, ordinary substitution, is defined in the language (that still contains all information about causal dependence) and not in the associated interleaving model.

A different approach to refining actions is taken in [GGM] and [Boudol a]. There again actions are assumed to be atomic, however they may now be refined when preserving atomicity. This requires to define a concept of atomicity for processes. In [Boudol a] two kinds of atomicity are proposed, corresponding with two kinds of refinement. In [GGM] this kind of refinement is carried out in an interleaving based model.

However, our results show that refinement of actions is possible without any restrictions when using causality based models and appropriate equivalence notions.

Acknowledgements

This research was initiated by a dicussion with Albert Meyer and Ernst–Rüdiger Olderog at ICALP 87 in Karlsruhe. Alex Rabinovich helped us by supplying the two systems considered in Example 7.6. Kim G. Larsen raised the question whether $\approx_h$ is the coarsest equivalence being preserved by refinement and respecting pomset bisimulation. Many thanks also to Ilaria Castellani, Rocco De Nicola and Frits Vaandrager for helpful discussions and comments, and to Gertrud Jacobs and Ingrid Filter for their patience and careful preparation of the manuscript.

References

[ADF] L. Aceto, R. De Nicola, A. Fantechi: *Testing Equivalences for Event Structures*, Mathematical Models for the Semantics of Parallelism, LNCS 280, Springer–Verlag, 1987

[AH] L. Aceto, M. Hennessy: *Towards Action–Refinement in Process Algebras*, Proc. LICS'89, IEEE Computer Society Press, Washington, pp 138–145, 1989

[AB] D. Austry, G. Boudol: *Algébre de processus et synchronisations,* Theoretical Computer Science, Vol. 30, No. 1, pp 91–131, 1984

[BT] J.A. Bergstra, J.V. Tucker: *Top–down Design and the Algebra of Communicating Processes*, Science of Computer Programming, Vol. 5, No. 2, pp 171–199, 1985

[BDKP] E. Best, R. Devillers, A. Kiehn, L. Pomello: *Fully Concurrent Bisimulation*, Technical Report LIT 202, Université Libre de Bruxelles, Laboratoire d' Informatique Theorique, 1989

[Boudol a] G. Boudol: *Atomic Actions (Note)*, Bulletin of the EATCS 38, pp 136–144, 1989

[Boudol b] G. Boudol: *Computations of Distributed Systems, Part 1: Flow Event structures and Flow Nets*, report INRIA Sophia Antipolis, to appear

[BC a] G. Boudol, I. Castellani: *On the Semantics of Concurrency: Partial Orders and Transition Systems*, Proc. TAPSOFT 87, Vol. I, LNCS 249, Springer–Verlag, pp 123–137, 1987

[BC b] G. Boudol, I. Castellani: *Permutation of Transitions: An Event Structure Semantics for CCS and SCCS*, Linear Time, Branching Time and Partial Order in Logics and Models for Concurrency, LNCS 354, Springer–Verlag, pp 411–427, 1989

[BGV] W. Brauer, R. Gold, W. Vogler: *Behaviour and Equivalence Preserving Refinements of Petri Nets*, Report, Institut für Informatik, Technische Universität München, 1990

[BHR] S.D. Brookes, C.A.R. Hoare, A.W. Roscoe: *A Theory of Communicating Sequential Processes*, Journal of the ACM, Vol. 31, No. 3, pp 560–599, 1984

[CDP] L. Castellano, G. De Michelis, L. Pomello: *Concurrency vs Interleaving: An Instructive Example*, Bulletin of the EATCS 31, pp 12–15, 1987

[DD a] P. Darondeau, P. Degano: *Causal Trees*, Proc. ICALP 89, LNCS 372, Springer–Verlag, pp 234–248, 1989

[DD b] Ph. Darondeau, P. Degano: *Event structures, Causal trees, and Refinements*, to appear in Proc. MFCS 90, LNCS, Springer–Verlag, 1990

[DDM a] P. Degano, R. De Nicola, U. Montanari: *Observational Equivalences for Concurrency Models*, Formal Description of Programming Concepts — III, Proc. of the third IFIP WG 2.2 working conference, Elsevier Science Publishers B.V. (North Holland), pp 105–129, 1987

[DDM b] P. Degano, R. De Nicola, U. Montanari: *A Distributed Operational Semantics for CCS Based on Condition/Event Systems*, Acta Informatica, Vol. 26, No. 1/2, pp 59–91, 1988

[DDM c] P. Degano, R. De Nicola, U. Montanari: *Partial Ordering Descriptions of Nondeterministic Concurrent Processes*, Linear Time, Branching Time and Partial Order in Logics and Models for Concurrency, LNCS 354, Springer–Verlag, pp 438–466, 1989

[DH] R. De Nicola, M. Hennessy: *Testing Equivalences for Processes*, Theoretical Computer Science, Vol. 34, pp 83–133, 1984

[Devillers] R. Devillers: *Maximality Preserving Bisimulation*, Technical Report LIT 214, Université Libre de Bruxelles, Laboratoire d' Informatique Theorique, 1990

[van Glabbeek a] R.J. van Glabbeek: *The Refinement Theorem for ST-Bisimulation Semantics*, Report CS–R9002, Centrum voor Wiskunde en Informatica, Amsterdam 1990; to appear in: Proceedings IFIP Working Conference on Programming Concepts and Methods, Israel at sea Gallilee 1990

[van Glabbeek b] R.J. van Glabbeek: *Comparative Concurrency Semantics and Refinement of Actions*, Ph. D. Thesis, Free University, Amsterdam 1990

[GG a] R.J. van Glabbeek, U. Goltz: *Equivalence Notions for Concurrent Systems and Refinement of Actions*, Arbeitspapiere der GMD 366, February 1989, Extended Abstract in Proc. MFCS 89, LNCS 379, Springer–Verlag, pp 237–248, 1989

[GG b] R.J. van Glabbeek, U. Goltz: *Refinement of Actions in Causality Based Models*, Stepwise Refinement of Distributed Systems: Models, Formalism, Correctness, LNCS 430, Springer–Verlag, pp 267–300, 1990

[GV] R.J. van Glabbeek, F.W. Vaandrager: *Petri Net Models for Algebraic Theories of Concurrency*, Proc. PARLE, Vol. II, LNCS 259, Springer–Verlag, pp 224–242, 1987

[GW] R.J. van Glabbeek, W.P. Weijland: *Refinement in Branching Time Semantics*, Report CS-R8922, Centrum voor Wiskunde en Informatica, Amsterdam 1989; in: J.W. de Bakker, 25 jaar semantiek, liber amicorum, Centrum voor Wiskunde en Informatica, Amsterdam 1989, pp 247–252; and in: Proceedings AMAST Conference, Iowa City, USA, pp 197–201, 1989

[GMM] R. Gorrieri, S.Marchetti, U. Montanari: *A^2CCS: A Simple Extension of CCS for Handling Atomic Actions*, Proc. CAAP'88, LNCS 299, Springer-Verlag, pp 258–270, 1988

[HM] M. Hennessy, R. Milner: *Algebraic Laws for Nondeterminism and Concurrency*, Journal of the ACM, Vol. 32, No. 1, pp 137–161, 1985

[Milne] G.J. Milne: *CIRCAL and the Representation of Communication, Concurrency and Time*, Transactions on Programming languages and Systems (ACM), Vol. 7, No. 2, pp 270–298, 1985

[Milner a] R. Milner: *A Calculus of Communicating Systems*, LNCS 92, Springer–Verlag, 1980

[Milner b] R. Milner: *Calculi for Synchrony and Asynchrony*, Theoretical Computer Science, Vol. 25, No. 3, pp 267–310, 1983

[NEL] M. Nielsen, U. Engberg, K.S. Larsen: *Fully Abstract Models for a Process Language with Refinement*, Linear Time, Branching Time and Partial Order in Logics and Models for Concurrency, LNCS 354, Springer-Verlag, pp 523–548, 1989

[NPW] M. Nielsen, G.D. Plotkin, G. Winskel: *Petri Nets, Event Structures and Domains, Part I*, Theoretical Computer Science, Vol. 13, No. 1, pp 85–108, 1981

[Park] D. Park: *Concurrency and Automata on Infinite Sequences*, Proc. 5th GI–Conference on Theoretical Computer Science, LNCS 104, Springer–Verlag, pp 167–183, 1981

[Petri] C.A. Petri: *Non-Sequential Processes*, Interner Bericht 77–05, GMD, Institut für Informationssystemforschung, 1977

[Pomello] L. Pomello: *Some Equivalence Notions for Concurrent Systems. An Overview*, in: Advances in Petri Nets 1985, LNCS 222, Springer–Verlag, pp 381–400, 1986

[Pratt] V.R. Pratt: *Modelling Concurrency with Partial Orders*, International Journal of Parallel Programming, Vol. 15, No. 1, pp 33–71, 1986

[Reisig] W. Reisig: *Petri Nets*, EATCS Monographs on Theoretical Computer Science 4, Springer–Verlag, 1985

[TV] D.A. Taubner, W. Vogler: *The Step Failure Semantics*, Proc. STACS 87, LNCS 247, Springer–Verlag, pp 348–359, 1987

[TRH] B.A. Trakhtenbrot, A. Rabinovich, J. Hirshfeld: *Nets of Processes*, Technical Report 97/88, Tel Aviv Univ., 1988, see also: A. Rabinovich, B.A. Trakhtenbrot: *Behavior Structures and Nets*, Fundamenta Informaticae, Vol. XI, No. 4, pp 357–404, 1988

[Vaandrager] F. Vaandrager: *An Explicit Representation of Equivalence Classes of the History Preserving Bisimulation*, Manuscript, CWI Amsterdam, 1989

[Vogler a] W. Vogler: *Failure Semantics Based on Interval Semiwords is a Congruence for Refinement*, Proc. STACS'90, LNCS 415, Springer-Verlag, pp 285–297, 1990

[Vogler b] W. Vogler: *Bisimulation and Action Refinement*, SFB–Bericht Nr. 342/10/90 A, Institut für Informatik, Technische Universität München, 1990

[Winskel] G. Winskel: *Event Structures*, Petri Nets: Applications and Relationships to Other Models of Concurrency, LNCS 255, Springer–Verlag, pp 325–392, 1987

CCS and Petri Nets[1]

Ursula Goltz
Gesellschaft für Mathematik und Datenverarbeitung
Postfach 1240, D–5205 Sankt Augustin 1

Abstract

In the usual semantics of CCS–like languages, parallelism is reduced to non–deterministic interleaving of actions. As an alternative semantic model for CCS with a clear distinction between concurrency and nondeterminism, Petri nets may be used. This paper gives an introduction to Petri net semantics for CCS. Two approaches are considered: a compositional approach where semantic operations are defined for Petri nets explicitly, and an operational approach using Plotkin–style transition rules which is particularly convenient for infinite processes. It is discussed which class of CCS programs is representable by finite nets.

1 Introduction

CCS [Milner 89] and similar calculi for concurrent systems are often refered to as *process algebras*. Besides CCS, the most prominent ones are CSP [Hoare 85] and ACP [Bergstra/Klop 84]. Process algebras offer a well–established theory for the specification and verification of concurrent systems. The strength of these approaches is their *compositionality*. Systems are composed from basic entities (*actions*) using composition operators like sequential composition, parallel composition or choice operators. This offers a well–structured representation and allows for modular construction of systems. Furthermore, this gives the possibility of using the structure of systems in verification procedures.

One of the most important operators in process algebras is the parallel composition. However, for reasons of simplicity and tractability, the semantic models in these calculi simulate independent parallel execution of components by arbitrary interleaving of their actions. Thus parallelism is reduced to nondeterministic choice and sequential composition.

1.1 Example

Consider the CCS processes $P = a|b$ and $Q = ab+ba$. In P, a and b are executed independently in parallel. In Q, either first a and then b is executed, or first b and then a.

However, the behaviour of both P and Q is formalised in the semantics of CCS for example by the synchronisation tree

[1]supported by the Esprit Basic Research Action No. 3148 DEMON (Design Methods Based on Nets).

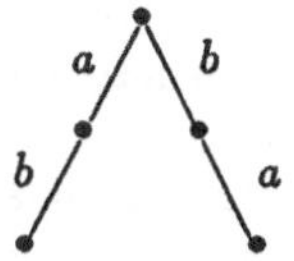

P and Q may not be distinguished in the usual semantics of CCS.

For many purposes, this socalled *interleaving semantics* is fully sufficient. However, from a theoretical point of view, it is intriguing to search for alternative semantic models where parallel composition may be modelled directly. Also it has been shown that for certain issues like *fairness*, the interleaving approach may sometimes not be faithful [Reisig 84]. Recently, it has been shown that a calculus for *refinement of actions* may be considered conveniently in more expressive models [Glabbeek/Goltz 90]. In the interleaving approach, actions have to be assumed to be atomic entities.

A lot of research has already been devoted to giving non–interleaved semantics to CCS–like languages. A rather complete list of references of this field was given in [Olderog et al. 88]. Most of these approaches are based on *Petri nets*, which offer a well–established theory for the representation of concurrency.

1.2 Example

The CCS processes $P = a|b$ and $Q = ab + ba$ from example 1.1 may be represented by the Petri nets

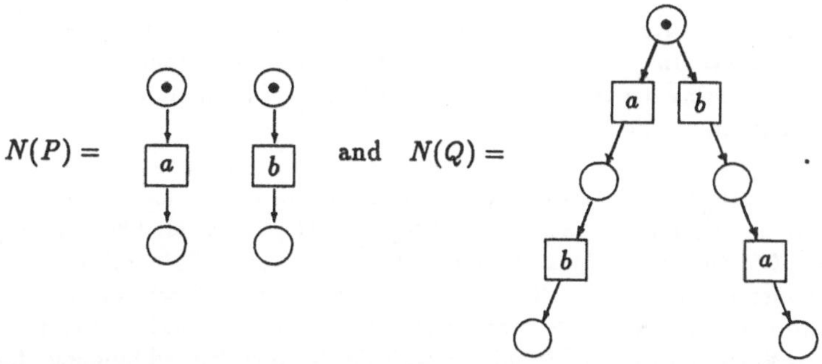

In the first net, the transitions labelled by a and b may occur independently of each other, whereas a and b may only be executed sequentially in the second net.

In the following, we give a short overview on the development of approaches for Petri net semantics of CCS (without claiming completeness).

A first attempt for a semantics of CCS using Petri nets was presented in [de Cindio et al. 83] where a subset of CCS (only bounded parallelism) was considered. In [Goltz/Mycroft 84], acyclic Petri nets called *occurrence nets* were used to model full CCS. This work was similar to and inspired by Winskel's semantics using *event structures* [Winskel 82] and uses constructions for occurrence nets similar to [Winskel 84]. Both occurrence nets and event structures represent infinite processes by infinite structures, even for simple recursive constructs like $\mu x(ax)$. It was observed in [Goltz/Mycroft 84] that many recursive CCS programs have natural representations as finite nets and it was tried to generate them by folding the infinite representations. These approaches gave a net semantics to CCS in a *compositional* style by defining operations like parallel composition or choice as operators on Petri nets.

[Degano et al. 86], [Olderog 87] and [Degano et al. 88a] presented a *structured operational net semantics* using Plotkin–style transition rules for full CCS (or extendable to full CCS). These approaches generate one–safe nets (places will never carry more than one token). Certain recursive expressions (like $\mu x(ax)$) are represented by finite (cyclic) nets. [Olderog 87] and [Degano et al. 88a] succeed to fully preserve concurrency in the modelling of choice and recursion and thus improve the approach of [Degano et al. 86]. An approach for a compositional semantics for ACP with one–safe nets was presented in [Glabbeek/Vaandrager 87]. However, it is not clear how to model recursive programs in this framework.

All approaches using one–safe nets need infinite net structures to represent processes with unboundedly growing parallelism like, for example, in $\mu x(ax|b)$. In [Goltz 88a, Goltz 88b], an approach was proposed for generating finite net representations for a class of CCS expressions with unbounded parallelism. The idea is to represent the growth of parallelism by arbitrarily large numbers of tokens on places, using place/transition–nets. This uses the full power of Petri nets, giving finite representations for infinite behaviours by means of the "token game". However, this is only possible for a restricted class of CCS programs, since full CCS is Turing powerful. In [Taubner 89] it has been shown that the language considered in [Goltz 88b] may not be extended, and a similar construction is investigated for another class of programs, not allowing recursively generated parallelism but with restriction and relabelling. Additionally, [Taubner 89] proposes a semantics for full CCS by using nets with individual tokens.

Petri net semantics were not only considered for abstract calculi where actions are just atomic entities, but also for languages like the concrete version of CSP [Hoare 78], where actions correspond to state space transformations.

In [Goltz/Reisig 85], a subset of 78–CSP was modelled by using individual tokens to code the information about data. In [Reisig 84], a structured operational semantics was given for the same subset of CSP, generating occurrence nets. In [Best 88] and [Degano et al. 88c], CSP programs with variables are modelled as one–safe nets.

In this paper, an introduction to the concepts of Petri net semantics for CCS is given. The presentation is mainly based on [Goltz 88a, Goltz 88b] and [Degano et al. 88a, Olderog 87]. We will only consider pure CCS; that is, actions will be abstract entities and we will not explain the treatment of data. After introducing basic notions of Petri nets (section 2), we consider finitary CCS (section 3) and show how to model all CCS operations except for recursion in Petri nets. Then we consider infinite processes (section 4). For simplicity, we consider a restricted language for infinite processes. We contrast the structured operational approach for Petri net semantics with a compositional approach defining Petri net operations explicitly. We conclude by discussing informally the relationship between the considered net semantics.

The paper is self–contained, however some familarity with basic concepts of CCS and Petri nets is assumed. All proofs are omitted, refering to the corresponding original papers.

2 Place/transition–systems and basic notions

In this section, we define the class of Petri nets we will use. For basic concepts and motivation we refer to [Reisig 85].

Usually, a net represents a system in the following form. The static structure of the system is represented as a net structure $N = (S, T, F)$ where S is a set of *places*, representing passive components of the system (i.e. positions of a local control), T is a set of *transitions*, representing activities, and the *flow relation* F represents the dependencies between active and passive components. A possible state of the system is represented by a *marking*, a distribution of *tokens* over places of the net. We will allow here that places may carry arbitrary many tokens to be able to represent also systems with infinite state space by finite net structures. The dynamic behaviour of the net is given by the *firing rule*. In our case, a transition may occur whenever all its preplaces (in terms of F) carry tokens. When it occurs it removes a token from each preplace and puts a token on each postplace.

Since we will use transitions to represent actions in CCS programs, we will label transitions by elements of *Act*. For the definition of composition operations, we distinguish a set of *initial places* in a net: these places will carry the initial marking.

For sake of simple definitions of composition operators, we slightly deviate from the usual notation for nets. We specify the flow relation implicitly, by considering labelled transitions of the form

(preset, action, postset).

We consider only transitions with non–empty pre– and postsets. $\mathcal{P}_+(S)$ denotes the set of non–empty subsets of a set S.

2.1 Definition

$N = (S, T, I)$ is called a *net* (*labelled over Act*) iff

- S is a set (of *places*),
- $T \subseteq \mathcal{P}_+(S) \times Act \times \mathcal{P}_+(S)$ (*transitions*),
- $I \subseteq S$ (*initial places*).

For $t \in T$, ${}^\bullet t := pr_1(t)$ denotes the *preset of t*, $t^\bullet := pr_3(t)$ denotes the *postset of t*; $l(t) := pr_2(t)$ denotes the *label of t* (where pr_i denotes the projection to the i–th component).

The usual net representation may be obtained by deriving the flow relation:

$$(x, y) \in F :\Longleftrightarrow x \in S, y \in T \text{ and } x \in {}^\bullet y \text{ or } x \in T, y \in S \text{ and } y \in x^\bullet.$$

We may then define the *pre*– and *postset of places* as usual:
${}^\bullet s := \{t \in T \mid tFs\}$, $s^\bullet := \{t \in T \mid sFt\}$.

We will need to refer to the sets of places without ingoing or without outgoing arcs.
Let ${}^\circ N := \{s \in S \mid {}^\bullet s = \emptyset\}$, $N^\circ := \{s \in S \mid s^\bullet = \emptyset\}$.
Note that in general ${}^\circ N \neq I$.

Nets are represented graphically as usual with circles for places, boxes for transitions (inscribed by the transition label), and arcs for the flow relation. The initial places are indicated by placing a token (a dot) on each of them.

For specifying the dynamic behaviour, we consider *markings* of a net to be multisets over the set S of places. A marking M specifies, for each place s, a number of tokens $M(s)$.

We will now define, for any marking M, which transitions are enabled by M and which transitions may be executed independently in one *step*. The usual firing rule is then obtained as a special case. Since we allow several tokens on places, we consequently allow transitions to occur concurrently with themselves, hence steps will be multisets over T.

We use the following notations for multisets.

$\mathbb{N}^S$ denotes the set of multisets over a set S.
$\mathbb{N}^S_+$ denotes the set of nonempty multisets over S.

Let $M, M' \in \mathbb{N}^S$.
$M \leq M'$ iff $\forall s \in S : M(s) \leq M'(s)$,
$M+M' \in \mathbb{N}^S$ is defined by $\forall s \in S : M+M'\ (s) = M(s)+M'(s)$,
$M-M' \in \mathbb{N}^S$, for $M' \leq M$, is defined by $\forall s \in S : M-M'\ (s) = M(s)-M'(s)$.

For defining the notion of a step, we extend the concept of the pre– and postset of a transition to multisets of transitions.

2.2 Definition Let $G \in \mathbb{N}^T$.

- The *preset of* $G, {}^\bullet G \in \mathbb{N}^S$, is defined by ${}^\bullet G(s) = \sum_{t \in T} {}^\bullet t(s) \cdot G(t)$ for all $s \in S$.
- The *postset of* $G, G^\bullet \in \mathbb{N}^S$, is defined by $G^\bullet(s) = \sum_{t \in T} t^\bullet(s) \cdot G(t)$ for all $s \in S$.

Note that we have used the characteristic mapping of ${}^\bullet t$ and $t^\bullet$ in this definition: ${}^\bullet t : S \to \{0,1\}$ and $t^\bullet : S \to \{0,1\}$.

Hence ${}^\bullet G$ specifies how many tokens are required by the multiset G of transitions; $G^\bullet$ specifies, how many tokens are produced by G. With these notions, it is now easy to define the notion of a step; a multiset of transitions may occur if there are enough tokens on the preplaces; the follower marking is obtained by removing the corresponding number of tokens from the preplaces and adding the corresponding number of tokens on the postplaces.

2.3 Definition Let $N = (S,T,I)$, let $G \in \mathbb{N}^T_+$, let $M, M' \in \mathbb{N}^S$.

G is called a *step from* M *to* M' ($M[G\rangle M'$) iff

- $M \geq {}^\bullet G$ (M *enables* G),
- $M' = M - {}^\bullet G + G^\bullet$.

Next, we consider the reachable markings of a net starting with an *initial marking* M_o. A net N with an initial marking $M_o \in \mathbb{N}^S$ is called a *place/transition–system* (*P/T–system*) and will be denoted by (N, M_o). Since we have distinguished initial places $I \subseteq S$, we will consider only initial markings M_0 with $M_0(s) = 0$ for $s \notin I$. Mostly, we will consider the initial marking I (each initial place carries exactly one token).

2.4 Definition Let (N, M_o) be a P/T–system.

The set of *reachable markings of* (N, M_o) is the smallest set, $[N, M_o\rangle$, such that $M_o \in [N, M_o\rangle$ and if $M \in [N, M_o\rangle$ and $\exists G$ with $M[G\rangle M'$ then $M' \in [N, M_o\rangle$.

A net with an initial marking is *one–safe* if places will never carry more than one token.

2.5 Definition

(N, M_o) is *one–safe* iff $\forall M \in [N, M_o\rangle, \forall s \in S : M(s) \leq 1$.

Next, we define a particularly simple class of nets with acyclic flow relation and only forward branched places.

2.6 Definition

$N = (S, T, I)$ is called an *occurrence net* iff

- the transitive closure of F is irreflexive (no cycles),
- $\forall s \in S : |^\bullet s| \leq 1$ (no backward-branched places),
- $\#$ is irreflexive, where for $x, y \in S \cup T$,
  $x \# y :\Longleftrightarrow \exists t, t' \in T$ with $t \neq t', {}^\bullet t \cap {}^\bullet t' \neq \emptyset, tF^* x$ and $t'F^* y$ (no self-conflicts),
- $\forall t \in T : \{t' \in T_N \mid t'F^* t\}$ is finite (axiom of finite causes),
- $I = {}^\circ N$.

Here F^* denotes the reflexive transitive closure of the flow relation F.

For comparing the behaviour of nets and CCS programs, we use labelled transition systems and the notion of (strong) bisimulation equivalence [Park 81, Milner 89].

2.7 Definition Let L be a set (of *labels*).

$\mathcal{A} = (St, \longrightarrow, q_o)$ is called a *transition system (labelled over L)* iff

- St is a set (of *states*),
- $\longrightarrow \subseteq St \times L \times St$ (*transition relation*),
- $q_o \in St$ (*initial state*).

For $(q, l, q') \in \longrightarrow$, we write $q \xrightarrow{l} q'$.

2.8 Definition

Two transition systems $\mathcal{A}_i = (St_i, \longrightarrow_i, q_i), i = 1, 2$, are *(strongly) bisimular* iff there exists a *bisimulation* R between $\mathcal{A}_1$ and $\mathcal{A}_2$, i.e. a relation $R \subseteq St_1 \times St_2$ with $(q_1, q_2) \in R$ and, for all $(p, q) \in R$,

- $p \xrightarrow{l}_1 p' \Longrightarrow \exists q'$ with $q \xrightarrow{l}_2 q'$ and $(p', q') \in R$,
- $q \xrightarrow{l}_2 q' \Longrightarrow \exists p'$ with $p \xrightarrow{l}_1 p'$ and $(p', q') \in R$.

We may now associate an interleaving semantics with a labelled P/T-system. We consider occurrences of single transitions and abstract from the names of transitions, keeping only the information about their labels.

2.9 Definition Let (N, M_o) be a P/T-system.

The *(interleaving) transition system of* (N, M_o), $\mathcal{A}_I(N, M_o)$, is defined as

$$\mathcal{A}_I(N, M_o) = (\mathbb{N}^S, \longrightarrow, M_o)$$

where $\longrightarrow \subseteq \mathbb{N}^S \times Act \times \mathbb{N}^S$ is defined by
$M \xrightarrow{a} M' :\Longleftrightarrow \exists t$ with $M[\{t\}\rangle M'$ and $l(t) = a$.

Essentially, $\mathcal{A}_I(N, M_o)$ corresponds to the usual notion of *case graph* [Reisig 85], replacing transition names at the vertices by transition labels.

Since we consider only interleavings of single transitions, we obtain, for example, bisimular transition systems for the nets $N(a|b)$ and $N(ab + ba)$ from example 1.2. More precise information about concurrent behaviour is provided when considering all possible steps, thus associating a *step transition system* with a P/T–system, where the arcs are labelled by multisets of actions.

However, this is still not sufficient to capture the precise information about causalities between action occurrences.

2.10 Example

Consider the CCS processes $P = a|b$ and $Q = a|b + ab$. In P, a and b are always executed independently in parallel, whereas they may be executed explicitly in sequence in Q. However, the corresponding nets

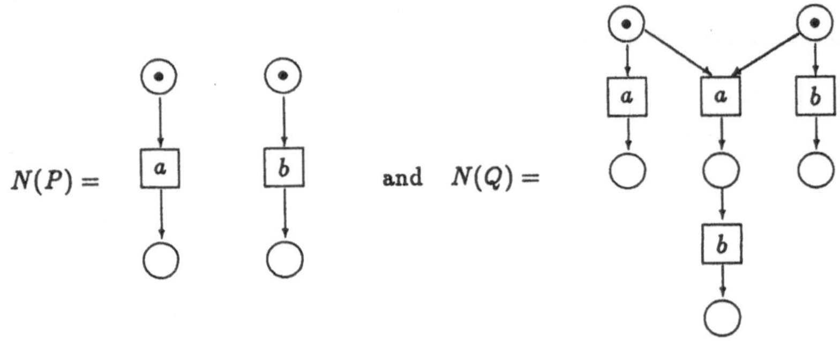

would have bisimular step transition systems.

In Petri net theory, the behaviour of systems with respect to causal dependencies may be captured precisely by the notion of *processes* of nets [Petri 77, Goltz/Reisig 83]. Processes of a net represent its possible executions as acyclic nets with unbranched places (special occurrence nets). Causal dependencies may then be derived from the flow relation. (The word *process* is used in net theory in a more specific sense than e.g. in CCS.)

2.11 Example

The net $N(Q)$ from example 2.10 has the processes

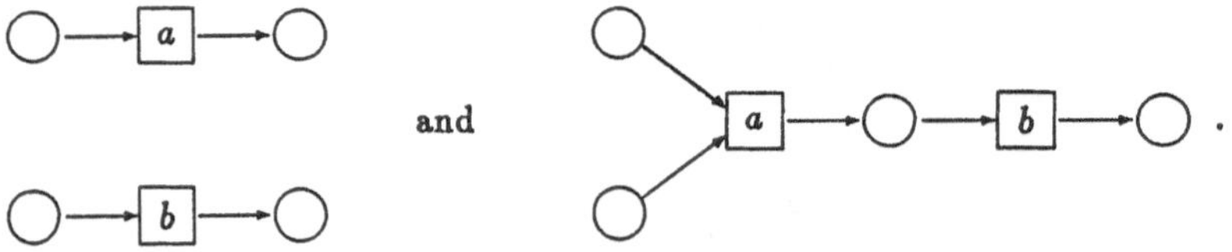

In the second process the occurrence of b causally depends on the occurrence of a; this process is not a process of $N(P)$.

Processes capture precisely the behaviour of nets with respect to causal dependencies, however they do not reflect the branching structure. In nets with labelled transitions, the timing of choices between alternative behaviours may not be recovered from the set of processes.

2.12 Example

Let $P = a(b + c)$ and $Q = ab + ac$.

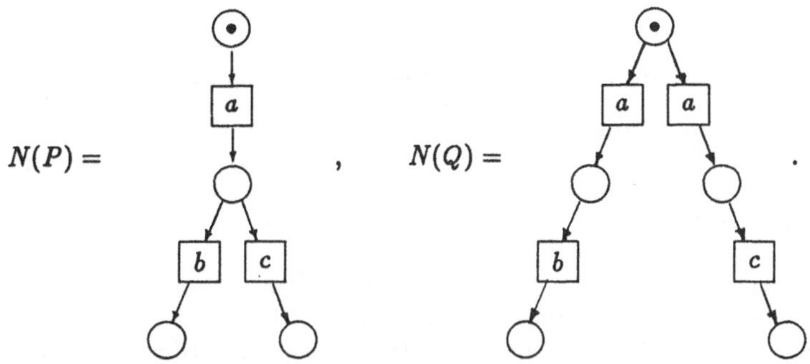

$N(P)$ and $N(Q)$ have the same set of processes.

Semantics and equivalence notions capturing both causalities and branching structure of systems are being investigated (see e.g. [Glabbeek 90]). A very precise equivalence has been proposed in [Rabinovich/Trakhtenbrot 88] and is now usually refered to as *history preserving bisimulation*. This notion has been defined for Petri nets in [Best et al. 89] under the name *fully concurrent bisimulation*. A very discriminating equivalence notion for Petri nets has been suggested in [Olderog 89]. It keeps track not only of causalities between transitions and the branching structure, but also of the places in nets. As a consequence, this equivalence implies equality of the sets of processes of the considered nets.

3 Finite behaviours

In this section, we will show how to give a compositional net semantics to CCS without recursion. The possibilities to extend this approach to infinite behaviours will be discussed in section 4.

3.1 CCS without recursion

Here we introduce the basic definitions and notations of CCS without recursion. For concepts and motivation we refer to [Milner 89]. We start by recalling the syntax of (pure) CCS.

Let Δ be a set of *names* (of actions), denoted by $a, b, \ldots$.

Let $\overline{\Delta} := \{\overline{a} \mid a \in \Delta\}$ (*conames*),
the mapping $a \mapsto \overline{a}$ is a bijection, extended by $\overline{\overline{a}} := a$.

Let τ be a special action name, $\tau \notin \Delta \cup \overline{\Delta}$.

Completementary actions a and $\overline{a}$ are those which will be allowed to communicate in a parallel composition, the result of a communication will then be an internal action not participating in any further communication. Internal actions have the special name τ.

In the following, τ–actions will be treated just like the visible actions in $\Delta \cup \overline{\Delta}$; we do not consider the problem of abstracting from internal actions. As a consequence, our net semantics will be faithful with respect to internal actions. For example, we will not use additional τ–actions in our definitions of composition operations for nets.

Let $Act := \Delta \cup \overline{\Delta} \cup \{\tau\}$ be the set of *actions*. We now define the set of *finitary CCS terms* (or *finitary CCS programs*) as follows.

3.1 Definition

The set *FCCS* of *finitary CCS terms* is defined by the following production system.

$$\mathbf{P} ::= \ nil \ \big| \ a.\mathbf{P} \ \big| \ \mathbf{P}|\mathbf{P} \ \big| \ \mathbf{P}+\mathbf{P} \ \big| \ \mathbf{P}[f] \ \big| \ \mathbf{P} \setminus a$$

where $a \in Act$ and
$f : Act \rightarrow Act$ with $f(\overline{a}) = \overline{f(a)}$ and $f(\tau) = \tau$.

We will apply brackets for uniqueness and the usual precedence rules: unary operators bind stronger than the binary ones. The dot in prefixing terms $a.P$ is often omitted and terms of the form $a.nil$ are abbreviated by a. For example, the term $((a.(b.nil)) + (c.nil))|(d.nil)$ is written as $(ab + c)|d$.

The intuitive meaning of the operators is as follows. *nil* is not able to perform any action. $a.P$ performs a and then behaves like P. In $P|Q, P$ and Q may proceed independently (usually modelled by arbitrary interleaving); complementary actions may be performed jointly as a τ–action. $P + Q$ behaves like P or like Q; as soon as one performs a first action the other is discarded. $P[f]$ behaves like P with actions renamed according to f. $P \setminus a$ behaves like P with the exception that a and $\overline{a}$ may not occur; in particular, this may be used to enforce communications in a parallel composition.

The meaning of the operations is usually formalised by associating a transition system with CCS where the transitions are labelled by actions. As states we take all FCCS terms. Transitions are then defined by structural rules in the style of Plotkin. Since only sequences of actions may be derived this yields an interleaving semantics; independent execution of parallel components is modelled by arbitrary interleaving of their actions.

3.2 Definition Let $P_o \in FCCS$.

The *transition system of* P_o is defined as

$$\mathcal{A}(P_o) := (FCCS, \longrightarrow, P_o)$$

where $\longrightarrow \subseteq FCCS \times Act \times FCCS$ is the relation generated by the rules in the following table (independently of P_o).

prefixing	$a.P \xrightarrow{a} P$	$(a \in Act)$	
sum	$\dfrac{P \xrightarrow{a} P'}{P+Q \xrightarrow{a} P'}$	$\dfrac{Q \xrightarrow{a} Q'}{P+Q \xrightarrow{a} Q'}$	
parallel composition	$\dfrac{P \xrightarrow{a} P'}{P\|Q \xrightarrow{a} P'\|Q}$	$\dfrac{Q \xrightarrow{a} Q'}{P\|Q \xrightarrow{a} P\|Q'}$	$\dfrac{P \xrightarrow{a} P',\ Q \xrightarrow{\overline{a}} Q'}{P\|Q \xrightarrow{\tau} P'\|Q'}$
renaming	$\dfrac{P \xrightarrow{a} P'}{P[f] \xrightarrow{f(a)} P'[f]}$		
restriction	$\dfrac{P \xrightarrow{b} P'}{P \setminus a \xrightarrow{b} P' \setminus a}$	$(b \notin \{a, \overline{a}\})$	

3.2 A compositional net semantics for finitary CCS

We will now give a net semantics to FCCS. In particular, we define a *compositional* semantics in the following sense. Assuming that we already have representations $[\![P]\!]$ and $[\![Q]\!]$ of the behaviour of P and Q, respectively, we want to infer the behaviour of a composed process P *op* Q by applying a semantical operator op' to $[\![P]\!]$ and $[\![Q]\!]$: $[\![P \; op \; Q]\!] = [\![P]\!] \; op' \; [\![Q]\!]$.

We will hence define composition operators for nets, corresponding to our intuitive understanding of the operations in FCCS. We may then associate a net with any FCCS term, simply by interpreting the syntactical operators by these semantical operators. The constructions presented here may be found e.g. in [Winskel 84], [Goltz/Mycroft 84], [Goltz 88a], [Glabbeek/Vaandrager 87].

We will apply *name–overloading*; we will use identical symbols for the operations on the syntactical and on the semantical level.

We start by defining a very simple net called *nil*.

3.3 Definition $nil := (\{s\}, \emptyset, \{s\})$, graphically .

The next operation models the prefixing operation.

3.4 Definition Let $a \in Act$, let $N = (S, T, I)$, let $s \notin S$.

Then $a.N := (\{s\} \cup S, \{(\{s\}, a, I)\} \cup T, \{s\})$.

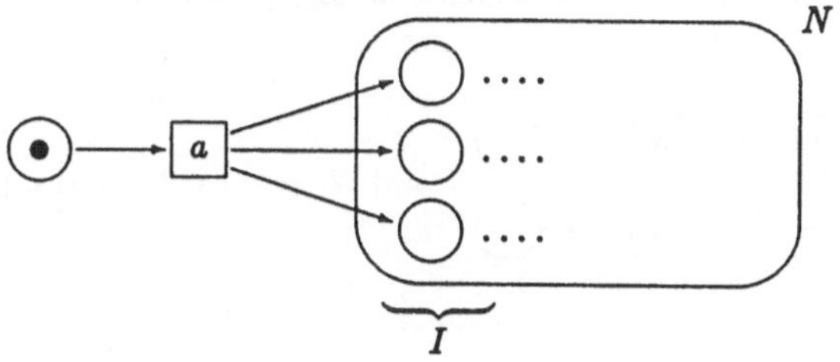

Note that names of places have no significance here; we will not distinguish isomorphic nets. Hence we may require disjoint sets of places for components of operations.

The definition of the parallel compositon of two nets should model our intuition that the two components are executed independently and that complementary actions may communicate, resulting in a joint τ–action. This may simply be modelled by the disjoint union of the two nets, enlarged by τ–transitions for all "syntactically" possible communications.

3.5 Definition Let $N_i = (S_i, T_i, I_i)$, $i = 1, 2$, with $S_1 \cap S_2 = \emptyset$.

Then $N_1 | N_2 := (S_1 \cup S_2, T_1 \cup T_2 \cup T, I_1 \cup I_2)$ where

$$T := \{({}^\bullet t_1 \cup {}^\bullet t_2, \tau, t_1^\bullet \cup t_2^\bullet) \mid t_1 \in T_1, t_2 \in T_2, l(t_1) = \overline{l(t_2)}\}.$$

3.6 Example

Let $N_1 =$ 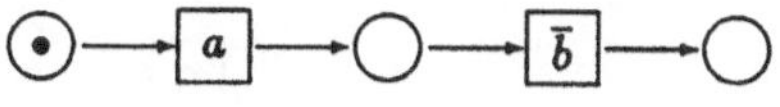

and $N_2 =$ 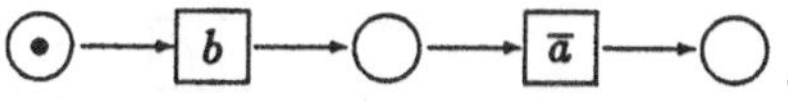.

Then $N_1 \mid N_2 =$

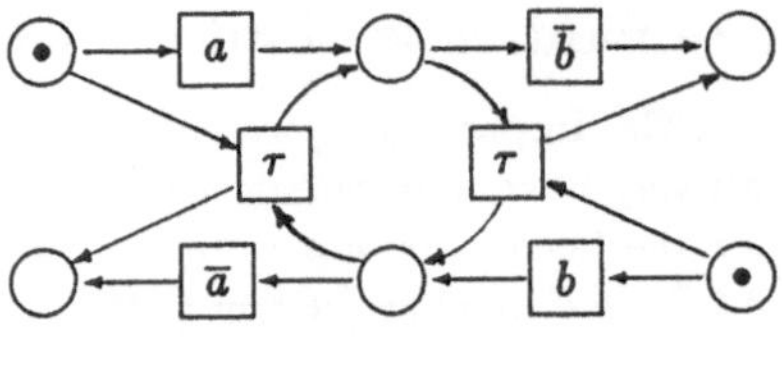

In case of communication possibilities, parallel composition may introduce cycles and backward branched places in nets.

Next, we will define the +–operation for nets. The net $N_1 + N_2$ should behave either like N_1 or like N_2. We will model this by merging the initial places of N_1 with the initial places of N_2.

3.7 Definition Let $N_i = (S_i, T_i, I_i)$, $i = 1, 2$, with $S_1 \cap S_2 = \emptyset$.

Then $N_1 + N_2 := (S_1' \cup S_2' \cup I, T_1' \cup T_2', I)$ where

$$S_i' := S_i - I_i, \ \ i = 1, 2,$$

$$I := I_1 \times I_2,$$

$$T_1' := \{(((({}^\bullet t \cap I_1) \times I_2) \cup ({}^\bullet t \cap S_1'), l(t), t^\bullet) \ \mid \ t \in T_1\},$$

$$T_2' := \{((I_1 \times ({}^\bullet t \cap I_2)) \cup ({}^\bullet t \cap S_2'), l(t), t^\bullet) \ \mid \ t \in T_2\}.$$

By using the cartesian product for initial places, we may disable all initial transitions of $N_1 + N_2$ in the part corresponding to N_2 whenever any transition in the part corresponding to N_1 occurs and vice versa. Initial parallelism in the components is fully preserved.

3.8 Example

Let $N_1 =$

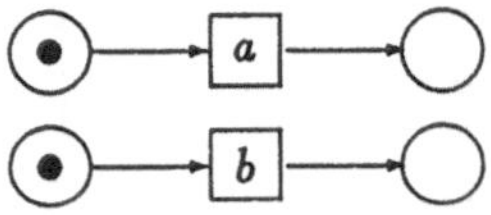

and $N_2 =$

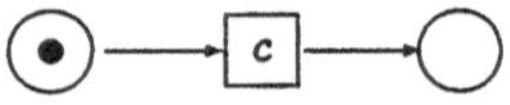

.

Then $N_1 + N_2 =$

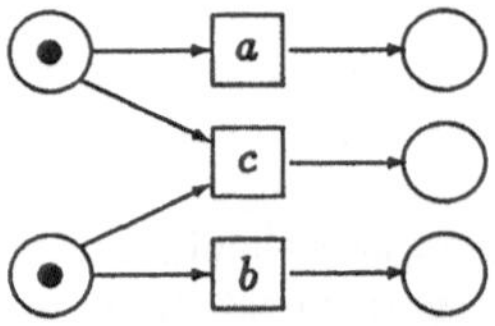

.

Note that this operation behaves not like the + of CCS for nets with ingoing arcs to initial places.

3.9 Example

Let $N_1 =$

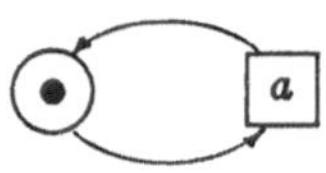

and $N_2 =$

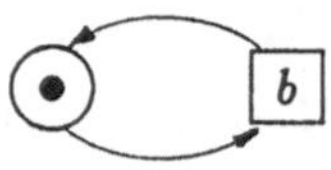

.

Then the sum of N_1 and N_2 should not be

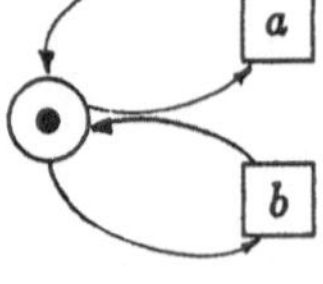

but rather behave like

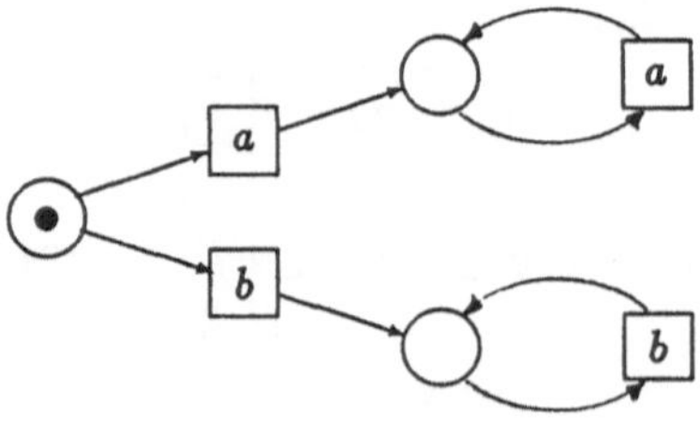

.

However, we will show that all nets N generated by our language will have the property $I \subseteq {}^\circ N$, i.e. initial places have no ingoing arcs.

Renaming is modelled simply by a corresponding relabelling.

3.10 Definition Let $N = (S,T,I)$, let $f : Act \rightarrow Act$.

Then $N[f] := (S, T[f], I)$ where

$$T[f] := \{({}^\bullet t, f(l(t)), t^\bullet) \mid t \in T\}.$$

Finally, restriction is modelled by removing the corresponding transitions.

3.11 Definition Let $N = (S,T,I), a \in \Delta$.

Then $N \setminus a := (S, T \setminus a, I)$ where

$$T \setminus a := T - l^{-1}(\{a, \overline{a}\}).$$

We may now associate a net with any FCCS program.

3.12 Definition Let $P \in FCCS$.

Then $N(P)$ is the net obtained by interpreting the operations in P with the net operations defined above.

We first observe that the generated net has the required property to guarantee correctness of the +–operation.

3.13 Proposition Let $P \in FCCS$, let $N(P) = (S,T,I)$.

Then $I \subseteq {}^\circ N(P)$.

By induction on the structure of P it may be shown that the net generated by P is one–safe. If P contains no possibilities for communication then the reachable part of $N(P)$ is an occurrence net.

The work of Boudol and Castellani on semantics for CCS, see e.g. [Boudol/Castellani 89], lead to defining a special class of nets, called *flow nets* [Boudol 89], which may be considered as a generalisation of occurrence nets. They allow "syntactic" cycles in the flow relation, however transitions will occur at most once in any execution. Flow nets are particularly tailored to allow the definition of CCS operations. In particular, the nets generated by FCCS are flow nets.

Finally, we should verify that the net semantics we have given is faithful with respect to the interleaving semantics. This may be done by showing that the usual semantics is retrievable from the net semantics. In fact, the interleaving transition system which we may associate with $N(P)$ is bisimulation equivalent with that of P.

3.14 Theorem [Goltz 88a]

For $P \in FCCS$, $\mathcal{A}(P) \approx \mathcal{A}_I(N(P))$.

4 Infinite behaviours

We will now discuss how to model recursive CCS programs with nets. A first possible approach is to extend the semantics in section 3 for dealing with recursion. This may be done by defining a *cpo* of nets and then using the usual fixpoint approach. For similar semantics based on occurrence nets, this has been carried out in the work of Winskel (see e.g. [Winskel 87]) and in [Goltz/Mycroft 84]. A slight complication is that we work with labelled structures. This requires a careful definition of the ordering in the cpo (see e.g. [Goltz/Mycroft 84]) or, alternatively, to keep track of the names of the transitions when defining the composition operations. For the class of nets which we used in section 3 (flow nets), this approach may be carried out similar as for *flow event structures* [Boudol/Castellani 89]. However, this kind of semantics will use infinite net structures to represent infinite behaviours.

When using nets, which in general have the power to model infinite behaviours by finite structures (via the token game), it is interesting to try to represent at least some CCS programs with infinite behaviours by finite nets. For example, we would like to represent the program $\mu x(ax)$, which executes an infinite sequence of a's, rather by the little net

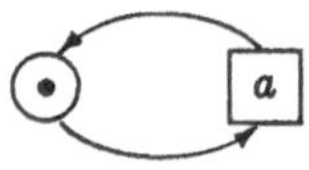

than by the infinite net

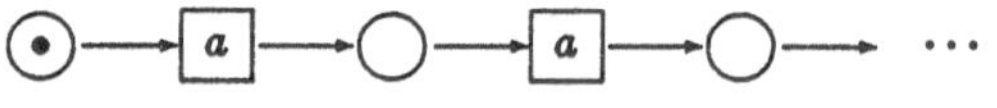

which would be generated by the fixpoint approach.

We will discuss two approaches here, which model CCS programs with recursion by nets and generate finite nets for a subset of CCS. The first one is a structured operational semantics which associates one–safe nets to arbitrary CCS programs and yields finite nets for a certain subclass [Degano et al. 88a, Olderog 87]. For simplicity, we present this approach here only for a restricted language. The second approach is a compositional semantics where recursion is modelled by a looping construct on nets [Goltz 88b]. This yields finite net representations even for certain programs with unbounded parallelism (which is not possible with one–safe nets). This approach is only feasable for a rather restricted class of CCS programs; it is for example not possible to add restriction. However, it yields insight in the respective power of place/transition–systems and of CCS operations. Furthermore, this approach gives an idea of how to add a looping construct to a compositional calculus of nets.

4.1 A subset of CCS with recursion

Throughout this section we will restrict ourselves to a subset of CCS with recursion but with a simplified choice operation. Furthermore we will not consider restriction and relabelling and we will require a rather strong version of guardedness in recursive expressions. Note that these assumptions are not necessary for the operational net semantics presented in 4.2; they will just simplify the presentation. However, we will show that most of these restrictions are essential for the representation of recursive programs by finite nets in 4.3.

We consider here a restricted version of the +–operation. We have already seen, when defining the semantical +–operation in section 3, that choice between two components is difficult if one of them contains initial parallelism. Consider again the expression $(a|b) + c$ (see example 3.8). If c occurs, a and b should be coincidently disabled. We will exclude this situation by considering only *guarded choice*; we require that all components of a choice start without concurrency by requiring that they are prefixed terms.

For uniformity, we introduce a general summation operation where each component must be a prefixed term. We will only consider finite sums here. *nil* and the usual prefixing operation may be obtained as special cases.

4.1 Definition Let *Var* be a set of *variables*, denoted by $x, y, \ldots$.

The set *RCCS* of *restricted (recursive) CCS terms* is then defined by the following production system.

$$\mathbf{P} ::= \mathbf{Q} \;\big|\; \mathbf{P}\,|\,\mathbf{P} \;\big|\; x \;\big|\; \mu x\, \mathbf{Q} \;\; (x \in \mathit{Var}),$$
$$\mathbf{Q} ::= \sum_{i=1}^{n} a_i\, \mathbf{P} \;\; (n \in \mathbb{N}, a_i \in \mathit{Act} \text{ for } 1 \le i \le n).$$

We will denote $\sum_{i=1}^{0} a_i P_i$ by *nil* and use the same precedence rules and abbreviations as in section 3.

A variable x is called *free* in a term P if x occurs outside the scope of an operator μx. RCCS terms without free variables are called *RCCS programs*.

Next we define the structured operational interleaving semantics of RCCS. Except for recursion, it coincides with the semantics for the corresponding subset of FCCS.

4.2 Definition Let $P_o \in RCCS$.

The *transition system of* P_o is defined as

$$\mathcal{A}(P_o) := (RCCS, \longrightarrow, P_o)$$

where $\longrightarrow \subseteq RCCS \times Act \times RCCS$ is the relation generated by the rules in the following table.

sum	$\sum_{i=1}^{n} a_i P_i \xrightarrow{a_j} P_j$	$(1 \le j \le n)$
parallel composition	$\dfrac{P \xrightarrow{a} P'}{P\|Q \xrightarrow{a} P'\|Q}$	$\dfrac{Q \xrightarrow{a} Q'}{P\|Q \xrightarrow{a} P\|Q'}$
	$\dfrac{P \xrightarrow{a} P',\; Q \xrightarrow{\bar{a}} Q'}{P\|Q \xrightarrow{\tau} P'\|Q'}$	
recursion	$\dfrac{P\{\mu x P/x\} \xrightarrow{a} P'}{\mu x P \xrightarrow{a} P'}$	
	where $\{Q/x\}$ denotes substitution of Q for all free occurrences of x (renaming bound variables when necessary)	

4.2 A structured operational net semantics

In this section, we will present the structured operational net semantics for CCS from [Olderog 87] and [Degano et al. 88a] for our subset of CCS. Both the handling of choice and recursion are simpler in our restricted language than in general. Restriction and relabelling may be added in a rather straightforward way.

The key idea (first introduced in [Degano et al. 85]) in this approach is to decompose a process P into a set of *sequential components* (sometimes called "grapes") which can be thought of as running in parallel. For example, the sequential components of $P|Q$ will be $P|$ and $|Q$, keeping the information that they occur in the context of a parallel composition. (We assumed here that P and Q do not contain any parallel operator; this could have required further decomposition.) We will represent sequential components by places in the net representation. If the corresponding place carries a token, the sequential component is locally enabled.

In general, actions will be represented by transitions of the form

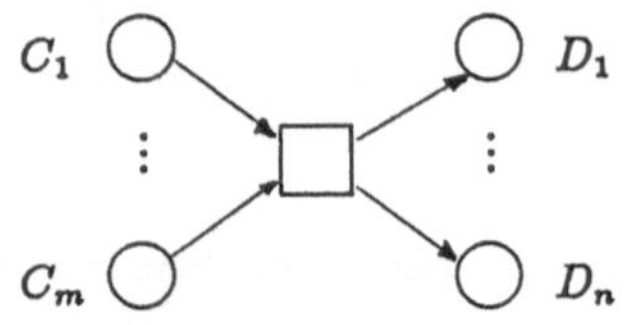

where $C_1, \ldots, C_m, D_1, \ldots D_n$ are sequential components. Note that communications are interactions between several sequential components of a system.

We start by defining syntactically the possible sequential components in our language. Exactly those processes without initial concurrency constitute sequential components.

4.3 Definition

The set SEQ of *sequential components of RCCS* is defined by the following production system.

$$\mathbf{C} ::= \mathbf{Q} \;\Big|\; \mathbf{C}| \;\Big|\; |\mathbf{C} \;\Big|\; x \;\Big|\; \mu x\, \mathbf{Q}\ (x \in Var)\,,$$

where $\mathbf{Q}$ stands for any RCCS term which is a sum.

Decomposition of processes into sets of sequential components is achieved by the *decomposition function.*

4.4 Definition

The *decomposition function* $dec : RCCS \rightarrow \mathcal{P}_{+}(SEQ)$ is defined by

- $dec(P_o) := \{P_o\}$ if P_o is not of the form $P|Q$,
- $dec(P|Q) := dec(P)| \cup |dec(Q)$,

for $P_o \in RCCS$.

$(\ )|$ and $|(\ )$ applied to sets of components are understood elementwise; that is

$$dec(P)| := \{C| \mid C \in dec(P)\},$$
$$|dec(P) := \{|C \mid C \in dec(P)\}.$$

We are now ready to define the net semantics for RCCS terms. As in the transition system semantics, we define the set of (local) states, the places, and the set of transitions uniformly for the whole language. For each term P_o we then choose a particular initial state (a marking) and we are then concerned only with the reachable part of the net.

4.5 Definition Let $P_o \in RCCS$.

Then $ON(P_o)$, the *(one-safe) net representation of* P_o is the net

$$ON(P_o) = (SEQ, T, dec(P_o))$$

where the set of transitions $T \subseteq \mathcal{P}_+(SEQ) \times Act \times \mathcal{P}_+(SEQ)$ is generated by the rules in the following table, writing $S_1 \xrightarrow{a} S_2$ for $(S_1, a, S_2) \in T$.

sum	$\{\sum_{i=1}^{n} a_i P_i\} \xrightarrow{a_j} dec(P_j)$	$(1 \leq j \leq n)$
parallel composition	$\dfrac{S \xrightarrow{a} S'}{S\| \xrightarrow{a} S'\|}$	$\dfrac{S \xrightarrow{a} S'}{\|S \xrightarrow{a} \|S'}$
	$\dfrac{S_1 \xrightarrow{a} S_1',\ S_2 \xrightarrow{\bar{a}} S_2'}{S_1\| \cup \|S_2 \xrightarrow{\tau} S_1'\| \cup \|S_2'}$	
recursion	$\dfrac{\{P\{\mu x P/x\}\} \xrightarrow{a} S}{\{\mu x P\} \xrightarrow{a} S}$	

Note that, for $\mu x P \in RCCS$, $P\{\mu x P/x\} \in SEQ$, since P is a sum.

4.6 Example

$ON(a\,|\,\bar{a}) =$

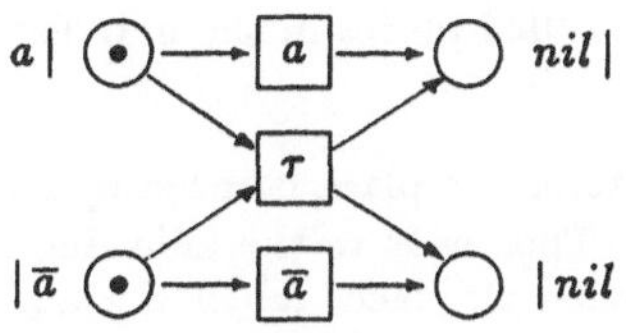

$ON(\mu x(ax)) =$

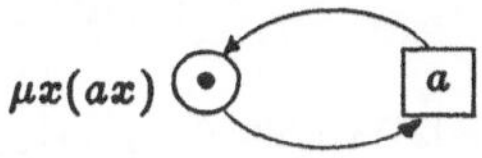

The nets we obtain are always one–safe.

4.7 Theorem [Degano et al. 88a, Olderog 87]

For $P \in RCCS$, $ON(P)$ is one–safe.

Certain CCS programs may not be represented as finite one–safe nets.

4.8 Example

Let $P = \mu x(a(bx|c))$.

$ON(P) =$

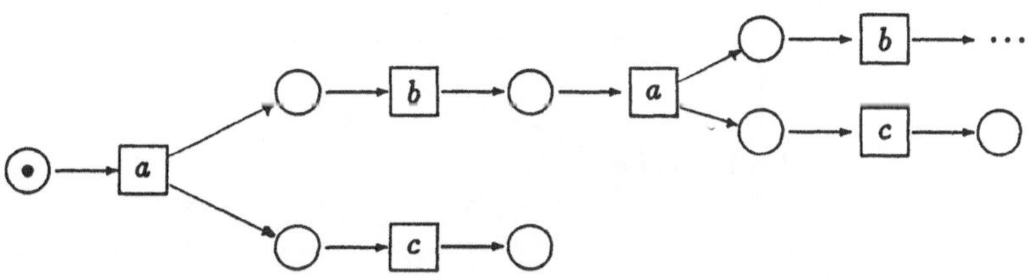

In P, more and more parallelism is generated by recursion. This may not be represented in a finite net with a bounded number of tokens.

Finally, we verify the consistency with the interleaving semantics.

4.9 Theorem [Degano et al. 88a, Olderog 87]

For $P \in RCCS$, $\mathcal{A}(P) \approx \mathcal{A}_I(ON(P))$.

[Degano et al. 88a] proves an even stronger result. A *step semantics* is associated with CCS and it is shown that the step transition system of the net coincides with this step semantics. This shows that indeed all possible parallelism is captured in the net semantics.

4.3 A compositional net semantics with finite place/transition–systems

We will now give a compositional net semantics to RCCS. For all operations except recursion, we could use the net operations defined in section 3.2. We will introduce a looping construction for nets which is sufficient for dealing with recursion under certain restrictions [Goltz 88a, Goltz 88b]. The idea is similar to a construction for the modelling of recursion in transition systems [Milner 84]. A slightly modified version of the Petri net construction presented here was investigated also in [Taubner 89].

We start by explaining informally the idea.

We will model variables as labelled places in the net. For example, the term x will be modelled as

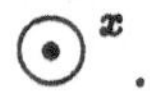

.

Whenever in the net for the term P a place labelled by x carries a token, this corresponds to a recursive call in the net for μxP. This leads to the following construction. The net for μxP is obtained from the net for P by removing all places labelled x and replacing each ingoing arc by arcs to the initial places of the net.

4.10 Example

We consider the term $\mu x(a(bx|c))$ which was represented as an infinite net in example 4.8 .

The term $a(bx|c)$ is represented as

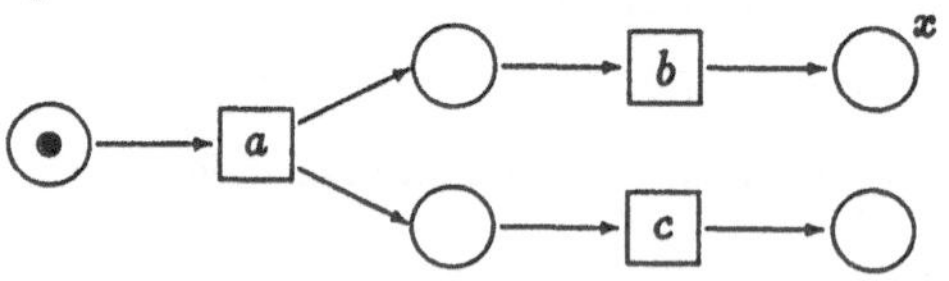

.

$\mu x(a(bx|c))$ is then represented by

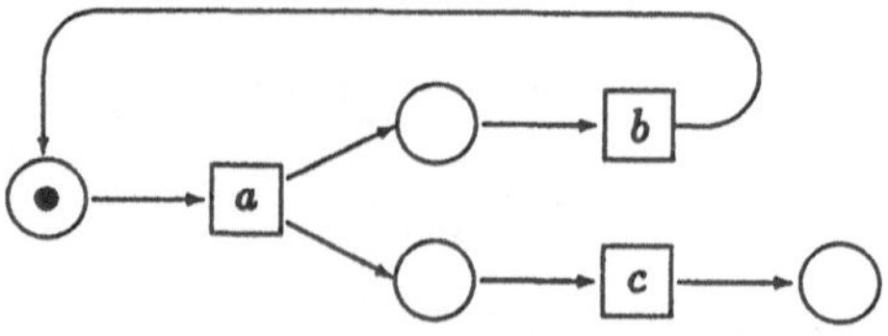

.

The labelled places are only used for the inductive construction of the net. As soon as a variable is bound, all places labelled by this variable are removed. Hence we have no problem with name clashes, and the net representation of an RCCS program will contain no labelled places.

Note that our construction already requires certain properties to be applicable. The variables in the recursive body need to be guarded. Furthermore, we may now obtain ingoing arcs to initial places, so we have to be careful with the +–operation. However, the restriction to guarded choice will avoid this problem. We will later show that this restriction is indeed necessary to guarantee correctness of the construction. Furthermore, we have to be more careful when communication is involved; this will be explained later.

We observe that we need multiple arcs or *arc weights* in nets for this construction.

4.11 Example Consider $\mu x(a(x|x))$.

$a(x|x) \; =$

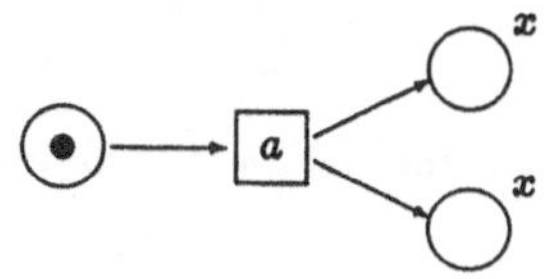

$\mu x(a(x|x)) \; =$

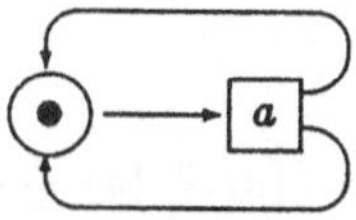

Hence we first expand our definition of a net slightly to deal with arc weights and with places labelled by variables. The pre– and postsets of transitions will now be multisets over places instead of sets of places.

4.12 Definition

$N = (S, T, I, L)$ is a *net* (*labelled over Act, with arc weights and places labelled over Var*) iff

- S is a set (of *places*),
- $T \subseteq \mathbb{N}_+^S \times Act \times \mathbb{N}_+^S$ (*transitions*),
- $I \subseteq S$ (*initial places*),
- $L : N^o - \longrightarrow Var$ (where $- \longrightarrow$ denotes a partial function).

L is a partial function from the set of places without outgoing arcs to the set of variables. This corresponds to the tail recursion in CCS and will be important for our looping construct. L will often be given by its graph, using set notation.

As before, ${}^\bullet t$ and $t^\bullet$ denote the pre– and postset of $t \in T$. However, this includes now the information about arc weights: ${}^\bullet t, t^\bullet \in \mathbb{N}^S$.

For the dynamic behaviour, we may apply the definition of a step and of the set of reachable markings as given in section 2. We only have to allow ${}^\bullet t, t^\bullet$ to be mappings from S into $\mathbb{N}$ instead of mappings from S into $\{0,1\}$.

Next, we define composition operations for nets modelling the operations of *RCCS*.

First, we define the general sum operation with guarded operands for nets.

4.13 Definition Let $N_i = (S_i, T_i, I_i, L_i), 1 \leq i \leq n$, let $S_i \cap S_j = \emptyset$ for $i \neq j$, let $s \notin \bigcup_{i=1}^{n} S_i$.

Then $\sum_{i=1}^{n} a_i N_i := (\{s\} \cup \bigcup_{i=1}^{n} S_i\ , \{(\{s\}, a_i, I_i) \mid 1 \leq i \leq n\} \cup \bigcup_{i=1}^{n} T_i\ , \{s\}\ , \bigcup_{i=1}^{n} L_i)$.

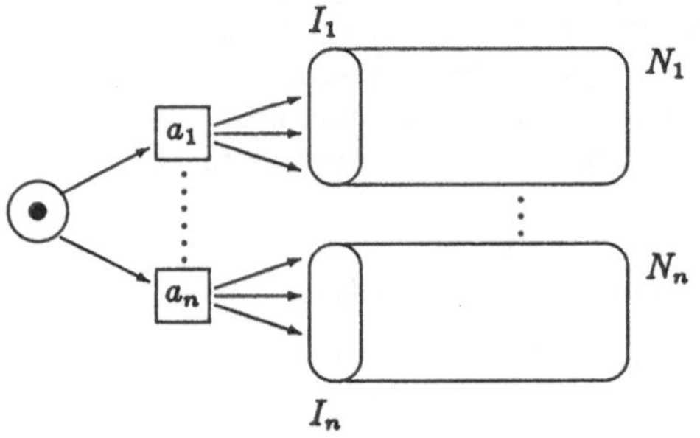

This operation may be obtained as a combination of prefixing with + (or as *nil* for $n = 0$), as defined in section 3.2.

As mentioned before, variables are represented by labelled places.

4.14 Definition Let $x \in Var$.

Then the net x is defined as $x := (\{s\}, \emptyset, \{s\}, \{(s, x)\})$.

The name-overloading might be confusing at first sight here; however we have just consequently applied our principle, seeing variables just like *nil* as operations of arity 0.

The parallel composition is defined just as in section 3.2. We only have to be a bit more careful, because we are dealing with multisets now for $^\bullet t$ and $t^\bullet$. We hence introduce first an operation for joining multisets over disjoint sets.

Let $M \in \mathbb{N}^S, M' \in \mathbb{N}^{S'}$ with $S \cap S' = \emptyset$.
Then $M \cup M' \in \mathbb{N}^{S \cup S'}$ is defined by

$$M \cup M'(s) := \begin{cases} M(s) & \text{iff } s \in S, \\ M'(s) & \text{iff } s \in S'. \end{cases}$$

Let O_S denote the *empty multiset over* S, $O_S(s) := 0$ for all $s \in S$.

4.15 Definition Let $N_i = (S_i, T_i, I_i, L_i), i = 1, 2$, let $S_1 \cap S_2 = \emptyset$.

Then $N_1 | N_2 := (S_1 \cup S_2, T_1' \cup T_2' \cup T, I_1 \cup I_2, L_1 \cup L_2)$ where

$$T_1' := \{(^\bullet t \cup O_{S_2}, l(t), t^\bullet \cup O_{S_2}) \mid t \in T_1\},$$
$$T_2' := \{(^\bullet t \cup O_{S_1}, l(t), t^\bullet \cup O_{S_1}) \mid t \in T_2\},$$
$$T := \{(^\bullet t_1 \cup {}^\bullet t_2, \tau, t_1^\bullet \cup t_2^\bullet) \mid t_1 \in T_1, t_2 \in T_2, l(t_1) = \overline{l(t_2)}\}.$$

Finally, we consider the construction for recursion. Essentially, $\mu x N$ will be obtained from the net N by removing all places labelled by x and replacing each ingoing arc by arcs to the initial places of N (note that only places without outgoing arcs may carry variables), as explained above. However, this is in general not sufficient to capture the intended behaviour, since new communication possibilities may arise when recursion generates parallelism.

4.16 Example Consider $P = \mu x(a\,\overline{a}\,(x|x))$.

The net for $a\,\overline{a}\,(x|x)$ is

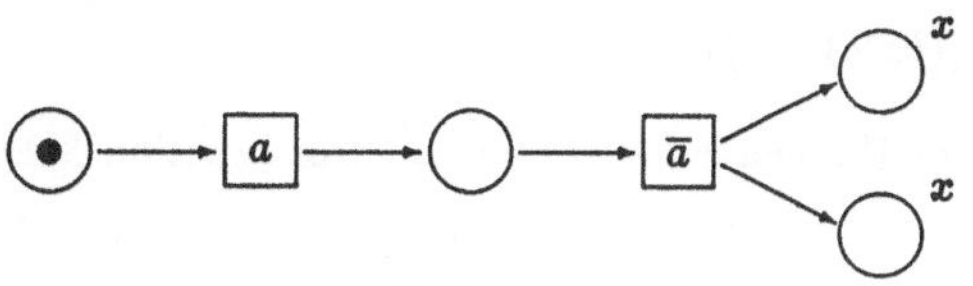

The construction explained above yields

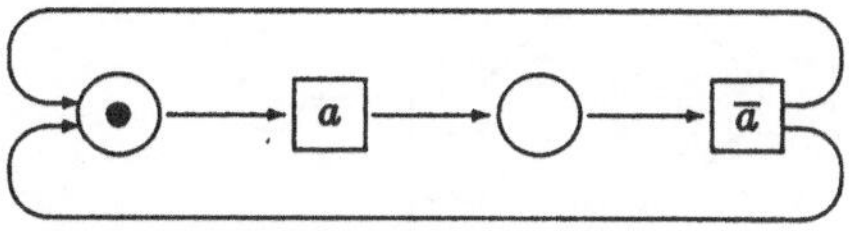

Consider the derivation

$$P \xrightarrow{a} \overline{a}(P|P) \xrightarrow{\overline{a}} P|P \xrightarrow{a} \overline{a}(P|P)|P \xrightarrow{\tau} (P|P)|\overline{a}(P|P)$$

(using the rules given in section 4.1). Then there is no transition corresponding to the τ–action in the constructed net.

Hence we first add all syntactically possible communications for recursion.

4.17 Definition Let $N = (S, T, I, L)$.

The *(syntactical) completion* of N is defined as $V(N) := (S, T \cup T', I, L)$ where

$$T' := \{({}^\bullet t_1 + {}^\bullet t_2, \tau, t_1^\bullet + t_2^\bullet) \mid t_1, t_2 \in T, l(t_1) = \overline{l(t_2)}\}.$$

Now we may implement recursion as explained above, using the complete version $V(N)$ instead of N.

4.18 Example

For $P = \mu x(a\,\overline{a}\,(x|x))$ from example 4.16, we obtain

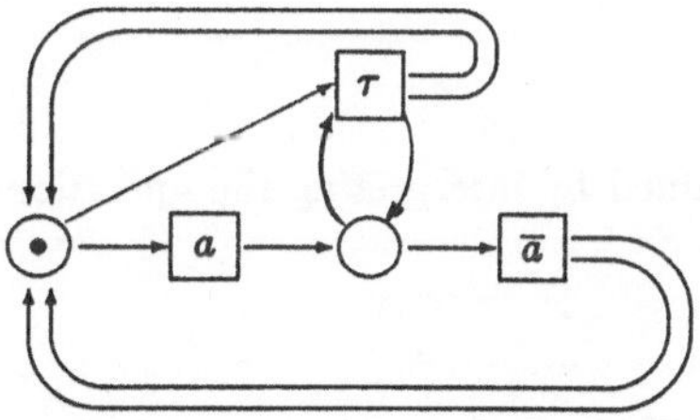

4.19 Definition Let N be obtained by a sum expression. Let $V(N) = (S, T, \{s\}, L)$.

Then $\mu x N := (S', T', \{s\}, L\lceil S')$ where

$$S' := S \setminus L^{-1}(x),$$

$$T' := \{({}^\bullet t\lceil S', l(t), t^\bullet\lceil S' + t^\bullet) \mid t \in T,\ t^\bullet(s') = \begin{cases} \#_x(t) & \text{iff } s' = s, \\ 0 & \text{otherwise} \end{cases} \text{ for } s' \in S',$$

with $\#_x(t) := \sum_{s \in L^{-1}(x)} t^\bullet(s)$ (the number of tokens produced by t on x–labelled places) $\}$.

We have defined this construction here only for the case that N is obtained as a sum and hence has exactly one initial place. For the general case, a definition is given in [Goltz 88a, 88b]. However, the restriction to guarded choice is essential.

4.20 Example Let $P = \mu x(a((bx|c) + d))$.

Using our constructions and the general +–operation from section 3.2, P would be represented as

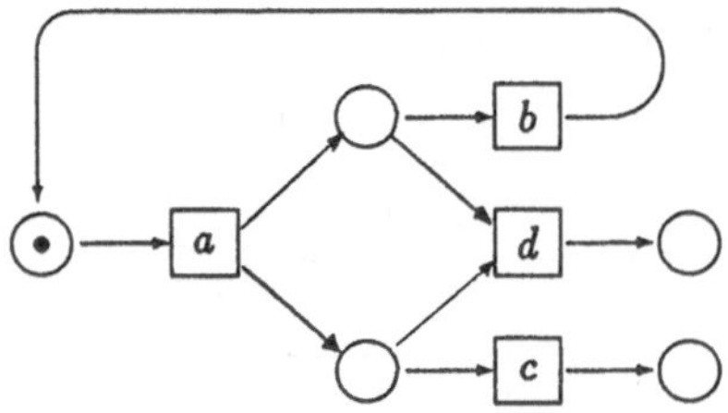

Now consider the following derivation of P:

$$P \xrightarrow{a} (bP|c) + d \xrightarrow{b} P|c \xrightarrow{a} ((bP|c) + d)|c \overset{\text{with the}}{\xrightarrow{\text{"inner"}c}} (bP|nil)|c$$

Next only b or c is possible.
Trying to simulate this in the net, we fire a, b, a again and then c, and arrive at a marking were d is enabled.

The problem lies in the initial parallelism of +–components inside recursion. Even when dublicating events corresponding to actions, it seems that no correct representation as a finite net is possible (correct with respect to causalities). To verify this is an open problem.

The construction may also not be extended to deal with restriction or relabelling nested with recursion. In fact, in [Taubner 89] it has been shown that adding either restriction or relabelling to the language with guarded choice would already yield Turing power, and hence this can not be modelled with finite nets as long as we do not use tokens with individualities.

All operations we have defined preserve finiteness of nets (a net is *finite* if $S \cup T$ is finite). Using these operations, we obtain a net semantics for RCCS which is consistent with the interleaving semantics of CCS.

4.21 Definition Let $P \in RCCS$.

Then $N(P)$ is the finite net obtained by interpreting the operations in P with the net operations defined above.

4.22 Theorem [Goltz 88a, 88b]

For $P \in RCCS$, $\mathcal{A}(P) \approx \mathcal{A}_I(N(P))$.

This net semantics coincides for non–recursive term with the net semantics defined in section 3.2.

4.4 Relationship of compositional and operational net semantics

We address — informally — the following two questions here.

- Do the presented net semantics coincide for non–recursive terms?
- How are the semantics related to each other for infinite processes?

Concerning the first question, one could perhaps expect that the two semantics, the compositional semantics and the operational semantics, yield isomorphic nets when considering only the reachable part of the nets generated operationally. However, this is not true.

4.23 Example Consider $P = a + a$.

$ON(P) =$ 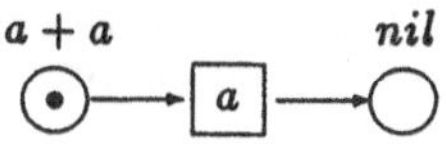

, but $N(P) =$ 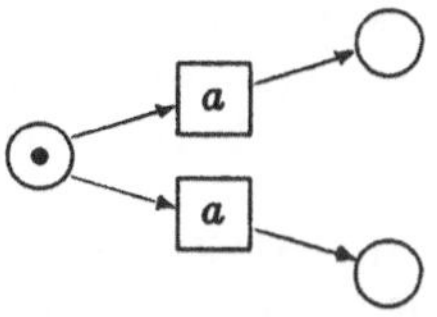

However, we can obtain isomorphic nets with a slightly modified operational semantics, keeping track of +–contexts. Such an operational semantics has been given and proved isomorphic to a compositional semantics (in terms of the generated event structures) in [Degano et al. 88b].

For infinite behaviours, a comparison of the two net semantics is more difficult. Both net semantics generate nets with cycles for certain CCS programs. However, the net semantics presented in section 4.3 contains "more cycles". One way to compare the semantics would be to "unfold" the generated nets into occurrence nets and to try to show, for $P \in RCCS$, that the unfoldings of $N(P)$ and $ON(P)$ (with a modified operational semantics as for finite processes) are isomorphic. For one–safe nets, the notion of unfolding is clear [Winskel 87], however for non–one–safe nets this notion still needs to be formalised.

A weaker result could be obtained by comparing the two semantics up to some notion of equivalence. However, we should then choose a rather strong notion of equivalence, keeping track of causalities and of the branching structure. As outlined in section 2, such equivalence notions are currently being investigated. The equivalence defined in [Olderog 89] has been applied in that paper to compare a compositional with an operational net semantics of a CCS–like language. However, only one–safe nets are considered. For recursion, it is shown that the operational semantics is preserved under substitution (up to equivalence). The treatment of infinite processes in the compositional approach is not considered explicitly.

Acknowledgements

Norbert Götz and Martin Steffen have given very helpful comments on a draft version of this paper. Special thanks also to Gertrud Jacobs and Ingrid Filter for the careful preparation of the manuscript.

References

[Bergstra/Klop 84] J.A. Bergstra, J.W. Klop: *Process Algebra for Synchronous Communication*, Information and Control, Vol. 60, No. 1–3, pp. 109–137, 1984

[Best 88] E. Best: *Weighted Basic Petri Nets*: Proc. Concurrency 88 (F.H. Vogt ed.), LNCS 335, Springer–Verlag, pp. 257–276, 1988

[Best et al. 89] E. Best, R. Devillers, A. Kiehn, L. Pomello: *Fully Concurrent Bisimulation*, Technical Report LIT 202, Université Libre de Bruxelles, Laboratoire d'Informatique Theorique, 1989

[Boudol 89] G. Boudol: *Computations of Distributed Systems, Part 1: Flow Event structures and Flow Nets*, report INRIA Sophia Antipolis, to appear

[**Boudol/Castellani 89**] G. Boudol, I. Castellani: *Permutation of Transitions: an Event Structure Semantics for CCS and SCCS*, Proc. REX School/Workshop on Linear Time, Branching Time and Partial Order in Logics and Models for Concurrency, Noortwijkerhout (J.W. de Bakker, W.-P. de Roever, G. Rozenberg, eds.), LNCS 354, Springer-Verlag, pp. 411–427, 1989

[**de Cindio et al. 83**] F. de Cindio, G. de Michelis, L. Pomello, C. Simone: *Milner's Communicating Systems and Petri Nets*, Selected Papers from the 3rd European Workshop on Application and Theory of Petri Nets, Springer Informatik Fachberichte 66, pp. 40–79, 1983

[**Degano et al. 85**] P. Degano, R. De Nicola, U. Montanari: *Partial Ordering Derivations for CCS*: Proc. FCT 85 (L. Budach, ed.), LNCS 199, Springer-Verlag, pp. 520–533, 1985

[**Degano et al. 86**] P. Degano, R. De Nicola, U. Montanari: *A New Operational Semantics for CCS based on Condition/Event Systems*, nota interna B4–42, Dept. of Computer Science, Univ. Pisa, 1986, see also: P. Degano, R. De Nicola, U. Monanari: *CCS is an (Augmented) Contact-Free C/E System*, Mathematical Models for the Semantics of Parallelism, Advanced School, Rome, LNCS 280, Springer-Verlag, pp. 144–164, 1987

[**Degano et al. 88a**] P. Degano, R. De Nicola, U. Montanari: *A Distributed Operational Semantics for CCS Based on Condition/Event Systems*, Acta Informatica 26, pp. 59–91, 1988

[**Degano et al. 88b**] P. Degano, R. De Nicola, U. Montanari: *On the Consistency of 'Truly Concurrent' Operational and Denotational Semantics*. Proc. Symposium on Logic in Computer Science (LICS) Edinburgh, pp. 133–141, 1988

[**Degano et al. 88c**] P. Degano, R. Gorrieri, S. Marchetti: *An Exercise in Concurrency: a CSP Process as a Condition/Event System*: Advances in Petri Nets 1988 (G. Rozenberg, ed.), LNCS 340, Springer-Verlag, pp. 85–105, 1988

[**Glabbeek 90**] R.J. van Glabbeek: *Comparative Concurrency Semantics and Refinement of Actions*, Dissertation, Vrije Universiteit te Amsterdam, 1990

[**Glabbeek/Goltz 90**] R.J. van Glabbeek, U. Goltz: *Refinement of Actions in Causality Based Models*, Proc. REX Workshop on Stepwise Refinement (J.W. de Bakker, W.-P. de Roever, G. Rozenberg, ed.), LNCS 430, Springer-Verlag, pp. 267–300, 1990

[**Glabbeek/Vaandrager 87**] R.J. van Glabbeek, F.W. Vaandrager: *Petri Net Models for Algebraic Theories of Concurrency*, Proc. PARLE, Vol. II, LNCS 259, Springer-Verlag, pp. 224–242, 1987

[**Goltz 88a**] U. Goltz: *Über die Darstellung von CCS-Programmen durch Petrinetze*, GMD-Bericht Nr. 172, Oldenbourg Verlag, 1988

[**Goltz 88b**] U. Goltz: *On Representing CCS Programs by Finite Petri Nets*, Proc. MFCS 88, LNCS 324, Springer-Verlag, pp. 339–350, 1988

[**Goltz/Mycroft 84**] U. Goltz, A. Mycroft: *On the Relationship of CCS and Petri Nets*, Proc. ICALP 84, LNCS 172, Springer-Verlag, pp. 196–208, 1984

[**Goltz/Reisig 83**] U. Goltz, W. Reisig: *The Non-Sequential Behaviour of Petri Nets*, Information and Control, Vol. 57, Nos. 2–3, pp. 125–147, 1983

[**Goltz/Reisig 85**] U. Goltz, W. Reisig: *CCS-Programs as Nets with Individual Tokens*, Advances in Petri Nets 1984, LNCS 188, Springer-Verlag, pp. 169–196, 1985

[**Hoare 85**] C.A.R. Hoare: *Communicating Sequential Processes*, Prentice Hall, 1985

[Milner 84] R. Milner: *A Complete Inference System for a Class of Regular Behaviours*, Journal of Computer and System Sciences, Vol. 28, pp. 439–466, 1984

[Milner 89] R. Milner: *Communication and Concurrency*, Prentice Hall, 1989

[Olderog 87] E.-R. Olderog: *Operational Petri Net Semantics for CCSP*, Advances in Petri Nets 1987, LNCS 266, Springer–Verlag, pp. 196–223, 1987

[Olderog 89] E.-R. Olderog: *Strong Bisimilarity on Nets: A New Concept for Comparing Net Semantics*, Proc. REX School/Workshop on Linear Time, Branching Time and Partial Order in Logics and Models for Concurrency, Noortwijkerhout (J.W. de Bakker, W.-P. de Roever, G. Rozenberg, eds.), LNCS 354, Springer–Verlag, pp. 549–573, 1989

[Olderog et al. 88] E.-R. Olderog, U. Goltz, R.J. van Glabbeek: *Combining Compositionality and Concurrency*, Summary of a GMD-Workshop, Königswinter March 1988, Arbeitspapiere der GMD 320, Sankt Augustin, 1988

[Park 81] D. Park: *Concurrency and Automata on Infinite Sequences*, Proc. Theoretical Computer Science (5th GI-Conference), LNCS 104, Springer–Verlag, pp. 167–183, 1981

[Petri 77] C.A. Petri: *Non-Sequential Processes*, Interner Bericht 77–05, GMD, Institut für Informationssystemforschung, 1977

[Rabinovich/Trakhtenbrot 88] A. Rabinovich, B.A. Trakhtenbrot: *Behaviour Structures and Nets*, Fundamenta Informaticae Vol. 11, No. 4, pp. 357–404, 1988

[Reisig 84] W. Reisig: *Partial Order Semantics versus Interleaving Semantics for CSP-like Languages and its Impact on Fairness*, Proc. ICALP 84, Antwerp (J. Paredaens, ed.), LNCS 172, Springer–Verlag, pp. 403–413, 1984

[Reisig 85] W. Reisig: *Petri Nets*, EATCS Monographs on Theoretical Computer Science Vol. 4, Springer–Verlag, 1985

[Taubner 89] D. Taubner: *Finite Representations of CCS and TCSP Programs by Automata and Petri Nets*, LNCS 369, Springer–Verlag, 1989

[Winskel 82] G. Winskel: *Event Structure Semantics for CCS and Related Languages*, Proc. ICALP 82, LNCS 224, Springer–Verlag, 1982

[Winskel 84] G. Winskel: *A New Definition of Morphism on Petri Nets*, Proc. STACS 84, LNCS 166, Springer–Verlag, pp.140–150, 1984

[Winskel 87] G. Winskel: *Event Structures*, Petri Nets: Applications and Relationships to Other Models of Concurrency, LNCS 255, Springer–Verlag, pp. 325–392, 1987

ABOUT FIXPOINTS FOR CONCURRENCY

Irène GUESSARIAN *

2, Place Jussieu, 75252 Paris Cedex 05, France - email: ig@litp.ibp.fr

Abstract : This paper recalls some fixpoint theorems in ordered algebraic structures and surveys some ways in which these theorems are applied in computer science. It also points out the shortcomings of the classical least fixpoint theory for domains such as nondeterministic or parallel programs, and shows how to overcome these liabilities by introducing better and more refined fixpoint tools.

1 - INTRODUCTION

The trend in Computer Science is to integrate more and more sophisticated tools in the programming language or even the underlying system, in order to give maximal flexibility to the user. One such tool is the use of recursion, which was initiated with LISP, and is now growing wider and wider. This comes from the fact that recursion allows one to express in a straightforward way the essential ideas of an algorithm, or a definition, without useless implementation details. However, if this straightforward recursive definition must then be converted into a complex imperative program, with lots of stack manipulations and book keeping, most of the gain is lost. So, once a recursive definition corresponding to a program, or describing a relation in a deductive data base, is given, usually in the form of a set of mutually recursive equations, we are interested in

1) finding the final state (e.g. result of a computation of the program, or elements belonging to the relation in the data base), which corresponds to a "stable state", namely a fixpoint of the set of recursive equations,

2) finding this stable state in the most effective and efficient way, i.e. computing the fixpoint as fast as possible and/or using as little space as possible.

The above mentioned two points form the core of the fixpoint theory, and in the past few years, researchers in domains going from semantics to data bases, and from automated proof theory to logic programming have been using various fixpoint theorems and implementations thereof. As we will see, nearly all the fixpoint techniques which are usable rely on an induction principle : they all compute the fixpoint by induction, using successive substitutions. Surprisingly enough, this very simple method leads to pretty efficient results and there is now a well established theory of least fixpoints of continuous functions which can be applied for stating and proving properties of programs, answering to queries, etc... [Scott, Van Emden-Kowalski, Gallaire-Minker-Nicolas, Guessarian, Tiuryn]. However, least fixpoints do not always suffice, or exist. In the case of logic programs, for instance, negations might be necessary, introducing non monotonicity, and

* Support from the PRC Mathématiques-Informatique is gratefully acknowledged.

the least fixpoint does no longer exist ; however, other fixpoints can be used [Apt-Blair-Walker, Makinson]. In the case of parallel or nondeterministic programs, least fixpoints are usually uninteresting or trivial, and one is then interested in various fixpoints, the greatest ones [Arnold-Nivat, Bergstra-Klop], other suitably chosen fixpoints [Darondeau-Gamatié, Rounds]. The problem then becomes : how to choose the right fixpoint, and once this choice is established, how to compute the chosen one. In the present paper, we try to improve the classical fixpoint tool and thus broaden the threshold of its applicability for parallel programs. To this end, we will study greatest or unique fixpoints, and their morphic images, which will apply in the case of parallel and non deterministic programs.

The present paper improves the results of [Guessarian 2], where only non-determinism was treated; we consider also here true concurrency.

2 - THE CLASSICAL LEAST FIXPOINT

We briefly recall here the classical Knaster-Tarski fixpoint theorem, and the constructive variant thereof, most widely used in computer science.

Fixpoint theorem 1(classical fixpoint theorem [Birkhoff, Tarski]): Let L be a complete lattice and $f : L \to L$ a monotone function; then f has a least fixpoint μf such that: $f(\mu f) = \mu f$ and for all $e \in L, f(e) = e \Rightarrow \mu f \leq e$.

However, this theorem is existential and non-constructive, whereas for Computer Science purposes, we need a constructive version of it, which will enable us to actually compute the least fixpoint. Recall first that:

(1) a c.p.o. E, or complete partial order, is a partially ordered set endowed with a least element $\perp$ and such that every chain has a least upper bound, and

(2) a function $f : E \to E$ is said to be *continuous* iff it preserves least upper bounds of nonempty chains, namely if

$$f(sup\{e_n / n \in N\}) = sup\{f(e_n) / n \in N\},$$

for all chains $\{e_n / n \in N\}$.

(3) a function $f : E \to E$ is said to be *strict* iff $f(\perp) = \perp$.

(4) a c.p.o. is said to be a complete semilattice iff every non empty subset has a greatest lower bound.

(5) for a signature Σ containing $\perp$, a Σ-algebra is said to be *complete* iff it is a c.p.o. and all the Σ-algebra operations are continuous.

Notice that we are in fact considering notions of ω-continuity and ω-completeness, but we are dropping the prefix ω which will be implicitly understood everywhere.

Fixpoint theorem 2 : Let E be a c.p.o., and $f : E \to E$ a continuous function; then f has a least fixpoint μf such that $f(\mu f) = \mu f$, and for all $e \in E$, $f(e) = e \Rightarrow e \geq \mu f$. Moreover, μf is computed by $\mu f = sup\{f^n(\perp) / n \in N\}$.

This second theorem effectively characterizes a fixpoint computable by induction ; the properties of the fixpoint can then also be proved by induction. This theorem provides the basis of most of the work done in semantics, algebraic semantics [Nivat, ADJ], denotational semantics [Scott, Rounds1], logic programming [Van Emden-Kowalski].

3 - ABOUT FIXPOINTS AND MORPHISMS

The fixpoint theory is most suited for describing the algebraic semantics of program schemes ; algebraic semantics is halfway in between denotational and operational semantics : on the one hand the fixpoint description captures the idea of denotational semantics, while on the other hand, the fixpoint computation corresponding to theorem 2 models the operational semantics [ADJ, Guessarian, Nivat].

3.1 - Fundamentals of fixpoint semantics

The basic idea is the following : given a program scheme S consisting of a set of recursive equations on a base signature Σ, we first solve S syntactically using theorem 2 in the Herbrand model, namely the free continuous Σ-algebra CT_Σ consisting of finite and infinite well formed Σ-trees. We thus obtain a generally infinite tree $T(S)$ which is the least fixpoint of S. We then interpret $T(S)$ in an arbitrary model A, by taking its image under a strict continuous morphism ϕ, which gives us the semantics of S in the model A; this image is the least fixpoint of the program $\phi(S)$ in the model A. The situation is illustrated by the following example.

Example 1 : Let $S : F(n) = g(n, F(p(n)))$, where $\Sigma = \{\perp, p, g\}$. Then $T(S)(n) = g(n, g(p(n), g(p^2(n), \ldots))) = sup\{g(n,\perp), g(n, g(p(n),\perp), \ldots\}$. Consider now as model $A = N \cup \{\perp_A\}$, with the discrete ordering having least element $\perp_A$. Define $p_A(n) = n-1$ and $g_A(n,m) =$ if $n=0$ then 0 else $n+m$, where $+$ and $-$ are the usual operations on N, and all functions are suitably extended to deal with $\perp_A$. Then $\phi(S)$ is the recursive definition $f(n) =$ if $n=0$ then 0 else $n + f(n-1)$. Let $\phi : CT_\Sigma \to A$ be the morphism defined by $\phi(\sigma) = \sigma_A$ for σ in Σ; we have $\phi(T(S))(n) = n(n+1)/2$, and $n \mapsto n(n+1)/2$ is indeed the least fixpoint of $\phi(S)$ in A, and provides us with the intended meaning of $\phi(S)$ in A.

More generally we have the following, stated for simplicity in the case of a single equation, but which holds for an arbitrary system of recursive equations.

Proposition 3 : Let Σ be a signature, $S : F = t(F)$ a recursive equation where $t(F)$ is a well-formed term on the signature $\Sigma \cup \{F\}$. Let A be a complete Σ-algebra and ϕ the morphism $\phi : CT_\Sigma \to A$ defined by: $\phi(\sigma) = \sigma_A$ for σ in Σ. Let $\phi(S)$ be the recursive equation $F = t_A(F)$, where t_A is deduced from t by substituting the σ_A's for the σ's. Let $\mu S'$ denote the least fixpoint of S' for S' in $\{S, \phi(S)\}$, then $\phi(\mu S) = \mu(\phi(S))$.

The proof is an immediate consequence of the freeness of CT_Σ. We identify the least solution of S with the corresponding least fixpoint. μS gives a syntactic description of the computations of S in the free model CT_Σ; to have an effective description of the computations in an actual model A, it is enough to use proposition 3, and take the image of μS under the morphism $\phi : CT_\Sigma \to A$.

3.2 - The parallel case

Unfortunately, for parallel or nondeterministic programs, the image of μS under ϕ does not necessarily yield the computations we are looking for, as shown by the:

Example 2: Let $S : F = a \cdot F + \tau \cdot F$ be a recursive definition on the signature $\Sigma = \{\perp, a, \tau, +\}$ and let $B = a^* \cup \{a^\omega\}$. Consider the algebra $A = \mathcal{P}(B)$, ordered by inclusion, with $\perp_A = \emptyset$, $\tau_A = id$, $+_A = \cup$, and $a_A(C) = \{a \cdot c / c \in C\}$. Then μS is the rational tree T defined by $T = a \cdot T + \tau \cdot T$ in CT_Σ; in the algebra A, however, we obtain $\phi(T) = \emptyset$, which is indeed the least fixpoint of $\phi(S) : F = a \cdot F \cup F$. This may be justified when dealing with deterministic programs, because $\phi(S)$ represents a loop; but it is no longer acceptable if we wish to model parallel and nondeterministic programs; in this latter case, τ would represent an invisible move, but we would nevertheless be interested in keeping some track of the infinite sequence of actions a. So, following [Arnold-Nivat] we would in the present case define the intended meaning of $x = ax$ in A as being its greatest fixpoint $\{a^\omega\}$ instead of its least fixpoint $\emptyset$. Similarly, the semantics of $x = ax \cup x$ in A will be its greatest fixpoint $a^* \cup \{a^\omega\}$ instead of its least fixpoint $\emptyset$. The same semantics is obtained in [Rounds 1] with slightly different tools.

Not even greatest fixpoints solve all problems, however:

Example 3: Consider the same signature as in example 2, and let $S : F(x) = a{\cdot}x+F(a{\cdot}x)$. Let A be defined as in example 2, then the greatest fixpoint of $\phi(S) : F(x) = a{\cdot}x \cup F(a{\cdot}x)$ is $a^+ \cup \{a^\omega\}$, and there has been some argumentation in the literature as to whether this might be attributed as semantics to $\phi(S)$ (see [Broy, Arnold-Nivat] for conflicting opinions). We consider that a^ω, which is *not* a limit of partial computations of $\phi(S)$, should therefore not be incorporated to its semantics, for the solace of preserving greatest fixpoints.

Combining examples 2 and 3 into:

$$S : \begin{cases} F(x) = a \cdot x + F(a \cdot x) \\ \quad G = a \cdot G + \tau \cdot G \end{cases}$$

shows that arbitrary fixpoints might be needed.

Note that the prefixing of an action is denoted by $\cdot$, but the $\cdot$ will be most often omitted in CT_Σ.

The problem, as illustrated by the previous examples, is to find a suitable way to translate the least fixpoint in the free model into the "right" fixpoint in the model A. The "right" fixpoint is supposed to take care of finite as well as infinite computations in A. So this problem amounts to studying alternate ways of transforming fixpoints by morphisms. Solutions have been proposed to this problem, but they basically amount to considering a case when the fixpoint is unique, as in the case of Greibach schemes [Arnold-Nivat], or guarded schemes [Kranakis, Bergstra-Klop], or contracting operators [Rounds]. These ideas will not apply because the scheme $\phi(S)$ will not be Greibach or guarded (example 3), or the operator corresponding to $\phi(S)$ will not be contracting in A (example 2). Example 2 also shows that we will not always be able to transform a least fixpoint into a greatest one via a closure operator: in that example, the closure of the empty set would have to be $a^* \cup \{a^\omega\}$, which is too demanding.

In the rest of this section, we will address an instance of the problem of transforming least (or unique) fixpoints via morphisms, which will be tailored for describing the semantics of communicating processes. Our formalism will be inspired from CCS (or ACP) - like languages [Milner, Bergstra-Klop].

3.3 - Fixpoints and morphisms for nondeterminism

Let A be an alphabet of unary action symbols, let NIL be a constant symbol representing deadlock (or termination), let τ be a distinguished symbol representing an invisible action and + be a binary symbol (representing nondeterministic choice). Let Σ be the signature $\Sigma = \Sigma_1 =< NIL, A, \tau, + >$, and let T_Σ (resp. CT_Σ) denote the set of finite (resp. finite and infinite) Σ-trees.

Let $S : F(x) = t(F)(x)$ be a recursive equation, with $t(F)(x) \in T_{\Sigma\cup\{F,x\}}$; t is thus a finite term on the signature Σ . For simplicity of notations we will assume we have a single recursive equation, the case of several mutually recursive equations would be similar. S is said to be *weakly guarded* (or weakly Greibach) iff it is not of the form $F(x) = F(t'(x))$.

Proposition 4: Let $S : F(x) = t(F)(x)$ be weakly guarded, then S has a unique fixpoint $T(S)$ in CT_Σ. $T(S)$ is thus also the least fixpoint of the operator $\lambda F.t(F)$, with the notations of [Rounds1].

The scheme S is recursive whereas for modelling CCS (or ACP) like processes we need only rational schemes of the form $F = t(F)$. We will keep this more general framework as long as it will not cost us any extra work. Our goal will be to use $T(S)$ to give the semantics of S in the classical model $\mathcal{P}(A^\infty)$ consisting of languages of finite and infinite words on the alphabet A, in a way which would render a good account of its operational semantics. We would like to define ϕ so as to obtain a mapping:

$$\phi : CT_\Sigma \longrightarrow \mathcal{P}(A^\infty) \tag{1}$$

where $\phi(T(S))$ would represent all the computations (i.e. possible finite or infinite sequences of actions of $T(S)$). Moreover, the semantics of NIL, $+$, τ in $\mathcal{P}(A^\infty)$ should satisfy:

$$\begin{gathered}\phi(NIL) = \varepsilon\,,\ \phi(T + T') = \phi(T) \cup \phi(T')\,,\\ \phi(aT) = a \cdot \phi(T)\,,\ \phi(\tau T) = \phi(T)\,.\end{gathered} \tag{2}$$

For T in CT_{Σ_1}, define $br(T)$ the set of maximal paths in T, i.e. the root to leaf (or infinite) sequences of pairs of node labels and node numbers along a path in T. We will thus have, for $b^1, \ldots, b^n$, in Σ_1, and $1, \ldots, n$ in N^*: $(b^1, 1) \cdots (b^n, n) \cdots \in br(T)$ iff $1 \ldots n \ldots$ is a maximal path in T and $b^n = T(n)$ is the label of node n in T. We can formally define $br(T)$ by induction on k, by letting $T = sup\{t_k / k \in N\}$, the t_k's being finite trees ordered by the relation "to be an initial subtree of".

Let then $\pi_A : \Sigma_1 \times N^* \rightarrow A$ be the projection morphism defined by:

$$\pi_A(b^n, n) = \begin{cases} b^n, & \text{if } b^n \in A; \\ \varepsilon, & \text{if } b^n \in \{\tau, +\}. \end{cases}$$

Define finally: $\phi(T) = \pi_A(br(T))$. $\phi(T)$ will provide us with the required mapping for the case when $\Sigma = \Sigma_1$. ϕ clearly satisfies the morphism requirements (2).

Theorem 5: Let

$$S : T = t(T) \tag{3}$$

be a left linear "à la CCS" recursion and $T(S)$ be the least fixpoint of S in CT_{Σ_1}. Then: (i) $\phi(T(S))$ is a fixpoint of the equation

$$X = \phi[t](X) \tag{4}$$

on $\mathcal{P}(A^\infty)$, where $\phi[t] : \mathcal{P}(A^\infty) \longrightarrow \mathcal{P}(A^\infty)$ is defined by induction on the depth of t by, for $X \subseteq \mathcal{P}(A^\infty)$:

$$\phi[t](X) = \begin{cases} X & \text{if } t(X) = X, \\ \varepsilon & \text{if } t(X) = NIL, \\ \phi[t_1](X) \cup \phi[t_2](X) & \text{if } t = t_1 + t_2, \\ a \cdot \phi[t_1](X) & \text{if } t = at_1, \\ \phi[t_1](X) & \text{if } t = \tau t_1 \ . \end{cases}$$

(ii) If moreover $\phi[t](X)$ is weakly guarded (or Greibach), then $\phi(T(S))$ is the greatest fixpoint of (4).

A term $\theta = \cup_{i=1}^n w_i X \cup U$ is said to be weakly guarded if at least one of the w_i's is different from ε, i.e. if θ is not of the form $X \cup U$. t is applied to (possibly infinite) terms in CT_{Σ_1}, whereas $\phi[t]$ is applied to (possibly infinite) sets of words in $\mathcal{P}(A^\infty)$. With the notations of [Guessarian], t would be denoted by $t_{CT_{\Sigma_1}}$, whereas $\phi[t]$ would be denoted by $t_{\mathcal{P}(A^\infty)}$.

Sketch of proof: (i) (3) will be translated into an equation involving $br(T)$, to which we will apply π_A, and this will yield the equation (4) we are looking for, namely $\phi(T) = \phi[t](\phi(T))$. ϕ is not continuous, but continuity is not needed because we only deal with a *finite* term t, and the corresponding $\phi(t)$ is also finite.

The proof of (ii) is more complicated, and needs an induction on the structure of t and intermediate results.

Theorem 5 also holds if S is a system of mutually recursive equations of the form:

$$S : \begin{cases} T_1 = t_1(T_1, \ldots, T_k) \\ \quad \vdots \\ T_k = t_k(T_1, \ldots, T_k) \end{cases} \tag{5}$$

Thus, for systems S of the form (3) or (5), on the signature $\Sigma_1 =< NIL, A, \tau, + >$, theorem 5 enables us to deduce the computations of S in an arbitrary model A from its syntactic computation in the free model CT_{Σ_1}, via the morphism ϕ defined by $\phi(T) = \pi_A(br(T))$. This yields, in that case, a clean semantics for parallel programs, based on initial algebras and morphisms.

3.4 - Extension to true concurrency

The case when $\Sigma = \Sigma_2 =< NIL, A, \tau, +, \|_\Delta >$, where $\|_\Delta$ is a binary symbol representing the Δ-synchronized shuffle [Rounds 1], i.e. actions in Δ are synchronized, and actions out of Δ are interleaved, is more complex. The idea is to decompose $\psi : CT_{\Sigma_2} \rightarrow \mathcal{P}(A^\infty)$ into $\psi = \phi \circ \theta$, where $\theta : CT_{\Sigma_2} \rightarrow CT_{\Sigma_1}$, and $\phi : CT_{\Sigma_1} \rightarrow \mathcal{P}(A^\infty)$; however, θ is neither monotone nor well defined, and $\phi_1 : CT_{\Sigma_2} \rightarrow CT_{\Sigma_1}/\!\sim$ has to be introduced, where $CT_{\Sigma_1}/\!\sim$ is a suitable factor of CT_{Σ_1}.

For technical reasons, we will consider signatures $\Sigma_2 =< NIL, A, \tau, +, \|_\Delta, \Omega, >$, and $\Sigma_1 =< NIL, A, \tau, +, \Omega >$, where Ω is a new symbol representing undefined, or "pending" computations, as in the theory of algebraic semantics [Guessarian], or, more recently, [Aceto-Hennessy]. The Δ-synchronized parallel composition $\|_\Delta$ is a combination of Milner's parallel composition and Rounds' [Rounds1] Δ-synchronized shuffle: it interleaves actions outside of Δ, and can either interleave or synchronize events in Δ. Formally, it satisfies the following expansion laws:

- if $p = \sum_{i\in I} a_i p_i$ and $q = \sum_{j\in J} b_j q_j$ then:

$$p \parallel_\Delta q = \sum_{i\in I} a_i \cdot (p_i \parallel_\Delta q) + \sum_{j\in J} b_j \cdot (p \parallel_\Delta q_j) + \sum_{a_i=\overline{b_j}\in\Delta} \tau \cdot (p_i \parallel_\Delta q_j) \quad (6)$$

- if $p = \sum_{i\in I} a_i p_i + \Omega$ and $q = \sum_{j\in J} b_j q_j$ or $q = \sum_{j\in J} b_j q_j + \Omega$ then

$$p \parallel_\Delta q = \sum_{i\in I} a_i \cdot (p_i \parallel_\Delta q) + \sum_{j\in J} b_j \cdot (p \parallel_\Delta q_j) + \sum_{a_i=\overline{b_j}\in\Delta} \tau \cdot (p_i \parallel_\Delta q_j) + \Omega \quad (6')$$

Remark: Our formalism could, modulo minor technical changes, also accomodate the cases of Rounds' Δ-synchronized shuffle; Milner's parallel composition $\parallel$ corresponds to $\parallel_A$. We could also allow for the usual restriction or hiding operators, the substitutions or renamings, and the sequential composition; of [Rounds1].

The first idea is to follow the same approach as in the case of the signature Σ_1, namely to try and interpret the trees of CT_{Σ_2} in the model CT_{Σ_1} in such a way that, if T is the solution to the equation $T = t(T)$, with t a term on the signature Σ_2, then $\phi_1(T)$ is the solution to the equation $T' = \phi_1[t](T')$, where $\phi_1[t]$ is a term on the signature Σ_1, suitably deduced from t. However, there can be no straightforward way to deduce $\phi_1[t]$ from t as shown by the following example:

Example 4: Let $S : T = (bT + bNIL) \parallel_\Delta bNIL$. S defines a left-linear recursion, hence its solution $T(S)$ is a regular tree in CT_{Σ_2}: the image of $T(S)$ under ϕ_1, however, is not regular, because $\phi_1(T(S))$ contains subtrees of the form $b^n NIL$, which are infinitely many. This example shows that we cannot apply the same method as in theorem 5.

We nevertheless will associate with each T in CT_{Σ_2} a tree $\phi_1(T)$ in CT_{Σ_1}; $\phi_1(T)$ will represent a "normal form" of T after elimination of the $\parallel_\Delta$'s. We then will apply a slight variation of ϕ to obtain $\psi(T) = \phi(\phi_1(T))$ in $\mathcal{P}(A^\infty)$. We finally will show that if $T = t(T)$, then, $\psi(T) = \phi(\phi_1(T))$ is a fixpoint of $X = \psi[t](X)$ in $\mathcal{P}(A^\infty)$, where $\psi[t]$ is deduced from t using the same method as in theorem 5.

CT_{Σ_2} will now contain an element Ω, representing the undefined process (or computations which are partial but will eventually terminate). Ω is the least element in CT_{Σ_2}, namely $\Omega \prec t$, for all t, and CT_{Σ_2} is ordered by the least ordering compatible with the operations in Σ_2, and having Ω as least element: i.e. $t \prec t'$ iff t' is deduced from t by substituting trees for occurrences of Ω. The relation t is an initial subtree of t' is now replaced by "$t \prec t'$", where Ω's indicate the cutpoints where branches of t can be extended into branches of t'.

We would like $\psi = \phi \circ \phi_1 \ : \ CT_{\Sigma_2} \to \mathcal{P}(A^\infty)$ to satisfy the equations (2) suitably extended in order to deal with the undefined element Ω and the parallel composition $\parallel_\Delta$, i.e.:

$$\begin{gathered}\psi(NIL) = \varepsilon\,,\ \psi(T+T') = \psi(T) \cup \psi(T')\,,\\ \psi(aT) = a \cdot \psi(T)\,,\ \psi(\tau T) = \psi(T)\,,\\ \psi(T \parallel_\Delta T') = \mathit{shuffle}_\Delta(\psi(T), \psi(T'))\,,\ \psi(\Omega) = \emptyset.\end{gathered} \quad (2')$$

where $shuffle_\Delta$ is defined below:

Definition 1: (i) For $w = a_1 \dots a_n, w' = a'_1 \dots a'_p$, two finite words in A^*,

$$shuffle_\Delta(\varepsilon, \varepsilon) = \varepsilon$$

$$shuffle_\Delta(w, w') = a_1 \cdot shuffle_\Delta(a_2 \dots a_n, a'_1 \dots a'_p) \cup a'_1 \cdot shuffle_\Delta(a_1 \dots a_n, a'_2 \dots a'_p) \cup S$$

where

$$S = \begin{cases} shuffle_\Delta(a_2 \dots a_n, a'_2 \dots a'_p) & \text{if } a_1 = \overline{a'_1} \in \Delta \\ \emptyset & \text{otherwise.} \end{cases}$$

(ii) For w, w' two infinite words in A^∞,

$$shuffle_\Delta(w, w') = adh\{\cup\{shuffle_\Delta(u, u'/u \text{ left factor of } w,\ u' \text{ left factor of } w'\}\}.$$

(iii) For L, L' two languages in $\mathcal{P}(A^\infty)$,

$$shuffle_\Delta(L, L') = \cup\{shuffle_\Delta(u, u'/u \in L, \text{ and } u' \in L'\}.$$

Recall that, for L a language in $\mathcal{P}(A^\infty)$, $adh(L)$ is the set of infinite words $w \in A^\omega$ such that all left factors of w belong to the set of left factors of L.

We now define formally $\phi_1(T)$ for T in CT_{Σ_2}. We first define $\phi'_1(T)$, which does not take into account the associativity and commutativity of $+$, and which will help us in understanding how ϕ_1 is defined.

Definition 2: (i) for t a finite tree in CT_{Σ_2}, $\phi'_1(t) \in CT_{\Sigma_1}$ is defined inductively as follows:

- if $t \in CT_{\Sigma_1}$, then $\phi'_1(t) = t$
- if $t = NIL \parallel_\Delta t'$, or $t = t' \parallel_\Delta NIL$, then $\phi'_1(t) = \phi'_1(t')$
- if $t = p + p' \parallel_\Delta q$, then $\phi'_1(t) = \phi'_1(p \parallel_\Delta q) + \phi'_1(p' \parallel_\Delta q)$
- if $t = p \parallel_\Delta q + q'$, then $\phi'_1(t) = \phi'_1(p \parallel_\Delta q) + \phi'_1(p \parallel_\Delta q')$
- if $t = ap \parallel_\Delta bq$ and $a \neq \bar{b}$, then $\phi'_1(t) = a \cdot \phi'_1(p \parallel_\Delta bq) + b \cdot \phi'_1(ap \parallel_\Delta q)$
- if $t = ap \parallel_\Delta bq$ and $a = \bar{b}$, then $\phi'_1(t) = (a \cdot \phi'_1(p \parallel_\Delta bq) + b \cdot \phi'_1(ap \parallel_\Delta q)) + \tau \cdot \phi'_1(p \parallel_\Delta q)$
- if $t = at' \parallel_\Delta \Omega$, then $\phi'_1(t) = a \cdot \phi'_1(t' \parallel_\Delta \Omega) + \Omega$
- if $t = \Omega \parallel_\Delta at'$, then $\phi'_1(t) = \Omega + a \cdot \phi'_1(\Omega \parallel_\Delta t')$

(ii) for $T = sup\{t_n / n \in N\}$ an infinite tree in CT_{Σ_2}, we define $\phi'_1(T) = sup\{\phi'_1(t_n)/ n \in N\}$.

Example 5: Let $\Delta = \{a, \bar{a}\}$, $t = aNIL \parallel_\Delta b^2 NIL$ and $T = aNIL \parallel_\Delta b\bar{a}b^\omega$; then:

$$\phi'_1(t) = ab^2NIL + b(abNIL + baNIL)$$

$$\phi'_1(T) = ab\bar{a}b^\omega + b((a\bar{a}b^\omega + \bar{a}T_1) + \tau b^\omega), \text{ where } T_1 = ab^\omega + bT_1$$

See Figure 1 in appendix 2.

Definition 2(ii) makes sense because CT_{Σ_1}, where $\Sigma_1 =< NIL, A, \tau, +, \Omega >$ is a c.p.o. for the ordering $\prec$ with least element Ω, and because of the following lemma:

Lemma 1: For t_1, t_2 finite trees in CT_{Σ_2} such that $t_1 \prec t_2$, $\phi'_1(t_1) \prec \phi'_1(t_2)$ in CT_{Σ_1}.

Proof: by induction on $(d(t_1), \delta(t_1))$, where $d(t)$ is the depth of t, and $\delta(t) = max\{d(t')+d(t'')/t' \parallel_\Delta t''$ is a subtree of $t\}$; the pair $(d(t_1), \delta(t_1))$ is ordered lexicographically, and the only non-trivial case is to check the inductive step when $t_1 = p \parallel_\Delta q$.

A different approach, requiring a slightly heavier technical machinery, but yielding in the end a simpler form for $\phi_1(t)$, is to take into account the associativity and commutativity of $+$.

Definition 3: (i) Let $\sim_{ac}$ be the congruence defined on T_{Σ_2} (the finite terms in CT_{Σ_2}) by the axioms:

$$\Omega \cdot p \sim_{ac} \Omega$$

$$(p+q)+r \sim_{ac} p+(q+r)$$

$$p+q \sim_{ac} q+p$$

for $p = \sum_{i\in I} a_i p_i + \Omega$ and $q = \sum_{j\in J} b_j q_j + \Omega$, with Ω omitted in $p \parallel_\Delta q$ if it is omitted in p and q.

(ii) $\sim_{ac}$ is extended to infinite terms $T, T' \in CT_{\Sigma_2}$ by: $T \sim_{ac} T'$ iff there exist increasing chains t_n and t'_n such that $T = sup\{t_n/n \in N\}$, $T' = sup\{t'_n/n \in N\}$ and $t_n \sim_{ac} t'_n$ for all n.

The restriction of the the congruence $\sim_{ac}$ on T_{Σ_1} (resp. CT_{Σ_1}), is also denoted by $\sim_{ac}$.

Remark 6: Definition 3 is *not* the standard way of extending $\sim_{ac}$ to infinite trees (cf. [Courcelle, Guessarian]). The standard way consists in:
1) Defining the preorder $\leq = (\prec \cup \sim_{ac})^*$ (the transitive closure of $\prec \cup \sim_{ac}$) on T_{Σ_2}.
2) Extending $\leq$ to CT_{Σ_2} by letting $T \leq T'$ iff $\forall t \prec T, \exists t' \prec T', T \leq T'$.
3) Letting $T \sim_1 T'$ iff $T \leq T'$ and $T' \leq T$ (for T, T' finite or infinite trees).
However, due to the particular form of $\sim_{ac}$, both extensions can be shown to be equivalent (see lemma 2 in appendix 1).
Then ϕ_1 can be defined more simply by:

Definition 4:(i) for t a finite tree in T_{Σ_2}, $\phi_1(t) \in T_{\Sigma_1}/\sim_{ac}$ is defined inductively as follows:
- if $t \in CT_{\Sigma_1}$, then $\phi_1(t) = [t]_{\sim_{ac}}$
- if $t = NIL \parallel_\Delta t'$, or $t = t' \parallel_\Delta NIL$, then $\phi_1(t) = \phi_1(t')$
- if $t = p \parallel_\Delta q$, with $p = \sum_{i\in I} a_i p_i + \Omega$, and $q = \sum_{j\in J} b_j q_j + \Omega$, then

$$\phi_1(t) = \sum_{i\in I} a_i \cdot \phi_1(p_i \parallel_\Delta q) + \sum_{j\in J} b_j \cdot \phi_1(p \parallel_\Delta q_j) + \sum_{a_i=\overline{b_j}\in\Delta} \tau \cdot \phi_1(p_i \parallel_\Delta q_j) + \Omega$$

(The Ω in $\phi_1(t)$ disappears if there is no Ω in neither p nor q).

(ii) for $T = sup\{t_n/n \in N\}$ an infinite tree in CT_{Σ_2}, we define $\phi_1(T) = sup\{\phi_1(t_n)/ n \in N\} \in CT_{\Sigma_1}/\sim_{ac}$.

Example 5 (continued): We now obtain:

$$\phi_1(T) = ab\bar{a}b^\omega + b(a\bar{a}b^\omega + \bar{a}T_1 + \tau b^\omega), \text{ where } T_1 = ab^\omega + bT_1$$

See Figure 2 in appendix 2.

Definition 4(i) makes sense because $t \sim_{ac} t'$ implies $\phi_1(t) = \phi_1(t')$, and definition 4(ii) makes sense because lemma 1 remains valid when replacing ϕ_1' by ϕ_1 and CT_{Σ_1} by $CT_{\Sigma_1}/\sim_{ac}$.

Remark: $\phi_1(t)$ can be considered to be a $\|_\Delta$-free normal form of t in CT_{Σ_2} with respect to the congruence $\sim$ defined as follows.

Definition 5: (i) Let $\sim$ be the congruence defined on T_{Σ_2} (the finite terms in CT_{Σ_2}) by the axioms:

$$\Omega \cdot p \sim \Omega$$

$$(p+q)+r \sim p+(q+r)$$

$$p+q \sim q+p$$

$$p \|_\Delta q \sim \sum_{i \in I} a_i \cdot (p_i \|_\Delta q) + \sum_{j \in J} b_j \cdot (p \|_\Delta q_j) + \sum_{a_i = \overline{b_j} \in \Delta} \tau \cdot (p_i \|_\Delta q_j) + \Omega$$

for $p = \sum_{i \in I} a_i p_i + \Omega$ and $q = \sum_{j \in J} b_j q_j + \Omega$, with Ω omitted in $p \|_\Delta q$ if it is omitted in p and q.

(ii) $\sim$ is extended to infinite terms $T, T' \in CT_{\Sigma_2}$ by: $T \sim T'$ iff there exist increasing chains t_n and t_n' such that $T = sup\{t_n/n \in N\}$, $T' = sup\{t_n'/n \in N\}$ and $t_n \sim t_n'$ for all n.

Lemma 2: For t, t' finite terms in $T_{\Sigma_2}, t \sim t'$ implies $t \approx t'$, where $\approx$ is a variant of Milner's bisimulation which is accomodated to deal with Ω [Aceto-Hennessy].

Proof: the axioms defining $\sim$ are obviously satisfied by $\approx$.

Conjecture: Lemma 2 is also true if T, T' are infinite trees in CT_{Σ_2}. This does not follow immediately from Lemma 2 because, if we allow for the additional axioms $p + p \equiv p$, then Lemma 2 is still true, but the conjecture is false as shown by the example (cf. [Aceto-Hennessy]): $T = a^\omega + \Omega = sup\{a^n\Omega + \Omega/n \in N\} = sup\{t_n/n \in N\}$, and $T' = \sum_{n \in N} a^n\Omega + \Omega = sup\{t_n'/n \in N\}$. Then $t_n' = (\sum_{p \in N} \Omega + a^n\Omega) + \Omega \equiv a^n\Omega + \Omega = t_n$ but T is not in bisimulation with T'.

Lemma 3: Let $t \in T_{\Sigma_2}$ and $T \in CT_{\Sigma_2}$, and assume T is a solution to $S : T = t(T)$, then $\phi_1(T)$ is also a solution to S modulo $\sim$, i.e. $\phi_1(T) \sim t(\phi_1(T))$.

Proof: by construction, for finite t_n's, $t_n \sim \phi_1(t_n)$, hence by definition, also $T = sup\{t_n/ n \in N\} \sim \phi_1(T) = sup\{\phi_1(t_n)/n \in N\}$. $\sim$ being a congruence, $T \sim \phi_1(T)$ implies $t(T) \sim t(\phi_1(T))$; whence finally $\phi_1(T) \sim T = t(T) \sim t(\phi_1(T))$.

Having defined $\phi_1 : CT_{\Sigma_2} \to CT_{\Sigma_1}/\sim$, we can now proceed to define $\psi : CT_{\Sigma_2} \to \mathcal{P}(A^\infty)$. We will need to first redefine $\phi : CT_{\Sigma_1} \to \mathcal{P}(A^\infty)$ to take into account the undefined element Ω. To this end, it suffices to extend the previously defined ϕ to trees possibly containing Ω by excluding paths ending with Ω from the set of maximal paths; we thus will not account for such paths in $\phi(T)$, intuitively, "only terminated paths count".

Lemma 4: For t, t' trees in CT_{Σ_1}, such that $t \sim t', \phi(t) = \phi(t')$.

Proof: By induction if t and t' are finite. By the definition of $\sim$ and of $br(t)$ for infinite t and t'.

ϕ can thus be factored through $\sim$ and we will define $\psi = (\phi/\sim) \circ \phi_1$. The commutative diagram of figure 3 in appendix 2 may help in clarifying the situation.

Corollary: For t, T in $CT_{\Sigma_2} : \phi \circ \phi'_1(T) = \phi \circ \phi'_1(t(\phi'_1(T)))$.

Proof: Immediate from Lemma 3 and 4.

Note the following fact:

Fact: We can identify a word w in A^∞ with a deterministic sequential process in CT_{Σ_2}: e.g. $a \cdot b$ will be identified with $abNIL$; then: for finite w, w' : $\mathit{shuffle}_\Delta(w, w') = \phi \circ \phi'_1(w \parallel_\Delta w')$ and similarly for infinite w, w'.

We can check that $\psi = (\phi/\sim) \circ \phi_1 = \phi \circ \phi'_1$ satisfies the equations (2′), and in particular that: $\psi(T \parallel_\Delta T') = \mathit{shuffle}_\Delta(\psi(T), \psi(T'))$.

Example 6: Let $S : F = aNIL \parallel_\Delta \bar{a}F$. $T(S)$ is depicted in figure 4, and $\psi(T(S))$ is the set of w such that, if $|w|_x$ denotes the number of occurrences of x in w:

- $|w|_a = |w|_{\bar{a}}$ if $|w|_{\bar{a}}$ is finite, and
- for each w' prefix of even length of w, $|w'|_a \leq |w'|_{\bar{a}}$.

Assume now that t is well guarded, namely all subterms of the form $t_1 \parallel_\Delta t_2$ (or $t_1 + t_2$) are such that $t_i = \Sigma a_k t_{i_k}$ for some a_k's, possibly equal to τ.

Then, letting $\psi = (\phi/\sim) \circ \phi_1 = \phi \circ \phi'_1$, we can show that, for T in CT_{Σ_2}, and t in T_{Σ_2}, $\psi(t(T))$ is defined by induction on the structure of t by:

$$\psi(t(T)) = \begin{cases} \psi(T) & \text{if } t(T) = T, \\ \varepsilon & \text{if } t = NIL\ , \\ \emptyset & \text{if } t = \Omega, \\ \psi(t_1(T)) \cup \psi(t_2(T)) & \text{if } t = t_1 + t_2, \\ a \cdot \psi(t_1(T)) & \text{if } t = at_1, \\ \mathit{shuffle}_\Delta(\psi(t_1(T)), \psi(t_2(T))) & \text{if } t = t_1 \parallel_\Delta t_2, \\ \psi(T) & \text{if } t = \tau t_1\ . \end{cases} \tag{7}$$

Whence the analog to theorem 5.

Theorem 7: Let $S : T = t(T)$ be a left linear recursion with t well guarded, and $T(S)$ be the least fixpoint of S in CT_{Σ_2}. Then $\psi(T(S))$ is a fixpoint of the corresponding equation

$$X = \psi[t](X) \tag{8}$$

on $\mathcal{P}(A^\infty)$, where $\psi[t] : \mathcal{P}(A^\infty) \to \mathcal{P}(A^\infty)$ is defined inductively by:

$$\psi[t](X) = \begin{cases} X & \text{if } t(X) = X, \\ \varepsilon & \text{if } t(X) = NIL, \\ \emptyset & \text{if } t = \Omega, \\ \psi[t_1](X) \cup \psi[t_2](X) & \text{if } t = t_1 + t_2, \\ a \cdot \psi[t_1](X) & \text{if } t = at_1, \\ \psi[t_1](X) & \text{if } t = \tau t_1, \\ \mathit{shuffle}_\Delta(\psi[t_1](X), \psi[t_2](X)) & \text{if } t = t_1 \parallel_\Delta t_2\ . \end{cases} \tag{9}$$

The difference with theorem 5 is twofold:

(i) the present theorem, with its proof, remains valid if S is not left linear, e.g. if we allow for sequential compositions;

(ii) we no longer ensure that $\psi(T(S))$ is the greatest fixpoint of (8), although we conjecture this is indeed the case when t is left-linear and well guarded.

Comparison with related work

The approach of [Rounds1] uses a metric instead of an ordering, and the model CT_{Σ_1} instead of $\mathcal{P}(A^\infty)$. The ordering approach seems to demand the introduction of an element Ω, and the corresponding congruence $\sim$: we could not define ϕ_1', ϕ_1 (or ψ) without the technical trick of introducing Ω.

One may wonder why we did not take, in the case of the signature Σ_2 a direct approach, as we did in the case of the signature Σ_1. The reason is that the détour via CT_{Σ_1} enables us to find an explicit and effective construction of the desired solution of the equation (8), by means of the syntactic solution $T(S)$ and the morphism ψ. One can construct directly (i.e. without passing via Σ_1) the equation (8), but then, one has no way to pick the right fixpoint of equation (8) which leads to the desired semantics.

4 - APPENDIX 1

Lemma 1: For $\theta, \theta' \in T_{\Sigma_2}/\sim_{ac}$, the following conditions are equivalent:

(i) $\forall t \in \theta, \exists t' \in \theta' : t \prec t'$

(ii) $\exists \in \theta, \exists t' \in \theta' : t \prec t'$

(iii) $\theta \leq \theta'$.

Proof: (iii) $\Rightarrow$ (i) $\Rightarrow$ (ii) are clear. (ii) $\Rightarrow$ (iii) is proven by induction on the number of applications of $\sim_{ac}$ in the sequence $t_0(\prec \cup \sim_{ac})^* t_0'$, where $t_0 \in \theta$ and $t_0' \in \theta'$.

Lemma 2: For $T, T' \in CT_{\Sigma_2}$ we have the following equivalences:

(i) $T \sim_{ac} T'$

(ii) $T \sim_1 T'$

(iii) $\forall t \prec T, \exists t' : t \sim_{ac} t' \prec T'$ and vice versa: $\forall t' \prec T', \exists t : t' \sim_{ac} t \prec T$.

Proof: (i) $\Rightarrow$ (ii): For $T = sup\{t_n/n \in N\}$, $T' = sup\{t_n'/n \in N\}$ and $\forall t \prec T$, $\exists t_n \prec T$, $t \prec t_n$, hence $\exists t' = t_n'$, $t \leq t'$, and vice versa (cf. remark 6 for the definition of $\sim_1$).

(ii) $\Rightarrow$ (i): Each t has a $\sim_{ac}$-normal form, where no two consecutive nodes are labeled by $+$, and the descendants of each node labeled by $+$ are ordered lexicographicallly. For t, t' in normal form, $t \leq t'$, i.e. $t(\prec \cup \sim_{ac})^* t'$ iff $t \prec t'$. Then, using normal forms together with rewritings according to $\sim_{ac}$, we can show that, for $T = sup\{t_n/n \in N\}$, $T' = sup\{t_n'/n \in N\}$, $T \sim_1 T'$ implies that: $\forall n, \exists m_n, p_n, t''_{m_n}$, such that: $t''_{m_n} \sim_{ac} t'_{m_n}$, $t_n \leq t'_{m_n} \leq t_{p_n}$ and $t_n \prec t''_{m_n} \prec t_{p_n}$, whence $T = sup\{t''_{m_n}/n \in N\}$, $T' = sup\{t'_{m_n}/n \in N\}$ and $t''_{m_n} \sim_{ac} t'_{m_n}, \forall n$.

Finally it is clear that: (i) $\Rightarrow$ (iii) $\Rightarrow$ (ii).

Corollary 3: $CT_{\Sigma_2}/\sim_{ac} = CT_{\Sigma_2}/\sim_1 = (T_{\Sigma_2}/\sim_{ac})^\infty$.

Recall that $(T_{\Sigma_2}/\sim_{ac})^\infty$ is the ideal completion of $T_{\Sigma_2}/\sim_{ac}$, and that $(CT_{\Sigma_2}/\sim) \subset (T_{\Sigma_2}/\sim)^\infty$, the inclusion being strict in general [Guessarian]. Here however, we can prove that:

1) $CT_{\Sigma_2}/\sim_{ac}$ is a c.p.o. and that every chain of $T_{\Sigma_2}/\sim_{ac}$ has a least upper bound in $CT_{\Sigma_2}/\sim_{ac}$ (by using lemma 1).

2) letting i be the canonical inclusion: $i : CT_{\Sigma_2}/\sim_{ac} \hookrightarrow (T_{\Sigma_2}/\sim_{ac})^\infty$, θ_n a chain in $T_{\Sigma_2}/\sim_{ac}$, θ the least upper bound of the θ_n's in $CT_{\Sigma_2}/\sim_{ac}$, and θ' the least upper

bound of the θ_n's in $(T_{\Sigma_2}/\sim_{ac})^\infty$, we have $i(\theta) \leq \theta'$, whence $i(\theta) = \theta'$ and the surjectivity of i which is thus an isomorphism.

Remark 4: $\sim_{ac}$ gives an example of a congruence slightly more general than the permutative congruences of [Courcelle] and for which Corollary 3 remains true.

Acknowledgments: I thank Philippe Darondeau: an informal discussion with him was the instigation for the problems herein considered, and his comments on the paper have been precious; I also thank A. Dupont who did a beautiful job of learning TEXwhile typing this paper.

5 - REFERENCES

[Aceto-Hennessy] L. Aceto, M. Hennessy, Termination, deadlock and divergence, to appear in J. Assoc. Comput. Mach..

[Apt] K. Apt, Efficient computing of least fixpoints, TR-88-33, Univ. Texas, Austin (1988).

[Apt-Blair-Walker] K.R. Apt, H. Blair, A. Walker, Towards a theory of declarative knowledge, presented at the Workshop on Deductive data bases and logic programming, Washington D.C. (August 1986).

[Arnold-Nivat] A. Arnold, M. Nivat, The metric space of infinite trees: Algebraic and Topological properties, Fund. Inform. 3 (1980), 445-476.

[Bergstra-Klop] J. Bergstra, J. Klop, Algebra of communicating processes, Proc. CWI Symposium Mathematics and Computer Science, J. de Bakker, M. Hazenwinkel and J. Lenstra, eds. (1986).

[Birkhoff] G. Birkhoff, Lattice theory, 3rd edition, Americ. Math. Soc., New-York (1979).

[Broy] M. Broy, On the Herbrand-Kleene universe for non deterministic computations, MFCS 84, LNCS 176, Springer-Verlag (1981), 214-222.

[Courcelle] B. Courcelle, Arbres infinis et systèmes d'équations, RAIRO Info. Théor. 13 (1979), 31-48.

[Darondeau-Gamatié] P. Darondeau, B. Gamatié, A fully observational model for infinite behaviors of communicating systems, to appear.

[van Emden-Kowalski] M.H. Van Emden, R.A. Kowalski, The Semantics of Predicate Logic as a Programming Language, Jour. Assoc. Comput. Mach. 23 (1976), 733-742.

[Gallaire-Minker-Nicolas] H. Gallaire, J. Minker, J. M. Nicolas, Logic and data bases: a deductive approach, Assoc. Comput. Mach. Comput. Surveys, 16 (1984), 153-185.

[ADJ] J. Goguen, J. Thatcher, E. Wagner, J. Wright, Initial algebra semantics and continuous algebras, J. Assoc. Comput. Mach. 24 (1977), 68-95.

[Guessarian] I. Guessarian, Algebraic Semantics, Lecture Notes in Comput. Sci. 99, Springer-Verlag, Berlin (1981).

[Guessarian 1] I. Guessarian, A note on fixpoint techniques in data base recursive logic programs, RAIRO Info. Théor. 22 (1988), 49-56.

[Guessarian 2] Improving fixpoint tools for computer science, IFIP'89 proceedings, G. Ritter ed., North-Holland (1989), 1109-1114.

[Kranakis] E. Kranakis, Existence and uniqueness Theorems in fixed point semantics, CWI Report (1987).

[Kraus-Lehmann-Magidor] S. Kraus, D. Lehmann, M. Magidor, Preferential models and cumulative logics, Submitted.

[Lassez-Nguyen-Sonenberg] J.-L. Lassez, V.L. Nguyen, E.A. Sonenberg, Fixed point theorems and semantics a folk tale, Infor. Proces. Letters 14 (1982), 112-116.

[Makinson] D. Makinson, General theory of cumulative inference, unpublished manuscript.

[Milner] R. Milner, A Calculus of Communicating systems, LNCS 92, Springer Verlag (1980).

[Nivat] M. Nivat, On the interpretation of recursive polyadic program schemes, Symp. Math. 15, Rome (1975), 255-281.

[Rounds] W. Rounds, Applications of topology to semantics of communicating processes, LNCS 197, Springer Verlag (1985), 360-372.

[Rounds 1] W. Rounds, On the relationships between Scott domains, synchronization trees, and metric spaces, Inf. and Control 66 (1985), 6-28.

[Scott] D. Scott, The lattice of flowdiagrams, Symp. on Semantics of Algorithmic Languages, Lect. Notes Math. 188, Springer Verlag, Berlin (1971), 311-366.

[Tiuryn] J. Tiuryn, Unique fixed points vs. least fixed points, Theor. Comput. Sci. 12 (1980), 229-254.

6 - APPENDIX 2

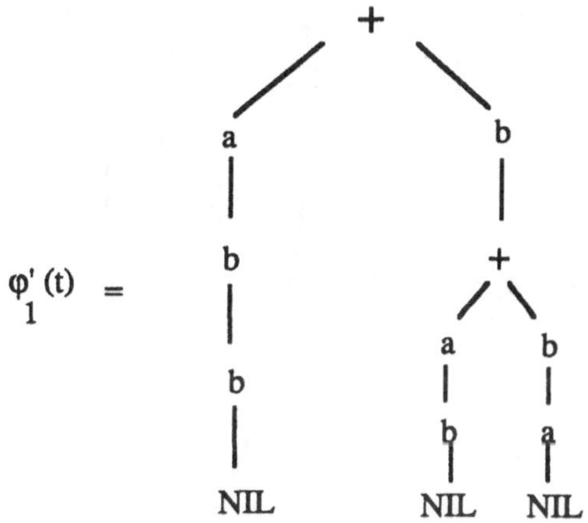

Fig. 1 a

$\varphi_1'(T) =$

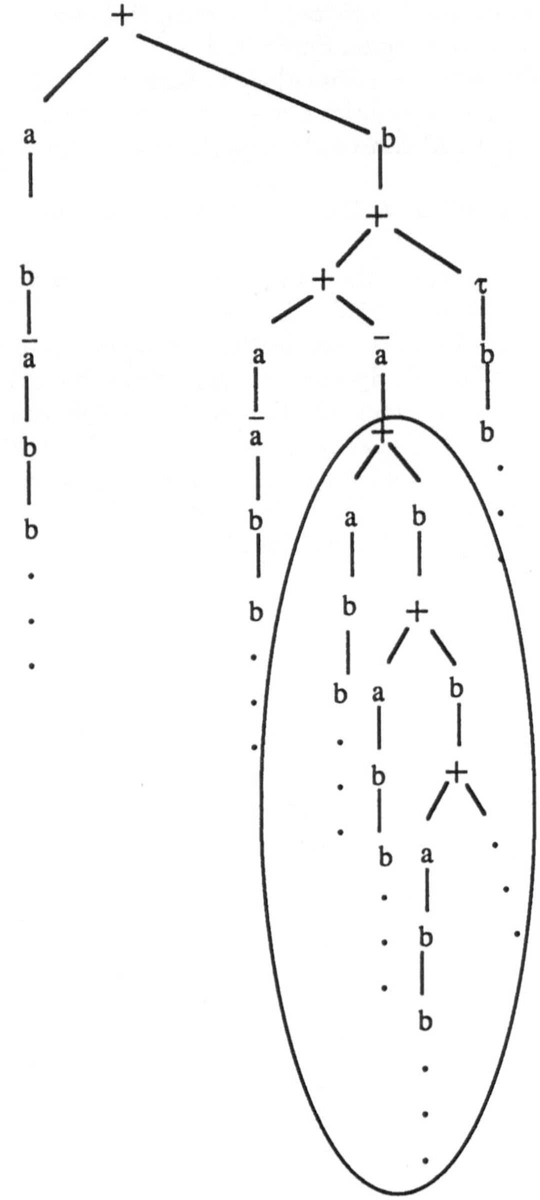

T_1 is circled

Figure 1 b

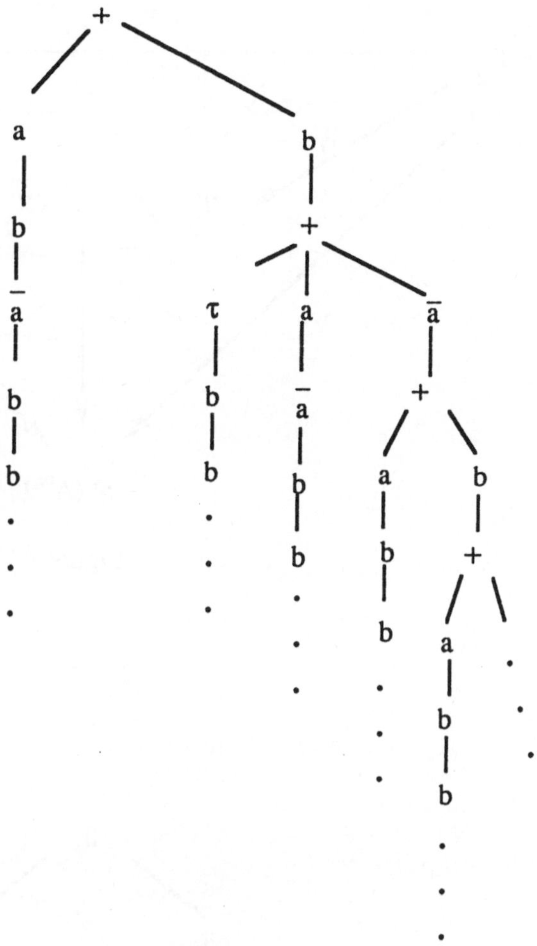

Figure 2

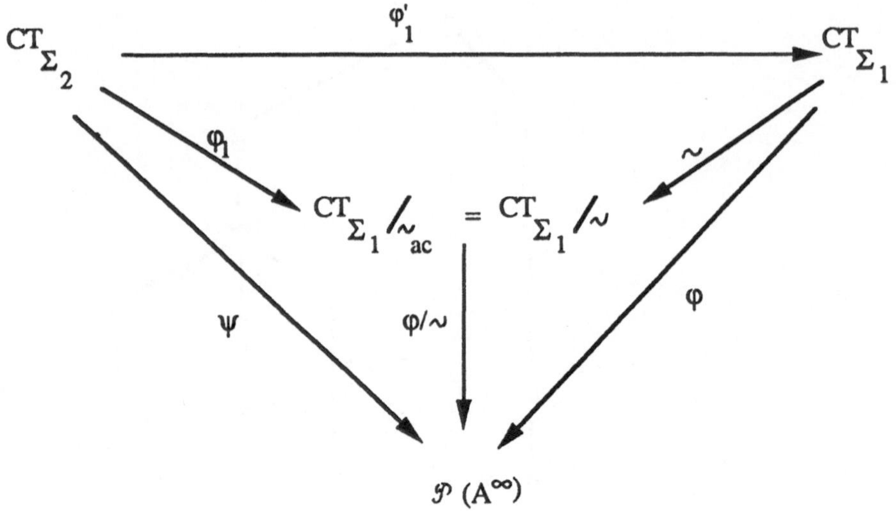

Figure 3

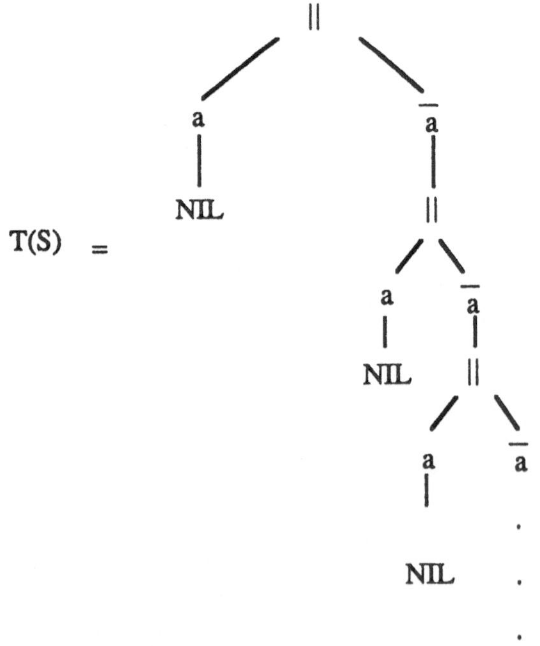

Figure 4

OBSERVERS, EXPERIMENTS, AND AGENTS: A COMPREHENSIVE APPROACH TO PARALLELISM

Stefano Kasangian, Mathematics Department, Milan University, Milan (Italy)
Anna Labella, Mathematics Department, Rome University La Sapienza, Rome (Italy)
Alberto Pettorossi, Electronics Department, Rome University Tor Vergata, Rome (Italy)

ABSTRACT

The aim of this paper is to introduce an enriched categorical approach which provides a unifying theory for many notions of parallelism and concurrency. Our constructions are based on a concept of observational equivalence induced by a set of *observers*, which perform *experiments* over agents. The outcome of those experiments is a set of computations together with an *agreement information*. In order to model parallel agents and their behaviours we use categories enriched over a bicategory. They provide an abstract framework with entities at three *levels*: i) observers at level 0, ii) experiments at level 1, and iii) computing agents at level 2. This comprehensive framework is parametric with respect to the nature of the observers, which may observe totally or partially ordered sets of actions in a discrete or continuous manner. The relationship between various models for parallelism can be expressed in terms of the change of the base bicategory of observers.

1. INTRODUCTION

Parallel processes and distributed computations have many facets, and a variety of approaches based on different intuitions have been proposed for providing their models and deepening their understanding. They range from Milner's SCCS-like calculi [Mil83], where the stress is on the notions of non-determinism and communication, to Petri Net Theory [Rei85], where *true concurrency* is taken into account. Many other approaches have been proposed, like, for instance, Traces Theory [Maz87], Event Structures [Win87], Labelled Event Structures [CFM83], Concurrent Histories [DeM87], and Pomsets [Pra86].

The need for a fruitful comparison among those models and possibly for a unifying theory has been felt for some time now, and it gave rise to several attempts in this direction. We may recall the *translation technique* [Wei83], by which two different models are related by translating terms of one model into terms of the other, and *the modal logic technique* (see, for instance, [LaT88]), by which the behaviours of computing agents are described by formulas of suitable modal calculi.

Other techniques are based on the construction of very rich algebraic structures, in which one may encode the different models of parallel computations to be compared (see, for example, [WiM87]).

Some other methods based on categorical techniques have been proposed in the literature. The

This work has been partially supported by the "Progetto Finalizzato Sistemi Informatici e Calcolo Parallelo", CNR, Italy.

reader may refer to the papers by Degano-Meseguer-Montanari [DMM89] and Winskel [Win85], where different kinds of Petri Nets theories are related via suitable functors. We have done some work along those lines [LaP86, KLP87, KaL90]. In particular, we have used enriched category theory for modelling various distributed computations.

In the present paper we develop a deeper analysis with respect to our previous work and we introduce a new framework, which encompasses most of the models we mentioned above. Our aim is to provide a mathematical foundation to a *comprehensive* approach to concurrency, which shares with SCCS-like systems some *metatheoretical* assumptions, as for instance, the partial inaccessibility of computing agents and hence the crucial relevance of the notion of observability. Indeed, we could say that this work attempts somehow to transform such metatheory into an actual mathematical theory.

We propose a categorical construction which is built from the definition of the bicategory of *observers* [Bén67]. By varying the observers we will get the different models of parallel computing agents we wish to compare. Observers are used for the description of sets of computations performed by the agents. From their observations we construct *structures of computations*, which can be viewed as categories *based on* the bicategory (actually, the 2-category) of observers.

In order to put into perspective the categorical tools we will use, let us recall some of the basic notions of Category Theory which have been adopted in the past for modelling computing agents and parallel processes. First of all, we mention Monoidal Categories [EiK65, Kel82] which were used in [MeM88] for providing an algebraic description of Petri Nets and in [Ben89] for modelling non-determinism and concurrency. Bicategories and 2-categories [Bén67] have been used for rewriting systems by Eilenberg, Street and others (see, for instance, [Pow90]). Enriched Categories, introduced in [EiK65], were used in Automata Theory to describe automata [Bet80, KKR83] and later in [KLP87, KaL90] to represent computing agents as categories enriched over monoidal categories of trees which in their turn represent computations. A recent application of enriched category theory in the mathematics of concurrency can be found in [CCM90]. The notion of categories based on a bicategory was introduced by [Wal81] and used in [BeK85] for modelling tree automata.

We now indicate some of the calculi for concurrency which will be modelled in the paper.
The first calculus is SCCS as presented in [Mil83], and it basically includes TCSP [BHR84]. In SCCS the rules introduced for the description of the agents behaviour are labelled by atomic actions. This fact corresponds to the assumption that it is possible to observe only one action at a time, and therefore, for the SCCS calculus it is adopted a system of *linearly ordered* observers.
Other calculi are the ones related to *true concurrency* as, for instance, the theory of Traces [Maz87], or the Event Structures [Win87]. They may be considered as algebraic approaches to the description of various kinds of Petri Nets [Pet62, Rei85], where many transition firings can take place at the same time, while some other firings can occur only in a sequential order. This corresponds to the assumption that it is possible to observe partial orders of firings, and therefore, for those calculi systems of *partially ordered* observers are adopted.

In Section 2 we introduce a theory of experiments and a three-level framework, which provides the general outline of our approach. Particular relevance will be placed on the notion of experiment performed by an observer, and the novel idea of associating two kinds of information with the experiments: i) the intrinsic information, called *extent*, and ii) the relational information, called *agreement* (see Figure 2 and 3 in Section 2).

In Section 3 we will present the categorical construction relative to the three-level framework and we will use the SCCS calculus [Mil83] as our running example. In Section 4 and 5 we will model the concatenation and the synchronization of computations and we will present the formal semantics of concurrent agents. In Section 6 we consider the case of Continuous Time agents [Car82], and in Section 7 we deal with the *true concurrency* case by examining Trace Theory [Mar87] and Event Structures [Win87].

2. THE THEORY OF EXPERIMENTS AND A THREE-LEVEL FRAMEWORK FOR CONCURRENT AGENTS

In our study about parallel computing agents we adopt a methodology similar to the one used in experimental sciences, where some objects of the real world are considered to be *measurement tools*, and they are used for performing experiments. The behaviour of those tools is assumed to be fully known, at least with respect to the notions of interest.
Analogously, our Theory of Experiments on concurrent agents begins by assuming the existence of a specified subset of computing agents, which is called *system of observers*. They are used as tools for experimenting and studying the behaviour of other agents. We assume that everything is known about the observers, at least with respect to the relevant notions of our theory. (The meaning of this hypothesis will be formalized below.)

Our Theory of Experiments is parametric with respect to a class of calculi for concurrency (see Figure 1).

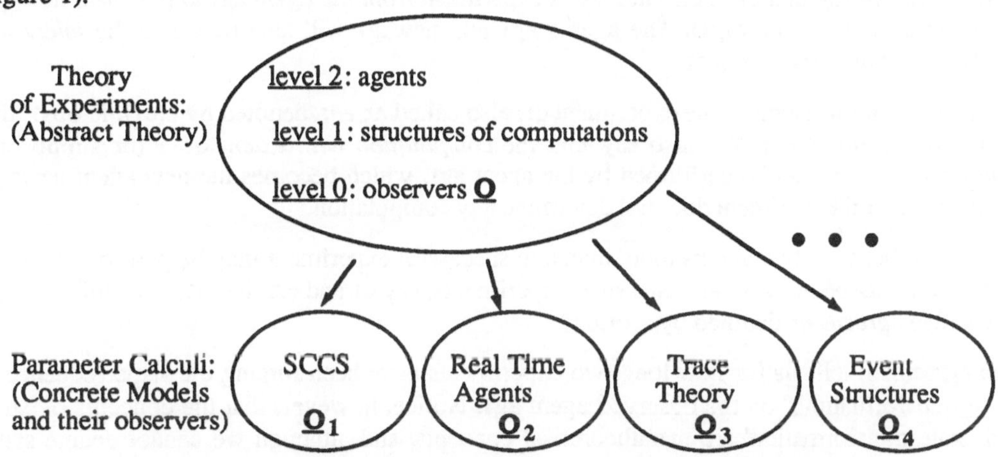

Figure 1. The Theory of Experiments and the Parameter Calculi.

A calculus of that class is a possible parameter of our theory if it satisfies the following minimal requirements. In the parameter calculus it should be possible to define:
i) a subset of computing agents which can be considered as the *system of observers*,
ii) a Hoare-like *synchronization*, denoted by ||, together with an *agents-reduction* relation, (whose reflexive and transitive closure is denoted by →), by which an agent-observer pair is reduced to a new agent-observer pair, and
iii) an observer, denoted by NIL, which is irreducible, that is, for any agent ag1 it does *not* exist any agent-observer pair p, different from ag1 || NIL, such that (ag1 || NIL) → p.

The observers are the objects of the category which is 'level 0' of the three-level framework in which we will formalize our Theory of Experiments.

Some extra assumptions on the parameter calculus for concurrency will be required for allowing the construction of our categorical models, and they will be indicated in the following sections, when needed. In particular, the system of observers will be required to be a sl-bicategory (see Section 3).

We consider that an *experiment* is an act of observing (that is, measuring) a computing agent via the joint activity of that agent and an *observer* (also called observing agent). In more formal terms, the experiment, say c1, on the agent ag1 using the observer obs1 is the *reduction* of the agent-observer pair (ag1 || obs1) to a new agent-observer pair, say (newag1 || newobs1).
This reduction may be a 'single-step' or a 'many steps' reduction, depending on how many intermediate agent-observer pairs come into existence during the experiment itself.
In general, this fact depends on the parameter calculus of concurrency we consider. Unless otherwise specified, we assume that an experiment is a *linearly ordered* sequence of countably or uncountably many agent-observer pairs, although the adopted calculus for concurrency may allow for a *branching* agents-reduction relation (that is, a relation which is *not* a function).

Experiments can be either *successful* or *unsuccessful*.
An experiment is *successful* iff the observing agent is reduced to the irreducible observer NIL. Thus, a successful experiment, say c1, on the agent ag1 performed by the observer obs1 can be viewed as the reduction: (ag1 || obs1) $\rightarrow$ (newag1 || NIL).

In this case we say that c1 is the successful experiment *from the agent* ag1 *to the agent* newag1, (or *between* ag1 and newag1). The agents ag1 and newag1 will also be called the *initial* and *final agent* of the experiment c1.

The *intrinsic* information of the experiment c1, also called *extent*, denoted by e(c1), is obs1, that is, the observing agent. We also say that the *computation with extent* obs1 (or simply, the *computation* obs1) can be performed by the agent ag1, which becomes the new agent newag1. An unsuccessful experiment does not determine any computation.

In general, between two agents more than one successful experiment may be performed, and in that case we associate with any two such experiments, say c1 and c2, the *relational* information, also called *agreement*, denoted by a(c1,c2).

The agreement tells us for how long two experiments have been forcing the same sequence of 'state transformations' on the observed agent ag1. Notice, however, that the concepts of 'state' and 'state transformation' are metatheoretical concepts, and although we cannot denote states and state transformations *within* our theory of experiments, the agreement captures in *theoretical* terms some information about the internal structure of the agents and their evolution during the experiments.

The set of all possible computations from ag1 to newag1 is assumed to be *structured* by the values of the agreement between the corresponding successful experiments. That structured set is called *structure of computations* and it will be modelled as a category *based on* [Wal81] the sl-bicategory of observers.

We will see that a structure of computations allows for a tree-like representation, where a root-to-leaf path is a computation and it is labelled by its extent. The agreement between any two computations determines the fusion of the corresponding paths, as it happens in a tree.

The structures of computations are the objects of the category which constitutes 'level 1' of the three-level abstract framework formalizing our Theory of Experiments (see Figure 2).

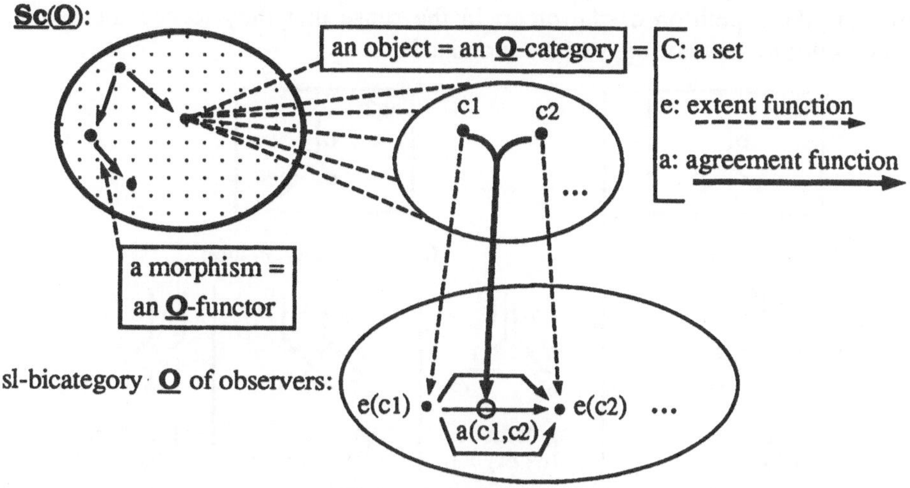

Figure 2. The level 1: the category **Sc(O)** of structures of computations.

Given the successful experiments c1 and c2, both from ag1 to newag1, using the observers obs1 and obs2, respectively, their agreement a(c1,c2) is identified with an observer which is a *common prefix* of obs1 and obs2, and whose actual definition depends on the parameter calculus of concurrency we consider. This agreement notion makes sense, because as we will see in the following section, it is assumed that the system of observers can be viewed as a *prefix closed* set of objects.
We also assume that for any successful experiment c1 performed by obs1, a(c1,c1) = obs1.

The agreement information allows us to define whether or not two experiments are identical. Given any two experiments ci and cj from the agent ag1 to the agent newag1 we say that they are *identical* (or they are *repetitions* of the same experiment) iff the observers involved are the same observer, say obs1, and a(ci,cj) = obs1.
We will assume that in a structure of computations no two computations exist such that they correspond to repetitions of the same experiment. This fact will be realized by the *skeletal property* of the category of the structure of computations (see below).

The agreement information allows also to express two different kinds of nondeterminism within agents, that is, the choice between *different* or *identical* alternatives. Indeed, a nondeterministic agent may undergo *different* successful experiments performed either by different observers or by the same observer. The following example will clarify the ideas.

Let us consider, for instance, the nondeterministic SCCS-like agent b:(r+b), where + is assumed to be neither commutative nor idempotent, so that, for instance, it is possible to identify the left and right occurrence of the summand r in the term r+r (see Figure 3). (For simplicity we did not write the 'terminator agent' 0, and we will do so also in the sequel). That agent may undergo two different successful experiments one performed by the observer b:r and the other by the observer b:b. The agreement between those two experiments is the 'common prefix' b.
If we consider the nondeterministic agent b:(r+r), it may undergo two different successful

experiments both performed by the same observer b:r. Those experiments have both intrinsic information b:r, while their agreement is *either* b if the two experiments force distinct state transformations due to the distinct copies of the summand r, *or* it is b:r if the two experiments are exactly one the repetition of the other, in the sense that they forced the same state transformations due to the same copy of the summand r.

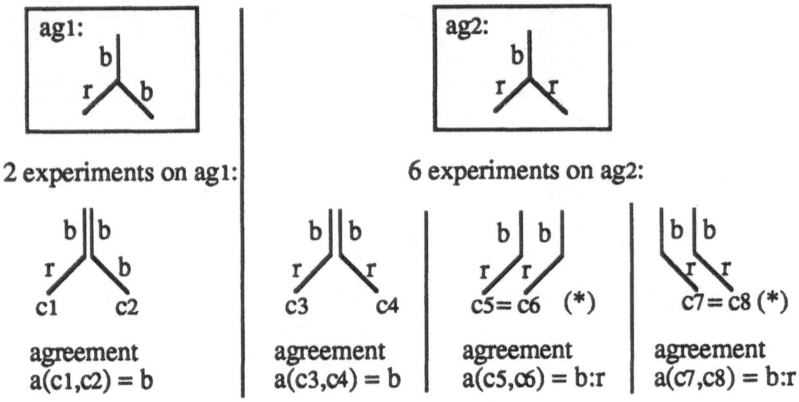

Figure 3. Experiments on SCCS-like agents.
(*) For i=5,7 ci and ci+1 are repetitions of the same experiment.

We also assume that observers are *fully known*. This fact can be formalized within our Theory of Experiments by the following two properties:

i) for any two observers obs1 and obs2, there exists a successful experiment c which reduces (obs1 || obs2) to (NIL || NIL) iff obs1 = obs2, and

ii) given the observer obs1 and any pair of successful experiments of the form:
c1: (obs1 || obs1) → (NIL || NIL) and c2: (obs1 || obs1) → (NIL || NIL) we have that:
a(c1,c2) = obs1, and therefore, they are repetitions of the same experiment.

Level 2 of our categorical framework is made out of *computing agents*, considered as black boxes. As already mentioned, we do not have access to their internal states or their states transformations. However, we can observe their computations by performing experiments using a given system of observers. When a successful experiment is performed, an agents-reduction process takes place, and it leads from a given agent to a new one.

As indicated in [KLP87, KL90], computing agents will be objects of a category enriched [Kel82] over a monoidal category of *structures of computations*, which is 'level 1'. We will associate to any two given agents the structure of computations which leads from the first agent (its domain) to the second one (its codomain).

As a reference to the reader we provide in Figure 4 below a pictorial representation of our Theory of Experiments and the three-level categorical framework.

Before closing this section we would like to make the following theoretical and metatheoretical remarks.

i) As one would expect, the observers which are objects at level 0, can be viewed as particular agents, that is, objects at level 2. Observers can also be viewed as objects at level 1, that is, as particular structures of computations.

ii) In our framework we can accommodate for a multi-level notion of *observational equivalence* among agents: a *lower level*, which is provided by the system of observers, so that we assume to be equivalent those agents whose computations cannot be distinguished by the experiments, and *higher levels*, which are provided by suitable equivalences which can be introduced among structures of computations, and therefore, among agents.

For instance, in the case of SCCS-like calculi, we may assume that agents which differ for the duration of their actions are equivalent at lower level, because the usual SCCS-like observers are not capable to distinguish them, while equivalences, like ag1+ag1 = ag1, can be introduced at higher levels.

Also various atomicities of actions (see, for instance, [BoC88]) can be taken into account by considering different observers and, thus, introducing various equivalences at lower level.

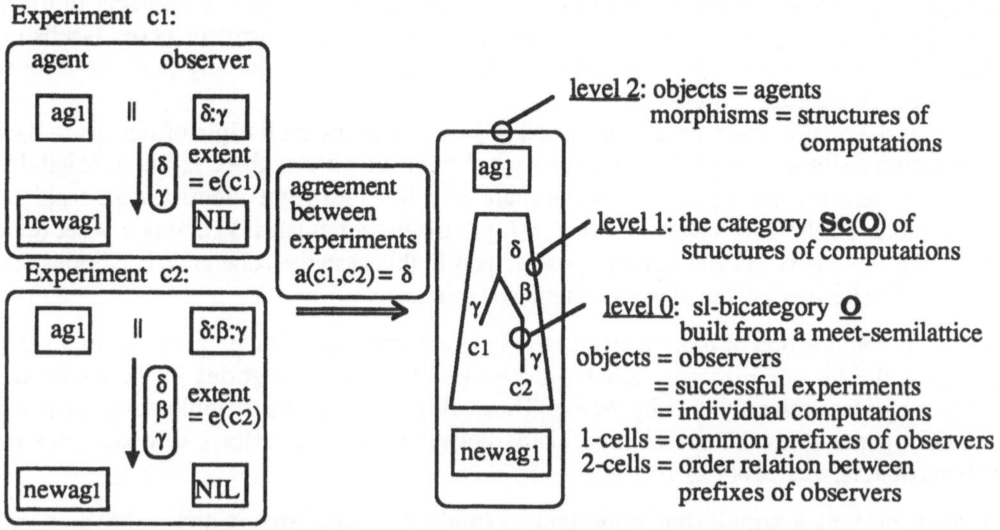

Figure 4. From experiments to a 3-level categorical framework for concurrency.

iii) In our Theory of Experiments we assume that for a suitable choice of the system of observers we can distinguish between the agent NIL and any other agent by performing experiments. For that hypothesis we need to take an optimistic approach with respect to the experiments, in the sense that if an experiment may be successful then it will be successful. (Recall that in general the agents-reduction relation is nondeterministic and it is possible for a given agent-observer pair to generate a successful or an unsuccessful experiment.)

iv) In the actual calculus of concurrency one chooses, it should be possible to determine whether or not an agent is equal (or equivalent) to a given one, otherwise we cannot determine the agents between which a successful experiment has taken place.

In order to determine the initial agent of an experiment we assume that agents are *reinitializable*, as it is the case for some classes of automata, so that two experiments may be said to be performed from the *same* initial agent.

We also assume that equivalent structures of computations which have equivalent final agents, induce the equivalence among the corresponding initial agents. Thus, the final agent of an experiment, say newag1, can be uniquely determined, up to a given equivalence, by performing experiments from newag1 itself to equivalent agents (or to the irreducible agent NIL). An analogous idea is behind the definition of bisimulation equivalence in SCCS-like calculi.

3. BASIC DEFINITIONS AND DISCRETE TIME SCCS-LIKE AGENTS

In this section we will introduce the basic definitions needed in our categorical constructions and we will use as running example the discrete-time agents, that is, TCSP or SCCS-like agents, whose atomic actions are taken from a given alphabet A. Other applications of our theory will be presented in the following sections.

We begin by presenting a structure by which the observing agents can be described. That structure is provided by the notion of bicategory [Bén67], which we now summarize, while the particular bicategories we will use are formally introduced in Definition 1 below.

A *bicategory* $\underline{\mathbf{B}}$ is a set of objects Ob($\underline{\mathbf{B}}$) together with, for each pair of objects (a,b), a *category* $\underline{\mathbf{B}}$(a,b). For any (a,b) the objects of $\underline{\mathbf{B}}$(a,b) are called morphisms of $\underline{\mathbf{B}}$ (or 1-cells of $\underline{\mathbf{B}}$), and they will be collectively denoted by morph($\underline{\mathbf{B}}$). Analogously, for any (a,b) the arrows of $\underline{\mathbf{B}}$(a,b) are called 2-cells of $\underline{\mathbf{B}}$.
For each object a of $\underline{\mathbf{B}}$ is given an identity 1-cell in $\underline{\mathbf{B}}$(a,a), and for each triple of objects (a,b,c) is given a composition functor. Further, for each 4-tuple of objects there is an associativity isomorphism, and for each pair of objects there is a left and right identity isomorphism satisfying suitable coherence conditions ([Ben67, p.5-6]. In particular, if $\underline{\mathbf{B}}$(a,b) is a poset (qua category), the bicategory is called locally posetal, and in this case the coherence conditions are trivially satisfied because all the diagrams involved commute.

REMARK. If composition of morphisms is strictly associative and the identities are strict w.r.t. composition, the bicategories are called 2-categories [KeS74]. Categories in their turn are special 2-categories with only identity 2-cells. Thus, with respect to the definition of a category, a bicategory generalizes the *set* of morphisms between any two objects to a *category* of morphisms (that is, a category of 1-cells).

Let us now present a simple but important example of bicategory, which motivates our Definition 1. This example motivated also the original notion of categories based on a bicategory [Wal81], which plays a central role in our categorical framework (see Definition 2).

EXAMPLE 1. Let us consider the lattice $\underline{\mathbf{T}}$ of open sets of a topological space T. From $\underline{\mathbf{T}}$ we can construct a bicategory whose objects are the elements of T. For any two objects u and v in $\underline{\mathbf{T}}$ the category $\underline{\mathbf{T}}$(u,v) has as objects (that is, 1-cells) the open sets contained in $u \cap v$ and as morphisms (that is, 2-cells) the inclusion among open sets. For any two 1-cells we define the composition as the intersection of open sets, and for any two 2-cells the composition is given by the transitivity of the inclusion. ■

Let us now give the formal definition of the kind of posetal bicategories (actually, 2-categories) we will consider in this paper.

DEFINITION 1. Given a meet-semilattice $(O,\le,\wedge,\perp)$, where O is the underlying set, $\le$ is the partial order over O, $\wedge$ is the meet operation, and $\perp$ is the bottom element, a *semilattice-bicategory* (called *sl-bicategory*, for short) $\underline{\mathbf{O}}$ is the following structure:

i) a set of objects Ob($\underline{\mathbf{O}}$), which coincides with O,
ii) for each pair of objects a and b, a poset $\underline{\mathbf{O}}$(a,b) (viewed as a category), defined by $\{k \mid k \in O \text{ and } k \le a \wedge b\}$. For each pair of objects a and b, the objects of $\underline{\mathbf{O}}$(a,b) are called 1-cells, and the arrows of $\underline{\mathbf{O}}$(a,b) are called 2-cells.
iii) For each triple of objects a, b, and c, an associative operation from pairs of 1-cells in $\underline{\mathbf{O}}(a,b)\times\underline{\mathbf{O}}(b,c)$ to a 1-cell in $\underline{\mathbf{O}}$(a,c), called *composition* of 1-cells, and defined by the meet operation $\wedge$,

iv) for each object a, an identity 1-cell, denoted by $\mathbf{1}_a$, in the category **O**(a,a), which is a itself (that is, the greatest object in **O**(a,a)). $\mathbf{1}_a$ is a left and right identity for the composition of 1-cells.

v) For each pair of 1-cells f and g, *at most* one 2-cell, defined by the relation f≤g, and

vi) for each pair of objects a and b and for each triple of 1-cells in **O**(a,b) an associative operation, called *vertical composition* of 2-cells, provided by the transitivity of the partial order ≤. ■

For each object a, there exists an identity 2-cell, denoted by $\mathbf{i}_a$, from $\mathbf{1}_a$ to $\mathbf{1}_a$, which is provided by the reflexivity of ≤. $\mathbf{i}_a$ is a left and right identity for the vertical composition.

Since sl-bicategories are used for modelling *observers* we have chosen the name **O** to denote sl-bicategories, instead of the name **B** usually adopted for bicategories.
By definition, for each pair of objects a and b we have that: **O**(a,b)=**O**(b,a).

We could have dispensed with the notion of bicategories, because sl-bicategories are in fact 2-categories. However, our choice is motivated by the fact that the replacement of sl-bicategories by general bicategories allows us to model observers of more sophisticated calculi for parallelism, like for instance, Labelled Event Structures [CFM83] and Pomsets [Pra86]. (These results will be presented in a forthcoming paper.)

The following simple example of sl-bicategory illustrates the above Definition 1.
EXAMPLE 2. Given the semilattice (O,≤,∧,⊥) which can be depicted as follows:

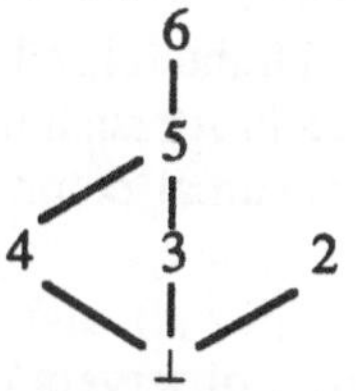

it can be viewed as a (usual) category whose objects are {⊥,2,3,4,5,6} and morphisms are those induced by the ≤ relation. This semilattice corresponds also to the sl-bicategory **O** such that the set of objects Ob(**O**) is the underlying set {⊥,2,3,4,5,6},
and **O**(6,5) is: **O**(5,4) is: **O**(5,3) is: **O**(5,2) is:

while the categories **O**(4,⊥), **O**(3,⊥), and **O**(2,⊥) have only one object: ⊥. In the pictures of the categories **O**(-,-), for simplicity reasons, we did not draw the identity 2-cells (which are loops on the 1-cells ⊥, 2, 3, 4, 5, and 6). For i = ⊥, 2, ..., 6 the category **O**(x,x) is the poset below (and including) x itself. Since **O**(x,y)= **O**(y,x), this completes the presentation of the categories between any two objects of **O**.

Let us also mention that in the usual bicategorical notation the category **O**(5,4), for instance, is depicted as follows:

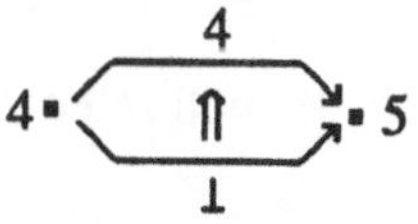

The single arrows between the objects 4 and 5 are the 1-cells: 4 and ⊥. The 2-cell between the

1-cells 4 and $\perp$ (denoted by the double arrow) means: $\perp \leq 4$.
For simplicity reasons, in the picture above we did not draw the 2-cells which are identities, that is, from a single arrow x to the same single arrow x we did not draw the double arrow meaning '$x \leq x$'.

In the following figure we represent the two categories **O**(4,5) and **O**(5,6), together with their composition, that is, the category **O**(4,6) with the two 1-cells $\perp$ and 4.
(Indeed, for each 1-cell x in **O**(5,6) we have: $\perp \wedge x = \perp$, $4 \wedge 4 = 4 \wedge 5 = 4$, and $4 \wedge 3 = 4 \wedge 2 = \perp$.)

O(4,5):

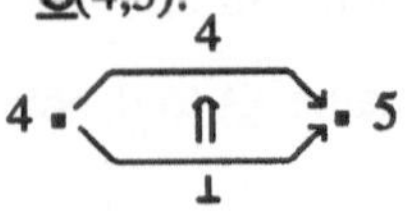

O(5,6):

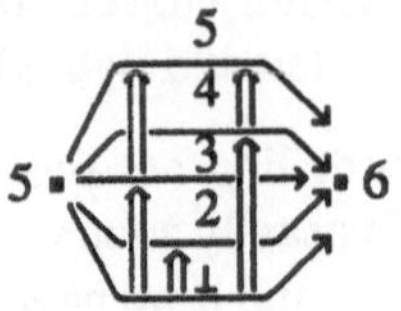

O(4,6):

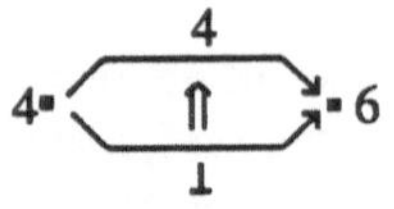

Within the category **O**(5,6) by vertical composition of $\perp \leq 4$ and $4 \leq 5$ (or $\perp \leq 3$ and $3 \leq 5$), we get the 2-cell $\perp \leq 5$ which may be represented as follows:

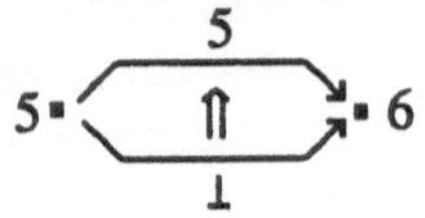

■

Let us now present the sl-bicategory **A** which is the base (that is, level 0) for the construction of our categorical models in the case of TCSP or SCCS-like agents.

We consider a set of atomic actions A with the related semilattice $(A^*, \leq, \wedge, \varepsilon)$ where A^* is the free monoid over A, $x \leq y$ iff there exists z in A^* such that $xz=y$, and $x \wedge y$ is the greatest element z such that $z \leq x$ and $z \leq y$ (that is, the maximal common prefix). The bottom element of the semilattice is the empty word ε.
A is the sl-bicategory associated with $(A^*, \leq, \wedge, \varepsilon)$, and, as any other sl-bicategory, it is referred to as the 'system of observers' (or simply, 'observers') **A**.

As we said in the previous sections, we assume that agents 'at level 2' manifest themselves by performing *computations* which are entities 'at level 1'. Any two agents P and Q are related by a *structured set of* (all possible) *computations* which: i) are performed by the agent P, ii) lead to the agent Q, and iii) are observed by the system **O** of observers 'at level 0'.
The structure of this set of computations is provided by two functions, the *extent* and the *agreement* function, called e and a, respectively. Thus, given a set C of computations, the corresponding structured set, called *structure of computations*, is the triple <C,e,a>, and it can be represented by using the following definition of **O**-*category* [Wal81], which refers to a sl-bicategory **O** of observers associated with the semilattice $(O, \leq, \wedge, \perp)$.

DEFINITION 2. An **O**-*category* (also called *category based on* **O**, or *enriched over* **O**) **C** is a triple <C,e,a>, where C is a set, and
i) e is a function, called *extent*, from C to Ob(**O**), and
ii) a is a function, called *agreement*, from $C \times C$ to morph(**O**), satisfying the following properties:
- $a(c_1,c_2)$ is an object of the category **O**$(e(c_1),e(c_2))$,
- for each element c in C, a(c,c) is the identity 1-cell $\mathbf{1}_{e(c)}$ for the object e(c) in **O**, and
- $a(c_1,c_2) \wedge a(c_2,c_3) \leq a(c_1,c_3)$.

O is called the *base bicategory* of **C**. Often we will refer to C as the set of *objects* of **C**, and C will also be denoted by Ob(**C**). ■

REMARKS. i) For each pair of elements c_1 and c_2 in C, $a(c_1,c_2)$ selects a 1-cell of

$\underline{\mathbf{O}}(e(c_1),e(c_2))$, say z, such that $z \le e(c_1) \wedge e(c_2)$. ii) For each element c in C a(c,c) selects the greatest object of the category $\underline{\mathbf{O}}(e(c),e(c))$, which is e(c) itself. ■

We say that an $\underline{\mathbf{O}}$-category $\underline{\mathbf{C}}$ is *symmetric* iff $a(c_1,c_2) = a(c_2,c_1)$.
This notion makes sense because for an sl-bicategory $\underline{\mathbf{O}}$ we have that: $\underline{\mathbf{O}}(c_1,c_2) = \underline{\mathbf{O}}(c_2,c_1)$ for each pair of objects c_1 and c_2.
We say that a symmetric $\underline{\mathbf{O}}$-category is *skeletal* iff for any two objects c_1, c_2 in C we have that: if $e(c_1)=e(c_2)=a(c_1,c_2)$ then $c_1=c_2$. (The reverse implication holds by Definition 2.)

The notion of skeletal symmetric $\underline{\mathbf{O}}$-categories is a key concept in this paper, and it will be used for modelling within our Theory of Experiments any structure of computations. Indeed, the structure of computations <C,e,a> will be represented by the skeletal symmetric $\underline{\mathbf{O}}$-category $\underline{\mathbf{C}}$, where $\underline{\mathbf{O}}$ is the sl-bicategory of observers by which experiments are performed.

Given the system of observers which is the sl-bicategory $\underline{\mathbf{A}}$ associated with $(A^*, \le, \wedge, \varepsilon)$, the function e of the structure of computations <C,e,a> associates with a computation c in C a word in A^*, that is, it gives to c a label in A^*. Thus, e can also be viewed as a labelling function.
Given any two computations c_1 and c_2, $a(c_1,c_2)$ is a 1-cell in $\underline{\mathbf{A}}(e(c_1),e(c_2))$, that is, an element in the partial order below (and including) $e(c_1) \wedge e(c_2)$. Thus, $a(c_1,c_2)$ is a common prefix of $e(c_1)$ and $e(c_2)$ (but, in general, it is *not* the maximal one).

Therefore, a structure of computations can be viewed as a set of labelled paths, whose initial subpaths are 'glued together' according to the identifications indicated by the agreement function. A structure of computations can be represented as a labelled tree, as the following example shows.

EXAMPLE 3. Given $C=\{c_1,c_2,c_3\}$, $A=\{\alpha,\beta,\gamma,\delta\}$, $e(c_1)=\alpha\beta\delta$, $e(c_2)=\alpha\beta\alpha$, $e(c_3)=\beta\gamma$, $a(c_1,c_2)=\alpha$, $a(c_2,c_3)=a(c_1,c_3)=\varepsilon$, and $a(c_i,c_i)=e(c_i)$ for i=1,2,3 we have the structure of computations $\underline{\mathbf{C}}$=<C,e,a> depicted in Figure 5. In that figure and in the following ones, the elements of the set C are written in 'leaf positions', because each of them may be considered as a path from the root to the corresponding leaf. For this reason we will often use the letter 'p' (short for path), possibly with subscripts, to denote the elements of the set C.

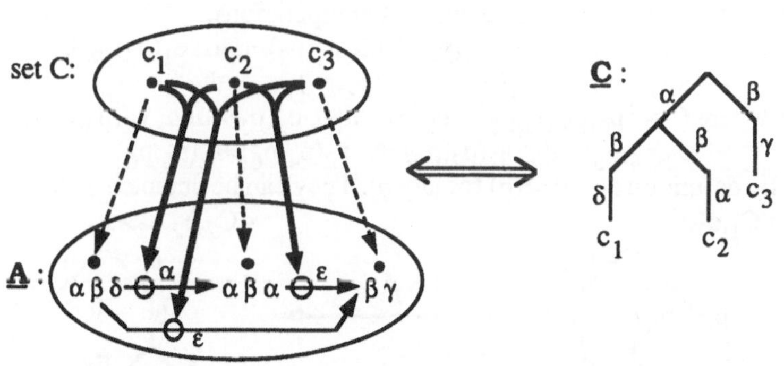

Figure 5. The structure of computations <C,e,a>.

■

Thus, we may say that in our categorical constructions the notion of a $\underline{\mathbf{O}}$-category, when $\underline{\mathbf{O}}$ is a sl-bicategory associated with a free monoid (which induces a partial order with a bottom element) coincides with the notion of a tree with labels taken from that monoid.

REMARK. With reference to Example 3, one should notice that if $e(c)=\alpha\beta$ for some computation c in C, we do *not* assume the existence of the elements x and y in C such that $e(x)=\alpha$, $e(y)=\beta$ and $a(c,x)=\alpha$. In that sense we say that in general the *factorization property* for a set of computations labelled over a free monoid is *not* assumed. ■

The key idea of our approach is the fact that we can generalize (as we will see later) the monoidal structure which is inherent to the system of observers in the special case of the bicategory **A**, to a generic sl-bicategory. This will provide a uniform framework for modelling various classes of concurrent agents.

Now, our modelling process continues by building a (usual) category, called **Sc(O)**, whose objects are structures of computations. The suitable notion of morphism in this category is provided by the following concept of **O**-functor.

DEFINITION 3. A **O**-*functor* f: $\mathbf{C}_1 \to \mathbf{C}_2$ between two **O**-categories $\mathbf{C}_1=<C_1,e_1,a_1>$ and $\mathbf{C}_2=<C_2,e_2,a_2>$ is a function from C_1 to C_2, also denoted by f, such that:
i) $e_1(c) = e_2(f(c))$ for any object c in C_1, and
ii) $a_1(c_1,c_2) \leq a_2(f(c_1),f(c_2))$, for any two objects c_1 and c_2 in C_1, where $\leq$ is the 2-cell in the sl-bicategory **O**. ■

Given a sl-bicategory **O** of observers, we may define the category **Sc(O)** of *structures of computations* as follows.

DEFINITION 4. The category **Sc(O)** has as objects *skeletal symmetric* **O**-categories, that is, structures of computations, and as morphisms **O**-functors. ■
The **O**-functors from $\mathbf{C}_1$ to $\mathbf{C}_2$ will be denoted by $\mathbf{Sc(O)}(\mathbf{C}_1,\mathbf{C}_2)$.

EXAMPLE 4. In the case of **A**-categories, structures of computations are trees whose root-to-leaf-paths (also called rl-paths) are labelled by words in A*. Morphisms between structures of computations are (total) functions from rl-paths into rl-paths which:
i) preserve labels (and obviously, their length as well), and
ii) do not separate in the codomain initial subpaths which are glued together in the domain by the agreement function, and in this sense we say that **A**-functors are *monotonic* w.r.t. the agreement.

Let us consider the following two structures of computations:
$<C_1,e_1,a_1>$ where $C_1=\{p_1,p_2,p_3\}$, $e_1(p_1)=\alpha\beta\delta$, $e_1(p_2)=\alpha\beta\alpha$, $e_1(p_3)=\beta\gamma$,
$a_1(p_1,p_2)=\alpha$, $a_1(p_1,p_3)=a_1(p_2,p_3)=\varepsilon$, and
$<C_2,e_2,a_2>$ where $C_2=\{p_4,p_5,p_6,p_7\}$, $e_2(p_4)=\alpha\beta\delta$, $e_2(p_5)=\alpha\beta\alpha$, $e_2(p_6)=\beta\gamma$, $e_2(p_7)=\beta\eta$,
$a_2(p_4,p_5)=\alpha\beta$, $a_2(p_7,p_6)=\beta$, $a_2(p_4,p_6)=a_2(p_5,p_6)=a_2(p_7,p_4)=a_2(p_7,p_5)=\varepsilon$.
(Recall that by definition $a(p,p)=e(p)$ for any p). They can be depicted as follows:

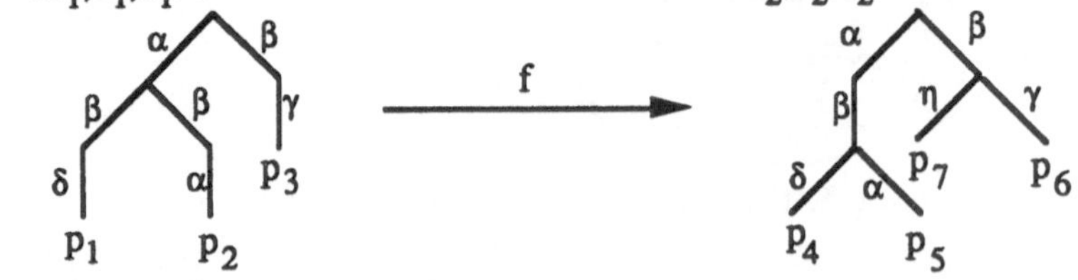

The function f: $C_1 \to C_2$, such that $f(p_1)=p_4$, $f(p_2)=p_5$, and $f(p_3)=p_6$ is a morphism between $<C_1,e_1,a_1>$ and $<C_2,e_2,a_2>$, because it is an **A**-functor. ■

Given the free monoid A* and the corresponding system of observers which is the sl-bicategory

A, **Sc(A)** is the category of skeletal symmetric **A**-categories, that is, the category of all trees whose root-to-leaf-paths are labelled by words in A*.
For simplicity, we call **Sc(A)** also **Trees**. We will feel free to call *trees* the objects of **Trees**, and we will denote them by $\mathbf{T}_1$, $\mathbf{T}_2$,... (instead of $\mathbf{C}_1$, $\mathbf{C}_2$,...).

The category **Trees** has sums. The sum of $\mathbf{T}_1 = <T_1,e_1,a_1>$ and $\mathbf{T}_2 = <T_2,e_2,a_2>$ is $\mathbf{T} = <T_1+T_2, e_1+e_2, a>$, where + denotes the disjoint union (that is, the coproduct in the category **Set**) and the agreement function is defined as follows:

$a(p_1,p_2) = a_i(p_1,p_2)$ if either p_1 and p_2 are both in T_1 or p_1 and p_2 are both in T_2
$= \varepsilon$ otherwise.

Thus, the sum of two trees can be represented by their gluing by the roots, as this picture shows:

The category **Trees** has products. The product $\mathbf{T} = <T,e,a>$ of the trees $\mathbf{T}_1 = <T_1,e_1,a_1>$ and $\mathbf{T}_2 = <T_2,e_2,a_2>$ is defined as follows: $T = \{<p_1,p_2> \mid p_1 \in T_1,\ p_2 \in T_2,\ e_1(p_1) = e_2(p_2)\}$,
$e(<p_1,p_2>) = e_1(p_1)$ (which is also equal to $e_2(p_2)$) for any $p_1 \in T_1$ and $p_2 \in T_2$, and
$a(<p_1,q_1>,<p_2,q_2>) = a_1(p_1,p_2) \wedge a_2(q_1,q_2)$ for any p_1, $p_2 \in T_1$, and q_1, $q_2 \in T_2$, where $\wedge$ is the meet operation in the base bicategory (in our case **A**).
For i=1,2 the projection π_i is defined by the equation: $\pi_i(<p_1,p_2>) = p_i$.

Since the definitions of sums and products do not depend on peculiarities of the bicategory **A** of the observers, we have that sums and products exist in any category **Sc(O)** of structures of computations.

4. MODELLING CONCATENATION AND SYNCHRONIZATION OF COMPUTATIONS

In this section we will provide a categorical model for two of the most important operations one can define on structures of computations, namely *concatenation* and *synchronization*.
Within the category **Trees** we can model the concatenation and synchronization of trees by introducing two functors, the first one induced by the concatenation of words in the monoid A* and the second one induced by a given partial synchronization operation $*$ from A*×A* to A*.
From the concatenation of words in A* we will get the functor ⊗: **A**×**A** → **A** which is a tensor product on **A**, and from the synchronization $*$ we will get the functor ✱: **A**×**A** → **A**, which is a homomorphism of bicategories. By lifting ⊗ and ✱ from the level of observers to the level of trees we get a functor [⊗]: **Trees**×**Trees** → **Trees**, and a monoidal functor [✱]: **Trees**×**Trees** → **Trees**, i.e. a functor enjoying an Interchange Property w.r.t. the tensor product [⊗] (see below).
In general, it will be the case that given a tensor product ⊗: **O**×**O** → **O**, it is possible to get a 'lifted' tensor product [⊗]: **Sc(O)**×**Sc(O)** → **Sc(O)**, as we will show in the case of **Trees**. However, the synchronization operation will be represented by a monoidal functor [✱]: **Sc(O)**×**Sc(O)** → **Sc(O)**, which in general is not induced by a functor ✱ defined at the level of observers.

The operations [⊗] and [✱] play a very important role in our theory, because they are the basis for the notion of *experiment*, in which computations as sequentially composed and synchronized.

Let us first introduce the following definition of homomorphism between sl-bicategories (see also [Bén67] for the general definition).

DEFINITION 5. Given the sl-bicategories $\underline{\mathbf{O}}_1=(O_1,\leq_1,\wedge_1,\perp_1)$ and $\underline{\mathbf{O}}_2=(O_2,\leq_2,\wedge_2,\perp_2)$, a *homomorphism* Φ: $\underline{\mathbf{O}}_1 \rightarrow \underline{\mathbf{O}}_2$ is given by:

i) a function F from $Ob(\underline{\mathbf{O}}_1)$ to $Ob(\underline{\mathbf{O}}_2)$,

ii) for any pair a and b in $Ob(\underline{\mathbf{O}}_1) \times Ob(\underline{\mathbf{O}}_1)$ a functor F[a,b] from $\underline{\mathbf{O}}_1(a,b)$ to $\underline{\mathbf{O}}_2(F(a),F(b))$,

iii) for any a in $Ob(\underline{\mathbf{O}}_1)$ $F[a,a](\mathbf{1}_a)=\mathbf{1}_{F(a)}$ (that is, F[a,a] maps the greatest object of $\underline{\mathbf{O}}_1(a,a)$ into the greatest object of $\underline{\mathbf{O}}_2(F(a),F(a))$), and

iv) for any triple of objects a, b, and c, and for any pair of 1-cells x and y in $\underline{\mathbf{O}}_1(a,b) \times \underline{\mathbf{O}}_1(b,c)$
$F[a,b](x) \wedge_2 F[b,c](y) = F[a,c](x \wedge_1 y)$. ■

In the above definition we did not state some extra conditions on the functors F[a,b]'s concerning their behaviour on 2-cells, which should have been given for general bicategories [Bén67]. Indeed those conditions are trivially satisfied for sl-bicategories.

We will define the concatenation of $\underline{\mathbf{A}}$-categories as a particular homomorphism from $\underline{\mathbf{Trees}} \times \underline{\mathbf{Trees}}$ to $\underline{\mathbf{Trees}}$, that is, a tensor product within the category $\underline{\mathbf{Trees}}$ of $\underline{\mathbf{A}}$-categories.

This tensor product, denoted by [⊗] is obtained by lifting a different tensor product, denoted by ⊗, in the bicategory $\underline{\mathbf{A}}$. ⊗ is defined in terms of concatenations of words in A*, which is denoted by $\cdot$, or simply by juxtaposition.

Let us begin by giving the definition of ⊗, where $\underline{\mathbf{A}} \times \underline{\mathbf{A}}$ is taken as a sl-bicategory in the canonical way starting from the sl-bicategory $\underline{\mathbf{A}}$.

DEFINITION 6. (*Concatenation of observers.*) The operation ⊗ from $\underline{\mathbf{A}} \times \underline{\mathbf{A}}$ to $\underline{\mathbf{A}}$ is defined as the following homomorphism between sl-bicategories: $\otimes(p_1,p_2) = p_1 \cdot p_2$ (thus, the function F of Definition 5 is taken to be the concatenation of words).

⊗ induces a functor $F[<p_1,q_1>,<p_2,q_2>]$ from $\underline{\mathbf{A}} \times \underline{\mathbf{A}}(<p_1,q_1>,<p_2,q_2>)$ to $\underline{\mathbf{A}}(p_1 \cdot q_1, p_2 \cdot q_2)$, such that: for any $k \leq p_1 \wedge p_2$ and $h \leq q_1 \wedge q_2$

$$
\begin{aligned}
F[<p_1,q_1>,<p_2,q_2>](k,h) &= k \cdot h && \text{if } p_1=p_2=k \\
&= k && \text{otherwise.}
\end{aligned}
$$
■

Thus the concatenation of two observers is simply 'one after the other'.

PROPOSITION 7. i) ⊗ is an homomorphism from $\underline{\mathbf{A}} \times \underline{\mathbf{A}}$ to $\underline{\mathbf{A}}$. ii) ⊗ is a tensor product.

PROOF. i) It is enough to check the Definition 5. ii) It is easy to show that ⊗ is associative and it has the bilateral identity which is the word ε of length 0. ■

The reader familiar with the literature on bicategories will realize that ⊗ is a global tensor product in the sense of [CaW82], but in our case ⊗ is not supposed to be symmetric.

DEFINITION 8. (*Concatenation of trees.*) In $\underline{\mathbf{Trees}}$ the concatenation [⊗] is defined as follows. For any two objects (that is, trees) $\underline{\mathbf{T}}_1=<T_1,e_1,a_1>$ and $\underline{\mathbf{T}}_2=<T_2,e_2,a_2>$:

$[\otimes](\underline{\mathbf{T}}_1,\underline{\mathbf{T}}_2) = <T_1 \times T_2, e_1 \cdot e_2, a_{12}>$ where for each p_1,p_2 in T_1 and q_1,q_2 in T_2 we have:

$$
\begin{aligned}
a_{12}(<p_1,q_1>,<p_2,q_2>) &= a_1(p_1,p_2) \cdot a_2(q_1,q_2) && \text{if } e_1(p_1) = e_1(p_2) = a_1(p_1,p_2) \\
&= a_1(p_1,p_2) && \text{otherwise.}
\end{aligned}
$$

For any two morphisms (that is, $\underline{\mathbf{A}}$-functors) f: $\underline{\mathbf{T}}_1 \rightarrow \underline{\mathbf{T}}_3$ and g: $\underline{\mathbf{T}}_2 \rightarrow \underline{\mathbf{T}}_4$, where $\underline{\mathbf{T}}_i=<T_i,e_i,a_i>$ for i=1,...,4, [⊗](f,g) is a morphism from $[\otimes](\underline{\mathbf{T}}_1,\underline{\mathbf{T}}_2)$ to $[\otimes](\underline{\mathbf{T}}_3,\underline{\mathbf{T}}_4)$, that is, from $<T_1 \times T_2, e_1 \cdot e_2, a_{12}>$ to $<T_3 \times T_4, e_3 \cdot e_4, a_{34}>$, such that:

for and p_1 in T_1 and p_2 in T_2 $[\otimes](f,g)(p_1,p_2)=<f(p_1),g(p_2)>$ in $T_3 \times T_4$. ■

Basically, $[\otimes](\underline{\mathbf{T}}_1,\underline{\mathbf{T}}_2)$ is the tree $\underline{\mathbf{T}}_1$ with a copy of $\underline{\mathbf{T}}_2$ below each of its leaves.

PROPOSITION 9. i) [$\otimes$] is a functor from **Trees**$\times$**Trees** to **Trees**. ii) [$\otimes$] is a tensor product.

PROOF. i) Routine. In particular, let us consider the **A**-functors f: $\mathbf{T_1} \to \mathbf{T_3}$ and g: $\mathbf{T_2} \to \mathbf{T_4}$. Let $\mathbf{T_i}$ be $<T_i,e_i,a_i>$ and p_i and q_i denote two paths in the tree $\mathbf{T_i}$ for i=1,...,4. It is required to check that if $p_3=f(p_1)$ and $q_3=f(q_1)$ and $p_4=g(p_2)$ and $q_4=g(q_2)$ then $a_{12}(<p_1,p_2>,<q_1,q_2>) \leq a_{34}(<p_3,p_4>,<q_3,q_4>)$, where a_{12} and a_{34} are the agreements in the trees $[\otimes](\mathbf{T_1},\mathbf{T_2})$ and $[\otimes](\mathbf{T_3},\mathbf{T_4})$, respectively. It is enough to show that: if $p_1=q_1$ then $p_3=q_3$.
Indeed, since $p_1=q_1$ we have that: $a_1(p_1,q_1) = e_1(p_1) = e_1(q_1) = e_3(p_3) = e_3(q_3)$. By definition of **A**-functor $a_1(p_1,q_1) \leq a_3(p_3,q_3)$. We also have that $a_3(p_3,q_3) \leq e_3(p_3)\wedge e_3(q_3)$ by definition of **A**-category. Thus, we have: $a_1(p_1,q_1) = a_3(p_3,q_3)$. Since our **A**-categories are skeletal we get: $p_3=q_3$.
ii) [$\otimes$] is associative and its bilateral identity is NIL=$<\{p\},e,a>$, where $e(p)=\varepsilon$ and $a(p,p)=\varepsilon$. ■
Thus, the category **Trees** is a monoidal category.

In the sequel for the tensor products $\otimes$ and [$\otimes$] we will feel free to use the infix notation, which will recall us that they are 'concatenation' operators.

PROPOSITION 10. **A** is isomorphic to a subcategory of **Trees**. It is a discrete subcategory, which is full. Thus, $\otimes$ is a restriction to **A** of the concatenation [$\otimes$].
The same holds for the generic bicategory of observers **O** which is a subcategory of **Sc(O)**.
PROOF. Any object w of an sl-bicategory **A** can be viewed as an **A**-category $<\{c\},e,a>$ where $e(c)=a(c,c)=w$. No morphism exists from an object w1 to a different object w2 in **Trees** because of condition i) of Definition 3. Only identity morphisms exist. ■

The operation [$\otimes$] concatenates structures of computations, that is, objects at level 1. However, [$\otimes$] can also be considered at level 2, where objects are agents and morphisms are structures of computations, because it simply corresponds to composition of morphisms. (See also Section 5.)

Now we are ready to define the synchronization of trees, which models the parallel composition (or synchronization) of computations, by 'lifting' a synchronization algebra [Win84] over the alphabet of actions A. Similar construction has been done in [KLP87].

DEFINITION 11. Given two strict monoidal categories $(\mathbf{M_1},\otimes_1,I_1)$ and $(\mathbf{M_2},\otimes_2,I_2)$ a functor F from $\mathbf{M_1}$ to $\mathbf{M_2}$ is said to be *monoidal* iff i) there exists a morphism from I_2 to $F(I_1)$ and ii) there exists a natural transformation τ which assigns to each pair of objects A and B in $\mathbf{M_1}$ a morphism from $F(A)\otimes_2F(B)$ to $F(A\otimes_1B)$ and τ well-behaves (see [EiK65, p.473]) w.r.t. the associativity and the identity of the tensor products.

PROPOSITION 12. A *partial* synchronization operation $*$: A$\times$A $\to$ A extends to a homomorphism between sl-bicategories $*$: **A**$\times$**A** $\to$ **A** and, successively, to a monoidal functor [$*$]: **Trees**$\times$**Trees** $\to$ **Trees**.
PROOF. We first define $*$: **A**$\times$**A** $\to$ **A** (We will also use the infix notation for $*$.) For any pair of objects of sl-bicategory **A** (that is, words in A*) $a=a_1a_2...a_n$ and $b=b_1b_2...b_m$ where $a_1,...,a_n,b_1...,b_m$ are elements of A,

$$* (a,b) = c_1...c_n \quad \text{if } n=m \text{ and } c_i=a_i*b_i \text{ for } i=1,...,n$$
$$= \varepsilon \quad \text{otherwise.}$$

Notice that $*$ may give a non-ε result only if the words to be synchronized have equal length.
For any pair of 1-cells $v \in Ob(\mathbf{A}(u,w))$ and $s \in Ob(\mathbf{A}(r,t))$,

$*[<u,r>,<w,t>](v,s) = (v * s) \wedge (u * r) \wedge (w * t)$.

Notice that in the above expression the term $(u * r) \wedge (w * t)$ is required because $v * s$ may not be an object of $\underline{\mathbf{A}}(u * r, w * t)$.

Consider, for instance, the case when $A=\{x\}$ and $x * x=x$. If $u=xx$, $w=r=t=x$ and $v=s=x$ we have: $v * s = x$, while $\underline{\mathbf{A}}(u * r, w * t) = \underline{\mathbf{A}}(\varepsilon,x)$ which is the poset $\{\varepsilon\}$.

For 2-cells we have: if $v_1 \leq v_2$ is a 2-cell in $\underline{\mathbf{A}}(u,w)$ and $s_1 \leq s_2$ is a 2-cell in $\underline{\mathbf{A}}(r,t)$ for some u, w, r, and $t \in Ob(\underline{\mathbf{A}})$ then $(*[<u,r>,<w,t>](v_1,s_1) \leq *[<u,r>,<w,t>](v_2,s_2))$ is a 2-cell in $\underline{\mathbf{A}}(*(u,r), *(w,t))$.

Let us now define the monoidal functor $[*]$, which models the parallel composition of two trees. We first consider the categories **Trees** and **Trees**×**Trees** as monoidal categories with respect to the tensor products $[\otimes]$ and $[\otimes]\times[\otimes]$, respectively.

On the objects the functor $[*]$ is defined as follows. (We will feel free to use the infix notation for $[*]$). Given the trees $\underline{\mathbf{T}}_i=<T_i,e_i,a_i>$ for i=1,2, $\underline{\mathbf{T}}_1[*]\underline{\mathbf{T}}_2$ is the tree $\underline{\mathbf{T}}=<T,e,a>$ such that:

- $T=\{<p_1,p_2> \mid (e(p_1) * e(p_2)) \neq \varepsilon$ or $e(p_1)=e(p_2)=\varepsilon$ with $p_i \in T_i$ for i=1,2$\}$ modulo skeletality,
- $e(<p_1,p_2>) = (e(p_1) * e(p_2))$, and
- $a(<p_1,q_1>,<p_2,q_2>)$ is the maximal common prefix w of $e(<p_1,q_1>)$ and $e(<p_2,q_2>)$ such that $|w| \leq |a(p_1,p_2)|$ and $|w| \leq |a(q_1,q_2)|$, where $|w|$ denotes the length of $w \in A^*$.

On the morphisms $[*]$ is defined as follows.

Given the morphisms f: $\underline{\mathbf{T}}_1 \to \underline{\mathbf{T}}_3$ and g: $\underline{\mathbf{T}}_2 \to \underline{\mathbf{T}}_4$, where $\underline{\mathbf{T}}_i=<T_i,e_i,a_i>$ for i=1,...,4, and p_1 in T_1, and p_2 in T_2 $[*](f,g)(p_1,p_2) = (f(p_1) * g(p_2))$. This is a good definition because $<f(p_1),g(p_2)> \in \underline{\mathbf{T}}_3 \times \underline{\mathbf{T}}_4$ iff $<p_1,p_2> \in \underline{\mathbf{T}}_1 \times \underline{\mathbf{T}}_2$. (Indeed f and g preserve the extent of paths and they are monotonic w.r.t. to the agreement).

One can easily check that $[*]$ is a monoidal functor w.r.t. the tensor product $[\otimes]$ [Kel82]. Indeed, NIL$[*]$NIL is isomorphic to NIL, and for any tree $\underline{\mathbf{T}}_1$, $\underline{\mathbf{T}}_2$, $\underline{\mathbf{T}}_3$, and $\underline{\mathbf{T}}_4$, there exists a $\underline{\mathbf{A}}$-functor from $(\underline{\mathbf{T}}_1[*]\underline{\mathbf{T}}_2)$ $[\otimes]$ $(\underline{\mathbf{T}}_3[*]\underline{\mathbf{T}}_4)$ to $(\underline{\mathbf{T}}_1[\otimes]\underline{\mathbf{T}}_2)$ $[*]$ $(\underline{\mathbf{T}}_3[\otimes]\underline{\mathbf{T}}_4)$ (Interchange Property). This $\underline{\mathbf{A}}$-functor generalizes the equality used by [MeM88, p. 156]. ■

Given a synchronization algebra, that is, a binary operation $*$ defined on a set A of actions, the above Proposition 12 allows us to synchronize two trees of actions according to the corresponding functor $[*]$. Thus, in particular, Proposition 12 allows us to build the categorical model for tree synchronization when $*$ is the Hoare-like synchronization $*_H$ (defined as: $\forall a \in A.\ a *_H a = a$, otherwise undefined) or any SCCS-like synchronization $*_{SCCS}$ (defined as: $\forall a,b \in A.\ \exists c \in A.\ a *_{SCCS} b = c$).

In the general case, when we need to synchronize two given structures of computations, that is, two objects in **Sc**(**O**) (not simply objects in **Trees**) we are required to have a monoidal functor, say $[\sigma]$, from **Sc**(**O**)×**Sc**(**O**) to **Sc**(**O**).

We will refer to $[\sigma]$ as a *synchronization between structures of computations*. However, it is not always the case that $[\sigma]$ can be obtained by lifting a synchronization algebra given at the level of the action alphabet, as we have done in the case of **Trees**.

Before closing this Section we state the following Theorem which will be useful for providing functorial connections between categories of different structures of computations, that is, between various **Sc**(**O**)'s when the sl-bicategory **O** of observers varies.

THEOREM 13. (*Change of the base bicategory of the observers.*) A homomorphism φ: **O** → **O'** between sl-bicategories induces a functor Φ: **Sc**(**O**) → **Sc**(**O'**).

PROOF. Φ on the objects is defined as follows. Given the **O**-category $\underline{\mathbf{C}}=<C,e,a>$, $\Phi(\underline{\mathbf{C}})$ is

<C',φe,φa>, where C' is C modulo skeletality, that is, C' is C/≈ where the equivalence relation ≈ is defined as follows: ∀ c_1,c_2 ∈ C. $c_1 \approx c_2$ iff $\varphi e(c_1) = \varphi e(c_2) = \varphi a(c_1,c_2)$).
Φ on the morphisms is defined as follows. Given the **O**-functor f: $\mathbf{C_1} \rightarrow \mathbf{C_2}$ between the **O**-categories $\mathbf{C_1}=<C_1,e_1,a_1>$ and $\mathbf{C_2}=<C_2,e_2,a_2>$, the functor Φ(f): $\mathbf{C_1}' \rightarrow \mathbf{C_2}'$, where $\mathbf{C_1}'=<C_1',e_1',a_1'>$ and $\mathbf{C_2}'=<C_2',e_2',a_2'>$, is the one induced by the function f' : $C_1' \rightarrow C_2'$ defined as follows: ∀ equivalence class [c] ∈ C_1'. f'([c])=[f(c)], where we use again f to denote the function $C_1 \rightarrow C_2$ induced by the functor f. Indeed it can be shown that:
- ∀ [c] ∈ C_1'. $e_1'([c])=e_2'(f'[c])$, and
- ∀ $[c_1],[c_2]$ ∈ C_1'. $a_1'([c_1],[c_2]) \leq' a_2'(f'[c_1],f'[c_2])$ where ≤' is the 2-cell in the sl-bicategory **O'**. The proof relies on the following facts:
- φ is a homomorphism of bicategories and preserves 2-cells,
- ∀ [c] ∈ C_1'. ∀ d ∈ [c]. $\varphi(e_1(d))=e_1'([c])$, and
- ∀ $[c_1],[c_2]$ ∈ C_1'. ∀ c ∈ $[c_1]$.∀ d ∈ $[c_2]$. $\varphi(a_1(c,d)) = a_1'([c_1],[c_2])$. ■

5. SEMANTICS FOR THE SYNCHRONIZATION OF AGENTS

In the previous Section we have constructed a categorical model for the synchronization operation over structures of computations, which corresponds to level 1 of our categorical framework. We now need to make a further step and we will define the model for the synchronization of computing agents at level 2.
Objects of that model will be computing agents, and between any two agents, say ag1 and ag2, there will be the structure of computations, which is derived from the successful experiments from ag1 to ag2. The synchronization operation [✱] defined on structures of computations at level 1 will be extended to an operation defined on agents.
As we have already done for constructing models at level 1 from those at level 0, we will apply the *enrichment construction* over a bicategory by defining a category **AG** of agents enriched over the monoidal category **Sc(O)** at level 1.

This approach is an extension of the one in [KLP87] in the sense that the enrichment construction over a monoidal category is an instance of the enrichment construction over a bicategory. Indeed, a generic monoidal category **M** can be regarded as a bicategory with one object, whose 1-cells are the objects of **M** and 2-cells are the morphisms of **M**. Analogously, a functor between two categories enriched over **M** is an instance of an **M**-functor, that is, a functor between categories based on **M**, considered as a bicategory.

DEFINITION 14. [Kel82] A category **AG** *enriched over* the strict monoidal category **Sc(O)**, with tensor product [⊗] and identity **I**, is a set of objects with a *hom-function* **AG**(-,-) from **AG**×**AG** to **Sc(O)** which assigns to each pair (a,b) of objects of **AG** an object of **Sc(O)** to be understood as the *hom-object* between a and b, such that for each triple of objects there exist: i) a *composition morphism* m[xyz]: **AG**(x,y) ⊗ **AG**(y,z) → **AG**(x,z), and ii) an *identity morphism* j(x): **I** → **AG**(x,x) which are subject to the associativity and unit axioms expressed by the commutativity of the following diagrams:

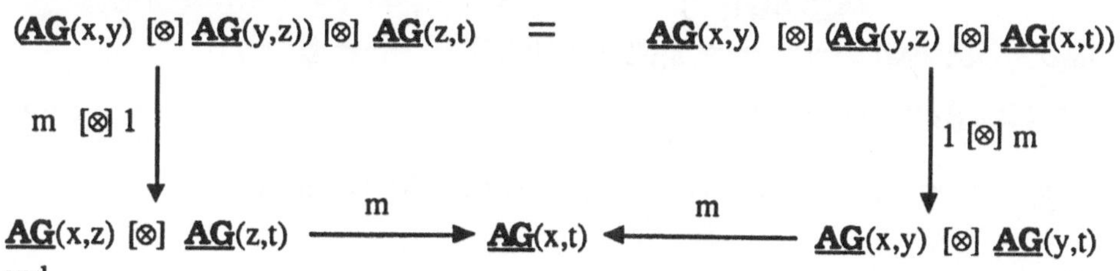

and

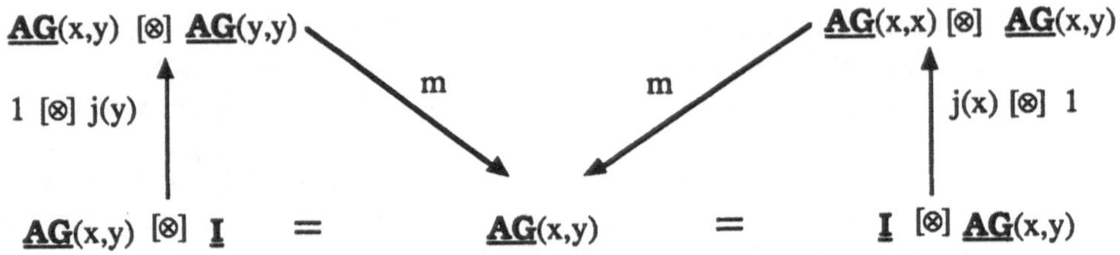

where m stands for m[...] with the suitable variables replacing dots. ■

Informally speaking, the composition morphism tells us that the structure of computations between the agents x and y concatenated with the one between the agents y and z is contained in the structure of computations between the agents x and z. Indeed, it may be the case that the structure of computations from x to z has more computations, because some of them may not be factorizable via y. The identity morphism tells us that the identity **I** of the tensor product is represented by a trivial computation from the agent x to itself.
As already mentioned, **AG** can be viewed as a **Sc(O)**-category.

DEFINITION 15. [Kel82] Given two **Sc(O)**-categories **AG1** and **AG2** a **Sc(O)**-functor F from **AG1** to **AG2** is a function from the objects of **AG1** to the objects of **AG2** such that there is a morphism F[x,y]: **AG1**(x,y) → **AG2**(F(x),F(y)), subject to the compatibility conditions w.r.t. composition and identities expressed by the commutativity of the following diagrams (where m and F stand for m[...] and F[...] with suitable variables replacing dots):

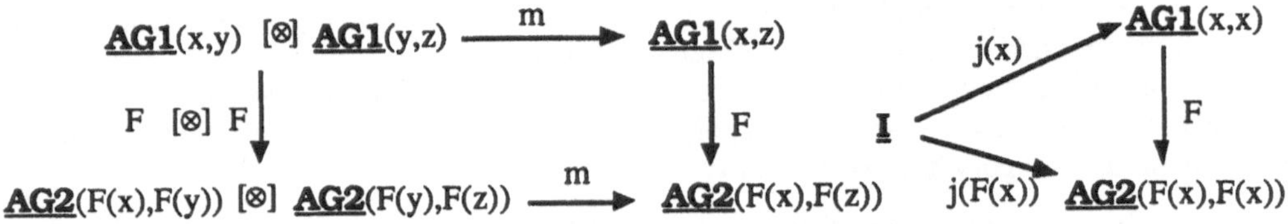

■

These diagrams basically say that the transformation via F of the concatenation of structures of computations is the concatenation of the transformed structures, and that the trivial computation is preserved under F.

DEFINITION 16. Given a *synchronization* [σ]: **Sc(O)**×**Sc(O)** → **Sc(O)** between structures of computations, a *semantics for* [σ] is a pair <**AG**, Σ>, where **AG** is **Sc(O)**-category (that is, a category of agents) and Σ is a **Sc(O)**-functor from **AG** $\times_\sigma$ **AG** to **AG**, where **AG** $\times_\sigma$ **AG** is the **Sc(O)**-category obtained as *effect* ([EiK65]) of the monoidal functor [σ] as follows.
Given the **Sc(O)**-category **AG**, we first get the category **AG**×**AG** which is a (**Sc(O)**×**Sc(O)**)-category. The category **AG** $\times_\sigma$ **AG** is obtained from **AG** × **AG** by changing the hom-function (**AG** × **AG**)(-,-) of **AG** × **AG** into the new hom-function (**AG** $\times_\sigma$ **AG**)(-,-) which is the composition of (**AG**×**AG**)(-,-) and [σ], as indicated by the following diagram:

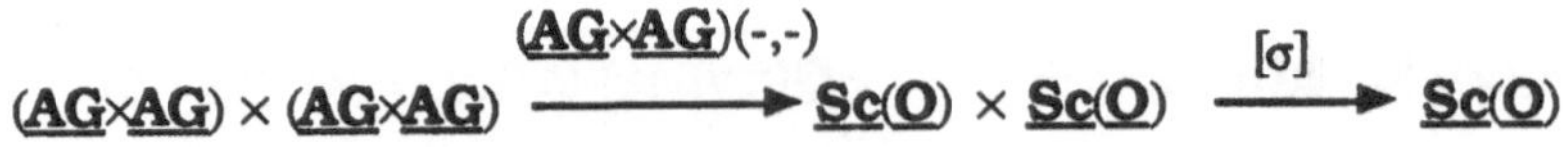

Thus, **AG** $\times_\sigma$ **AG** is a **Sc(O)**-category. ■

The following picture represents the effect construction and the **Sc(O)**-functor Σ.

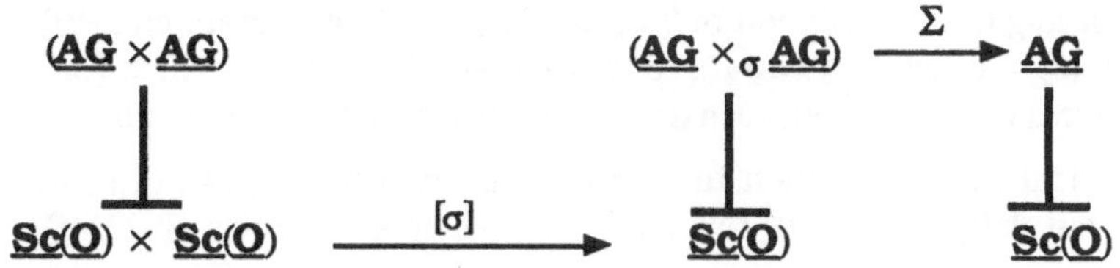

(⊥ denotes the enrichment.)

Given two structures of computations $\underline{C}_1$ and $\underline{C}_2$ in **Sc(O)**, the functor Σ allows us to define the agents in **AG** which are the domain and the codomain of the structure of computation obtained by synchronizing $\underline{C}_1$ and $\underline{C}_2$.
In particular, if the system of observers **O** is the bicategory **A** and [σ] is [✱], the functor Σ allows us to define the agent which is the synchronization of two given agents of a SCCS-like calculus. Indeed, as the following Theorem shows Milner's agents and their behaviour trees [Mil80, p.12] can be viewed as a category of agents in our sense (see also [KLP87]). (For sake of simplicity we consider here only behaviour trees with paths of finite length and without equivalence relations defined on them, like, for instance, those concerning the silent action τ).

THEOREM 17. **Trees** can be considered as a **Trees**-category. There exists a **Trees**-functor Σ such that <**Trees**, Σ> is a semantics for the functor [✱] derived from a synchronization algebra ✱: A*×A* → A*, where A is the alphabet of actions.
PROOF. **Trees** can be viewed as a category enriched over itself by considering between any two trees $\underline{T}_1$=<T_1,e_1,a_1> and $\underline{T}_2$=<T_2,e_2,a_2> the hom-object made out of the tree-like initial part of $\underline{T}_2$, which includes all paths from the root of $\underline{T}_2$ to a copy of $\underline{T}_1$. Thus, the hom-object is the structure of computations each of which leads from the agent $\underline{T}_2$ to the agent $\underline{T}_1$. (See Figure 6.)

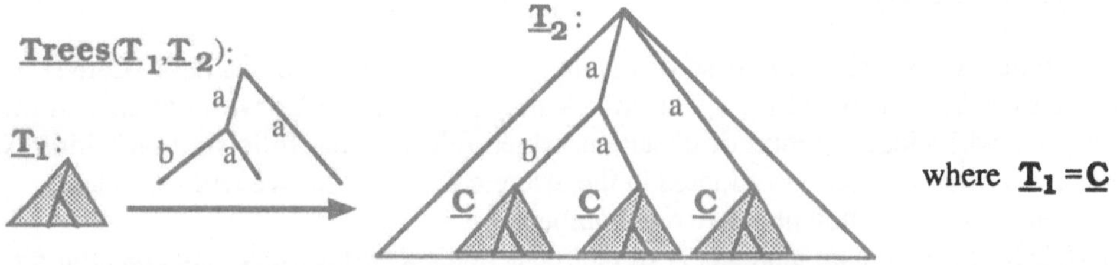

Figure 6. **Trees** as a category enriched over itself: the tree **Trees($\underline{T}_1$,$\underline{T}_2$)** from $\underline{T}_1$ to $\underline{T}_2$.

In formal terms, between $\underline{T}_1$ and $\underline{T}_2$ we consider the tree **Trees($\underline{T}_1$,$\underline{T}_2$)** = <T,e,a>, where:
- T ={π_{sC} | ∃ s∈A*. ∃ a tree $\underline{C}$ s.t. π_{sC} is an isomorphism from $\underline{T}_1$ to $\underline{C}$=<C,e_C,a_C>, where:
  - C is a maximal subset of paths in $\underline{T}_2$ satisfying the following two conditions:
    i) for each path p∈C $s \leq e_2(p)$, and
    ii) for each pair of paths $p_1,p_2 \in C$ $s \leq a_2(p_1,p_2)$, and
    $e_C(p)$ and $a_C(p_1,p_2)$ are defined by the following equations:
  - $e_2(p) = s \cdot e_C(p)$, where · denotes the concatenation of words, and
  - $a_2(p_1,p_2) = s \cdot a_C(p_1,p_2)$} modulo skeletality,
- $e(\pi_{sC}) = s$, and for any pair of isomorphisms π_1, π_2 in T we have:
- $a(\pi_1,\pi_2) = a(p_1,p_2)$, where p_i is any path of $\underline{T}_2$ in the image of π_i for i=1,2.

In Figure 6 there are 3 isomorphisms corresponding to s = ab, aa, a.

Notice that, according to the definition of **Trees**($\mathbf{T}_1$,$\mathbf{T}_2$), **Trees**(a+b, c:(a+b)) = <{p},e,a> where e(p) = a(p,p) = c, while **Trees**(a+b, c:(a+b+a)) = <∅,∅,∅>, where for simplicity the trees in the argument positions have been denoted using a SCCS-like notation.

Given any monoidal synchronization functor [✱] and two trees $\mathbf{T}_1$=<T_1,e_1,a_1> and $\mathbf{T}_2$ = <T_2,e_2,a_2> we can define a **Trees**-functor Σ on objects as follows: $\mathbf{T}_1$ Σ $\mathbf{T}_2$ = <T,e,a>, where:

- T=$T_1 \times T_2$ modulo the relation induced by skeletality condition,
- e(<p_1,p_2>) is the maximal word w = w_1[✱]w_2, where w_i is a prefix of $e_i(p_i)$ for i=1,2, (recall that a word w can be viewed as the tree <{p},e,a>, where e(p)=a(p,p)=w), and
- a(<p_1,q_1>,<p_2,q_2>) is the maximal common prefix w of e(<p_1,q_1>) and e(<p_2,q_2>) such that $|w| \le |a(p_1,p_2)|$ and $|w| \le |a(q_1,q_2)|$.

The definition of Σ on the hom-objects is simply given by the synchronization functor [✱]. Intuitively speaking, the synchronization of two trees using Σ is obtained by first synchronizing any two paths one for each tree *as long as possible starting from the root* using the given synchronization algebra ∗, and then by computing the agreement between the resulting paths using [✱], as defined above. ■

REMARK. In **Trees** we have the following two different structures of computations (and, consequently, two different agents can be defined when considering **Trees** enriched over itself):
i) NIL=<{p},e,a>, where e(p)=a(p,p)=ε, which is the identity of the tensor product [⊗], and
ii) δ=<∅,∅,∅>. For NIL one successful experiment only can be performed and it has extent ε, while for δ no successful experiment exists. We may say that δ corresponds to a complete disaster, in the sense that δ[⊗]**T** = **T**[⊗]δ = δ for any **T** in **Trees**. More details and examples are given in [KLP87, KaL90]. ■

6. CONTINUOUS TREES

In this Section we consider the case of *continuous time agents* à la Cardelli [Car82] and we construct a categorical model for agents which may perform actions with *duration* in time. In this case we will adopt a notion of observers which relies on the following definition (which extends the notion of observers adopted in the discrete time case, as we will see below).
Let R^+ denote the set of non negative real numbers.
DEFINITION 18. Given an alphabet A of atomic actions, a *partial piecewise constant function* (*partial pc-function* or *pc-function*, for short) f is a function from R^+ to A defined over a bounded interval $[0,t) \subseteq R^+$, such that for any $a \in A$ $f^{-1}(a)$ is the union of finitely many intervals of the form [r,s), with r and s non-negative reals. ■
The condition of the boundedness of the interval [0,t) may be released for modelling Cardelli's agents with actions of indefinite duration (see [Car82], p.103).

PROPOSITION 19. The set CA of partial piecewise constant functions is a meet-semilattice where: i) f≤g iff dom(f) ⊆ dom(g) and if x ∈ dom(f) then f(x)=g(x),
ii) f ∧ g is defined as follows: - dom(f∧g) = [0,t) where t is s.t.
∀x<t both f(x) and g(x) are defined and f(x)=g(x), and
if f(t) and g(t) are both defined then f(t)≠g(t),
- if x ⊆ dom(f∧g) then (f∧g)(x) = f(x), and
iii) the bottom element ⊥ is the empty function defined in the empty interval [0,0). ■

The meet of the pc-functions f and g of Figure 7 is the pc-function h such that $dom(h)=[0,t_2)$, $h^{-1}(\alpha) = [0,t_1)$, $h^{-1}(\beta) = [t_1,t_2)$.

PROPOSITION 20. **CA** =(CA,≤,∧,⊥) is an sl-bicategory. ■

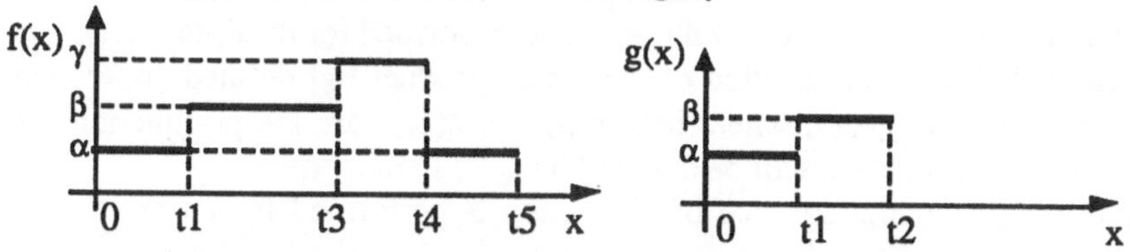

Figure 7. Two piecewise constant functions f and g. (Assume that if i<j then $t_i<t_j$).
$dom(f)=[0,t_5)$, $f^{-1}(\alpha)=[0,t_1)\cup[t_4,t_5)$, $f^{-1}(\beta)=[t_1,t_3)$, $f^{-1}(\gamma)=[t_3,t_4)$.
$dom(g)=[0,t_2)$, $g^{-1}(\alpha)=[0,t_1)$, $g^{-1}(\beta)=[t_1,t_2)$.

CA will be used as the system of observers for real time agents. The system of observers **A** for discrete time agents which we have introduced in the previous section, can be defined as **CA** by considering each sequence of actions, that is, words in A*, as a partial pc-function from the *natural numbers* to A, defined on an initial segment [0,n) for some n. In this sense **A** turns out to be a discrete version of **CA**.

Let **Sc(CA)** be the category of skeletal symmetric categories based on **CA**. **Sc(CA)** can be described as the category of all trees whose root-to-leaf paths are labelled by partial piecewise constant functions. Also the agreement between any two paths is a partial piecewise-constant function (see Figure 8 below, where for each path in the tree the labelling functions have been represented by the corresponding Greek letters). In analogy to the discrete case **Sc(CA)** will also be called **CTrees** (short for Continuous Trees).

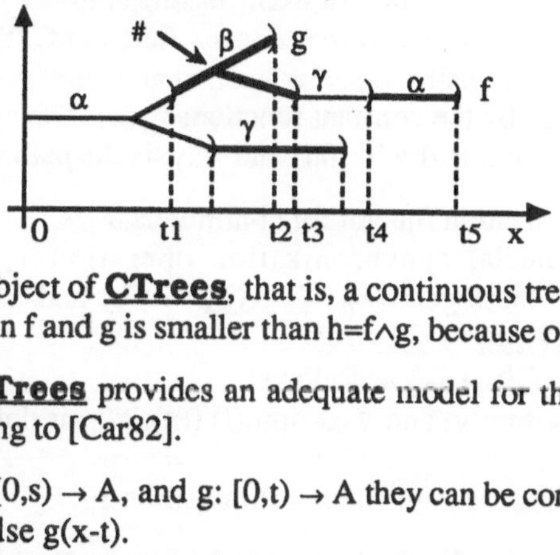

Figure 8. An object of **CTrees**, that is, a continuous tree with 3 paths.
The agreement between f and g is smaller than h=f∧g, because of the *choice point* in #.

We will now show that **CTrees** provides an adequate model for the computations performed by real time agents according to [Car82].

Given two pc-functions f: [0,s) → A, and g: [0,t) → A they can be concatenated as follows:
$(f\cdot g)(x) =$ if x<t then f(x) else g(x-t).

PROPOSITION 21. The concatenation of pc-functions defines a tensor product on the sl-bicategory **CA**, namely ⊗: **CA**×**CA** → **CA**.

PROOF. Analogous to the proof of Proposition 7. The identity of the tensor product ⊗ is the empty function ⊥. ■

The concatenation [⊗] of continuous trees in **CTrees** can be defined as for **Trees** (see Definition 8).

PROPOSITION 22. i) [⊗] is a functor from **CTrees**×**CTrees** to **CTrees**. ii) [⊗] is a tensor product. Thus, **CTrees** is a monoidal category.

PROOF. (See the proof of Proposition 9) The identity for [⊗] is the tree CNIL=<{p},e,a> where e(p)=a(p,p)=⊥. ■

In [Car82] the following two concatenation operators for continuous trees are defined:

i) α[t]:_ (prefixing a continuous tree by the action α performed for the duration t).
It can be modelled by the restriction of the tensor product [⊗] defined above, when the left operand is the tree <{p},e,a>, where both e(p) and a(p,p) are the pc-function assuming the value α in [0,t). This function will be denoted by $f_\alpha(t)$ in the sequel.

ii) α(t):_ (prefixing a continuous tree by the action α performed for an arbitrary duration x, $0<x\leq t$).
It can be defined as a restriction of a functor **CTrees**×**CTrees** → **CTrees** (and this definition will be given in a forthcoming paper), but it can also be defined as follows.
Let us consider the subcategory **cCA** of **CA** of the partial *constant functions*, that is, pc-functions which take one value only. **cCA** can be considered as a discrete subcategory of **CTrees** (see Proposition 10).
We define a functor P from **cCA** to **CTrees** by assuming $P(f_\alpha(t))$=<dom($f_\alpha(t)$),e,a>, where for any x and y in [0,t) we have that: i) e(x)=f_α restricted to [0,x), and ii) a(x,y) = e(x) ∧ e(y).
The functor P produces a tree with an infinite number of paths. At the end of each of them a copy of the second tree to be concatenated is attached. The behaviour of the functor P corresponds to the fact that the duration of the action α in α(t):_ may be any positive real smaller than t. Thus, we have:

$$\underline{\mathbf{cCA}} \times \underline{\mathbf{CTrees}} \xrightarrow{P\times 1} \underline{\mathbf{CTrees}} \times \underline{\mathbf{CTrees}} \xrightarrow{[\otimes]} \underline{\mathbf{CTrees}}$$

which gives the required functor modeling the a(t):_ operator of [Car82].

Notice that in our approach the definition of α(t):_ has been given in terms of the definition of α[t]:_ in the sense that the path labelled by the constant function $f_\alpha(t)$ in the tree modelling α[t]:_ has been replaced by a *set* of paths one for each real value x in [0,t) such that the path corresponding to x is labelled by the constant functions $f_\alpha(x)$. The agreement between the paths with labels $f_\alpha(x)$ and $f_\alpha(y)$, for x and y in [0,t) and x≤y, is the path with label $f_\alpha(x)$.

We now define the synchronization functor for continuous trees.

PROPOSITION 23. A partial synchronization operation ∗: A×A → A extends to a homomorphism between sl-bicategories ✱: **CA**×**CA** → **CA** and, successively, to a monoidal functor [✱]: **CTrees**×**CTrees** → **CTrees**.

PROOF. We define ✱ : **CA**×**CA** → **CA** as follows:

dom(f✱ g) = *if* dom(f)=dom(g) and ∀ x∈dom(f) f(x)∗g(x) is defined *then* dom(f) *else* ∅.

(f✱ g)(x) = f(x)∗g(x).

The rest of the proof is analogous to the one of Proposition 12. ■

Now we may define a semantics for the functor [✱] in analogy with what we have done in the discrete-time case in the previous Section.

Indeed, it is possible to consider the category **CTrees** as a category of agents, that is, **CTrees** can be viewed as a **CTrees**-category, and it is possible to define a **CTrees**-functor Σ from **CTrees**$\times_*$**CTrees** to **CTrees**. <**CTrees**, Σ> provides the semantics for any given synchronization functor between structures of computations in **CTrees**.

A theorem corresponding to Theorem 17 holds when replacing **Trees** by **CTrees**.

Before closing this section on the construction of a categorical model for real time agents [Car82], we would like to make the following remarks.

i) In [Car82, p.100] (see the axioms α[][]→ and α()()→) the operational behaviour of the agent α(t):p is obtained from the one of α[t]:p by adding all 'shorter sub-behaviours' corresponding to the agent α[x]:p for $0<x<t$, and then the axiom $p+p=p$ is used for eliminating the multiplicity of common sub-behaviours.
In our framework we have followed the same approach, but the agreement notion eliminates the multiplicity of common sub-behaviours, and the continuous tree corresponding to α(t):p is indeed a standard continuous tree with the property of having infinitely many paths.
Thus, the problem of giving an explicit axiomatization of the behaviour of α(t):p w.r.t. the synchronization functor Σ (see the conditional axioms FT1-FT4 in [Car82]) is avoided.

ii) The agent which performs the action α for an indefinite duration [Car82, p.103] can be modelled by using the constant function $f_\alpha(\infty)$ and the functor P.

7. ABOUT TRUE CONCURRENCY

In this section we will consider two of the most common approaches to *true concurrency*, the Trace Theory and the Event Structures, and we will show the way in which they can be considered as particular instances of our categorical constructions by a suitable choice of the sl-bicategory of observers.

Let us first consider Mazurkiewicz's Trace Theory. For the relevant definitions the reader may refer to [Maz87].
We can associate to every *elementary net system* (or simply, *net*) N a set of *firing sequences* (and the corresponding *firing traces*) over a concurrent alphabet, and this set represents the behaviour of the net N.

For the net N a *concurrent alphabet* is defined as the pair <A,D>, where A is the set of *events* occurring in N, and D is a symmetric and reflexive binary relation on A, which is called *dependency relation.* Notice that in Trace Theory labels are not taken into account, in the sense that different events have different names.
Given <A,D> we can consider the so-called *independence relation* $I = A^2 \setminus D$ between any two events in N. This relation yields a congruence relation ≡ on A^* as the minimal one generated by I, as formalized in the following definition.
DEFINITION 24. A *monoid of traces* on a set A of events with the symmetric and irreflexive relation I is the monoid $(A^*,\cdot,\varepsilon)/\equiv$, where ≡ is the following congruence relation:
$s \equiv t$ iff ∃ a sequence $<w_0,w_1, \ldots,w_n>$ such that: i) $s=w_0$, ii) $t=w_n$, and
iii) $\forall\, i\in \{0,\ldots,n-1\}\ \exists\, u_i,v_i \in A^*$ such that $w_i = u_i abv_i$, $w_{i+1} = u_i bav_i$, and $(a,b)\in I$.
A trace is an equivalence class of the relation ≡. The trace to which the word w belongs is denoted by [w]. ■

PROPOSITION 25. $A^*/\equiv$ is a meet-semilattice and therefore, an sl-bicategory, which we called **TO** (short for trace-observers).
PROOF. $(A^*/\equiv, \leq, \wedge, [\varepsilon])$ is a semilattice, where given the traces [u] and [v] we have:
$[u] \leq [v]$ iff $\forall\, u_i$ in [u]. $\exists\, v_j$ in [v] such that u_i is a *prefix* of v_j.
The meet of the two traces [u] and [v] is the trace [w] such that w is a maximal word in the set $\{w_{ij} \mid w_{ij}$ prefix of u_i and w_{ij} prefix of v_j and $u_i \in [u]$ and $v_j \in [v]\}$. It is easy to see that for any choice of w we indeed get the same trace [w].
The bottom element is [ε], because the empty string is a prefix of every string. ■
A trace-observer is an element of **TO**, that is, a trace.

Traces can also be viewed as posets. They represent *conflict-free* parts of the behaviour of an elementary net system N, and they correspond to prefixes of *processes* [Maz87]. Linearizations of traces represent observations made by trace-observers which are total orders (see also Proposition 29).

Given two traces [m] and [n] we define their *concatenation* [m]⊗[n] to be the trace [m·n], where · denotes the concatenation of words.
PROPOSITION 26. The sl-bicategory **TO** is equipped with a tensor product given by ⊗.
PROOF. Routine (see Proposition 7). ■

As we have done in the case of **Trees**, we can now consider our structures of computations 'at level 1'. They are categories based on **TO**, and hence, we may introduce the category **Sc(TO)**. A category based on **TO** is, as usual, a triple <X,e,a>. With each element x_i in X we associate an object of **TO**, that is, the trace $e(x_i)$, and with any pair of elements x_i and x_j we associate their agreement $a(x_i,x_j)$ which is a trace smaller than $e(x_i) \wedge e(x_j)$.
The tensor product ⊗ can be lifted to the tensor product [⊗] in the monoidal category **Sc(TO)**, the identity element being the **TO**-category TNIL=<{p},e,a>, where e(p)=a(p,p)=[ε].

Referring to an elementary net system N and an initial marking M_0, we can define 'level 2', that is, a category, say **Net**, enriched over **Sc(TO)**. The objects of **Net** are the markings (finitely) reachable from M_0, and the hom-object between any two reachable markings M_1 and M_2, is the **TO**-category denoting the tree whose paths are labelled by *firing traces* leading from M_1 to M_2. These firing traces are conflict-free [Maz87], and the agreement between any two firing traces is their maximal initial common trace. This agreement trace cannot be extended without resolving a conflict in the net N. (The notion of agreement between two traces is indeed a novelty of our approach.)

Let us now consider the problem of modelling the synchronization of traces. Mazurkiewicz's definition considers that operation between sets of traces. If those sets are over the same alphabet, we obtain a Hoare-like synchronization, because in that case, according to the definition in [Maz87, p.302], only two equal traces can be synchronized giving as result one of the two. Obviously, this operation can be defined using the synchronization algebra from A×A to A which is the diagonal.

DEFINITION 27. Given two traces [n] and [m] their *synchronization* à la Hoare is defined as follows: [n]✱[m] = [n] if [n]=[m]
[ε] if [n]≠[m]. ■

PROPOSITION 28. We can extend ✱ to a homomorphism: **TO**×**TO** → **TO** and to a monoidal functor [✱]: **Sc(TO)**×**Sc(TO)** → **Sc(TO)**.
PROOF. It is similar to the one of Proposition 12, where now ✱ is defined as in Definition 27. Given two structures of computations, that is, **TO**-categories $\mathbf{T_i}$=<T_i,e_i,a_i> for i=1,2, we define: [✱]($\mathbf{T_1}$,$\mathbf{T_2}$) to be the tree **T**=<T,e,a> such that:
- $T=\{\langle p_1,p_2\rangle \mid e(p_1) = e(p_2)$ with $p_i \in T_i$ for i=1,2$\}$ modulo skeletality,
- $e(\langle p_1,p_2\rangle) = e(p_1)$ (=$e(p_2)$), and
- $a(\langle p_1,p_2\rangle,\langle p_1',p_2'\rangle) = a(p_1,p_1') \wedge a(p_2,p_2')$, where p_i, $p_i' \in \mathbf{T_i}$, for i=1,2.
On the morphisms [✱] is defined as presented in the proof of Proposition 12. Given the morphisms f: $\mathbf{T_1} \to \mathbf{T_3}$ and g: $\mathbf{T_2} \to \mathbf{T_4}$, where $\mathbf{T_i}$=<T_i,e_i,a_i> for i=1,…,4, and p_1 in T_1, and p_2 in T_2 [✱](f,g)(p_1,p_2) = f(p_1)✱ g(p_2).

It is easy to check that [✱] is a monoidal functor w.r.t. the tensor product [⊗].
Indeed, (TNIL[✱]TNIL) is isomorphic to TNIL, and the Interchange Property holds, that is, for any structure of computations $\underline{\mathbf{T}}_1$, $\underline{\mathbf{T}}_2$, $\underline{\mathbf{T}}_3$, and $\underline{\mathbf{T}}_4$, there exists a $\underline{\mathbf{TO}}$-functor from $(\underline{\mathbf{T}}_1[*]\underline{\mathbf{T}}_2)\,[\otimes]\,(\underline{\mathbf{T}}_3[*]\underline{\mathbf{T}}_4)$ to $(\underline{\mathbf{T}}_1[\otimes]\underline{\mathbf{T}}_2)\,[*]\,(\underline{\mathbf{T}}_3[\otimes]\underline{\mathbf{T}}_4)$. ■

Given the alphabet of events A and the independence relation I we can consider the categories $\underline{\mathbf{Sc}}(\underline{\mathbf{A}})$ (that is, $\underline{\mathbf{Trees}}$) and $\underline{\mathbf{Sc}}(\underline{\mathbf{TO}})$.
There is a natural monoid homomorphism between A* and A*/≡, which is induced by the congruence ≡. This homomorphism extends to a morphism of sl-bicategories g: $\underline{\mathbf{A}} \to \underline{\mathbf{TO}}$.
By Theorem 13 we get from g a functor tr: $\underline{\mathbf{Sc}}(\underline{\mathbf{A}}) \to \underline{\mathbf{Sc}}(\underline{\mathbf{TO}})$. Thus, tr($\underline{\mathbf{T}}$) is the $\underline{\mathbf{TO}}$-category $<tr(T), tr(e_T), tr(a_T)>$ corresponding to a given $\underline{\mathbf{A}}$-category $\underline{\mathbf{T}}=<T,e_T,a_T>$. We have: tr(T)=T (recall Theorem 13). Basically, tr transforms the words which label the paths of a tree into the corresponding traces (see Figure 9 below, where for each path $p \in T$ we have denoted by [p] the corresponding path in tr(T)).

Let us consider the functor in: $\underline{\mathbf{Sc}}(\underline{\mathbf{TO}}) \to \underline{\mathbf{Sc}}(\underline{\mathbf{A}})$, called *interleaving* functor, defined as follows:
- given the $\underline{\mathbf{TO}}$-category $\underline{\mathbf{Z}}=<Z,e_Z,a_Z>$ (that is, a tree labelled by traces in A*/≡), in($\underline{\mathbf{Z}}$) is the $\underline{\mathbf{A}}$-category (that is, a tree labelled by words in A*) $\underline{\mathbf{Z}}'=<Z',e_Z',a_Z'>$ such that:
  - $Z' = \{<p,s> \mid p \in Z,\ s \in e_Z(p)\}$,
  - $e_Z'(<p,s>) = s$, and
  - $a_Z'(<p_1,s_1>,<p_2,s_2>) = (s_1 \wedge s_2)$ restricted to the length of $a_Z(p_1,p_2)$ (the meet ∧ being in $\underline{\mathbf{A}}$),
- given the $\underline{\mathbf{TO}}$-functor f: $\underline{\mathbf{Z}}_1 \to \underline{\mathbf{Z}}_2$, in(f): in($\underline{\mathbf{Z}}_1$) → in($\underline{\mathbf{Z}}_2$) is the $\underline{\mathbf{A}}$-functor defined such that: in(f)(<p,s>) = <f(p),s> (where f here denotes also the function corresponding to the functor f).

The conditions for in(f) to be an $\underline{\mathbf{A}}$-functor as stated in Definition 3, are satisfied. In particular, notice that in(f) preserves the extents of paths. (See also Figure 9, where tr($\underline{\mathbf{T}}$) and in(tr($\underline{\mathbf{T}}$)) play the role of $\underline{\mathbf{Z}}$ and $\underline{\mathbf{Z}}'$, respectively, w.r.t. the above definition of the functor 'in'.)
Informally speaking, given a tree labelled by traces the functor 'in' constructs a tree labelled by all strings belonging to these traces by realizing the corresponding interleavings w.r.t. ≡.
The agreement between two paths with labels s_1 and s_2 is the maximal initial common substring of s_1 and s_2, which is not longer than the agreement of the corresponding traces.

PROPOSITION 29. tr is the left adjoint for in.
PROOF. Let us consider an $\underline{\mathbf{A}}$-category $\underline{\mathbf{T}}=<T,e_T,a_T>$ and a $\underline{\mathbf{TO}}$-category $\underline{\mathbf{Z}}=<Z,e_Z,a_Z>$.
Let tr($\underline{\mathbf{T}}$) be $<tr(T),tr(e_T),tr(a_T)>$ and in($\underline{\mathbf{Z}}$) be $<in(Z),in(e_Z),in(a_Z)>$.
Recall that: i) tr(T)=T, and ii) [p] denotes the path in tr(T) corresponding to the path p in T.
Given k: $\underline{\mathbf{T}} \to$ in($\underline{\mathbf{Z}}$) we may define k' : tr($\underline{\mathbf{T}}$) → $\underline{\mathbf{Z}}$ as follows:

$$k'([p]) =_{def} \pi_1(k(p)) \text{ for any } p \in T.$$

Viceversa, given h: tr($\underline{\mathbf{T}}$) → $\underline{\mathbf{Z}}$ we may define $\underline{h}$: $\underline{\mathbf{T}} \to$ in($\underline{\mathbf{Z}}$) as follows:

$$\underline{h}(t) =_{def} <h([p]), e_T(p)> \text{ for any } p \in T.$$

Thus, we have:

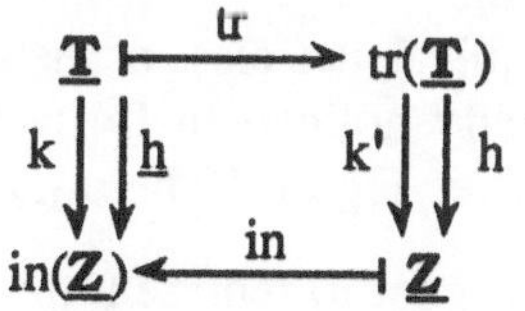

One can easily show that indeed k' is a $\underline{\mathbf{TO}}$-functor, because:
i) $(tr(e_T))([p]) = e_Z(k'([p]))$, and ii) $(tr(a_T))([p],[q]) \le a_Z(k'([p]),k'([q]))$, and $\underline{h}$ is an $\underline{\mathbf{A}}$-functor, because: i) $e_T(p) = (in(e_Z))(\underline{h}(p))$, and ii) $a_T(p,q) \le in(a_Z)(\underline{h}(p),\underline{h}(q))$.
We have that $\underline{(k')} = k$, and $(\underline{h})' = h$. The naturality conditions are easily checked. ■

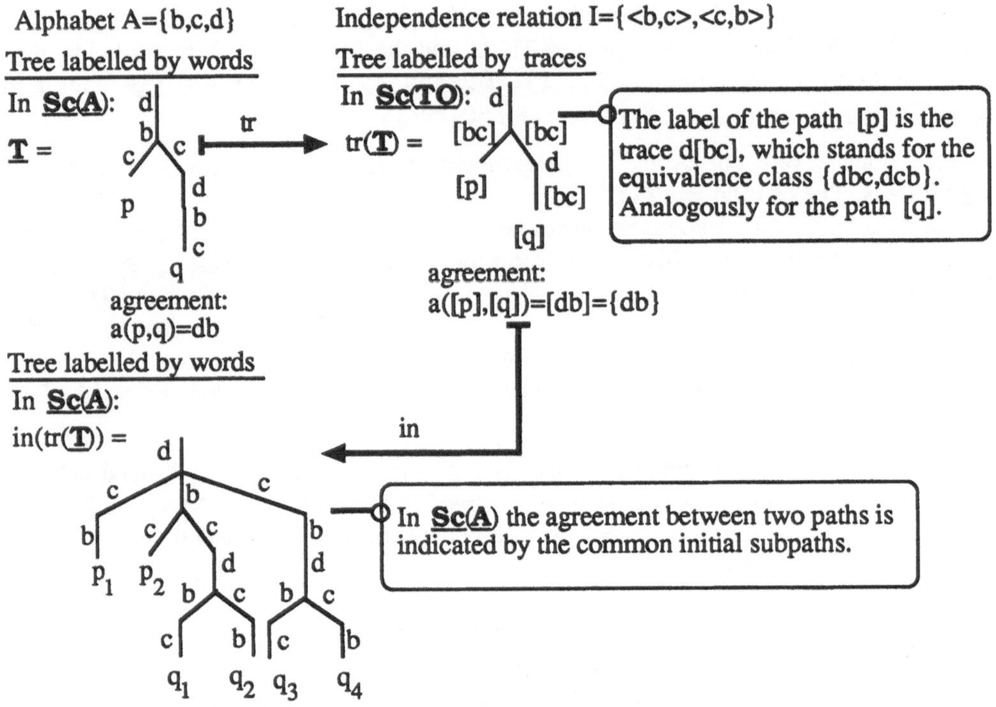

Figure 9. The functors tr and in.

Let us now consider the Event Structures approach [NPW81, Win87] to the description of parallel computations and we will show that the relevant notions of this theory can be reconstructed within our categorical framework by a suitable choice of the bicategory of observers.

We consider the classes of nets as axiomatically defined in [NPW81]. In that paper it is shown that for any contact-free *transition net* N with initial marking M_0 it is possible to construct an equivalent *occurrence net* $O[N,M_0]$, which basically corresponds to the 'unfolding' of N.
This construction relies on the definition of an equivalence relation among *sequences of transitions* which lead from the initial marking M_0 to the firing of a given transition.
The relevant part of that equivalence is generated by the relation which says that if the sequences of transitions 't_1 followed by t_2' and 't_2 followed by t_1' both lead from a reachable marking M_i to the same marking M_j then they are equivalent. In that case we say that the transitions (also called *events*) t_1 and t_2 are *concurrent.*
This equivalence is also a congruence w.r.t. the concatenation of sequences of transitions which, so to speak, agree on the joining marking.
In $O[N,M_0]$ each transition (or event) t is an equivalence class of the sequences of transitions in N which cause t starting from M_0. As already noticed in [NPW81], $O[N,M_0]$ may have *forward conflicts,* but not *backward conflicts.* (See Figure 10 below.)

Differently from [NPW81], we assume that in order to represent the actions performed by the computing agents *action names* are associated with the transitions of the given net N.
It is also assumed that in the net N no two transitions have the same action names, but since N may have cycles, the occurrence net $O[N,M_0]$ may have two transitions with the same name.

However, a unique name p can be associated with each transition t of $O[N,M_0]$ by choosing p to be the pair <a,n> where a is the action name corresponding to t and n is a natural number indicating how many times the transition t is encountered in a 'breadth-first and left-to-right' visit of $O[N,M_0]$.

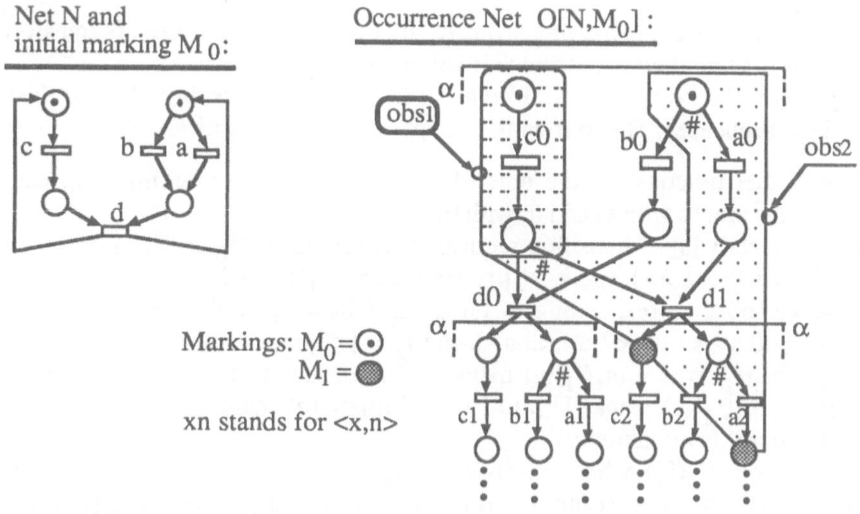

1. In # forward conflicts should be resolved.
2. Any computation over N from M_0 is a conflict-free part of $O[N,M_0]$ between M_0 and a reachable marking. (See for instance, obs2 from M_0 to M_1.)
3. The agreement of any two computations where c fires at least once, includes the observer obs1.
4. Below α the occurrence net repeats itself.

Figure 10. A net N, two markings M_0 (initial) and M_1, and the occurrence net $O[N,M_0]$.

Let us now define the sl-bicategory **ESO**, which is the system of *event-structure observers* for a given transition net N with initial marking M_0 and action names taken from a given set A.

DEFINITION 30. An *event-structure observer* (or *es-observer*, for short), that is, an object of **ESO**, is an equivalence class of partial piecewise-constant functions from the natural numbers to A, each function in the class being defined on the initial segment [0,n) for some n, and the equivalence relation being the reflexive and transitive closure of the following one:

$f \approx g$ iff for some k, a, and b we have: g(k)=a and g(k+1)=b and
$f = (g \setminus \{<k,a>,<k+1,b>\}) \cup \{<k,b>,<k+1,a>\}$ and
a and b are action names of *concurrent* events in the above specified sense. ■

PROPOSITION 31. For any given net N and initial marking M_0 the corresponding category **ESO** is a meet-semilattice, and therefore a sl-bicategory.

PROOF. We define an order $\leq$ among es-observers in **ESO** as follows.

Let $f_i \leq g_j$ mean '$dom(f_i) \subseteq dom(g_j)$ and if $k \in dom(f_i)$ then $f_i(k)=g_j(k)$'.

$[f] \leq [g]$ iff $\forall f_i \in [f]\ \exists g_j \in [g]$ such that $f_i \leq g_j$.

$[f] \wedge [g] = [h]$, h is a maximal function in $\{h_{ij} \mid h_{ij} \leq f_i$ and $h_{ij} \leq g_j$ and $f_i \in [f]$ and $g_j \in [g]\}$.

The empty function is the bottom element. ■

It easy to see that given the occurrence net $O[N,M_0]$, an equivalence class [s] of transition

sequences which lead from a reachable marking M_1 to another reachable marking M_2, corresponds to an es-observer [f] in the following sense:
$\forall\ s_i \in [s].\ \exists\ f_i \in [f].\ m(f_i)=s_i$ where m is a function from natural numbers to natural numbers such that for each action name $a \in A$ occurring in f_i m monotonically renumbers the occurrences of a.
In other words, $\forall\ a \in A$ the increasing sequence $f_i^{-1}(a)$ of natural numbers is transformed by m into a sequence of natural numbers which is still increasing.
Conversely, an es-observer can be viewed as a monotonic renumbering of an equivalence class [s] of transition sequences. The following example will clarify the ideas.

EXAMPLE 5. Let us consider the nets of Figure 10 and the markings M_0 and M_1. The concurrent events are: (c with a) and (c with b).
The equivalence class [s] of transition sequences leading from M_0 to M_1 is $\{s_1,s_2\}$ where s_1 = {<a,0>,<c,0>,<d,1>,<a,2>} and s_2 = {<c,0>,<a,0>,<d,1>,<a,2>}.
The es-observer obs2 corresponding to [s] is the following equivalence class of partial pc-functions f_1 = {<0,a>,<1,c>,<2,d>,<3,a>} and f_2 = {<0,c>,<1,a>,<2,d>,<3,a>}.
We have $s_1 = m_1(f_1)$ where $m_1(f_1)(a)$ maps the increasing sequence [0,3] into the increasing sequence [0,2], $m_1(f_1)(c)$ maps [1] into [0], and $m_1(f_1)(d)$ maps [2] into [1]. Thus, for each event a, b and d, m_1 is monotonic.
Analogously, $s_2 = m_2(f_2)$ where $m_2(f_2)(a)$ maps the increasing sequence [1,3] into the increasing sequence [0,2], $m_1(f_1)(c)$ maps [0] into [0], and $m_1(f_1)(d)$ maps [2] into [1]. Thus, for each event m_2 also is monotonic. ■

The *concatenation* of the es-observers [f] and [g] is defined by the equivalence class of the concatenation of two functions, one in [f] and the other in [g] (see Section 6). This concatenation gives us a tensor product for the sl-bicategory **ESO**.

Level 1 of our categorical framework is the category of structures of computations, each structure being an **ESO**-category, which can be viewed as a tree whose paths are labelled by es-observers. The agreement between two paths is an es-observer smaller than the two es-observers labelling those paths.
Thus, given $O[N,M_0]$ and two reachable markings M_1 and M_2, we may consider between them the tree whose paths are labelled by the equivalence classes of transition sequences leading from M_1 to M_2. The agreement between any two paths is the longest equivalence class of transition sequences which is a prefix of those labelling the two paths and which does *not* resolve any *forward conflict* in $O[N,M_0]$ (see [NPW81]).

Let us now recall the definition of prime event structure and then state the correspondence of Theorem 32.
$\langle E,\leq,\#\rangle$ is said to be a *prime event structure* [NPW81] iff
i) E is a set of so-called *events*,
ii) $\leq$ and # are two binary relations on E such that $\leq \cap \# = \emptyset$,
iii) $\leq$ is a partial order such that $\forall e \in E.\ \{e' \mid e' \leq e\}$ is finite, and
iv) # is symmetric, irreflexive, and hereditary (that is, if e#e' and e'≤e" then e#e").
For a prime event structure we can define a *concurrency* relation $co =_{def} (E \times E) \setminus (\leq \cup \geq \cup \#)$. It is symmetric and irreflexive.

THEOREM 32. An **ESO**-category is a finite prime event structure and viceversa.
PROOF. Let us consider the **ESO**-category $\langle X,e,a\rangle$. Let X be the set $\{x_i \mid i \in I\}$ for some suitable index set I, and $e(x_i)$ be the es-observer $[f]_i$.

<X,e,a> can be considered as the prime event structure $\langle P,\leq_P,\#_P\rangle$, where:
- P is the set Q divided by the equivalence relation ρ, where Q is the disjoint union for all $i\in I$ of all equivalence classes $[g_k]_i$ which are es-observers smaller or equal to $[f]_i$, and ρ is the following equivalence relation:
  $\forall$ i,j $\in$ I. $\forall$ es-observers $[g_k]_i$, $[h_m]_j$. $[g_k]_i \,\rho\, [h_m]_j$ iff $([g_k]_i=[h_m]_j$ and $[g_k]_i\leq a(x_i,x_j))$,
- $\leq_P$ is the partial order induced on P by the partial orders, one for each index $i\in I$. (The partial order for the index i is the one which exists among the es-observers $[g_k]_i$ smaller or equal to $[f]_i$).
- $\#_P$ is defined as follows:
  $\forall$ i,j $\in$ I. $[g_k]_i \#_P [h_m]_j$ iff ($i\neq j$ *and* not($[g_k]_i\leq a(x_i,x_j)$) *and* not($[h_m]_j\leq a(x_i,x_j)$)).

It is easy to see that all axioms of the prime event structures are satisfied. (See the Example 6 below.)
Viceversa, any given finite prime event structure $\langle A,\leq_A,\#_A\rangle$ can be considered as an **ESO**-category <X,e,a> as follows. Take a maximal configuration C_i. (Recall that a configuration is a subset of A such that: i) *if* a,b $\in C_i$ *then* not(a $\#_A$ b), and ii) *if* b $\in C_i$ and a $\leq_A$b *then* a $\in C_i$.)
Let us associate with any C_i of cardinality n the es-observer $[f]_i$ where f is a pc-function from [0,n) to A such that it induces a total order compatible with the partial order of C_i. The set of all es-observers $[f]_i$'s for all choices of the C_i's gives us the required **ESO**-category.
The agreement between two es-observers is defined by the es-observer corresponding to the intersection of the corresponding maximal configurations. ■

EXAMPLE 6. Let us consider the following net with transitions A={a,b,c,d} together with its initial marking:

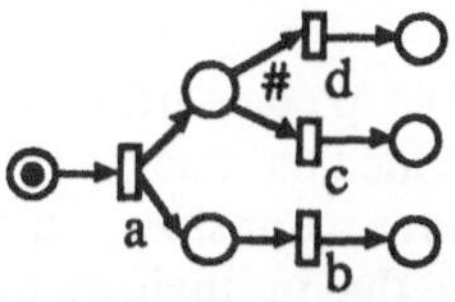

For this net we may consider the sl-bicategory **ESO**, and the following **ESO**-category <X,e,a>: X={p,q}, e(p)=[abc], e(q)=[abd], a(p,q)=[ab]. (For simplicity, we have denoted es-observers by sequences of transitions in square brackets.) Notice that [abc]=[acb] and [abd]=[adb].
<X,e,a> can be viewed as a prime event structure $\langle P,\leq_P,\#_P\rangle$, where P={[ε], [a], [ab], [ac], [ad], [abc], [abd]}, $\leq_P$ is the prefix relation, and [ac]$\#_P$[ad], [ac]$\#_P$[abd], [ad]$\#_P$[abc], and [abc]$\#_P$[abd]. ■

A prime event structure $\langle E,\leq,\#\rangle$ is said to be conflict-free iff the relation # is empty.
COROLLARY 33. An es-observer is a conflict-free finite prime event structure. ■

PROPOSITION 34. The sl-bicategory of the es-observers **ESO** and the sl-bicategory of traces **TO** associated with the same occurrence net $O[N,M_0]$ are isomorphic.
PROOF. Immediate. ■

8. CONCLUSIONS

In previous papers we described distributed computations and synchronization of agents using an enriched categorical approach. We introduced a two-level framework by making a distinction between a *world of computations* and a *world of agents*, whose categorical descriptions were respectively, monoidal categories and categories enriched over them. This approach allowed us to make explicit the relationship between the *agents*, whose internal structure was assumed to be unknown, and their *behaviours*, which consist in the computations they perform. However, we were left with the problem of justifying the structure of those computations.

In this paper we have studied this problem and we have proposed a solution by assuming that the computations performed by agents can be observed by a *system of observers* which perform experiments on the agents themselves. We have defined an abstract theory of parallelism, called Theory of Experiments, in which observers can be modelled, and we have added to our two-level framework the 0-level, which is the level of observers.

We have shown that various concrete calculi, like SCCS, Real-Time Agents, Trace Theory, and Event Structures can be understood as particular instances of our Theory of Experiments by considering suitable bicategories of observers. Thus, our categorical approach can also be viewed as a unifying theory for understanding and comparing those different calculi.

One of the advantages of our framework is that the models for the above mentioned calculi, can be constructed in a uniform way, by defining 'at level 0' a sl-bicategory **O** of observers, and 'at level 1' the monoidal category **Sc(O)**, whose objects are categories based on **O**, which denote the structures of computations. **Sc(O)** corresponds to our world of computations and it has been used, as suggested in [KLP87], as a base category for defining 'level 2', where objects are computing agents and between any two agents there is a structure of computations.
It is worth mentioning that from a categorical point of view observers can also be considered as particular structures of computations and particular agents as well, as required by our Theory of Experiments.

Using our techniques we have been able to construct a model for Real-Time Agents, which was not given in [Car82] and we have provided the categorical correspondences between the various models for parallelism mentioned above. (Consider, for instance, Propositions 29 and 34, and the simple examples provided by the inclusions of **A** into **CA** or into **TO**.) These correspondences, already partially explored in [Win85], are now explained in a uniform way by the notion of 'change of base bicategory' (see Theorem 13), that is, the change of the bicategory of observers.

We believe that more sophisticated calculi for parallelism and concurrency, like the Labelled Event Structures [CFM83] and Pomsets [Pra86], can also be modelled in our framework at the expense of considering as observers general bicategories, instead of sl-bicategories. Some results in this direction will be published in a forthcoming paper.

ACKNOWLEDGEMENTS

We would like to thank our University Departments for the support given to us during this joint research project. Many thanks to Irène Guessarian for the invitation to the Ecole de Printemps (La Roche-Posay, France). We are grateful to the lecturers and to the participants for the many stimulating conversations and suggestions.

REFERENCES

[BeD88] Best, E. and Devillers, R.: "Sequential and Concurrent Behaviour in Petri Net Theory", Theoretical Computer Science, Vol. 55, 1(1988), 87-136.

[Bén67] Bénabou, J.: "Introduction to Bicategories", in LNM 47, Springer Verlag, Berlin (1967), 1-77.

[Ben89] Benson, D.B.: "Some Foundations for Distributed and Concurrent Computations", Fundamenta Informatiicae, 12(4) (1989), 427-486.

[BeK85] Bergstra, J.A. and Klop, J.W.: "Algebra of Communicating Processes with Abstraction". Theoretical Computer Science, Vol.37, No.1 (1985), 77-121.

[BeK85] Betti, R., and Kasangian, S.: "Tree Automata and Enriched Category Theory" Rend. Ist. Mat. Univ. Trieste, XVII (1985), 71-78.

[Bet80] Betti, R.: "Automi e Categorie Chiuse", Boll.Un. Matem. Ital. (5) 17-13 (1980), 44-58.

[BoC88] Boudol, L., and Castellani, I.: "Concurrency and Atomicity", Theoretical Computer Science, 59 (1988), 1-60.

[BHR84] Brookes, S. D., Hoare, C.A.R., and Roscoe, A.W.: "A Theory of Communicating Sequential Processes" J.A.C.M. 31, 3 (1984), 560-599.

[Car82] Cardelli, L.: "Real Time Agents" Proc. ICALP 1982, LNCS n. 140 (1982), 94-106.

[CaW87] Carboni, A. and Walters, R.F.C.: "Cartesian Bicategories I" J. Pure Applied Algebra 49, (1987), 11-32.

[CCM90] Casley, R., Crew, R.F., Meseguer, J., and Pratt, V.: "Temporal Structures" Category Theory and Computer Science, LNCS n.389 Springer Verlag, Berlin (1989), 21-51.

[CFM83] Castellani, I., Franceschi, P., and Montanari, U.: "Labelled Event Structures: A Model for Observable Concurrency" Proc. IFI TC2 Working Conference on Formal Description of Programming Concepts II Garmisch (D. Bjørner, ed.) North Holland (1983), 383-400.

[DDM87] Degano, P. De Nicola, R. and Montanari, U.: "Observational Equivalences for Concurrent Models", Working Conf. on Formal Description of Programming Concepts, Ebberup (Denmark), 25-28 August 1986, (M. Wirsing, ed.), (1987), 105-132.

[DMM89] Degano, P., Meseguer, J., and Montanari, U.: "Axiomatizing Net Computations and Processes", Fourth Annual Symposium on Logic in Computer Science, IEEE Computer Society Press, (1989), 175-185.

[DeM87] Degano, P. and Montanari, U.: "Concurrent Histories: A Basis for Observing Distributed Systems", Journal of Computer and System Science, 34 (1987), 422-461.

[DeH84] De Nicola, R. and Hennessy, M.: "Testing Equivalences for Processes" Theoretical Computer Science, 34 (1984), 83-133.

[DeN87] De Nicola, R.: "Extensional Equivalences for Transition Systems", Acta Informatica 24, (1987), 211-237.

[EiK65] Eilenberg, S. and Kelly, G.M.: "Closed Categories" Proc. of the Conference on Categorical Algebra, La Jolla 1965, Springer Verlag (1966), 421-562.

[Hoa78] Hoare, C.A.R.: "Communicating Sequential Processes" Communications A.C.M. Vol.21, n.8, (1978), 666-677.

[KaL90] Kasangian, S. and Labella, A.:"Enriched Categorical Semantics for Distributed Calculi" (to appear in Journal of Pure and Applied Algebra) (1990).

[KKR] Kasangian, S., Kelly, G.M., and Rossi, F.: "Cofibrations and the Realization of Nondeterministic Automata", Cahiers de Topologie et Géométrie Differentielle. XXIV 1 (1983), 23-46.

[KLP87] Kasangian, S., Labella, A. and Pettorossi, A.: "Enriched Categories for Local and Interaction Calculi", LNCS 283, Springer Verlag, Berlin (1987), 57-70.

[Kel82] Kelly, G.M.: "Basic Concepts of Enriched Category Theory", Cambridge University Press, Cambridge (1982).

[KeS74] Kelly, G.M. and Street, R.H.: "Review of the Elements of 2-categories", Lecture Notes in Mathematics, no.420 (1974), 75-103.

[LaT88] Larsen, G., and Thomsen, B.: "A Modal Process Logic", Third Annual Symposium on Logic in Computer Science, IEEE Computer Society Press, Edinburgh, Scotland (1988), 203-210.

[LaP86] Labella, A. and Pettorossi, A.: "Categorical Models of Process Cooperation" Proc. Category Theory and Computer Programming, Guildford, U.K., September 1985, LNCS n. 240, Springer Verlag, Berlin (1986), 282-298.

[Law73] Lawvere, F.W.: "Metric Spaces, Generalized Logic, and Closed Categories" Rendiconti del Seminario Matematico e Fisico, Milano 43 (1973), 135-166.

[Maz87] Mazurkiewicz, A.: "Trace theory" in LNCS 255, Springer Verlag (1987), 279-324.

[MeM88] Meseguer, J., and Montanari, U.:"Petri Nets are Monoids: A New Algebraic Foundation for Net Theory" Proc. 3rd Annual Symposium on Logic in Computer Science, June 5-8, 1988, Edinburgh (Scotland), 155-164.

[Mil80] Milner, R.: "A Calculus of Communicating Systems", LNCS 92, Springer Verlag, Berlin (1980).

[Mil83] Milner, R.: "Calculi for Synchrony and Asynchrony" Theoretical Computer Science, Vol.25 (1983), 267-310.

[NPW81] Nielsen, M., Plotkin, G., and Winskel, G.: "Petri Nets, Event Structures, and Domains", Theoretical Computer Science 13 (1981), 85-108.

[Pow89] Power, A.J.:"An Abstract Formulation for Rewriting Systems" Category Theory and Computer Science, LNCS n.389 Springer Verlag, Berlin (1989), 300-312.

[Pet62] Petri, C. A: "Fundamentals of a Theory of Asynchronous Information Flow" in: Proc. of IFIP Congress 1962, North Holland, Amsterdam (1962).

[Pra86] Pratt, V.: "Modelling Concurrency with Partial Orders" International Journal of Parallel Programming, v.15, 1(1986), 33-71.

[Rei85] Reisig, W.:"Petri Nets: An Introduction" EATCS Monographs on Theoretical Computer Science, Vol.4, Springer Verlag (1985).

[Wal81] Walters, R.F.C.:"Sheaves and Cauchy-Complete Categories" Cahiers de Top. et Géom. Diff. 22. (1981), 283-286.

[Wei83] Wei Li: "An Operational Approach to Semantics and Translation for Concurrent Programming Languages", Ph.D. Thesis in Computer Science, Edinburgh University, Edinburgh (Scotland) (1983).

[WiM87] Winkowski, J., and Maggiolo-Schettini, A.: "An Algebra of Processes" Journal of Computer and System Science, 35 (1987), 206-228.

[Win84] Winskel, G.: "Synchronization Trees" Theoretical Computer Sci., 34 (1984), 33-82.

[Win85] Winskel, G.: "Category Theory and Models for Parallel Computations" in: Category Theory and Computer Programming, LNCS 240, Springer Verlag (1985), 266-281.

[Win87] Winskel, G.: "Event Structures" in LNCS 255, Springer Verlag (1987), 325-392.

Action versus State based Logics for Transition Systems

Rocco De Nicola
IEI - CNR
Via S. Maria, 46 I-56126 Pisa
ITALY
DENICOLA@ICNUCEVM.CNUCE.CNR.IT

Frits Vaandrager
CWI
P.O. Box 4079, 1009 AB Amsterdam
THE NETHERLANDS
FRITSV@CWI.NL

Abstract

A temporal logic based on actions rather than on states is presented and interpreted over labelled transition systems. It is proved that it has essentially the same power as CTL^*, a temporal logic interpreted over Kripke structures. The relationship between the two logics is established by introducing two mappings from Kripke structures to labelled transition systems and viceversa and two transformation functions between the two logics which preserve truth. A branching time version of the action based logic is also introduced. This new logic for transition systems can play an important role as an intermediate between Hennessy-Milner Logic and the modal μ-calculus. It is sufficiently expressive to describe safety and liveness properties but permits model checking in linear time.

1. Introduction

Labelled Transition Systems (LTS's) and Kripke Structures (KS's) are two types of structures which have proven to be basic for many applications in computer science, especially for modelling reactive and concurrent systems. On one hand, LTS's have been more widely used to interpret process algebra languages like CCS and other languages for the description of communicating systems. On the other hand, KS's form the common model for interpreting many temporal and modal logics which are used as tools for specifying properties of communicating systems. The two types of structures are very similar and both can be seen as generalizations of state automata: in LTS's transitions are labelled to describe the actions which cause a state change while in KS's states are labelled to describe how they are modified by the transitions.

In spite of their similarity and, we might say, their complementarity, the two models have mostly been considered as alternative to each other and there are strong advocates standing on each side. For example,

Note: The research has been partially supported by Esprit Basic Research Action Program, Project 3011 CEDISYS and by CNR Progetto Finalizzato Sistemi Informatici e Calcolo Parallelo, project LAMBRUSCO.

due to the "experienced" easiness in formulating properties of systems in terms of their states, Lamport "...decide(d) to base an axiomatic system for describing concurrent programs upon states rather than operations." [Lam83]. Actually, very interesting logics like CTL and CTL* interpreted over KS's have been put forward [EH83, ES89] and have been thoroughly investigated [BCG88]; also, sophisticated and efficient tools have been developed for them [CES86]. For LTS's, on the other hand, Hennessy an Milner which were more interested in properly describing the actual behaviour of communicating systems, did define a new logic, now known as HML [HM85]. More recently, due to the success of process algebras, other, more expressive, logics interpreted over LTS's have been proposed (see e.g. [Lar88, Sti89, DV90]) and tools have been developed to support reasoning with them [CPS90].

Still, one might say that modal and temporal logics for computer science and the associated complexity issue have been more thoroughly investigated in the setting of Kripke structures and that combinators for transition systems and the issue of behavioural equivalence, as the basis for defining process algebras, have received more attention in the setting of Labelled Transition Systems.

The point we want to make with this paper is that there is really no need for taking a definite standing between LTS's and KS's as semantic models. For example, our results will enable one to use ones favorite process algebra to describe system behaviour as an LTS and to use CTL* to specify the requirement the system has to comply with. The model checker for CTL* or (better) for its branching time subset CTL can then be used to check whether a given process satisfies the required properties.

We will introduce an action based version of CTL* interpreted over LTS's (we will call it ACTL*) which is the natural analogue of CTL* in a setting where transitions are labelled. The new logics contains relativized modalities (e.g. $X_a\varphi$ - to be read "the next transition is labelled with an action a and the subsequent path satisfies φ"-) as demanded by the interpretation model and is more expressive than HML. Together with the new logic, we will introduce two transformation functions from KS's to LTS's and viceversa which preserve essential properties of systems. In correspondence of the two transformation functions, we will define two mappings between the logics, one from CTL* to ACTL* and the other in the opposite direction, which, in combination with the functions on the models, preserve truth. We will prove that, if $\mathcal{A}$ is an LTS, $\mathcal{K}$ is a KS , the $\mathfrak{ks}$'s and the $\mathfrak{lts}$'s are the transformation functions, and the two $\models$'s are the satisfaction relation, we have:

- $\mathcal{A}, \rho \models \varphi$ iff $\mathfrak{ks}(\mathcal{A}), \mathfrak{ks}(\rho) \models \mathfrak{ks}(\varphi)$

and

- $\mathcal{K}, \rho \models \varphi$ iff $\mathfrak{lts}(\mathcal{K}), \mathfrak{lts}(\rho) \models \mathfrak{lts}(\varphi)$.

Thus, one might say that the two logics are essentially equivalent.

Like it has been done for CTL*, we will introduce a branching time subset of ACTL* which we will call ACTL. Moreover, we will present a linear time translation from ACTL to CTL. This permits linear model checking for ACTL via reduction to CTL model checking. Also ACTL appears to be rather expressive and we argue that it can be used to express various interesting properties of concurrent systems. We will conclude the paper with a brief discussion on the discriminative power of ACTL without next time operators, be them relativized or not. We will argue that this restricted logic induces on transition systems the same equivalence as the divergence sensitive version of the branching bisimulation equivalence of [GW89] as presented in [DV90].

As mentioned above, our results about ACTL permit equipping verification tools for process algebras with a model checker which is linear in the size of the formula being checked; at the best of our knowledge almost all existing tools rely on model checking variants of the μ-calculus and the algorithm for this is exponential in the size of formulae. A type of work similar to ours in this respect is presented in [JKP90]. These authors do stick to CTL as a logic for LTS's but substantially change its satisfaction relation; in a sense they have a relativized satisfaction relation ($<a, s> \models \varphi$) instead of our relativized modality ($X_a\ \varphi$). The expressive power of the two languages seems similar, but our satisfaction relation is more immediate. It is also worth mentioning that our transformation from LTS's to KS's is linear while theirs is quadratic. Besides, they do not consider invisible actions and we have not been able to generalize their approach to systems with silent steps in a way that would preserve some behavioural equivalence.

We think that our new logic for transition systems can play an important role as an intermediate between HML and the modal μ-calculus. It is well known that HML is not expressive enough and that model checking for the modal μ-calculus requires exponential time. ACTL is sufficiently expressive to describe safety and liveness properties but permits model checking in linear time.

2. ACTL*: A logic for Labelled Transition Systems

In this section, we introduce our action based logic and elaborate upon its expressivity. Firstly, we provide the necessary definitions about labelled transition systems and their runs. Then, we describe the logic and introduce auxiliary modalities which will be useful in the sequel.

Definition 2.1. (*Labelled Transition Systems*)
A *labelled transition system* (or *LTS*) is a structure $\mathcal{A} = (S, A, \rightarrow)$ where:

• S is a set of *states*;

• A is a finite, non-empty set of *actions*; the *silent action* τ is not in A;

• $\rightarrow\ \subseteq S \times (A \cup \{\tau\}) \times S$ is the *transition relation*; an element $(r,\alpha,s) \in\ \rightarrow$ is called a *transition*, and is usually written as $r{-}\alpha{\rightarrow}s$.

We let $A_\tau = A \cup \{\tau\}$; $A_\varepsilon = A \cup \{\varepsilon\}$, $\varepsilon \notin A_\tau$. Moreover, we let r, s, ... range over states; a, b, ... over A; α, β, ... over A_τ and k, ... over A_ε. ♦

Remark 2.2. (*Finiteness assumptions are not essential*)
The assumption that the set A of actions is finite and non-empty is made for technical reasons. The results of this paper can be generalized to arbitrary sets of actions if either one is willing to use infinitary disjunctions in the logics or to restrict attention to those LTS's for which the set of labels which actually occur in transitions is finite. ♦

Definition 2.3. (*Notation for strings*)
Let K be any set. K^* stands for the set of finite sequences of elements of K; K^ω denotes the set of infinite sequences of elements of K; K^∞ stands for $K^\omega \cup K^*$. Concatenation of sequences is denoted by juxtaposition; λ denotes the empty sequence; $|\pi|$ denotes the length of a sequence π. ♦

Definition 2.4. (*Paths and runs over LTS's*)

Let $\mathcal{A}$ = (S, A, →) be a LTS.

• A sequence (s_0,α_0,s_1) (s_1,α_1,s_2)... $\in \rightarrow^\infty$ is called a *path* from s_0; if a path cannot be extended anymore because it is either infinite or ends in a state without outgoing transitions, it is called a *fullpath*.

• a *run* from s ∈ S is a pair ρ = (s,π), where π is a path from s; we write first(ρ) = s and path(ρ) = π; moreover, if π is finite then last(ρ) denotes the last state of π; a *maximal run* is a run whose second element is a fullpath;

• with $\rho < \theta$ and $\rho \leq \theta$ we indicate that run θ is a proper suffix, respectively a suffix, of run ρ;

• concatenation of runs is denoted by juxtaposition; concatenation is a partial operation: ρθ is only defined if ρ is a finite run and last(ρ)=first(θ).

• we write $run_{\mathcal{A}}(s)$, or just run(s), for the set of runs from s and $\mu run_{\mathcal{A}}(s)$, or just μrun(s), for the set of maximal runs from s;

• we write $run_{\mathcal{A}}$ and $\mu run_{\mathcal{A}}$ for the set of runs resp. maximal runs in $\mathcal{A}$.

We let π, ... range over paths and ρ, σ, ... over runs. ♦

Definition 2.5. (*ACTL***: an Action based Computation Tree Logic*)

The syntax of the logic *ACTL** *(Action based CTL***)* is defined by the following grammar where we let φ, φ', ... range over ACTL*-formulas:

$$\varphi ::= T \mid \neg\varphi \mid \varphi\wedge\varphi' \mid \exists\varphi \mid \varphi U \varphi' \mid X\varphi \mid X_a\varphi.$$ ♦

Definition 2.6. (*Satisfaction relations for ACTL**)

Let $\mathcal{A}$ = (S, A, →) be a LTS. *Satisfaction* of an ACTL*-formula φ by a run ρ, notation $\mathcal{A},\rho \models \varphi$ or just $\rho \models \varphi$, is defined inductively by:

• $\rho \models T$ always;

• $\rho \models \neg\varphi$ iff $\rho \not\models \varphi$;

• $\rho \models \varphi\wedge\varphi'$ iff $\rho \models \varphi$ and $\rho \models \varphi'$;

• $\rho \models \exists\varphi$ iff there exists a run $\theta \in \mu run(first(\rho))$ such that $\theta \models \varphi$;

• $\rho \models \varphi U \varphi'$ iff there exists a θ with $\rho \leq \theta$ such that $\theta \models \varphi'$ and for all $\rho \leq \eta < \theta$: $\eta \models \varphi$;

• $\rho \models X\varphi$ iff there exist s, α, s', θ such that $\rho = (s,(s,\alpha,s'))\theta$ and $\theta \models \varphi$;

• $\rho \models X_a\varphi$ iff there exist s, s', θ such that $\rho = (s,(s,a,s'))\theta$ and $\theta \models \varphi$.

For s ∈ S and φ ∈ L we define $s \models \varphi$ iff $(s, \lambda) \models \varphi$. ♦

Notation 2.7. (*Auxiliary notation for ACTL**)

We write

• F for ¬T,

• $\varphi \vee \varphi'$ for $\neg(\neg\varphi \wedge \neg\varphi')$,

• $\vee\{\varphi_i \mid i \in \{i1,..,in\}\}$ for $\varphi_{i1} \vee .. \vee \varphi_{in}$ (by convention $\vee\{\varphi_i \mid i \in \emptyset\} = F$),

• $\varphi \Rightarrow \varphi'$ for $\neg\varphi\vee\varphi'$,

• $\forall\varphi$ for $\neg\exists\neg\varphi$,

• $F\varphi$ for $T\, U\, \varphi$,

• $G\varphi$ for $\neg F \neg\varphi$,

• $X_\tau\, \varphi$ for $X\varphi \wedge \neg(\vee\{X_a\, \varphi \mid a \in A\})$. ♦

In order to define more powerful modalities which will significantly shorten our notation, we introduce a tiny auxiliary logic of actions.

Definition 2.8. *(Action formulas)*
The collection *Afor* of *action formulas* over A is defined by the following grammar where we let χ, χ', range over action formulas:

$$\chi ::= a\in A \mid \neg\chi \mid \chi\wedge\chi'.$$

We write T for $\neg(a_0\wedge\neg a_0)$ where a_0 is some arbitrarily chosen action. Also, we use the abbreviations F, $\varphi\vee\varphi'$, etc. that were introduced for ACTL*. ♦

Definition 2.9. *(Satisfaction relations for Afor)*
Satisfaction of an action formula χ by an action a, notation $a \models \chi$, is defined inductively by:

- $a \models b$ iff $a = b$;
- $a \models \neg\chi$ iff $a \not\models \chi$;
- $a \models \chi\wedge\chi'$ iff $a \models \chi$ and $a \models \chi'$. ♦

Definition 2.10. *(Derived modalities)*
By using the notion of action formulas we can introduce a number of very useful modalities. We will write

- $X_\chi\, \varphi$ for $\vee\{X_a\, \varphi \mid a\in A \text{ and } a \models \chi\}$,
- $\varphi\, {}_\chi U_{\chi'}\, \varphi'$ for $(\varphi\wedge(X_\tau T \vee X_\chi T))\; U\; (\varphi \wedge X_{\chi'}\, \varphi')$,
- $\varphi\, {}_\chi U\, \varphi'$ for $(\varphi\wedge(X_\tau T \vee X_\chi\, T))\; U\; \varphi'$,
- $\varphi\, \langle a\rangle\, \varphi'$ for $\exists(\varphi\, {}_F U_a\, \varphi')$,
- $\varphi\, \langle\varepsilon\rangle \varphi'$ for $\exists(\varphi\, {}_F U\, \varphi')$,
- $\langle k\rangle\, \varphi$ for $T\, \langle k\rangle\, \varphi$,
- $[k]\, \varphi$ for $\neg\, \langle k\rangle \neg\varphi$. ♦

Intuitively, a path satisfies $X_\chi\, \varphi$ if it starts with a visible action that satisfies χ and moreover the remainder of the path satisfies φ. A path satisfies $\varphi\, {}_\chi U_{\chi'}\, \varphi'$ if eventually it contains a visible transition whose label satisfies χ' with a remainder satisfying φ', whereas at any moment before this event φ holds and all visible labels satisfy χ. A path satisfies $\varphi\, {}_\chi U\, \varphi'$ if some suffix satisfies φ' and at any moment before φ holds and all visible actions satisfy χ. Please, note that $\varphi\, {}_T U\, \varphi'$ is equivalent to $\varphi\, U\, \varphi'$. The logic ACTL* is more expressive than the Hennessy-Milner logic with until operators that was introduced in [DV90]; these modalities are just the modalities $\varphi\, \langle a\rangle\, \varphi'$ and $\varphi\, \langle\varepsilon\rangle\varphi'$ as defined above. The formula $\varphi\, \langle a\rangle\, \varphi'$ holds in a state if it is possible to do some τ-transitions followed by an a-step such that after the a-step φ' holds and at any moment before φ holds. The formula $\varphi\, \langle\varepsilon\rangle\varphi'$ is valid if after zero or more τ-steps φ' holds and at any moment before φ holds. Our diamond operator $\langle a\rangle\varphi$ is slightly different from the diamond operator in the standard Hennessy-Milner Logic (HML) of [HM85]. Our modality requires that there exists a path consisting of a number of τ's followed by an a-transition such that φ holds immediately after the a-step, whereas in standard HML it is allowed to have an additional number of τ-steps between the a-step and the φ-state. The diamond operator $\langle a\rangle\varphi$ of standard HML is rendered by our $\langle a\rangle\langle\varepsilon\rangle\varphi$. Finally, we introduce the modality $[k]\, \varphi$, which is the dual of $\langle k\rangle\, \varphi$.

Example 2.11. (*Expressivity of ACTL**)
$ACTL^*$ allows us to express in a concise way interesting properties of reactive systems. For instance, a one bit buffer will satisfy the following property

$$\forall G([in0]\ (\forall\ (T\ {}_{\neg(in0 \vee in1 \vee out1)}U_{out0}\ T)))$$

which expresses that always after a 0 is placed in the buffer eventually the buffer will release it; moreover, as long as this event has not yet occurred, no bit will be accepted by the buffer and also no 1 will be released. ♦

3. CTL*: a logic for Kripke Structures

Those readers who are familiar with the logic CTL^* will have realized that the logic $ACTL^*$ resembles it very closely. In this section, we will recall the definitions of CTL^* and of the Kripke structures which serve as models for it; this will allow us to investigate, later on in the paper, the relationships between the two logics more closely.

Definition 3.1. (*Kripke structures*)
A *Kripke structure* (or *KS*) is a 4-tuple $\mathcal{K} = (S, \mathbf{AP}, \mathcal{L}, \rightarrow)$ where:
- S is a set of *states*;
- **AP** is a finite, nonempty set of *atomic proposition names* ranged over by p, q, ...;
- $\mathcal{L}: S \rightarrow 2^{\mathbf{AP}}$ is the *proposition labelling*;
- $\rightarrow\ \subseteq S \times S$ is the *transition relation*; an element $(r,s) \in\ \rightarrow$ is called a *transition* and is usually written as $r \rightarrow s$.

The notations for runs that were introduced for LTS's carry over to Kripke structures in the obvious way. The only difference is that transitions are now no longer triples but pairs. ♦

Definition 3.2. (*CTL**)
The syntax the logic CTL* is defined by the following grammar where we let φ, φ', ... range over CTL* formulas and p over atomic proposition names:

$$\varphi ::= p \mid \neg\varphi \mid \varphi\wedge\varphi' \mid \exists\varphi \mid \varphi U \varphi' \mid X\varphi.$$

We write T for $\neg(p_0\wedge\neg p_0)$ where p_0 is some arbitrarily chosen atomic proposition name. Also, we use the abbreviations F, $\varphi\vee\varphi'$, etc. that were introduced for the logic $ACTL^*$. ♦

Definition 3.3. (*Satisfaction relation for CTL**)
Let $\mathcal{K} = (S, \mathbf{AP}, \mathcal{L}, \rightarrow)$ be a Kripke structure. *Satisfaction* of a CTL* formula φ by a run ρ, notation $\mathcal{K}, \rho \models \varphi$ or just $\rho \models \varphi$, is defined inductively by:
- $\rho \models p$ iff $p \in \mathcal{L}(first(\rho))$;
- $\rho \models \neg\varphi$ iff $\rho \not\models \varphi$;

- $\rho \models \varphi \wedge \varphi'$ iff $\rho \models \varphi$ and $\rho \models \varphi'$;
- $\rho \models \exists\varphi$ iff there exists a run $\theta \in \mu run(first(\rho))$ such that $\theta \models \varphi$;
- $\rho \models \varphi U \varphi'$ iff there exists a θ with $\rho \leq \theta$ such that $\theta \models \varphi'$ and for all $\rho \leq \eta < \theta$: $\eta \models \varphi$;
- $\rho \models X\varphi$ iff there exist s, s', θ such that $\rho = (s,(s,s'))\theta$ and $\theta \models \varphi$.

For $s \in S$ and $\varphi \in$ CTL* we define $s \models \varphi$ iff $(s, \lambda) \models \varphi$. ♦

For the sake of clarity, please notice that the above relation, which is the standard satisfaction relation for CTL* (see e.g. [ES89]), was called *satisfaction with respect to maximal paths* in [DV90] and it was there written as $\rho \models_{\mu} \varphi$.

4. Actions vs States: relating ACTL* and CTL*

To relate the two logics presented in the previous sections, we will need some preliminary work which allows us to relate the different structures on which they are interpreted, namely Kripke structures and Labelled Transition Systems. We will make use of two (slightly modified) transformation functions introduced in [DV90b]. For both constructions, the generated system has almost the same structure as that of the original one. The first construction builds a Kripke structure from a labelled transition system by splitting transitions labelled by visible actions and creating a new states for each of them, labelled with the label of the original transition. The second construction builds a transition system from a Kripke structure by labellling the original transitions with the set of atomic propositions labelling their target state and by splitting all the original states to avoid that atomic propositions associated to states without incoming transitions be lost. Together with the two tranformation functions on the modelling structures we will present two transformation functions for the two logics and will then prove that truth of logical formula is preserved by them.

Definition 4.1. (*From LTS's to KS's*)
Let $\mathcal{A} = (S, A, \rightarrow)$ be a LTS and $\perp$ be fresh symbol not in A. The KS, $\mathbf{ks}(\mathcal{A})$, is defined as $(S', \mathbf{AP}, \mathcal{L}, \rightarrow')$ where

- $S' = S \cup \{(r,a,s) \mid a \in A \text{ and } r \xrightarrow{a} s\}$;
- $\mathbf{AP} = A \cup \{\perp\}$;
- $\rightarrow' = \{(r,s) \mid r \xrightarrow{\tau} s\} \cup \{(r,(r,a,s)) \mid r \xrightarrow{a} s\} \cup \{((r,a,s),s) \mid r \xrightarrow{a} s\}$;
- For $r, s \in S$ and $a \in A$: $\mathcal{L}(s) = \{\perp\}$ and $\mathcal{L}((r,a,s)) = \{a\}$.

The mapping can be adapted in the obvious way to runs; it is sufficient to replace each transition (r,a,s) by the pair of transitions (r,(r,a,s)) ((r,a,s),s). ♦

Mapping $\mathbf{ks}$ is nothing more than the composition of the mappings $\mathbf{tr}_2$ and KS as presented in [DV90b]. Essentially, what $\mathbf{ks}$ does is to introduce an intermediate state for each visible transition in the LTS, and to label the fresh states with the label of the transition and the old ones with $\{\perp\}$ while forgetting the label of the transitions.

In correspondence of the mapping from LTS's to KS's, we have a mapping from ACTL* formulae to CTL* formulae which preserves truth.

Definition 4.2. *(From ACTL* to CTL*)*
The mapping $\mathfrak{ks}$: ACTL*→CTL* is inductively defined by:

- $\mathfrak{ks}(T) = T$,
- $\mathfrak{ks}(\neg\varphi) = \neg\,\mathfrak{ks}(\varphi)$,
- $\mathfrak{ks}(\varphi\wedge\varphi') = \mathfrak{ks}(\varphi)\wedge\mathfrak{ks}(\varphi')$,
- $\mathfrak{ks}(\exists\varphi) = \exists\,\mathfrak{ks}(\varphi)$,
- $\mathfrak{ks}(\varphi U\varphi') = (\bot\Rightarrow\mathfrak{ks}(\varphi))\,U\,(\bot\wedge\mathfrak{ks}(\varphi'))$,
- $\mathfrak{ks}(X\varphi) = X((\bot\wedge\mathfrak{ks}(\varphi))\vee\bigvee\{(a\wedge X(\mathfrak{ks}(\varphi)))\mid a\in A\})$,
- $\mathfrak{ks}(X_a\,\varphi) = X(a\wedge X(\mathfrak{ks}(\varphi)))$. ♦

Theorem 4.3. *($\mathfrak{ks}$'s preserve truth)*
Let $\mathcal{A}$ be a LTS, let ρ be a run of $\mathcal{A}$ and let φ be an ACTL*-formula, then:

$\mathcal{A},\rho \models \varphi$ iff $\mathfrak{ks}(\mathcal{A}),\mathfrak{ks}(\rho) \models \mathfrak{ks}(\varphi)$. ♦

The translation $\mathfrak{ks}$ is linear in the size of the formulas, except for the case of the X-modality which can cause an exponential blowup. Note however that by replacing in ACTL* the X-modality by the relativized modality X_τ, which would mean no loss in expressivity since X can be defined in terms of the modalities X_τ and X_a, it becomes easy to give a linear version of $\mathfrak{ks}$ by defining:

$\mathfrak{ks}(X_\tau\,\varphi) = X(\bot\wedge\mathfrak{ks}(\varphi))$.

Somewhat arbitrarily, we have decided to use X in ACTL* instead of X_τ because otherwise the reverse translation $\mathfrak{lts}$: CTL*→ACTL* which we present below would not be linear anymore.

Definition 4.4. *(From KS's to LTS's)*
Let $\mathcal{K} = (S, AP, \mathcal{L}, \rightarrow)$ be a Kripke structure. The LTS $\mathfrak{lts}(\mathcal{K})$ is defined as $(S', A', \rightarrow')$ where

- $S' = S \cup \{\underline{s} \mid s\in S\}$;
- $A' = 2^{AP} \cup \{\bot\}$ (we assume ⊥ is a fresh symbol);
- $\rightarrow' = \{(s, \bot, \underline{s}) \mid s\in S\} \cup$
  $\{(\underline{s}, \mathcal{L}(s), s) \mid s\in S\} \cup$
  $\{(r, \tau, s) \mid r,s\in S, r\rightarrow s \text{ and } \mathcal{L}(r)=\mathcal{L}(s)\} \cup$
  $\{(r, \mathcal{L}(s), s) \mid r,s\in S, r\rightarrow s \text{ and } \mathcal{L}(r)\neq\mathcal{L}(s)\}$.

The mapping can be easily adapted to runs by defining:

$\mathfrak{lts}(s0, (s0,s1)(s1,s2)\ldots) = (s0, (s0,L1,s1)\,(s1,L2,s2)\ldots)$

where $Ln{+}1 =_{def}$ **if** $\mathcal{L}(sn{+}1)=\mathcal{L}(sn)$ **then** τ **else** $\mathcal{L}(sn{+}1)$. ♦

The above transformation $\mathfrak{lts}$ is the result of a minor modification of the transformation LTSo$\mathfrak{tr}$ of [DV90b]. We could not directly use transformation $\mathfrak{tr}$ here because in general it does not preserve all the essential information in a Kripke structure. The modification that we presented above uses an idea which was also exploited in the definition of transformation $\mathfrak{ks}$: just like $\mathfrak{ks}$ splits each (visible) transition into two consecutive transitions, the transformation lts splits each state into two adjacent states.

We now present the translation function lts from CTL^* to our new logic $ACTL^*$. It is the identity function for all operators but for atomic propositions.

Definition 4.5. (*From CTL^* to $ACTL^*$*)
The mapping lts: $CTL^* \rightarrow ACTL^*$ is inductively defined by:

- $\mathit{lts}(p) \quad = <\!\bot\!> (\vee \{<\!\alpha\!> T \mid p \in \alpha \subseteq AP\})$,
- $\mathit{lts}(\neg\varphi) \quad = \neg\, \mathit{lts}(\varphi)$,
- $\mathit{lts}(\varphi \wedge \varphi') \quad = \mathit{lts}(\varphi) \wedge \mathit{lts}(\varphi')$,
- $\mathit{lts}(\exists\varphi) \quad = \exists\, \mathit{lts}(\varphi)$,
- $\mathit{lts}(\varphi U \varphi') \quad = \mathit{lts}(\varphi)\, U\, \mathit{lts}(\varphi')$,
- $\mathit{lts}(X\varphi) \quad = X\, \mathit{lts}(\varphi)$. ♦

We recall from Definition 2.10, that $<\!\bot\!>\varphi$ means that there exists a path containing any number of silent moves and then a transition labelled by $\bot$ which leads to a state satisfying φ, formally we have: $<\!\bot\!>\varphi \equiv \exists ((X_\tau T)\, U\, (X_\bot \varphi))$.

Theorem 4.6. (*lts's preserve truth*)
Let $\mathcal{K}$ be a Kripke structure, let ρ be a run of $\mathcal{K}$ and let φ be a CTL^*-formula, then:

$\mathcal{K},\rho \models \varphi$ iff $\mathit{lts}(\mathcal{K}),\mathit{lts}(\rho) \models \mathit{lts}(\varphi)$. ♦

The huge disjunction which we need in Definition 4.5 in order to deal with atomic proposition names results from a kind of mismatch between LTS's and Kripke structures: transitions in LTS's are labelled just by actions, whereas states in KS's are labelled with sets of atomic proposition names. Had we used a slightly different type of LTS's which allowed sets of actions to occur as label rather than single actions, it would have been natural to equip the logic $ACTL^*$ with modalities X_p for p an element of a transition label. In that case the translation lts could have been simplified even further by defining:

$\mathit{lts}(p) = <\!\bot\!> <\!p\!> T$.

The translation ks would not be more complicated in this approach. In this paper we have chosen not to label transitions with sets of actions, but just with actions, in order to preserve more closely the connection with the LTS's semantics of a wide variety of process description languages.

Now we have defined a translation ks from LTS's to KS's and another translation lts from KS's to LTS's, a natural question to ask is what are the relationships between a LTS $\mathcal{A}$ and the LTS $\mathit{lts}(\mathit{ks}(\mathcal{A}))$, or between a KS $\mathcal{K}$ and the KS $\mathit{ks}(\mathit{lts}(\mathcal{K}))$. It is not hard to see that, for instance, $\mathcal{A}$ and $\mathit{lts}(\mathit{ks}(\mathcal{A}))$ are not directly related via some behavioural equivalence like trace equivalence or bisimulation equivalence. Although we still think that there exist interesting behavioural relationships, we have decided not to adress these issues in the present paper.

5. ACTL: a new branching time logic for LTS's

In the previous sections we have introduced the logic $ACTL^*$ and shown that it is a very expressive logic which is equivalent to CTL^* in the sense that model checking for $ACTL^*$ can be reduced to model checking for CTL^* and vice versa. However, since model checking for CTL^* is in PSPACE [EL87], and because of our polynomial reduction of model checking for CTL^* to model checking for $ACTL^*$, this means that model checking for $ACTL^*$ is in PSPACE.

The branching time logic CTL is a subset of CTL^* which has an efficient model checking algorithm with complexity $O((|S| + |\rightarrow|) \times |\varphi|)$ [CES86]. Moreover an efficient implementation exists in the Extended Model Checker (EMC), developed at CMU. Therefore it becomes interesting to look for subsets of $ACTL^*$ which can be translated effieciently to CTL. Of course one should aim at having this subsets as large as possible in order not to loose too much of the expressive power of $ACTL^*$. In this section we present the logic ACTL which is essentially a subset of $ACTL^*$ and which has the desired properties mentioned above. However, before we come to ACTL, we will first define the logic CTL to which it is closely related.

Definition 5.1. (*CTL*)
The set of formulas CTL is defined as the smallest set of state formulas such that:
- if $p \in \mathbf{AP}$, then p is a state formula;
- if φ and φ' are state formulas, then $\neg\varphi$ and $\varphi\wedge\varphi'$ are state formulas;
- if π is a path formula, then $\exists\pi$ is a state formula;
- if φ and φ' are state formulas, then $X\varphi$ and $\varphi U\varphi'$ are path formulas;
- if π is a path formula, then so is $\neg\pi$.

We let φ,... range over CTL state formulas and π,... over CTL path formulas. ♦

Clearly, CTL is just a subset of CTL^*. Thus the definition of the satisfaction relation for CTL^* carries over to CTL. Now here comes our proposal for ACTL:

Definition 5.2. (*ACTL*)
The set of formulas ACTL is defined as the smallest set of state formulas such that:
- T is a state formula;
- if φ and φ' are state formulas, then $\neg\varphi$ and $\varphi\wedge\varphi'$ are state formulas;
- if π is a path formula, then $\exists\pi$ is a state formula;
- if φ and φ' are state formulas and χ and χ' are action formulas, then $X_\chi\varphi$, $X_\tau\varphi$, $\varphi\, {}_\chi U_{\chi'}\, \varphi'$ and $\varphi\, {}_\chi U\, \varphi'$ are path formulas;
- if π is a path formula, then so is $\neg\pi$.

Again, we let φ,... range over state formulas and π,... over path formulas. ♦

The modalities $X_\chi\varphi$, $\varphi\, {}_\chi U_{\chi'}\, \varphi'$ and $\varphi\, {}_\chi U\, \varphi'$ used above can be seen as compact notation for $ACTL^*$ formulae, thus ACTL is a proper subset of $ACTL^*$ and it inherits the satisfaction relation from $ACTL^*$.

For translating ACTL to CTL we cannot just use the mapping $ks: ACTL^* \rightarrow CTL^*$, restricted to ACTL and with the understanding that modalities like $X_\chi\varphi$ are expanded to $ACTL^*$. For instance, consider the

ACTL formula of the form $X_\chi\ \varphi$; if we expand notation, we obtain an ACTL* formula of the form $\vee\{X_a\ \varphi \mid a \in A \text{ and } a \models \chi\}$. Mapping $\mathfrak{ks}$ will translate this to a CTL* formula $\vee\{X(a \wedge X(\mathfrak{ks}(\varphi))) \mid a \in A \text{ and } a \models \chi\}$ which is not a CTL formula; indeed, in CTL no conjunction or disjuntion of X-modalities is allowed. Thus we have to modify the mapping $\mathfrak{ks}$. The reader may check that the mapping $\mathfrak{ks}'$ which is defined below does yield CTL formulas.

Definition 5.3. (*From ACTL to CTL*)
The mapping $\mathfrak{ks}'$: ACTL$\to$CTL is inductively defined by:

- $\mathfrak{ks}'(T) = T$,
- $\mathfrak{ks}'(\neg\varphi) = \neg\,\mathfrak{ks}'(\varphi)$,
- $\mathfrak{ks}'(\varphi\wedge\varphi') = \mathfrak{ks}'(\varphi) \wedge \mathfrak{ks}'(\varphi')$,
- $\mathfrak{ks}'(\exists\pi) = \exists\,\mathfrak{ks}'(\pi)$,
- $\mathfrak{ks}'(\varphi\ {}_\chi U_{\chi'}\ \varphi') = ((\bot \wedge \mathfrak{ks}'(\varphi)) \vee (\neg\bot \wedge \chi))\ U\ (\neg\bot \wedge \exists((\neg\bot \wedge \chi')\ U\ (\bot \wedge \mathfrak{ks}'(\varphi'))))$,
- $\mathfrak{ks}'(\varphi\ {}_\chi U\ \varphi') = ((\bot \wedge \mathfrak{ks}'(\varphi)) \vee (\neg\bot \wedge \chi))\ U\ (\bot \wedge \mathfrak{ks}'(\varphi'))$,
- $\mathfrak{ks}'(X_\chi\varphi) = X(\neg\bot \wedge \chi \wedge \exists X(\mathfrak{ks}'(\varphi)))$,
- $\mathfrak{ks}'(X_\tau\varphi) = X(\bot \wedge \mathfrak{ks}'(\varphi))$,
- $\mathfrak{ks}'(\neg\pi) = \neg\,\mathfrak{ks}'(\pi)$. ♦

The key result about $\mathfrak{ks}'$ is that it preserves truth. An interesting propery is that the size of $\mathfrak{ks}'(\varphi)$ is linear in the size of φ.

Theorem 5.4. (*$\mathfrak{ks}$ and $\mathfrak{ks}'$ together preserve truth*)
Let $\mathcal{A}$ be a LTS, let s be a state of $\mathcal{A}$ and let φ be an ACTL-formula. Then:

$$\mathcal{A}, s \models \varphi \quad \text{iff} \quad \mathfrak{ks}(\mathcal{A}), s \models \mathfrak{ks}'(\varphi). \qquad ♦$$

As a corollary of the above theorem, we have that there exists a model checking algorithm for ACTL with time complexity $O((|S|+|\to|) \times |\varphi|)$. Indeed, if we let $\mathcal{A}$ be a finite LTS, s be a state of $\mathcal{A}$ and φ be an ACTL-formula, Theorem 5.4 says that in order to determine whether $\mathcal{A}, s \models \varphi$ it suffices to check whether $\mathfrak{ks}(\mathcal{A}), s \models \mathfrak{ks}'(\varphi)$. We can easily compute $\mathfrak{ks}(\mathcal{A})$ in $O(|S|+|\to|)$-time and the number of states and transitions of $\mathfrak{ks}(\mathcal{A})$ will be of order $|S|+|\to|$. The formula $\mathfrak{ks}'(\varphi)$ can be computed in $O(|\varphi|)$-time and its size will be of order $|\varphi|$. Next, we can apply the model checking algorithm for CTL of [CES86] which will terminate in $O((|S|+|\to|) \times |\varphi|)$-time.

ACTL is still a rather expressive logic in which safety and liveness properties can be formulated. The formula of Example 2.11 for instance is an ACTL formula. Also the next proposition shows that, given our design objective to find a subset of ACTL* which can be translated into CTL, we have still managed to preserve expressiveness: in combination with Theorem 4.6 and Theorem 5.4, the proposition says that ACTL is just as expressive as CTL in the setting with transformations $\mathfrak{lts}$ and $\mathfrak{ks}$ between KS's and LTS's.

Proposition 5.5. (*ACTL has the same expressive power of CTL*)
Let φ be a CTL formula. Then $\mathfrak{lts}(\varphi)$ is an ACTL formula. ♦

An interesting feature of the mapping $\mathfrak{ks}'$ is that it maps all formulae without the relativized next time operators into formulae of CTL which do not cointain the next operator. This fact allows us to conclude this section and the paper with a few remarks about the relationships between the equivalence induced on LTS's by our new logics and the (divergence sensitive version of the) branching bisimulation equivalence of [GW89].

In fact, by exploiting the results of [DV90] about the correspondence between the equivalence induced by CTL- X and branching bisimulation equivalence and by relying on Theorem 5.4 above, we can deduce that ACTL-$\{X_\chi, X_\tau\}$ induces on finite LTS's the same identifications as divergence sensitive branching bisimulation equivalence. Due to the way the transformation function $\mathfrak{ks}$ from ACTL* to CTL* is defined, we cannot use the same chain of reasoning to prove that also the equivalence induced by ACTL*- $\{X, X_a\}$ coincides with branching bisimulation. It is, however, possible to define, in the same vein of $\mathfrak{ks}'$, a new mapping $\mathfrak{ks}''$ to CTL*-X from ACTL* without next operators but with the relativized until modalities $_{\chi}U_{\chi'}$; and this would enable us to conclude that also the richer logics is in full agreement with divergence sensitive branching bisimulation equivalence.

6. References

[BCG88] M.C. Browne, E.M. Clarke & O. Grümberg: Characterizing Finite Kripke Structures in Propositional Temporal Logic. *Theoret. Comp. Sci.*, **59** (1,2), 1988, pp. 115-131.

[CES89] E.M. Clarke, E.A. Emerson & A.P. Sistla: Automatic Verification of Finite State Concurrent Systems using Temporal Logic Specifications. *ACM Toplas*, **8** (2), 1986, pp. 244-263.

[CLM89] E.M. Clarke, D.E. Long & K.L. Macmillan: Compositional Model Checking. In *Proceedings 4th Annual Symposium on Logic in Computer Science (LICS)*, Asilomar, California, IEEE Computer Society Press, Washington, 1989, pp. 353-362.

[CPS88] Cleaveland, R., Parrow, J., Steffen, B. The Concurrency Workbench. In *Automatic Verification Methods for Finite State Systems* (J. Sifakis, ed.) Lecture Notes in Computer Science **407**, Springer-Verlag, 1990, pp. 24-37.

[DV90a] R. De Nicola, & F.W. Vaandrager: Three Logics for Branching Bisimulations (Extended Abstract) in Proc. of the 5th Annual Symposium on Logic in Computer Science (*LICS '90*), Philadelphia, USA, June 1990, IEEE Computer Society Press, Los Alamitos, CA, 1990, pp. 118-129.

[DV90b] R. De Nicola, & F.W. Vaandrager: Three Logics for Branching Bisimulations, CWI Report CS-R9012, 1990.

[EH86] E.A.Emerson & J.Y. Halpern: "Sometimes" and "Not Never" Revisited: on Branching Time versus Linear Time Temporal Logic. *Journal of ACM*, **33**, 1, 1986, pp. 151-178.

[EL87] E.A. Emerson & C.L. Lei: Modalities for Model Checking: Branching Time Strikes Back. *Science of Computer Programming*, **6**, 1987.

[ES89] E. A. Emerson & J. Srinivasan: Branching Time Temporal Logic. In *Linear Time, Branching Time and Partial Order in Logics and Models for Concurrency*, (de Bakker, de Roever and Rozenberg, eds.) Lecture Notes in Computer Science **354**, Springer-Verlag, 1989, pp. 123-172.

[GV90] J.F. Groote & F.W. Vaandrager: An Efficient Algorithm for Branching Bisimulation and Stuttering Equivalence.In *Proceedings ICALP '90*, Warwick, Lecture Notes in Computer Science, Springer-Verlag, 1990.

[GW89] R.J. van Glabbeek & W.P. Weijland: Branching Time and Abstraction in Bisimulation Semantics (extended abstract). In *Information Processing '89* (G.X. Ritter, ed.), Elsevier Science Publishers B.V. (North Holland), 1989, pp. 613-618.

[HM85] M. Hennessy & R. Milner: Algebraic Laws for Nondeterminism and Concurrency. *Journal of ACM*, **32**, 1985, pp. 137-161.

[JKP90] B. Jonsson, A.H. Khan & J. Parrow: Implementing a model checking algorithm by adapting existing automated tools. In *Automatic Verification Methods for Finite State Systems* (J. Sifakis, ed.) Lecture Notes in Computer Science **407**, Springer-Verlag, 1990, pp. 179-188.

[Lam83] L. Lamport: What Good Is Temporal Logic? , *Information Processing '83* (R.E.A. Mason, ed.) Elsevier Science Publishers B.V. (North Holland), 1983, pp. 657-668.

[Lar88] K.G. Larsen: Proof Systems for Hennessy-Milner Logic with Recursion, in proceeding *CAAP '88* (M. Dauchet & M. Nivat eds) Lecture Notes in Computer Science **299**, Springer-Verlag, 1988.

[Sti89] C. Stirling: Temporal Logics for CCS, in *Linear Time, Branching Time and Partial Order in Logics and Models for Concurrency*, (de Bakker, de Roever and Rozenberg, eds.) Lecture Notes in Computer Science **354**, Springer-Verlag, 1989, pp. 660-672.

Approaching Fair Computations by Ultra Metrics

Lutz Priese*
L.I.T.P., Université de Paris 7, Paris, France

Abstract

In this lecture I present some results of Philippe Darondeau, Doris Nolte, Serge Yoccoz and me on the connection of fairness, Π_3^0-sets and ultra metrics.

1 Introduction

A semantic of non-deterministic or concurrent programs has been presented in the framework of metric spaces, see, e.g., Arnold and Nivat [AN80] or DeBakker and Meyer [BM85]. Degano and Montanari [DM84] have been the first who expressed fairness properties as convergence criteria in metric spaces. They defined a simple concurrent programming language in the style of Milner's CCS [M80] and proved that a computation c is weakly (strongly) fair iff the initial segments of c form a Cauchy sequence in some appropriate metric space.

These ideas have been adapted by Costa [C85] who presented metric characterizations of fair computations in CCS. Costa and Hennessy put the question, whether this research can be generalized to transition systems. Note, that in a transition system a state is an atomic object whilst in CCS states bear structure s.t. one may tell from a state which objects are still 'live', etc.

We will show that this approach can indeed be generalized to transition systems, even for very abstract notions of fairness that include all known fairness concepts of the literature to my knowledge. Further this technique may be applied to reduce the logical complexity of some known fairness concept from Π_3^0 to Π_2^0.

The following results have been developed in a common research by Philippe Darondeau, Doris Nolte, Serge Yoccoz and me. In this lecture of the Spring School I present some (more or less) new proofs, that are slightly more general than those in [PN90] or [DNPY90].

2 Some Ultra Metrics on Σ^∞

We present a few methods how to construct ultra metrics on Σ^∞ that will be applied in the sequel.

*Permanent address: Universität Paderborn, 4790 Paderborn, Germany

Definition 1.
$\Sigma \subseteq I\!N$ denotes a recursive nonempty set (alphabet) of letters, not necessarily finite, Σ^* denotes the set of all finite words, and Σ^ω of all infinite words, over Σ.
$\Sigma^\infty := \Sigma^\omega \cup \Sigma^*$. λ denotes the empty letter or word.
$|w|$ denotes the length of $w \in \Sigma^\infty$, where $|w| := \omega$ for $w \in \Sigma^\omega$ holds.
We identify $w \in \Sigma^\infty$ with a finite or infinite sequence $w = w(1)w(2)\ldots w(|w|)$ or mapping $w : I\!N^\infty \to \Sigma$, i.e. $w : \{1, 2, \ldots, |w|\} \to \Sigma$.

$$w[n,m] := \begin{cases} w(n)\ldots w(m) & \text{iff } n \le m \le |w|, \\ w(n)\ldots w(|w|) & \text{iff } n \le |w| < m, \\ \lambda & \text{otherwise} \end{cases}$$

is the infix (factor) of w from n to m.
Thus $w[n, |w|]$ is a suffix (right factor) and $w[1, n]$ an prefix (left factor) of w.

$w_1 \le w_2$ iff $\exists w_3 : w_1 w_3 = w_2$,
$w_1 \subseteq w_2$ iff $\exists w_3, w_4 : w_3 w_1 w_4 = w_2$,
$w_1 \sqcap w_2 := sup\{n; w_1[1,n] = w_2[1,n] \text{ and } |w_1| \ge n \text{ and } |w_2| \ge n\}$
is the length of the greatest common left factor of both w_1 and w_2.

Definition 2.
A measure is a function $f : \Sigma^\infty \times I\!N \to I\!N$ s.t. $f(w,n) = f(w,|w|)$ for all $n \ge |w|$.
A measure is called
finite iff $f(w,n) = f(w[1,n],n)$ holds $\forall w, n$.
monotonic iff $n' \ge n \Rightarrow f(w,n') \ge f(w,n)$ holds $\forall w, n, n'$.
For any measure f we denote by $\hat{f}$ the function $\hat{f} : \Sigma^\infty \times I\!N \to I\!N$ defined as

$$\hat{f}(w,n) := \min\{f(w,l); l \ge n\}.$$

The following lemma is obvious:

Lemma 1: For any measure f the following holds:

- $\hat{f}$ is also a measure,
- f is monotonic iff $f = \hat{f}$,
- f is finite iff $w_1[0,n] = w_2[0,n] \Rightarrow f(w_1,n) = f(w_2,n)\ \forall w_1, w_2, n$.

Thus $\hat{f}$ is the monotonic closure of f and finiteness may also be regarded as a kind of a symmetry property.

Definition 3.
The Baire ultra metric on Σ^∞ is defined as

$$\delta(w_1,w_2) := \begin{cases} 0 & \text{if } w_1 = w_2, \\ ((w_1 \sqcap w_2) + 1)^{-1} & \text{otherwise.} \end{cases}$$

For any measure f we define

$$d_f(w_1,w_2) := \begin{cases} 0 & \text{if } w_1 = w_2, \\ \max(f(w_1, w_1 \sqcap w_2) + 1)^{-1}, (f(w_2, w_1 \sqcap w_2) + 1)^{-1}) & \text{otherwise.} \end{cases}$$

Theorem 1:
(1) δ is an ultra metric on Σ^∞.
(2) If f is a finite and monotonic measure then d_f is an ultra metric on Σ^∞.
(3) If f is a finite measure then $d_{\hat{f}}$ is an ultra metric on Σ^∞.

Proof:
(1): Note that the set $\{w_1 \sqcap w_2, w_1 \sqcap w_3, w_2 \sqcap w_3\}$ contains at most two different values, namely the maximal value and both non-maximal values have to coincide. Thus

$$w_1 \sqcap w_2 \geq \min(w_1 \sqcap w_3, w_2 \sqcap w_3), \qquad (i)$$

which implies the strong triangle inequality for δ.

(2): Let f be finite and monotonic.

We prove $\forall w_1, w_2, w_3$:

$$f(w_1, w_1 \sqcap w_2) \geq \min(f(w_1, w_1 \sqcap w_3), f(w_3, w_2 \sqcap w_3)). \qquad (ii)$$

Case 1: $w_1 \sqcap w_3 = w_2 \sqcap w_3 \leq w_1 \sqcap w_2$.
Thus $f(w_1, w_1 \sqcap w_2) \geq f(w_1, w_1 \sqcap w_3)$, by monotonicity.

Case 2: $w_1 \sqcap w_2 = w_1 \sqcap w_3 \leq w_2 \sqcap w_3$.
Thus $f(w_1, w_1 \sqcap w_2) = f(w_1, w_1, \sqcap w_3)$.

Case 3: $w_1 \sqcap w_2 = w_2 \sqcap w_3 \leq w_1 \sqcap w_3$.
Thus $f(w_1, w_1 \sqcap w_2) = f(w_2, w_1 \sqcap w_2) = f(w_2, w_2 \sqcap w_3) = f(w_3, w_2 \sqcap w_3)$.

As $f(x, x \sqcap y) = f(y, x \sqcap y)$ for finite f, (ii) implies the strong triangle inequality for d_f easily.

(3): Let f be only finite. Thus $\hat{f}$ is monotonic but not finite itself in general. However, we again prove $\forall w_1, w_2, w_3$:

$$\hat{f}(w_1, w_1 \sqcap w_2) \geq \min(\hat{f}(w_1, w_1 \sqcap w_3), \hat{f}(w_3, w_2 \sqcap w_3)). \qquad (iii)$$

Cases 1 and 2 are as above.

Case 3: $w_1 \sqcap w_2 = w_2 \sqcap w_3 \leq w_1 \sqcap w_3$.
If $\hat{f}(w_1, w_1 \sqcap w_2) \geq \hat{f}(w_1, w_1 \sqcap w_3)$ we are done.
Thus we suppose $f_o := \hat{f}(w_1, w_1 \sqcap w_2) < \hat{f}(w_1, w_1 \sqcap w_3)$. This implies

$$f_o = \min\{f(w_1, l); l \geq w_1 \sqcap w_2\} = f(w_1, l_o), \text{ with } w_1 \sqcap w_2 = w_2 \sqcap w_3 \leq l_o.$$

Thus $l_o < w_1 \sqcap w_3$, as $l_o \geq w_1 \sqcap w_3$ implies $\hat{f}(w_1, w_1 \sqcap w_3) = f(w_1, l_o) = \hat{f}(w_1, w_1 \sqcap w_2)$.
Thus $w_2 \sqcap w_3 \leq l_o < w_1 \sqcap w_3$, and by finiteness of f we conclude

$$\hat{f}(w_1, w_1 \sqcap w_2) = f_o = f(w_1, l_o) = f(w_3, l_o) geq \hat{f}(w_3, w_2 \sqcap w_3).$$

This proves (iii).
By writing (iii) with w_2 instead of w_1 we also conclude

$$\hat{f}(w_2, w_1 \sqcap w_2) \geq \min(\hat{f}(w_2, w_2 \sqcap w_3), \hat{f}(w_3, w_1 \sqcap w_3)). \qquad (iv)$$

(iii) and (iv) immediately prove the strong triangle inequality for $d_{\hat{f}}$. □

It should be noted that finiteness is the essential property that allows us to define metrics, not monotonicity, as is clarified in the following lemma.

Lemma 2:
There exists a monotonic measure f s.t. d_f is not a metric.

Proof:
$\Sigma := \{a, b\}, f(w, n) := \#_a w + \min(|w|, n)$ is a monotonic measure. $\#_a w$ denotes the number of occurrences of a's in w.

For $w_1 := b^3, w_2 = a^3, w_3 := b^2 a$ there holds:
$d_f(w_1, w_2) = 1 > 1/3 + 1/2 = d_f(w_1, w_3) + d_f(w_2, w_3)$. □

In the sequel we need the logical complexity of metrics and sets of functions and integers. Therefore we use the standard Π^0_n, Σ^0_n complexity classes.

Definition 4.
A relation $R \subseteq (I\!N^\infty)^k \times I\!N^m$ is called recursive iff there exists a Turing machine, M_R, that decides whether $R(p_1, \ldots, p_k, x_1, \ldots, x_m)$ holds given $x_1, \ldots x_m \in I\!N$ as inputs and $p_1, \ldots p_m \in I\!N^\infty$ as oracles to M_R.

A relation $R \subseteq (I\!N^\infty)^k \times I\!N^m$ is called $\Sigma^0_n(\Pi^0_n)$ iff it is defined by

$$R(p_1, \ldots p_k, x_1, \ldots, x_m) \;\rtimes \exists y_1 : \forall y_2 : \ldots : \overset{\forall}{\exists} y_n : P(p_1, \ldots, p_k, x_1, \ldots, x_m, y_1, \ldots y_n)$$

$$\text{(respectively:} \qquad \rtimes \forall y_1 : \exists x_2 : \ldots : \overset{\forall}{\exists} y_n : P(p_1, \ldots, p_k, x_1, \ldots, x_m, y_1, \ldots y_n))$$

with an recursive predicate P, where the quantifiers range over integers.

A set $M \subseteq (I\!N^\infty)^k \times I\!N^m$ is called recursive, Σ^0_n, Π^0_n, resp., iff it's characteristic predicate $M(p_1, \ldots, p_k, x_1, \ldots, x_m) : \rtimes (p_1, \ldots p_k, x_1, \ldots, x_m) \in M$ is recursive, Σ^0_n, Π^0_n, respectively.

A predicate (set) is called Δ^0_n iff it is Π^0_n and Σ^0_n.

A metric $d : \Sigma^\infty \times \Sigma^\infty \to I\!R$ is called recursive, $\Sigma^0_n, \Pi^0_n, \Delta^0_n$, respectively (in some f, R) iff the predicate $D \subseteq (I\!N^\infty)^2 \times I\!N$ defined by $D(u, v, N) : \rtimes d(u, v) < 1/N$ is recursive, $\Sigma^0_n, \Pi^0_n, \Delta^0_n$, respectively (for recursive f, R). d is called recursive, Σ^0_n, etc. on $\mathcal{K}$ for a set $\mathcal{K}$ iff $D(u, v, N)$ is recursive, Σ^0_n, etc. for values $(u, v) \in \mathcal{K}, N \in I\!N$.

Any oracle $p \in I\!N^\infty$ is written as an input on additional read-only tapes of M_R with special endmarkers for finite oracles p. As a consequence, predicates as $|p| = i$ or $p(i) = j$ are thus decidable by M_R for any oracle p.

Lemma 3:
(1) The Baire ultra metric δ is recursive.
(2) For a finite and monotonic measure f the ultra metric d_f is recursive in f on $(\Sigma^\omega \times \Sigma^*) \cup (\Sigma^* \times \Sigma^\omega)$.
(3) For a finite measure f the ultra metric $d_{\hat{f}}$ is Π^0_1 in f on $\Sigma^\infty \times \Sigma^\infty$ and on $(\Sigma^\omega \times \Sigma^*)$

$\cup (\Sigma^* \times \Sigma^\omega)$, but recursive in f on $\Sigma^* \times \Sigma^*$.

Proof: $\forall u, v, w \in \Sigma^\infty, N \in I\!N$:

(1): $\delta(u,v) < 1/N \asymp u \sqcap v \geq N \asymp \forall i \leq N : u(i) = v(i)$ and $|u| \geq i$.

(2): $\max(1/(f(u, u \sqcap v)+1), 1/(f(v, u \sqcap v)+1)) < 1/N$
$\asymp f(u, u \sqcap v) \geq N$ and $f(v, u \sqcap v) \geq N$
$\asymp \exists i : i = u \sqcap v$ and $f(u,i) \geq N$ and $f(v,i) \geq N$ $\quad (\in \Sigma_1^0)$
$\asymp \forall i : i = u \sqcap v \rightarrow f(u,i) \geq N$ and $f(v,i) \geq N$ $\quad (\in \Pi_1^0)$
is thus Δ_1^0 in f and thus recursive in f, as
$i = u \sqcap v \asymp \forall i' \leq i : u(i') = v(i')$ and $u(i+1) \neq v(i+1)$ or $|u| = i$ is recursive.

Thus $d(u,v) < 1/N$ is recursive on $(\Sigma^\omega \times \Sigma^*) \cup (\Sigma^* \times \Sigma^\omega)$, as for such values $u = v$ is impossible.

(3): $d_{\hat{f}}(u,v) < 1/N \asymp \hat{f}(u, u \sqcap v) \geq N$ and $\hat{f}(v, u \sqcap v) \geq N$ or $u = v$
$\asymp \forall l : ((l \geq u \sqcap v \Rightarrow (f(u,l) \geq N$ and $f(v,l) \geq N)))$ or $(u(l) = v(l) \forall l))$
is Π_1^0 in f and recursive in f for $u, v \in \Sigma^*$. □

This result is not surprising. For finite, but non-monotonic f we had to use $\hat{f}$ to construct a metric. In contrast to f, $\hat{f}$ is nor longer finite but needs an inspection of the 'future', i.e. $\hat{f}(w,u)$ depends also on the 'future of w after u', i.e. on $w[1,u]$ and $w[u,|w|]$. Due to this inspection of the future we cannot expect $d_{\hat{f}}$ to be recursive in f on infinite words.

In the sequel we need a further method to define a metric with some inspection of the future of some number theoretical predicates. We have already identified mappings $p : I\!N \rightarrow I\!N$ with infinite words over $I\!N$, i.e. $I\!N^{I\!N} = I\!N^\omega$. Further we will identify finite sequences with numbers:

Definition 5.
Let $<,>: I\!N^2 \rightarrow I\!N$ denote the standard recursive and bijective Cantor coding of $I\!N^2$ into $I\!N$ with recursive decoding functions φ_1, φ_2 .

$<>_k: I\!N^k \rightarrow I\!N$ is defined inductively by
$<>_1$:=id, and $<w>_{k+1} := <w(1), <w(2) \ldots w(k+1)>_k>$.

Let φ_i^k denote the decoding functions of $<>_k$ s.t. $\varphi_i^k(<w>)$ equals $w(i)$ for $w \in I\!N^k$ and $i \leq k$, and 0 otherwise.

The Goedel coding $<>: I\!N^* \rightarrow I\!N$ is defined by

$$<w> := \begin{cases} 0 & \text{if } w = \lambda, \\ <|w|, <w>_{|w|}> +1 & \text{otherwise,} \end{cases}$$

and $(\,)_i : I\!N \rightarrow I\!N$ are defined by

$$(w)_i := \begin{cases} \varphi_1(w) & \text{if } i = 0, \\ \varphi_i^{\varphi_1(w)}(\varphi_2(w)) & \text{otherwise.} \end{cases}$$

The restriction $\restriction : I\!N^\infty \times I\!N \rightarrow I\!N$ is defined as $p \restriction k := <p[1,k]>$,
and the length $||: I\!N \rightarrow I\!N$ is defined as $|n| := \varphi_1(n)$.

The following is known.

Lemma 4:

(1) The mappings $<>, ()_i, \upharpoonright, ||$ are recursive.
(2) $<>: I\!N^* \rightarrow I\!N$ is bijective.
(3) $\forall w \in I\!N^\infty : i \in I\!N$:

$$(<w>)_i = \begin{cases} |w| & \text{for } i = 0, \\ w(i) & \text{for } 0 < i \leq |w|, \\ 0 & \text{for } i > |w|. \end{cases}$$

As a consequence we frequently identify $N =< I\!N^* >$ with $I\!N^*$.

Definition 6.
For any predicate $R \subseteq I\!N^2$ define $f_R : I\!N^\infty \times I\!N \rightarrow I\!N$ by

$$f_R(p,n) := \max\{i \leq \min(|p|,n); \forall i' \leq i : \forall k : \min(|p|,n) \leq k \leq |p| : R(p \upharpoonright k, i')\}.$$

Lemma 5: For any predicate $R \subseteq I\!N^2$ the following holds:

(1) f_R is a monotonic (but not finite) measure,
(2) d_{f_R} is an ultra metric on $I\!N^\infty$,
(3) d_{f_R} is Π_1^0 in R, but recursive in R on $I\!N^* \times I\!N^*$.

Proof:
(1) is obvious.
(2): We only show the strong triangle inequality:

$$d_{f_R}(u,v) \leq \max(d_{f_R}(u,w), d_{f_R}(v,w)).$$

Case 1: $u \sqcap w = v \sqcap w \leq u \sqcap v$.
Thus $f_R(u, u \sqcap v) \geq f_R(u, u \sqcap w)$ and $f_R(v, u \sqcap v) \geq f_R(v, v \sqcap w)$ by monotonicity.

Case 2: $u \sqcap v = v \sqcap w \leq u \sqcup w$.
Thus $f_R(v, u \sqcap v) = f_R(v, v \sqcap w)$.
$f_R(u, u \sqcap v) \geq \min(f_R(u, u \sqcap w), f_R(w, v \sqcap w))$ is seen as follows:
Suppose $f_R(u, u \sqcap v) < f_R(u, u \sqcap w)$.
For $I := f_R(u, u \sqcap v) + 1$ this implies:

- $I \leq f_R(u, u \sqcap w) \leq u \sqcap w$,
- $\exists k_o \geq u \sqcap v : \neg R(u \upharpoonright k_o, I)$, as $f_R(u, u \sqcap v) = I - 1$,
- $\forall k \geq u \sqcap w : R(u \upharpoonright k, I)$, as $f_R(u, u \sqcap w) \geq I$ by assumption.

Thus there exists $k_o : u \sqcap v \leq k_o < u \sqcap w : \neg R(u \upharpoonright k_o, I)$.
As $w \upharpoonright k_o = u \upharpoonright k_o$ for $k_o \leq u \sqcap w$, we conclude: $\neg R(w \upharpoonright k_o, I)$.
Thus $f_R(w, u \sqcap v) < I$, and $f_R(w, u \sqcap v) = f_R(w, v \sqcap w) \leq f_R(u, u \sqcap v) = I - 1$.

Case 3: $u \sqcap v = u \sqcap w$.
As case 2, interchange u and v.

(3): $d_{f_R}(u,v) < 1/N \iff (f_R(u, u \sqcap v) \geq N$ and $f_R(v, u \sqcap v) \geq N)$ or $u = v$.
$f_R(u, u \sqcap v) \geq N \iff |u| \geq N$ and $\forall i' \leq N : \forall k : \min(|u|, u \sqcap v) \leq k \leq |u| : R(u \upharpoonright k, i')$
is Π_1^0 in R, as $|u| = \omega$ may hold. □

3 Cluster Points

In this chapter we research sets of infinite words or, equivalently, sets of functions from $\mathbb{N}$ to $\mathbb{N}$ that can be approximated by measures.

Definition 7.
A set $M \subseteq \Sigma^\omega$ is called ($f-$) approximated iff $p \in M \Leftrightarrow \lim_{n \to \omega} f(p,n) = \omega$ holds for some measure f.
$U_f := \{p \in \Sigma^\infty; \lim_{n \to \omega} f(p,n) = \omega\}$.

Lemma 6: For any measure f the following holds:

(1) $U_f \subseteq \Sigma^\omega$,
(2) $U_f = U_{\hat{f}}$,
(3) M is f-approximated $\iff M = U_f \iff M = U_{\hat{f}}$.

Proof:
(1): As $f(p,n) = f(p,|p|)$ for $p \in \Sigma^*$ and $n > |p|$, we conclude $\lim_{n \to \omega} f(p,n) = f(p,|p|) < \omega$ for $p \in \Sigma^*$. Thus $U_f \subseteq \Sigma^\omega$.
(2): $\lim_{n \to \omega} f(w,n) = \omega \iff \lim_{n \to \omega} \min\{f(w,l), l \geq n\} = \omega \iff \lim_{n \to \omega} \hat{f}(w,n) = \omega$.
(3): just restates (1) and (2). □

It should be noted that the property $f(p,n) = f(p,|p|)$ $\forall n \geq |p|$ was just stated for a measure to ensure lemma 6. The simple fact that $U_f \subseteq \Sigma^\omega$ will simplify further theorems. E.g., it will allow us to identify cluster points and Cauchy-sequences.

Definition 8.
For any metric d on Σ^∞, and any $K \subseteq \Sigma^\infty$, define

- $CP_d(K) := \{p \in \Sigma^\infty; \forall N : \exists p_N \in K : p \neq p_N$ and $d(p, p_N) < 1/N\}$,
  the set of cluster points of K,
- $CS_d := \{p \in \Sigma^\omega; \{p[1,n]\}_{n \in \mathbb{N}}$ is a non-stationary d-Cauchy sequence$\}$,
- $LIM_d := \{p \in \Sigma^\omega; p = \lim^d_{n \to \omega} p[1,n]\}$.

Although all three concepts usually differ in general metric spaces they will coincide for finite measures:

Theorem 2:
For any finite measure f :

$$U_{\hat{f}} = CP_{d_{\hat{f}}}(\Sigma^*) = CS_{d_{\hat{f}}} = LIM_{d_{\hat{f}}}.$$

For any predicate $R \subseteq \mathbb{N}^2$:

$$U_{f_R} = CP_{d_{f_R}}(\mathbb{N}) = CS_{d_{f_R}} = LIM_{d_{f_R}}.$$

Proof:
We need $\lim_{n\to\omega} f_R(p[1,n],n) = \omega \leftrightarrow \lim_{n\to\omega} f_R(p,n) = \omega$:

$f_R(p[1,n],n) \to \omega$
$\leftrightarrow \forall N : \exists n_N \geq N : \forall n \geq n_N : f_R(p[1,n],n) \geq N$
$\leftrightarrow \forall N : \exists n_N \geq N : \forall n \geq n_N : N \leq |p[1,n]| \ \wedge \forall i' \leq N : \forall k = |p[1,n]| : R(p \restriction k, i')$
$\leftrightarrow \forall N : \exists n_N \geq N : \forall i' \leq N : \forall n \geq n_N : R(p \restriction n, i') \wedge |p| = \omega$
$\leftrightarrow \forall N : \exists n_N \geq N : f_R(p, n_N) \geq N$
$\leftrightarrow f_R(p,n) \to \omega.$

For a finite measure f the above equality holds trivially. Let g denote f_R or $\hat{f}$. Thus :

$p \in U_g \leftrightarrow g(p,n) \to \omega \leftrightarrow g(p,n) \to \omega \wedge g(p[1,n],n) \to \omega$
$\leftrightarrow |p| = \omega \ \wedge \ \lim^{d_g}_{n\to\omega} p[1,n] = p \ > \ \{p[1,n]\}_n$ is a non-stationary d_g Cauchy sequence
$> \ p \in CP_{d_g}(\mathbb{N}^*) \ > \ \forall N : \exists n_N : g(p, n_N) \geq N \leftrightarrow g(p,n) \to \omega$. □

Lemma 7:

(1) U_f is Π^0_3 in f,
(2) $CP_d(\Sigma^*)$ is Π^0_2 in d.

Proof:
(1): $\lim_{n\to\omega} f(p,n) = \omega \leftrightarrow \forall N : \exists n_N : \forall i \geq n_N : f(p,i) \geq N$ is Π^0_3 in f.

(2): $p \in CP_d(\Sigma^*) \leftrightarrow \forall N : \exists p_N \in \Sigma^* : d(p,p_N) \leq 1/N$ and $p_N \neq p \leftrightarrow \forall N \in \mathbb{N} : \exists n_N \in \mathbb{N} :$
$n_N \in \Sigma^* \ \wedge \ \overline{d}(p,n_N) < 1/N \ \wedge \ p \neq n_N,$
where $n_N \in \Sigma^* \ : \leftrightarrow \forall i \leq (n_N)_o : (n_N)_i \in \Sigma$ is recursive,
$\overline{d}(p,n_N) := d(p, (n_N)_1 \ldots (n_N)_{(n_N)_o})$ is recursive in d, and
$p \neq n_N : \leftrightarrow \exists i \leq |p| : p(i) \neq (n_N)_i$ is Σ^0_1, as $|p| = \omega$ may hold.

Thus $CP_d(\Sigma^*)$ is Π^0_2 in d. □

Lemma 7 involves a whole program of research:

Many important sets M in mathematics and computer science are U_f for some recursive measure f. Thus they are Π^0_3. However, if in addition some finite, monotonic, recursive measure f' can be found s. t. $M = U_{f'}$ we know in addition

$$M = CP_{d_{f'}}(\Sigma^*)$$

by theorem 2 and lemma 1, (2). Thus, by lemma 3, (2), $d_{f'}$ is recursive and by lemma 7 M is thus Π^0_2.

Consequence:
Finding a finite, monotonic and recursive measure reduces complexity of U_f from *Π^0_3 to Π^0_2*.

4 Applications

4.1 Π_3^0-Sets of Functions

There are many interesting examples of approximated sets due to the fact, that any Π_3^0 set of functions is approximated.

Theorem 3:
For any Π_3^0 set $M \subseteq \Sigma^\omega$ exists a recursive measure f s.t. $M = U_f$.

Proof:
It is known in recursion theory that Σ_1^0 sets of functions are characterized by formulae $\exists k : R(p \restriction k)$, with recursive R. Further $\{f : I\!N \to I\!N; \forall j : \exists k \leq j : f(k) = 0\}$ is Σ_2^0-complete. Combining both results it is seen that any Π_3^0 set $M$is characterized by a recursive predicate $R \subseteq I\!N^2$ as $M = \{p : I\!N \to I\!N; \forall i : \exists j : \forall k \geq j : R(p \restriction k, i)\}$. Thus, $p \in M$ iff $lim_{n \to \omega} f_R(p, n) = \omega$, compare definition 6. I.e., $M = U_{f_R}$.

For $M \subseteq \Sigma^\omega$, just note that $\Sigma \subseteq I\!N$ is recursive. Thus $M = \{p : I\!N \to I\!N; \forall i : p(i) \in \Sigma \wedge \forall i : \exists j : \forall k \geq j : R(p \restriction k, i)\} = \{p : I\!N \to I\!N; \forall i : \exists j : \forall k \geq j : R^+(p \restriction k, i)\} = U_{f_{R^+}}$,
where $R^+(n, m) : \Leftrightarrow R(n, m) \wedge p(m) \in \Sigma$. □

As a consequence, Π_3^0, approximated, cluster points, Cauchy-sequences and limites are just equivalent notions for subsets of Σ^ω.

4.2 Abstract Fairness

Now regard any fairness concept of the literature in any wanted model used anywhere. An infinite computation in some model usually is called fair if some objects that are infinitely often enabled during that computation have to be used also (infinitely often) during that computation.

As infinite computations we regard here functions $p : I\!N \to I\!N$ together with an predicate C s.t. $C(p)$ holds iff p is (a coding of) an allowed infinite computation in the used model. Standard models for computations are infinite, recursive, labelled transition systems. Here C becomes an Π_1^0 predicate telling us that a computation is a finite or infinite directed path. Further, the fact that p is fair is described by a $\forall(\exists^\omega \Rightarrow \exists^\omega)$-formula : for all objects : if they are infinitely often enabled (in p) they have to occur (infinitely often) in p. Again, in all models I know, the used predicates 'o is a coding of an enabled object', etc. are recursive such that this formula is again Π_3^0. Note that $\forall(\exists^\omega \Rightarrow \exists^\omega) \equiv \forall(\exists\forall \vee \forall\exists) \equiv \forall\exists\forall$.

Thus, any fairness condition of the literature leads usually to fair computations that are described by Π_3^0 predicates.

As a consequence all those fair computations can be described as limites of Cauchy-sequences of their own finite prefixes in an adequate ultra metric. This remark fulfills the program of Degano, Montanari and Costa who started to describe strong and weak fair computations in CCS as convergence criteria in some (ultra) metrics.

On the other hand, any Π_3^0 set is characterized as $\forall i : \exists j : \forall k \leq j : R(p \upharpoonright k, i)$ or equivalently as $\forall i : (\exists^\omega k : \neg R(p \upharpoonright k, i)) \Rightarrow (\exists^\omega 0 = 1))$.

Thus any Π_3^0 set defines a fairness condition itself, where $\neg R(p \upharpoonright k, i)$ reads that i is enabled at $p(k)$ and occurrence is always false.
As a consequence we thus claim that Π_3^0 sets of functions and fairness notions just coincide. This fact was pointed to us by Philippe Darondeau and Serge Yoccoz. However, they used much more complicated proofs than here. It is the characterization of Π_3^0 sets by formulae of the form $\forall i : \exists j : \forall k \leq j : R(p \upharpoonright k, i)$ that allows for such a smooth approach.

4.3 Π_2^0-Fairness

With the previous remark, Π_3^0 sets and abstract fairness conditions coincide. However, there are some fairness conditions that are Π_2^0. For example weak fairness is of the form: $\forall$ objects o: (o almost always enabled in $p \Rightarrow o$ occurs in p) $\equiv \forall(\forall^\omega \Rightarrow \exists) \equiv \forall\forall\exists\exists \in \Pi_2^0$. Weak fairness will be treated in the following paragraph.

But also several strong fairness concepts of [PRW87] defined in finite transition systems are Π_2^0. This may be shown by defining a finite, monotonic and recursive measure f s.t. p is fair iff $p \in U_f (\in \Pi_2^0)$ according to our results in chapter 3.

A finite labelled transition systems, T, is a finite multigraph with possibly several different edges connecting the same two nodes and a labelling function $\phi : E_T \rightarrow \Sigma$ that adds labels (a letter of Σ) to the edges of T (E_T). Thus a labelled finite transition systems is just a nondeterministic automaton without final states and without an initial state.

For any edge e in T $^\bullet e$ denotes the state where e starts from and $e^\bullet$ the state where e ends. A directed path p is thus a finite or infinite word $p \in E_T^\infty$ s.t. $p(n)^\bullet = {}^\bullet p(n+1)$ $\forall n < |p|$. For a finite path q we denote $^\bullet q(1)$ by $^\bullet q$ and $q(|q|)^\bullet$ by $q^\bullet$.

An infinite directed path p in T is called

edge-fair iff any edge e of T, s.t. $^\bullet e$ is infinitely often a touched state of p, has to be used by p infinitely often,

path-fair iff any finite path q in T, s. t. $^\bullet q$ is touched infinitely often in p, has to be a sub-path of p,

word-fair iff the labelling $\phi(q)$ of any finite path q in T, s. t. $^\bullet q$ is touched infinitely often in p, has to be an infix (factor) of the labelling $\phi(p)$ of p.

For further detail, see [PR88], or [PRW87].

By $E^*(p \upharpoonright n)$ we denote the set of finite paths that 'can be seen from $^\bullet p(n)$', i.e.:
$E^*(p \upharpoonright n) = \{q \in E_T^*; \exists r \in E_T^* : {}^\bullet r = {}^\bullet p(n) \text{ and } r^\bullet = {}^\bullet q\}$.
Further, $E(p \upharpoonright n) := E^*(p \upharpoonright n) \cap E_T$.

It should be noted that for a finite transition system any infinite path p has to run in some closely connected part T_o ultimatively, i.e. $p[m_p, |p|]$ runs in T_o. For any edge-fair path p the edges infinitely often touched by p and those in $\bigcap_{n \geq m_p} E(p \restriction n)$ thus coincide. For any path-fair (word-fair) path p the finite paths (their labellings) that are touched infinitely often by p and $\bigcap_{n \geq m_p} E^*(p \restriction n)(\phi(\bigcap_{n \geq m_p} E^*(p \restriction n))$, respectively) thus coincide.

These considerations allow to define finite, monotonic, recursive measures f for all mentioned fairness concepts for finite transition systems:

for $n \leq |p|$:
$f_{\text{edge-fair}}(p, n) := \sup\{k; E(p \restriction n) \subseteq p[k, n]\}$,
$f_{\text{path-fair}}(p, n) := \sup\{k; E^*(p \restriction n) \cap E_T^k \subseteq p[1, n]\}$,
$f_{\text{word-fair}}(p, n) := \sup\{k; \phi(E^*(p \restriction n)) \cap \Sigma^k \subseteq \phi(p[1, n])\}$,

and $f_{\dots}(p, n) := f_{\dots}(p, |p|)$ for $n > |p|$.

An easy exercise shows that p is x-fair $\Join$ $\lim_{n \to w} f_{x\text{-fair}}(p, n) = \omega$ for $x \in$ {edge, path, word}.

Thus edge-, path- and word-fairness are Π_2^0 predicates.

4.4 Weak Fairness

Weak Fairness is usually defined as a negative property : no object shall be enabled almost always. A positive version will be seen to be equivalent: Any object that is enabled almost always has to occur (at least once). Again we assume that the predicates 'enabled', 'occurs', etc. are recursive. Thus, a path p of some transition system T is

weakly fair iff $C_T(p) \wedge \forall o : (\exists j : \forall k \geq j : o$ is x-enabled at $p(j) \Rightarrow \exists k : o$ occurs at $p(k)$)

$\equiv \forall(\exists\forall \Rightarrow \exists) \equiv \forall\forall\exists\exists \in \Pi_2^0$, as $C_T(p)$ just describes that p is an infinite path in T and is thus Π_1^0. Obviously, the negative version is also Π_2^0 ,as $\neg(\exists\forall^\omega) \equiv \forall\exists^\omega \equiv \forall\forall\exists$.

Now let M be any Π_2^0 set of functions. As Π_2^0 sets are just complements of Σ_2^0 sets we know of the existence of a recursive predicate $R_M \subseteq I\!N$ s.t. $p \in M \Join \exists^\omega k : R_M(p \restriction k)$. Thus, M is already a weak fairness concept in the negative version if we define 'enabledness' as $\neg R_M$.

Define $f_M : I\!N^\infty \times I\!N \to I\!N$ by $f_M(p, n) := \max\{j \leq n; R_M(p \restriction j)\}$.

f_M is a finite and monotonic measure and $f_M(p, n) \geq N$ is recursive. This doesn't imply that the ultra metric $d_M := d_{f_M}$ is also recursive on $I\!N^\infty$, just because $p = p'$ is not recursive on $I\!N^\infty$. But d_M is recursive on $(I\!N^\omega \times I\!N^*) \cup (I\!N^* \times I\!N^\omega)$. Further:

$p \in U_{f_M} \Join f_M(p, n) \to \omega \Join \forall N : \exists n_N : \forall n \geq n_N : f_M(p, n) \geq N \Join$
$\forall N : \exists n_N : \forall n \geq n_N : \exists j : N \leq j \leq n : R_M(p \restriction j) \Join \forall N : \exists j \geq N : R_M(p \restriction j) \Join p \in M$.

Thus we know

$$M = U_{f_M} = CP_{d_M}(I\!N) = LIM_{d_M} = CS_{d_M}.$$

Of course, even for a recursive metric d CS_d and LIM_d are Π_3^0 in general, but CP_d has to be Π_2^0.
Putting everything together we know:

Π_2^0 sets of functions, sets of weakly fair computations, and cluster points in $\mathbb{N}^\omega$ of metrics that are recursive on $(\mathbb{N}^\omega \times \mathbb{N}) \cup (\mathbb{N} \times \mathbb{N}^\omega)$ coincide .

4.5 A Universal Finite Transition System T_0 For Fairness

Let $P^{xf}(T)(P^{xf}_{weak}(T))$ denote the sets of all (weakly) x-fair infinite paths in some model T, where x stands for some fairness notion defined by some recursive predicates telling which objects are enabled and do occur.

Let T_0 be the finite transition system with one state and two edges looping on that state with labels 0 and 1. Using the homomorphism $\psi : \mathbb{N}^\omega \rightarrow P^\omega_{T_0}$ with $\psi(n) := 0^n1$, the set of functions $\mathbb{N}^\omega$ is identified with the '1-fair' computations in T_0, where the edge 1 has to be used infinitely often. As this fairness property is easily expressed as a Σ_1^0 predicate, we conclude that any Π_3^0 set of functions coincides with $P^{xf}(T_0)$ and any Π_2^0 set of functions coincides with $P^{yf}_{weak}(T_0)$ for appropriate fairness concepts xf and yf.

4.6 Main Consequence

All together we have shown:

(1) For any $M \subseteq \mathbb{N}^\omega$ the following is equivalent:

- $M \in \Pi_3^0$
- $M = P^{xf}(T)$ for some xf, T
- $M = P^{xf}(T_0)$ for some xf
- $M = LIM_d$ for some Π_1^0 metric d on $\mathbb{N}^\infty$
- $M = LIM_d$ for some Π_1^0 ultra metric d that is recursive on $\mathbb{N}^*$
- $M = CP_d(\mathbb{N})$ for some Σ_2^0 metric on $\mathbb{N}^\infty$
- $M = CP_d(\mathbb{N})$ for some Π_1^0 ultra metric that is recursive on $\mathbb{N}^*$.

(2) For any $M \subseteq \mathbb{N}^\omega$ the following is equivalent:

- $M \in \Pi_2^0$
- $M = P^{xf}_{weak}(T)$ for some xf, T
- $M = P^{xf}_{weak}(T_0)$ for some xf

- $M = CP_d(\mathbb{N})$ for some Π_1^0 ultra metric d on $\mathbb{N}^\infty$ that is recursive on $(\mathbb{N}^\omega \times \mathbb{N}^*) \cup (\mathbb{N}^* \times \mathbb{N}^\omega)$

4.7 Fair Languages

The x-fair language of T consists of all infinite words of Σ^ω that are labellings of x-fair paths, i.e.

$$L^{xf}(T) := \phi(P^{xf}(T)).$$

As an important fact, $L^{xf}(T)$ leaves the arithmetical hierarchy as a quantifier <u>over functions</u> is required:

$$w \in L^{xf}(T) \rtimes \exists p \in E^\omega : \ p \text{ is } x\text{-fair and } w = \phi(p).$$

Thus fair languages are examples of sets above Π_n^0.

Nevertheless, if we regard again finite labelled transition systems as our model T we will be able to show for all fairness concepts as mentioned in [PR88] or [PRW87]that their fair languages are sets of cluster points of some ultra metric and thus Π_3^0 again. This application is shown in detail in [PN90].

4.8 Open Problems

Our technique doesn't apply to fair languages in infinite transition systems. Of course, fair languages of arbitrary recursive infinite transition systems should be Σ_1^1 complete. Thus there arises the question whether for some interesting classes of infinite transition systems the fair languages may be Π_3^0 or just characterized as sets of cluster points of some metrics (rather complicated in the arithmetical hierarchy).

The previous results suggest some result like "any Π_{2n+1}^0 set is a set of cluster points of some Π_{2n-1}^0 metric", or similar. However, I cannot see how to generalize these presented methods to higher classes.

It might be true that any Π_3^0 set M may be characterized as LIM_d with a recursive metric on $\mathbb{N}^\infty$. However, for such a metric d $LIM_d \neq CP_d(\mathbb{N})$ has to hold in general, as $\Pi_3^0 \neq \Pi_2^0$, such that our presented methods cannot work.

Acknowledgement

I would like to thank Gerardo Costa, Pierpaolo Degano, Philippe Darondeau, Alain Louveau, Ugo Montanari, Maurice Nivat, Doris Nolte and Serge Yoccoz for valuable discussions. The proofs, as presented here, have been developed by the author during a longer visit at the LITP, Paris, from others proofs as presented by Philippe and Serge and by Doris and myself. Two more detailed papers by Priese, Nolte on fair languages and by Darondeau, Nolte, Priese,

Yoccoz on Π_3^0 sets are in preparation. Thus, these results on the connection of fairness, Π_3^0-sets and ultra metrics are common results of Philippe Darondeau, Doris Nolte, Serge Yoccoz and me.

References

AN80 A. Arnold, M. Nivat. Metric interpretations of infinite trees and semantics of non deterministic programs. TCS 11, pp 181-205, 1980.

C85 G. Costa. A metric characterization of fair computations in CCS. LNCS 186, pp. 239-251, 1985.

BM87 J.W. deBakker, J.J. Meyer. Order and metric in the stream semantics of elemental concurrency. Acta Informatica, 1987.

DNPY90 Ph. Darondeau, D. Nolte, L. Priese, S. Yoccoz, Fairness, Distances and Degrees, to appear

DM84 P. Degano, U. Montanari. Liveness properties as convergence in metric spaces. STACS 84, pp 31-38, 1984.

M80 R. Milner. A calculus of communicating systems, LNCS 92, 1980.

P88 L. Priese. Fairness. EATCS-Bulletin 35, pp 171-181, 1988.

PN90 L. Priese, D. Nolte. Strong fairness, metric spaces and logical complexity. Reihe Theoretische Informatik, Universität-GH Paderborn, Bericht 65, 1990.

PRW87 L. Priese, R. Rehrmann, Ul Willecke-Klemme. Some results on fairness - the regular case. LNCS 1987.

On Distributed Languages and Models for Distributed Computation

(Extended Abstract)

Brigitte Rozoy
L.R.I. bât. 490
91 405 Orsay Cedex
France

Abstract :

This paper may be seen as proposing a tentative synthesis of various models of parallelism : we establish representation results for three kinds of Models for Distributed Systems, **Labelled Transition Systems, Labelled Event Structures** and **Distributed Languages**. For that purpose, we introduce a new representation model for concurrent systems, the **Distributed Languages**. Based on Words and Equivalence Relations, they are generalizations of the Trace Languages and model the behaviour of any asynchronous concurrent system.

Résumé :

Nous proposons ici une synthèse de plusieurs modèles classiquement utilisés pour la description et l'étude des systèmes distribués, à savoir les modèles à base d'états et de transitions, ceux qui reposent sur des actions et des relations d'ordre partiel, et enfin ceux qui utilisent des mots et des classes d'équivalence de mots. Pour ce faire, nous introduisons un nouveau modèle, celui des langages distribués, qui est une généralisation du monoïde des traces et permet de décrire les exécutions de tout système distribué. Puis nous prouvons des théorèmes de représentation entre des classes bien choisies de systèmes de transitions, de structures d'évènements, et cette nouvelle classe de langages distribués.

The work presented in this paper has been partially carried within the Esprit Basic Research Action "Demon" and the PRC "C³", CNRS.

0 INTRODUCTION

A lot of models are currently used in order to describe the running of distributed systems. When looking accurately at them, we can assert that they more or less belong to one of three general categories : they are based either on states, events, or words.

- State Based Models : At the dawn of parallelism were problems dealing with distribution of tasks and synchronization of machines. Starting with multi-processing organizations, this view of systems has slowly given way to a conception whereby machines only communicate through messages along channels. The methods used for specification and validation of communications protocols has been essentially based on *states and transitions* from states to states. This research method is thus called *Transition Systems* and is to be found in various guises in many writings. As it is particularly adapted to machine description, it has been used in a lot of situations. Such are for example Petri Nets, Finite States Automata, Bounded Channel Networks, Fifo Files, etc... See for example J.Sifakis [27] , A.Arnold-M.Nivat [2-3], [18], or A.Mazurkiewicz [14-15] for transition systems, R.Prinoth [20] and P.Starke [28] for connexions with other models.
- Events Based Models : The second pole to be identified is linked with a series of works which may be grouped under the generic heading of "Partial Order Semantic". This method essentially involves considering that the description of the system running entails taking into accounts events, that is actions occurring more or less independently at various locations, points of a network, nods of a graph, etc... Such events are considered to be partially abstracted from their nature, their origin, and from many other elements which may characterize them; only certain links connecting or separating them are retained. These are mainly causal relation ships : if an event is the consequence of an other one, then it necessarily occurs after it; if, on the other hand, they are totally independent, then no relation can bring them together, and the model must account for this independence. Using Partial Order Sets, the first attempt of "event based" model has probably been performed by L.Lamport [13], and intensively studied since ([5], [6], [8], [9]), whereas the event structure model has been introduced by G.Winskel ([31] [32] [33]). This *Event Structure* model is based on events, seen as occurrences of actions; it emphasizes relationships between these actions, and describe them by two relations, an order and a conflict one. Moreover, event structures arise naturally in the theory of Petri nets and Domains ([21], [22], [17]).
- Words Based Models : The last classical description for the running of such distributed systems is well known under the denomination of the *"interleaving point of view"*. Given an alphabet, its letters can be viewed as the actions associated with a distributed system. A word may be then used to represent a possible firing sequence; thus a language describes the behaviour of the system in

terms of possible sequences of actions that it can exhibit. But, in a distributed environment, the first problem lays in the fact that no one is never able to assert neither that a particular execution has really been performed nor even what is the real meaning of this notion. The second problem has to be found in the feeling that words do not seem to capture independency, causality, non-determinism... Thus the interleaving models, and consequently classical tools on words and formal languages, have been under suspicions for a long time. This contradiction has been partially removed by trace languages, that use a *commutability relation.* Such a commutability relation on the alphabet of actions may be viewed as capturing the causal independence (*concurrency*) of a pair of actions as and when they occur adjacent to each other. Hence with the help of this framework, the tools and techniques of formal language theory can be applied to the study of distributed systems. The pioneering effort in this approach to the study of distributed systems in due to Mazurkiewicz ([14] [15] [16]) who defined a formalism called *Trace Languages* or *Free Partially Commutative Monoid.* This theory is well-developed ([1], [7], [10], [19], [29]). But in a way it may be considered as too restrictive : it models concurrency for independent transactions in a data base but is to weak to express more general problems, such as the "Producer and Consumer" example.

The first aim of this paper is to introduce a new widest word based model, namely *Distributed Languages.* These languages are generalizations of usual trace languages, but are built in order to possibly model the behaviour of any asynchronous distributed system. Then *the second aim* of the paper *is to yield to facts some equivalences between the three point of view* : it may be seen as proposing a tentative synthesis of these various models. Subject to well choose axioms, we will show that they three are equivalent and that we can move freely from one to the other, keeping there major properties.

Finally, we can be briefly outlined as follows the ideas underlying our presentation of models and leading to constructions of equivalence between them :

- We are looking for three equivalent models respectively based on states and transitions, events and order relations, words and equivalence relations.
- The conditions to be placed on the models have to be as less restrictive as possible, in order to give an account for a large family of problems.
- Either the well known classical models have to be restrictions of our three models, or they have at least to be easily deductible from them.
- The basic properties of distributed systems, such as concurrency, non determinism, choice, and so on, have to be explicitly represented.

As a consequence of the two first points, on one hand, formulations, constructions and proofs will be technical and difficult, but on the other hand we can assert that any problem in a distributed asynchronous system may be expressed with the help of such tools.

In order to follow the last point, we will focus on event structures, where the basic properties of distributed systems are clearly expressed through a partial order relation and a conflict relation.

This choice of event structures as reference model is deeply influenced by the strong connexions that they admit with Domains and another special kinds of PoSets[1], the C.P.O. or Completely Coherent Prime Algebraic PoSets. These PoSets have been frequently and intensively used in semantics of languages[2] : they allow to solve fix-point equations and then to provide semantics of recursive constructs. Thus, first starting with an event structure, we will look for construction of states, to get a transition system, and for construction of words, to get a distributed language; moreover, these constructions will have to preserve the well known usual PoSets properties. Second, we will try to recover the event structure from the transition system and the distributed language. Namely we are looking for representation theorems between the three kinds of models. As such representation theorems exists between Event Structures, Petri Nets, Domains and Coherent Prime Algebraic PoSets, we get then a wide picture of the matter.

1 POSETS AND LABELLED EVENT STRUCTURES

In that paragraph, we give the basic definitions regarding PoSets, Labelled Event Structures[3] and their configurations. Latter on, this will allow us to construct a canonical Labelled Transition System[4] associated to a given Labelled Event Structure.

As asserted before, partial order relations have been frequently used in order to provide semantics for languages in sequential systems; we will use them again for distributed systems; in that case, the partial order relation will not capture the sequentiality, but the causality. We shall first recall some *classical definitions and notations regarding PoSets.*

1.0 Definitions regarding PoSets.

Let $(Z, <)$ be a PoSet, u be an element and X be a subset of Z. An *immediate predecessor* of an u is an element v such that $v < u$, $v \neq u$, and for any v', $v < v' < u$ implies $v'=v$ or $v'=u$. We denote it by $v <\!\!\cdot\, u$. The sets $\downarrow X$ and $\uparrow X$ will denote respectively the *past* and the *future* of the set X, that is $\downarrow X = \{z \in Z \mid \exists x \in X : z<x\}$ and $\uparrow X = \{z \in Z \mid \exists x \in X : x<z\}$. If X admits an upper bound in Z, that is if there exists an element z in Z such that $y<z$ for any y in X, X is said to be *bounded, or consistent*. It is said to be *pair-wise bounded*, or *pair-wise consistent* if any pair x, y of elements in X is bounded. If every pair x, y of elements in X admits a bound *in* X, then X is said to be *directed*. If it exists, $\sqcup X$, $\sqcap X$,

[1] PoSet : Partial Order Set.
[2] C.P.O. will be formally described in the next paragraph.
[3] L.E.S. : Labelled Event Structures.
[4] L.T.S. : Labelled Transition System.

will denote the *least upper bound*, respectively the *greatest lower bound* of X. In case X= {x,y}, we will write $x \sqcup y$ and $x \sqcap y$ instead of $\sqcup\{x,y\}$ and $\sqcap\{x,y\}$.

The PoSet (Z, <) is said to be a *Complete Partial Order* (C.P.O.) iff it admits a least element and if every directed subset admits a least upper bound. It is *bounded complete or consistently complete* iff every bounded subset admits a least upper bound. It is said to be *finitely coherent* if every finite pair-wise bounded subset of Z admits a least upper bound[5]. For a C.P.O., some elements may happen to be essential, in the sense that they may allow to reconstruct the whole PoSet starting only from them : such elements are called *compact and prime elements*. An element u is said to be *compact* iff : whenever $X \subset Z$ is directed and $u < \sqcup X$, then u<v for some v in X. An element u is said to be a *prime* iff : whenever $X \subset Z$ is such that $\sqcup X$ exists and $u < \sqcup X$, then u<v for some v in X. For any u in Z, C(u) and PR(u) will denote respectively the set of compact and prime elements bounded by u, whereas C(Z) and PR(Z) will respectively be the set of compact and prime elements of the whole PoSet (Z,<). The PoSet is said to be *algebraic* iff every element u in Z is the least upper bound of C(u). A *Scott-domain* is an algebraic PoSet with a countable set of compact elements. Finally a PoSet is said to be *prime algebraic* iff every element u in Z is the least upper bound of PR(u).

♦

As we restrict our study to observable runnings of distributed systems, thus to finite sets and finite firing sequences, we will be interested in finitary, prime algebraic and finitely coherent posets only, and in their prime elements. This will be done through finitary event structures.

In distributed systems, our purpose is to give an account of concurrency as well as to causality. That will be performed by two binary relations. Basically an *Event Structure Model* is a Partially Ordered Set of event occurrences together with a symmetric and irreflexive *conflict relation*. The partial ordering relation is meant to capture causal dependency. The conflict relation models non-determinism (choice) so that two events that are in conflict cannot both occur in any stretch of behaviour. Consequently two events that are neither ordered nor in conflict may occur concurrently (i.e. with no order). Thus, in an event structure, basic phenomena of a sequence, non-determinism and concurrency, are represented in an explicit and clearly separated fashion. By labelling the events with the actions taken from some alphabet we get *Labelled Event Structures*.

1.1 Definition - Conflict Relations and Event Structures

Let (E, <) be a partially ordered set.

---

[5] Note that we consider only finitary coherence and not complete coherence : we deal here with observable states and events only; that leads to finite subsets and words, and thus to coherence and not complete coherence. An analogous theory for complete coherence needs infinite words or infinite firing sequences; it has been performed in a particular case in [11].

(i) A *conflict relation* on (E, <) is any irreflexive and symmetric relation # that satisfies $\forall$ e, f, g $\in$ E, (e # f and e < g) $\Rightarrow$ (g # f). The conflict will be said to be an *inherited* relation with respect to the order relation <.
(ii) A *labelling function* ℓ from E onto A is a surjective application from a set E on a set A.
(iii) A *Labelled Event Structure* is a 5-uple ES=(E, <, #, ℓ, A), where (E ,<) is a partially ordered set, # is a conflict relation, and ℓ is a labelling function from E onto A. Elements in E are called *events*. The event structure is said to be *finitary* if any element admits a finite past[6].

♦

Note that the fact for two events to be in conflict implies that they do not have a common bound. Otherwise e'#e", e'<e, e"<e would imply e#e, which contradicts the fact that # is irreflexive. A running of such a system is not implicitly included in its formulation. Such a description has to be understood as the whole collection of occurrences of action that may eventually arise under the restriction of partial order (causality) and conflict. We give below an example of an event structure. The events have been settled in order to model a situation where a producer communicates items via an unbounded buffer to a consumer.
The producer can stop after producing zero, one, or more items. Both the producer and the consumer are assumed to work in a sequential fashion.

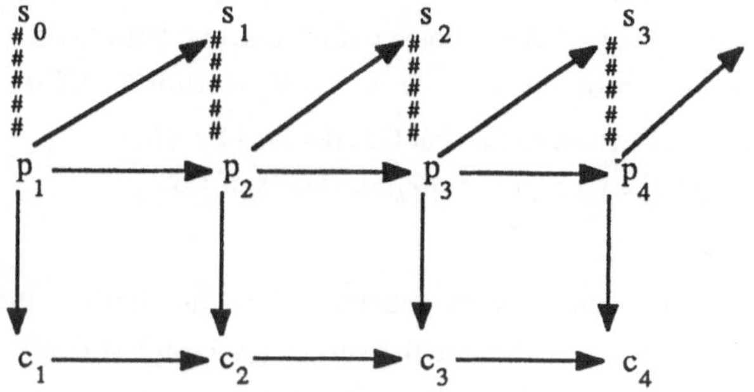

The set of events is $E=\{p_1,p_2,p_3,\ldots,s_0,s_1,s_2,s_3,\ldots,c_1,c_2,c_3,\ldots\}$ where p stands for "produce", c for "consume" and s for "stop". The alphabet of actions is {p,c,s}, with the obvious labelling function $\ell(x_i)=x$. The partial order relation is shown with the help of the corresponding Hass diagram; it is the transitive and reflexive closure of : $\forall i\ p_i<p_{i+1}$, $p_i<c_i$, $p_i<s_i$, $c_i<c_{i+1}$. Finally, the conflict relation is shown with the help of the closure under inheritance (condition (i) in def.1.1) of the minimal conflict relation : $\forall i\ p_{i+1}\#s_i$.
In the figure, we have shown only the minimal elements for the causality relation (as directed arcs) as well as for the conflict relation (as #### lines). Thus $p_1<c_2$ because $p_1<c_1$ and $c_1<c_2$.

---

[6] From now on and unless otherwise stated, every event structure that we encounter will be assumed to be finitary.

Moreover, $s_1\#p_3$ because $s_1\#p_2$ and $p_2<p_3$. The conflict relation may be understood as the fact that two events e' and e" that are in conflict will never occur together in the same execution of the system.
We want now to move from a labelled event structure to a labelled transition system, and for that define a notion that give an account of the states of the distributed system expressed by the event structure. In a lot of formalisms related to distributed algorithms or based on Lamport-like representation, such global states are refereed to as "consistent cuts"; for event structures, the classical notion is that of "*configurations*" : global states are viewed as possible finite subsets of events, called *configurations*. The intuitive idea underlying these configurations is simply that a configuration is a structured collection of events that have been performed; such global states carry the weight of their whole history, and consequently their number is infinite as soon as so is the set of events. Opposite to the high complexity due to this high number of states, the running of the system will be easy to describe : the transitions between global states will simply be defined latter on by the fact that, when performing an event, the system changes its configuration (global state) to another one by adding an event.

1.2 Definition - Configurations

Let $ES=(E,<,\#,\ell,A)$ be a labelled event structure and C be a subset of E. Then:
(i) C is said to be *conflict-free* iff $\# \cap (C\times C)=\emptyset$; C is said to be *left-closed* [7] iff $\downarrow C\subset C$
(ii) A *configuration* is any subset that is both conflict-free and left-closed.
(iii) An event e is said to be *enabled at a configuration* C, iff ($e \notin C$) and ($C\cup\{e\}$ is a configuration). The set of events enabled at C is denoted by $\mathcal{E}(C)$.
(iv) We denote by $\mathcal{C}_{ES}$ *the set of finite configurations* of ES.

♦

For the producer and consumer event structure given just before, the sets $\{p_1\}$, $\{p_1,c_1,s_1\}$, $\{p_i \mid i\in N\}$ are configurations, whereas the subset $\{p_1,c_1,c_2\}$ is conflict-free but not closed in the past, and $\{p_1,p_2,s_1\}$ is left-closed but not conflict-free (conflict between p_2 and s_1). In a partially commutative monoid, for an independency relation $\theta=\{(a,c), (c,a)\}$ on the alphabet $\{a,b,c\}$, the set $\{[a], [c], [acb], [acba], [acbc]\}$ is a configuration, whereas $\{[a], [b], [ab]\}$ is not.
With the subset inclusion as partial order relation, *the PoSet of configurations of an event structure* admits a lot of nice properties, namely it *is a finitary prime algebraic finitely coherent PoSet* ([17], [25]). We will not use them directly, but establish a rather equivalent formulation through associated (infinite) transition systems, that are more convenient to define related distributed languages; however and clearly, the structural properties of these transition systems are the exact translation of the analogous properties on this PoSet of (finite) configurations. To define these

---
[7] or closed into the past.

transition systems, the second task is to look at transitions from one configuration to another; that will be done in setting that "some event has occurred". These transitions satisfy a lot of technical properties, that will later be basic for the definition of our class of transition systems.

1.3 Definition

Let LES= $(E,<,\#,\ell,A)$ be a Labelled Event Structure, and $S=\mathscr{C}(E)$ be its set of finite configurations. The transition relation " $\longrightarrow$ " between configurations is defined in $S{\times}E{\times}S$ by :

$$\forall\ C\ \forall\ C' \in S \quad \forall e \in E \quad (C,e,C') \in \longrightarrow \quad \Leftrightarrow \quad C'=C\cup\{e\} \text{ and } e \notin C$$

♦

With the previous example of producer and consumer, a subset C of events is a configuration iff $C=\emptyset$, or $C=\{s_0\}$ or $\exists\ i,j$: $C=\{p_1...p_j\}$, or $C=\{p_1...p_j,s_j\}$, or $C=\{p_1...p_j,c_1,...c_i\}$, or $C=\{p_1,...p_j,c_1,...c_i,s_j\}$ with $i \leqslant j$ The transitions are of one of the following form : $\emptyset \rightarrow p_1 \rightarrow \{p_1\}$, $\emptyset \rightarrow s_0 \rightarrow \{s_0\}$, $\{p_1...p_j\} \rightarrow p_{j+1} \rightarrow \{p_1...p_{j+1}\}$, $\{p_1...p_j\} \rightarrow c_1 \rightarrow \{p_1...p_j,c_1\}$, $\{p_1...p_j\} \rightarrow s_j \rightarrow \{p_1...p_j,s_j\}$, $\{p_1...p_j,s_j\} \rightarrow c_1 \rightarrow \{p_1...p_j,s_j,c_1\}$, $\{p_1,...p_j,c_1,...c_i\} \rightarrow p_{j+1} \rightarrow \{p_1...p_j,p_{j+1},c_1,...c_i\}$, $\{p_1,...p_j,c_1,...c_i\} \rightarrow s_j \rightarrow \{p_1...p_j,s_j,c_1,...c_i\}$, $\{p_1,...p_j,c_1,...c_i\} \rightarrow c_{i+1} \rightarrow \{p_1...p_j,c_1,...c_i,c_{i+1}\}$ if $i<j$, $\{p_1,...p_j,c_1,...c_i,s_j\} \rightarrow c_{i+1} \rightarrow \{p_1,...p_j,c_1,...c_i,s_j\}$ if $i<j$. As settled before, this transition relation between configurations will be shown to satisfy a family of properties that we will examined now. Technically, they express the fact that we will require $(S, \longrightarrow^*)$ to be a prime algebraic finitely coherent PoSet and they derive in a rather straightforward way from properties of set inclusion. Latter on, they will turn to be necessary and sufficient conditions that allow the recovering of an event structure starting with a transition system. Intuitively, they may be paraphrased and interpreted as follows : first of all, the property $\mathscr{CS}_0$ expresses the fact that the transition relation between configurations has to admit a reflexive and transitive closure which is an order relation, in order to recover the PoSet $(E,<)$. Property $\mathscr{CS}_1$ limits the set of global states to the set of reachable ones. Property $\mathscr{CS}_2$ expresses some kind of determinism[8]. Properties $\mathscr{CS}_3$ and $\mathscr{CS}_4$ are often refereed to as the forward and the backward diamond properties[9]. They expresses concurrency by setting that, if two actions such as a', a" are concurrent and enabled at a state s, then s may immediately and equivalently be followed by a' then by a", or by a" then by a'; moreover, the resulting state s.a'.a"≈ s.a".a' is necessarily contained in the past of any system having performed these actions. Finally, the last property $\mathscr{CS}_5$ is a kind of generalisation of $\mathscr{CS}_3$ to several concurrent actions.

---

[8] The strong determinism expressed by this property may more or less be removed. See [24] for the details.

[9] As it is done by A. Mazurkiewicz, who has defined them in his first papers on traces.

1.4 Lemma and Axioms $\mathfrak{C}\mathcal{S}$.

Let LES= (E,<, #, ℓ, A) be a Labelled Event Structure, S= $\mathcal{C}$(E) be its set of finite configurations, and "$\longrightarrow$" be the transition relation between configurations defined in 1.3. Then the following properties are satisfied :[10]

$\mathfrak{C}\mathcal{S}_0$: The relation $\xrightarrow{+}$ in $Sx(A)^+xS$ is acyclic : $\forall$ s,s' $\in$ S $(s \xrightarrow{+} s' \Rightarrow s \neq s')$

$\mathfrak{C}\mathcal{S}_1$: $S = \uparrow s_0$

$\mathfrak{C}\mathcal{S}_2$: $\forall$ s, s', s" $\in$ S $\forall$ a, b $\in$ A, $(s \xrightarrow{a} s'$ and $s \xrightarrow{b} s") \Rightarrow (a=b \Leftrightarrow s'=s")$

$\mathfrak{C}\mathcal{S}_3$: $\forall$ s, s_1, s_2 $\in$ S , $\forall$ a_1, a_2 $\in$ A,
$(s \xrightarrow{a_1} s_1$, $s \xrightarrow{a_2} s_2$, $s_1 \neq s_2$ and $\exists$ s $s_i \xrightarrow{*} s$ (i=1,2) $\Rightarrow$ ($\exists$ $s'=s_1 \sqcup s_2$ and $s_1 \xrightarrow{a_2} s'$, $s_1 \xrightarrow{a_1} s'$).

$\mathfrak{C}\mathcal{S}_4$ $\forall$ s , s_1, s_2 $\in$ S , $\forall$ a_1, a_2 $\in$ A , $(s_1 \xrightarrow{a_1} s$, $s_2 \xrightarrow{a_2} s$, $s_1 \neq s_2$) $\Rightarrow$ ($\exists$ $s'=s_1 s_2$ and $s' \xrightarrow{a_1} s_2$, $s' \xrightarrow{a_2} s_1$)

$\mathfrak{C}\mathcal{S}_5$: $\forall n \in \mathbb{N}$, $\forall s \in S$, $\forall$ $s_1, s_2, \ldots, s_n \in S$, $\forall a_1, a_2, \ldots, a_n \in A$, ($\forall$ i $s \xrightarrow{a_i} s_i$ and $\forall$ i, j $\exists$ s_{ij} (k=i,j) $s_k \xrightarrow{*} s_{ij}$ $\Rightarrow$ $\exists$s $\forall$ i $s_i \xrightarrow{*} s$)

The properties $\mathfrak{C}\mathcal{S}_0$, $\mathfrak{C}\mathcal{S}_1$, $\mathfrak{C}\mathcal{S}_2$, $\mathfrak{C}\mathcal{S}_3$, $\mathfrak{C}\mathcal{S}_4$, $\mathfrak{C}\mathcal{S}_5$, are referred to as "$\mathfrak{C}\mathcal{S}$ axioms"

♦

The transition relation between configurations define what we will call a transition system, and the properties that we will generally require on transition systems will be exactly these previous one. Let us now start with a transition system satisfying these properties ("$\mathfrak{C}\mathcal{S}$ axioms") and try to reconstruct a labelled event structure.

2 DISTRIBUTED LABELLED TRANSITION SYSTEMS

In order to model distributed systems, the second possibility is classically performed by **Transition Systems**, where basic elements are states and transitions from one state to another. First we give a general definition for transition systems; it will be strengthened latter on.

---

10 For a relation $\longrightarrow$ in SxAxS, $\longrightarrow^+$ and $\longrightarrow^*$ will denote respectively a kind of irreflexixe-transitive and reflexive-transitive closure of $\longrightarrow$. They are defined inductively on (SxA^+xS) and (SxA^*xS), starting with $s \xrightarrow{a} s' \Leftrightarrow (s,a,s') \in \longrightarrow$, or $s \xrightarrow{\varepsilon} s' \Leftrightarrow s=s'$, and $s \xrightarrow{wa} s' \Leftrightarrow s \xrightarrow{w} s"$ and $s" \xrightarrow{a} s'$.

2.1 Definition

A *Labelled Transition System* is a 6-uple TS= (S, A', s_0 , ⟶, ℓ, A), where S, A, A' are sets, ⟶ is a subset of SxA'xS, s_0 is an element of S, ℓ is a surjective application from A' onto A.

♦

The sets S, A', A are referred to respectively as the set of states (S), the alphabet of transitions (A'), and the alphabet of actions (A). The subset "⟶ " of SxA'xS is called set of transitions, s_0 is the initial state, and ℓ the labelling function. A running of such a system is classically understood as a sequence $(s_0, a_1, s_1), (s_1, a_2, s_2), \ldots, (s_{n-1}, a_n, s_n)$ of transitions, starting in the initial state.

In order to be associated to distributed computations, those systems often satisfy various axioms, depending on the considered problem. As our aim is the equivalence between event structures and transition systems, we will choose the "$\mathfrak{C}\mathcal{S}$ axioms" defined in 1.4. They have already been interpreted above.

2.2 Definition : Distributed Labelled Transition System.

A *Distributed Labelled Transition System* is a labelled transition system TS= (S, A', s_0 , ⟶, ℓ, A) satisfying the "$\mathfrak{C}\mathcal{S}$ axioms" defined in 1.4 .

♦

By lemma 1.4, it is obvious that the construction of the first paragraph, starting with an event structure, leads to such a distributed labelled transition system.

2.3 Definition : function Δ.

Let LES=(E,<, #, ℓ, A) be a Labelled Event Structure, S= $\mathfrak{C}$(E) be the set of its finite configurations, ⟶ be the transition relation between configuration (def. 1.3). Then the *Distributed Labelled Transition System associated to LES* is defined as

$$\Delta(\text{LES}) = (S, E, \longrightarrow, \emptyset, \ell, A)$$

♦

With again our example of producer and consumer, we get a transition system where the set of states and the transitions have been described above; the alphabet of actions is A= {p, c, s}, and the labelling function ℓ satisfies : $\forall i$ $\ell(c_i)=c$, $\ell(p_i)=p$, $\ell(s_i)=s$.

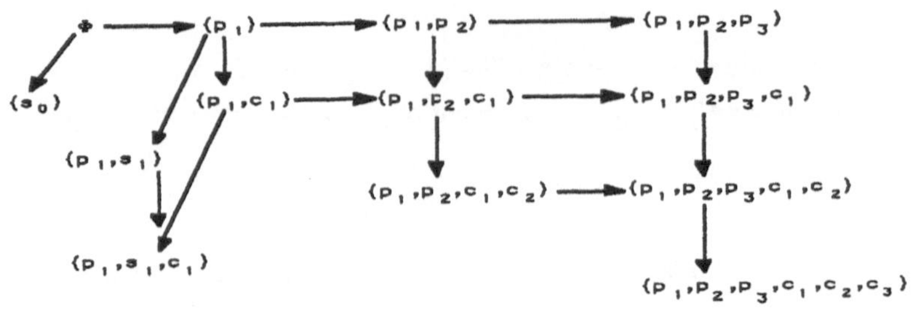

As our purpose is always the equivalence between the models, we have now to move in the other direction : from transition systems to event structures. It will be a little bit difficult, but the problem of recovering an event structure from its domains of configurations is a rather classical one[11]. The construction settled here can be viewed as one adaptation of this general setting in a slightly distinct axiomatization.

The problem lies in the determination of "events". Let us look again at the producer and consumer example. Two distinct transitions such that $\{p_1,p_2,c_1\} \rightarrow p_3 \rightarrow \{p_1,p_2,p_3,c_1\}$ and $\{p_1,p_2,c_1,c_2\} \rightarrow p_3 \rightarrow \{p_1,p_2,p_3,c_1,c_2\}$ have clearly to be interpreted as the third production and thus to be associated to the same "event" p_3 : this production is clearly "independent" of the consumptions. To express such an idea, we will first gather in a single equivalence class these two transitions together with the transition $\{p_1,p_2\} \rightarrow p_3 \rightarrow \{p_1,p_2,p_3\}$; second, we will choose for each class some canonical element, which will lead to the corresponding event. That is performed through the following notion of equivalence of transitions and that of prime elements (def. 1.0). We set here a quick construction without proof, but it is really a tricky and rather hard work to be done. Its complete description may be found in [24]. First, we consider the PoSet $(S, \longrightarrow^*)$ associated to a distributed labelled transition systems : its prime elements may be characterized with the help of immediate predecessors; this technical and difficult key point is settled down in the following lemma, and leads to the required properties of finitary prime algebraicity and finitely coherence for the PoSet $(S, \longrightarrow^*)$.

2.4 Lemma.

Let LES= $(S, A', \longrightarrow, s_0, \ell, A)$ be a Distributed Labelled Transition System and $\longrightarrow^*$ be the order relation[12] defined as the transitive and reflexive closure of the transition relation $\longrightarrow$. Then the set of prime elements for $(S, \longrightarrow^*)$ is the subset of elements of S that admits exactly

[11] The ideas of such construction have already been achieved in a different way by Winskel for trees, and by Nielsen, Plotkin and Winskel, who have shown how to recover an Event Structure from its domain of configurations.

[12] The fact for $\longrightarrow^*$ to be an order relation derives in a straightforward way from lemma 1.4.

one immediate predecessor for the order relation, and $(S, \longrightarrow^*)$ is a finitary prime algebraic and finitely coherent PoSet.

♦

As a consequence of this lemma, we may associate to a prime element p a single immediate predecessor p'= pred(p) in S and a single letter der(p)= a in A', such that (p', a, p) is a transition. Thus the application der is well defined on the set PR(S) of prime elements, and will be used as a labelling function latter on.

2.4 Definitions : Equivalence between transitions.

Let LES= $(S, A', \longrightarrow, s_0, \ell, A)$ be a Distributed Labelled Transition System. For any prime element p of $(S, \longrightarrow^*)$, denote by der(p) the single letter a of A' such that (p', a, p) belongs to $\longrightarrow$. The binary relations « and ≡ are defined on the set $\longrightarrow$ of transitions by (s, a, s') « (t, a, t') iff s=ts' and t'=t⊔ s', and ≡ is the reflexive and transitive closure of (« ∪ »).

♦

With our famous producer and consumer example, we get $(\{p_1,p_2\}, p_3, \{p_1,p_2,p_3\})$ « $(\{p_1,p_2,c_1\}, p_3, \{p_1,p_2,p_3,c_1\})$ « $(\{p_1,p_2,c_1,c_2\}, p_3, \{p_1, p_2,p_3,c_1,c_2\})$, and the relation ≡ is equal to (« ∪ »). In general, the relation « is an order relation among transitions, and ≡ is an equivalence. As suggested before, an event may be interpreted as an equivalence class for ≡, as is for example p_3 in previous case. Moreover, it may be proved that any equivalence class admits a least element (p', a, p) for the order «, and that p is a prime element. As the prime elements are convenient objects for the description of the PoSet $(S, \longrightarrow^*)$, due to its prime algebraicity, we shall identify any equivalence class with the single prime corresponding to its least element.

2.5 Lemma

Let LES= $(S, A', \longrightarrow, s_0, \ell, A)$ be a Distributed Labelled Transition System, and $\mathcal{C}$ be a class for ≡. Then $\mathcal{C}$ admits a least element (p', a, p) for « and p is a prime. Moreover (p', a, p) is the single transition of the class with p as prime. Conversly, for any prime element p, there exists a single class $\mathcal{C}$ such that (p', a, p) belongs to $\mathcal{C}$, and is moreover its least element.

♦

This characterisation of prime elements leads to the construction of the event structure associated to the transition system : the event will be exactly the prime elements, whereas the order and the conflict relations derive directly from the transition relation $\longrightarrow$.

2.6 Lemma

Let LTS=(S, A', ⟶, s_0, ℓ, A) be a distributed labelled transition system. Set E= PR(S) and define a relation < in ExE as the restriction to E of the order $\longrightarrow^*$ in SxS. Define a relation # in E×E by setting e" # e' ⇔ ∀e ∈ S not(e'$\longrightarrow^*$e and e$\longrightarrow^*$e). Last define a function ℓ" : E ⟶ A as ℓ"=ℓ∘<u>der</u>, where <u>der</u> is the function defined in 2.4. Then (E,<) is a finitary PoSet, # is a conflict relation on (E, <), and ℓ" is a labelling function from E onto A.

♦

As a consequence of this lemma, we get that (PR(S), <, #, ℓ", A) is a Labelled Event Structure, which will be canonically associated to the original labelled transition system.

2.7 Definition : function ∇.

Let LTS=(S, A', ⟶, s_0, ℓ, A) be a distributed labelled transition system; define the relations <, # and the function ℓ" as in 2.6. Then the *Labelled Event Structure associated to LTS* is defined as

$$\nabla(LTS)= (E, <, \#, \ell", A)$$

♦

In previous example, the event structure associated to Δ("Producer and Consumer") is exactly the original model. Let now LTS= (S, A, ⟶, s_0, Id, A) be the labelled transition system pictured below, with S={o, p, q, r, s, t, u, v, w, x, y, z}, A={e, f, g, h} and the customary graphical conventions; the transitions are given by : (o,e,v), (o,f,y), (o,g,u), (o,h,p), (p,g,t), (q,g,r), u,h,t), (t,h,r), (p,h,q), (r,h,s), (y,g,x), (u,f,x), (y,e,w), (v,f,w), (w,f,z)

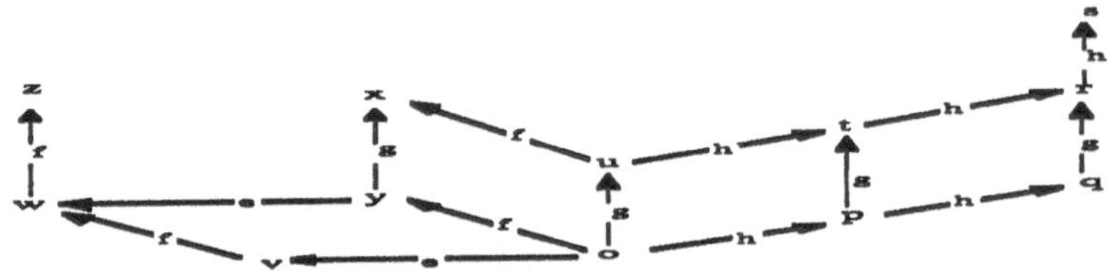

LTS

Its image by ∇ is the labelled event structure LES= (E, <, #, ℓ", A), where E={p, q, s, u, v, y, z }, ℓ"(p)= ℓ"(q)= ℓ"(s)= h, ℓ"(u)=g, ℓ"(v)=e, ℓ"(y)= ℓ"(z)=f, the order relation is given by v<z, y<z, p<q<s, u<s, and the conflict one by {v,z} # {p,u,q,s} and y # {p,q,s}.

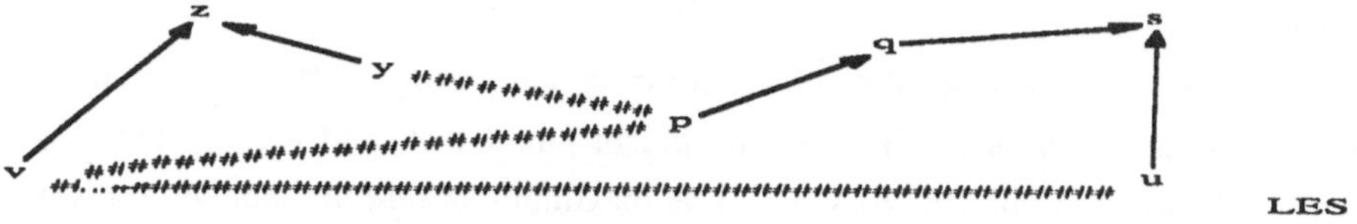

The notable result in that construction is that Δ **does not deteriorate anything inside the set of finite configurations** and that ∇ eventually creates new names for transitions, but **preserves the set of states, the structures of the set of transitions, and the alphabet of actions.** We get that $\nabla c \Delta$ is an isomorphism between labelled event structures. This notion will be defined formally below, in order to express the natural idea that two event structures are isomorphic iff there exist bijective mappings between their sets of events and their alphabets, that preserve the order, the conflict, and the labelling. The situation is slightly different for $\Delta o \nabla$, the reason being that the mapping Δ get rise to an intermediary set of events, PR(S), which was not placed in a prominent position through the initial system. The result will be a set of names of transitions in general largest that the initial one, though the projections on the set of actions, remain without alteration. We get that the image of a labelled transition system by $\nabla o \Delta$ is the largest labelled transition system that preserves the structure and that can be associated to the original one. Again we define below formally these ideas with the help of a semi-order relation on the family of transition systems. This semi-order put in formal words the following considerations : up to a renaming, the set of states and actions remain without alteration, the alphabet A' of names of transitions of the largest system is larger than that of the smallest one, and the transition relation of the largest system derives in a straightforward way from the transition relation of the smallest one.

2.8 Definition.

Two labelled event structures $(E,<,\#,\ell,A)$ and $(E',<',\#',\ell',A')$ are said to be *isomorphic* if there exist two bijective mappings $f{:}E \longrightarrow E'$ and $\alpha{:}A \longrightarrow A'$ such that $\ell' o f = \alpha o \ell$, $e<e' \Leftrightarrow f(e)<'f(e')$, and $e\#e' \Leftrightarrow f(e)\#'f(e')$.

Let $LTS_1=(S_1, A'_1, \longrightarrow^1, s_1, \ell_1, A_1)$ and $LTS_2=(S_2, A'_2, \longrightarrow^2, s_2, \ell_2, A_2)$ be two labelled transition systems. We will say that *LTS_1 is smaller than LTS_2*, denoted by $LTS_1 \ll LTS_2$, if there exist bijective mappings : $f : S_2 \longrightarrow S_1$, $\Pi : A_2 \longrightarrow A_1$, and a surjective mapping : $\Pi' : A'_2 \longrightarrow A'_1$, such that : (i) $f(s_2)=s_1$ (ii) $\ell_1 o \Pi' = \Pi o \ell_2$ (iii) $\forall s, s' \in S_2$, $\forall a'_2 \in A'_2$, $(s,a'_2,s') \in \longrightarrow^2 \ \Rightarrow \ (f(s),\Pi'(a'_2),f(s')) \in \longrightarrow^1$ (iv) $\forall s, s' \in S_1$, $\forall a'_1 \in A'_1$, $(s,a'_1,s') \in \longrightarrow^1 \ \Rightarrow \exists a'_2 \in \Pi'^{1}(a'_1) : (f^{-1}(s),a'_2,f^{-1}(s')) \ \in \ \longrightarrow^2$

♦

2.8 Theorem [13]

Let $\mathcal{LCS}$ be the family of labelled transition systems and $\mathcal{LES}$ be the family of finitary event structures. Then $\nabla \circ \Delta$ is an isomorphism on $\mathcal{LES}$, and for any labelled transition system, up to an isomorphism, $\Delta \circ \nabla$(LTS) is maximum among the labelled transition systems that bound LTS.

♦

Thus we have been able to closely link distributed transition systems and labelled event structure by representation results. Our purpose now is to deal with words : for Petri nets, the natural idea is to study the language of firing sequences; when starting with transitions systems, this will turn to the study of paths from one state to another. Following that idea, the purpose of the following paragraph is to axiomatize languages deriving from a distributed transition systems.

3 DISTRIBUTED LANGUAGES

The idea behind a language for expressing concurrent behaviours is : if two actions a and b act concurrently, then sequences such that a.b and b.a are equivalent. The trace monoid was constructed in that way, starting with a relation defined on the alphabet. But, as mentioned earlier, it may be considered as too restrictive, being unable to express the immutable "Producer and Consumer" example ! Consider a processor that is able to produce an unbounded number of items, and then to stop, whereas another processor consummates these items. As they act independently, the only constraint is that an item cannot be consummated before being produced : we have to deal with the context where they act. For symbolizing this problem, we make use of letters "p", "c" and "s", which respectively stands for "produce", "consume" and "stop". The idea that we want to traduce is at least that two words are equivalent if they both are associated to the same possible execution of the system; this at least required that they both belong or not to the associated language in $\{p,c,s\}^*$:

$$L = \{ w \mid |w|_s \leq 1 \quad w_i = s \Rightarrow \forall j > i \quad w_j = c, \qquad \forall w' \subset w \quad |w'|_p \geqslant |w'|_c \}$$

For example "p.c.p.s.c" and "p.p.c.s.c" are equivalent, whereas "p.c.p.s.c" and "c.p.p.s.c" are not ! The letters "p" and "c" eventually commute, but not in every context.

We are looking for **some commutation relation $\approx$ on the whole set A***, relation that possibly **depends on the context.** Moreover, we want to built with it a model such that $A^*/\approx$

[13]An analogous result in a restricted case can be found in a [25] .

will get the structure of a prime algebraic coherent PoSet w.r.t. the prefix relation, as it is the case for the trace monoids, and more generally for the set of firing sequences constructed with event structures. Thus the first task is to precise ad-hoc axioms that have to satisfy such equivalence relations . We give them just below : they have been clearly built in order to fit with the axioms $\mathfrak{C}\mathcal{S}$ (lemma 1.4) of distributed labelled transition systems. Thus the intuition underlying them is a direct translation of that given for transition systems; for $\mathcal{D}_0$, $\mathcal{D}_1$, $\mathcal{D}_2$, the equivalence relation fit well with the right concatenation; for $\mathcal{D}_3$, $\mathcal{D}_4$, if two actions such that a', a" are concurrent in the context w, that is after the prefix w, then w.a'.a" is equivalent to w.a".a', as were for example p.c.p.<u>c.p</u> and p.c.p.<u>p.c</u> in the producer and consumer example; this is nothing else that the diamond properties. Their interpretations and technical justifications will become clear later, through the representation theorems.

3.1 Axioms $\mathcal{D}(A,\approx)$ [14]

Let A be a finite alphabet, $\approx$ be an equivalence relation on A^*, and define the *"concurrency axioms"* for equivalence relations as follows :

<u>Axiom $\mathcal{D}_0$</u> : $\forall$ w', w" $\in A^*$, $\forall$ a $\in$ A   w'$\approx$w" $\Rightarrow$ w'a$\approx$w"a

<u>Axiom $\mathcal{D}_1$</u> : $\forall$ w $\in A^*$ w$\approx\varepsilon$ $\Rightarrow$ w$=\varepsilon$

<u>Axiom $\mathcal{D}_2$</u> : $\forall$ w',w" $\in A^*$, $\forall$ a',a" $\in$ A (w'a'$\approx$w"a") $\Rightarrow$ (a'=a" $\Leftrightarrow$ w'$\approx$w")

<u>Axiom $\mathcal{D}_3$</u> : $\forall$ w,w',w" $\in A^*$, $\forall$ a',a" $\in$ A

(w'$\approx$wa', w"$\approx$wa" and $\exists$ t', t" $\in A^*$: w't'$\approx$w"t") $\Rightarrow$ w'a"$\approx$w"a'

<u>Axiom $\mathcal{D}_4$</u> : $\forall$ w',w" $\in A^*$, $\forall$ a',a" $\in$ A

(a'$\neq$a" and w'a'$\approx$w"a") $\Rightarrow$ ($\exists$ w $\in A^*$: wa"$\approx$w' and wa'$\approx$w")

<u>Axiom $\mathcal{D}_5$</u> : $\forall$ $w_1 \dots w_n \in A^*$ $\forall$ $a_1,\dots,a_n$ in A ($a_i \neq a_j$) $\forall$ w' $\in A^*$

($\forall$i $w_i \approx w'a_i$ and $\forall$i $\forall$j $\exists w_{ij}$ $\exists x_{ij}$ $\exists x_{ji}$: $[w_{ij}] = [w_i][x_{ij}] = [w_j][x_{ji}]$)

$\Rightarrow$ ($\exists$ w $\in A^*$: $[w] = \sqcup \{ [w_i] \mid i=1\dots n \}$)

♦

3.2 Definitions

A *Distributed Equivalence Relation* is an equivalence relation satisfying axioms $\mathcal{D}_0$ to $\mathcal{D}_5$, and a *Distributed Congruence* is a distributed equivalence relation that is a congruence.

A *Distributed Language* L is any subset of $A^*/\approx$, the quotient of A^* by a distributed equivalence relation.

A *Distributed Monoid* is the quotient of the free monoid A^* by a distributed congruence.

♦

[14] For a word w, [w] is the equivalence class of w for $\approx$. The symbol of least upper bound $\sqcup$ in axiom $\mathcal{D}_5$ is justified by the fact that axioms $\mathcal{D}_0$ to $\mathcal{D}_4$ implies that the prefix relation (defined by : $[w]<[w'] \Leftrightarrow \exists$ x : $[wx]=[w']$) is an order relation.

The first notable example is again the previous "Producer and Consumer" model. There, the equivalence relation $\approx$ is the congruence generated by $w.x.y \approx w.y.x$ iff ($x=c$, $y=p$, and $|w|_p > |w|_c$). The second well known example is the Trace Monoid, which is defined with a congruence generated by a commutativity relation on the alphabet A. The third one is the language of executions of a distributed network of communicating machines, that is to say equivalence classes of firing sequences (see [23], [24], where we called it "histories").

We have now to account for these definition, by proving representation theorems with both the Event Structures and the Transition Systems.[15]

First, when starting from a distributed labelled transition system $(S, A', \longrightarrow, s_0, \ell, A)$, the idea is to define and study the language of firing sequences, that is the language of paths from one state to another. Let s be a state and w be some word (path) such that $s_0 \rightarrow^{w} \rightarrow s$. As axiom $\mathfrak{C}\mathcal{S}_2$ is satisfied, we can assert that, when starting from s_0 with w, we obtain a single state, s : the natural idea is to associated to this "s" the whole set of words w such that $s_0 \rightarrow^{w} \rightarrow s$; in that way, we would get a partition of A'^*, and therefore an equivalence relation. For example, with $S = \{s_0, s_1, s_2, s_3, s_4, s_5, s_6, s_7\}$ and the transitions $\{(s_0,b,s_1), (s_1,b,s_2), (s_3,b,s_4), (s_4,b,s_5), (s_2,c,s_5), (s_1,c,s_4), (s_0,c,s_3), (s_6,c,s_7), (s_2,a,s_6), (s_5,a,s_7)\}$, the set {bbac, bbca, bcba, cbba} will be associated to state s_7. Unfortunately this is not always suitable : the set A' is very often an infinite one, and can not be viewed as an alphabet ! Thus we will project any w of A'^* on A^* : we dwell here on the part held by the labelling function $\ell : A' \longrightarrow A$, and require this function to satisfy well choose constraints, in order to retain equivalence relation's properties. The following considerations are devoted to this task.

3.3 Definitions

The labelling function ℓ is said to be *finite* if so is the set A , and *nice* if :

$$\forall s, s', s'' \in S \quad s' \neq s''$$
$$(\exists e' \exists e'' \in A : \quad (s,e',s') \in \longrightarrow \quad \text{and} \quad (s,e'',s'') \in \longrightarrow) \quad \Rightarrow \quad \ell(e') \neq \ell(e'')$$

$\mathcal{L}\mathfrak{C}\mathcal{S}_a$ will denote the class of distributed labelled transition system provided with a nice and finite labelling function.

♦

We will see latter that distributed labelled transition system provided with a nice and finite labelling function will give rise to distributed languages. Conversly, the problem of finding a distributed labelled transition system canonically associated to any distributed language may be done in a rather straightforward way. Let $\approx$ be a distributed equivalence relation and L be a distributed language. Then the prefix relation $[w]<[w'] \Leftrightarrow \exists x : [w.x]=[w']$ is an order relation; we will

---

[15] For a restricted case, the relationship between trace languages and event structures has first been observed in [25] and [26]. The prime algebraicity of trace posets has also been noted in [29].

denote by Pref(L) the set $\{[w] \mid \exists\, w' \in L : [w]<[w']\}$ and use it to construct the distributed labelled transition system associated to L.

3.4 Proposition

Let L be a distributed language, set S=Pref(L), A'=A , $\ell=Id_A$, $s_0=[\varepsilon]$ and $\longrightarrow = \{([w], a, [wa]) \mid a \in A, ([w], [wa]) \in S\times S\}$. Then (S, A,$\longrightarrow$, $[\varepsilon]$, Id, A) is a distributed labelled transition system, provided with a finite and nice labelling.

♦

As a direct consequence of lemma 2.4, we obtain in particular that (Pref(L), $\longrightarrow^*$) is a finitary prime algebraic and finitely coherent PoSet. Conversely, we have to associate distributed languages to any distributed labelled transition systems. As suggested before, we will do it only for transition system provided with a finite and nice labelling.

3.5 Lemma

Set $\forall s \in S$ $W(s)=\{w \in A^* \mid \exists\, w' \in A'^* : \ell(w')=w$ and $s_0 \xrightarrow{w'} s\}$. If the labelling function ℓ is nice, then we get : $s\neq s' \Rightarrow W(s)\cap W(s')=\emptyset$.

♦

3.6 Proposition

Let LTS=(S, A', $\longrightarrow$, s_0, ℓ, A) be in $\mathcal{LCS}_a$ and define the equivalence relation $\approx$ on A^* by : $w'\approx w''$ iff ($w'=w''$ or $\exists\, s \in S$: $\{w', w''\}\subset W(s)$). Then $\approx$ is a distributed equivalence relation. Moreover, $\{[w] \mid \exists\, s \in S : w \in W(s)\}$ is a distributed language ordered by the prefix relation and, when viewed as PoSet, isomorphic to S, the set of states.

♦

The question of course is : what can be done for distributed labelled transition systems (S, A', $\longrightarrow$, s_0, ℓ, A)that are not in $\mathcal{LCS}_a$ (not provided with a finite and nice labelling) ? As axioms for transition systems and major properties do not depend on the labelling function ℓ nor on the alphabet A , one hope is to find some other finite alphabet A" and a nice labelling function, such that (S, A',$\longrightarrow$,s_0, ℓ', A") will be in $\mathcal{LCS}_a$; clearly, it will not be possible if the number of immediate successors of the states is not bounded. In other cases and till now, only the following partial result holds :

3.7 Lemma

Let us call *degree* of the transition system the maximum of $\{card(s^\bullet) \mid s \in S\}$, where $s^\bullet = \{s' \in S \mid \exists\, a' \in A' : (s,a',s') \in \longrightarrow\}$. Then, if the system degree is equal to 2, there exists a nice and finite labelling function $\ell : A' \longrightarrow A$, such that card(A)=2 ; moreover, the construction of the labelling function can be effectively performed.[16]

♦

Thus we are able to move forth and back between a restricted class of transition systems and our distributed languages. Clearly the passage from a transition system to a distributed language loose the events A', but nothing from the alphabet of actions A, whereas the converse does not forget anything from an original prefix closed language. Let us finally summarize all these constructions in the following definitions and representation results.

3.8 Definition : function Γ and Φ.

Let LTS be in the family $\mathcal{LTS}_a$ of labelled transition systems provided with a finite and nice labelling function, and L be in the family $\mathcal{PDL}$ of distributed languages. Then Γ(LTS) is defined in $\mathcal{PDL}$ as in proposition 3.6 and Φ(L) is defined in $\mathcal{LTS}_a$ as in proposition 3.4.

♦

4 REPRESENTATION RESULTS

4.1 Theorem

Let $\mathcal{PDL}$ denote the class of Prefix Closed Distributed Languages and $\mathcal{LTS}_a$ the class of Distributed Labelled Transition Systems provided with a nice and finite labelling function.
Then $\Gamma \circ \Phi$ is the identity on $\mathcal{PDL}$, and $\Phi \circ \Gamma$ is an isomorphism on $\mathcal{LTS}_a$.

♦

If we want now to express the whole family of connexions between event structures, transition systems and distributed languages, we have to use representation theorem 2.8, and to consider the restriction made on the family of labelled transition systems through the labelling. Coming back to the beginning, we carry easily this labelling restriction on event structures, and obtain the following definitions and technical notions :

---

[16] Following this result, its seems natural to conjecture similar one for other degrees. It is indeed not true as soon as the degree equal 3 : a counter example due to Brochet shows that we may need at least 4 letters. Thus another conjecture is the existence of some finite nice labelling for any system of finite degree, but the question is really hard, and is actually studied in Lyon by Assous, Charreton, Pouzet. See [4, 24, 25]. H.J. Hoogeboom and G.Rozenberg, in Leiden, have also considered a restricted case of such a similar labelling problem.

4.2 Definition

Let $(E,<,\#,\ell,A)$ be a labelled event structure. The *concurrency* relation **co** is defined on ExE as the complementary of both conflict and order relation :

$$e' \text{ co } e'' \Leftrightarrow \text{not } (e'<e'' \text{ or } e''<e' \text{ or } e'\#e'')$$

The *immediate conflict* relation $\#_\mu$ is defined by :

$$e' \#_\mu e'' \Leftrightarrow e'\#e'' \text{ and } (\forall e<e' \;\; e \# e'' \Rightarrow e=e') \text{ and } (\forall e<e'' \;\; e \# e' \Rightarrow e=e'')$$

The *degree* of the event structure is defined as :

$$\text{Max}\{\text{card}(E') \mid E'\subset E \text{ and } \forall e',e'' \in E' \;\; e' \text{ co } e'' \text{ or } e' \#_\mu e''\}$$

♦

The conformity of the two degrees notions respectively on event structures and transition systems is correct, as settled in the next lemma :

4.3 Lemma

Let LES and LTS be respectively a labelled event structure and a distributed labelled transition system. Then degree(LTS)=degree(Δ(LTS)) and degree(LES)=degree(∇(LES)).

♦

Thus we may carry the restrictions of labelling functions from transition systems to event structures and vice versa.

4.4 Definition

Let LES= $(E,<,\#,\ell,A)$ be a labelled event structure. The labelling function ℓ is said to be *finite and nice* if A is finite and if ℓ satisfies :

$$\forall e',e'' \in E \;\; (e' \text{ co } e'' \text{ or } e' \#_\mu e'') \Rightarrow \ell(e') \neq \ell(e'')$$

$\mathcal{LES}_a$ will denote the class of finitary labelled event structure provided with a nice and finite labelling function.

♦

Due to lemma 4.3, it clear that the mappings Δ and ∇ between labelled transition systems and labelled event structures preserve the finite and nice labelling properties : under previous hypothesis, $\Delta(\mathcal{LTS}a)\subset \mathcal{LES}a$ and $\nabla(\mathcal{LES}a)\subset \mathcal{LTS}a$. We are now able to jump over transition systems, and obtain the following required representation result.

4.5 Theorem

Let $\mathcal{PDL}$ denotes the class of Prefix Closed Distributed Languages and $\mathcal{LES}_a$ the class of Finitary Labelled Event Structures provided with a nice and finite labelling function. Then $\nabla\circ\Phi\circ\Gamma\circ\Delta$ and $\Gamma\circ\Delta\circ\nabla\circ\Phi$ are isomorphisms on $\mathcal{LES}_a$ and $\mathcal{PDL}$ respectively.

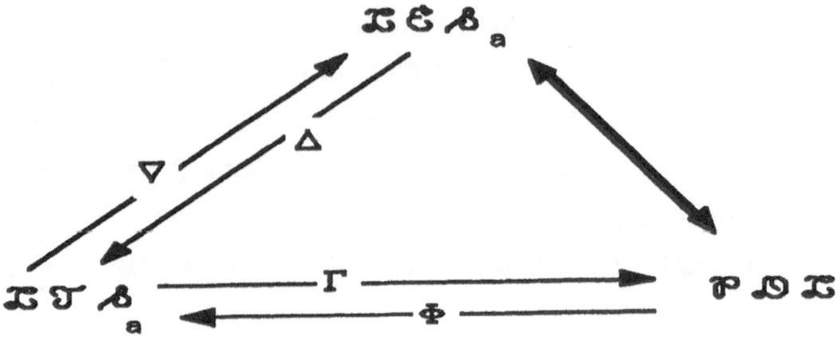

Therefore, *most of the properties available on event structures carry on on distributed languages,* and that in a straightforward way. That is in particular the reason why we obtain that distributed languages are finitary prime algebraic and finitely coherent PoSets, for the prefix relation as partial order relation[17].

In conclusion, we may assert that the major results of this work are : first to yield to facts the equivalence of different points of view, and second to introduce the new notion of Distributed Languages. Subject to well choose axioms, we get three equivalent models and we can move freely from one to the other, keeping there major properties.

The main conclusion is thus the possibility of expressing concurrency either through languages ***associated with an equivalence relation,*** *as well as through other well known possible models which are proved to be, in a meaning, equivalent to previous one : we are speaking of* ***Labelled Event Structures*** *and* ***Distributed Labelled Transition Systems.***

Acknowledgements : the author is indebted to Antoni Mazurkiewicz, Grzegorz Rozenberg, and P.S.Thiagarajan, for introducing her to Event Structures and Transition Systems, as well as for numerous debates about it.

---

[17] An analogous work is to be tried on infinite languages, in order to recover domains and complete coherence. It has already been done in [11] for the particular case of partially commutative languages.

REFERENCES

[1] I.J. AALBERSBERG - G. ROZENBERG, Theory of Traces, T.C.S. 60 (1988) p.1-82

[2] A. ARNOLD, Construction et analyse des systèmes de transitions : le système MEC, Proc.1th Col, C3 Angoulême 1985, A.Arnold ed. Bordeaux Univ. France.

[3] A. ARNOLD - An extension of the notion of traces and of asynchronous automata, T.R. 89-96, Bordeaux University.

[4] R.ASSOUS- C.CHARRETTON, Nice Labelling of Event Structures, Bull. EATCS n°41, 1990 June, p.184-190.

[5] G. BOUDOL - I. CASTELLANI, Semantics of Concurrency : Partial Orders and Transition Systems, Techn. Rep. 550 (1987) I.N.R.I.A. Sophia Antipolis, France and TAPSOFT 87, Lect. Notes in Comp. Sci. 249, p.123-137.

[6] I. CASTELLANI - P. FRANCESCHI - U. MONTANARI, Labelled Event Structures : A Model for Observable Concurrency, Proc. I.F.I.P. TC 2 , Formal Description of Programming Concepts II (D.Bjorner ed.) Garmisch-Partenkirchen (1982) North-Holland Amsterdam , p.383-400.

[7] R. CORI - D. PERRIN, Automates et commutations partielles, Rairo Inf. theor. Vol.19 n°1 (1985) p. 21-32.

[8] P. DEGANO - U. MONTANARI, Distributed Systems, Partial Ordering of Events and Event Structures, in: Control Flow and Data Flow: Concepts of Distributed Programming, NATO ASI Series F, Vol.14 , M. Broy ed. (1985) p.7-106.

[9] C. FERNANDEZ - M. NIELSEN - P.S. THIAGARAJAN, Notions of Realizable Non-Sequential Process, Fund. Infor. IX (1986) p.421-454.

[10] M.P. FLE - G. ROUCAIROL, A Language Theoretic Approach to Serialisation Problem in Concurrent Systems, Lect. Notes in Comp. Sci. 199 (1985) p.128-145.

[11] P. GASTIN, B.ROZOY,Infinitary Partially Commutative Monoids, T.R. 89-24 (1989) L.I.T.P. Paris 7 Univ. France.

[12] H.J. HOOGEBOOM, G. ROZENBERG, Diamond Properties of State Spaces of Elementary Net Systems, T.R. 89-18, Leiden University, Holland.

[13] L. LAMPORT, Time, Clocks and the Ordering of Events in a Distributed System, Comm. A.C.M. Vol.21 n°7 (1978) p.558-565.

[14] A. MAZURKIEWICZ, Traces, Histories and Graphs : Instances of Process Monoids, Lect. Notes in Comp. Sci. 176 (1984) p.115-133.

[15] A. MAZURKIEWICZ, Semantics of Concurrent Systems : a Modular Fixed Point Trace Approach, Lect. Notes in Comp. Sci. 188 (1985) p.353-375.

[16] A. MAZURKIEWICZ, Trace Theory, Paper n°16 , Advanced Course on Petri Nets, Bad Honnef (1986).

[17] M. NIELSEN - G. PLOTKIN - G. WINSKEL, Petri Nets, Event Structures and Domains, Theor. Comp. Sci. 13 (1981) p. 85-108.

[18] M. NIVAT Behaviours of Synchronized Systems of Processes, Tech. Rep.64 (1981) L.I.T.P. Paris 7 Univ. France.

[19] D. PERRIN, Partial Commutations, ICALP 89, L.N.C.S. 372 (1989) p.637-651.

[20] R. PRINOTH, An Algorithm to Construct Distributed Systems from State Machines, Protocol Specification Testing Verification, North Holland P.C. C.Sunshine ed. (1982) p.261-282.

[21] G. ROZENBERG, Behaviour of Elementary Net Systems, Paper n°7 , Advanced Course on Petri Nets , Bad Honnef (1986).

[22] G. ROZENBERG - P.S. THIAGARAJAN, Petri Nets : Basic Notions, Structure, Behaviour, Lect. Notes in Comp. Sci. 224 (1986) p. 585-668.

[23] B. ROZOY, Termination for Distributed Systems : Model and Cost, Computer and Artificial Intelligence 88-1, Inst. of Techn. Cybern. Slovak Acad. of Sciences

[24] B. ROZOY, Un Modèle pour le Parallélisme : le Monoïde Distribué, thèse d'état, Tech. Rep. 1 (1987) L.I.U.C. Caen Univ. France.

[25] B. ROZOY - P.S. THIAGARAJAN, Trace Monoids and Event Structures, Tech. Rep. 47 (1987) L.I.T.P. Paris 7 Univ. France, to appear in T.C.S.

[26] M.W. SHIELDS, Concurrent Machines, The Computer Journal Vol.28 n°5 (1985) p.449-465.

[27] J. SIFAKIS, A Unified Approach for Studying the Properties of Transition Systems, Theor. Comp. Sci. 18 (1982) p.227-258.

[28] P.H. STARKE, Multiprocessor Systems and Their Concurrency, Journal of Information Processing and Cybernetics E.I.K. Vol.20 n°4 (1984) p.207-227, Abstract in : L.N.C.S.

[29] P.H. STARKE, Traces and Semiwords, Lect. Notes in Comp. Sci. 208 (1985) p.332-349.

[30] P.S. THIAGARAJAN, Some Behavioural Aspects of Net Theory, L.N.C.S. 317 (1988) p.630-653.

[31] G. WINSKEL, Events in Computation, Ph.D. Thesis (1980) Edinburgh Univ. England.

[32] G. WINSKEL, Categories of Models for Concurrency, L.N.C.S.197 (1984).

[33] G. WINSKEL, Event Structures, L.N.C.S. 255, p.325-392.

Vol. 408: M. Leeser, G. Brown (Eds.),Hardware Specification, Verification and Synthesis: Mathematical Aspects. Proceedings, 1989. VI, 402 pages. 1990.

Vol. 409: A. Buchmann, O. Günther, T. R. Smith, Y.-F. Wang (Eds.), Design and Implementation of Large Spatial Databases. Proceedings, 1989. IX, 364 pages. 1990.

Vol. 410: F. Pichler, R. Moreno-Diaz (Eds.), Computer Aided Systems Theory – EUROCAST '89. Proceedings, 1989. VII, 427 pages. 1990.

Vol. 411: M. Nagl (Ed.), Graph-Theoretic Concepts in Computer Science. Proceedings, 1989. VII, 374 pages. 1990.

Vol. 412: L. B. Almeida, C. J. Wellekens (Eds.), Neural Networks. Proceedings, 1990. IX, 276 pages. 1990,

Vol. 413: R. Lenz, Group Theoretical Methods in Image Processing. VIII, 139 pages. 1990.

Vol. 414: A.Kreczmar, A. Salwicki, M. Warpechowski, LOGLAN '88 – Report on the Programming Language. X, 133 pages. 1990.

Vol. 415: C. Choffrut, T. Lengauer (Eds.), STACS 90. Proceedings, 1990. VI, 312 pages. 1990.

Vol. 416: F. Bancilhon, C. Thanos, D. Tsichritzis (Eds.), Advances in Database Technology – EDBT '90. Proceedings, 1990. IX, 452 pages. 1990.

Vol. 417: P. Martin-Löf, G. Mints (Eds.), COLOG-88. International Conference on Computer Logic. Proceedings, 1988. VI, 338 pages. 1990.

Vol. 418: K. H. Bläsius, U. Hedtstück, C.-R. Rollinger (Eds.), Sorts and Types in Artificial Intelligence. Proceedings, 1989. VIII, 307 pages. 1990. (Subseries LNAI).

Vol. 419: K. Weichselberger, S. Pöhlmann, A Methodology for Uncertainty in Knowledge-Based Systems. VIII, 136 pages. 1990 (Subseries LNAI).

Vol. 420: Z. Michalewicz (Ed.), Statistical and Scientific Database Management, V SSDBM. Proceedings, 1990. V, 256 pages. 1990.

Vol. 421: T. Onodera, S. Kawai, A Formal Model of Visualization in Computer Graphics Systems. X, 100 pages. 1990.

Vol. 422: B. Nebel, Reasoning and Revision in Hybrid Representation Systems. XII, 270 pages. 1990 (Subseries LNAI).

Vol. 423: L. E. Deimel (Ed.), Software Engineering Education. Proceedings, 1990. VI, 164 pages. 1990.

Vol. 424: G. Rozenberg (Ed.), Advances in Petri Nets 1989. VI, 524 pages. 1990.

Vol. 425: C. H. Bergman, R. D. Maddux, D. L. Pigozzi (Eds.), Algebraic Logic and Universal Algebra in Computer Science. Proceedings, 1988. XI, 292 pages. 1990.

Vol. 426: N. Houbak, SIL – a Simulation Language. VII, 192 pages. 1990.

Vol. 427: O. Faugeras (Ed.), Computer Vision – ECCV 90. Proceedings, 1990. XII, 619 pages. 1990.

Vol. 428: D. Bjørner, C. A. R. Hoare, H. Langmaack (Eds.), VDM '90. VDM and Z – Formal Methods in Software Development. Proceedings, 1990. XVII, 580 pages. 1990.

Vol. 429: A. Miola (Ed.), Design and Implementation of Symbolic Computation Systems. Proceedings, 1990. XII, 284 pages. 1990.

Vol. 430: J. W. de Bakker, W.-P. de Roever, G. Rozenberg (Eds.), Stepwise Refinement of Distributed Systems. Models, Formalisms, Correctness. Proceedings, 1989. X, 808 pages. 1990.

Vol. 431: A. Arnold (Ed.), CAAP '90. Proceedings, 1990. VI, 285 pages. 1990.

Vol. 432: N. Jones (Ed.), ESOP '90. Proceedings, 1990. IX, 436 pages. 1990.

Vol. 433: W. Schröder-Preikschat, W. Zimmer (Eds.), Progress in Distributed Operating Systems and Distributed Systems Management. Proceedings, 1989. V, 206 pages. 1990.

Vol. 434: J.-J. Quisquater, J. Vandewalle (Eds.), Advances in Cryptology – EUROCRYPT '89. Proceedings, 1989. X, 710 pages. 1990.

Vol. 435: G. Brassard (Ed.), Advances in Cryptology – CRYPTO '89. Proceedings, 1989. XIII, 634 pages. 1990.

Vol. 436: B. Steinholtz, A. Sølvberg, L. Bergman (Eds.), Advanced Information Systems Engineering. Proceedings, 1990. X, 392 pages. 1990.

Vol. 437: D. Kumar (Ed.), Current Trends in SNePS – Semantic Network Processing System. Proceedings, 1989. VII, 162 pages. 1990. (Subseries LNAI).

Vol. 438: D. H. Norrie, H.-W. Six (Eds.), Computer Assisted Learning – ICCAL '90. Proceedings, 1990. VII, 467 pages. 1990.

Vol. 439: P. Gorny, M. Tauber (Eds.), Visualization in Human-Computer Interaction. Proceedings, 1988. VI, 274 pages. 1990.

Vol. 440: E.Börger, H. Kleine Büning, M. M. Richter (Eds.), CSL '89. Proceedings, 1989. VI, 437 pages. 1990.

Vol. 441: T. Ito, R. H. Halstead, Jr. (Eds.), Parallel Lisp: Languages and Systems. Proceedings, 1989. XII, 364 pages. 1990.

Vol. 442: M. Main, A. Melton, M. Mislove, D. Schmidt (Eds.), Mathematical Foundations of Programming Semantics. Proceedings, 1989. VI, 439 pages. 1990.

Vol. 443: M. S. Paterson (Ed.), Automata, Languages and Programming. Proceedings, 1990. IX, 781 pages. 1990.

Vol. 444: S. Ramani, R. Chandrasekar, K. S. R. Anjaneyulu (Eds.), Knowledge Based Computer Systems. Proceedings, 1989. X, 546 pages. 1990. (Subseries LNAI).

Vol. 445: A. J. M. van Gasteren, On the Shape of Mathematical Arguments. VIII, 181 pages. 1990.

Vol. 446: L. Plümer, Termination Proofs for Logic Programs. VIII, 142 pages. 1990. (Subseries LNAI).

Vol. 447: J. R. Gilbert, R. Karlsson (Eds.), SWAT 90. 2nd Scandinavian Workshop on Algorithm Theory. Proceedings, 1990. VI, 417 pages. 1990.

Vol. 448: B. Simons, A. Spector (Eds.), Fault-Tolerant Distributed Computing. VI, 298 pages. 1990.

Vol. 449: M. E. Stickel (Ed.), 10th International Conference on Automated Deduction. Proceedings, 1990. XVI, 688 pages. 1990. (Subseries LNAI).

Vol. 450: T. Asano, T. Ibaraki, H. Imai, T. Nishizeki (Eds.), Algorithms. Proceedings, 1990. VIII, 479 pages. 1990.

Vol. 451: V. Mařík, O. Štěpánková, Z. Zdráhal (Eds.), Artificial Intelligence in Higher Education. Proceedings, 1989. IX, 247 pages. 1990. (Subseries LNAI).

Vol. 452: B. Rovan (Ed.), Mathematical Foundations of Computer Science 1990. Proceedings, 1990. VIII, 544 pages. 1990.

Vol. 453: J. Seberry, J. Pieprzyk (Eds.), Advances in Cryptology – AUSCRYPT '90. Proceedings, 1990. IX, 462 pages. 1990.

Vol. 454: V. Diekert, Combinatorics on Traces. XII, 165 pages. 1990.

Vol. 455: C. A. Floudas, P. M. Pardalos, A Collection of Test Problems for Constrained Global Optimization Algorithms. XIV, 180 pages. 1990.

Vol. 456: P. Deransart, J. Maluszyński (Eds.), Programming Language Implementation and Logic Programming. Proceedings, 1990. VIII, 401 pages. 1990.

Vol. 457: H. Burkhart (Ed.), CONPAR '90 – VAPP IV. Proceedings, 1990. XIV, 900 pages. 1990.

Vol. 458: J. C. M. Baeten, J. W. Klop (Eds.), CONCUR '90. Proceedings, 1990. VII, 537 pages. 1990.

Vol. 459: R. Studer (Ed.), Natural Language and Logic. Proceedings, 1989. VII, 252 pages. 1990. (Subseries LNAI).

Vol. 460: J. Uhl, H. A. Schmid, A Systematic Catalogue of Reusable Abstract Data Types. XII, 344 pages. 1990.

Vol. 461: P. Deransart, M. Jourdan (Eds.), Attribute Grammars and their Applications. Proceedings, 1990. VIII, 358 pages. 1990.

Vol. 462: G. Gottlob, W. Nejdl (Eds.), Expert Systems in Engineering. Proceedings, 1990. IX, 260 pages. 1990. (Subseries LNAI).

Vol. 463: H. Kirchner, W. Wechler (Eds.), Algebraic and Logic Programming. Proceedings, 1990. VII, 386 pages. 1990.

Vol. 464: J. Dassow, J. Kelemen (Eds.), Aspects and Prospects of Theoretical Computer Science. Proceedings, 1990. VI, 298 pages. 1990.

Vol. 466: A. Blaser (Ed.), Database Systems of the 90s. Proceedings, 1990. VIII, 334 pages. 1990.

Vol. 467: F. Long (Ed.), Software Engineering Environments. Proceedings, 1989. VI, 313 pages. 1990.

Vol. 468: S. G. Akl, F. Fiala, W. W. Koczkodaj (Eds.), Advances in Computing and Information – ICCI '90. Proceedings, 1990. VII, 529 pages. 1990.

Vol. 469: I. Guessarian (Ed.), Semantics of Systems of Concurrent Processes. Proceedings, 1990. V, 456 pages. 1990.